P9-AGI-282

Google Analytics Demystified

Fourth Edition

Google Analytics Demystified

Fourth Edition

Alexa L. Mokalis

Joel J. Davis

Copyright © 2018 by Alexa L. Mokalis and Joel J. Davis

All rights reserved. No part of this book or any digital representation of this book shall be reproduced, stored in a retrieval system, or transmitted by any means, electronic, mechanical, photocopying, recording, scanning, or otherwise without written permission from the copyright holder, except as permitted under Sections 107 or 108 of the 1976 United States Copyright Act. No patent liability is assumed with respect to the use of the information contained herein. Although every precaution has been taken in the preparation of this book, the publisher and author assume no responsibility for errors or omissions. Requests for reprint permission or other correspondence with the author should be directed to gad4ed@gmail.com.

ISBN-13: 978-1545486917

ISBN-10: 1545486913

Trademarks. This book makes descriptive reference to trademarks that may be owned by others. All terms mentioned in this book that are known to be trademarks or service marks have been appropriately capitalized. Use of a term in this book should not be regarded as affecting the validity of any trademark or service mark and, additionally, should not be viewed as an intention of trademark infringement. The use of such trademarks within this book is not an assertion of ownership of such trademarks by the author or publisher and is not intended to represent or imply the existence of an association between the author or publisher and the lawful owners of such trademarks. The author is not associated with any product, vendor, organization or individual mentioned in this book.

Limit of Liability/Disclaimer of Warranty. Every effort has been made to make this book as complete and as accurate as possible, but no warranty of fitness is implied. The publisher and author make no representations or warranties with respect to the accuracy or completeness of the contents of this work and specifically disclaim all warranties, including without limitation, warranties of fitness for a particular purpose. No warranty may be created or extended by sales or promotional materials. The information, guidance, suggestions, and strategies provided are on an "as is" basis. The author and the publisher shall have neither liability nor responsibility to any person or entity with respect to any loss or damages arising from the information or application of information contained in this book. This work is sold with the understanding that neither the publisher nor the author is engaged in rendering legal, accounting, advertising, marketing, digital design, or other professional services. If professional assistance is required, the services of a competent professional person should be sought. Organizations, individuals and websites referred to in this work are provided for information only and should not be interpreted as an endorsement of the organization or any advise or materials the organization may provide. Readers should be aware that digital references listed in this work may no longer be active or may have changed and that Google Analytics terminology, organization and displays may have changed since the date of publication.

Data. All data is fictitious and is presented for instructional purposes only. Data presented is not intended to be interpreted as an indication of actual performance. Travel and Tour is a fictitious company and is presented for instructional purposes only.

For Mom, Dad, Niko, & Kyle.
For their everlasting love, support & loyalty.

For Danna, Kyle and McKenna.
For the joy they bring.

In order to minimize environmental impact by reducing waste, *Google Analytics Demystified* is printed on-demand. When an order is placed, a book is printed. Given this approach, there is a *very slight* chance that there may be a printing problem. If this is the case, we apologize and, if you purchased from Amazon, we encourage you to request a free replacement. To contact Amazon by email, phone, or chat, click the "Contact Us" button from any Help page at `http://www.amazon.com/help`. If you can't access this feature, use one of the Amazon.com customer service phone numbers: U.S. and Canada (1-866-216-1072) or International (1-206-266-2992).

We are always interested in your comments and suggestions. Please feel free to send them to: gad4ed@gmail.com.

Brief Contents

Detailed Contents

Section V: The Audience Menu

Section VI: The Behavior Menu

Section VII: Segments

Section VIII: Goals

Section IX: Tracking Downloads

Section X: Events

Appendix: Pageviews, Events, and Ecommerce With Global Site Tag

Index

Every website and blog begins with a set of assumptions. We use our best judgment to make decisions related to content, navigation, and visitor flow and behaviors. Once the property is up and running, we have three options:

- We can let the property continue as is and hope for the best (very dangerous).

    Or ...

- We can rely on our judgment or best guess to plan revisions (still dangerous).

    Or ...

- We can monitor visitor characteristics and behaviors to determine the best way to reduce weaknesses and increase strengths (very beneficial).

If you are currently taking the latter approach and are using the full range of Google Analytics to inform your judgment, then congratulations. On the other hand, if you are not familiar with Google Analytics, or if you would like to improve how you use and apply Google Analytics to making better strategic decisions, then this book is definitely for you.

What Google Analytics can do for you

Simply put, Google Analytics helps you work smarter (not harder) so that you can increase the success of your digital property. In this book, we focus on the application of Google Analytics to websites and blogs, for which Google Analytics allows you to answer questions such as:

- How are visitors finding my site and what do they do when they arrive? What are the most common entrance pages? What are the most common exit pages?

- Which content do my visitors find most interesting and motivating? How much of my content is actually being consumed? What do visitors do after they read my content?

- How easily can site visitors find what they are looking for? Is my site content aligned with the search terms visitors use to find content?

- What are the strengths and weaknesses of site interaction? What can I do to improve visitors' experience and facilitate interaction?

- How effective are my campaigns? What efforts result in positive outcomes and help accomplish my goals? How can I make my campaigns more effective?

- How do visitor characteristics, site usage, and other aspects of site engagement influence my site transactions?

- How can I conduct tests to optimize my site's layout, content, organization, and navigation?

- How can I identify and examine the characteristics and behaviors of key sub-groups of site visitors?

- How can I monitor and evaluate important site interactions such as downloads, video viewing, and page scrolling?

- How can I create custom data tables to help me better understand site strengths and weaknesses?

And best of all, not only will Google Analytics help you answer these questions, it will do so for free as long as your website or blog has less than 10 million hits per month.

Moving through the book

Many of the chapters provide stand-alone instruction, so if there is a particular topic of interest you can immediately turn to that chapter. However, the concepts and exercises in the book have been sequenced to allow ideas to build over the course of the book. As a result, we suggest that you move through the book sequentially.

Required technical skills

Our approach to Google Analytics is detailed but not overly technical. While it is important to understand the "what" of Google Analytics, our focus and emphasis is on the "why." We try to help you not only see what the data "is," but we also try to help you extend your skills so that you are better able to determine what the data "means." The ability to draw meaning from Google Analytics data should help you make more informed, better strategic decisions. This, in turn, should lead to higher levels of success for your own digital properties. Nevertheless, your active engagement in learning Google Analytics and extending this learning to your own website does require a basic set of technical skills. We assume that you or others that you can turn to can do the following prior to starting with Chapter One:

- transfer files to and from your computer to an external server

- open a web page and modify the source code

Let's get started.

Approach

Google Analytics Demystified takes a four-step approach to helping you get the most from your time invested in learning Google Analytics. This approach also mirrors the path you can take in using Google Analytics to improve the success of your own digital properties.

The first step is "Question." Google Analytics works best when you have one or more specific questions in mind. In other words, what problem do you need to solve or what do you need to learn in order to improve on your prior success? Given the importance of this starting point, we place the discussion of Google Analytics data in the context of the strategic question(s) the data best answers.

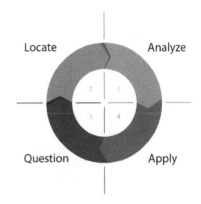

The second step is "Locate." Once you know what you need to learn, the challenge becomes locating the relevant data. Here, we take a step by step visual approach to helping you learn how and where to access Google Analytics data.

The third step is "Analyze." Once you've located the relevant data, you need to be able to infer what the data means and determine the implications of your analysis for future actions. Given the importance of this critical step, we accompany discussions of data location with case studies and actual data to show you how to make the leap from data examination to data meaning.

The final step is "Apply." Here you relate the prior analysis to your initial question(s) and determine the strategic action most likely to make a positive impact on your digital property. Many of our discussions take you through this final step.

Organization

Google Analytics Demystified presents sixteen sections of content, organized as follows:

- *Section I* consists of five chapters that help you get your website up and running so that it can be tracked by Google Analytics, be registered with Google search, and have activated key data collection parameters.

- A prerequisite to the useful acquisition of Google Analytics data is that all administrative functions be understood and completed prior to a significant amount of data being collected. The three chapters in *Section II* help you understand Google Analytics account structure and how to apply this structure to ensure that data is being collected and disseminated in the most efficient manner.

- Google Analytics filters allow you to specify the types of data included in your data reports. Filters provide a powerful way to reduce the effort required to examine important segments of data and, as a consequence, they make an important contribution to strategic decision-making. The first three chapters in *Section III* show you how to create and apply filters. The last chapter in this section provides step-by-step directions for using filters to eliminate spam from your reported data.

- All Google Analytics reports are organized around the principles of dimensions and metrics. *Section IV* helps you understand the characteristics and application of dimensions and metrics to analytics data collection and reporting.

- Google Analytics provides extensive data with regard to the characteristics of individuals who visit your website or blog. You can learn their demographics and interests, the technology they use to begin and continue engagement, where they are located, their frequency/recency of sessions, and how they move through your site page by page. The six chapters in *Section V* help you to understand the full range of audience specific data and the application of this data to strategic decision-making.

  - Google Analytics Audience data helps you see the characteristics of individuals who visit your website or blog. Google Analytics Behavior data provides a complimentary perspective where the focus is on explaining what visitors do after they arrive. The five chapters in *Section VI* help you understand the range of behavior-related data and the application of this data to strategic decision-making.

– *Sections VII* and *VIII* focus on tools and techniques that both broaden and deepen your analytics data and the data's subsequent application to decision-making. These sections explore segmentation, custom segments and goal creation and application.

– *Sections XI to XIII* continue the explanation of core analytics data.

One of the most powerful aspects of Google Analytics is the ability to track the origin of website users and to relate various origins to the broad range of data provided, including page interactions, goal conversions, conversion paths, user characteristics, and transactions. The six chapters in *Section XI* help you better understand how to find and apply this data to your own strategic decision-making.

Section XII focuses on the analysis of ecommerce data, helping you to understand the types of information available and the strategic insights this information provides.

Attribution is the process by which you assign a value to each of your visitors' touchpoints in order to determine the relative contribution of each touch point to a final conversion such as a purchase or other site interaction. The four chapters in *Section XIII* lead you through the process of working with and applying attribution models.

– *Section XIV* explains how to use Google Analytics to conduct content- and design-related experiments.

– *Section XV* discusses how move beyond aggregated data in order to track, analyze and apply data collected on the level of individual users.

– *Section XVI* addresses topics related to ongoing data management: alerts, short-cuts, data exports, dashboards, custom reports, calculated measures and intelligence questions. This section can be read any time after you are familiar with Google Analytics data.

Section XVI is followed by an appendix which presents chapters modified to explain the impact and application of the new tracking code provided by Google Analytics (see page *vi*).

The book concludes with a comprehensive index.

A Note on Google Analytics Tracking Code

Google Analytics uses a small snippet of JavaScript to communicate with your website or other digital property. This script, [1] which needs to appear on each monitored page of your site, sends data on visitors' behaviors, characteristics, and site performance to Google Analytics for processing and ultimately for display in your Google Analytics reports.

Until fall 2017, Universal Analytics (also referred to as "analytics.js") was the script required for communication between your site and Google Analytics. This is likely the script that you used if you've already placed a Google Analytics tracking script on your site. The Universal Analytics script is of the form shown below:

```
<script>
(function(i,s,o,g,r,a,m){i['GoogleAnalyticsObject']=r;i[r]=i[r]||function(){
(i[r].q=i[r].q||[]).push(arguments)},i[r].l=1*new Date();a=s.createElement(o),
m=s.getElementsByTagName(o)[0];a.async=1;a.src=g;m.parentNode.insertBefore(a,m)})
(window,document,'script','//www.google-analytics.com/analytics.js','ga');
ga('create', 'UA-54675304-1', 'auto');
ga('send', 'pageview');
</script>
```

Google released a new tracking code script in Fall, 2017. This script, named Global Site Tag (also referred to as "gtag.js"), is designed to replace the Universal Analytics script and is of the form shown below:

```
<!-- Global site tag (gtag.js) - Google Analytics -->
<script async src="https://www.googletagmanager.com/gtag/js?id=UA-41714766-4"></script>
<script>
  window.dataLayer = window.dataLayer || [];
  function gtag(){dataLayer.push(arguments);}
  gtag('js', new Date());
  gtag('config', 'UA-41714766-4');
</script>
```

---

[1] For this discussion the terms "script," "tracking script" and "tracking code" refer to the same thing.

Google explains the rationale behind this new script as follows:

> "gtag.js is the web tagging library that works for Google's site measurement, conversion tracking, and remarketing products – giving you better control while making implementation easier. By using gtag.js, you will be able to benefit from the latest dynamic features and integrations as they become available."

Don't panic if you've already placed the Universal Analytics tracking code on your site. Industry analysts believe that the Universal Analytics script should remain fully functional for quite a few more years. You can continue using this script on the pages where it is already installed. If you want to continue using the Universal Analytics script on new pages that you add to your site, then just copy the script from an existing page and paste it into the new page.

It's necessary to copy and paste the Universal Analytics tracking code from an existing site page because when you generate your tracking code from within Google Analytics, you will likely be given the gtag.js script as this tracking code is being rolled out to all Google Analytics users. As a result, an alternative to copying/pasting the Universal Analytics code is to use gtag.js on new site pages, as it is compatible with Universal Analytics. This will give you a head start on migrating to the Global Site Tag script. Importantly, some of your site pages can have Universal Analytics script while others can have the new Global Site Tag script. We simply recommend against putting both the Universal Analytics and Global Site Tag scripts on the same page. However (and this is a crucial however), Global Site Tag has changed the way in which the following types of data are sent to Google Analytics:

- Pageview tracking
- Event tracking
- Ecommerce tracking
- Custom dimension/metric tracking
- Client/User ID tracking
- User timings
- Exception tracking

The Global Site Tag also does not support content experiments, tasks, and custom plugins. If you are interested in content experiments, you might consider using the more powerful Google Optimize, which offers a WYSIWYG editor, multivariate test capabilities, and the ability to still run a redirect test if desired.[2] Thus, if you use the Global Site Tag script on any site pages that perform any of the above functions, you will need to use the new gtag.js format for sending information to Google Analytics rather than the analytics.js format.[3] On the other hand, if you are using the analytics.js script to perform any of the above functions, you can leave the script and functions as they are. They will continue to work as they have in the past.

---

[2] For support in using Google Optimize see Joel Davis, *Google Optimize Demystified.*

[3] Directions for migrating these analytics features to the Global Site Tag environment can be found at https://developers.google.com/analytics/devguides/collection/gtagjs/migration.

How does all of this impact this book's content?

We're aware that at this point most readers will continue to use Universal Analytics while some (but fewer) others may decide to use the Global Site Tag script. Fortunately, the Google Analytics reports generated by both scripts are identical, so the explanatory portions of this book will be relevant to all Google Analytics users regardless of the script they are using. Additionally, Chapter 1 provides directions for placing both types of scripts on your site.

With regard to directions for using each script for more advanced situations:

- Our discussions of pageview monitoring, event tracking, and ecommerce are customized to each script. The relevant chapters (Chapters 33, 36 – 44, 51) in the main portion of the book provide guidance for using Universal Analytics for these functions. These same chapters have also been rewritten and presented in the appendix. Here, guidance is provided for using the Global Site Tag to accomplish these same functions. We've placed reminders throughout the book to guide you to the appropriate chapters.

A Note on Data Examples

We think that individuals learn best when the discussion and examples are consistent and concrete. All of the examples throughout the book relate to two ecommerce websites: the Google Store (see page *x*) and Travel & Tour, where site visitors have the opportunity to "purchase" a vacation to either the Bahamas or Mexico. Of course, no real vacations are purchased and no payment is received.

You can view the site at:

http://www.googleanalyticsdemystified.com/xqanqeon

The incorporation of ecommerce into both sites allows us to show you how to use transactions as a terminal event. As such, you can improve your analytical and strategic skills by using Google Analytics to answer questions such as:

- Are some referral sources more important than others in facilitating transactions?

- To what extent are new versus returning site visitors different with regard to transactions?

- How do site visitors move through the site on the way to a transaction? What site characteristics facilitate a transaction? What site characteristics reduce the opportunity for a successful transaction?

- Do transactions differ by browser? By geography?

- How effective are my marketing or other communications in facilitating and encouraging transactions?

Learning how to answer these and related questions will serve you well even if your site or blog is not engaged in ecommerce. Let's say, for example, that you have a website or blog where terminal events relate to content consumption. The prior questions and the skills you'll acquire in addressing these questions still apply - simply substitute "content consumption" for transactions. The skills you learn using ecommerce data should be generalizable to whatever terminal events are appropriate to your website or blog.

A Note on Enhanced Ecommerce

Enhanced Ecommerce is an advanced form of ecommerce tracking:. This data collection option allows a deeper understanding of shopping and purchasing behaviors, product and category economic performance, and merchandising success. However, the use of Enhanced Ecommerce does require a considerable level of expertise in shopping cart and product data management and integration. Since we believe that relatively few readers of *Google Analytics Demystified* are likely to implement Enhanced Ecommerce, we direct those interested to the following resources.

The three sources below provide explanations and direction for enacting Enhanced Ecommerce within the Universal Analytics framework.

Better Data, Better Decisions: Enhanced Ecommerce Boosts Shopping Analytics	`http://analytics.blogspot.ie/2014/05/better-data-better-decisions-enhanced.html`
Overview of Enhanced Ecommerce	`https://support.google.com/analytics/answer/6014841`
Enhanced Ecommerce (UA) Developer Guide	`https://developers.google.com/tag-manager/enhanced-ecommerce`

The two sources below provide explanations and direction for enacting Enhanced Ecommerce within the Global Site Tag framework.

Enhanced Ecommerce with gtag.js	`https://developers.google.com/analytics/devguides/collection/gtagjs/enhanced-ecommerce`
Ecommerce with gtag.js	`https://support.google.com/analytics/answer/7475631`

Google Store Data

Learning Google Analytics can at times be both intimidating and scary, especially when accompanied by the fear that the process will somehow "mess up" your actual analytics data. Google has recognized this problem and has made available data from its store (i.e., the Google Merchandise Store, http://store.google.com) for you to explore and play with. This demo account "includes all the major features you would typically implement, like AdWords linking, Goals and Enhanced Ecommerce. The result is a fully functional account, with real business data."[4]

Once you are ready, you can register for access to the data by doing the following:

1. Make certain that you are signed into your Google Analytics account. (If you don't have an account yet, follow the directions in Section I and then complete these steps.)

2. You register for Google Merchandise Store data at:

   https://support.google.com/analytics/answer/6367342#access

   Use this link to access the registration page.

2. Find the section of the page labeled **Access the Demo Account.**

3. Click on the link labeled **>>>ACCESS DEMO ACCOUNT<<<**

4. You will be redirected to the display of Google Merchandise Store data.

---

[4] *Introducing the Google Analytics Demo Account* at
https://analytics.googleblog.com/2016/08/introducing-google-analytics-demo.html

Section I:
Getting Started

The five chapters in this section help you get your website up and running with Google Analytics. Feel free to skip any steps that you have already accomplished or that are not relevant to your unique situation.

- Chapter 1 shows you how to register your site with Google Analytics and how to incorporate the Google Analytics tracking code into your site. Both the Universal Analytics and Global Site Tag codes are addressed.

- Chapter 2 verifies that your site is operational and that Google Analytics is collecting and reporting data.

- Chapter 3 registers your site with Google search.

- Chapter 4 shows you how to inform Google Analytics that you want to collect and view the demographics and interests of site visitors and, if necessary, to communicate to Google that your site engages in ecommerce.

- Chapter 5 discusses data generation.

1
First Steps

This first set of activities gets your website tracked by Google Analytics. Please feel free to skip any steps that you've already accomplished or are that not relevant to your particular situation. The steps to follow are:

- Make certain that you have a Google account, such as that used for Gmail or Google+.

- Register your website with Google Analytics.

- Obtain your unique Google Analytics Tracking Code (GATC).

- Add GATC to each page of your website.

- Upload your revised website.

The chapter ends with a note on advanced implementation procedures.

If needed, create a Google account

A Google account is required for access to Google Analytics. If you already have a Google account, such as that used for Gmail or Google+, then skip this step. Otherwise, you'll need to create an account.

Creating a new Google account is very simple. You just respond to the questions asked at:

`https://accounts.google.com/SignUp`

Google will now associate all of your Google Analytics activities with this account. Remember to be signed into this account when you want to access Google Analytics.

Register your website with Google Analytics

Now it's time for you sign up for Google Analytics, which will allow Google to collect and report data from your site. **Before visiting the Google Analytics entry page, make certain that you are signed into Google with the email account that you want associated with Google Analytics**. Then, create a Google Analytics account as follows:

1. Go to the Google Analytics main page at: http://www.google.com/analytics/

    Click the **Sign In** link on the top right-hand side of the page. Then select "Analytics" from the pull-down menu.

2. On the next page, click the **SIGN UP** button on the right side of the page.

3. You'll now see where you let Google Analytics know your site specifics. The **Website** box is highlighted on the top of the page. Leave this box as is.

4. Scroll down (if necessary) to **Setting up your account**.

5. In the "Account Name" text box beneath **Setting up your account**, type in the name that you will use to identify your Google Analytics master account.

6. Scroll down (if necessary) to **Setting up your property**. In Google Analytics, a web property is the total set of pages on which your tracking code is installed. Every property has a unique ID, which you will receive later in the registration process. Name your property in the **Website Name** text box.

7. The next text box (labeled **Website URL**) asks for your website URL. Type in the full URL (including the subdirectory, if any) at which your website resides. This is the path by which you access the home page of your site. Thus, for my site, I would type in:

    http://www.googleanalyticsdemystified.com/xqanqeon/

8. Choose the appropriate **Industry category**.

9. Select your country and time zone from the next pair of pull-down menus.

10. Select or unselect the four boxes on the bottom of the page.

11. Click on the blue **Get Tracking ID** button.

12. **Accept** the terms of service. You should then see a "Success" message on the top of the page.

Obtain your unique Google Analytics Tracking Code (GATC)

After you've successfully completed the registration process, you'll be taken to the page that provides your unique Google Analytics tracking code. As we discussed earlier (see pages *vi* to *viii*) you will see either the Universal Analytics or Global Site Tag script. The Universal Analytics script is presented as shown on the top of page 5.

"**Website tracking**
This is the Universal Analytics tracking code for this property.
To get all the benefits of Universal Analytics for this property, copy and paste this code into every webpage you want to track."

Our Universal Analytics tracking code is shown below.

```
<script>
(function(i,s,o,g,r,a,m){i['GoogleAnalyticsObject']=r;i[r]=i[r]||function(){
(i[r].q=i[r].q||[]).push(arguments)},i[r].l=1*new Date();a=s.createElement(o),
m=s.getElementsByTagName(o)[0];a.async=1;a.src=g;m.parentNode.insertBefore(a,m)})
(window,document,'script','//www.google-analytics.com/analytics.js','ga');
ga('create', 'UA-54675304-1', 'auto');
ga('send', 'pageview');
</script>
```

On the other hand you might see the Global Site Tag script, as shown below.

"**Global Site Tag (gtag.js)**
This is the Global Site Tag (gtag.js) tracking code for this property. Copy and paste this code as the first item into the <HEAD> of every webpage you want to track. If you already have a Global Site Tag on your page, simply add the *config* line from the snippet below to your existing Global Site Tag."

Our Global Site Tag tracking code is shown below.

```
<!-- Global site tag (gtag.js) - Google Analytics -->
<script async src="https://www.googletagmanager.com/gtag/js?id=UA-41714766-4"></script>
<script>
  window.dataLayer = window.dataLayer || [];
  function gtag(){dataLayer.push(arguments);}
  gtag('js', new Date());
  gtag('config', 'UA-41714766-4');
</script>
```

In both cases, your tracking code will look identical to mine **except** that you will see your unique tracking number, which starts with "UA". Note that both versions of the tracking code are only intended for use on the website you described in the registration process. A different implementation of the code is required for mobile or app tracking; and for different websites or blogs you may wish to track. In this book, we address the most common implementation of Google Analytics: website or blog data collection for a single domain.

If you need but don't have access to the code at a later date, you can retrieve your Google Analytics tracking code from the Google Analytics site as follows:

1. Make certain that you are signed into the Google account associated with your website. Then, go to the Google Analytics home page at:

   http://www.google.com/analytics/

   Click the **Sign In** link on the top right-hand side of the page. Then select "Analytics" from the pull-down menu.

2. On the next page, click on **Admin,** which can be found on the bottom of the left-hand menu.

3. The next page will display three columns, indicating an account, property, and view. Make certain that the left and center columns display the account and property for which you want to retrieve the GATC. If not, use the Account and/or Property pull-down menus to select the desired account and property. In the middle column is a link labeled **Tracking Info**. Click on this link to reveal a new submenu. From this new menu select the top link, labeled **Tracking Code**. When this link is selected, your tracking code will be displayed.

Add GATC to each page of your website

You now need to paste your tracking code into the HTML of every page that you want to track via Google Analytics. You do this as follows for *each* page of your website:

1. Copy or have available the Google Analytics tracking script in your computer's memory.

2. Open the target page in your HTML editing program.[5]

3. Look at the HTML source code for the page. You'll notice two HTML tags labeled **<head>** and **</head>** near the top of the page's HTML code.

   Go to Step 4a if you are using the Universal Analytics tracking code. Go to Step 4b if you are using the Global Site Tag tracking code. Note that 4a differs from 4b in terms of tracking code placement. Once the code is pasted into the page's HTML continue with Step 5.

4a. Paste the Universal Analytics tracking code just *prior to the closing* **</head>** tag, as shown on the top of page 7. Note that the closing head tag is identified by the "/" in front of "head".

---

[5] Do not use Microsoft Word for HTML editing. If you do not have access to an HTML editor we suggest the use of Brackets, which can be downloaded for free from http://brackets.io/. Select the "Download Brackets without Extract" option.

```
<script>
(function(i,s,o,g,r,a,m){i['GoogleAnalyticsObject']=r;i[r]=i[r]||function(){
(i[r].q=i[r].q||[]).push(arguments)},i[r].l=1*new Date();a=s.createElement(o),
m=s.getElementsByTagName(o)[0];a.async=1;a.src=g;m.parentNode.insertBefore(a,})
(window,document,'script','//www.google-analytics.com/analytics.js','ga');
ga('create', 'UA-54675304-1', 'auto');
ga('send', 'pageview');
</script>

</head>
```

4b. Paste the Global Site Tag tracking code just *after to the opening* **<head>** tag, as shown below. Note that the opening head tag is identified by the *absence* of a "/" in front of "head".

```
<head>

<!-- Global site tag (gtag.js) - Google Analytics -->
<script async src="https://www.googletagmanager.com/gtag/js?id=UA-41714766-4"></script>
<script>
  window.dataLayer = window.dataLayer || [];
  function gtag(){dataLayer.push(arguments);}
  gtag('js', new Date());
  gtag('config', 'UA-41714766-4');
</script>
```

5. Save the page without changing its name.

Upload your site

Google Analytics will only collect data from pages that are live, as opposed to running locally from your desktop. As a result, make certain to re-upload all of your pages (which should now contain the tracking code) to your server. Chapter 2 shows you how to confirm that Google Analytics is receiving data from your revised site pages.

Advanced implementations

There is no real limit to how you can employ Google Analytics' data collection and reporting capabilities. While this book focuses on the fundamentals, let's take a look at what might lie ahead.

Expanding beyond a website: The Measurement Protocol

Most individuals and companies will use Google Analytics to monitor website or mobile app visitors and visitor behaviors. But, these are only two sources of data.

Google Analytics data collection is not limited to websites and mobile apps. Google Analytics can receive, process and report data from _any_ internet-connected device, such as a kiosk, an online point-of-sale system, or an e-commerce platform. You'll send the data from all of these devices to Google Analytics via the _Measurement Protocol_, a "standard set of rules for collecting and sending hits to Google Analytics."

If the need arises, you can begin to learn more about the Measurement Protocol at: https://developers.google.com/analytics/devguides/collection/protocol/v1/.[6]

Cross-domain tracking

The standard Google Analytics tracking code assumes that you are tracking behaviors generated at a single domain, in my case:

http://www.googleanalyticsdemystified.com/

But some websites have a more complex structure involving the use of subdomains or subdirectories. If you are using the most current version of the Google Analytics tracking code (Universal Analytics) then no additional configuration is needed to achieve the following:

- _Subdomains._ A website might use the subdomain http://reviews.site.com to present book reviews and the subdomain http://promotions.site.com to communicate individual promotions. Google Analytics can combine data from both subdomains into the same report.

- _Subdirectories._ A website might place different content in different folders or subdirectories. Here, the domain name remains the same but it is followed by the name of the subdirectory. For example, instead of using a subdomain (as in the prior example) a website might instead place all of the content related to book reviews in a single subdirectory: http://www.site.com/reviews. Google Analytics can collect and report data for the subdirectory in a separate report as if it were a single site.

Some businesses use a complex setup, where two sites (a source domain and a destination domain) need to share a single unique client ID between them. These sites may exhibit one or more of the following characteristics:

- _The use of 3rd-party shopping carts_ - where an online store is has one domain name and a shopping cart is hosted on another domain.

---

[6] See also _Google Analytics Measurement Protocol & Hit Builder_ at
https://www.optimizesmart.com/understanding-universal-analytics-measurement-protocol/.

- *The use of multiple top-level domains* - where data needs to be collected and combined (in a single report) from two or more domains that you own.

- *The use of iFrame content* - where the transfer between two domains is done by opening a new window or by providing content in an iFrame of a second domain.[7]

Google Analytics can handle all of these situations, but you'll need to customize your tracking code.

User IDs: Tracking Visitors Across Multiple Devices

Imagine that Carolyn is visiting your website via her laptop and then later in the day via her mobile phone. Without User ID, Google Analytics would record two sessions initiated by two separate individuals. Google Analytics' User ID feature allows you to connect multiple devices, sessions, and engagement data to the same visitors. So, with User ID, you would know that Carolyn initiated both sessions.

> ✅ To implement the Google Analytics User ID feature, you must be able to generate your own unique IDs, consistently assign IDs to users, and include these IDs wherever you send data to Google Analytics. For example, you might ask a site visitor to create an account and then (regardless of the device used to visit the site) sign/log in whenever visiting. Use of the User ID feature also requires that you enable this feature in your Google Analytics account and then create a User ID view to analyze User ID data.[8]

Google Tag Manager

We believe that the process of modifying your HTML will help you best understand not only how Google Analytics works, but how modifications to this code result in different types of data collection. However, an alternative to directly creating and changing some of your HTML code is Google Tag Manager.

A tag is a small snippet of code that when added to your site, allows you to measure traffic and visitor behavior. Google Tag Manager keeps track of the tags and tag-firing triggers that define what tags should be make available and the conditions under which the tag's availability occurs.[9] According to Google, the "Google Tag Manager is a tag management system that allows you to quickly and easily update:

---

[7] *Tracking Multiple Domains* at
https://developers.google.com/analytics/devguides/collection/gajs/gaTrackingSite.
Additional information on cross-domain tracking and tracking code customization can be found at *Set Up Cross Domain Tracking* at https://support.google.com/analytics/answer/1034342.

[8] For additional guidance on User IDs see *About User ID Views* at
https://support.google.com/analytics/answer/3123669.
[9] *About Tags and Tag Management* at https://www.google.com/analytics/tag-manager/faq/.

- *tags and code snippets on your website or mobile app,* such as those intended for traffic analysis and marketing optimization. Here, you can add and update AdWords, Google Analytics, Floodlight, and 3rd party or custom tags from the Tag Manager user interface instead of [directly] editing site code, and

- *configuration and flag values of mobile apps.* Instead of rebuilding and deploying new mobile app binaries, you can use the Tag Manager interface to change configuration values (such as timeouts, ad positioning, game play dynamics) and turn on flag-enabled features."[10]

Google Tag Manager is free to use. You can learn more about Google Tag Manager at the Google Analytics Academy at https://analyticsacademy.withgoogle.com/course/5. You can register for Google Tag Manager at https://www.google.com/analytics/tag-manager/ .

External Configuration: Management API

Most companies will configure their Google Analytics account from within the Google Analytics site. Larger companies with extensive data sets may however, find it more efficient to configure their account externally, that is, not from within the Google Analytics website. This can be accomplished via the Management API.

The Google Analytics Management API allows for [external] access to your Google Analytics configuration data. As a result, you can build applications to more efficiently manage large or complex Google Analytics accounts. Large companies with many properties can automate account setup.[11]

Merging Online and Offline Data (Data Import)

It is often advantageous to combine data from offline sources with online data. You can, for example, turn separate CRM data, ecommerce data, and Google Analytics data into a single comprehensive view of your business. This can help you organize, analyze and act upon this unified data view in ways that are better aligned with your specific and unique business needs.[12]

> ✅ Data Import lets you send Google Analytics data from external sources and combine it with data you collect via Google Analytics. You can then use Google Analytics to organize and analyze all of your data in ways that better reflect your business.

---

[10] *Google Tag Manager Overview* at https://support.google.com/tagmanager/answer/6102821.

[11] *Analytics Management API* at https://developers.google.com/analytics/devguides/config/mgmt/v3/.

2

Verifying Data Collection

We now need to confirm that Google Analytics is tracking visits and visitor behaviors.

Make certain that you are signed into the Google account associated with your website. Then visit the Google Analytics home page at: http://www.google.com/analytics. Click the **Sign In** link on the top right-hand side of the page. Then select "Analytics" from the pull-down menu.

Selecting the desired property and view

There are two ways to select the desired property and view.

Top of Page Navigation

When you sign-in to Google Analytics account you'll see menu options on the left-hand side of the page and summary charts on the remainder of the page. On the top of the page you'll see the current property and view (see opposite for an example where the property is "My Travel Website" and the view is "All Web Site Data").

There is a downward facing arrow to the right of the property name. Clicking on this arrow will display all properties and views associated with your account (as illustrated below). Just select the desired account, property and view.

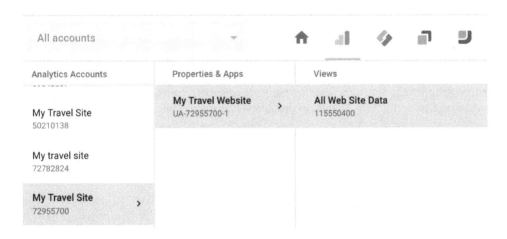

Properties, Views and Summary Metrics

Next to the top of page listing of the current property and view is the Google Analytics icon. The icon is to the left of the listing (see opposite).

All accounts > My Travel Website
All Web Site Data ▾

Clicking on this icon will take you to a different display (see below). Here, you can select a View by clicking on its name. Keep in mind that a display will sometimes be collapsed where only the account name is shown, as in "Account2" below. If this is the case, click on the folder icon to expand the display.

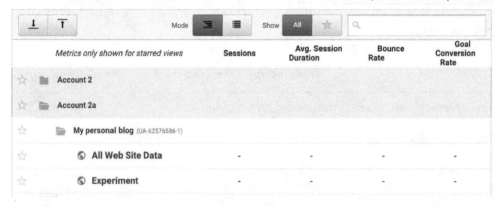

Nov 11, 2017 - Nov 17, 2017 ▾

Metrics only shown for starred views	Sessions	Avg. Session Duration	Bounce Rate	Goal Conversion Rate
☆ 📁 Account 2				
☆ 📁 Account 2a				
☆ 📁 My personal blog (UA-62576586-1)				
☆ 🌐 All Web Site Data	-	-	-	-
☆ 🌐 Experiment	-	-	-	-

You'll notice that the above display does not present any summary data for the views in Account 2a. Data can be requested by clicking on the star to the left of the desired account, property and/or view.

Clicking on your data view name (in my case, **All Web Site Data)** takes you to the home page for that view. Before proceeding, always confirm that the desired property and view are displayed on the top of the page.

Viewing your data in real-time

We want to confirm that we placed the tracking code correctly and that each site page is sending data to Google Analytics. This can be accomplished by clicking on the **Real-Time** menu option on the left-hand side of the page and then on the **Overview** link from the newly revealed menu. This brings up the Real-Time display shown on page 13.

Note that **Top Active Pages** is blank because no one is visiting our site right now. When I visit my home page in another browser tab this display changes to indicate that someone is on this page (see figure below). The URL of my home page is shown beneath the **Active Page** heading.

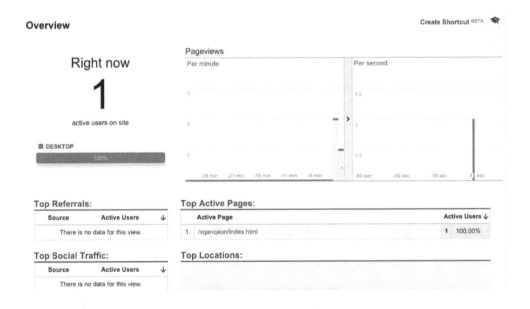

You can confirm that your code is working correctly by visiting each of your website's pages and then checking the Real-Time display. If the page you are visiting is displayed beneath the **Active Page** heading than all is working fine. If the page is not displayed, then recheck that the correct GATC is available and placed correctly on the page.

3

Registering Your Site With Google Search

You improve the chances of your site showing up in Google search results when you explicitly bring the site to Google's attention. The easiest way to accomplish this is to manually submit your site's primary URL through the following steps.

1. Visit Google Search Console at:

    https://www.google.com/webmasters/tools/submit-url

    You should see the screen shown below:

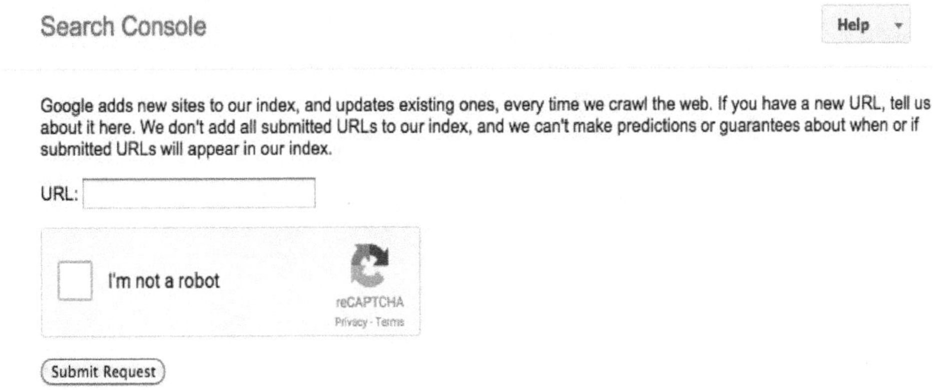

Search Console   Help ▾

Google adds new sites to our index, and updates existing ones, every time we crawl the web. If you have a new URL, tell us about it here. We don't add all submitted URLs to our index, and we can't make predictions or guarantees about when or if submitted URLs will appear in our index.

URL: [_____]

[ ] I'm not a robot   reCAPTCHA
                              Privacy - Terms

(Submit Request)

3. Type the full URL to your site in the box labeled URL. In my case, I would type:

    http://www.googleanalyticsdemystified.com/xqanqeon/

4. Check the box next to **I'm not a robot**.

5. Click **Submit Request**. If all has gone well, you should see a confirmation message that reads: "Your request has been received and will be processed shortly."

4

Activating Ecommerce and Demographic/Interests Data Collection

Google Analytics needs to be informed if a site is engaged in ecommerce in order to process purchase and related information. It also needs for you to explicitly acknowledge that you want to collect and view the demographics and interests of site visitors. Both of these tasks are easy to accomplish. (Note: If your site does not use ecommerce, then skip to the discussion of demographics/interests later in this chapter.)

Ecommerce

We inform Google Analytics of our engagement in ecommerce as follows:

1. Visit the Google Analytics site at:

    http://www.google.com/analytics

    Sign in, if necessary, using the Google account associated with your website.

2. Your home page appears next. Click **Admin**, which appears on the very bottom of the left-hand side menu options (see below).

3.   The next page will display three columns indicating an account, property, and view. Make certain that the desired account, property and view are displayed. (If not, change the display using the pull-down menus). The far right column contains a link labeled **Ecommerce Settings**.

4.   Click on the **Ecommerce Settings** link to reveal a new page. Beneath **Enable Ecommerce** is a slider bar labeled, "Status". Click on this bar to turn it "On".

5.   Decide if *Related Products* applies to your situation. Google Analytics can automatically generate a list of related products per product for your ecommerce-enabled property based on transaction data. You can use this data to improve product bundling, merchandizing, remarketing, and email campaigns. Toggle the **Enable Related Products** bar to either "Off" or "On" depending upon your unique circumstances. You can read more about Related Products at:

     https://support.google.com/analytics/answer/6223409

6.   Click **Next Step**.

7.   Leave **Enhanced Ecommerce Settings** set to "Off" unless you have the knowledge and resources to take advantage of this feature. When done, press **Submit**. You will then see a message noting "Success" on the top of the page. Click on **Home** on the top of the page to return to your Google Analytics home page.

Demographics and Interests

Two steps are required for registration and access to demographic and interest data.

First, you must agree to *Advertising Reporting Features* as follows:

-   Log into Google Analytics (if necessary). Select **Admin** from the left-hand side menu options. On the next page displayed, make certain that the correct account and property are selected.

-   Click on **Tracking Info** in the middle Property column. From the newly displayed menu options click on **Data Collection**.

-   The bottom block of text on the next page refers to Advertising Reporting Features (see below). Toggle the Off/On switch to "On".

Advertising Reporting Features
Enables data collection for Advertising Reporting features like Audience Demographics and Interests Reporting, DoubleClick Campaign Manager reporting, DoubleClick Bid Manager reporting, and Google Display Network Impression Reporting that help you better understand your users. Learn more

-   Press **Save**, after which you will see "Success."

Second, you enable data collection, as follows:

- Log into Google Analytics (if necessary). Select **Admin** from the left-hand side menu options. On the next page displayed, make certain that the correct account and property are selected.

- Click on **Property Settings** in the middle Property column.

- Scroll down the next page to "Advertising Features. Enable Demographics and Interest Reports" (see below). Toggle the Off/On switch to "On".

-

Advertising Features

Enable Demographics and Interest Reports (?)
Demographics and Interest Reports make Age, Gender, and Interest data available so you can better understand who your users are. To see this data, you may need to enable Advertising Features first. Learn more

`ON`

- Press **Save** on the bottom of the page, after which you will see "Success."

Finally, you need to update your website or blog's privacy policy. Google notes that you are not allowed to merge "personally-identifiable information with non-personally identifiable information collected through any Google advertising product or feature unless you have robust notice of, and the user's prior affirmative (i.e., opt-in) consent to, that merger. [Further] you are required to notify your visitors by disclosing the following information in your privacy policy:

- The Google Analytics Advertising Features you've implemented.

- How you and third-party vendors use first-party cookies (such as the Google Analytics cookie) or other first-party identifiers, and third-party cookies (such as Google advertising cookies) or other third-party identifiers together.

- How visitors can opt-out of the Google Analytics Advertising Features you use, including through Ads Settings, Ad Settings for mobile apps, or any other available means (for example, the NAI's consumer opt-out)."[13]

---

[13] See *Policy Features for Google Analytics Advertising Features* at https://support.google.com/analytics/answer/2700409.

Populating Your Site With Data

We will soon lead you through an examination of the types of data available through Google Analytics. This examination and accompanying discussion will be much more meaningful if you are able to apply the discussion to your own data. As a result, it would be valuable for you to populate your site with data if none currently exists. You can do this using one or both of the approaches described below.

- Populate your site with data yourself. Here, using your Chrome browser, visit the site and view one or more pages. Clear your browser history after every three or so visits in order to obtain a mix of new and returning users. Do this twenty or thirty times. Your visit can originate either through direct access by typing the desired site page into your browser or by using Google search results, if available.

- Ask your friends/others at your company to populate the site with data. You can use email or social media to display/send links to your site. Some links can go to the home page while other links may go directly to other pages. Encourage the use of different links. You can also provide your friends with a search term that they can use to find and access your site via search results.

You can check to see if data is accumulating by doing the following.

Log into your Google Analytics account and on make certain that the correct account, property and view is displayed on the top of your home page. Then, in the left-hand column, click on **Audience** and then **Overview**. This will take you to your **Audience Overview** page, as illustrated on the top of page 22. Note that the session count of 17 is reported along with other summary data, such as four users.[14] If all works as expected, you should see a page that resembles the image on the next page, only reporting your website's data. If there is a session count and other data on this page, congratulations, your site is operational and Google Analytics is collecting data. If there is no data, wait a day and check again. If there is still no data then repeat the steps outlined in Chapter 2 to make certain that your GATC is operating properly.

---

[14] For the moment, think of a "session" as a visit to your site and a "user" as a site visitor. More precise definitions are presented later in the book.

Google Analytics Demystified

Section II:
Account Management

A prerequisite to the useful acquisition of Google Analytics data is that all administrative functions be understood and completed prior to a significant amount of data being collected. The chapters in this section help you understand Google Analytics account structure and how to apply this structure to ensure that data is being collected and disseminated in the most efficient manner.

- Chapter 6 introduces you to Google Analytics account structure, and explains the characteristics and inter-relationships of accounts, properties, and views.

- Chapter 7 shows you how to create and modify accounts, properties, and views.

- Chapter 8 explains how to give others access to your data.

Accounts, Properties, and Views

So far, you have at least one Google Analytics account, property and view. This chapter explains accounts, properties, and views; their relationship to each other; and how to expand your options in terms of multiple accounts, properties, and views.

Let's begin with a look at the account, property, and view hierarchy. Then, we'll see how to organize accounts and properties to best meet different types of advertising or business situations.

The account, property, and view hierarchy

Google Analytics is organized around a hierarchy of accounts, properties and views. Any single account can have one or more properties and each property, in turn, can have one or more views. The figure shown below provides a real-life example and also shows how any single Google user ID (such as the e-mail address you use to log into Google Analytics) can have multiple accounts, each of which in turn can have multiple properties and views.

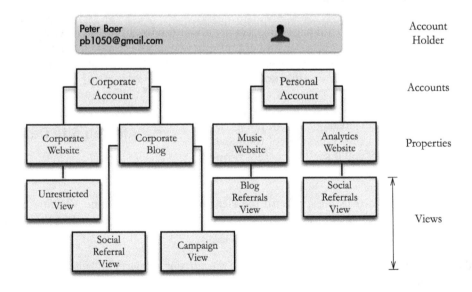

Let's look at this structure.

- Peter is the account holder. He uses his Google ID **pb1050@gmail.com** to log into various Google properties, including Google Analytics.

- Peter has access to two accounts at Google Analytics. These accounts reflect his two roles. Since Peter is the analytics manager for his company, the first account he has access to collects data relevant to his company's website. Peter also has a personal account, which he manages.

- Peter's company uses Google Analytics to help evaluate two of its digital properties. One property is the corporate website and the second property is the corporate blog. Peter also uses Google Analytics to help him collect information on two of his personal digital endeavors: a music website and an analytics website. Since the company and personal accounts are set up separately, the data from the two never intermix.

- The chart shows the views, or ways of looking at the data, collected by Google Analytics for each of the properties. One view is shown for the corporate website and two views are shown for the corporate blog. More views are used, but they are omitted so that the amount of clutter in the chart is minimized. Some of the views associated with Peter's music blog and analytics blog are also shown.

With this in mind, the following sections explain the characteristics of accounts, properties, and views.

What is an account?

As indicated in the figure on page 25, accounts are at the top of the hierarchy. A Google Analytics account is a way to name and organize how you collect data from one or more properties. Every Google Analytics user has access to at least one account: either the one they created themselves or one that someone else gave them access to.

When you sign-in to Google Analytics, you'll see menu options on the left-hand side of the page and summary charts on the remainder of the page. On the top of the page, you'll see the current property and view.

There is a downward facing arrow to the right of the property name. Clicking on this arrow will display all properties and views associated with your. Just select the desired account, property and view.

Alternatively, next to the top of page listing of the current property and view is the Google Analytics icon. The icon is to the left of the listing (see above).

Clicking on this icon will take you to a different display (see below). Here, you can select a View by clicking on its name. Keep in mind that a display will sometimes be collapsed, where only the account name is shown, as in "Account 2" below. If this is the case, click on the folder icon to expand the display.

Nov 11, 2017 - Nov 17, 2017 ⌄

You'll notice that the above display does not present any summary data for the views in Account 2a. Data can be requested by clicking on the star to the left of the desired account, property and/or view.

Clicking on your data view name (in my case, **All Web Site Data)** takes you to the home page for that view. Confirm that the desired property and view are displayed on the top of the page.

We have several accounts, two of which are shown opposite. "My Travel Site" is used for instructional purposes while "Personal Accounts" monitors our personal digital properties.

As noted earlier, if the properties associated with an account are not displayed, clicking on the folder icon to the left of the account name will display all of the properties associated with that account, as shown opposite. In our case, one property is associated with the account set up for this book ("My Travel Site/My Travel Website"). In addition, two properties are associated with my "Personal Accounts." One property monitors our website activity and the other monitors our Wordpress blog.

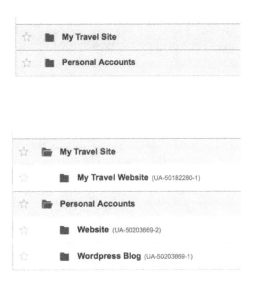

A property can be a website, a mobile application, a blog -- any page or screen that receives traffic via the web. Within any Google Analytics account, you can create one or more properties from which you want to collect visitor data. Google Analytics generates the unique tracking code that collects data from each property. As we saw earlier, I have two properties associated with my account labeled "Personal Accounts."

You can tell the relationship between properties and accounts by looking at the Google Analytics identification number that follows each property name. Every account has a unique identification number and, as a result, different identification numbers keep the accounts separate. In my case (as illustrated in the screen capture shown on the top of this page), the primary identification number for "My Travel Site" is "UA-50182280" while the primary identification number for "Personal Accounts" is "UA-50203869". The dashed digit at the end of the identification number is the unique property identifier. Within "Personal Accounts," for example, my blog is one property associated with this account (indicated by the "-1"), while my website is another property within the account (indicated by use of the same account number but followed by a "-2" at the end of the identification number).

> When setting up properties within accounts, **never** assign the same property to more than one account as this will seriously affect data integrity and the validity of subsequent analyses.

Google Analytics allows you to move a property from one account to another.[15] Here, Google notes that "Moving properties lets you keep your Analytics implementation current with your business. You might be reorganizing after a merger, after an internal restructuring, after hiring a new agency."

You move a property from a *source* account to a *destination* account, as follows:[16]

1. Sign in to your Google Analytics account.

2. Select the **Admin** link from the bottom of the left-hand side menu options.

3. In the "Account" column, use the menu to select the account that contains the property you want to move.

4. In the "Property" column, select the property you want to move.

---

[15] Source for this section is *Move a Property* at https://support.google.com/analytics/answer/6370521.

[16] To move a property, you must have Manage Users and Edit permissions for both the source and destination accounts. Permissions are discussed in Chapter 8.

5. Click **Property Settings**, then click **Move property**.

6. Select the destination account.

7. Choose your permissions settings, either:

    •   *Keep existing property and view permissions.* The current set of user permissions is copied along with the property, and the property will not inherit permissions from the destination account.

    •   *Replace existing property and view permissions with permissions of the destination account.* The property will inherit permissions from the destination account.

8. Click **Move**.

9. Confirm data processing, then click **Save**.

Moving a property from one account to another provides a powerful way to reorganize your data collection and reporting procedures. Keep the following in mind, however, whenever planning a property move.

If the source account no longer contains properties after the move, you can delete the source account. An empty source account still counts against the maximum number of Google Analytics accounts you can have.

-   The Tracking ID (e.g., UA-12345-1) does not change, so there's no need to retag anything. The source account does not reuse the ID, so the Tracking ID remains unique throughout your Google Analytics environment.

-   When you move a property, you have two options for how to handle permissions:

    •   *Replace existing property and view permissions with permissions of the destination account.* The property and its views will inherit permissions from the destination account.

    •   *Keep existing property and view permissions.* The current property and view permissions are copied along with the property. Users who have account-level access in the source account will have property-level access in the destination account.

-   All reporting data associated with a property is moved (not copied) to the destination account.

-   Property settings remain intact when you move a property, as do other settings and associated objects like User-ID, Remarketing Audiences and Dynamic Attributes, Custom Definitions, Data Import, and Custom Tables.

- All views associated with a property are moved, and all the view settings remain intact. In addition, any assets associated with the view are moved, including dashboards, custom reports, annotations, segments, and goals.

- Filters that are applied to any of the property's views are copied to the destination account. If Analytics detects an exact match in the destination account (filter name and configuration), then the filter is not copied, and the filter in the destination account is applied. Filters are never removed from the source account.

Relationship between accounts and properties

You can use a one-to-one relationship of *one account/one property*, or you can use a one-to-many relationship of *one account/many properties*. You can also have multiple Google Analytics accounts (as I do), where each of which contains one or more properties.

One Account/One Property

This is the simplest configuration. Here, you've associated a single account with your Google identity and you've created one property to be tracked within that account. This is comparable to having just one corporate website or one corporate blog that you want to track. Your current Google Analytics configuration uses this approach.

One Account/Multiple Properties

Imagine that your situation is a bit more complex: you want to track multiple properties within a single account. This is the situation described for my Personal Accounts on the prior page where two properties (Website, Wordpress Blog) are reported within the single account.

Multiple Accounts

If you manage Google Analytics for multiple websites that belong to multiple clients, you can create a separate Google Analytics account for each client with as many properties and views as necessary within each account. This type of organization lets you give your clients access to their unique accounts, and ensures that clients are not able to view one another's data.

Once you have set up your accounts and properties, it then becomes necessary to decide the characteristics of the data you want to view. This is where **Views** come in.

What is a view?

Views determine the specific data you see for a property. Whenever you set up a property, Google Analytics sets up an unfiltered view for that property's data, which by default is labeled **All Web Site Data**. An unfiltered view means that 100% of the data collected is shown in all of that view's reports.

But, this does not have to be the case. Google Analytics allows up to 50 views for each property and these views can be added at any time. Why, though, would you need more than the unfiltered, complete data view? There are several reasons.

First, you can manage data reporting by using different views to display different data sets. You could, for example, use different views in the same account to:

- allow you to specifically focus on visitor and behavior data from one subdomain;

- look more closely at visitor and behavior data associated with a specific part of the site (for example, a subdirectory, page, or group of pages);

- limit a Google Analytics users' access to a subset of data.

You still may not need 50 views, but there are some views that you should be certain to create for each property. It's a good idea to create these views early in the process, as the data reported in a view includes only the data collected since the view was created. If, for example, you create a new view on June 1, then you can examine data from June 1 forward, but you will not be able to see any data collected prior to June 1 in that view.

Most views are created by adding filters; a filter defines the types of data that are included and excluded from a particular view. For now, let's identify the different types of alternative views and filters that underlie good analytics practice. The next two chapters will take you through the steps required to create new accounts, properties, and views with and without filters.

Ideally, since views do not report historical data, all four views should be created at the time you initiate analytics data collection. Views only report data onwards from the date they were created. New views will not display any data created prior their creation.

There are four views that every property should have.

View 1: Raw, unfiltered data

This is the view we just discussed. It is the easiest to set up because there are no filters. This default view presents 100% of all data collected. This view is important because it is your backup should anything "bad" happen to the other views. For example, if any of your other views have issues with your Google Analytics setup, you will be able to refer to your raw data to get to the bottom of the issue, or if you inappropriately apply a filter to another view, this view will help you recover data that would have been lost.

View 2: Eliminate irrelevant sources of traffic

It's likely that a significant amount of traffic is generated by you or other individuals whose behaviors and characteristics are of no interest. This might include others who work for your company or vendors who are working on the site. Creating this view results in data reports that provide only the traffic you consider relevant, while excluding any traffic you consider irrelevant. You can apply one or more filters to create this view.

View 3: Filters test view

As much as we all try to avoid error, it is nevertheless the case that nearly everyone working with Google Analytics has at one time made a mistake in applying filters. When an erroneous filter is applied to a working view, the results can be devastating, as filtered data cannot be recovered. While this view doesn't eliminate inappropriate or erroneous filters, it does eliminate the disaster associated with these filters. This view is a place to try out new filters before they are applied to View 2 or another working view. Try out your new filters here and monitor the results for a week or so. If all seems to be working fine, then apply this filter to the working file, delete this view with its filter, and create a new replacement view file, which can be used the next time you want to try out a new filter.

View 4: Experimental test view

This view is similar in intent to View 3. It is a place for you to test actions related to goals, funnels, custom variables, and other approaches to customizing Google Analytics. (These topics will be discussed in later chapters.) Try out your ideas here before incorporating them into your working view. As with View 3, monitor the results for a week or so. If all seems to be working fine, then apply your new customizations to the working file. Then, when necessary, delete this file and create a new experimental file to allow for the evaluation of future customization attempts.

7
Managing Accounts, Properties, and Views

Chapter 6 introduced you to the concepts of accounts, properties, and views. This chapter helps you learn how to create new accounts, properties and views. The examples in this chapter are for practice rather than actual data collection, so you can delete all of your work when you are done with this chapter. No existing data will be affected.

The activities in this chapter will help you learn how to execute the most common functions related to accounts, properties and views. You will learn how to:

- Create a new Google Analytics account and property

- Add a second property to an account

- Rename an existing view

- Duplicate an existing view

- Delete an existing view

- Create an entirely new view

- Delete an existing property

- Delete an existing account

Accessing administrative functions

Login to Google Analytics using the appropriate email address.

You create new accounts, properties and views, as well as manage these items via the Google Analytics administrator page. To access the administrator's page, click the **Admin** link after you have logged into Google Analytics and reached your home page.

Three columns of information are displayed whenever you access this page through the **Admin** link. The left-hand column is labeled **Account**, the middle column is labeled **Property** and the right-hand column is labeled **View** (see below). Your administrator page should look similar to mine, except that your own accounts, properties and views will be displayed. Make certain that the desired account, property and view are displayed. If not, use the pull-down menus to select your choices.

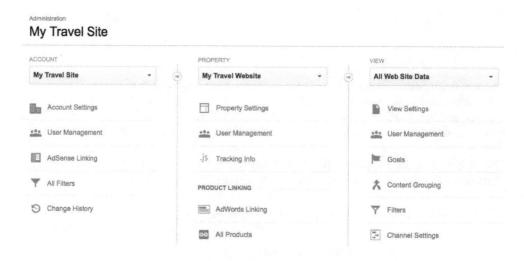

With this in mind, let's create a new account with an associated property.

Create a new account and associated property

Your new account will have the following characteristics:

      Account name: Account 2

      Property name: My personal blog

      View name: Leave as default - All Web Site Data

      Website: www.chapter7.net

You begin by pulling down the menu beneath **Account** on the top left-hand side of the page. This is where the names of your accounts are shown (see left-hand column on the top of page 35).

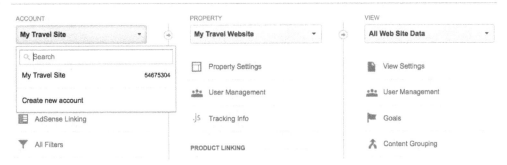

Select **Create new account** from the menu choices. This will take you to the "Account Creation" page. The steps you follow to create a new account and property are the same as those you followed to set up your initial account and property. See if you can complete this process on your own (using the parameters shown below). When you are

done and subsequently return to your start page (by pressing the **Home** icon on the top of the page), you should see the figure shown opposite. Remember, if nothing appears below "Account 2" you can click on the folder icon to reveal the property and view.

> ✅ If **All Web Site Data** is not displayed, click on the file folder icon next to **My personal blog.**

If you are having trouble creating this new account and property, follow the directions below after you select **Create new account** from the **Account** pull-down menu.

1. You'll see the page where you let Google Analytics know the parameters for data collection. On the top of the page, the **Website** box is highlighted. Leave this box checked.

2. Scroll down (if necessary) to **Setting up your account**.

3. In the box beneath **Setting up your account,** type in the name that you want to use to identify your Google Analytics account. This box is labeled "Account Name." Name your account "Account 2."

4. Scroll down (if necessary) to **Setting up your property**. You'll recall that, a web property is the total set of pages on which your tracking code is installed. Every property has a unique ID that you will receive later in the registration process. Name your property "My personal blog".

5. Beneath the property name is a text box labeled "Website URL." This is the full URL path by which you access the home page of your site. For this exercise type in "www.chapter7.net".

6. Choose "Other" for **Industry category**.

7. Select the appropriate country and time zone from the next pair of pull-down menus.

8. Leave the four boxes on the bottom of the page checked.

9. Click **Get Tracking ID**.

10. **Accept** the terms of service. You should then see the **Success** notification.

If you've successfully followed these steps, you should see the figure shown on the middle of page 35 when you click on the **Home** link or icon, which is on the top of the page.

Add a second property to the account

The procedure for adding an additional property to an account is very similar to adding a new account. Let's add a second property to the "Account 2" account called "My personal website". As before, click on **Admin** to go to the administrator's page (if you are not already there). Make certain that "Account 2" is displayed in the account column (the left-hand column). If it is not displayed, then use the pull-down menu to select it.

Now, pull down the property name menu and select **Create new property**, as shown below.

See if you can create a new property named "My personal website" at URL www.account2a.net. If you are successful you should see the figure shown opposite when you return to your home page. Remember that you can see the view(s) associated with each property by clicking on the file folder icon next to the view name.

If you are having difficulty, follow the directions below after you have selected **Create new property**.

1. On the top of the page, the **Website** box is highlighted. Leave this as it is.

2. Scroll down (if necessary) to **Setting up your property**. Your website name is: "My personal website."

3. The website URL is: "www.account2a.net."

4. Choose "Other" for **Industry category**.

5. Select the appropriate country and time zone from the next pair of pull-down menus.

6. Click **Get Tracking ID**. You should then see the **Success** notification.

7. On the tracking code page, click on the **Home** link or icon on the top left-hand side of the page to return to your starting home page.

If you followed these steps successfully, you should see the figure shown opposite, which lists the two properties in your new account.

Rename an existing view

One view, "All Web Site Data", already exists for the property "My personal website" in "Account 2". Based on the prior example, try to rename this view to "View 1: Unfiltered".

If you are having difficulty, follow these steps:

1. Click on **Admin** to go to the administrator's page.

2. Use the pull-down menus to make certain that the account is "Account 2", the property is "My personal website", and the view is "All Web Site Data", as shown below.

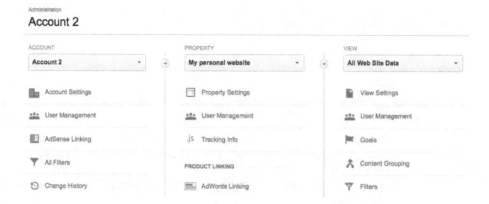

3. Click on **View Settings** in the right-most **View** column.

4. On the next page, in the **View Name** box, delete "All Web Site Data" and type "View 1: Unfiltered" as shown below.

5. Scroll to the bottom of the page and press **Save.** A message on the top of the page should indicate that the renaming process was a "Success."

6. Click on the **Home** link or icon on the top left side of the page to return to the main home page where you should see the account, property, and view shown opposite.

After the prior step, "My personal website" has one view. We now want to duplicate this view. The new view should be named "View 2: Filtered". See if you can use the **View Settings** on the **Admin** page link to accomplish this. If you are having difficulty, follow these steps:

1. From whatever page you are on, click on **Admin** to go to the administrator page.

2. Use the pull-down menus to make certain that the account is "Account 2", the property is "My personal website", and the view is "View 1: Unfiltered", as shown below.

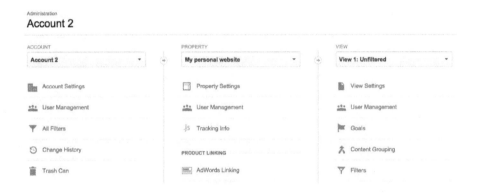

3. Click on **View Settings** in the right-most **View** column.

4. A new page will be displayed. On the top, right-hand side of the page, press **Copy view.**

5. On the top of the next page, delete the contents of the **New View Name** text box and then name the view "View 2: Filtered." Then press **Copy view.** A message on the top of the page should indicate that the duplication process was a "Success."

6. Click on the **Home** link or icon on the top left side of the page to return to the home page. If all has gone well you should see the figure opposite.

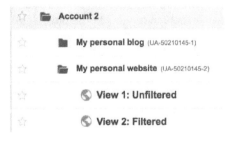

Two views now exist for the property "My personal website" in "Account 2". Based on the prior example, try to delete the view labeled "View 2: Filtered". If you are having difficulty, follow these steps.

1. From whatever page you are on, click on **Admin** to go to the administrator's page.

2. Use the pull-down menus to make certain that the account is "Account 2", the property is "My personal website", and the view is "View 2: Filtered", as shown below.

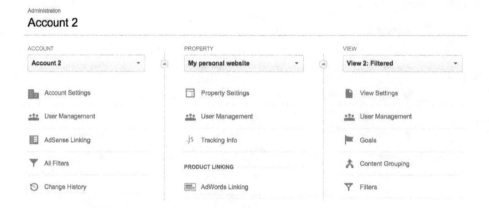

3. Click on **View Settings** in the right-most **View** column.

4. On the next page press **Move to Trash Can** (on the top, right-hand side of the page).

5. On the next page confirm that you want to delete this view by pressing **Trash View.**

6. Click on the **Home** link or icon on the top left side of the next page to return to your home page. If all has gone well, you should see the display shown opposite.

✅ The Trash Can is a temporary holding area for accounts, properties, and views before they are deleted. Account, properties, and views moved to the Trash Can are held for 35 days before they are permanently deleted. After 35 days in the Trash Can, an entity is permanently deleted.

Let's create an entirely new view that will have the following characteristics: the account is "Account 2", the property is "My personal website", and the view name is "New View". See if you can use the **View Settings** link on the **Admin** page to accomplish this. If you are having difficulty, follow these steps:

1. From whatever page you are on, click on **Admin** to go to the administrator's page.

2. Use the pull-down menus to make certain that the account is "Account 2", the property is "My personal website", and the view is "View 1: Unfiltered".

3. Use the pull-down menu in the **View** column to display **Create new view**, as shown below. Click on this link.

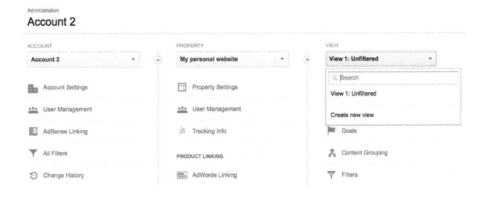

4. On the next page, leave **Website** highlighted.

5. Beneath **Setting up your view** is a text box labeled "Reporting View Name." Type "New View" into this box. Then, confirm the country and time zone.

6. Click **Create view** on the bottom of the page. You will then be informed that the process has been a "Success." You should then see the new view name listed in the **View** column.

7. Click on the **Home** link or icon on the top left side of the page to return to the start page. If all has gone well you should see the view listed in the appropriate property.

Delete an existing property

You delete a property similarly to the way you delete a view. See if you can apply what you learned earlier about deleting a view to deleting the "My personal blog" property. If you are having trouble, just follow the steps beginning on page 42.

1. From whatever page you are on, click on **Admin**.

2. Use the pull-down menus to make certain that the account is "Account 2" and the Property is "My personal blog". There is only one view associated with this property: "All Website Data".

3. Click on **Property Settings** in the middle **Property** column.

4. On the top, right-hand side of the next page select **Move to Trash Can.**

5. On the next page, confirm that you want to delete this property.

6. You'll then see the page shown below. Note that the display has defaulted to our remaining property.

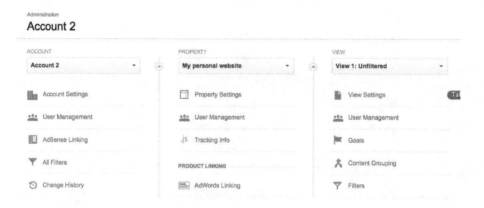

Delete an existing account

Finally, let's work through the steps required to delete the account you created earlier in this chapter.

You delete an account the same way you delete a view. If we wanted to delete the "Account2" account, we would do the following:

1. From whatever page you are on, click on **Admin** to go to the administrator's page.

2. Use the pull-down menus to make certain that the Account is "Account 2," as shown on the top of page 43.

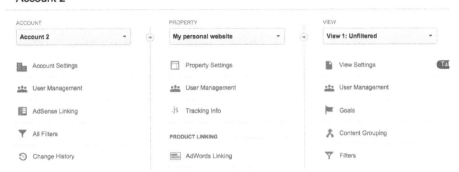

ACCOUNT	PROPERTY	VIEW
Account 2 ▾	My personal website ▾	View 1: Unfiltered ▾
Account Settings	Property Settings	View Settings
User Management	User Management	User Management
AdSense Linking	.js Tracking Info	Goals
All Filters	**PRODUCT LINKING**	Content Grouping
Change History	AdWords Linking	Filters

3. In the Account column, click on the top link, **Account Settings**.

4. When the next page is displayed, press **Move to Trash Can.**

5. On the next page confirm that you want to delete this account.

6. Click on the **Home** icon to return to your home page.

8

Permissions

As the administrator of your account(s), you have complete and unrestricted access to all account functions. You can create and delete accounts, properties, and views and can determine what data is made available within various reports and views. You can also manage the format in which data appears.

In large companies, it is often necessary to share access to a Google Analytics account, property or view with others at the company. However, it is dangerous to allow everyone with access to manipulate account settings and property/view data. As a result, Google Analytics allows you to assign an individual the appropriately restricted level of access and interaction. Every individual you want to add must have a Google ID such as a Google email address.

Your first decision is to determine at what level you want to grant access. You can grant someone access at the account, property or view level. As you think about access levels, keep in mind that Google Analytics uses hierarchies to determine ultimate level of access. An individual given access at the account level, for example, has the potential for access to all properties and views within that account. Similarly, an individual with property level access will have access to all views within that property. Finally, an individual with view access will have access only to that single view. As a general rule, you want to assign the lowest level of access that will allow the desired level of viewing and interaction.

There are three levels of permission access, which from highest to lowest are:

- **Edit**: Individuals with this level of access can perform administrative and report-related functions (e.g., add/edit/delete accounts, properties, views, filters, goals, etc., but not manage users) and see report data. These individuals also have the ability to engage in all the behaviors listed under **Collaborate** and **Read & Analyze**.

- **Collaborate**: Individuals with this level of access can create personal assets and share them. (*Assets* are tools that you create and use in Google Analytics to help you customize data analysis.) Individuals can also collaborate on shared assets, for example, edit a dashboard or annotation. These individuals also have the ability to engage in all the behaviors listed under **Read & Analyze**.

- **Read & Analyze**: Individuals with this level of access can see report and configuration data; can manipulate data within reports (e.g., filter a table, add a secondary dimension, create a segment); can create personal assets and share them; and can see shared assets. Individuals with this lowest level of access cannot collaborate on shared assets or perform any data editing.

Independent of level of access, you must also decide whether or not an individual will be allowed to **Manage Other Users**. An individual with this permission can add or delete others at different levels of access and can assign permission to edit, collaborate, or read and analyze. This individual can even delete you from the account - so be very careful to whom you give this permission.

Assigning permissions

You assign permissions via the administrator's page, which you access by clicking **Admin** on the bottom of any page (after you have logged into your Analytics account). Make certain that you have the desired account, property and view showing in the pull-down menus.

As shown below, all three columns on this page display an option for assigning permissions. Select **User Management** (the second link in each column) in the Account column if you want to assign permission at the account level. Select **User Management** in the Property column if you want to assign permission at the property level. Select **User Management** in the View column if you want to assign permission for just one specific view. All **User Management** additions, changes and deletions follow the same procedure regardless of the level selected.

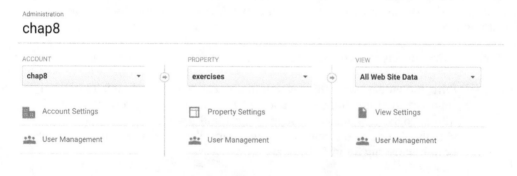

Creating permissions at the account level

Let's add a new user with permissions at the account level.

First, we need to make certain that the desired account is the currently active account. We do this by checking the information in the upper left-hand corner of the display.

Clicking on **User Management** at the account level, that is, the second link in the far left-hand column on the administrator's page, takes us to the user management interface shown below where a list of all those with permissions is displayed. At the moment I am the only individual with permission to access this account. My name, email address and permission level are all displayed.

Now we'll add a new user to the account by clicking on the "+" sign in the upper right hand corner of the display. This brings up the overlay shown below.

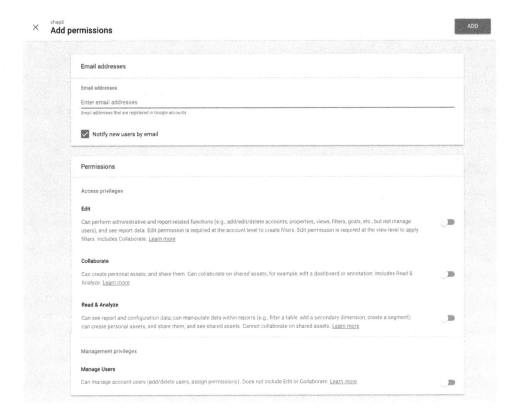

The top of the form allows us to enter the individual's email address which in this case is "joeljay1050@gmail. com." Next, we'll use the slider bars to assign privileges. This new user will have permission at the **Edit** level, which includes **Collaborate** and **Read & Analyze**. Keep in mind that since we are setting permissions at the account level, this new individual will have Edit permissions for all properties and views within this account. (In other words, assigning permission at a higher level automatically grants permission at all lower levels.) Finally, we will not give this person permission to Manage Users, so this slider bar is not activated.

After all the appropriate information is entered we finish the process by clicking **Add** on the top of the display. We then see that the new user is now listed along with the level of permission (see below).

We can now click on the **"X"** on the top of the page to return to the administrator's page.

The permissions hierarchy

We follow the exact same steps to add a new user with permission at the property level. We'll add user permissionschapter9@gmail.com. When done, note how all the appropriate permissions are displayed, except now we are on the property level as opposed to the account level.

After this individual is added to permissions, we can return to the main administrator's page. There, when we select **User Management** from the Account options we see a different permissions page, as shown below.

Notice how the new user lacks permission at the account level (as indicated by **"None"** being displayed beneath "Permissions"). Clicking on the individual's line in the listing brings up a display that details the permissions relevant to this individual.

Confirming permissions

We've discussed how granting permission at the account level grants permission to all associated properties and views. We can confirm this outcome by clicking on the information icon on the right-hand side of an individual's listing. (The information icon is the small circle with an "i".) This brings up a display where you can see all of the permissions granted to the individual (see below).

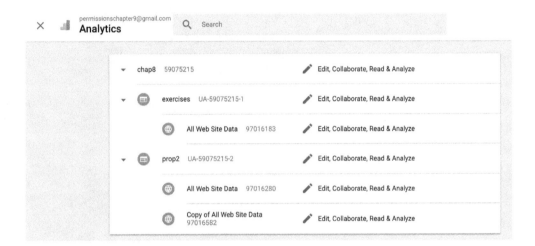

Modifying permissions

We can change the level of permission for any individual by clicking on the individual's listing and then modifying the slider bars (as described earlier).

We can delete a user by clicking on the three dots at the far right-hand side of an individual's listing. This bring up the option to "Remove Access." Clicking here brings up the overlay shown on page 50 where you can confirm the deletion.

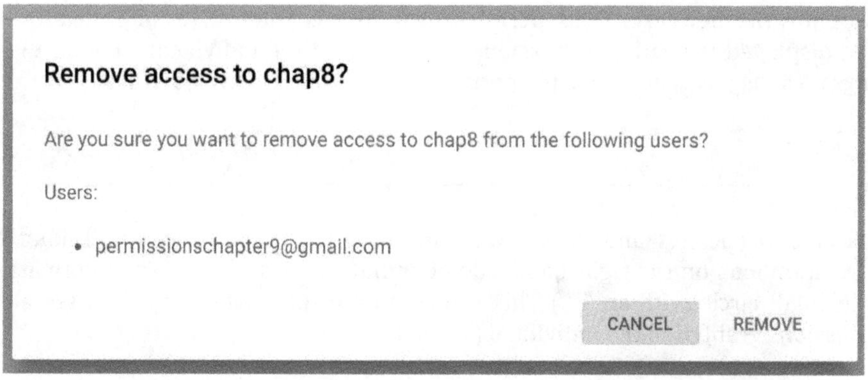

Remove access to chap8?

Are you sure you want to remove access to chap8 from the following users?

Users:

- permissionschapter9@gmail.com

CANCEL   REMOVE

Section III:
Predefined and Custom Filters

Google Analytics filters allow you to specify the types of data included in the different views associated with a particular property. Filters accomplish this by restricting the data available within the view to which they are applied. A view with no filter presents all data collected for a property, while a view with one or more filters presents only a subset of the data. In this case, the specific characteristics of the data are defined by the characteristics of the filter(s) applied. Filters provide a powerful way to reduce the effort required to examine important segments of data and, as a consequence, they make an important contribution to strategic decision-making.

- Chapter 9 discusses predefined filters: a small but powerful set of filters that Google Analytics has made available to reduce the effort in filter creation.

- Chapter 10 discusses regular expressions: the syntax used to move you beyond predefined filters to the creation of more flexible, extensive, and complex filters.

- Chapter 11 provides direction for the use of custom filters.

- Chapter 12 discusses the application of filters to a significant website problem: referral spam. Here, we present procedures to reduce/eliminate data that can significantly distort your interpretation of key data trends and outcomes.

Views With Predefined Filters

Every time you create a new property, Google Analytics creates an unedited (unfiltered) view of the data. Unless you rename it, this view is called **All Web Site Data**. By now, you should know how to rename and perform additional manipulations to this and other views as well as how to add additional views to a property.

The views you've dealt with so far have been unfiltered. This means that all of the data collected by Google Analytics is present in the view. There are circumstances, however, where you will only want to view important subsets of the total data file. Here, you can create any number of additional views to assist in strategic decision-making and site evaluation/revision. Pages 31-32, for example, provide a description of the four views every website should have. Beyond these views, you might set up one view that only reports visitors from organic search and another view that only reports data from individuals referred to your site through your Wordpress blog.

The use and effect of filters in the creation of views is illustrated below. Imagine that you currently have one view: an unfiltered view that includes all website visitors. Now you want to easily see the behaviors of site visitors who come to the site via a social platform such as YouTube or Facebook. You name this view "Social". Google Analytics monitors all of your website visitors and places their data in the unrestricted view. However, you can also apply a "Social Referral" filter to all the data coming into Google Analytics so that the "Social" view will only contain data generated by the individuals of interest; in this case, those that arrive via a social platform.

All website visitors from different referral sources

Social Referral Filter

Only website visitors from a social referral

Appear in "Unrestricted" view

Appear in "Social" view

As you can see, you restrict the data displayed in a view by applying one or more filters, which can either be predefined or custom.

It is important to remember that any filter you apply to a view begins on the day the filter was applied and continues until the filter is removed. Google Analytics does not apply filters to historical data, nor does it remove filter effects should the filter later be removed.

Filter options are near limitless, so it is recommended that any filtered view of your data have a clear strategic grounding. You might, for example, want to create a view that allows an individual to see only a subset of the total data set. Or, you might create views to reflect users behaviors such a visits to a specific subdomain, subdirectory, portions of the website or even specific pages.

This chapter and the next focus on predefined filters. This is followed in Chapters 11 to 12 by a discussion of regular expressions and custom filters.

What are predefined filters?

Predefined filters are Google's attempt to simplify your life. A predefined filter consists of three parts:

- The decision whether to *include* or *exclude* specified data.

- The *source* of the included/excluded data. Sources can be traffic from a specific ISP domain; from a specific IP address; to a specific hostname; or to a specific sub-directory.

- How the *source* of the data is to be *identified*. Here, the options are: equal to, begins with, ends with, and contains.

These characteristics work together to permit you to create a view that precisely defines a restricted data set, for example:

- You find that your Google Analytics data make little sense, in great part because the data include all of the behaviors of those in your company who visit the website through their computers while at work. You can create a view, which collects and reports data on all website visitors *except* those who come to the site through the company's IP address.

- Imagine that you create a YouTube channel as a means of (hopefully) driving traffic to your website. While you want the data generated by those referred by YouTube to be included in the total data set, you also want to examine the behaviors of these individuals independently. You can accomplish this by creating a view that includes only those individuals who come from a domain containing "youtube.com".

- You have a subdirectory on your site named "/historical archives" for which you want to examine traffic and other behaviors independent of other site data. You can accomplish this by creating a view, which only includes data generated by traffic to the subdirectory.

Creating a filtered view of your data using predefined filters is a straightforward process that should begin only after you identify a strategic rationale for creating the view.

Let's work though each of the prior examples to see how predefined views are created. But first, if you want to follow the outlined steps, you'll need to create a new account, property and view, as follows:

Account name: **Account 2**

Property name: **My personal website**

View name: Rename default to **View 1: Unfiltered**

Website: www.chapter11.org

Refer to Chapter 7 if you are unsure how to do this.

Eliminate data whose source is the company IP address

This case illustrates a situation where you find that your Google Analytics data make little sense, in great part because the data include the behaviors of those in your company who visit the website though their computers while at work. As a result, you want to filter out traffic from your company IP address from all views except the master file, which is labeled **View 1: Unfiltered.** This is a two-step process where we first create the new view and then apply the filter to the view.

We begin by creating a new view, which we'll label **View 2: Company IP Excluded**. Similar to the examples discussed earlier, we create a new view through these steps:

1. Sign into Google Analytics with the email associated with your travel website. Once you have access, click on **Admin** to go to the administrator's page.

2. Use the pull-down menus to make certain that the account is "Account 2", the property is "My personal website", and the view is "View 1: Unfiltered" (as shown below). Next, use the pull-down the menu in the View column to select **Create new view**.

3. On the next page, leave **Website** highlighted.

4. In the text box labeled **Reporting View Name**, type in "View 2: Company IP Excluded", as shown below.

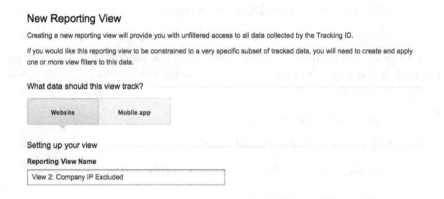

5. Use the pull-down menus on the bottom of the page to indicate country and time zone.

6. Press **Create view.** You should be informed that the view creation was a "Success."

7. Click on the **Home** link or icon on the top left side of the page to return to your home page. If all has gone well you should see the figure opposite.

Next, we need to add a predefined filter to this view to inform Google Analytics that when reporting data in this view, it should ignore all individuals who arrive at our site through the company IP address. We accomplish this as follows.

1. From whatever page you are on, click on **Admin** to go to the administrator's page.

2. Use the pull-down menus to make certain that the account is "Account2", the property is "My personal website", and the view is "View 2: Company IP Excluded".

3. Click on **Filters** in the right-most **VIEW** column. The next screen lists all of the filters currently associated with view (if any) and is the starting point for the creation of new filters for the selected view.

4. On the next page, click on **+Add Filter**.

5. On the top of the next page select **Create new Filter**.

6. Let's name this filter "Company IP Excluded". Type this name into the text box labeled **Filter Name**.

7. We'll use a predefined filter. Select this option.

8. Use the three drop down menus to select: **Exclude, traffic from the IP addresses,** and **that begin with.** Type "46.249.223" in the **IP address** box. These three numbers represent the beginning of the IP address assigned to our company. (We're assuming that our company is the exclusive user of this IP address.)[17]

9. When you are done, and your screen looks like that shown below, press **Save**.

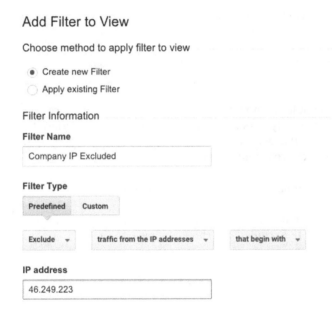

If you were successful, the confirmation page shown on the top of page 58 will appear. This page should list the filter you just created.

Whenever you select this view, you will see data generated by all those who came to your site **except** for those visiting the site through the company's network as specified by the IP address.

---

[17] You'll follow this same procedure for you own digital property. Simply substitute your company's IP address for the example IP address used in Step 8.

Rank	▾	Filter Name	Filter Type	
1		Company IP Excluded	Exclude	remove

+ ADD FILTER   🔍 Search

Filtering for YouTube referrals

Now let's set up a filtered view that reports the behaviors only of those users who arrive at the site via a YouTube referral, keeping in mind that we also want to simultaneously filter out individuals arriving through our company IP address. As a result, we need to apply two filters to this view.

Similar to the previous example, our first task is to create a new view, which we'll label "YouTube Referrals/Company IP Excluded." The steps are:

1. From whatever page you are on, click on **Admin** to go to the administrator's page.

2. Use the pull-down menus to make certain that the Account is "Account 2", the Property is "My personal website", and the View is "View 1: Unfiltered". Next, as you did in the last example, use the pull-down the menu in the View column and then select **Create new view**.

3. On the next page, leave **Website** highlighted.

4. In the text box labeled **Reporting View Name**, type in "YouTube Referral/ Company IP Excluded", as shown below.

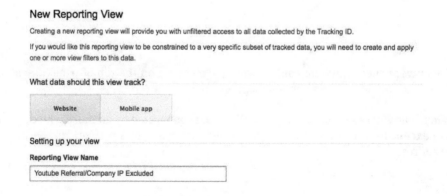

5. Use the pull-down menus on the bottom of the page to indicate country and time zone.

6. Press **Create view.** You should be informed that view creation was successful.

7. The next page displayed is your administrator's page. Your new view should be displayed in the View column, as shown below.

Now we need to add two predefined filters to this view to inform Google Analytics that when reporting data in this view, the data display should *include* only those individuals who arrive at our site through a YouTube referral but simultaneously *exclude* from this display any who are connected to the internet via our company IP address.

Since we have already created a company IP filter, we can apply that filter to this view rather than creating this filter from scratch. This process is as follows:

1. Access the Administrator's Page to make certain that the **YouTube Referral/ Company IP Excluded** view is displayed, as shown above.

2. In the View column, click on **Filters**.

3. On the next page, click on **+Add Filter**.

4. On the next page, click on **Apply Existing Filter**.

5. On the next page, in the box labeled **Available Filters,** highlight **Company IP Excluded**. Press **Add** to place this filter in the **Selected Filters** column. Press **Save**. You'll then see the Company IP filter added to this view, as shown below.

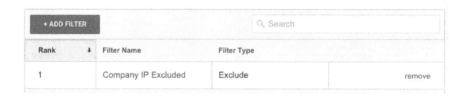

A second predefined filter can now be added to this view to *include* only those individuals who were sent to our site via youtube.com. The steps to follow are:

1. Click on **Admin** to go to the administrator's page.

2. Use the pull-down menus to make certain that the account is "Account 2," the property is "My personal website," and the view is "YouTube Referral/Company IP Excluded."

3. Click on **Filters** in the right-most **VIEW** column.

4. On the next page, click on **+Add Filter**.

5. On the top of the next page, choose **Create New Filter**.

6. Select predefined filter. Use the text box to name this filter "YouTube Only".

7. Use the three drop-down menus to select: **Include only, traffic from the ISP domain,** and **that contain**. Type "youtube.com" in the **ISP Domain** text box and leave **Case Sensitive** unchecked (see below).

(Note that Google Analytics allows you to verify some types of predefined filters. This filter is one that can be verified. The verification process is described in the Addendum to this chapter.)

8. When you are done and your screen looks like the one above, press **Save**. Your confirmation page should resemble that shown below, noting that both filters have been applied to the view.

In the prior example, the view's filtering procedures would first eliminate those individuals coming to the site through the company IP address and then, for those remaining, select (include) only those who were referred by YouTube. In this particular case, order does not matter but you should always be sensitive to order effects.

When you have multiple filters associated with a view, the filter application order is set by first selecting **Filters** from the Admin View column and then selecting **Assign Filter Order**. The next page displayed allows you to move filter application either up or down in the sequence.

We address filter order in more detail when we discuss custom filters in Chapter 11.

Examine behaviors specific to a subdirectory

Imagine that you have a subdirectory on your site named "/Historic archives" for which you want to examine traffic and other behaviors independent of other site data. You can accomplish this by creating a view that only includes metrics associated with traffic within this subdirectory. Let's create this view, again filtering out all individuals who came to the site via the company IP address.

Similar to the prior example, our first task is to create a new view, which we'll label "Historic Archives/Company IP Excluded." The steps are:

1. From whatever page you are on, click on **Admin** to go to the administrator's page.

2. Use the pull-down menus to make certain that the Account is "Account 2", the Property is "My personal website", and the View is "View 1: Unfiltered". Next, similar to what you did in the last example, pull-down the menu in the View column and then select **Create new view**.

3. On the next page, leave **Website** highlighted.

4. In the text box labeled **Reporting View Name**, type in "Historic Archives/Company IP Excluded", as shown on the top of page 62.

New Reporting View

Creating a new reporting view will provide you with unfiltered access to all data collected by the Tracking ID.

If you would like this reporting view to be constrained to a very specific subset of tracked data, you will need to create and apply one or more view filters to this data.

What data should this view track?

Setting up your view

Reporting View Name

Historic Archives/Company IP Excluded

5. Use the pull-down menus to indicate the correct country and time zone.

6. Press **Create view.**

7. The next page displayed is your administrator's page. Your new view should be displayed in the **View** column, as shown below.

Next we need to add two predefined filters to this view to inform Google Analytics that when reporting data in this view, the report should *include* only traffic to the targeted subdirectory but simultaneously *exclude* from this report any who are connected to the Internet via our company IP address.

Since we have already created a company IP filter, we can apply that filter to this view rather than creating this filter anew from scratch. The process is as follows:

1. Access the Administrator's Page to make certain that the **Historic Archives/ Company IP Excluded** view is displayed, as shown above.

2. In the View column, click on **Filters**.

3. On the next page, click on **+Add Filter**.

4. On the next page, click on **Apply Existing Filter**.

5. On the next page, in the box labeled **Available Filters,** highlight **Company IP Excluded**. Press **Add** to place this filter in the **Selected Filters** column. Press **Save**. You'll then see the Company IP filter added to this view, as shown on the top of page 63.

A second predefined filter can now be added to this view to *include* only those individuals who visited the "/Historic archives/" subdirectory. The steps to follow are:

1. From whatever page you are on, click on **Admin**.

2. Use the pull-down menus to make certain that the account is "Account2", the property is "My personal website", and the view is "Historic Archives/Company IP Excluded".

3. Click on **Filters** in the right-most **VIEW** column.

4. On the next page, click on **+Add Filter**.

5. On the top of the next page, choose **Create New Filter**.

6. Let's name this filter "Historic Archives".

7. We'll use a predefined filter. Click on this option.

8. Use the three drop down menus to select: **Include only, traffic to the sub-directories, which begin with**. Type "/Historic archives" in the **Subdirectory** text box. Leave **Case Sensitive** unchecked (see below).

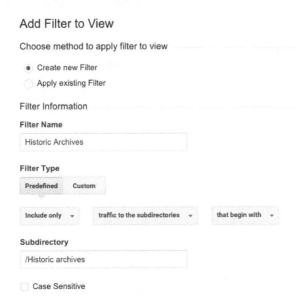

9. When you are done and your screen looks like the one on page 63, press **Save**. Your confirmation page should resemble that shown below.

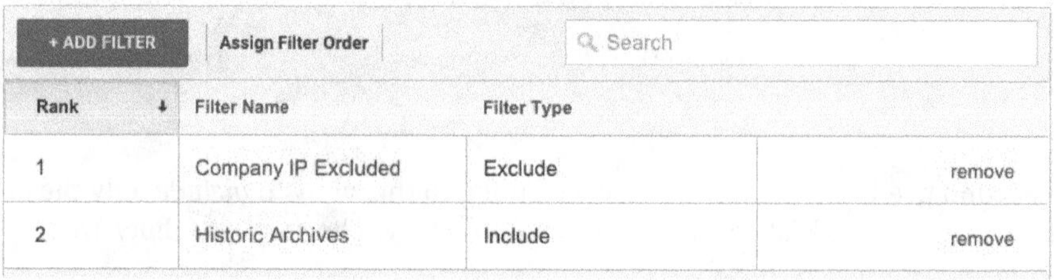

+ ADD FILTER	Assign Filter Order		Q Search	
Rank ↓	Filter Name	Filter Type		
1	Company IP Excluded	Exclude		remove
2	Historic Archives	Include		remove

Chapter Addendum: Filter Verification

Filters provide a powerful way to manage the data communicated in any particular view. The ultimate integrity of the data displayed, however, is directly related to the accuracy of any applied filter(s). Fortunately, Google Analytics provides a way to verify a filter prior to its implementation. This increases the probability that the data you *think* you are examining is actually the data you *are* examining.

Filter verification examines data from the preceding seven days in the selected view and then determines how the data would have been modified had the filter been in place at the start of the period. Unfortunately, this verification process has several limitations.

-   Filter verification uses a calculated sample of your full data set. Because of this, the results of the verification process may not be accurate or there may not be enough available data for examination. The latter case may cause you to receive a verification "error" even though the filter is configured properly.

-   Google's privacy policy prohibits the verification of any filters using Geo-based metrics, for example, Country and IP address.

-   Verification will not work (i.e., will return an "error") when placed on a newly created view that has not yet begun to collect data.[18]

The verification procedure is the same for predefined and custom filters (which are discussed in Chapter 11.) Let's see how verification works for both Include and Exclude filters using this scenario:

> Imagine that I have created a special section of my site with travel offers not available to the general public. All of the special offers are within the /specialsale subdirectory of the site, which individuals can only enter with a special code that was sent via email. I want to

---

[18] It is for this reason that we recommend maintaining an "experimental" view against which planned filters, etc. can be tested (see page 32). The procedure would be to create and verify the filter using the data in the experimental view and then, if all works as planned, the test filter will be cancelled and then recreated and applied against the desired view.

examine the metrics associated with traffic to this subdirectory in isolation of other site-related analytics *and* I do not want this data combined with data generated by traffic outside of this subdirectory. As a result, I need two different views with filters. One view will present the data only from traffic to the /specialsale directory (this would be an Include filter), while a second view would present my website data without incorporating data from traffic to the /specialsale directory (this would be an Exclude filter).

Verifying Include Filters

We first create the appropriate Include filter (see below). The application of this filter allows us to view analytics metrics only for traffic to the /specialsale directory.

Add Filter to View

Choose method to apply filter to view

- ● Create new Filter
- ○ Apply existing Filter

Filter Information

Filter Name

Visit Specialsale

Filter Type

| Predefined | Custom |

| Include only ▾ | traffic to the subdirectories ▾ | that contain ▾ |

Subdirectory

/specialsale

☐ Case Sensitive

Filter Verification ?

Verify this filter   See how this filter would affect the current view's data, based on traffic from the previous 7 days.

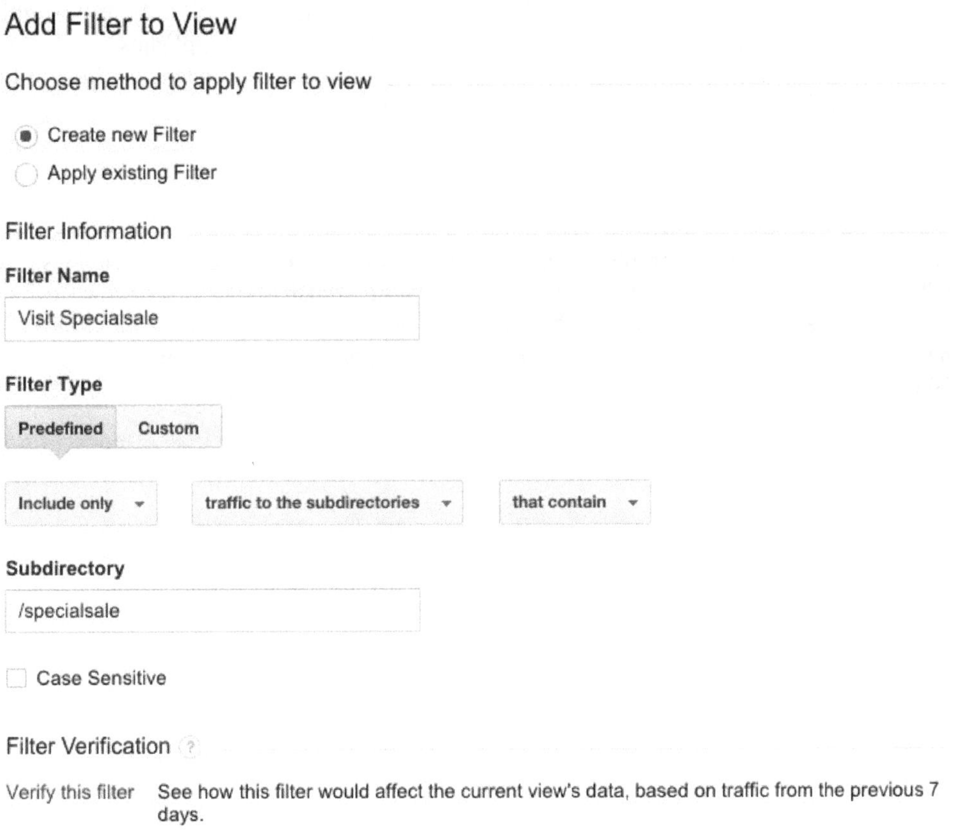

We click on the **Verify this filter** link after the filter's characteristics have been defined. This results (for my data) in the display shown on the top of page 66.

Before filter applied				After filter applied			
Page	Sessions	Pageviews	Screen Views	Page	Sessions	Pageviews	Screen Views
/xqanqeon/	21	28	0	/xqanqeon/specialsale/inf...	10	15	0
/xqanqeon/contact.html	1	12	0				
/xqanqeon/purchase.html	3	9	0				
/xqanqeon/specialsale/inf...	10	15	0				

The left-hand side of the table shows the records that would be affected prior to the filter taking effect. Notice that the last row on the left-hand side contains the target subdirectory. The records on the right-hand side display the data that would be reported by the view after the filter is applied. As you can see, the filter accomplishes our Include goal as only traffic to the /specialsale directory is included in the view's "After filter applied" data set.

Verifying Exclude Filters

Similar to the previous example, we first create the appropriate Exclude filter. This filter will allow the view to present analytics metrics for all website traffic *except* for traffic to the /specialsale directory. The filter looks just like the preceding example, only here we've changed the filter's name and the filter parameter from Include to Exclude (see below).

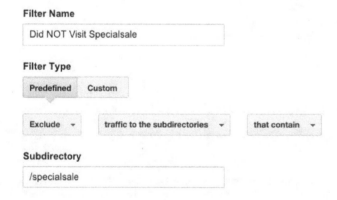

Next, we click on the **Verify this filter** link. The table shown on the top of page 67 is displayed.

Before filter applied				After filter applied			
Page	Sessions	Pageviews	Screen Views	Page	Sessions	Pageviews	Screen Views
/xqanqeon/specialsale/inf…	10	15	0				

The left-hand side of the table shows the records that would be affected prior to the filter taking effect. The presence of the /specialsale directory in this column indicates that the filter has targeted the proper data set. The records on the right-hand side display the data that would be reported by the view after the filter is applied. As you can see, this section is blank, indicating that the filter is working by eliminating metrics associated with traffic to the /specialsale directory.

10
Regular Expressions

Chapter 9 described predefined filters, an easy and powerful way to filter data within a property's view. Custom filters are even more flexible and powerful, but this flexibility and power comes with a cost: increased complexity.

Custom filters are more complex because they typically rely on the use of *regular expressions* (also known as regex) to communicate the filter's desired characteristics. A regular expression is a pattern of letters and/or numbers and/or special characters, which are applied to one or more pieces of data collected on your behalf by Google Analytics. If the pattern matches, the regular expression returns a "hit" or positive result.

The logic behind regular expressions is similar to that of a Google search. At its most basic level, you type in a word or phrase and the search engine returns "hits" that contain that word or phrase. A search for "yoghurt", for example, brings up the following, all of which contain the word "yoghurt":

Yogurt - Wikipedia, the free encyclopedia
en.wikipedia.org/wiki/Yogurt ▾
Yogurt or **yoghurt** or yoghourt (/ ˈjoʊɡərt/ or / ˈjɒɡərt/; from Turkish: yoğurt; other spellings listed below) is a fermented milk product (soy milk, nut milks such as ...
Lactobacillus delbrueckii - Frozen yogurt - Streptococcus thermophilus - Raita

Yoghurt - Simple English Wikipedia, the free encyclopedia
simple.wikipedia.org/wiki/**Yoghurt** ▾
Yogurt, or **yoghurt**, is a dairy product made by bacterial fermentation of milk. The lactose in the milk becomes lactic acid when it is fermented. Lactic acid acts on ...

News for **yoghurt**

Bill Granger recipe: Spiced salmon and spinach toasts with garlic **yoghurt**
The Independent - 5 days ago
Bursting with greens, protein and healthy oils, this will wipe away any traces of cocktails and leave your body a temple.

Regex expressions work in the same way, except there is more flexibility (and somewhat greater complexity) in how the search is defined. Within the context of Google Analytics, you will use regex expressions not to search the Internet, but rather to search and examine your data. Data that matches the regex expression are considered "hits" and are either included or excluded from a property's view depending upon your instructions.

This chapter focuses on the regex expressions you're most likely to use. The next chapter shows you how to apply these expressions when creating custom filters for Google Analytics views.

The regex expression "OR"

Most search engines allow you to use the word "or" as part of your search request. Thus, rather than doing multiple sequential searches (for example: guitar then violin, then viola), you do just one search using the "or" connector: guitar or violin or viola. The results of this latter search contain all the hits of guitar, violin or viola.

Regex doesn't use the word "or" but rather the pipe symbol: | . Thus, a regex search for "guitar", "violin" or "viola" would be: **guitar|violin|viola**. Note that there are no blank spaces.

Let's try this out. Visit the website Regex Pal at: `http://regexpal.com/`. Click on the **Original Regexpal** link on the top left-hand side of the page.

You'll see two boxes on the top of the page, where the smaller top box says **Regular Expression** and the box beneath says **Test String**. Begin by typing the following into the **Test String** box:

oboe
oboes
clarinet
harp
harps
mandolin
trumpet
harpist
harpsichord

Now we want to write a regex expression that will "hit" only the words "harp" or "oboe".

> ✅ Keep in mind that when using this site, a "hit" only occurs when the **entire** word is highlighted in the **Test String** box.

In the top **Regular Expression** box we type the regex expression: **harp|oboe**, which means "consider a hit positive when you find any sequence of letters which in its *entirety* is either 'harp' or 'oboe'." (You can ignore the other characters in this box.) When this is done, notice how harp and oboe, our two targets, are *fully* highlighted in the lower box. Importantly, these are the only words that are fully highlighted. This means our "or" regex expression worked.

The prior example also illustrates how the execution of any regex statement is quite literal. Since we have told it to look for "harp" or "oboe" then "harps", "harpist" and "harpsichord" are rightfully excluded from the list of hits. We can tell they are not considered a "hit" because they are not fully highlighted. Finally, there is no limit to the number of "or" commands that can appear in a single regex expression. If we change the prior regex to: **harp|oboe|trumpet** at Regex Pal, then all three terms would be fully highlighted.

Regex optional characters

Imagine that we still want to process items in the list provided in the previous section:

oboe
oboes
clarinet
harp
harps
mandolin
trumpet
harpist
harpsichord

However, now we not only want to "hit" oboe and harp but in addition we want to "hit" oboes and harps.

The less than ideal way to accomplish this would be to use a string of "or" statements, for example: **oboe|oboes|harp|harps**. While this would accomplish our goal, long strings of "or" statements become cumbersome and their length increases the potential for error. A shorter and more efficient way to identify these four words would be to use the regex quantifier indicated by a question mark: **?**

A **?** in a regular expression is translated to mean "the character or group of characters immediately preceding the **?** are optional - they may occur zero or one time in order for a hit to occur."

- The **?** can apply to just a single character. The regex expression **colou?r** will find both "color" (the u is found 0 times) and colour (where the u is found 1 time).

- The **?** can apply to a group of characters contained within a set of parentheses where the **?** follows the closing parenthesis. **Dec(ember)?** matches both Dec and December. Similarly, you can use multiple question marks in a single regex expression as in **Oct(ober)? 10(th)?** that matches Oct 10, October 10, Oct 10th, and October 10th.

Now let's apply this to our list where we apply the **?** to a single character. We begin with the "or" statement used in the prior section: **oboe|harp**. We then add the **s?** to the end of each word, which translates to mean "find the character string 'oboe', which may or may not end in an 's' or find the character string 'harp' which may or may not end in an 's'." Try this statement (**oboes?|harps?**) at Regex Pal to see that it fully hits (highlights) only the four target words of interest: oboe, oboes, harp, and harps.

As indicated earlier, the **?** can also be used to communicate that everything within a set of parentheses is optional. Consider the following list:

mother
father
grandmother
grandfather
great grandmother
great grandfather
step mother
step father

Let's work through the steps for using regex to identify all the items on the list. Here, it might be helpful to paste the above list into regex pal, typing in the sequence of regex statements discussed below.

A simple "or" statement will "hit" just mother and father:

mother|father

Next, we add the optional **(grand)?** to additionally "hit" grandmother and grandfather:

(grand)?(mother|father)

Note that because the addition of "grand" is marked as optional, mother and father alone are still considered a "hit."

Finally, we can add two additional optional elements to "hit" the four remaining items on the list. Any of the three approaches shown below will accomplish this.

(step)?(great)?(grand)?(mother|father)

((step)?|(great)?)(grand)?(mother|father)

(step |great)?(grand)?(mother|father)

Notice how in all three examples we added a space after "step" and "grand" to mirror the spaces shown on the list.

Think about the mathematical expression 10*(7+5). In the same way that this mathematical statement means 10*7 plus 10*5, the use of parentheses in regular expressions makes certain that the characters outside of the parentheses are applied equally and consistently to the characters inside the parentheses. When coupled with the | symbol, parentheses provide significant control over what terms are considered a "hit."

If, for example, we wanted to match alternative (mis)spellings of "pharmacy" we would use the regex expression **(ph|f|fh|)armacy**, which would match "pharmacy", "farmacy" and "fharmacy".

Finally, note that we can use an empty | in our list of matching options to indicate that the target string alone should be considered a hit. Imagine, for example, that we want to match "bicycle", "tricycle" and "cycle" but not "unicycle" or "motorcycle". The regex statement **.*cycle** would not work as this would match all of the terms. The statement **(bi|tri)cycle** would not work because it would hit "bicycle" and "tricycle" but not "cycle". The solution is **(bi|tri|)cycle** where we add a third empty "Or" option after "tri". This regex statement would be interpreted as: "a hit is considered to be 'bi' plus 'cycle' (i.e., bicycle), or a hit is considered to be 'tri' plus 'cycle' (i.e., tricycle), or a hit is considered to be nothing plus 'cycle' (i.e., cycle)." Just the three target terms are selected.

Regex wildcard characters

Imagine that we want to identify individuals who use specific search terms via our website's search engine. We could use an "or" statement, but this would require that we know in advance all of the possible terms a person could use and then string these terms together in one incredibly long regex "or" statement. There is a better way.

The **.*** combination of symbols in regex is translated to mean "find anything or nothing that appears in this position in any piece of data that we are searching." Let's try this at Regex Pal.

Begin by typing the following into the **Test String** box (making certain that the top box is empty):

autoharp
autoharps
harpsichord
harpsichords
harpist
harpists
harp
harps
vibraharp

Now we want to write a regex expression that "hits" all of these listed terms as they are all relevant to harps. So, in the top box (labeled **Regular Expression**) we type the regex expression **harp.*** which means "consider a hit positive when you find any string of letters that starts with 'harp' no matter what, if anything, is on the end of the word." When this is done, notice how all six words beginning with "harp" but with different endings, are fully highlighted in the **Test String** box. Pretty good, but not perfect. We need to expand our regex expression to include "consider a hit positive when you find any string of letters that contains 'harp' no matter what, if anything, is on the beginning or end of the word." We accomplish this by also adding the wildcard command **.*** to the beginning of our search term "harp", changing the regex statement in the **Regular Expression** box to **.*harp.***. Change your regex statement at Regex Pal. Notice how all the words in the list are now fully highlighted, indicating that we have "hit" all of the target terms.

Combining regex "OR" and wildcard expressions

Imagine that we are an ecommerce site, selling a wide range of merchandise. Two products - bicycles and tricycles - are important parts of our business. As a result, we want to create a view in which we can look at those who have visited our site and those who have used our site search engine to search for these products. We'll once again use Regex Pal to work through the logic of how this can be accomplished. Type the following list in the **Test String** box at Regex Tester. These are the search terms that we want to capture. (Note that there are some intentional misspellings as these might also appear as search terms.) Make certain that the **Regular Expression** box is empty.

bicycle
bicycles
bike
bikes
biking
motorbike
motorbikes
biker
tricycle
tricycles
bicyclist
bicyclists
bicycl
cycl
bikr
tricycl

First we have to look at the characteristics of the target terms. It appears that the words, even the misspelled ones, fall into two groups: those that refer to cycles and those that refer to bikes. As a result, we could create a regex statement that uses wildcards and "or" to locate target terms. The regex statement would be **.*cycle.*|.*bike.***. This would be interpreted to mean "consider a hit positive when you find any string of letters that contains 'cycle' no matter what, if anything, is on the beginning or end of the word **or** consider a hit positive when you find any string of letters that contains 'bike', no matter what, if anything, is on the beginning or end of the word." Type the regex statement **.*cycle.*|.*bike.*** in the **Regular Expression** box at Regex Pal and see which words are fully highlighted.

The **.*cycle.*|.*bike.*** statement found those words, which had "cycle" or "bike" fully spelled out, but it missed important terms without this full spelling, for example, bicyclist and biking. Our regex statement was too restrictive. We can make the statement less restrictive by reducing the required number of matches in the search terms, for example, we can change the original regex statement to **.*cycl.*|.*bik.*** by dropping the final "e" on the end of each word. This revised regex statement would be interpreted to mean "consider a hit positive when you find any string of letters that contains 'cycl', no matter what, if anything, is on the beginning or end of the word **or** consider a hit positive when you find any string of letters that contains 'bik', no matter what, if anything, is on the beginning or end of the word." Type the regex statement **.*cycl.*|.*bik.*** in the **Regular Expression** box at Regex Pal and see which words are fully highlighted. Note that now all target terms, including the misspelled ones, have been successfully found.

Literals: Escape characters

We've seen that regex statements use some common symbols (such as the period and asterisk) as instructions. The period in the **.*** command, for example, does not mean "end of sentence" but rather provides direction for how the data is to be examined. There are times, however, when you want a period or other symbol in a regex statement to be read literally, that is, in its everyday meaning. This might occur, for example, when want a regex statement to evaluate a URL that contains periods.

Imagine that we have a subdirectory on our site named `www.mysite.com/content`. Within this directory there are a number of subdirectories, for example:

`www.mysite.com/content/history`
`www.mysite.com/content/science`
`www.mysite.com/content/music`
`www.mysite.com/content/programming`

We want to identify all individuals who viewed any content, not caring about the specific subject matter of the content. We can begin with this regex statement:

www.mysite.com/content/.*

The end of the statement is intended to mean "find anything or nothing that comes at this point in the URL." Unfortunately, we can't consider this regex statement correct (nor would it work as we intended) because the periods earlier in the URL (between www and mysite, and between mysite and com) would be interpreted as a regex instruction and not part of the URL. Fortunately, there is an easy way to fix this. Whenever you want regex to interpret a restricted letter or symbol literally and not as a command, precede that character with a backward slash: \ . Thus, if we want to find all instances of content viewing at this URL, the regex instruction would need to have a \ before each period:

www\.mysite\.com/content/.*

We can test this regex statement at Regex Pal. First, type the prior regex statement into the **Regular Expression** box. Then type the following list in the **Test String** box:

www.mysite.com/control
www.mysite.com/content/history
www.mysite.com/content/math
www.mysite.com/history
www.mysite.com/math

Notice how our proposed regex statement matches only the URLs of interest.

Numeric and alphabetical spans

Imagine that our travel website uses the following approach to label the tour purchase confirmation page:

-    all confirmation pages begin with `thanks_p`

-    the number of tour days is indicated by a number (currently 2, 10 or 15)

-    the country is indicated by a letter (m for Mexico, b for Bahamas)

Thus the confirmation page `thanks_p2m` would indicate a two day tour to Mexico while `thanks_p15b` would indicate a fifteen day tour to the Bahamas. Six combinations are therefore available, as shown below:

thanks_p2m
thanks_p10m
thanks_p15m
thanks_p2b
thanks_p10b
thanks_p15b

We can use the regex commands discussed earlier in this chapter to accomplish the following:

Find any Mexico purchase:	**thanks_p(2|10|15)m**
Find any two day purchase:	**thanks_p2(m|b)**
Find any purchase:	**thanks_p(2|10|15)(m|b)**

The prior approaches work well because the number of days and countries are limited.

Imagine, though, that we can sell a tour consisting of any number of days between 2 and 59. It would be too time consuming to type every number between 2 and 59 in an "or" statement. Instead we can use brackets **[ ]** to indicate a span of numbers. The command **[2-9]**, for example, would indicate that we want to match any number between 2 and 9. Thus, if we wanted to identify all Mexican tours of between 2 and 9 days the regex statement would be: **thanks_p[2-9]m**.

We can count sequentially to higher numbers by using multiple brackets. We could, for example, count from 20 to 49 as follows: **[2-4][0-9]**. This would be interpreted to mean "start counting by combining 2 and 0 (which gives 20), keep going by combining 2 with the remaining numbers (21, 22, etc.), then do the same with 3 (30, 31, etc.) and finally do the same with 4 (40, 41, etc.)."

The prior worked because all of our target numbers had the same number of digits. When the digits in the target range have different numbers of digits, we need to separate our numeric spans with an "or" command, as shown below:

Count from 0 to 19	**[0-9]|1[0-9]**
Count from 0 to 119	**[0-9]|[1-9][0-9]|1[0-1][0-9]**

With this in mind, we can now identify all Mexican tour purchases regardless of the specific number of days between 2 and 59 , as follows: **thanks_p[2-9]|[1-5][0-9]m**.

Brackets can also be used to indicate a span of letters. The regex command **[a-h]**, for example, would match all letters between "a" and "h". Imagine that we sold tours to multiple locations using a single letter to indicate the country or region (i.e., b for Bahamas, c for Caribbean, d for Denmark, etc.) and that the letters used are between "c" and "w." Using regex letter spans, we can now identify all five day purchased tours, regardless of country, with the regex command **thanks_p5[c-w]**

Additional regex commands

The regex commands we've discussed so far should serve nearly all your needs. While there are a significant number of additional commands, those which might be useful in more specialized circumstances are shown.

[^]   A compliment box enables a single character not within a character list or range to be matched.

^   The caret anchor matches the beginning of the line.

$ The dollar anchor matches the end of the line.

The application of these commands to string search and evaluation is shown below.

[hc]at   *hat* and *cat* are positive matches

[^b]at   any three letter word ending in "at" except *bat* is a positive match

^[hc]at   *hat* and *cat* are positive matches but only at the beginning of a line

[hc]at$ *hat* and *cat* are positive matches but only at the end of a line

11

Views With Custom Filters

Chapter 9 demonstrated the contribution that predefined filters can make to data views and subsequent strategic decision-making. A predefined filter grounded by strategic information needs can provide the specific insights required for positive website revision and improvement. The restricted and predefined parameters of these filters make them very easy to use while maintaining significant power.

Custom filters provide greater flexibility and range of parameters versus predefined filters. However, along with this greater power comes a bit more difficulty in use. When using custom filters, you need to do all the configuration work. Thus, while the use of custom filters can be challenging, mastering their implementation provides significant advanced control over the data that appear in your views.

The greater range of options for custom filters is reflected in the custom filter form, shown below, after we select the **Custom** tab. Note how the number of options has expanded beyond just **Include** and **Exclude** configurations.

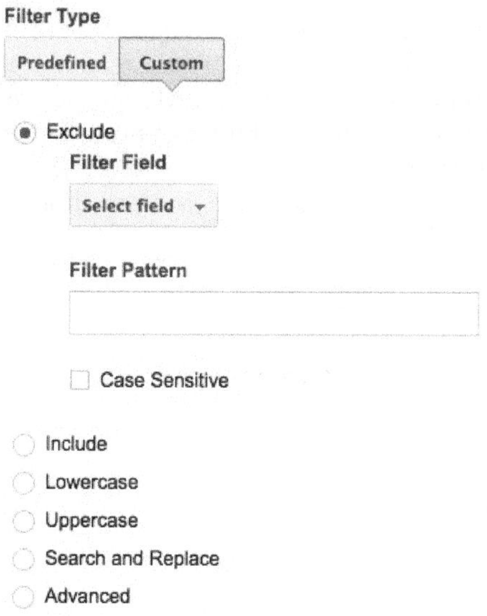

Filter Type

| Predefined | Custom |

◉ Exclude
Filter Field
Select field ▾

Filter Pattern

☐ Case Sensitive

○ Include
○ Lowercase
○ Uppercase
○ Search and Replace
○ Advanced

Let's take a closer look at each of the custom filter options.

The logic underlying 'include' and 'exclude' custom filters is the same as that for predefined filters. You use include and exclude parameters when you want to examine data views that reflect one or more characteristics or behaviors of the tracked visitor. As we saw in Chapter 10, predefined filters allow you to include or exclude based on one of four characteristics:

- traffic from the ISP domain

- traffic from the IP addresses

- traffic to the subdirectories

- traffic to the hostname

Custom filters greatly expand this list. For a complete listing and definitions of all include and exclude characteristics available for use in custom filters, see *Data Filters for Views: Custom Filter Fields* at:

https://support.google.com/analytics/answer/1034380

You begin the creation of custom filters in exactly the same way as predefined filters.

1. Click on **Admin** to go to the administrator's page.

2. Use the pull-down menus to make certain that your desired **Account**, **Property** and **View** are displayed. Remember, similar to predefined filters, the filters you create will be added to whatever view is displayed. So, if you do not want to apply a new custom filter to the current view, then either select a different view or create a new view before proceeding.

3. Click on **Filters** in the right-most **VIEW** column.

4. On the next page, click on **+Add Filter**.

5. Select **Create New Filter**.

6. Select **Custom Filter**.

Let's try some examples using Include and Exclude.

Case 1

Imagine that we have set up our website so that some content is free, while other premium content is available only for a fee. We want to look more closely at those individuals who pay for premium content in order to try to increase the proportion of site visitors who pay for access. We can create a view that includes only these individuals.

This view reflects an ecommerce transaction for which we have assigned the internal item code "99". To create a view with an associated filter that includes only the behaviors and characteristics of individuals with this ecommerce item code, we would (on the filter creation page):

- name the filter "Bought Content".

- check **Include**

- select "Ecommerce Item Code" from the **Filter Field** box[19]

- type "99" in the **Filter Pattern** box.

We leave **Case sensitive** unchecked and the custom filter is complete, as shown below.

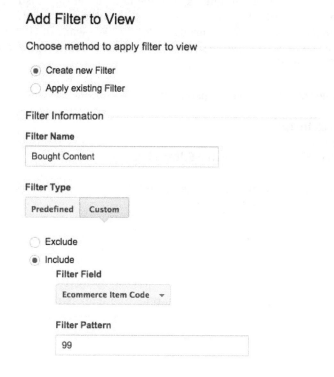

---

[19] The Filter Field pull-down menu has a search box on the very top of the menu. You can always use this function to find a particular metric rather than scrolling through all the Filter Field options.

We can then verify the filter, if desired. Finally, pressing the **Save** button saves our new filter and displays the confirmation page shown below. The filter has been added to the current view.

Case 2

Imagine that one of our site goals is to have visitors sign up for our newsletter. The sign-up page allows users to select "Sign-Up Now" or "Sign-Up Later". Those who select "Sign-Up Later" are taken to one of nine pages depending upon the reason selected for deferment. Each page is titled with the word "Defer" plus the numeric identifier for the reason, as in: "Defer1," "Defer2" through "Defer9". We want to create a view that combines all those who defer sign-up, ignoring the specific reason for deferment. We would create the filter as follows:

- name the filter "Defer Registration"

- check **Include**

- select "Page Title" from the **Filter Field** box

- use regex to identify the target page titles in the **Filter Pattern** box. In this case the regex is: **.*Defer[1-9]**

We leave **Case sensitive** unchecked and the custom filter is complete, as shown on the top of the page 83.

We can verify the filter, if desired. Finally, pressing the **Save** button saves our filter and then displays the filter creation confirmation. The filter has been added to the current view.

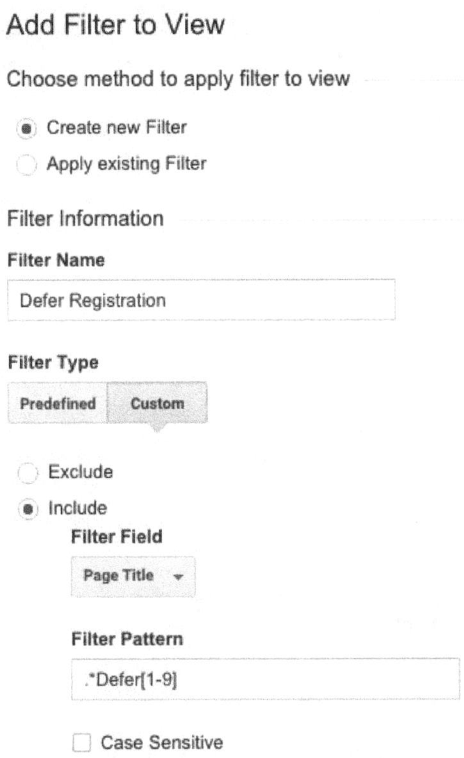

Add Filter to View

Choose method to apply filter to view

- ◉ Create new Filter
- ○ Apply existing Filter

Filter Information

Filter Name

Defer Registration

Filter Type

| Predefined | Custom |

- ○ Exclude
- ◉ Include

Filter Field

Page Title ▾

Filter Pattern

.*Defer[1-9]

☐ Case Sensitive

Case 3

Imagine that California is an important region for our sales efforts and, as a result, it is crucial that we understand the behaviors and characteristics of Californians who visit our website. We can create a view with an associated filter that includes only these individuals. On the filter creation page we would:

- name the filter "Californians"

- check **Include**

- select "Region" from the **Filter Field** box

- type "California" in the **Filter Pattern** box.

We leave **Case sensitive** unchecked and the custom filter is complete, as shown on the top of page 84.

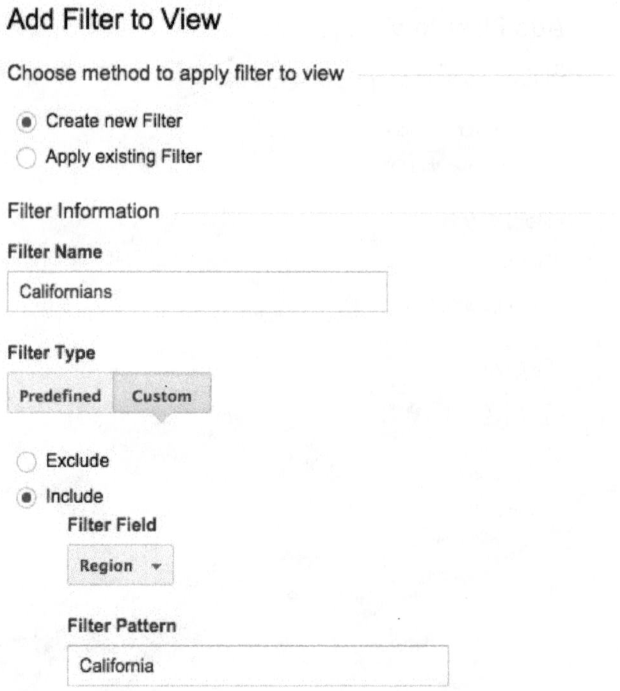

Add Filter to View

Choose method to apply filter to view

- (●) Create new Filter
- ( ) Apply existing Filter

Filter Information

Filter Name

Californians

Filter Type

Predefined	Custom

- ( ) Exclude
- (●) Include

    Filter Field

    | Region ▾ |

    Filter Pattern

    | California |

We can verify the filter, if desired. Finally, pressing the **Save** button saves your filter and then displays the filter creation confirmation. The filter has been added to the current view.

Case 4

Let's take Case 3 one step further. Imagine that instead of only being interested in Californians in the view, we are instead interested in looking at Californians and New Yorkers together in the **same** view. Thus, the view will consist of individuals who live in **either** California **or** New York. You might think that this could be accomplished by setting up two filters for the view, one filter that selects (includes) individuals who live in California and a second filter that selects individuals who live in New York. This won't work, however, because of the sequential way in which Google Analytics applies multiple filters to a single view.

Imagine that you take the dual filter approach in which the California filter is applied first, followed by the New York filter. The chart shown on the top of page 85 displays the last seven people who visited the website and where they live.

Person	Residence
1	California
2	New York
3	Maine
4	California
5	New York
6	Idaho
7	California

Applying the California filter first would eliminate persons 2, 3, 5, 6 as follows:

Person	Residence
1	California
~~2~~	~~New York~~
~~3~~	~~Maine~~
4	California
~~5~~	~~New York~~
~~6~~	~~Idaho~~
7	California

Unfortunately, this includes the two people from New York, whom we want to remain in the view. Reversing the order of the filters also doesn't work. As shown below, applying the New York filter first eliminates Californians 1, 4, and 7.

Person	Residence
~~1~~	~~California~~
2	New York
~~3~~	~~Maine~~
~~4~~	~~California~~
5	New York
~~6~~	~~Idaho~~
~~7~~	~~California~~

The solution to the problem lies in telling Google Analytics that you are want it to select either California or New York on the first (and only) pass through the data. As discussed in Chapter 10, this is accomplished by using the regex "or" symbol | as shown in the figure on the top of 86.

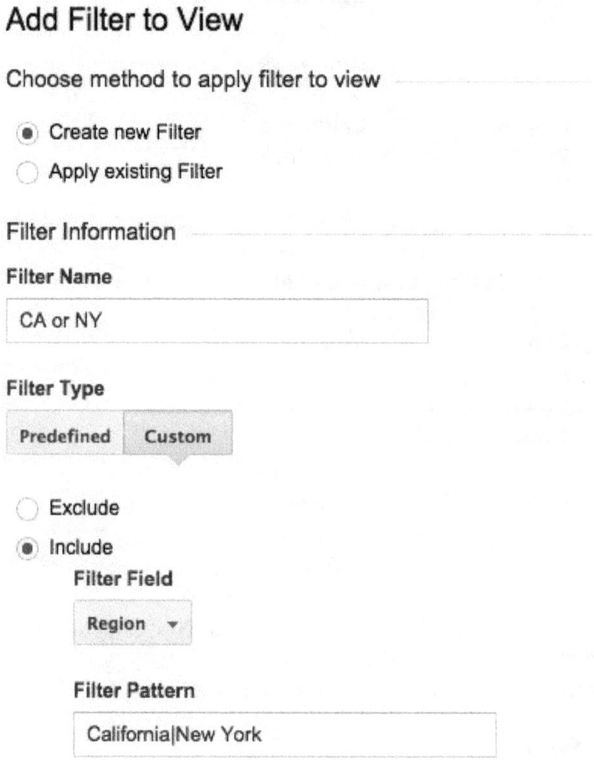

Add Filter to View

Choose method to apply filter to view

- (•) Create new Filter
- ( ) Apply existing Filter

Filter Information

Filter Name

> CA or NY

Filter Type

| Predefined | Custom |

- ( ) Exclude
- (•) Include

    Filter Field

    | Region ▾ |

    Filter Pattern

    > California|New York

We can verify the filter, if desired. Finally, pressing the **Save** button saves your filter and then displays the filter creation confirmation. The filter has been added to the current view.

Case 5

We've discussed the importance of filtering out the data generated by company employees before drawing insights from data collected by Google Analytics. We saw a simple example of how to do this using predefined filters. This situation is different, however, as our company uses a *range* of IP addresses and, as a result, we want to filter out all of the IP addresses used by the company. The company IP address range is 63.212.171.1 to 63.212.171.23.

To create a view that excludes the behaviors and characteristics of individuals accessing the web site through any of the company IP addresses we would:

-   name the filter "Company IP Filtered"

-   check "Exclude"

- select "IP Address" from the **Filter Field** box

- type the range of IP addresses in the **Filter Pattern** box.

In order to accomplish this last step, we need to use regex to define the range of IP addresses, which can be accomplished at the generator provided by Analytics Market at:

http://www.analyticsmarket.com/freetools/ipregex

When we type in the minimum and maximum values for our IP range, the generator returns this regex statement:

^63\.212\.171\.([1-9]|1[0-9]|2[0-3])$

This code is then copied and pasted in the **Filter Pattern** box.[20]

We leave **Case sensitive** unchecked and the custom filter is complete, as shown below.

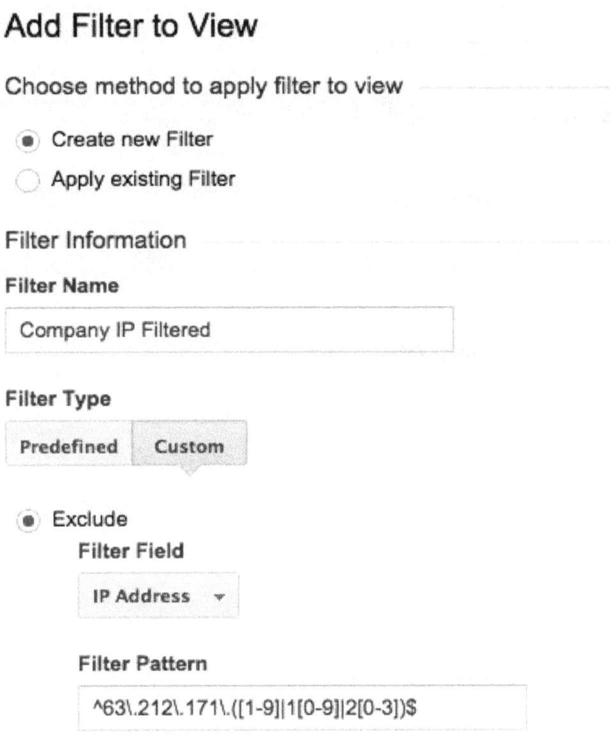

Add Filter to View

Choose method to apply filter to view

- ● Create new Filter
- ○ Apply existing Filter

Filter Information

Filter Name

```
Company IP Filtered
```

Filter Type

| Predefined | Custom |

- ● Exclude

    Filter Field

    IP Address ▾

    Filter Pattern

    ^63\.212\.171\.([1-9]|1[0-9]|2[0-3])$

---

[20] Note how the regex statement uses the \ to identify literal regex characters, in this case the period between each block of numbers.

Google's privacy policy prevents this filter from being verified. Pressing the **Save** button saves your filter and then displays the filter creation confirmation. The filter has been added to the current view.

Case 6

Earlier we discussed how we would form a regex statement to identify individuals who used a variety of terms in our internal search engine to search for bicycles and related items. Google Analytics' custom filters can help us identify those who used these terms on an external search engine (such as Google or Bing) prior to arriving at our site.

To create a view that includes the behaviors and characteristics of individuals who were referred to our site via the use of targeted search engine terms, we would:

- name the filter "Search term related to bike or cycle"

- check **Include**

- select "Search Term" from the **Filter Field** box

- type **.*cycl.*|.*bik.*** in the **Filter Pattern** box.

We leave **Case sensitive** unchecked and the custom filter is complete, as shown below.

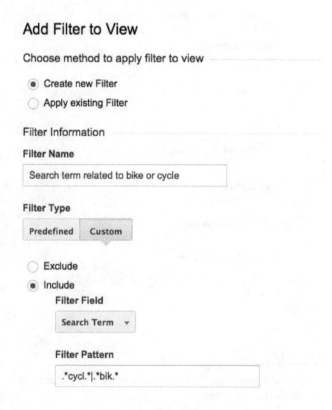

We can verify the filter, if desired. Finally, pressing the **Save** button saves your filter and then displays the filter creation confirmation. The filter has been added to the current view.

Different individuals often take different approaches when typing a website page's URL. When I first set up one of my websites, site visitors used each of the following URLs to reach the purchase page:

> http://www.Classmatandread.net/462Site/purchase.html
>
> http://www.classmatandread.net/462Site/Purchase.html
>
> http://www.classmatandread.net/462site/purchase.html
>
> http://www.classmatandread.net/462site/Purchase.html
>
> http://www.classmatandread.Net/462site/Purchase.html

All of these URLs work the same way and direct site users to the same page; they differ only in terms of capitalization. However, because Google Analytics is case sensitive (and treats the same item differently when it is in upper versus lower case) each different approach resulted in a different reported page view, significantly complicating data review and analysis.

There is no strategic reason to create different pageviews since the underlying intent of all consumers is the same: to reach the purchase page. Fortunately, you can apply a custom filter to your data to transform all requested URLs to either all upper case or all lowercase resulting in one single, consistent URL in your reports.

The approach to creating this filter is the same as the prior custom filters. Once you tell Google Analytics that you want to create a new filter, provide a name, and indicate custom filter, you would:

- name the filter, in this case "All Lowercase"

- check **Lowercase**

- select "Request URL" in the **Filter Field** box

We leave **Case sensitive** unchecked and the custom filter is complete, as shown on the top of page 90.

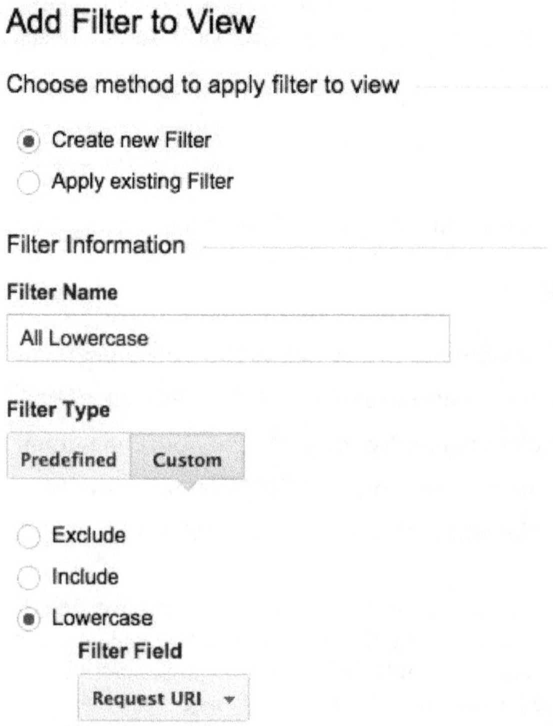

Add Filter to View

Choose method to apply filter to view

- ◉ Create new Filter
- ◯ Apply existing Filter

Filter Information

Filter Name

| All Lowercase |

Filter Type

| Predefined | **Custom** |

- ◯ Exclude
- ◯ Include
- ◉ Lowercase

   Filter Field

   | Request URI ▾ |

Finally, note that this transformation is available for a wide range of data, as reflected in the options shown in the **Filter Field** pull-down menu.

Search and replace

The search and replace function allows you to substitute one term for another. This function works the same way in Google Analytics as it does in your word processing program. For example, when writing a document you can decide to replace all instances of "U.S." with "United States". The logic is identical for search and replace custom filters.

While search and replace filters have a wide range of applications, they are typically used to replace internal codes with explanatory labels or to merge different URLs into a single URL. Let's take a closer look at these two applications of search and replace.

Case 1

Almost all ecommerce sites assign department numbers to products, for example:

http://www.bestguitarstrings.com/546/aquila-strings

http://www.bestguitarstrings.com/546/arunez-strings

http://www.bestguitarstrings.com/446/elixr-strings

While these codes are useful internally, they require those viewing the company's Google Analytics reports to have memorized or look up the codes. It would facilitate data analysis and application if the Google Analytics reports automatically translated the department numeric code within each URL into a textual descriptor. This can be accomplished as follows:

- Name the filter "Dept1"

- Check "Search and Replace"

- Select "Request URL" in the **Filter Field** box

- Type "546" in the **Search String** field as this is the piece of data that is to be replaced

- Type "classical" in the **Replace String** field as this is the new label

We leave **Case sensitive** unchecked and the custom filter is complete, as shown below.

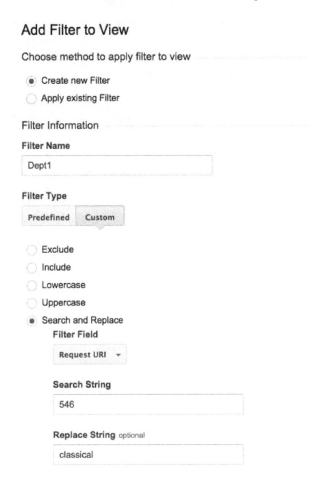

Since there are two department numbers that we want to replace, we would add a second search and replace custom filter to this view. This filter would replace "446" with "bass". When both filters are applied URLs of the form:

http://www.bestguitarstrings.com/546/aquila-strings

http://www.bestguitarstrings.com/446/elixr-strings

would now appear in Google Analytics reports as:

http://www.bestguitarstrings.com/classical/aquila-strings

http://www.bestguitarstrings.com/bass/elixr-strings

Case 2

Another common use case for the Search and Replace filter is to turn multiple URLs into one single URL. Imagine that you have multiple pages of cooking content on your website, where each piece of content is referred to by a unique URL within the "cooking" folder, as follows:

example.com/content/cooking/cooking+in+june

example.com/content/cooking/may+treats

example.com/content/cooking/fab+fish+bbq

example.com/content/cooking/bravura+brownies+and+cakes

You might find it useful to create a URL that reports site visitors' interactions with **any** cooking-related content. The search and replace function can accomplish this by standardizing the end of the specified cooking-related URLs. This would be done as follows:

- Name the filter "Cooking Content"

- Check **Search and Replace**

- Select "Request URL" in the **Filter Field** box

- Type **example\.com/content/cooking/.*** in the **Search String** field. The **.*** at the end of the search string tells Google to find anything that appears in this position.

- Type **example\.com/content/cooking** in the **Replace String** field as this is the new label.

We leave **Case sensitive** unchecked and the custom filter is complete, as shown on page 93.

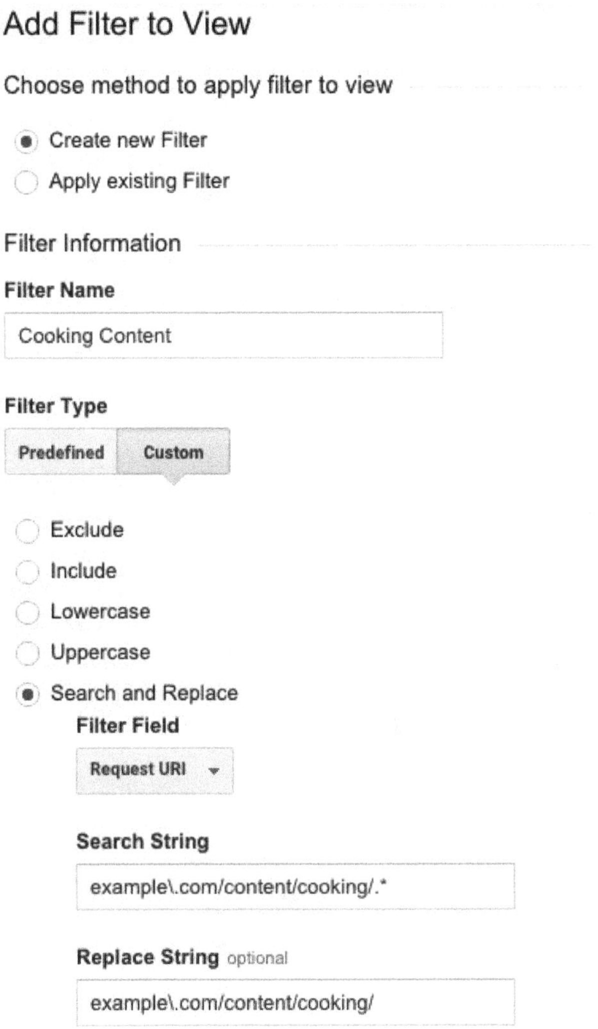

Add Filter to View

Choose method to apply filter to view

- ● Create new Filter
- ○ Apply existing Filter

Filter Information

Filter Name

Cooking Content

Filter Type

Predefined	Custom

- ○ Exclude
- ○ Include
- ○ Lowercase
- ○ Uppercase
- ● Search and Replace

   Filter Field

   Request URI ▾

   Search String

   example\.com/content/cooking/.*

   Replace String optional

   example\.com/content/cooking/

Google Analytics Demystified

12

Using Filters to Reduce Referral Spam

A website or blog with little or no traffic is generally of little benefit to its owner. As a result, website and blog owners expend a great deal of time, energy and money to increase site traffic. Google Analytics can help site owners evaluate their success in obtaining traffic from different sources, but only when the data being reported accurately reflect *real* site visitor behaviors.

Why wouldn't traffic data being reported by Google Analytics be accurate? Blame the referral spammers. The trail left by these potentially malicious individuals significantly distorts the referral data reported by Google Analytics and tends to skew major metrics such as ecommerce conversion rate, bounce rate, and average session duration.

Consider my website. After I log into Google Analytics, I select the appropriate data view (from my analytics home page's options) and then, from the menu on the left-hand side of the data display, I select **Acquisition > All Traffic > Channels**.[21] The table shown below reports my data for August, 2015.

Default Channel Grouping	Acquisition			Behavior			Conversions eCommerce ▾	
	Sessions ↓	% New Sessions	New Users	Bounce Rate	Pages / Session	Avg. Session Duration	Ecommerce Conversion Rate	Transactions
	751 % of Total: 100.00% (751)	93.34% Avg for View: 93.34% (0.00%)	701 % of Total: 100.00% (701)	64.98% Avg for View: 64.98% (0.00%)	1.52 Avg for View: 1.52 (0.00%)	00:00:53 Avg for View: 00:00:53 (0.00%)	2.13% Avg for View: 2.13% (0.00%)	16 % of Total: 100.00% (16)
1. Referral	372 (49.53%)	98.92%	368 (52.50%)	44.62%	1.49	00:01:02	0.00%	0 (0.00%)
2. Direct	369 (49.13%)	89.16%	329 (46.93%)	85.37%	1.48	00:00:44	4.34%	16(100.00%)
3. Organic Search	6 (0.80%)	66.67%	4 (0.57%)	83.33%	3.17	00:00:08	0.00%	0 (0.00%)
4. (Other)	4 (0.53%)	0.00%	0 (0.00%)	50.00%	6.25	00:02:41	0.00%	0 (0.00%)

---

[21] We use this nomenclature throughout the book. **Acquisition > All Traffic > Channels** means select the **Acquisition** menu option (from the left-hand side menu). Then from the new menu select the **All Traffic** option. Finally, from the new menu select the **Channels** option.

Four types of site traffic are reported in the first column of the table. We'll focus on direct and referral traffic where:

- *Direct* traffic represents sessions in which a visitor typed my website URL directly into his/her browser or who came to my site via a bookmark.

- *Referral* represents traffic sent to my website from other websites not identified as social.

My site traffic appears very promising with regard to sessions generated by direct and referral traffic. Looking at the first column of data, we can see that I have 369 sessions initiated via direct access to my site and 372 sessions initiated via referral from other sites. These levels of traffic are especially positive as each represents a large increase over the prior month. (This comparative data is not shown in the table.) It looks as if my efforts to reach out and increase referral traffic are finally starting to pay off. But something looks odd, as there are *no* transactions associated with any referral traffic (see last table column) significantly reducing my overall ecommerce conversion rate. Is my conclusion regarding the positive trend in referral traffic valid?

We can look more closely at the specific sources of referral traffic by clicking on the **Referral** link in the previous table.[22] The table shown below appears.

Source ?	Acquisition			Behavior			Conversions
	Sessions ↓ ?	% New Sessions ?	New Users ?	Bounce Rate ?	Pages / Session ?	Avg. Session Duration ?	Ecommerce Conversion Rate ?
	372 % of Total: 49.53% (751)	98.92% Avg for View: 93.34% (5.98%)	368 % of Total: 52.50% (701)	44.62% Avg for View: 64.98% (-31.33%)	1.49 Avg for View: 1.52 (-2.06%)	00:01:02 Avg for View: 00:00:53 (17.31%)	0.00% Avg for View: 2.13% (-100.00%)
1. free-share-buttons.com	114 (30.65%)	100.00%	114 (30.98%)	14.04%	1.86	00:01:16	0.00%
2. guardlink.org	109 (29.30%)	100.00%	109 (29.62%)	100.00%	1.00	00:00:00	0.00%
3. site4.free-share-buttons.com	45 (12.10%)	100.00%	45 (12.23%)	0.00%	2.00	00:01:29	0.00%
4. site3.free-share-buttons.com	31 (8.33%)	100.00%	31 (8.42%)	0.00%	2.00	00:01:35	0.00%
5. pornhub-forum.ga	15 (4.03%)	100.00%	15 (4.08%)	100.00%	1.00	00:00:00	0.00%
6. buy-cheap-online.info	14 (3.76%)	100.00%	14 (3.80%)	100.00%	1.00	00:00:00	0.00%
7. www.event-tracking.com	13 (3.49%)	100.00%	13 (3.53%)	0.00%	0.00	00:00:00	0.00%
8. free-social-buttons.com	12 (3.23%)	100.00%	12 (3.26%)	0.00%	2.00	00:07:55	0.00%
9. www.Get-Free-Traffic-Now.com	10 (2.69%)	100.00%	10 (2.72%)	100.00%	1.00	00:00:00	0.00%
10. site6.free-share-buttons.com	4 (1.08%)	100.00%	4 (1.09%)	0.00%	2.00	00:07:55	0.00%

---

[22] This is a common outcome in Google Analytics. Clicking on a link in a table almost always brings up more detailed information related to that link's relevant metric.

What is happening? I have referral traffic from sites I've never heard of and with URLs that spoof real web sites. Additionally, I know that I have no content that would be of interest to porn sites (as shown in line 5 of the table). In fact, all of the referral traffic shown in the report is spam referral traffic. *There is a complete absence of legitimate referral traffic.* My conclusion that referral traffic is moving in the right direction appears to be fundamentally flawed as *none* of the referral traffic reported by Google Analytics represents real visitor behaviors.

Let's take a closer look at why this is happening. Then we'll see how to significantly reduce/eliminate spam referral traffic from your Google Analytics reports.

Where does referral spam come from?

There are two sources of referral spam: bots and ghosts.

- A web bot (also know as a web crawler or spider) is an automated piece of software that collects information from web servers at incredibly fast speeds. Many bots are not malicious and simply retrieve information regarding the content and structure of a website. "Good" bots, such as Google's and Bing's bots, are ways in which these search engines obtain information that is translated into search results. These bots announce themselves to your server and obey the rules provided in your site or server's `robots.txt` file. Other bots do not play by the rules. These bots do not announce themselves and thus inappropriately show up as visitors in your Google Analytics reports.

- Ghost referral spam is more prevalent than bot-related spam and is thus more likely to skew your analytics reports. Ghost referral spam occurs when a company uses automated systems to send visitor data *directly* to Google Analytics *without ever* actually visiting your site. Ghost spammers use computers to systematically generate Google Analytics account numbers and when a match is found session data is sent directly to Google's servers. This session data is recorded as a bounce with 0:00 time spent on site.

In both cases you might ask "Why do these spammers bother?" The answer is money.

All of these spammers hope that you will click on the link that appears in your Google Analytics referral report (such as that shown on page 98). Alternatively, they might benefit from public web server data in which their links appear. In any case, if they are a pay per click company, they are paid once their link is clicked. Or, more dangerously, clicking on the link may allow malware to be placed on your computer. As a result, you should never, ever click on these links unless you are running powerful and current virus protection. Even then, satisfying your curiosity may prove dangerous.

We can eliminate almost all referral spam through the use of custom filters. Since these filters are applied on the View level, **we recommend that you create a new "clean" view rather than combine filtered and unfiltered data in an existing view**. Chapter 28 will show you how to remove referral spam from existing data as well as illustrate with actual data why this is so important.

The next section describes how to reduce/eliminate bot-related referral spam before it shows up in your Google Analytics reports. This is followed by a section with suggestions for reducing/eliminating ghost spam. When you have completed both sections, you will have requested Google to filter for bots and you will have created and applied several custom filters to the same view.[23]

Steps to reduce bot-related referral spam

Bot-related referral spam can be significantly reduced/eliminated by using Google's filtering ability and the use of a custom filter.

Activating the Google Analytics Bot Filter

Google Analytics provides a first defense against referral spam by offering a filter designed to exclude hits from known bots and spiders. You activate this filter from your Google Analytics administration page, as follows:

1. Sign into your Google Analytics account (if necessary). From the Home page click on **Admin**. On the next page, make certain that the correct account, property, and view are displayed.

2. The top option in the View column is **View Settings**. Click on this option.

3. The next page displays the view's current settings. Scroll down the page (if necessary) until you see "Bot Filtering" (see below). Check the box to "Exclude all hits from known bots and spiders."

Bot Filtering
☐ Exclude all hits from known bots and spiders

4. Scroll (if necessary) to the bottom of the page and press **Save**. You'll then see a confirmation "Success" message. Google's bot filter will now be active.

Create Several Custom Filters: Exclude Bot Spammers

These filters are designed to supplement Google's attempts to eliminate bot-initiated spam from your analytics reports. Each filter is a custom filter that will exclude the behaviors of major known spammers from a data view. Because there are so many spammers, several filters need to be applied to the same view. We'll use the filters developed by Ben Travis,[24] who has provided a great service to the analytics community by creating the necessary regex. The first filter is created as follows:

---

[23] The described approach will significantly reduce referral spam beginning on the date the filters are applied. We discuss how to remove referral spam from data already collected in Chapter 28.

[24] Ben Travis at https://viget.com/about/team/btravis.

1. Sign into your Google Analytics account (if necessary). From the Home page click on **Admin**. On the next page, make certain that the correct account, property, and view are displayed.

2. Select **Filters** from the options displayed in the View column. Select **+Add Filter** on the next page.

3. On the newly displayed filter creation page, name the filter "Exclude Referrer Bot Spam #1" and select "Custom Filter."

4. Check **Exclude.**

5. Select "Campaign Source" from the pull down menu. Keep the browser page at Google Analytics open.

6. In another browser (or browser window) visit Ben Travis' Vignet blog at:

    https://viget.com/advance/removing-referral-spam-from-google-analytics

7. Scroll down to the middle of the page until you see a dark text box labeled "Featured Regular Expressions." Copy the regex expression in the text box. Leave your browser open to this page.

8. Return to your filter creation page at Google Analytics. Paste the regex expression you just copied in the **Filter Pattern** text box.

7. Leave **Case Sensitive** unchecked. The filter is now complete as shown below. Click **Save**. The Filter Summary page lists the new filter.

Now, follow the same steps as just described in order to create a new filter. Name this new filter "Exclude Referrer Bot Spam #2". Here, though, cut and paste the regex from "Update #1" (on Ben Travis' blog page) into the **Filter Pattern** text box.

Finally, follow the same procedure for any remaining regex updates on Ben Travis' blog page. At the time of this publication, there were five additional updates, which require the creation of five additional filters.

Steps to reduce ghost referral spam

The two filters created in this section reduce or eliminate ghost referral spam data from your analytics reports by capitalizing on the limitations of the approach used by ghost spammers.

Create Custom Filter: Include Only Legitimate Hostnames

Spammers send spam to random Google Analytics account IDs. Working IDs accept the spam. Since the process is random, spammers don't know the hostname of the website corresponding to a specific Google Analytics property. This means that it is possible to filter out fake referral data by creating a filter that only allows traffic sent to legitimate hostnames. The drawback of this approach is that it is easy to accidentally filter out legitimate data if relevant hostnames are not included in the filter. If, for example, an individual views a page of my site through Google Translate, this will be reported as coming from hostname `translate.googleusercontent.com`. If I want to preserve the data generated by this visit, then I need to include this hostname in the filter.

Given the level of detail required for this filter, we suggest that you try your approach on an experimental view prior to its application to working views.

The first step in creating this filter requires you to identify all legitimate hostnames for your site or blog. You can accomplish this by logging into your Google Analytics account and selecting (clicking on) the appropriate view from the Home page. The view's data will then be displayed. Then, from the options on the left-hand side of the page select **Audience > Technology > Network**. On the top of the newly displayed table are two data display options, **Service Provider** and **Hostname** (see below). Click on **Hostname**.

A table similar to that shown on the top of page 101 will be displayed.

Hostname ?	Acquisition			Behavior			
	Sessions ? ↓	% New Sessions ?	New Users ?	Bounce Rate ?	Pages / Session ?	Avg. Session Duration ?
Hostname	**542** % of Total: 35.52% (1,526)	**52.03%** Avg for View: 82.96% (-37.29%)	**282** % of Total: 22.27% (1,266)	**56.64%** Avg for View: 70.64% (-19.82%)	**2.86** Avg for View: 1.78 (60.69%)	**00:02:50** Avg for View: 00:01:18 (118.47%)
1. www.googleanalyticsdemystified.com	**411** (75.83%)	57.66%	237 (84.04%)	50.12%	3.15	00:03:13
2. co.lumb.co	**58** (10.70%)	1.72%	1 (0.35%)	96.55%	1.03	00:00:01
3. googleanalyticsdemystified.com	**32** (5.90%)	68.75%	22 (7.80%)	62.50%	3.28	00:02:58
4. www.classmatandread.net	**12** (2.21%)	33.33%	4 (1.42%)	25.00%	4.08	00:09:17
5. forum.topic55850388.darodar.com	**5** (0.92%)	0.00%	0 (0.00%)	60.00%	1.80	00:00:00

With regard to my site, the hostnames shown in lines 1 and 3 are valid. All other host-names are invalid and will need to be filtered out. Your data table should list your own domain name as well as any other hostnames that provide real data. You can use this information to make a list of all relevant (legitimate) hostnames.

Once you have created the list of relevant hostnames, the second step requires you to identify any hostnames that you think are valid, but which may not appear on your Google Analytics hostname report. In my case, this includes translate.googleuser content.com. and two other services: PayPal and YouTube. Your additional host-names (if any) will vary.

The third step generates a regular expressions statement that includes all valid host-names. In my case this statement is:

.*googleanalyticsdemystified.*|.*googleusercontent.*|.*paypal.*|.*youtube.*

Notice how we separate each hostname with the regex "or" symbol: **|**.

Finally, we create a custom filter that Includes only the valid hostname domains, as follows:

1. Sign into your Google Analytics account (if necessary). From the Home page, click on **Admin**. On the next page, make certain that the correct account, property, and view are displayed.

2. Select **Filters** from the options displayed in the View column. Select **+Add Filter** on the next page.

3. On the next page, name the filter "Hostname" and select "Custom Filter".

4. Check **Include.**

5. Select "Hostname" from the **Filter Field** box

6. Paste your hostnames regex expression in the **Filter Pattern** box. (My expression is shown in the example.) Remember that Google Analytics restricts the number of characters in this box to 255.

7. Leave **Case Sensitive** unchecked. The filter is now complete as shown below. Click **Save**. The Filter summary page now lists the new filter.

Create Custom Filter: Page Titles

The second ghost referral filter takes advantage of the inability of spammers to read your pages' titles.[25]

Page titles are an important way for you to help site visitors navigate your site, as a page's title is displayed on the top of the browser window. You indicate a page's title in the HTML code, as shown below, where the page title is placed between the **<title>** and **</title>** tags.

<title>Xqanqeon - Buy a tour</title>

This filter uses page titles to confirm that the data being generated is actually valid data. Blackmore Ops notes that "if you look closely into your Google Analytics reports, you will see that ghost Google Analytics referral spam shows 'Page Title' as '(not set)' In fact, this is not really '(not set)', it's a NULL value."

---

[25] This solution is proposed by Blackmore Ops, *Three Effective Solutions for Google Analytics Referral Spam* at http://www.blackmoreops.com/2015/05/06/effective-solutions-for-google-analytics-referral-spam/.

Why does this happen?

We discussed earlier how Google Analytics ghost referral spammers send fake data by using your tracking ID without visiting your website. Because the IDs are randomly generated, it is almost impossible for the spammers to include page title information. Instead, they leave page title information set to NULL. When Google Analytics gets this fake data, it sets the NULL page title to (not set).

Assuming that you have given every page on your site a title, then filtering for NULL page titles becomes a very effective way to reduce/eliminate ghost referral spam. Once this you are certain that every website or blog page has a title, do the following:

1. Sign into your Google Analytics account (if necessary). From the Home page, click on **Admin**. On the next page, make certain that the correct account, property, and view are displayed.

2. Select **Filters** from the options displayed in the View column. Select **+ New Filter** on the next page.

3. On the next page, name the filter "Page Title Not Set" and select "Custom Filter."

4. Check **Exclude.**

5. Select "Page Title" from the **Filter Field** box.

6. Paste your regex expression **^$** in the **Filter Pattern** box. (This is the expression for NULL.)

7. Leave **Case Sensitive** unchecked. The custom filter is now complete as shown below. Click **Save**. The Filter summary page now lists the new filter.

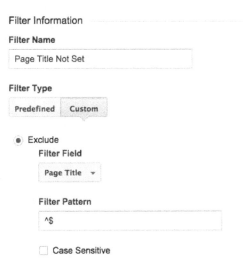

Section IV:
Data Characteristics

All Google Analytics reports are organized around the principles of dimensions and metrics. The chapter in this section will help you understand the characteristics and application of dimensions and metrics to analytics data collection and reporting.

Chapter 13 defines and explains dimensions and metrics and their use in Google Analytics reports.

Metrics and Dimensions

Google Analytics organizes and reports data in terms of dimensions, values, and metrics. It is important to understand what each of these terms represents prior to interpreting your Google Analytics reports.

Google Analytics defines a dimension as "a descriptive attribute or characteristic of an object that can be given different values." Metrics are defined as the "individual elements of a dimension that can be measured as a sum or a ratio." Given that these definitions are a bit obtuse, it might help you to understand dimensions and metrics if we first discuss these concepts outside the context of Google Analytics.

Examples of a dimension and a metric

Think about students at a university. One dimension that describes students is "Academic Status." This dimension has five different values: Freshman, Sophomore, Junior, Senior, or Graduate Student. We use metrics to describe a specific characteristic or aspect of a dimension's values, as shown in the table below, where we describe the average grade point average of each type of student (as defined by the dimension's values) living in a particular dorm.

Dimension: Academic Status of Students in Dorm X

Values	Grade Point Average
Freshman	2.3
Sophomore	2.6
Junior	2.7
Senior	3.0
Graduate	3.7

The table illustrates how to distinguish dimensions, values and metrics. A dimension can be thought of as the overall category and is typically the table descriptor or label for the first column of information. In this case, the dimension is "Academic Status." Values are divisions of the dimension and typically occur in the first column of a table. The values in this table are Freshman, Sophomore, etc. Metrics are the actual numbers that appear in a labeled column of the table, typically beginning in the second column of a data table. The label "Grade Point Average" indicates that this is the metric being reported.

We are not limited to the selection of a single metric to describe a dimension's values. Let's keep our dimension and its values constant with the previous example, but change the metric. Imagine that we wanted to obtain insights into the eating habits of the students living in our fictitious dorm. We could select a range of relevant metrics to provide these insights. We could, for example, take a look at the last week and the total number of meals consumed and report:

- the percentage of meals cooked at home (that is, in the dorm),

- the percentage of meals purchased at a fast food restaurant, and

- the average cost of a meal.

All three of these metrics are reported in the table below, where the trend is for students to cook at home more, eat less fast food, and spend more per meal as they increase in academic status.

Dimension: Academic Status of Students in Dorm X

Values	Metrics		
	Percent Meals Cooked at Home	Percent Meals at Fast Food Rest.	Ave. Cost/Meal
Freshman	22.3%	43.2%	$3.23
Sophomore	24.6	40.1	3.78
Junior	34.7	31.9	4.33
Senior	43.0	23.3	4.75
Graduate	63.7	11.9	6.01

Finally, the table illustrates how the use of multiple related metrics to describe a single dimension provides greater insights than that provided by each metric alone. This is the advantage of selecting multiple related metrics to describe the values within a single dimension.

With this in mind, let's now look at how dimensions, values and metrics are presented in Google Analytics.

Dimensions and metrics in Google Analytics

The table shown on the top of page 109 focuses on the types of individuals responsible for sessions on my website. The dimension is **User Type**; the dimension's values are the user classifications. In this case, **New** and **Returning**, and the metrics are the data that appear in each of the columns. We can see, for example, that new users are responsible for significantly more sessions (1,223 sessions or 82.97% of all sessions) versus returning users (251 sessions or 17.03% of all sessions). Also note that since **User Type** must either be **New** or **Returning**, the combined percentages of these two dimension values equals 100%.

User Type	Acquisition			Behavior		
	Sessions ↓	% New Sessions	New Users	Bounce Rate	Pages / Session	Avg. Session Duration
	1,474 % of Total: 100.00% (1,474)	**82.97%** Site Avg: 82.97% (0.00%)	**1,223** % of Total: 100.00% (1,223)	**33.58%** Site Avg: 33.58% (0.00%)	**2.49** Site Avg: 2.49 (0.00%)	**00:00:47** Site Avg: 00:00:47 (0.00%)
1. New Visitor	**1,223** (82.97%)	100.00%	1,223 (100.00%)	31.73%	2.41	00:00:31
2. Returning Visitor	**251** (17.03%)	0.00%	0 (0.00%)	42.63%	2.92	00:02:02

Similar to our student example, we are not limited to examining just one metric for any particular dimension. Google Analytics allows a broad range of options for metric selection. The table below, for example, maintains the **User Type** dimension, but changes the metrics to more detailed site related behaviors, in this case adding **Pages Per Session** and **Average Session Duration**.

User Type	Sessions ↓	Pages / Session	Avg. Session Duration	Bounce Rate
	1,474 % of Total: 100.00% (1,474)	**2.49** Site Avg: 2.49 (0.00%)	**00:00:47** Site Avg: 00:00:47 (0.00%)	**33.58%** Site Avg: 33.58% (0.00%)
1. New Visitor	**1,223** (82.97%)	2.41	00:00:31	31.73%
2. Returning Visitor	**251** (17.03%)	2.92	00:02:02	42.63%

Simultaneous examination of two dimensions

By default, Google Analytics' tables initially report a single dimension with multiple relevant metrics. These tables provide valuable insights. Insights can be even deeper, however, when two dimensions are examined simultaneously.[26]

Let's begin with the **New and Returning User** chart displayed earlier and shown again on the top of page 110.

---

[26] In this chapter we only discuss the value of examining two dimensions at the same time. We discuss how to generate these two dimensional tables later in the book in the context of data exploration.

User Type	Acquisition			Behavior		
	Sessions ↓	% New Sessions	New Users	Bounce Rate	Pages / Session	Avg. Session Duration
	1,474 % of Total: 100.00% (1,474)	**82.97%** Site Avg: 82.97% (0.00%)	**1,223** % of Total: 100.00% (1,223)	**33.58%** Site Avg: 33.58% (0.00%)	**2.49** Site Avg: 2.49 (0.00%)	**00:00:47** Site Avg: 00:00:47 (0.00%)
1. New Visitor	**1,223** (82.97%)	100.00%	**1,223**(100.00%)	31.73%	2.41	00:00:31
2. Returning Visitor	**251** (17.03%)	0.00%	**0** (0.00%)	42.63%	2.92	00:02:02

This chart provides important insights into the relative proportion of new and returning users and their site behaviors, but the table cannot answer additional relevant questions, for example: How are new and returning users accessing my site? This latter question can be answered, however, by adding a second dimension - **Source** - to the prior table.

We'll look at new and returning users separately. The table shown below lists only **New Visitors** in the first column (representing one value of the dimension **User Type**) and lists source used to access my site in the second column. (**Source** is the second dimension and its values are shown in this column). The data in the table indicate that the vast majority of new users access my site directly (763 sessions or 62.39%), with Facebook and Wordpress accounting for the majority of remaining sessions.

- Facebook accounts for 157 sessions or 12.84%.

- Wordpress accounts for 60 sessions or 4.91%

User Type	Source	Acquisition		
		Sessions ↓	% New Sessions	New Users
		1,223 % of Total: 82.97% (1,474)	**100.00%** Site Avg: 82.97% (20.52%)	**1,223** % of Total: 100.00% (1,223)
1. New Visitor	(direct)	**763** (62.39%)	100.00%	763 (62.39%)
2. New Visitor	Facebook	**157** (12.84%)	100.00%	157 (12.84%)
3. New Visitor	Wordpress	**60** (4.91%)	100.00%	60 (4.91%)
4. New Visitor	Press	**54** (4.42%)	100.00%	54 (4.42%)

Now let's look at **Returning Visitors** to see if the pattern of site access is similar or different from that of new visitors. The data is shown in the table below.

User Type	Source	Acquisition		
		Sessions ↓	% New Sessions	New Users
		251 % of Total: 17.03% (1,474)	**0.00%** Site Avg: 82.97% (-100.00%)	**0** % of Total: 0.00% (1,223)
1. Returning Visitor	(direct)	**79** (31.47%)	0.00%	0 (0.00%)
2. Returning Visitor	TransTest	**24** (9.56%)	0.00%	0 (0.00%)
3. Returning Visitor	Internal	**23** (9.16%)	0.00%	0 (0.00%)
4. Returning Visitor	Facebook	**16** (6.37%)	0.00%	0 (0.00%)
5. Returning Visitor	google	**16** (6.37%)	0.00%	0 (0.00%)
6. Returning Visitor	Wordpress	**16** (6.37%)	0.00%	0 (0.00%)

In fact, the pattern of site access for returning visitors is both similar and different to new visitors. Similar to new visitors, direct access is still the most common way to access the site, but the relative percentage of this type of access is much lower for returning visitors versus new visitors. Facebook and Wordpress also account for site access, but these, too, are at lower levels for returning users versus new users. The specific values of the second dimension (**Source**) of the two lists are also not identical. The overall conclusion is that while direct access is the dominant form of site access for both new and returning users, beyond this, new and returning site users appear to have different preferences for site access.

This insight would not have been possible had we not examined the two dimensions simultaneously.

Dimension and metric combinations

The use of simultaneous dimensions has the potential to provide insights beyond those available when examining each dimension separately. However, even Google Analytics has its limitations.

Every dimension and metric has a *scope*, which is defined in terms of users, sessions, or interactions. In the Google Analytics basic data model, a user interacts with content over a period of time and any subsequent engagement is broken down into a hierarchy.

The diagram shown below illustrates this model for a single site visitor, where each block represents the number of user sessions and interactions from that visitor. Each level in the model is defined as follows:

A **user (visitor)** is the individual who visits the site.

A **session (visit)** is the period of time during which the visitor is active on the site.

An **interaction (hit)** is the activity initiated by a site visitor. Interactions can include things such as a pageview, an event (e.g. click on a movie button) or a transaction.

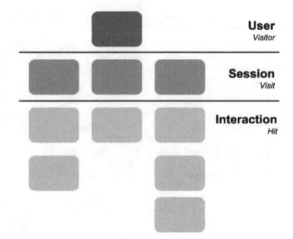

Each of these three levels defines a specific scope of user engagement. This distinction is important in Google Analytics because you may want to perform an analysis of your data at a particular scope. You might, for example, want to measure the number of sessions where users removed an item from their shopping cart. For this particular case, you would be doing a session-level analysis that includes each session during which an item was removed from a cart, even if the sessions are from the same user. On the other hand, you might want to measure the number of unique users who removed items from their shopping cart at any time, regardless of session. For this example, you would be doing a user-level analysis.[27]

Not every metric can be combined with every dimension and not all dimensions can be combined with each other. In most cases, it only makes sense to combine dimensions and metrics that share the same scope, for example:

- **Sessions** is a session-based metric so it can only be used with session-level dimensions like **source** or **city**. It wouldn't be logical to combine **sessions** with an action-level (or, hit-level) dimension like **page**.

[27] *Overview of the Google Analytics Data Model* at
http://analyticsacademy.withgoogle.com/course02/assets/html/GoogleAnalyticsAcademy-PlatformPrinciples-Lesson1.3-OverviewoftheGoogleAnalyticsdatamodel-Resource.html.

- The **count of visits** is a session-based metric so it can only be used with session-level dimensions such as **traffic source** or **geographic location**. It wouldn't be logical to combine the **count of visits** metric with a hit-level dimension like **page title**.[28]

Fortunately, Google has provided an interactive page to help you identify valid metric/ dimension combinations. The page can be found at:

https://developers.google.com/analytics/devguides/reporting/core/dimsmets.

[28] See Google Analytics Academy *Platform Principles* at
https://analyticsacademy.withgoogle.com/course02/assets/html/GoogleAnalyticsAcademy-PlatformPrinciples-Lesson4.2-TextLesson.html and *Dimensions and Metrics* at
https://support.google.com/analytics/answer/1033861?hl=en#ValidDimensionMetricCombinati
ons.

Section V:
The Audience Menu

Google Analytics provides extensive data with regard to the characteristics of individuals who visit your website or blog. You can learn their demographics and interests, the technology they use to begin and continue engagement, where they are located, their frequency/recency of sessions, and how they move through your site page by page. The chapters in this section help you to understand the full range of audience specific data and the application of this data to strategic decision-making.

- Google Analytics provides audience data through overviews or focused reports. Chapters 14 through 16 introduce you to the Audience Overview report.

- Chapter 17 presents a detailed discussion of additional data provided through the Audience Menu with the exception of Users Flow (discussed in Chapter 18) and Cohorts and Benchmarks (discussed in Chapter 19).

- Chapter 20 presents a discussion of the new Lifetime Value report feature, currently in beta.

Audience Menu: Top Graph

Your home page is the first page you see after you sign into Google Analytics. Menu options for accessing your analytics data are on the left-hand side of the page. The right-hand side of the page contains Google curated data charts, for example: real-time data, traffic sources, user locations, sessions, pages visited, and active users over time. You may also see data relevant to goals and ecommerce if these are active on your site.

Before proceeding to your data, make certain that the correct account, property and view is selected as indicated on the top, left-hand side of the page. Should you need to change the current settings, just click on the Google Analytics icon on the top, far left-hand side of the page and then select the desired property and view from the newly displayed list. When all is correct, click on **Audience** and then **Overview** in the left-hand side menu to display **Audience Overview** data.

As we move through this chapter, keep in mind that the data presentation techniques discussed in the context of audience data can be applied to almost all Google Analytics reports.

Checking the date range

Prior to examining this or any other data, always be certain that the date range is correct, that is, that it spans the entire range of data collection in which you are interested. By default, Google Analytics only reports data for the prior 30 days.

The date range can be found in the upper right-hand corner of any data reporting page, as shown below.

If you want to change this date range, click on the downward facing arrow next to the ending date. Once the calendars appear, you can use the pull-down menu next to "Date Range" to select a standard period or you can use the calendar or date boxes to select the beginning and end of the desired date range (see the top of page 118). In the latter case, make certain that the pull-down menu beneath the initial date range says **Custom**.

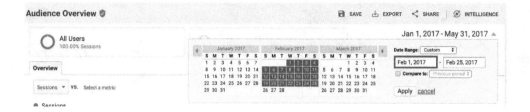

Click **Apply** when done and all data displayed in the current session will be drawn from the date range you specified.

The top graph

By default, the top graph shows the number of site sessions taking place each day within the selected date range, which in this case is January 1, 2017 to May 31, 2017 (see below). The line graph in this example shows that there are several distinct time periods underlying site sessions, with sessions spiking early in the year.[29]

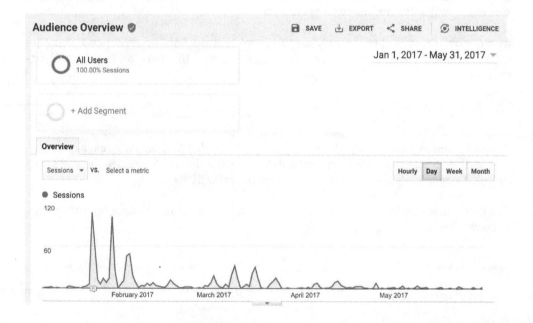

Placing your cursor over any point on the line graph displays detailed information for that date, as reflected in the chart shown on the top of page 119. Here, we learn that 107 sessions occurred on January 18, 2017.

---

[29] Sessions and other key metrics related to the Audience Menu are defined in this chapter's addendum.

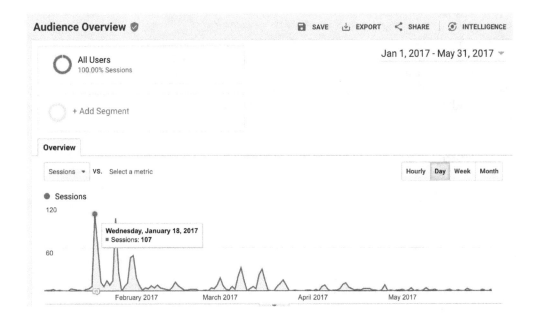

Sample rate

All of the data reflected in the prior and subsequent data displays reflect my full data set. We can confirm this by clicking on the green shield next to the report name (i.e., **Audience Overview**). This brings up the message, which reads: "This report is based on 100% of sessions."

However, when a very large number of sessions underlie a report, it is possible that Google Analytics may present data based on only a sample (or subset) of the data. When this occurs, you will see a message at the top of the report, which says, "This report is based on [number] of sessions." When you view a sampled report, you have the option to adjust the sampling rate in order to increase accuracy and affect how quickly the report loads. You can use the pull-down menu to select either **Faster response** or **Greater precision**. Your data automatically refreshes using the new setting. Your preference is saved across all of your reports, but resets after you close your current analytics session.[30]

---

[30] *Adjusting the Sampling Rate in Reports* at
https://support.google.com/analytics/answer/1733979?hl=en.

Changing how reported data is grouped

The menu options on the top right-hand side of the graph provide you with data grouping options. You can ask for data to be reported hourly (for restricted date periods), by the day (as in the prior chart), week or month. Just click on the desired time grouping. The chart below presents the same data as the prior chart, only this time, grouped by week.

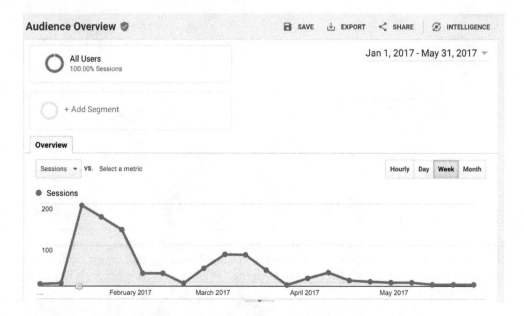

Changing the data displayed in the line graph

The display of site sessions is not the only metric that can be displayed in the line graph. Beneath **Overview** on the top left-hand side of the graph is a pull-down menu, currently (by default) labeled **Sessions**. You can select to chart any of the available metrics (see below).

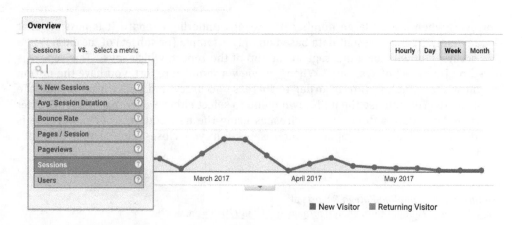

These metrics can be charted by your desired time period. The chart below, for example, displays **Pageviews** by **Month**.

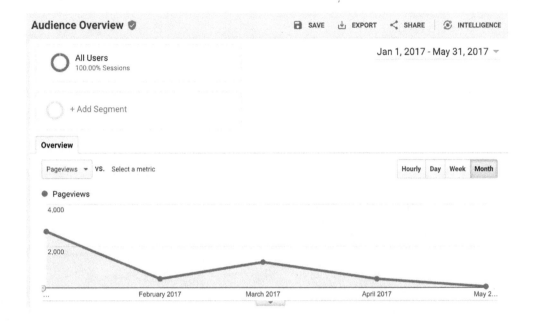

You can annotate any chart, that is, leave a note for yourself and others viewing the chart. Your annotation might be used, for example, to explain a rapid rise or fall in data trends or the start and end of an email campaign.

There are two ways to annotate a chart: directly through the chart or through Administrative options.

Placing an Annotation Directly on the Chart

To annotate a chart, first click on the small downward facing arrow on the bottom center of the chart. Next, click (in the chart) to locate the date you want to annotate and then click on **+Create new annotation** located on the bottom right-hand side of the chart. It is easiest to accomplish this by charting your data using the **Day** option. Our target date is January 18, 2017. When this is done, you should see a screen resembling that shown on the top of page 122.

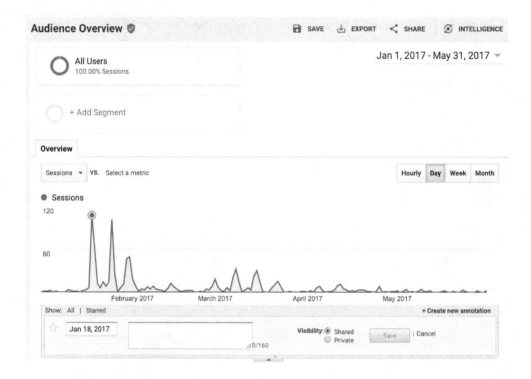

Check the date in the date text box. If the incorrect date is showing, then just click on the text box and then either type in or use the pull-down calendar to select the date for the annotation. Now, click whether you want the annotation to be shared or private and then type your annotation into the text box. Click **Save** when you are done (or click **Cancel** if you change your mind). Saved annotations result in a small annotation symbol on the target date (see below). You can close the annotation box by clicking on the upward facing arrow beneath the line graph.

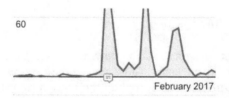

At any point thereafter, clicking on the annotation symbol displays the corresponding annotation, as shown below.

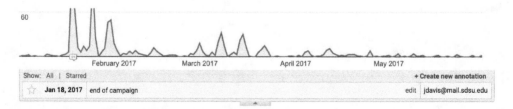

Google Analytics Demystified

Finally, notice the information provided on the lower right-hand side of the annotation. My email address appears because I created the annotation. In addition, the **Edit** link allows me to edit any attribute of the annotation or even delete the entire annotation.

Placing an Annotation Through the Administrative Menu

Annotations can also be placed using the appropriate link in the Administrative menu. The link appears near the bottom of the View column, as shown below.

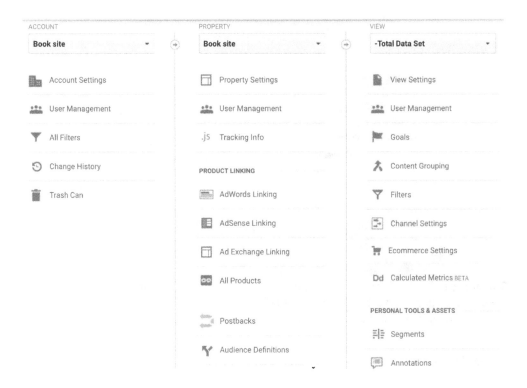

Clicking on this link brings up the summary page for all annotations associated with the current view. The summary page below shows the annotation created in the prior section.

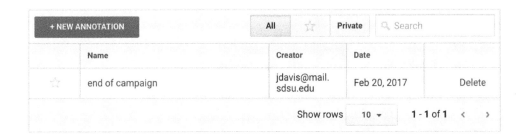

A click on the **+ NEW ANNOTATION** button displays the annotation creation page, as shown below.

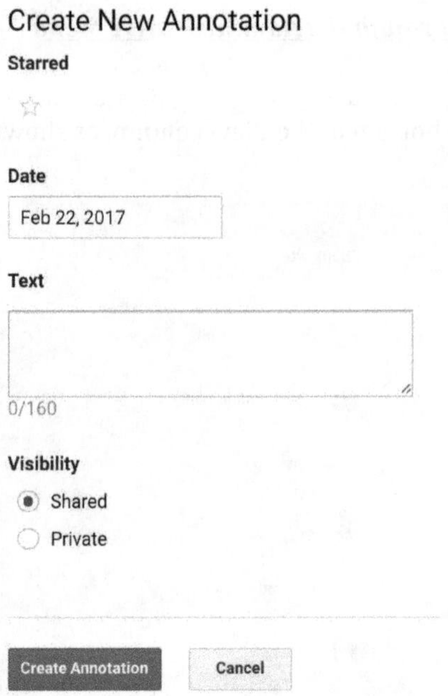

Create New Annotation

Starred

☆

Date

Feb 22, 2017

Text

0/160

Visibility

⦿ Shared

◯ Private

Create Annotation   Cancel

This form requests information identical to that described in the prior section. When completed, click on **CREATE ANNOTATION**, which will add the annotation to the appropriate date in the chart.

Simultaneously charting two metrics

You are not restricted to charting only one metric at a time. As described earlier, you use the pull-down menu on the top left-hand side of the line graph to select your primary metric. Next to this menu is the option to **Select a (second) metric**. Clicking on this link brings up a second pull-down menu, which lists all the remaining metrics for the type of data being examined, in this case audience data (see the top of page 125).

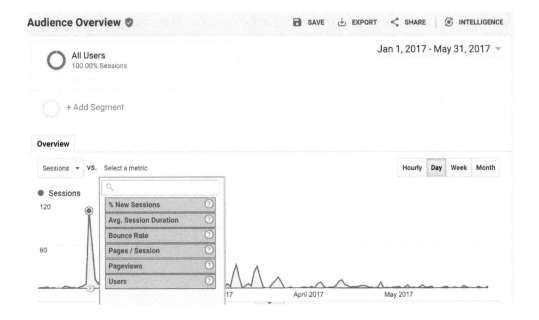

Selecting a metric from this second pull-down menu adds the data for this second metric to your chart. The chart below, for example, simultaneously charts **Pageviews** and **Average Session Duration**. Note that each metric is presented in a different shade, and that the scales for each metric are on opposite sides of the chart. The scale for **Pageviews** is on the left-hand side of the chart, while the scale for the second variable, **Average Session Duration**, is located on the right-hand side of the chart.

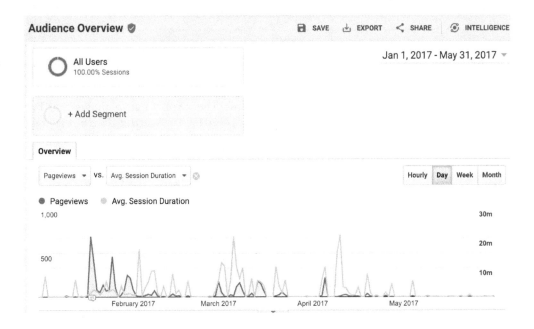

As before, putting your cursor over any specific date now brings up the data for both metrics for that date, as shown below.

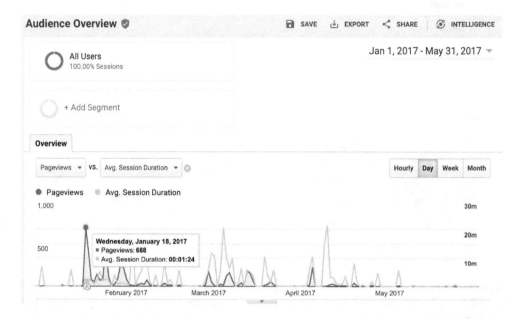

Clicking on the small "x" next to your second metric eliminates that metric from the display.

Comparing metrics for two date ranges

We can compare a metric across two different time periods. The procedure for accomplishing this begins with the date range shown on the top of any data-reporting page. First select your target date range by using either the calendar or date boxes to indicate start and end dates. Make certain that you have highlighted the appropriate start/end date box when selecting starting and ending dates. The display below shows that I've selected the period February 1, 2017 to February 14, 2017. The starting date box is highlighted.

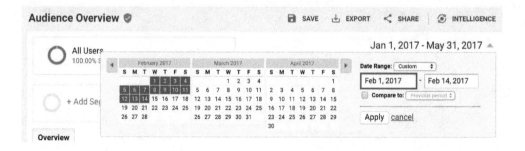

Beneath the target date range boxes is a box labeled **Compare to**. Select this box and change the pull-down menu to its right to **Custom**. The calendar will change to display two date ranges, noting by color which dates have already been selected for the two time periods (see below). Note that Google Analytics will by default select a comparison time frame equal in length to the first (target) time frame.

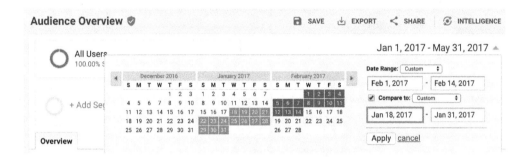

If you are satisfied with the two date ranges, then click **Apply**. If this does not suit your needs, then you can always change your comparison date range.

- To set the comparison start date, click in the left-hand date box beneath **Compare to** and then use the calendar to set the start date. (Note: The date box may not highlight when you click in it.) Once you select the date via the calendar, the date in the start box will change to the selected date.

- To set the comparison end date, click in the right-hand date box beneath **Compare to** and then use the calendar to set the end date. (Note: the date box may not highlight when you click in it.) Once you select the date via the calendar, the date in the end box will change to the selected date.

We'll select February 1, 2017 to February 10, 2017 for our first range and February 11, 2017 to March 31, 2017 as our second date range. When done, and the screen looks like that shown below, we click **Apply**. Note that the date ranges are not equivalent in length.

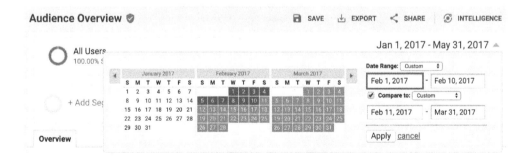

The line chart has now changed, where the metric **Sessions** is displayed for the two selected time periods, as shown on the top of page 128.

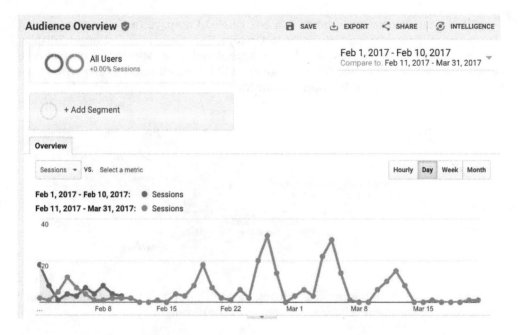

When looking at a line graph, the order in which the two dates are entered makes no difference since one line is simply superimposed over the other. However, the order of entry *does* make a difference in numeric tables, which compare data across two time periods.

> ✅ Keep in mind that the second date range entered becomes the *frame of reference* for the comparison of data trends.

The display shown below is the result of entering February 1, 2017 to February 10, 2017 as our first date range, and February 11, 2017 to March 31, 2017 as our second date range. Notice how both numbers are negative, indicating that site sessions and number of users in the first time period were significantly lower than in the second time period.

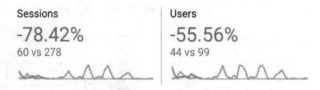

Sessions	Users
-78.42%	-55.56%
60 vs 278	44 vs 99

The display shown below takes the opposite approach. Here, the time period February 11, 2017 to March 31, 2017 was entered first while February 1, 2017 to February 10, 2017 was entered as the "Compare to" time frame. Notice how the direction of the comparison is reversed, indicating that the sessions in the first time period were significantly higher than those in the second period.

The data is the same in both cases (as seen in the numbers beneath the percentages), but the interpretation's perspective is different. As a result, always make certain that you understand the direction of the comparison when examining data across two time periods.

Chapter Addendum: Definitions of Key Audience Metrics

Google Analytics provides a core set of metrics with regard to users, sessions, and pageviews. These metrics are defined as follows:

Users

The User metric reports the number of unique individuals who have had at least one session within the selected date range. This metric includes both new and returning individuals.

Sessions

Google notes that "The concept of a session in Google Analytics is important to understand because many features, reports, and metrics depend on how Analytics calculates sessions." Google Analytics defines a session as "a group of interactions that take place on your website within a given time frame. For example a single session can contain multiple pageviews, events, social interactions, custom variables, and ecommerce transactions."[31]

Time and activity both contribute to when Google Analytics considers a session to begin and end. There are three circumstances, which define session stop time. Sessions end:

- After 30 minutes of inactivity

- At midnight

- If a user arrives via one campaign, leaves, and then comes back via a different campaign.

The impact of these events is illustrated in the following description of Mary's behaviors, where an "x" in the "New Session" column indicates that the behavior results in a new session being counted. Thus, over a three-day period, Mary was responsible for six site sessions due to periods of activity and inactivity.

---

[31] *How Sessions Are Calculated in Analytics* at
https://support.google.com/analytics/answer/2731565?hl=en

Day	Time	Behavior	New Session
Monday	9:00	Mary visits for the first time	x
	9:25	Mary's infant starts to cry. Mary's computer stays on the website as Mary leaves to tend to her daughter.	
	9:56	*It's been more than 30 minutes since Mary viewed a page. Google Analytics ends the current session.*	
	11:30	It took a long time to get Mary's daughter to stop crying. Mary comes back to her computer and to your website. She begins to view pages on the website.	x
	11:45	Mary leaves the your website to surf elsewhere.	
	19:30	Mary returns to your website.	x
	20:05	Bedtime for Mary	
Tuesday	6:00	Mary returns to the website by typing the URL directly into her browser.	x
	6:20	Mary leaves the website to surf elsewhere.	
	11:42	Mary sees your Adwords ad and returns to your website by clicking on the ad. *Since the campaign source has changed, Google Analytics considers this the start of a new session.*	x
Wednesday	00:01	*Given the time, Google Analytics considers this the start of a new session.*	x

Google Analytics allows you to set the time limit that controls when a session is considered to have ended. Keep your strategic goals in mind when deciding what the revised session limit should be. A website with significant content, long blog entries, etc. may required longer session periods while sites with less or very simple content may require shorter session periods.

Session settings are altered on the property level. To access this function, click on **Admin** from any page and then make certain that the desired account, property and view are displayed. In the property column, click on **Tracking Info** and then on the next menu click on **Session Settings.** The page shown below will be displayed.

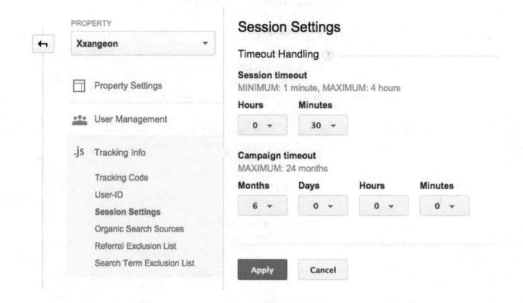

Provide the new timeout limits for sessions and/or campaigns by using the pull-down menus and then press **Apply**.

Google Analytics will not apply new session or campaign timeout directions to historical data. As a result, it is best to create a new View (with annotation) if these parameters are changed, so that session characteristics are consistent across the entire time period being examined.

Percent new sessions

This is an estimate of the percent of first time (new) sessions during the selected time period. In the prior example Mary would have accounted for multiple sessions but only one new session when we consider the total week in which her visits took place.

Average session duration

Average session duration is calculated as the total duration of all sessions divided by the total number of sessions. Thus, if in a particular time period all site users spent 5,000 minutes on your site distributed across 2,000 sessions, the average session duration would be 2.5 minutes (5000 ÷ 2000).

An individual's visit duration is calculated differently depending on whether or not there are *engagement hits* (such as playing a video) on the last page of a visit.

When there are no engagement hits, Google tracks the amount of time spent from the beginning of viewing the first page loaded upon entering the site to the beginning of viewing the last page seen before leaving the site, as illustrated in the following figure. Thus, in this example, the total session time would be 20 minutes (12:00 to 12:20).

NO PAGE ENGAGEMENT

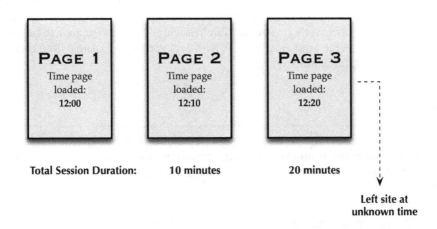

When there is an engagement hit on the last page viewed, Google tracks the amount of time spent from the beginning of viewing the first page loaded upon entering the site to the start of engagement on the final page viewed, as shown below. In this case, total session time is 25 minutes, calculated by subtracting the time of the initial page load (12:00) from the time of the final engagement (12:25).

ENGAGEMENT ON
FINAL PAGE

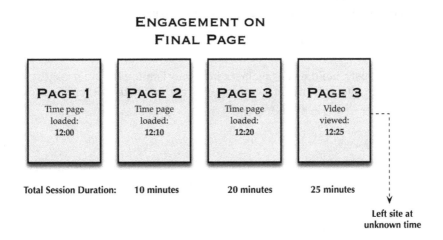

The prior examples illustrated how Google Analytics' calculation of session duration requires a start and stop time. Thus, an individual must view at least two pages or have an initial page view with an engagement hit in order for session duration to be calculated. An individual without a second page view or engagement on the first page viewed is considered to have spent no time on site and so session duration will be zero for that individual *regardless of how long that individual actually spent on the first page viewed*. Thus, it might be beneficial to build in some form of engagement (for example, a "read more" link), in order to get a more accurate reflection of session length. Building engagement into a page will also affect bounce rate, as described in the next section.

Finally, as session duration is an average, the calculation should be used directionally and with caution. Odd or skewed distributions can result in an overall average that does not represent your site user's typical session behavior. The metric can also be skewed if your site is designed for long engagement with just your entry page as the focus of behavior (as in a blog, for example).

Bounce rate

Bounce Rate is the percentage of single-page sessions, that is, sessions in which a site visitor leaves your site from the first page viewed without interacting with that or any other page. As with the other measures, Bounce Rate needs to be interpreted within the context of your site.

- A high bounce rate on a large, multipage site may indicate problems with landing page design or content. Here, individuals may be arriving at your site expecting but not finding specific content, or the landing page may be too confusing, cluttered or otherwise off-putting.

- A high bounce rate on a blog may be acceptable, however. Imagine, for example, that Denise comes to your blog and spends ten minutes reading your latest blog post. She's impressed and decides to return often. She leaves with a good attitude, but without any interaction with the page and without viewing any additional pages. Denise would be counted as a "bounce" and her time on site would be recorded as "0:00".

As noted previously, building engagement into your landing (or other pages) will reduce the bounce rate and will provide a more accurate estimate of those sessions without engagement or multiple page views.

Pageviews

Pageviews is the total number of pages (which contain the Google Analytics tracking code) viewed during all sessions by all users. This measure is subject to inflation due to the way that duplicate page views are handled. If, for example, a visitor clicks reload after reaching a particular page, this is counted as an additional pageview and two pageviews would be recorded. Similarly, if a user navigates to a different page on the site and then returns to the original page, a second pageview is then recorded even though the original page had already been seen.

Pages Per Session is the average number of pages viewed during a session on your site, keeping in mind that repeated views of a single page are counted in this calculation. Thus, if in a particular period there are 2000 total pageviews and 1,000 sessions, the average pages per session would be 2.0 (2000 ÷ 1000).

This calculation should be used directionally and with caution as it may not always represent your site user's *typical* behavior. Consider the following four site visitors:

	Number of Pageviews	Number of Sessions	Average Pages Per Per Session
Max	15	5	3.0
Ken	27	9	3.0
Sally	12	4	3.0
Candice	35	1	35.0
TOTAL	**89**	**19**	**4.7**

Google Analytics would calculate the pages per visit metric as 4.7 (89 pageviews divided by 19 visits), which is significantly higher than the *typical* pages per visit.

15

Audience Menu: Middle of Page Data

The metrics and charts in the center of the **Audience Overview** page (see below) provide summary information for key audience metrics within a selected time period. The data below relates to my website activity from January 1, 2014 to May 4, 2014.

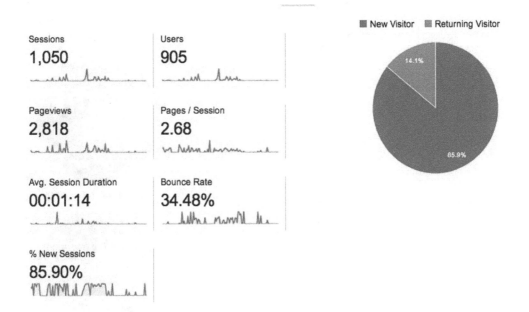

Each of these metrics was defined in Chapter 13. Note that clicking on any of the line graphs in this block brings detailed information on that metric up to the line graph shown on the top of the page (as discussed in Chapter 13). Clicking on the small line graph beneath **% New Sessions,** for example, changes the metric displayed in the top line graph to **% New Sessions.**

You'll recall from Chapter 13 that we can simultaneously examine two different time periods. When two time periods are selected, the data in this summary chart is changed to facilitate this comparison.

Imagine that we want to compare this set of metrics across two time periods: January 1, 2014 to February 28, 2014 and March 1, 2014 to May 4, 2014. The parameters used for creating this comparison are shown on the top of the following page.

The display then reports the comparative summary metrics for each time period, as shown below.

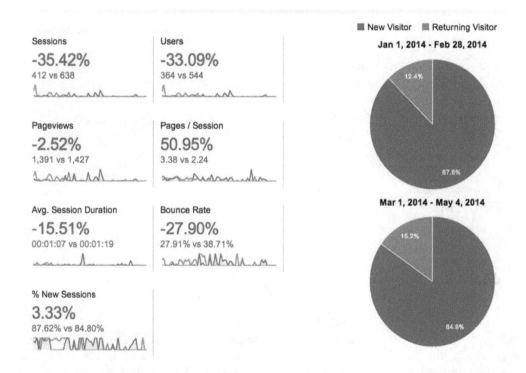

The percentages compare time period one to time period two, where a negative percentage typically indicates *lower* (or worse) numbers for period one versus period two, and a positive percentage indicates *higher* (or better) numbers for period one versus period two. Thus, in this example, period one (January to February) had 35.42% fewer sessions than period two (March to May). There were 412 versus 638 sessions. The positive percentage for average number of pages viewed per session (Pages/Session) indicates a higher average number of pages viewed per session in period one versus period two (3.38 versus 2.24 pages). The exception to this interpretation is bounce rate, where a negative number indicates that the bounce rate was better (i.e., lower) in period one versus period two.

16

Audience Menu:
Bottom of Page Data

The links and charts on the bottom of the **Audience Overview** page provide access to detailed audience descriptive dimensions and metrics, as shown below.

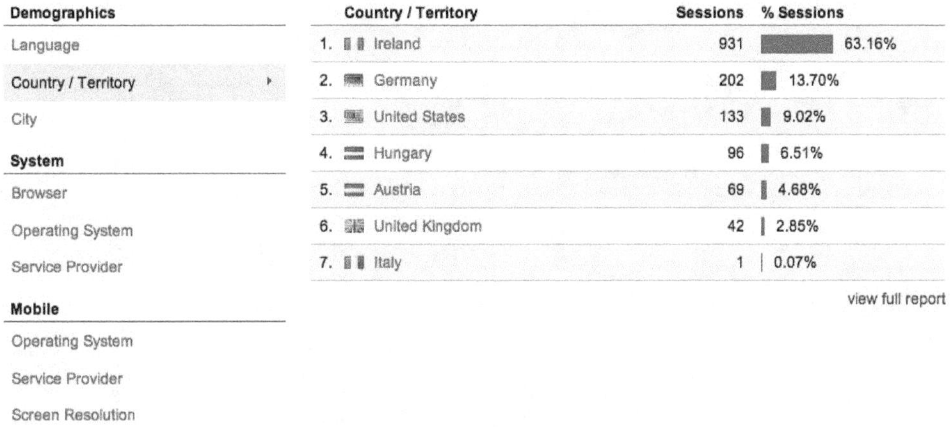

Demographics		Country / Territory	Sessions	% Sessions
Language		1. ▮▮ Ireland	931	▬▬▬ 63.16%
Country / Territory	▸	2. ▦ Germany	202	▮ 13.70%
City		3. ▤ United States	133	▮ 9.02%
System		4. ▭ Hungary	96	▮ 6.51%
Browser		5. ▭ Austria	69	▮ 4.68%
Operating System		6. ▦ United Kingdom	42	│ 2.85%
Service Provider		7. ▮▮ Italy	1	│ 0.07%
Mobile				view full report
Operating System				
Service Provider				
Screen Resolution				

Dimensions, organized into three large groups (Demographics, System, and Mobile), are shown on the left-hand side of the page. Each dimension is clickable, where a click brings up more detailed dimensions, values and metrics related to the selected dimension. The chart on the right-hand side of the page above, for example, tells me the countries in which my sessions originate and the percentage of sessions from each country. This chart was generated when I clicked on the **Country/Territory** link.

We have two options for exploring the data in more detail. First, we can click on active links within the table. Selecting any link within the table brings up a new page with a diverse range of information available for the selected dimension and value. Second, we can click on the **View Full Report** link beneath the table, which provides a detailed tabular report on the selected dimension.

Clicking a link in the table

Selecting a link in the **Audience Overview** bottom of page, right-hand table takes you to a new page, which provides greater detail on the selected dimension's value. The map and table shown below, for example, are displayed when I click on "Ireland" in the summary table on the bottom right-hand side of the **Audience Overview** page.

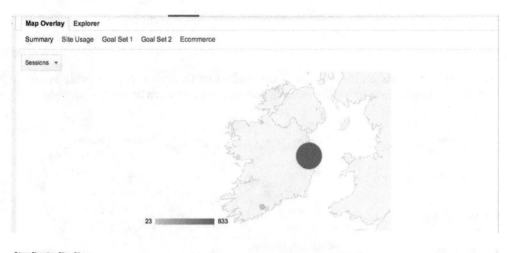

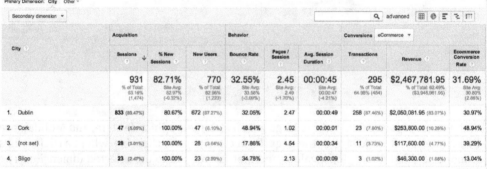

City	Acquisition			Behavior			Conversions eCommerce ▾		
	Sessions ↓	% New Sessions	New Users	Bounce Rate	Pages / Session	Avg. Session Duration	Transactions	Revenue	Ecommerce Conversion Rate
	931 % of Total: 63.16% (1,474)	82.71% Site Avg: 82.97% (-0.32%)	770 % of Total: 82.96% (1,223)	32.55% Site Avg: 33.58% (-3.09%)	2.45 Site Avg: 2.49 (-1.70%)	00:00:45 Site Avg: 00:00:47 (-4.21%)	295 % of Total: 64.95% (454)	$2,467,781.95 % of Total: 62.49% ($3,946,961.95)	31.69% Site Avg: 30.80% (2.88%)
1. Dublin	833 (89.47%)	80.67%	672 (87.27%)	32.05%	2.47	00:00:49	258 (87.46%)	$2,050,081.95 (83.07%)	30.97%
2. Cork	47 (5.05%)	100.00%	47 (6.10%)	48.94%	1.02	00:00:01	23 (7.80%)	$253,800.00 (10.28%)	48.94%
3. (not set)	28 (3.01%)	100.00%	28 (3.64%)	17.86%	4.54	00:00:34	11 (3.73%)	$117,600.00 (4.77%)	39.29%
4. Sligo	23 (2.47%)	100.00%	23 (2.99%)	34.78%	2.13	00:00:09	3 (1.02%)	$46,300.00 (1.88%)	13.04%

We'll look at each data report separately.

The top map[32]

The location of the circles in the map informs me of the cities (in this case, those in Ireland) in which my sessions originate; while the size of the circles indicates the *relative* number of sessions that come from each city. The larger the circle, the larger the city's number of sessions.

---

[32] The map is displayed whenever geography is the dimension of interest. Otherwise, line graphs are displayed.

The map is interactive. Rolling your cursor over any of the cities displays the relevant data for that city, in this case the data is related to sessions. Sessions are displayed in the cursor roll-over because this is the default metric shown in the pull-down menu in the upper left-hand corner.

You are not restricted to the variables shown on the initial map, keeping in mind that all data will be restricted to the dimension value that brought you to this page: in this case, Ireland. The figure shown below illustrates your options for alternative metric selection.

Selecting **Average Order Value** from the pull-down menu changes the map and displays this new information in the same format as the initial **Session**s map (see the top of page 142). Now, however, the circles and data have changed to report **Average Order Value.**

The bottom table

The table below is displayed beneath the map.

The first two sections of this table (labeled **Acquisition** and **Behavior**) report six of the metrics we've seen before on the **Audience Overview** page, except now the data is reported (organized) by city in tabular/numeric format.[33] Only Irish cities are shown because this page was generated when I selected "Ireland" from the table on the **Audience Overview** page. The last block of columns relates to website conversions, in this case, ecommerce transactions. The data in this block is selectable through the pull-down menu next to **Conversions** on the top right-hand side of the chart.

- **Transactions:** reports the absolute number and percentage of all transactions for each value listed in the first column. In this case, Dublin accounts for 258 of 295 total Irish transactions (87.49%).

---

[33] Note that "not set" in line three of the table indicates that Google Analytics was unable to determine the exact city.

- **Revenue:** reports the amount of sales generated and the overall percentage of sales. In this case, Dublin accounts for just over two million dollars in sales (or 83.07% of all sales).

- **Ecommerce Conversion Rate:** reports the percentage of all sessions that resulted in a sale. In this case, 30.97% of all site sessions from Dublin resulted in a sale.

Charts in this format allow you to easily compare the performance of each metric to the overall dimension averages or totals shown in the top row of the table. This is an important comparison because it provides insights into how specific metrics either exceed or lag behind the average, thereby identifying areas of website or blog strength and weakness.

The numeric table on page 142, for example, indicates that there is a significant difference in the bounce rate among visitors from different Irish cities. When using the overall Irish bounce percentage (32.55%) as the frame of reference, it is clear that the bounce rate in Cork (48.94%) is much higher than average. We would want to try to determine why this is the case in order to reduce this bounce rate. Additionally, the ecommerce conversion rate in Sligo (13.04%) is considerably below the overall average (31.69%). We would want to determine why this was occurring and plan a response that would increase this specific conversion rate.

Note that the number of dimensions reportable in this table varies depending upon the depth of detail collected by Google Analytics. The prior chart was generated directly from the Ireland link on the **Audience Overview** page. Note that on the very top of the table (in the left-hand corner) the **Primary Dimension** of **City** is highlighted and alone. This indicates that this is the only detail available for Ireland.

Clicking on the United States link from the table on the **Audience Overview** page brings up a different level of detail. Selecting this link first reports data by state, as illustrated below. (Note that Google Analytics defines states as "Regions.")

Now there are more options next to **Primary Dimension**. Data for the United States is available on the **City** and **Metro** level. All cities or metro areas can be shown in the same table (by clicking on either **City** or **Metro** as shown in the following two tables.)

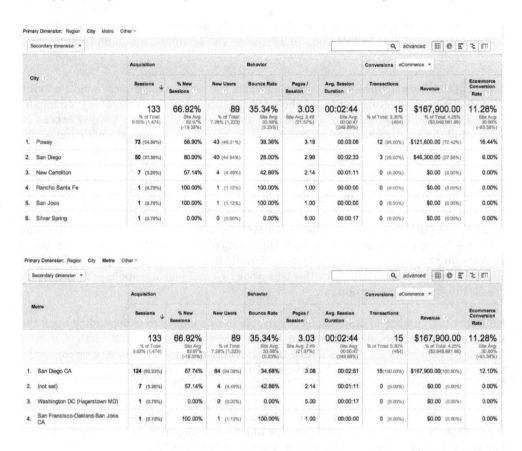

Finally, note that items shown in the first column are also interactive links. Clicking on any of these links will display additional relevant information, if available.

Changing dimensions and metrics in the bottom table

Acquisition, **Behavior** and **Conversions** are the default metrics displayed at the bottom-of-page table. You are not limited to these metrics, however.

Immediately beneath the tab labeled **Map Overlay** on the top of the map are alternative display options. **Summary** is already selected as the default (see the top of page 145). Note that the options shown on your display may be different than that shown in the example. **Site Usage** will always be an available option. **Ecommerce** and **Goal Sets** appear only after these options have been activated.

Clicking on **Site Usage** changes the dimensions and metrics presented in the bottom of page table (see below). Now all metrics relate to site usage behaviors.

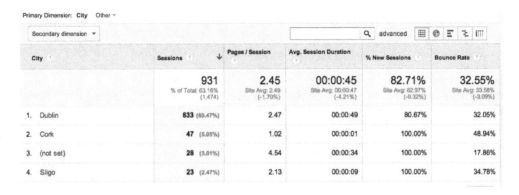

Similarly, selecting **Ecommerce** displays ecommerce metrics in the bottom of page table (see below).

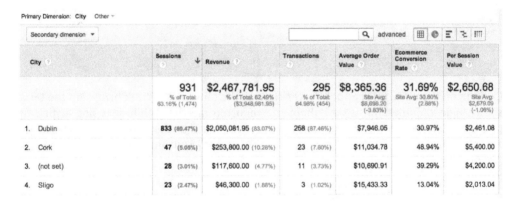

Secondary dimensions

Most numeric tables allow you to add a secondary dimension to the basic analysis. The secondary dimension option, when available, can be found in the upper left-hand corner of a numeric table. Secondary dimensions are accessed via a pull-down menu, which by default is labeled **Secondary dimension** (see table above). Pulling down this menu brings up a range of additional dimensions and metrics, which can be added to the primary analysis (see table on the top of page 146).

Let's try to determine how browser and type of access (mobile versus desktop) affect transactions and sales. We begin on the **Audience Overview** page, selecting **Browser** to bring up the listing of browsers used to access my site (see below).

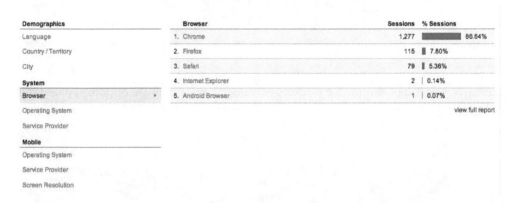

Clicking on the **view full report** (lower right in the table above) link brings up the table shown below. Something is odd about the reported metrics. While it is not surprising that one browser type may dominate, it is surprising that there were **no** transactions among those using Firefox, Internet Explorer or an Android browser (granted, the sample size for the latter two is small).

We can look more deeply into this data by selecting **Device Category** from the **Secondary Dimension** pull-down menu (see below).

When this is done, the table shown below is displayed. The metrics in this table provide important direction for site revision and future site success. With regard to Firefox, all sessions originated from desktops, but there were no transactions. Is there something on our site that is not working with Firefox, in particular, the purchase page? With regard to Safari and Android, these sessions originated on a mobile devise and again there were no transactions. To what extent is our site optimized for mobile, and what, in particular on our site, might not be working with mobile devices?

Alternative table formats

As we saw earlier, the table shown on the top of page 148 is the primary display once Ireland is selected as the dimension value of interest. Note that in the upper-right hand corner above the chart is a series of icons.

City ?	Sessions ? ↓	Revenue ?	Transactions ?	Average Order Value ?	Ecommerce Conversion Rate ?	Per Session Value ?
	931 % of Total: 63.16% (1,474)	**$2,467,781.95** % of Total: 62.49% ($3,948,981.95)	**295** % of Total: 64.98% (454)	**$8,365.36** Site Avg: $8,698.20 (-3.83%)	**31.69%** Site Avg: 30.80% (2.88%)	**$2,650.68** Site Avg: $2,679.09 (-1.06%)
1. Dublin	**833** (89.47%)	$2,050,081.95 (83.07%)	258 (87.46%)	$7,946.05	30.97%	$2,461.08
2. Cork	**47** (5.05%)	$253,800.00 (10.28%)	23 (7.80%)	$11,034.78	48.94%	$5,400.00
3. (not set)	**28** (3.01%)	$117,600.00 (4.77%)	11 (3.73%)	$10,690.91	39.29%	$4,200.00
4. Sligo	**23** (2.47%)	$46,300.00 (1.88%)	3 (1.02%)	$15,433.33	13.04%	$2,013.04

Each of these icons (see below for a larger visual) allows you to alter both what data are displayed and the format of the display.

The box icon on the far left represents the default view. Selection of this icon presents the data in tabular format, as shown in the table at the top of this page.

The next icon, the circle, allows you to turn any set of available metrics into a numeric table and pie chart, again keeping in mind that the data displayed are restricted to only that which is relevant to your selected dimension. My selection of this icon displays the table and pie chart shown below. Similar to prior data displays, the default view displays sessions. I've also selected the same metric for both the tabular and pie displays, allowing the pie chart to display the tabular data.

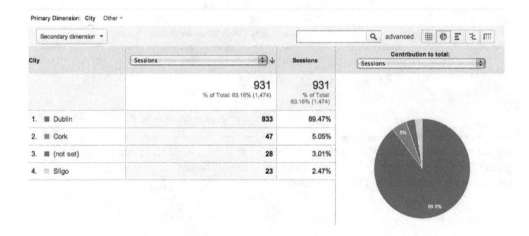

Google Analytics Demystified

The data display can be changed by using the pull-down menus. The chart below, for example, illustrates what happens when both displays are set to **Transactions**.

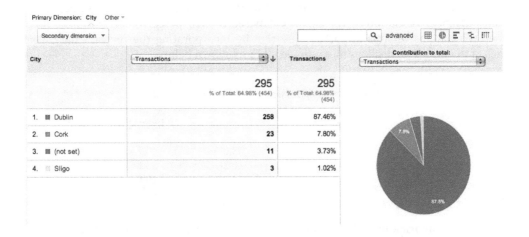

This chart would be interpreted as follows:

- There were 295 total transactions in Irish cities.

- 258 of these transactions originated in Dublin. This represents 87.46% of all Irish transactions.

The previous examples selected the same metric to be displayed in both the numeric table and pie chart. In this circumstance, the pie chart simply presents an alternative display to the numeric table. This does not have to be the case, however.

We can use this charting option to examine the relationship between two metrics by selecting different metrics for the numeric and pie chart. The chart shown below, for example, displays the number of sessions in the first column and revenue in both the second numeric column and the pie chart. We select these measures by using the pull-down menus.

While all of this data is available in the original numeric table, conducting an analysis that focuses on just two metrics makes it easier to identify and answer important strategic questions. Given the prior two displays, we might ask: What is the relationship between sessions and revenue; that is, are some cities over-performing or underperforming when their percent contribution to sessions is compared to their percent contribution to revenue? We can answer this important question by incorporating the relevant data from each of the prior two displays into a single table, as shown below.

Relationship of Sessions and Revenue in Irish Cities

City	% Sessions	% Revenue	Index[34]
Dublin	87.46%	83.07%	95
Cork	7.80	10.28	132
Sligo	1.02	1.88	184

This chart is informative. While Dublin accounts for the vast majority of both sessions and revenue, the relationship between these two measures (as reflected in the relatively lower index) is "off." Dublin's revenue is a bit less than you would expect given its percentage of sessions. The remaining two cities are over-performing, that is, they are generating more revenue than their percentage of sessions would predict. Thus, we are faced with two important yet different strategic questions:

- How do we increase the revenue per session in Dublin?

- How do we increase sessions in Cork and Sligo to capitalize on the relatively greater revenue generated per session?

The next icon, the bars, allows you to turn any set of available metrics into a bar chart, again keeping in mind that the data displayed is restricted to only that which is relevant to your selected dimension. Selection of this icon displays the table and bar chart for sessions shown on the top of page 151.

---

[34] An index compares the size of one group to another through division. The index for Dublin, for example, is calculated by dividing Dublin's revenue percentage by the session percentage and then multiplying the outcome by 100. An index of 100 is average. The more an index lies above or below 100, the greater the difference in size between the two measures.

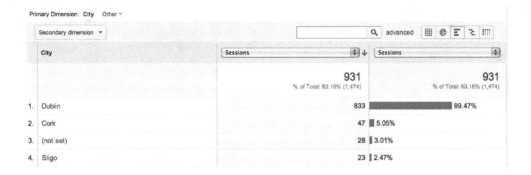

As with the earlier displays, you can report the data for one or two metrics through use of the pull-down menus.

The next icon, the over/under bars, allows you to turn any set of available metrics into a bar chart that compares each value's metric to the overall average, noting the percentage by which that metric is over or under the average. Selection of this icon displays a table and bar chart similar to that shown below.

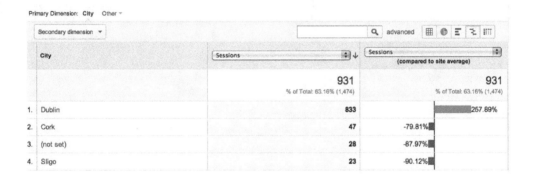

Finally, the icon on the far right allows you to cross-tabulate the data. Personally, I've found little use for this data display.

The Full Audience Menu

The left-hand side of almost every Google Analytics report page contains menu options that allow you to access data across a broad range of categories. We'll examine each of these throughout the book. For now, let's finish looking at **Audience** data.

Clicking on the **Audience** link opens a menu of additional audience dimensions (see opposite). Many of the dimensions have one or more data reporting options and metrics.[35]

We've already looked at the data presented when the **Overview** option is selected. Let's now take a look at the data provided by the other options, leaving **Users Flow** for Chapter 18, **Cohort Analysis** and **Bench-marking** for Chapter 19, and **Lifetime Value** (in beta) for Chapter 20. **User Explorer** is discussed in this chapter and in greater detail in Chapter 60.[36]

---

[35] Note that "Behavior" menu options get a bit confusing because there are actually two of these. One appears as an option in this **Audience** menu while the other heads its own major menu section. The data reported via each option are quite different. We discuss the first option in this chapter. Section VI discusses the full **Behavior** menu and its options.

[36] **Audiences** is likely to have only specialized appeal to readers and so we've eliminated discussion of this data report. If you are interested, you can find a discussion of Audiences set-up and data reporting at:
  Create and Edit Audiences (https://support.google.com/analytics/answer/2611404) and *Create Audiences from Segments* (https://support.google.com/analytics/answer/6015314).

Google Analytics defines an *active user* as "a user that has had at least one session on your website or app within the time frame set. This includes new and returning users." Note, that although the metric in the Active User report is labeled "active user" its meaning is the same as "user".

The active users report is accessed through the **Audience > Active Users** link on the left-hand side of any report page. When this link is selected, the "1 Day Active Users" line graph is displayed along with summary information for four pre-specified time periods (shown beneath the line chart). The "1 Day Active Users" line chart shown below, for example, displays day by day active users for my selected time period of May 12, 2015 to June 10, 2015.

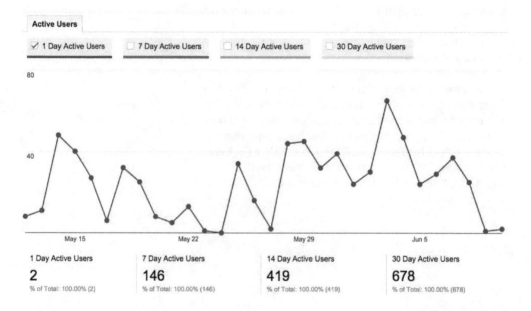

This time period was set using the calendar on the top of the data presentation page, as shown below.

Let's look at the line graph first.

The data displayed in the line graph is controlled by both the date range you set prior to data display, and the time frame selected from the options on the top of the chart. As noted earlier, the line chart shown on page 154 displays "1 Day Active Users" for the time frame I specified prior to data reporting. Changing the time period to March 12 to June 10, 2015, for example, changes the chart to that shown below. Note that while the time frame has changed, the chart still plots active users by day, since that is the option selected on the top of the chart.

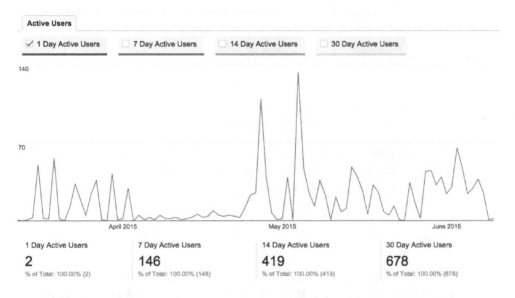

As you can see, the data displayed in the line graph is controlled by the options on the top of the line graph. Selecting the first three options from above the line chart displays the chart shown below.

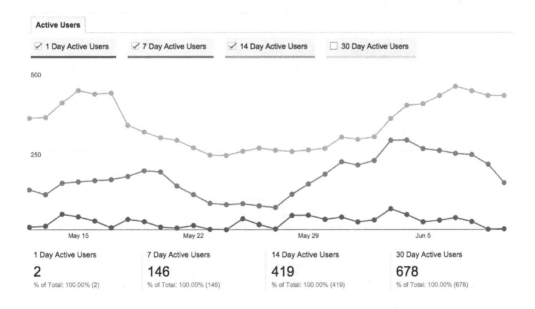

You've likely noticed that in all of the prior manipulations of the line chart, the data on the bottom of the chart remained the same. This is because the data provided is calculated *relative to the end date* of your specified date range. Thus, for example, this data would remain the same for all of the following date ranges because the end date is the same:

March 12, 2015 to June 10, 2015
March 12, 2014 to June 10, 2015
June 1, 2015 to June 10, 2015
June 10, 2015 to June 10, 2015

With this in mind, active users for all of the prior time periods would be defined as follows:

- *1-Day Active Users* are the number of unique new and returning users who initiated sessions on June 10, 2015 (the last day of the date range).

- *7-Day Active Users* are the number of unique new and returning users who initiated sessions from June 4 through June 10, 2015 (the last 7 days of the date range based on the range's end date).

- *14-Day Active Users* are the number of unique new and returning users who initiated sessions from May 28 through June 10, 2015 (the last 14 days of the date range based on the range's end date).

- *30-Day Active Users* are the number of unique users who initiated sessions from May 14 through June 10, 2015 (the entire 30 days based on the range's end date).

Finally, while the data presented beneath the line chart is determined by the end date of your date range, you can see the 1, 7, 14 or 30 day active user total for any date in your date range by hovering your mouse over one of the points in the line graph, as shown below.

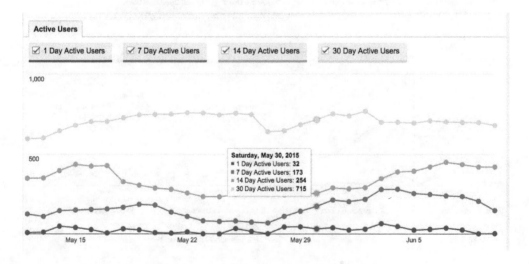

There are two circumstances in which I've found active user data useful. First, it provides a quick overview of the trend in website usage. I can use the line graph to see if traffic is growing, declining, or staying the same; and I can use the summary data to see if traffic is approaching or exceeding the traffic goals that I set for specific time periods. Second, the data can be used to quickly see the short- and longer-term effects of any marketing campaigns initiated to drive traffic to the site.

Demographics and interests[37]

Under certain circumstances, Google Analytics will provide estimates of your website users' demographics and interests. You can obtain this data by clicking on the relevant link beneath either the **Audience > Demographics** or **Audience > Interests** links, where the dimensions display the following values and metrics:

- Demographics
    Overview (overview of traffic by age and gender)
    Age (traffic by age ranges)
    Gender (traffic by gender)

- Interests
    Overview (overview of traffic by affinity and other categories)
    Affinity Categories (behavior by affinity categories)
    In-Market Categories (behavior by in-market categories)
    Other Categories (behavior by other interest categories)

These reports have the potential to help you understand the characteristics of the individuals who initiate site sessions, and as a result, can contribute to strategic planning. You can, for example, examine your analytics data by these demographic or interest characteristics to better understand the differences in age or interests between converting and non-converting users.

Similar to other data collected by Google Analytics, cookies play a key role in data collection for demographic and interest metrics. These cookies represent multiple, complimentary approaches to estimating demographic information.

- When individuals visit a website that has partnered with the Google Display Network, Google uses cookies to store a number in their browser to remember their visits. This number uniquely identifies a web browser on a specific computer, not a specific person. Browsers may be associated with a demographic

---

[37] Data in this section is adapted from: *Reach people of specific age and gender* at https://www.google.com/analytics/web/?hl=en#report/visitors-demographics-overview/a41714766w71256007p74402499/; *Reach people interested in your products or services* at https://support.google.com/adwords/answer/2497941?hl=en&utm_id=ad; *Overview of Demographics & Interests reports* at https://support.google.com/analytics/answer/2799357?hl=en); and pages linked from *About the audience reports* at https://support.google.com/analytics/answer/1012034?hl=en&ref_topic=1007027.

category (such as gender or age range) based on visited sites. In addition, some sites, such as social networking sites, provide Google with the demographic information that people volunteered to share. Google may also use demographics derived from Google profiles.

Think about Sara, who loves to garden. Many of the gardening sites and blogs on the Google Display Network that Sara visits have a majority of female visitors. Based on this, Sarah's browser would be added to the "female" demographic category. Thus, if Sara uses this browser to visit your site, then Google will count her visit as generated by a female.

- Google predicts an individual's interests from his or her web browsing behaviors. When someone visits a Google partner website, Google uses the content of the page or website as well as data from third-party companies to associate interests with a visitor's anonymous cookie ID, taking into account how often that individual visits sites of different categories. In addition, Google may use information that people provide to these partner websites about interests.

  Google places visitors in an interest category for 30 days, but this can change depending on the sites they visit. Imagine, for example, how a gardening enthusiast would most likely visit gardening-related sites over long periods of time. If that person then moves on to another interest (such as cooking) and is no longer reading as many pages about gardening but is reading a lot of pages related to cooking, Google will update the person's profile to remove gardening and include cooking. If, however, the gardening enthusiast continues to visit gardening websites for a long period of time, he or she will likely be included in that interest category for a longer period of time.

Things to keep in mind[38]

Google Analytics' demographic and interest information should always be used directionally rather than definitively. This is the case for four reasons:

- Google may not actually know the real age and interests of the vast majority of your site users.

  You can see the accuracy of Google's classifications by using the browser you use most often online and then taking a look at your own Google Ads settings at:

  https://www.google.com/settings/ads

  Is your description accurate? The profile and interests associated with the Safari browser on my personal computer have me classified as a 55 to 64 year old woman who is interested in rap music and fitness, all of which (needless to say) don't apply. The profile and interests associated with the Firefox browser

---

[38] *Demographics and Interest Reports in Google Analytics* at
http://www.seerinteractive.com/blog/demographics-and-interest-reports-in-google-analytics.

on my personal computer classify me as a 35 to 44 year old male interested in East Asian and electronic music (all of which, again, are inaccurate descriptors).

- Data thresholds are applied to demographic and interest reports, which means that not all of the user data may be available, so you may be viewing partial and perhaps nonrepresentative data.

  Google explains thresholds as follows: "Thresholds are applied to prevent any-one viewing a report from inferring the demographics or interests of individual users. When a report contains *Age*, *Gender*, or *Interest Category* (as a primary or secondary dimension, or as part of an applied segment), a threshold may be applied and some data may be withheld from the report. For example, if there are fewer than *N* instances of *Gender=male* in a report, then data for the *male* dimension may be withheld. If a threshold has been applied to a report, you will see a notice below the report title."[39]

- Your website users may have opted out of having data collected in their Google Ads Settings. There may also be other ways of opting out of having this data collected that could also impact what is reported by Google Analytics. Again, you may only have partial data, which should be used with caution.

- Data from users who are not logged into their Google account when browsing might not be recorded.

How accurate is the data?

Given that not all data is displayed in the demographics and interest reports *and* that a great deal of the data is estimated, it is important to understand data accuracy prior to its application to strategic planning. Overall, it appears that demographic and interest data accuracy increases along with sample size, so be very careful about using this data when it reflects a relatively low number of sessions.

Starting demographic and interest data collection

If you have not done so already, follow the steps outlined in Chapter 4 (pages 17-19) to begin the process of demographic/interest data collection. Keep in mind that demo-graphic and interest metrics, subject to data thresholds, will typically start to appear in your reports in about a day or so.

Demographic Metrics

Demographic data is accessed through **Audience > Demographics**.

---

[39] *Demographics and Interests Data Collection and Thresholds* at
https://support.google.com/analytics/answer/2954071?hl=en&utm_id=ad#thresholds.

The **Audience > Demographics > Overview** menu option provides summative demographic information for your site. By default, demographic information for site sessions is initially displayed, as shown below.

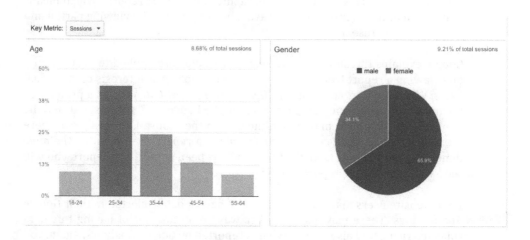

In my case, the greatest number of sessions is estimated to be associated with 25 to 34 year olds (the second column from the left), while the fewest number of sessions is associated with those aged 55 to 64 (the far right column). With regard to gender: men are much more likely to engage in site sessions versus women. Finally, note that due to sampling, the data represents only 9.21% of total site sessions (see top right-hand side of figure).

Sessions is the default display, as indicated in the pull-down menu labeled **Key Metric** (on the top left-hand-side of the figure). Selecting a different metric changes the display to show age and gender distributions for the new metric.

The **Audience > Demographics > Age** menu option displays a table similar to that shown below, where age is the organizing dimension. By default, the table will order the age groups in terms of each group's number of sessions. You can reorder the age groups chronologically by clicking twice in the top left-hand box labeled Age.

Let's focus on ecommerce by selecting Ecommerce from beneath the Explorer tab on the top of the Google Analytics report page (see below).

When we do so, the table shown below is presented.

Age	Sessions	Revenue	Transactions	Average Order Value	Ecommerce Conversion Rate	Per Session Value
	347 % of Total: 6.56% (5,286)	$238,500.00 % of Total: 26.72% ($892,500.00)	53 % of Total: 34.19% (155)	$4,500.00 Avg for View: $5,758.06 (-21.85%)	15.27% Avg for View: 2.93% (420.89%)	$687.32 Avg for View: $188.84 (307.08%)
1. 18-24	26 (7.49%)	$23,000.00 (9.64%)	5 (9.43%)	$4,600.00	19.23%	$884.62
2. 25-34	156 (44.96%)	$98,000.00 (41.09%)	20 (37.74%)	$4,900.00	12.82%	$628.21
3. 35-44	97 (27.95%)	$70,000.00 (29.35%)	16 (30.19%)	$4,375.00	16.49%	$721.65
4. 45-54	44 (12.68%)	$30,000.00 (12.58%)	7 (13.21%)	$4,285.71	15.91%	$681.82
5. 55-64	24 (6.92%)	$17,500.00 (7.34%)	5 (9.43%)	$3,500.00	20.83%	$729.17

Notice how the Ecommerce Conversion Rate is highest in the 55 to 64 year old group. It might be beneficial to attract more of these individuals to our site, as they are most likely to make a purchase. However, we might also want to try and raise this group's Average Order Value, as it is the lowest among the age groups.

Selecting **Audience > Demographics > Gender** displays a table identical to that shown when **Audience > Demographics > Age** is selected, except now the data is presented for men and women (see below). Here, we can see in greater detail how men are currently more important to our site's success than women. Men are more likely to initiate site sessions and they have a substantially higher Ecommerce conversion rate. Together, these factors result in men generating significantly more revenue compared to women.

The **Secondary Dimension** pull-down menu on the top left-hand side of each table allows us to create a table that examines and reports two dimensions simultaneously. The table shown below, for example, treats age as the primary dimension and gender as the secondary dimension. Here, we can see that:

- The skew to men (as indicated in the previous table) is not true for all age groups. While there are about equal numbers of sessions initiated by men versus women in the 18 to 24 and 25 to 34 year old groups, it is the older groups that skew male. In fact, we have *no* female site visitors aged 45 and above.

- Conversion rates vary across age/gender groups. 18 to 24 year old women and 55 to 64 year old men have the highest Ecommerce conversion rates.

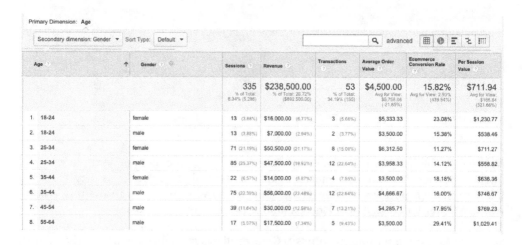

Interest Metrics

Interest group and related data is accessed through **Audience > Interests > Overview**. This menu option brings up three summary tables, each of which classifies site sessions in slightly different ways. Two of the tables are shown on the next page.

Key Metric: Sessions ▼

Affinity Category (reach)			9.33% of total sessions
7.13%		Technophiles	
5.78%		Movie Lovers	
5.24%		TV Lovers	
4.97%		Shutterbugs	
4.38%		News Junkies & Avid Readers/Entertainment & Celebrity News Junkies	
4.36%		Business Professionals	
3.82%		Travel Buffs	
3.14%		News Junkies & Avid Readers	
3.12%		Mobile Enthusiasts	
2.95%		Music Lovers	

In-Market Segment			8.57% of total sessions
4.69%		Business Services/Advertising & Marketing Services	
4.61%		Employment	
4.12%		Software/Business & Productivity Software	
3.53%		Business Services/Business Technology/Web Services/Web Design & Development	
3.38%		Financial Services/Investment Services	
3.38%		Travel/Hotels & Accommodations	
3.28%		Business Services/Advertising & Marketing Services/SEO & SEM Services	
3.16%		Dating Services	
2.76%		Real Estate/Residential Properties	
2.74%		Education/Post-Secondary Education	

- *Affinity Categories* estimate an individual's overall interests, passions, and life-style as reflected in their long-term online search/browsing patterns. Google explains these categories as follows: "Affinity audiences consist of aggregated consumers who have demonstrated a qualified interest in a particular topic ... Our more than 80 segments have been [created] using rich data points and past online behaviors of consumers, taking into account how many times a consumer visits a site and for how long."[40]

- *In-Market Audiences* are composed of individuals who are searching and comparing your product/service. Google describes these individuals as those who are "are actively researching or comparing products and services across Google Display Network publisher and partner sites and YouTube. To qualify someone as being in-market for a specific product or service, Google takes into account clicks on related ads and subsequent conversions, along with the content of the sites and pages they visit and the recency and frequency of the visits."[41]

- The *Other Category* table (not shown in the image above) provides a more focused view of the type of content in which site users are interested when compared to the Affinity Categories.

Clicking on any of the links beneath **Audience > Interests** displays acquisition, behavior and ecommerce metrics for the category selected. The table shown on the top of page 164, for example, is displayed when I select **Audience > Interests > Affinity Categories.**

---

[40] *Affinity Audiences* at https://www.thinkwithgoogle.com/products/affinity-audiences.html.

[41] *In-Market Audiences* at https://www.thinkwithgoogle.com/products/in-market-audiences-gdn.html.

Google Analytics Demystified   163

Affinity Category (reach)	Acquisition			Behavior			Conversions eCommerce ▼		
	Sessions ↓	% New Sessions	New Users	Bounce Rate	Pages / Session	Avg. Session Duration	Transactions	Revenue	Ecommerce Conversion Rate
	493 % of Total: 9.33% (5,268)	**63.49%** Avg for View: 84.34% (-24.72%)	**313** % of Total: 7.02% (4,458)	**55.58%** Avg for View: 79.46% (-30.05%)	**2.85** Avg for View: 1.53 (86.59%)	**00:02:01** Avg for View: 00:00:56 (113.67%)	**68** % of Total: 43.87% (155)	**$322,000.00** % of Total: 36.08% ($892,500.00)	**13.79%** Avg for View: 2.93% (370.39%)
1. Technophiles	370 (7.13%)	67.30%	249 (7.31%)	58.11%	2.72	00:01:58	55 (7.81%)	$245,500.00 (7.82%)	14.86%
2. Movie Lovers	300 (5.78%)	63.00%	189 (5.55%)	59.33%	2.63	00:01:58	33 (4.69%)	$166,000.00 (5.14%)	11.00%
3. TV Lovers	272 (5.24%)	70.96%	193 (5.66%)	58.09%	2.78	00:01:58	34 (4.83%)	$158,000.00 (4.89%)	12.50%
4. Shutterbugs	258 (4.97%)	61.24%	158 (4.64%)	59.69%	2.73	00:01:56	37 (5.26%)	$180,000.00 (5.57%)	14.34%
5. News Junkies & Avid Readers/Entertainment & Celebrity News Junkies	227 (4.38%)	61.67%	140 (4.11%)	61.67%	2.70	00:01:56	32 (4.55%)	$148,500.00 (4.60%)	14.10%
6. Business Professionals	226 (4.36%)	58.85%	133 (3.90%)	61.50%	2.64	00:01:54	31 (4.40%)	$125,500.00 (3.86%)	13.72%
7. Travel Buffs	198 (3.82%)	64.14%	127 (3.73%)	62.63%	2.59	00:02:02	24 (3.41%)	$103,500.00 (3.20%)	12.12%
8. News Junkies & Avid Readers	163 (3.14%)	68.10%	111 (3.26%)	54.80%	2.67	00:02:00	22 (3.12%)	$107,500.00 (3.33%)	13.50%
9. Mobile Enthusiasts	162 (3.12%)	69.75%	113 (3.32%)	50.62%	2.98	00:01:46	30 (4.26%)	$133,000.00 (4.12%)	18.52%
10. Music Lovers	153 (2.95%)	67.32%	103 (3.02%)	52.94%	3.25	00:01:52	25 (3.55%)	$110,000.00 (3.40%)	16.34%

User Explorer

By default, Google Analytics treats each distinct browser as representing a different user. Imagine, for example, that John visits your website via his laptop in the morning and then visits again later in the day via his mobile phone. Google Analytics would associate these visits with two different users.

Individuals and businesses that hope to correct this situation can use the Google Analytics User ID function, which allows you to associate visitor data from multiple devices and different sessions. If, for example, we assign John a unique user ID on his first visit to our website, we can use this ID to identify him when he visits via his phone. As a result, his multiple sessions on different devices will all be associated with the same unique individual, in this case John. Google goes on the explain how "when you implement the User ID, you can identify related actions and devices and connect these seemingly independent data points. That same search on a phone, purchase on a laptop, and re-engagement on a tablet that previously looked like three unrelated actions on unrelated devices can now be understood as three related actions on related devices. This gives context to your analysis and so you can get a holistic view of your users and their behaviors.

The User ID feature relies on you - not Google - to create, assign and maintain the User ID. Here, Google notes that in order "to implement the User ID, you must be able to generate your own unique IDs, consistently assign IDs to users, and include these IDs wherever you send data to Analytics. For example, you could send the unique IDs generated by your own authentication system to Analytics as values for the User ID. Any engagement, like link clicks and page or screen navigation, that happen while a unique ID is assigned can be sent and connected in Analytics via the User ID."[42]

---

[42] https://support.google.com/analytics/answer/3123662?hl=en

The **Audience > Behavior > User-ID Coverage** report presents the distribution of assigned User IDs among all traffic. You can use this report to see the total number of sessions and compare the proportion in which users are assigned a User ID to the proportion in which users aren't assigned a User ID. (Note that this report is only available in Views in which you have set up the User ID feature.[43]

An example **Audience > Behavior > User-ID Coverage** report is shown below, where it is noted that all (100%) of our site sessions were unassigned; that is, did not use the User ID feature.

Note the pull down menu (currently labeled "Sessions") on the top, middle of the display. This menu (See below) allows you to look at the use the User ID in the context of other metrics.

Finally, when using this report, keep in mind that the report only gives you an overview of how much of your traffic has a User ID assigned (or not). This report does not provide any data or details about users and sessions in which a user ID is assigned. Use the **User-ID Coverage** report in conjunction with a User ID filtered view to get a more in-depth analysis of how users with an assigned user ID engage with your content.[44]

Geography

Clicking on the **Audience > Geo** link brings up options to view either language or location information. These links lead to the same information as that generated through the **Audience Overview** page.

---

[43] Set up the User ID at https://support.google.com/analytics/answer/3123666

[44] User ID Coverage Report at https://support.google.com/analytics/answer/3123670

Keep the following in mind when interpreting this data:

- Language spoken is inferred from the user's browser locale.

- Location is derived from mapping IP addresses to geographic locations. City location may not be accurate for visits from mobile devices.

Finally, it is possible that you will see "(not set)" in these reports. In this context "(not set)" means that Google Analytics could not determine where someone was located.

Behavior

Clicking on the **Audience > Behavior** link brings up three options: **New Vs. Returning, Frequency & Recency**, and **Engagement.**

New Vs. Returning

The **Audience Overview** page we looked at earlier presented summary information for Sessions, Users and % New Sessions. The **Audience > Behavior > New Vs. Returning** option provides another perspective on these metrics.

When this option is selected from the left-hand menu, the first thing we see is the standard reporting table with metrics reported individually for new and returning visitors (see below).

This table always has the potential to provide important strategic insights. In my case, there is some depressing news for my travel agency website. First, new visitors generate almost all of my ses-sions. Repeat business is almost nonexistent. Second, the behaviors of new visitors versus returning visitors are quite different. Unfortunately for our travel agency, returning visitors have a higher bounce rate and are much less likely to make a purchase (as reflected in the Ecommerce Conversion Rate column). Clearly, something needs to be done to address this situation. The business cannot be successful without returning visitors. Why aren't people coming back? When they do come back, why aren't they staying and buying? Both of these questions need an immediate answer.

In situations such as this, it is often beneficial to use the charting options on the top of the table to focus on one or two specific metrics. The first chart below uses the over/under chart option and the pull-down menus to focus on the relative size of new to returning website visitors. This chart makes it easy to see that almost all of my traffic is from new visitors. The second chart below simultaneously displays both sessions and ecommerce conversion rate for new versus returning visitors. As with the first chart, this approach makes the differences between the two groups much easier to see.

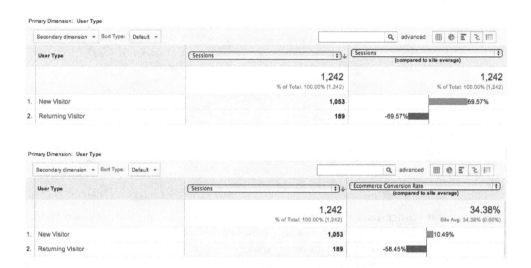

Frequency & Recency

This report lets you see the extent to which your site is able to maintain user interest over time using sessions as the classifying metric. **Audience > Behavior > Frequency & Recency** allows you to see the number of single and multiple sessions taking place within a specified time frame and how many days, if any, have elapsed between the first and subsequent sessions.

Clicking on the **Audience > Behavior > Frequency & Recency** option first displays a distribution of sessions (**Count of Sessions**) within your specified time period, as shown on the top of page 168. A **Count of Sessions** equal to one (in the first column) indicates a single session, that is, a session without a return to the site. Here, you can see that the news for my website is quite disappointing. The overwhelming majority of site visitors had only a single session: 665 out of a total 1,135 sessions were a single session. Among the remainder, very few sessions were two or more by the same individual.

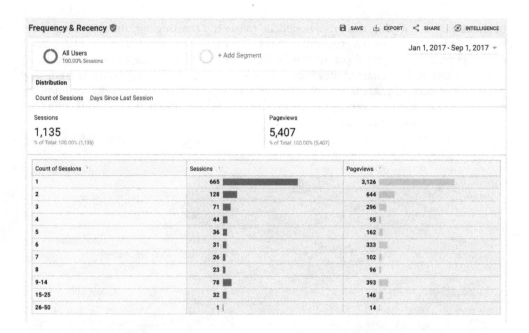

Clicking on **Days Since Last Session** on the top of the chart changes the data view to that shown below. A **Days Since Last Session** equal to zero indicates a new user. A **Days Since Last Session** equal to one indicates that a user visited and then returned on the next day. Here we can see that site users make up their minds very quickly - they either never come back after their first session or they initiate another session very quickly. Few site visitors initiate a session after a time lag (from first visit) of two or more days.

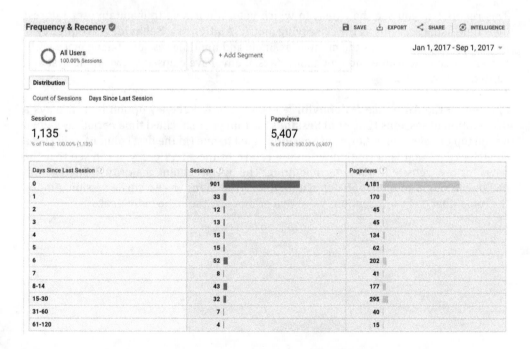

Engagement

The last **Audience > Behavior** metric is **Engagement**, which reports how much time people spend on your site (reported as Session Duration) and how many pages they view (reported as Page Depth).

The chart of **Session Duration** is shown below. Nearly half of all site sessions are 10 seconds or less (i.e., 503 sessions out of 1,135).

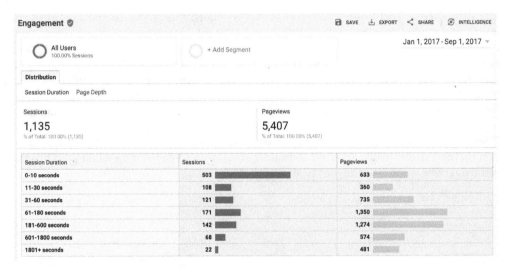

The news from the **Page Depth** report (below) is no more encouraging. The majority of site sessions end after a viewing just one or two pages.

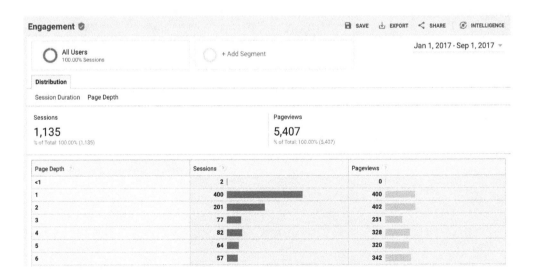

The **Audience > Technology** link provides the opportunity to view two technology-related aspects of user behavior: **Browser & OS** and **Network**. Note that links to this information also appear on the **Audience Overview** page.

Browser and OS Report

The **Audience > Technology > Browser & OS** report allows you to see the different browsers people use to reach your site, along with information about the systems that run those browsers. Google notes that "this information is helpful when you are making design decisions about your site. For example, if the bulk of your visitors are using screen resolutions of 1024 x 768 and above, you can design for the additional viewing area. With information about which browsers visitors use and whether they maintain recent versions of Flash, you can scope your testing to cover the most likely population."

Selecting the **Audience > Technology > Browser & OS** report first brings up information on the various browsers used to initiate sessions on your site (see below). Chrome is the overwhelming favorite for my site.

Note that links to additional, related information (Operating System, Screen Resolution, Screen Colors, Flash version, and Java Support via the Other pull-down menu) run across the top of the table. Clicking on any of these links brings up a table with the relevant information. Selecting Screen Resolution, for example, displays the table shown on the top of page 171.

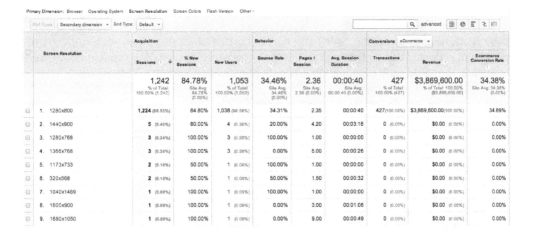

Screen Resolution	Acquisition			Behavior				Conversions eCommerce ˅		
	Sessions ↓	% New Sessions	New Users	Bounce Rate	Pages / Session	Avg. Session Duration	Transactions	Revenue	Ecommerce Conversion Rate
	1,242 % of Total: 100.00% (1,242)	84.78% Site Avg: 84.78% (0.00%)	1,053 % of Total: 100.00% (1,053)	34.46% Site Avg: 34.46% (0.00%)	2.36 Site Avg: 2.36 (0.00%)	00:00:40 Site Avg: 00:00:40 (0.00%)	427 % of Total: 100.00% (427)	$3,869,600.00 % of Total: 100.00% ($3,869,600.00)	34.38% Site Avg: 34.38% (0.00%)
1. 1280x800	1,224 (98.55%)	84.80%	1,038 (98.58%)	34.31%	2.35	00:00:40	427(100.00%)	$3,869,600.00(100.00%)	34.89%
2. 1440x900	5 (0.40%)	80.00%	4 (0.38%)	20.00%	4.20	00:03:18	0 (0.00%)	$0.00 (0.00%)	0.00%
3. 1280x768	3 (0.24%)	100.00%	3 (0.28%)	100.00%	1.00	00:00:00	0 (0.00%)	$0.00 (0.00%)	0.00%
4. 1366x768	3 (0.24%)	100.00%	3 (0.28%)	0.00%	5.00	00:00:26	0 (0.00%)	$0.00 (0.00%)	0.00%
5. 1173x733	2 (0.16%)	50.00%	1 (0.09%)	100.00%	1.00	00:00:00	0 (0.00%)	$0.00 (0.00%)	0.00%
6. 320x568	2 (0.16%)	50.00%	1 (0.09%)	50.00%	1.50	00:00:32	0 (0.00%)	$0.00 (0.00%)	0.00%
7. 1040x1469	1 (0.08%)	100.00%	1 (0.09%)	100.00%	1.00	00:00:00	0 (0.00%)	$0.00 (0.00%)	0.00%
8. 1600x900	1 (0.08%)	100.00%	1 (0.09%)	0.00%	3.00	00:01:06	0 (0.00%)	$0.00 (0.00%)	0.00%
9. 1680x1050	1 (0.08%)	100.00%	1 (0.09%)	0.00%	9.00	00:00:49	0 (0.00%)	$0.00 (0.00%)	0.00%

Network Report

The **Audience > Technology > Network** report lets you see which service providers account for the most sessions and the domain to which they are connected. Google notes that "having insight into which service providers your visitors use can help you design your site's content. For example, if your site offers video content and you see that visitors are evenly distributed among providers that offer a variety of connection speeds, you can offer them a choice of video quality (720p and 360p). If the bulk of your visitors use providers that offer high connection speeds, you can offer high-definition video, along with higher resolution graphics and a higher quality audio-compression format."

Selecting **Audience > Technology > Network** provides the names of the networks individuals used to initiate sessions on your site. The table below displays the most common networks used to access my site.

Service Provider	Acquisition			Behavior				Conversions eCommerce ˅		
	Sessions ↓	% New Sessions	New Users	Bounce Rate	Pages / Session	Avg. Session Duration	Transactions	Revenue	Ecommerce Conversion Rate
	1,242 % of Total: 100.00% (1,242)	84.78% Site Avg: 84.78% (0.00%)	1,053 % of Total: 100.00% (1,053)	34.46% Site Avg: 34.46% (0.00%)	2.36 Site Avg: 2.36 (0.00%)	00:00:40 Site Avg: 00:00:40 (0.00%)	427 % of Total: 100.00% (427)	$3,869,600.00 % of Total: 100.00% ($3,869,600.00)	34.38% Site Avg: 34.38% (0.00%)
1. subscriber block 2	262 (21.10%)	91.60%	240 (22.79%)	35.88%	1.88	00:00:37	106 (24.82%)	$963,700.00 (24.90%)	40.46%
2. kabel deutschland breitband customer 20	199 (16.02%)	90.95%	181 (17.19%)	31.16%	2.15	00:00:11	86 (20.14%)	$800,600.00 (20.69%)	43.22%
3. hutchison 3g ireland ltd.	133 (10.71%)	87.22%	116 (11.02%)	34.59%	2.11	00:00:29	60 (14.05%)	$498,800.00 (12.89%)	45.11%
4. subscriber block 1	122 (9.82%)	73.77%	90 (8.55%)	36.89%	2.59	00:00:31	37 (8.67%)	$340,300.00 (8.79%)	30.33%
5. hutchison 3g ireland limited	113 (9.10%)	75.22%	85 (9.07%)	18.58%	3.12	00:00:45	39 (9.13%)	$285,500.00 (7.38%)	34.51%

Selecting **Hostname** from the top of the table changes the display to report the hostname(s) or domain(s) that visitors used to reach your site. Google notes that "Typically this is your site's domain. For example, if you host your blog on mysite.example.com, then your hostname report will contain mysite.example.com. In some cases, your website might be hosted on other domains, such as when you create a mirror (copy) of your site to host on a domain in another country (e.g. mysite.example.uk). In addition, if someone copies a page from your website directly without modifying any of the source code (including the tracking code) and places that page on their own website, your reports will reflect traffic to that page from that hostname as well. You can use view filters to ensure that only traffic from allowed hosts reaches your reports."[45]

Additionally, as we discussed in terms of referral spam (see pages 100 to 103) the Hostname report provides valuable information, which can be used to create referral spam filters.

Mobile[46]

The **Audience > Mobile** menu provides two types of reports: **Overview** and **Devices**. The **Audience > Mobile > Overview** report classifies sessions on the basis of the type of device used to access your site. The **Audience > Mobile > Devices** report provides significant detail *about* the mobile devices that were used by people engaged in site sessions.

The **Audience > Mobile > Overview** report is organized around three device category dimensions, defined as follows:

- **Desktop:** contains towers, laptops, netbooks and game consoles such as Playstation 3 and the Nintendo Wii/Wii U.

- **Mobile Phones:** covers smart phones and hand held game consoles such as the Nintendo 3DS and PlayStation Vita.

- **Tablets:** includes standard iPads, Google Nexus, Galaxy Tabs, and also e-readers such as the Kindle Fire.

The table shown below is displayed when I select the **Audience > Mobile > Overview** report. As you can see, almost all my site sessions are initiated via desktop. Almost no sessions are through mobile or tablets.

Device Category	Acquisition			Behavior			Conversions eCommerce		
	Sessions	% New Sessions	New Users	Bounce Rate	Pages / Session	Avg. Session Duration	Transactions	Revenue	Ecommerce Conversion Rate
	774 % of Total: 100.00% (774)	87.21% Avg for View: 87.21% (0.00%)	675 % of Total: 100.00% (675)	75.32% Avg for View: 75.32% (0.00%)	1.55 Avg for View: 1.55 (0.00%)	00:01:05 Avg for View: 00:01:05 (0.00%)	52 % of Total: 100.00% (52)	$356,000.00 % of Total: 100.00% ($356,000.00)	6.72% Avg for View: 6.72% (0.00%)
1. desktop	744 (96.12%)	89.52%	666 (98.67%)	77.82%	1.45	00:01:03	39 (75.00%)	$262,500.00 (73.74%)	5.24%
2. mobile	27 (3.49%)	29.63%	8 (1.19%)	3.70%	4.37	00:01:52	13 (25.00%)	$93,500.00 (26.26%)	48.15%
3. tablet	3 (0.39%)	33.33%	1 (0.15%)	100.00%	1.00	00:00:00	0 (0.00%)	$0.00 (0.00%)	0.00%

---

[45] *Hostname* at https://support.google.com/analytics/answer/1032966?hl=en.

[46] *Audience: Mobile* at https://support.google.com/analytics/answer/1011360?hl=en; *What You Can Learn From Google Analytics Mobile Reports* at http://searchenginewatch.com/article/2308358/What-You-Can-Learn-From-Google-Analytics-Mobile-Reports.

The **Audience > Mobile > Mobile Devices** report is shown below. By default, the initial set of data displays the names of the mobile devices used to access your site. In this case, three mobile devices were identified as being used for site sessions. But, more data is available.

When you look across the top of the report, you can see that you can also view information related to: Mobile Device Branding, Service Provider, Mobile Input Selector (e.g., touchscreen, joystick, stylus), Operating System and Screen Resolution via the Other pull-down menu.

Google points out that "understanding mobile traffic to your site can give you an indication of whether you need to design your site to accommodate both mobile and computer traffic, or whether the traffic justifies a *separate* mobile site. For example, while mobile visits may represent only a few percent of your overall visitors, you might find that they convert at a higher rate and that the average value of mobile transactions is higher. In this case, a site devoted exclusively to mobile platforms (streamlined content, simpler navigation) might further encourage transactions via smart phones."

18

The Audience Menu: Users Flow

Audience > Users Flow provides a graphical representation of the paths individuals take through your site. **Users Flow** identifies how sessions begin, move through different pages, and then ultimately end. The table shown below appears when I select **Audience > Users Flow** from my colleague's travel site.

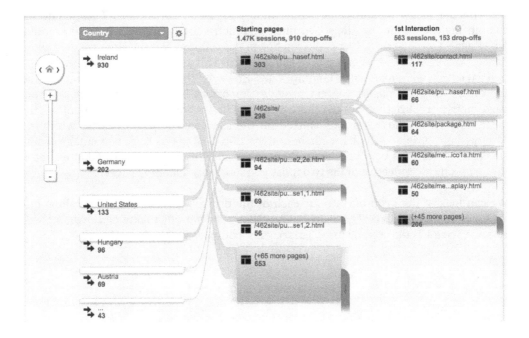

The default chart uses **Country** as the organizing dimension (see the top of the first column). Beneath **Country** is a list of all country sources of sessions: Ireland initiated the greatest number of sessions (930) followed by Germany (202) and the United States (133).

The chart is composed of different sized boxes and grey bands. The boxes in the "Starting pages" and subsequent columns contain page URLs from my website. The size of the individual boxes indicates the relative number of sessions occurring on any individual page. The larger the box, the greater the number of sessions. The grey bands show connections between the values of your organizing dimension (in this case different countries) and pages of your site or between two site pages. The larger the grey band, the greater the connection between two items.

You can see the exact size of the relationship by placing your cursor over any grey band, as shown below. The pop-up window indicates that 16.2% of all site traffic involved sessions originating in Ireland and starting on the site's purchasef.html page.

The "Starting pages" column rank orders landing pages for site sessions. The data in this column indicates that the site's two most common starting pages are an alternative home page (purchasef.html, the top box in the column) and the site's regular home page (/462site/, the second box in the column). This is good news, as these are the two pages that were planned as landing pages. However, the information provided at the top of the "Starting pages" column provides important but disturbing news. Starting page metrics report that overall there were 1,470 sessions with 916 drop-offs. This means that of all those sessions started on the site (on any page) nearly two-thirds "dropped off" or left without any further interaction. Losing this large percentage of sessions at the outset is very bad news. What we need to determine is: To what extent is this drop-off rate reflective of the two most frequently used landing pages?

We can look at the drop-off rate for each of the primary landing pages by rolling our cursor over the page box. The chart below examines drop-offs taking place when purchasef.html is the landing page. This page is a disaster with a drop-off rate of 87.5%.

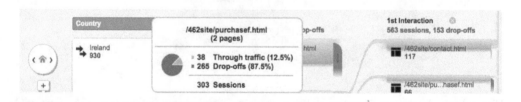

Fortunately, as indicated in the chart on the top of page 177, the drop-off problem appears to be confined to our purchasef.html page. The drop-off rate for the regular home page is only 23.5%. Clearly, it is in the site's best interest to eliminate traffic to the purchasef.html page.

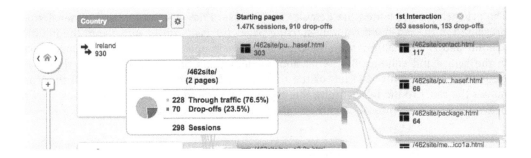

The default users flow chart shown on page 175 displayed all of the countries from which sessions originated. We can simplify the display, however, by selecting one individual country to focus upon. This is accomplished by clicking on the country of interest (in this case the United States) and selecting **View only this segment**, as shown below.

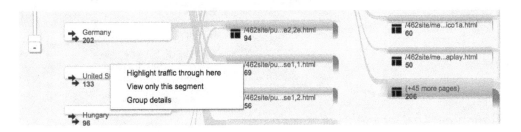

When this is done, all traffic *except that* which originated in the United States is eliminated from the chart (see below).

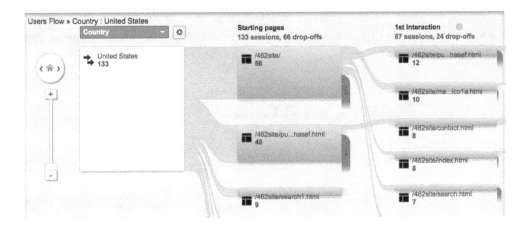

The prior charts presented the default view for users flow: the organizing dimension is presented in the left-hand column, starting pages for visits to the site are in the middle column, and 1st interactions with the site (i.e., where people go from the landing page) are in the right-hand column. But, what about interactions that take place after the first? Notice the circle icon to the left of the first column. Clicking on the arrows in the icon moves the chart to the left or right, thereby displaying additional interactions, as shown below where the 2nd interaction now appears.

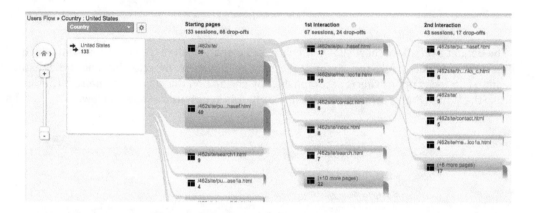

Changing the organizing dimension

There are times when you may want to look at user flow in terms of dimensions other than country. This can be done via the pull-down menu (see below). We might, for example, want to examine the behaviors of those who came to the site via a social network or from a particular city. Let's use the latter as our example.

We begin by choosing **City** as our organizing dimension from the pull-down menu (see below).

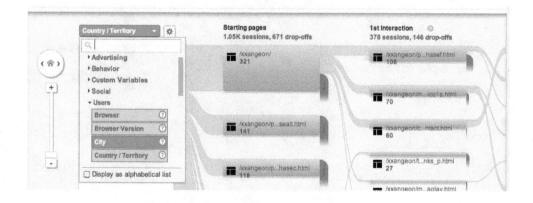

Selecting **City** results in the chart shown below, where city names are shown in the first column as the values of our selected dimension.

Let's imagine that I want to reduce the complexity of the chart by focusing on just those sessions that originated in San Diego. There are two ways to accomplish this.

First, clicking on the box labeled "San Diego" brings up a pop-up window with three options (see below).

Selecting the **Highlight traffic through here** option keeps all of the reported data from the original chart, but now, all traffic *not* through San Diego is faded out, and all traffic that *is* through San Diego is highlighted. This is illustrated in the chart shown on the top of page 180. Clicking once again on "San Diego" and selecting **Clear Highlighting** from the pop-up menu brings the chart back to its original form.

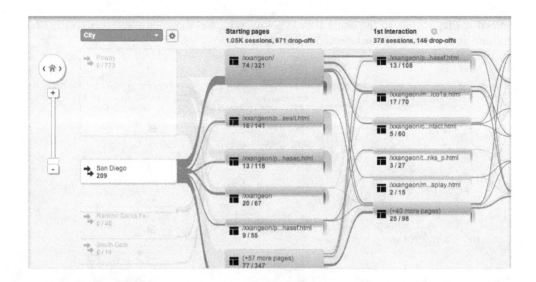

Alternatively, I can eliminate all data not of interest. Once again, I begin by clicking on San Diego, only this time, I select **View only this segment.** When this option is chosen, the chart changes to display only sessions initiated in San Diego (see below).

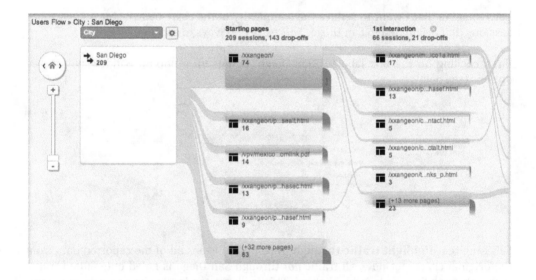

✔ The two pop-up menu options ("Highlight traffic through here" and "View only this segment") can be applied to any item shown in a box on the chart. As a result, you can perform detailed analyses of session paths focusing on any page listed as the start page or subsequent interaction.

There may be times when you want to examine a subset of the data in one chart, but this subset consists of two or three elements rather than just one. You might, for example, want to look at user flow for two cities in different parts of California. The **Users Flow** options allow this to be done easily and quickly. Let's illustrate this by focusing on the desire to examine user flow for just two California cities: San Diego and San Francisco.

We begin with the standard Users Flow chart organized by city, as shown below.

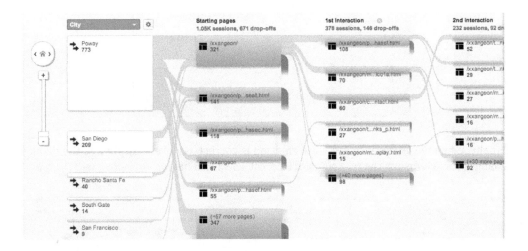

Next, we indicate that we want to examine just these two cities. We do this by clicking on the small gear symbol to the left of **City** (see below).

When this is done the popup window shown below appears.

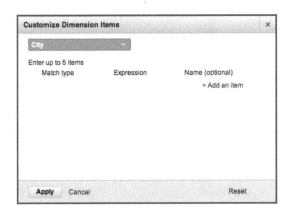

We begin by clicking on **+Add an item**. On the new line displayed we leave **Match type** set to the default **Equals** and we type San Diego into the **Expression** box. We then do the same for San Francisco. When we are done, the information provided in the window is as shown below.

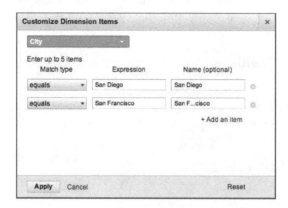

Finally, when we are sure that the information is correct, we press **Apply** and the display changes to include just the two cities of interest, as shown below.

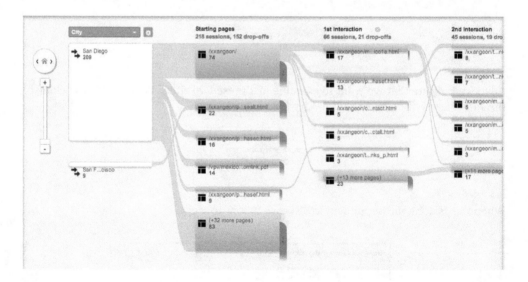

Users flow and strategic questions

The prior discussion illustrated how users flow charts can provide important insights into how individuals start, move through and end site sessions. Users flow charts can also help you answer strategic questions that can lead to improved site design and organization.

Let's look at the data from a travel website based in Germany. Imagine that the site's owners have spent a great deal of time and money creating videos for this travel site. These videos, which appear on the `mediaplay.html` page are designed to highlight the benefits of vacation travel and to "push" people toward the purchase page after they have landed on the site home page (`/index.html/`). The owner's want the purchase page to be viewed immediately after the videos are seen. Thus, the strategic goal is to have:

- sessions begin on the site home page
- the 1st interaction be the video page
- the 2nd interaction be the purchase page

The users flow chart can help us determine the extent to which this strategic goal is being realized.

We begin by clicking on Germany in the first column and then **View only this segment** in the pop-up window to isolate only sessions originating from Germany. Next, we click on our home page (`index.html`) in the "Starting pages" column. When the pop-up window appears we select **Highlight traffic through here**. When this is done the chart shown below is displayed.

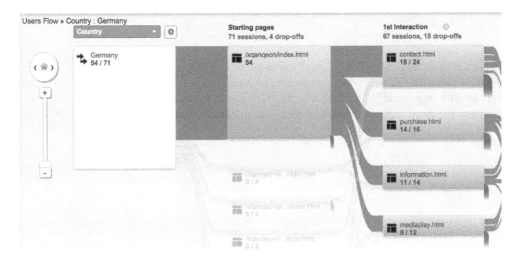

Two positive indicators appear. First, the majority of site sessions (54 out of 71) begin on my home page - exactly where the site's owners want them to start. So, the first part of the goal is being achieved. Additionally, there are very few drop-offs from the page (only 4 out of 71).

Next, there is good and bad news to be found. The bad news appears when we examine the flow from the home page to `mediaplay.html` in the 1st Interaction column (`mediaplay.html` is in the last position). Hovering my mouse over the grey band that connects the home page to `mediaplay.html` displays the chart shown on the top of page 184. There are relatively few sessions that move in the desired direction from the home page to the video page (17% or 9 out of 54). So, the goal to have the video page viewed immediately after the home page appears not to be realized. We'll need to examine the home page with an eye to revising content and design in order to remedy this situation.

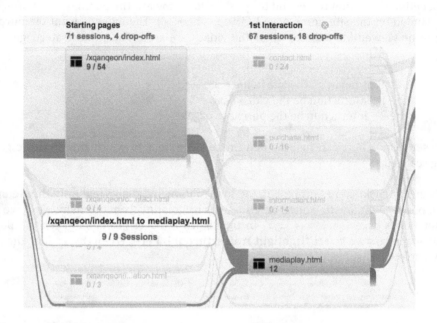

The good news appears when I hover my mouse over the green mediaplay.html box (see below). There is relatively little drop-off from this page (25% or 3 out of 12 sessions) and so this page does appear to successfully move people through the site once they arrive at the page. But, are they moving to the purchase page?

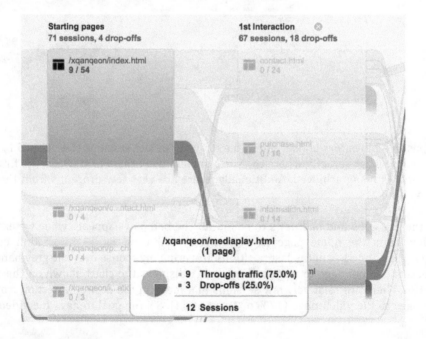

The last part of the strategic goal wants people view the videos on the video page immediately prior to arriving at the purchase page. We can explore how well the site accomplished this part of the goal by looking at where people go after they view the video page (which is immediately after they enter the site). This is determined by first identifying the total number of people viewing the video page (from any Starting page) and then tracking where they go after the video page by following the grey bands to 2nd Interaction pages. We accomplish this through the chart shown below.

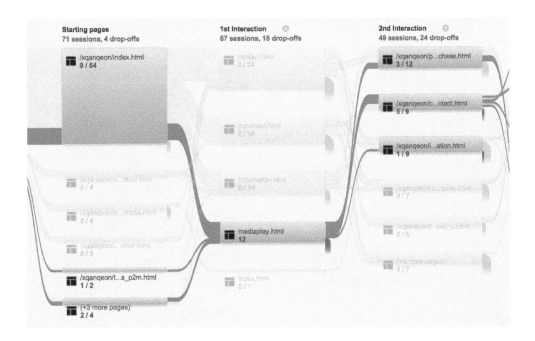

We can see that twelve people in total viewed the mediaplay.html page as their 1st Interaction. Then, these individuals went to view one of three pages: the purchase page (the top box in the 2nd Interaction column), the contact page (the middle box in the 2nd Interaction column), and the more information page (the bottom box in the 2nd Interaction column). The numbers within each box tell a sad story. They indicate that the video page is not leading site visitors to the purchase page. In fact, of the people who do move on to the 2nd Interaction from the video page, more visit the contact page then the purchase page. Once again, the current flow indicates that the site needs to: 1) determine what is lacking/confusing on the video page that is motivating people to use the contact form and 2) more explicitly encourage people to view the purchase page after the video page.

19

The Audience Menu: Cohorts and Benchmarks

Cohort analysis

A cohort is "a group of people who share a common characteristic or experience within a defined period."[47] Everyone born on June 7, 1948, for example, would be a member of this date's birth cohort. Similarly, every student who graduates in June, 2016 would be a member of the "Class of 2016" cohort. Finally, all those who attended the Woodstock Music Festival would be members of the Woodstock cohort. At present, Google Analytics defines a cohort as a group of individuals all of who initiated their *first* session on your website or blog on the same day.

Honestly, I haven't found a great deal of use for cohort analysis, except for the limited instance in which I want to track a group of individuals who are all the target of a specific marketing or communication campaign. The data is complex and difficult to apply and the way in which day-to-day data is presented encourages you to spend a considerable amount of time examining/explaining micro changes in trends that in reality may represent just the normal ebb and flow of website traffic and engagement. All of this can lead to inappropriate actions designed to capitalize on (incorrectly) perceived positive and negative trends. So, if you want to skip this section, I think that you can do so without harm. If you are interested, we'll first explain how to access, read, and interpret cohort reports. Then, we'll discuss what I think are significant cautions/caveats in viewing and applying user retention metrics to strategic decision-making.

Cohort analysis is currently in beta test and is available to most Google Analytics accounts. When available, cohort reports can be accessed via the **Audience > Cohort Analysis** link from the left-hand side of any report page. When this link is selected, the display shown on the top of page 188 is presented.

---

[47] *Cohort Study* at https://en.wikipedia.org/wiki/Cohort_study.

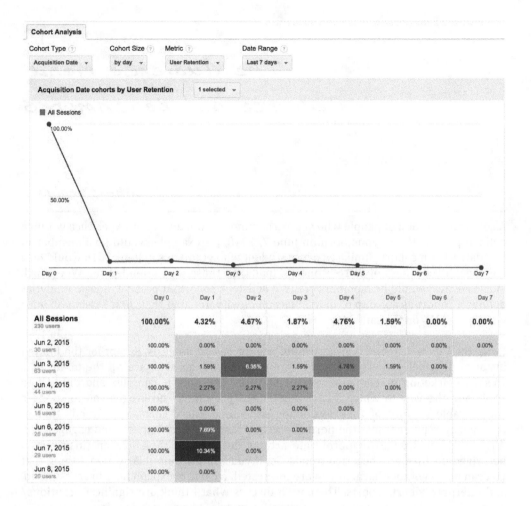

There are three parts to this report:

- Display options, found on the very top of the report just below the Cohort Analysis tab.

- Cohort averages and metrics, found in the table on the bottom of the report.

- A line graph, found in the middle of the report that charts cohort averages and other summary data.

Display Options

There are four display options at the top of the report (see the figure on the top of page 189).

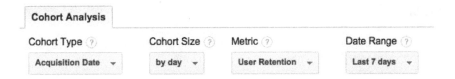

- **Cohort Type** specifies the criteria used to define the cohort. "Acquisition Date" is the only criteria available at the time of this writing. As a result, individuals are assigned to a cohort based on the day they initiated their *first* session on your site.

- **Metric** provides a pull-down menu that allows you to select the specific metric being reported (see below). The default option is "User Retention", which we will discuss in more detail shortly.

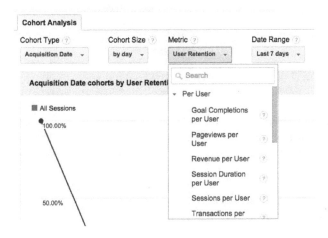

The metric selected via this menu selects the data displayed in both the line graph and the individual metrics displayed beneath the line graph.

- The remaining two options, **Cohort Size** and **Date Range,** work in tandem with each other and allow you to specify the time-related criteria to be used to display cohort data in both the line graph and the data report.

  Selecting **Cohort Size** *by day* allows you to set the **Date Range** and subsequent data display to the last 7, 14, 21, or 30 days prior to today's date.

  Selecting **Cohort Size** *by week* allows you to set the **Date Range** and subsequent data display to the last week or 3, 6, 9 or 12 weeks prior to today's date.

  Selecting **Cohort Size** *by month* allows you to set the **Date Range** and subsequent data display to the last 1, 2 or 3 months prior to today's date.

The Data Display

The bottom-of-the-report data display shows the activity of each cohort from the time of the first session through subsequent time periods.

- When Cohort Size is set to "day" then a new cohort is formed every day and cohort behaviors are reported on a daily basis starting with the day after the first session (see below for daily User Retention reporting).

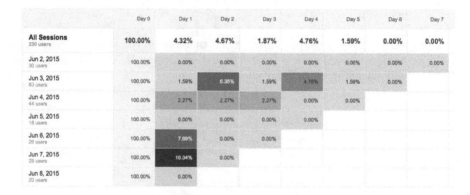

- When Cohort Size is set to "week", then a new cohort is formed each week and cohort behaviors are reported starting with the first week after the end of the initial week's first session (see below for weekly User Retention reporting).

Google Analytics Demystified

- When Cohort Size is set to "month", then a new cohort is formed each month; and cohort behaviors are reported starting with the first month after the end of the initial month's first session (see below for monthly User Retention reporting).

	Month 0	Month 1	Month 2	Month 3
All Sessions 7 users	100.00%	42.86%	0.00%	0.00%
Mar 1, 2015 - Mar 31, 2015 0 users	0.00%	0.00%	0.00%	0.00%
Apr 1, 2015 - Apr 30, 2015 0 users	0.00%	0.00%	0.00%	
May 1, 2015 - May 31, 2015 7 users	100.00%	42.86%		

Let's look at several metrics to see how this data is interpreted. We'll look first at User Retention (by day) for the past seven days. The data is shown below.

	Day 0	Day 1	Day 2	Day 3	Day 4	Day 5	Day 6	Day 7
All Sessions 230 users	100.00%	4.32%	4.67%	1.87%	4.76%	1.59%	0.00%	0.00%
Jun 2, 2015 30 users	100.00%	0.00%	0.00%	0.00%	0.00%	0.00%	0.00%	0.00%
Jun 3, 2015 63 users	100.00%	1.59%	6.35%	1.59%	4.76%	1.59%	0.00%	
Jun 4, 2015 44 users	100.00%	2.27%	2.27%	2.27%	0.00%	0.00%		
Jun 5, 2015 18 users	100.00%	0.00%	0.00%	0.00%	0.00%			
Jun 6, 2015 26 users	100.00%	7.69%	0.00%	0.00%				
Jun 7, 2015 29 users	100.00%	10.34%	0.00%					
Jun 8, 2015 20 users	100.00%	0.00%						

The first column, "All Sessions", lists each date during the prior seven days. Each date defines a different cohort. Thirty users, for example, are in the June 2, 2015 cohort as this is the day these users had their first session with our site. 63 users comprise the second cohort, those who had their first session on our site on June 3, 2015.

The top row of the table presents a weighted average of User Retention, the metric selected for this chart. Looking across this row we can see that *on average*, 4.32% of those who visited our site came back the next day (Day 1) and 4.67% of those who visited our site two days ago came back again (Day 2). No one returned after six or more days (Days 6 and 7).

Each individual shaded row in the prior chart provides cohort-specific data. The interpretation of "Day 1", "Day 2" etc. in terms of a specific calendar date is dependent upon the date of first interaction. Let's use the calendar shown to the right to illustrate this phenomenon and the interpretation of dates and data.

June

S	M	T	W	T	F	S
		1	2	3	4	5	6
7	8	9	10	11	12	13
14	15	16	17	18	19	20
21	22	23	24	25	26	27
28	29	30

- The first row of the table (directly beneath the averages) provides data for the cohort whose first site session was on June 2, 2015. The zeros across the row indicate that none of these individuals returned to the site within the following seven days (June 3 to June 9).

- The second row of the table provides data for the cohort whose first site interaction was on June 3, 2015. Of these individuals, 1.59% returned the next day (Day 1, June 4), 6.36% returned two days later (Day 2, June 5), 1.59% returned three days later (Day 3, June 6), 4.76% returned four days later (Day 4, June 7) and 1.59% returned five days later (Day 5, June 8). No one returned six days later.

- The third row of the table provides data for the cohort whose first site interaction was on June 4, 2015. Since their day of first session differs from the prior cohort, the days associated with each cell in the table are all one day later. Of these individuals, 2.27% returned one day later (Day 1, June 5), two days later (Day 2, June 6), and three days later (Day 3, June 7). No one returned four or five days later.

The shading in the table is intended to help you see days when there were significantly higher levels of the metric being reported. The darker the shading, the more the metric differs from the remainder of the data.

The interpretation is similar for other charts that use daily reporting, but with other metrics. Changing the metric to Sessions, for example, generates the table displayed on the top of page 193 where:

- The All Sessions line presents summary data, but this time we are seeing sums rather than averages. Over the week noted in the chart, there were 238 total sessions. Of the individuals who took part in these sessions 14 returned one day after their initial session, 10 returned two days after their initial session, etc.

- We interpret the individual cohort lines in exactly the same way as the prior chart. The second row of the table, for example, provides data for the cohort whose first site interaction was on June 3, 2015. Of these individuals, one returned the next day (Day 1, June 4), nine returned two days later (Day 2, June 5), one returned three days later (Day 3, June 6), five returned four days later (Day 4, June 7) and two returned five days later (Day 5, June 8). No one returned six days later.

	Day 0	Day 1	Day 2	Day 3	Day 4	Day 5	Day 6	Day 7
All Sessions 238 users	238	14	10	3	5	2	0	0
Jun 2, 2015 30 users	30	0	0	0	0	0	0	0
Jun 3, 2015 63 users	66	1	9	1	5	2	0	
Jun 4, 2015 44 users	44	3	1	2	0	0		
Jun 5, 2015 18 users	18	0	0	0	0			
Jun 6, 2015 26 users	26	4	0	0				
Jun 7, 2015 29 users	29	6	0					
Jun 8, 2015 20 users	25	0						

We use the same approach to data interpretation when the reporting period changes. The table below, for example, reports User Retention by month.

	Month 0	Month 1	Month 2	Month 3
All Sessions 1,338 users	100.00%	0.48%	0.00%	0.00%
Mar 1, 2015 - Mar 31, 2015 292 users	100.00%	0.68%	0.00%	0.00%
Apr 1, 2015 - Apr 30, 2015 296 users	100.00%	0.00%	0.00%	
May 1, 2015 - May 31, 2015 750 users	100.00%	0.40%		

This chart would be interpreted as follows:

-   The "All Sessions" line indicates that, on average, .48% of all users whose first site session was between March 1 and May 31, 2015 returned the month following their first interaction. No one returned to the site in the second or third month after his or her first interaction.

-   The first row of the table (directly beneath the All Sessions summary) provides data for the cohort whose first site interaction was anytime during March. Of these individuals, .68% returned the next month (Month 1, April). No one returned at any time two or three months after their first site visit in March.

-   The second row of the table provides data for the cohort whose first site interaction was anytime during April. None of these individuals returned to the site at any time during the next one or two months after their first site visit.

-   The last row of the table provides data for the cohort whose first site interaction was anytime during May. Of these individuals, .40% returned the next month (Month 1, June).

The chart below shows revenue by month.

	Month 0	Month 1	Month 2	Month 3
All Sessions 1,338 users	$212,500.00	$0.00	$0.00	$0.00
Mar 1, 2015 - Mar 31, 2015 292 users	$24,500.00	$0.00	$0.00	$0.00
Apr 1, 2015 - Apr 30, 2015 296 users	$39,000.00	$0.00	$0.00	
May 1, 2015 - May 31, 2015 750 users	$149,000.00	$0.00		

This chart would be interpreted as follows:

- Over the course of the three months, all site sessions initiated by these three cohorts resulted in $212,500 in sales. The majority of these sales took place in May. All sales took place during the month of users' initial visit (Month 0). No additional sales were accounted for by anyone in these three cohorts during a month after their first visit.

- The first row of the table (directly beneath the All Sessions summary) provides data for the cohort whose first site interaction was anytime during March. These individuals spent $24,500 in March. They did not make any purchases in any subsequent month.

- The second row of the table provides data for the cohort whose first site interaction was anytime during April. These individuals spent $39,000 in April. They did not make any purchases in any subsequent month.

- The last row of the table provides data for the cohort whose first site interaction was anytime during May. These individuals spent $149,000 in May. They did not make any purchases in the next month.

As you can see, there is a significant amount of data available. Thus, should you decide to use these reports, your approach should focus on using this data to address your own specific and explicit website strategic goals.

The Line Graph

The line graph provides a visual display of the data trend with regard to the metric and time period selected. By default, the graph is comprised of the data shown in the summary line of the data report. The graph shown on the top of page 195, for example, shows the graph of User Retention for a seven-day period. Note that while the dots on the graph communicate the data shown in the top (summary) line of the table, the dots are not necessarily over the appropriate data point.

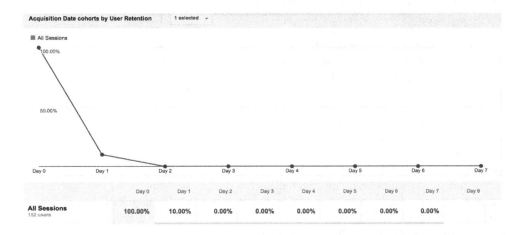

	Day 0	Day 1	Day 2	Day 3	Day 4	Day 5	Day 6	Day 7	Day 8
All Sessions 152 users	100.00%	10.00%	0.00%	0.00%	0.00%	0.00%	0.00%	0.00%	

You are not limited to plotting the data on the top summary line of a data table, as in the chart above. Let's leave the metric of interest "User Retention" but change the reporting period to weekly. On the top of the line graph is a pull-down menu, which, by default, is set to "1 selected." Pulling-down this menu reveals the date(s) used to define each cohort. Selecting just two of the weeks allows me to change the line graph so that only the selected weeks are displayed (see chart below).

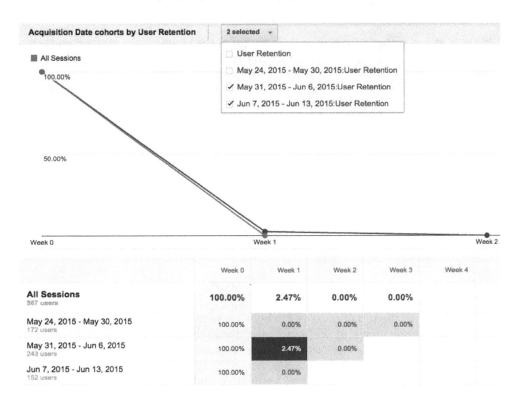

	Week 0	Week 1	Week 2	Week 3	Week 4
All Sessions 567 users	100.00%	2.47%	0.00%	0.00%	
May 24, 2015 - May 30, 2015 172 users	100.00%	0.00%	0.00%	0.00%	
May 31, 2015 - Jun 6, 2015 243 users	100.00%	2.47%	0.00%		
Jun 7, 2015 - Jun 13, 2015 152 users	100.00%	0.00%			

Caution When Interpreting User Retention Metrics

Many websites and blogs find that their success is in great part influenced by their ability to successfully encourage repeat visits. The ability to monitor the frequency of repeat visits among a cohort of new visitors is the key insight provided by user retention metrics. The ambiguity in the interpretation of this data can, however, lead to ineffective or damaging strategic decisions and actions. Let's use a simplified example to illustrate this.

Imagine that your strategic goal is to have new visitors return to the site within four days of their initial visit. Using the cohort analysis report, you find that on June 1, 2015 there were four visitors to your site named Alex, Bailey, Connor, and Dylan. When you look at this cohort on a day-to-day basis for the four days after their first visit, the data might look as shown below. The chart indicates that 25% of the initial four users (one out of four) came back on each of the four days after the day of initial visit (which is labeled "Day 0"). From this, you might conclude that your retention rate is only 25% and that significant work should be done to increase this rate of user retention. But would you be right?

	Day 0	Day 1	Day 2	Day 3	Day 4
June 1, 2015 4 users	100%	25%	25%	25%	25%

Let's look at one scenario by adding the name(s) of the people who returned on each of the four days after the initial visit. This chart is shown below, and we see that Alex is solely responsible for the 25% return percentage. If this is the case, then user retention might indeed be a problem as three of the four initial visitors (Bailey, Connor and Dylan) did not return within four days of their initial visit.

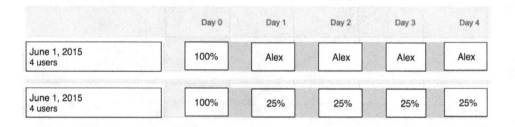

	Day 0	Day 1	Day 2	Day 3	Day 4
June 1, 2015 4 users	100%	Alex	Alex	Alex	Alex
June 1, 2015 4 users	100%	25%	25%	25%	25%

Now let's look at an equally plausible scenario by again adding the names of the people who returned on each of the days four days after the cohort's initial day of visit. This chart is shown on the top of page 197, where we see that every member of the cohort returned within four days of the initial visit. Some individuals just took longer than others to return. However, because only one returned per day the percentage shown within each column would remain at 25%. *But, 100% of new visitors returned within four days.* Your strategic goal is being met very successfully. Nothing needs to be done - everything is working - and any changes to the site might, in fact, negatively affect levels of user retention.

	Day 0	Day 1	Day 2	Day 3	Day 4
June 1, 2015 4 users	100%	Alex	Bailey	Connor	Dylan
June 1, 2015 4 users	100%	25%	25%	25%	25%

The reported user retention percentage in the Google Analytics cohort table, 25% user retention per day, is identical for the two scenarios, but the underlying cause for this percentage is very different across the scenarios. Thus, use this data cautiously, and try to determine using supplemental techniques (such as log-ins, cookies, custom measures) the causes for the reported percentages prior to enacting any significant changes in strategy, design, or execution.

Benchmarking

Benchmarking allows you to compare your own website or blog performance to other websites of similar size, industry, and function. While these comparisons are interesting, it is only appropriate if your website shares similar goals and objectives with the sites comprising the benchmark sample. Since this cannot be explicitly verified, we recommend that this data only be used directionally and as a jumping-off point for further exploration of Google Analytics data. We've also found that benchmark data is typically more meaningful when longer periods for data analysis are selected: for example, three months versus three weeks.

Google Analytics provides benchmarking data to analytics accounts that have agreed to share their data anonymously with Google. You provide the consent to share your data either during the account creation process or by visiting **Account Settings** via your Google Analytics administrator page. In both cases, you indicate your consent by checking the Benchmarking box, as shown below.

☑ Benchmarking RECOMMENDED
Contribute anonymous data to an aggregate data set to enable features like benchmarking and publication that can help you understand data trends. All identifiable information about your website is removed and combined with other anonymous data before it is shared with others.

Benchmarking data can be viewed via the **Audience > Benchmarking** menu options: Channels, Locations, and Devices. Selecting **Audience > Benchmarking > Channels** brings up the display shown on page 198. Let's use this display to discuss the three components of every benchmarking report.

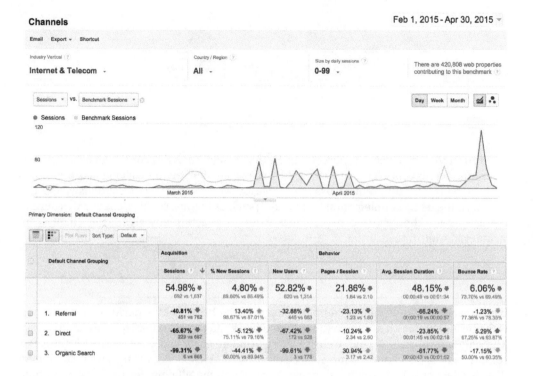

Default Channel Grouping	Acquisition			Behavior		
	Sessions	% New Sessions	New Users	Pages / Session	Avg. Session Duration	Bounce Rate
	54.98% 692 vs 1,637	4.80% 89.60% vs 85.49%	52.82% 820 vs 1,314	21.86% 1.64 vs 2.10	48.15% 00:00:49 vs 00:01:34	6.06% 73.70% vs 69.49%
1. Referral	-40.81% 451 vs 762	13.40% 98.67% vs 87.01%	-32.88% 445 vs 663	-23.13% 1.23 vs 1.60	-66.24% 00:00:19 vs 00:00:57	-1.23% 77.38% vs 78.35%
2. Direct	-65.67% 229 vs 667	-5.12% 75.11% vs 79.16%	-67.42% 172 vs 528	-10.24% 2.34 vs 2.60	-23.85% 00:01:45 vs 00:02:18	5.29% 67.25% vs 63.87%
3. Organic Search	-99.31% 6 vs 865	-44.41% 50.00% vs 89.94%	-99.61% 3 vs 778	30.94% 3.17 vs 2.42	-61.77% 00:00:43 vs 00:01:52	-17.15% 50.00% vs 60.35%

The Benchmark Parameters

The top section of the report allows you to set the benchmarking parameters. You should always set these prior to data analysis. This is the line of menu options in the above figure currently set to "Internet & Telecom," "All" and " 0-99". The first pull-down menu (labeled "Industry Vertical") allows you to select the industry to be used as the benchmark (see below). Google Analytics provides over 1,600 options. If scrolling through menus is too laborious or time consuming, you can find your benchmark industry quickly by using the search box on the top of the pull-down menu.

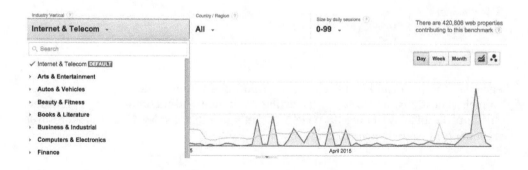

We'll set our benchmark industry to "Travel Agencies & Services", as shown below. Note that when this is done, the number of web properties (as shown in the upper right-hand corner) is updated to reflect the change in industry.

The middle pull-down menu is labeled "Country/Region". This menu option (see below) allows you to set the geographic coverage of the benchmark properties. You can select entire countries and, when data is available, you can select states, regions, or cities.

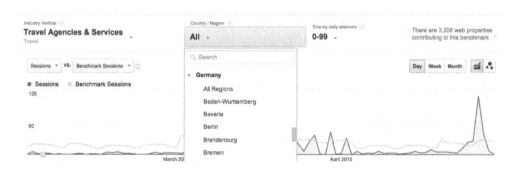

We'll select "United States: All Regions", which changes the display to that shown below. Note, once again, that the number of web properties comprising the benchmark sample has been updated and, in this case, significantly reduced. Always pay attention to this figure prior to beginning data analysis. The smaller the sample, the more dangerous it becomes to take strategic actions based on benchmarking data.

The last pull-down menu, labeled "Size by daily sessions", allows you to restrict the benchmark data to web properties that have traffic patterns similar to your own. The menu options are shown below. We'll leave the default, 0 - 99, alone as this range is the most appropriate to our site. We're now ready to examine the line chart.

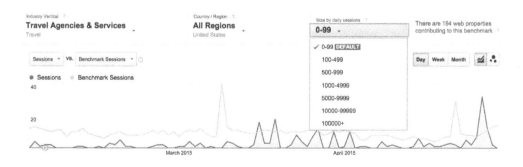

Benchmarking Line Chart

By default, the line graph displays the trend in sessions for your website or blog versus the web properties comprising the benchmark sample. The line graph for my site is shown below.

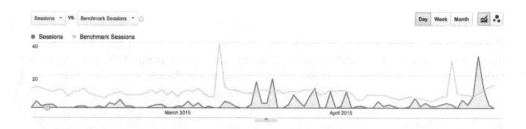

Your goal in examining these and other line charts is to look for overall trends rather than focusing on individual fluctuations in the data. In my case, I notice that the number of sessions is relatively stable for the benchmark data (ignoring the two spikes), while my trend in sessions is much more erratic. I might want to see how to maintain more consistency in website traffic.

The two pull-down menus at the top of the line chart allow you to change the metrics displayed in the chart. While either menu can display your own or benchmark metrics, data analysis is facilitated when you are consistent in selection. You might, for example, always use the left-hand menu to display our own metrics, while the right-hand menu is used to display metrics for the benchmark sample. Additionally, while you can set these menus to whatever metrics you desire, we've found that the data become very difficult to interpret when each menu selects a different metric. As a result, data analysis is facilitated when the same metric is selected in each menu, as shown below.

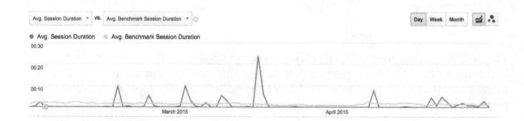

Benchmarking Data Display

The bottom-of-the-page data display provides a numeric comparison of your site's characteristics to the benchmark sample. Six metrics are always reported (see table on the top of page 201):

- *Acquisition:* Sessions, % New Sessions, and New Users

- *Behavior:* Pages/Session, Average Session Duration, and Bounce Rate

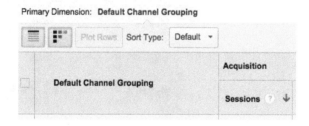

Acquisition			Behavior		
Sessions ↓	% New Sessions	New Users	Pages / Session	Avg. Session Duration	Bounce Rate
72.55% ▼	1.00% ▲	72.27% ▼	10.79% ▼	4.71% ▼	2.17% ▼
235 vs 856	80.00% vs 79.21%	188 vs 678	2.04 vs 2.29	00:01:24 vs 00:01:28	68.51% vs 67.06%
-67.57% ▼	22.52% ▲	-60.26% ▼	-38.93% ▼	-66.04% ▼	11.70% ▲
120 vs 370	100.00% vs 81.62%	120 vs 302	1.20 vs 1.96	00:00:19 vs 00:00:57	80.00% vs 71.62%

Each cell of the table presents both your own and the benchmark data. The top row of the table provides the overall average for the dimension you are using to organize the data (i.e., channels, locations, or devices). In the rows beneath the average, red shaded cells indicate metrics where your website is significantly underperforming versus the benchmark, while green shaded cells indicate areas where you are significantly outperforming the benchmark. The darker the shading, the greater the discrepancy between your own and benchmark performance. Finally, each cell contains a red or green arrow to confirm the direction of difference.

Above every table are two display options beneath "Primary Dimension", as shown below.

Selecting the icon on the far left eliminates the underlying data leaving only the percentage differences displayed in the numeric table. The second icon removes shading from the cells. Either or both may be selected to alter the table's data display.

When examining the data in any chart, be certain that you are only paying attention to large percentage differences for which the underlying data show meaningful differences. Let's illustrate this with the data tables generated from each of the **Audience > Benchmark** options. Selecting **Audience > Benchmark > Channels** from the left-hand side menu of any report page organizes the data by channel and creates the table shown on the top of page 202.

Default Channel Grouping	Acquisition			Behavior		
	Sessions ↓	% New Sessions	New Users	Pages / Session	Avg. Session Duration	Bounce Rate
	72.55% ⬇ 235 vs 856	1.00% ⬆ 80.00% vs 79.21%	72.27% ⬇ 188 vs 678	10.79% ⬇ 2.04 vs 2.29	4.71% ⬇ 00:01:24 vs 00:01:28	2.17% ⬇ 68.51% vs 67.06%
1. Referral	-67.57% ⬇ 120 vs 370	22.52% ⬆ 100.00% vs 81.62%	-60.26% ⬇ 120 vs 302	-38.93% ⬇ 1.20 vs 1.96	-66.04% ⬇ 00:00:19 vs 00:00:57	11.70% ⬆ 80.00% vs 71.62%
2. Direct	-69.66% ⬇ 108 vs 356	-19.10% ⬇ 62.04% vs 76.69%	-75.46% ⬇ 67 vs 273	37.57% ⬆ 2.81 vs 2.04	72.24% ⬆ 00:02:34 vs 00:01:30	-25.25% ⬇ 56.48% vs 75.56%
3. Organic Search	-99.78% ⬇ 1 vs 454	35.52% ⬆ 100.00% vs 73.79%	-99.70% ⬇ 1 vs 335	177.31% ⬆ 7.00 vs 2.52	11.13% ⬆ 00:02:01 vs 00:01:49	-100.00% ⬇ 0.00% vs 87.27%
4. Social	-100.00% ⬇ 0 vs 6	-100.00% ⬇ 0.00% vs 83.33%	-100.00% ⬇ 0 vs 5	-100.00% ⬇ 0.00 vs 2.00	-100.00% ⬇ 00:00:00 vs 00:01:04	-100.00% ⬇ 0.00% vs 66.67%

Since there is so much data contained in this table, let's look at just the half that shows the Acquisition metrics. This data is provided in the chart below.

Default Channel Grouping	Acquisition		
	Sessions ↓	% New Sessions	New Users
	72.55% ⬇ 235 vs 856	1.00% ⬆ 80.00% vs 79.21%	72.27% ⬇ 188 vs 678
1. Referral	-67.57% ⬇ 120 vs 370	22.52% ⬆ 100.00% vs 81.62%	-60.26% ⬇ 120 vs 302
2. Direct	-69.66% ⬇ 108 vs 356	-19.10% ⬇ 62.04% vs 76.69%	-75.46% ⬇ 67 vs 273
3. Organic Search	-99.78% ⬇ 1 vs 454	35.52% ⬆ 100.00% vs 73.79%	-99.70% ⬇ 1 vs 335
4. Social	-100.00% ⬇ 0 vs 6	-100.00% ⬇ 0.00% vs 83.33%	-100.00% ⬇ 0 vs 5

The following conclusions can be drawn, assuming that there is comparability in terms of strategic goals between my website and the benchmark sample:

- Overall, my count of sessions is significantly below that of the benchmark sample (72.55% fewer sessions). This difference is worth noting given the difference in the absolute number of sessions (235 versus 856). Importantly, this low level of sessions reinforces our impression from other **Audience** measures, where our session level has been consistently low over time.

  My deficit in terms of session number extends across all four reported channels, but is especially noteworthy for Organic Search, where we have only one session generated through this channel versus 454 for the benchmark sample. Since this is an important channel for the benchmark channel (and by extension our competitors), we should at least have an internal discussion related to extending our marketing efforts into this channel. Success in this channel might help to address the problem with the low number of overall sessions.

We ignore the difference between our own site's performance and that of the benchmark sample in terms of sessions generated by the Social channel. This is not an important channel for our competitors (with only 6 total sessions). However, given that our competitors are ignoring this channel, we should at least consider extending our efforts into this channel as a way of distinguishing ourselves from our competitors as we (can perhaps) take ownership of this channel as a way of generating additional website traffic.

- Overall, both our site and the benchmark sample rely on new sessions to generate site traffic (80.0% versus 79.21% are new sessions for our site and the benchmark sample, respectively). Our percentage of new sessions by channel does not appear to be meaningfully different from that of the benchmark sample for Referral and Direct traffic. We ignore the differences in the remaining two channels since our percentage of new sessions (100%) for Organic Search is based on only one session for our website while the percentage for Social is based on zero sessions. In both cases, the sample size is much too low for the calculated percentage differences to be meaningful.

- Since most of the sessions for both our site and the competition are comprised of new sessions, the interpretation of the New Users column is identical to that of the Sessions column.

The remaining two **Audience > Benchmark** options change the organizing dimension keeping the metrics the same as in the prior **Audience > Benchmark > Channels** option. Selecting **Audience > Benchmark > Location** changes the organizing dimension to the country or other areas you selected in the Country/Region pull-down menu. The following table is displayed for our site. Note that only the United States is shown, as this was the only country selected for the benchmark sample.

Country	Acquisition			Behavior		
	Sessions ↓	% New Sessions	New Users	Pages / Session	Avg. Session Duration	Bounce Rate
	72.55% ▼	1.00% ▲	72.27% ▼	10.79% ▼	4.71% ▼	2.17% ▼
	235 vs 856	80.00% vs 79.21%	188 vs 678	2.04 vs 2.29	00:01:24 vs 00:01:26	68.51% vs 67.06%
1. ▇ United States	-72.55% ▼	1.00% ▲	-72.27% ▼	-10.79% ▼	-4.71% ▼	2.17% ▲
	235 vs 856	80.00% vs 79.21%	188 vs 678	2.04 vs 2.29	00:01:24 vs 00:01:26	68.51% vs 67.06%

Selecting **Audience > Benchmark > Devices** changes the organizing dimension to devices used to access the site, as shown below.

Device Category	Acquisition			Behavior		
	Sessions ↓	% New Sessions	New Users	Pages / Session	Avg. Session Duration	Bounce Rate
	72.55% ▼	1.00% ▲	72.27% ▼	10.79% ▼	4.71% ▼	2.17% ▼
	235 vs 856	80.00% vs 79.21%	188 vs 678	2.04 vs 2.29	00:01:24 vs 00:01:28	68.51% vs 67.06%
1. tablet	-25.00% ▼	-11.11% ▼	-33.33% ▼	-69.23% ▼	-100.00% ▼	33.33% ▲
	3 vs 4	66.67% vs 75.00%	2 vs 3	1.00 vs 3.25	00:00:00 vs 00:08:04	100.00% vs 75.00%
2. desktop	-60.92% ▼	0.18% ▲	-60.85% ▼	-8.58% ▼	0.80% ▲	-3.66% ▼
	229 vs 586	80.35% vs 80.20%	184 vs 470	2.04 vs 2.24	00:01:26 vs 00:01:25	68.56% vs 71.16%
3. mobile	-99.19% ▼	-2.62% ▼	-99.21% ▼	46.83% ▲	-67.54% ▼	-44.29% ▼
	3 vs 371	66.67% vs 68.46%	2 vs 254	3.00 vs 2.04	00:00:27 vs 00:01:22	33.33% vs 59.84%

Let's look more closely at the Behavior data from this table (see below).

Device Category	Behavior		
	Pages / Session	Avg. Session Duration	Bounce Rate
	10.79% ⬇ 2.04 vs 2.29	**4.71%** ⬇ 00:01:24 vs 00:01:28	**2.17%** ⬇ 68.51% vs 67.06%
1. tablet	**-69.23%** ⬇ 1.00 vs 3.25	**-100.00%** ⬇ 00:00:00 vs 00:06:04	**33.33%** ⬆ 100.00% vs 75.00%
2. desktop	**-8.58%** ⬇ 2.04 vs 2.24	**0.80%** ⬆ 00:01:26 vs 00:01:25	**-3.66%** ⬇ 68.56% vs 71.16%
3. mobile	**46.83%** ⬆ 3.00 vs 2.04	**-67.54%** ⬇ 00:00:27 vs 00:01:22	**-44.29%** ⬇ 33.33% vs 59.84%

Overall, the good news is that all three of our behavior measures are in line with those of the Benchmark sample. There are no real, meaningful differences in terms of Pages/ Session (2.04 versus 2.29), Average Session Duration (1:24 versus 1:28), and Bounce Rate (68.51% versus 67.06%). The latter metric, however, should still be a matter of concern, even though it is in line with the benchmark sample. A bounce rate this high needs to be reduced.

The conclusion drawn from the overall benchmark sample - that we are doing as well as the benchmark and so, by inference, all is well - masks important differences across device types.

- Access to our site via a tablet appears to be a disaster, both in an absolute sense and in comparison to the benchmark sample. Our number of Pages/Session and Average Session Duration are very low and competitively weak and our Bounce Rate is significantly higher than the benchmark sample. Clearly, one of our strategic priorities needs to determine (and then fix) the underlying causes. We can use the **Audience > Mobile > Devices** report to see in more detail where the problems lie.

- The site seems to be working well (i.e., in line with the benchmark sample) for site access via desktop.

- The data reported for mobile devices is contradictory. While Pages/ Session and Bounce Rate are both at better levels than the benchmark sample, Average Session Duration appears to be shorter. We can once again use the **Audience > Mobile > Devices** report in an attempt to understand these contradictory outcomes.

20
The Audience Menu:
Lifetime Value

This chapter explains the functions and capabilities of the Google Analytics Lifetime Value Report (LTV), which was in beta at the time this book was published. The **Audience > Lifetime Value** report allows you to assess the value of your customers relative to your business, based on their lifetime performance.

Let's begin with an introduction to the Lifetime Value Report, followed by an overview of each of the report's key elements.

Lifetime Value Report: Overview

Satisfied customers will continue to shop from their favorite online retailer, just as satisfied readers will continue to consume content from their favorite blogs. The Lifetime Value Report is a powerful tool you can use to evaluate this satisfaction in the form of projected revenue (sales) those customers may generate. In other words, this report assigns a cumulative value to your customers across their entire relationship with your business.

You can, for example, view the lifetime value of your customers acquired through email or paid search. "With that information in hand, you can determine a profitable allocation of marketing resources to the acquisition of those users."[48]

The Lifetime Value report is accessed through **Audience > Lifetime Value** on the left-hand side of any report page. The table shown on the next page appears when I select **Audience > Lifetime Value** from our travel site.

---

[48] Google, *Lifetime Value* at https://support.google.com/analytics/answer/6182550.

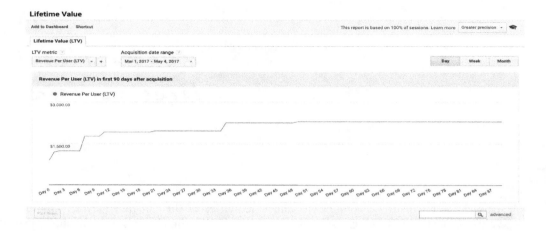

Acquisition date range

Acquisition date range refers to the duration during which website users were acquired.

We can choose to use the predefined date range options or we can create our own custom date range, either of which can be accomplished via the Date Range option shown on the right-hand side of the figure below. If we want look at users acquired during the most recent single day, we can set our acquisition date to yesterday. We do so by clicking **Acquisition Date Range > Date Range > Yesterday**

If we want to look at users acquired from the previous week, we can set our acquisition date range to **Acquisition Date Range > Last Week** (see image on page 208).

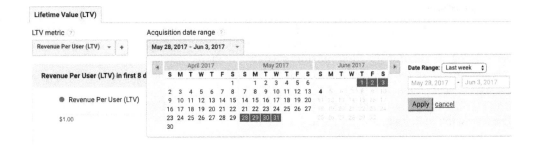

Likewise, if we want our report to evaluate all users acquired in the past month, we can set our acquisition date range to **Acquisition Date Range > Last 30 Days**.

We can also set a custom acquisition date range. In the example shown below, we looked at all website users acquired between March 6th and May 4th, which reflected our campaign launch date through our campaign end date. Any user acquired during this period will be included in our Lifetime Value report.

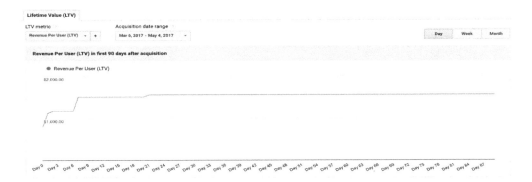

The LTV report provides a variety of metrics that help you evaluate how your website is performing in relation to your business goals. *Lifetime value is calculated using the cumulative sum of the selected metric value divided by the total number of users acquired during the acquisition date range.*[49]

The following metrics are available in the report[50]:

- Appviews Per User (LTV): the cumulative average appviews per user.

- Goal Completions Per User (LTV): the cumulative average goal completions per user.

- Pageviews Per User (LTV): cumulative average pageviews per user.

- Revenue Per User (LTV): the cumulative average revenue per user.

- Session Duration Per User (LTV): the cumulative average session duration (in seconds) per user.

- Sessions Per User (LTV): the cumulative average transactions per user.

- Transactions Per User (LTV): the cumulative average transactions per user.

You can access these different metrics by clicking the dropdown menu under LTV metric, as shown in the image on the next page.

---

[49] Adapted from Google Analytics at https://support.google.com/analytics answer/6182550.

[50] The following article provides an example of how each of the metrics listed above is calculated and applied to a business example: *https://www.optimizesmart.com/measuring-customers-lifetime-value-in-google-analytics-for-mobile-app-users/.*

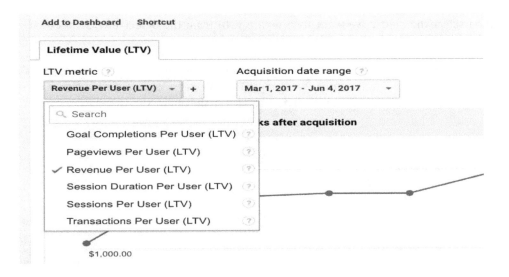

In the example shown here, we have selected Revenue Per User (LTV) as our metric.

Compare metric

The Lifetime Value report also allows us to compare our LTV metrics against one another in order to evaluate the relative performance of different elements of our website, campaign, etc. We can, for example, compare customers gained through social to those who came from email, in order to evaluate which source brought the highest-value customers.

To compare LTV metrics against one another, we will click on the **+** button next to the LTV metric.

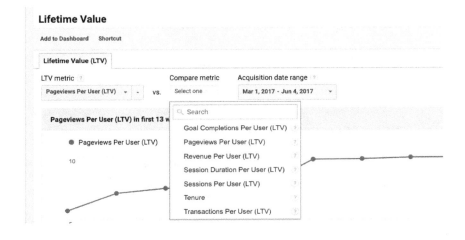

We then select the metric we want to compare it to from the **Select one** drop down menu.

Let's look at an example. Perhaps our business is interested in looking at Revenue Per User (LTV) relative to Transactions Per User (LTV). We set a custom acquisition date range to March 1st – June 4th. Our report would look like the image shown below.

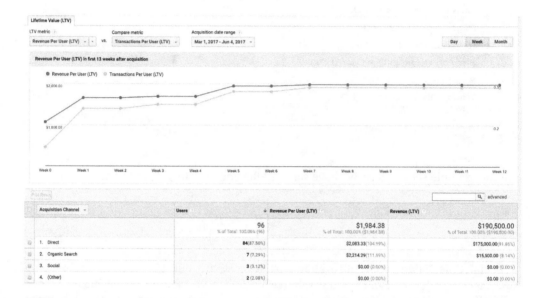

Based on this report, we see that as Transactions Per User (LTV) increased, so did Revenue Per User (LTV). We also see a plateau in both LTV metrics after Week 5 of our campaign. As a business, this pattern may be worth investigating in order to determine why transactions and revenue stopped increasing after Week 5.

To delete the Compare Metric from your report, simply press the – button next to the LTV metric. This will revert your report back to evaluating just one LTV metric.

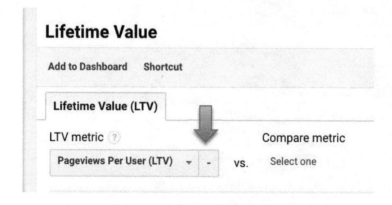

It's often useful to put Lifetime Value metrics in the context of dimensions in which we are also interested. We can do use by using the **Dimensions** element of the Lifetime Value report.

For example, if we are looking at Transactions Per User (LTV), we may also be interested in knowing which channel delivered the most transactions per user. We would select **Acquisition Channel** from the dimension drop down menu (see below).

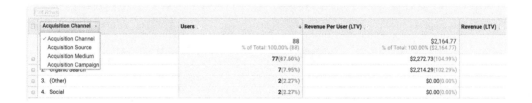

Let's look at another example. Let's say we are now interested in how our customers have interacted with our website; so we look at Session Duration Per User (LTV). We may also want to better understand which medium fosters the longest session durations; so we would select **Acquisition Medium** from the dimension drop down menu.

✅ You cannot apply secondary or custom dimensions to the Lifetime Value report.

The graph component of the Lifetime Value report *illustrates the lifetime value per user for the LTV metrics over a period of 90 days, in increments of days, weeks, or months.* The graph below shows the cumulative average pageviews in the first 30 days after acquisition.

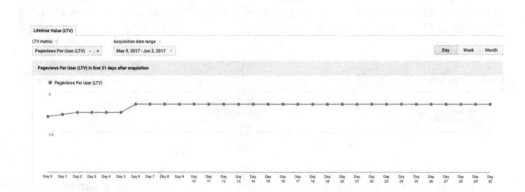

As illustrated in the graph above, **Day 0** shows the cumulative average pageviews of users on the day of acquisition. **Day 29** shows the cumulative average pageviews of users on the 29th day after acquisition.

If you would like the graph to reflect one data point for each week, instead of one data point for each day, you can change the x-axis to illustrate such. We accomplish this by clicking on the **Week** tab next to the Acquisition date range.

If done successfully, your graph should look like my example shown below, except with your digital property's data:

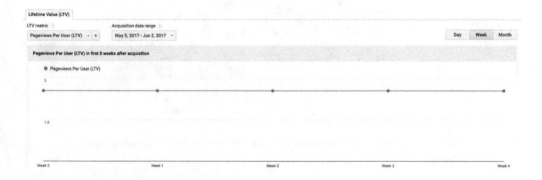

The table component of the Lifetime Value report illustrates the data tablularly, rather than graphically.

The LTV metrics in the table are distributed based on the dimension we choose to evaluate. For example, in the table below, we looked at Sessions Per User LTV (metric) and Acquisition Medium (dimension) over the last 30 days (date range).

Acquisition Medium ▾			Users	↓ Sessions Per User (LTV)	Sessions (LTV)
			13	1.46	19
			% of Total: 100.00% (13)	% of Total: 100.00% (1.46)	% of Total: 100.00% (19)
	1.	(none)	12(92.31%)	1.50(102.63%)	18(94.74%)
	2.	referral	1 (7.69%)	1.00(68.42%)	1 (5.26%)

The table in the Lifetime Value report will always present the following pieces of information:

- The number of users you acquired during the Acquisition Date Range

- Two aspects of the metric you selected for the report

For example, continuing on with our example from above, let's say we are looking at Sessions Per User LTV. The table will show us:

- Sessions per User (LTV): Average sessions per user over lifetime

- Sessions (LTV): Total sessions for all users over lifetime

Sessions Per User (LTV) ?	Sessions (LTV) ?
1.46	19
% of Total: 100.00% (1.46)	% of Total: 100.00% (19)
1.00(68.42%)	1 (5.26%)
1.50(102.63%)	18(94.74%)

Let's look at another example. Perhaps we're interested in Revenue Per User (LTV) and the channels in which our users came to our site. Our table would look like that shown below:

Acquisition Channel ▾	Users	↓ Revenue Per User (LTV)	Revenue (LTV)
	44 % of Total: 100.00% (44)	$159.09 % of Total: 100.00% ($159.09)	$7,000.00 % of Total: 100.00% ($7,000.00)
1. Direct	40 (90.91%)	$175.00 (110.00%)	$7,000.00 (100.00%)
2. (Other)	2 (4.55%)	$0.00 (0.00%)	$0.00 (0.00%)
3. Social	2 (4.55%)	$0.00 (0.00%)	$0.00 (0.00%)

The table has provided us with the following the number of users we acquired during our date range (44 users) as well as the following two metrics:

- Revenue per User (LTV): Average revenue per user over lifetime

- Revenue (LTV): Total revenue for all users over lifetime

Regardless of which LTV metric and acquisition dimension you are looking at together, the Lifetime Value report will always provide you with three such pieces of data.

In sum, whether you are trying to determine whether a certain campaign is more effective, or whether a certain medium more efficient, the Lifetime Value report will allow you to evaluate the value of your customers over time and the overall effectiveness of your campaigns.

Section VI:
The Behavior Menu

Google Analytics **Audience** data helps you see the characteristics of individuals who visit your website or blog. Google Analytics **Behavior** data provides a complimentary perspective where the focus is on explaining what visitors do after they arrive. The chapters in this section help you understand the range of behavior-related data and the application of this data to strategic decision-making.

- Google Analytics provides behavior data through overviews or focused reports. Chapter 21 discusses the Behavior Overview while Chapters 22 through 25 address specific metrics (behavior flow, site content, site search, site speed, and in-page analytics, respectively).

Together, the chapters in this section show you different ways to access, manipulate, and strategically apply Google Analytics Behavior data.

21

The Behavior Menu: Overview

Google Analytics provides multiple perspectives on how users interact with different pages on your site. The **Users Flow** chart, discussed earlier, shows the pages users interact with and the order in which these interactions take place. Beyond this approach to the data, Google Analytics also provides you with detailed information on how site users interact with each page of your site as well as with your site as a whole. This information is available through the **Behavior** menu (see below).

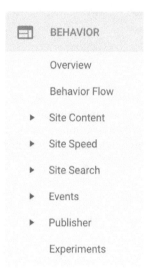

This chapter focuses on the **Overview** report. The next chapter addresses **Site Content** and **Site Search**. Chapter 23 discusses **Behavior Flow**. **Site Speed** is discussed in Chapter 24. **In-Page Analytics** (formerly part of the Behavior menu) are discussed in Chapter 25.[51] We'll return to this menu later in the book when we discuss **Events** (Section X) and **Experiments** (Section XIV).

Behavior Overview

Data presented in the **Behavior > Overview** report is formatted in the same way as the **Audience > Overview** page, except that now the data focuses on users' interactions with site pages rather than on the characteristics of users themselves.

---

[51] We do not address **Publisher,** which may be used by only a few purchasers of this book.

Top of Page

By default, the chart on the top of the page shows the trend in **Pageviews** over your selected time period. As with the **Audience Overview**, you can modify the time period by which the data is grouped and presented. The chart below, for example, shows my website's trend in pageviews between January 1, 2017 and May 4, 2017, as indicated by the date in the upper right-hand corner.

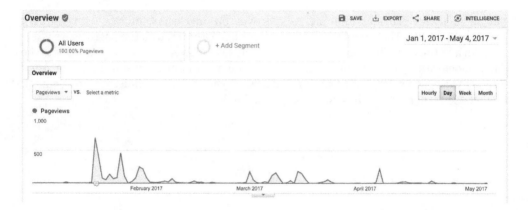

You are not limited to charting pageviews. The pull-down menu on the top left-hand side of the chart allows you to chart other page interaction metrics, as shown below. Each of these new metrics is defined in the addendum to this chapter.

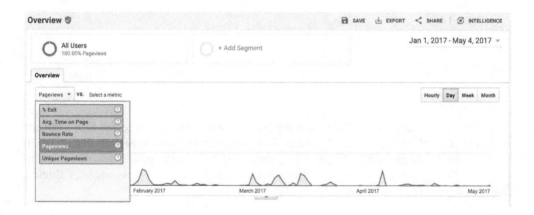

The chart shown on the top of page 219, for example, shows the **Average Time on Page**.

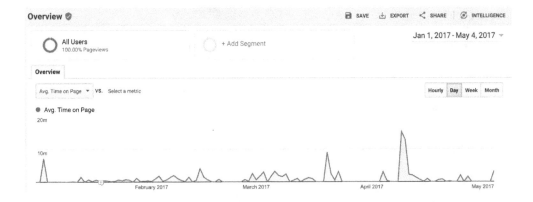

Similar to the **Audience Overview** chart, you can examine two metrics simultaneously. Imagine, for example, that you wanted to know how the trend in site users is related to users' average time on page. You can either (a) generate and compare the metrics in individual charts, or (b) display both metrics on the same chart. This latter approach is accomplished by selecting **Pageviews** from the drop-down menu and **Ave. Time on Page** from the **Select a Metric** menu. This generates the chart shown below.

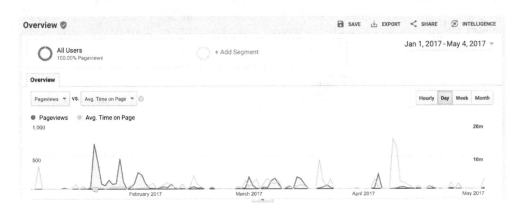

Finally, note that any annotations made to charts when using other menu options also appear on this line chart. Of course, you can always add new annotations to this chart by following the same procedure you used to add annotations to the **Audience Overview** chart discussed earlier.

Middle of the Page

The metrics and charts in the center of the **Behavior > Overview** page provide summary information for key page and content interaction metrics within the selected time period (see table on the top of page 220). The metrics are the same as those available through the pull-down menus in the top of page line chart.

Pageviews	Unique Pageviews	Avg. Time on Page
4,799	**2,939**	**00:00:46**

Bounce Rate	% Exit
32.60%	**18.84%**

Similar to the **Audience Overview** display, clicking on any of the line graphs in this block brings detailed information on that metric up to the line graph shown on the top of the report page. Clicking on the small line graph beneath **Unique Pageviews**, for example, changes the metric displayed in the top line graph to **Unique Pageviews**.

Bottom of the Page

The bottom of the **Behavior > Overview** report allows you to examine data in terms of site content (Page and Page Title), site search terms, and event categories (see the left-hand side of the table shown below). The default view for Site Content is **Page** (shown below), which uses pageviews to rank order site pages from greatest to least pageviews. Note that this display uses URLs to describe each page.

Site Content		Page		Pageviews	% Pageviews
Page	▸	1. /xqanqeon/index.html		1,602	33.38%
Page Title		2. /xqanqeon/purchase.html		883	18.40%
Site Search		3. /xqanqeon/information.html		524	10.92%
Search Term		4. /xqanqeon/mediaplay.html		427	8.90%
Events		5. /xqanqeon/contact.html		227	4.73%
Event Category		6. /xqanqeon/events1.html		221	4.61%
		7. /xqanqeon/thanks_p2m.html		160	3.33%
		8. /xqanqeon/chapter54a.html		87	1.81%
		9. /xqanqeon/thanks_p15m.html		83	1.73%
		10. /xqanqeon/events2.html		79	1.65%

view full report

URLs can be difficult to interpret so Google Analytics provides two options to facilitate interpretation. First, between each URL and its pageview count is a small icon. Clicking on this icon displays a new window that shows the actual website page. The second option changes the display from URLs to page titles (see table on the top of page 221). This is done by selecting the **Page Title** option beneath Site Content on the left-hand side of the report. (This latter approach only works, however, if you provide a page title in the page's HTML code.)

Site Content		Page Title	Pageviews	% Pageviews
Page		1. Xqanqeon - Home Page Welcome	1,602	33.38%
Page Title	▶	2. Xqanqeon - Buy a tour	889	18.52%
Site Search		3. Xqanqeon - More Information	657	13.69%
Search Term		4. Xqanqeon - Videos	427	8.90%
Events		5. (not set)	311	6.48%
Event Category		6. Xqanqeon - Contact	227	4.73%
		7. Purchase Thanks - 2 Day Tour	201	4.19%
		8. Purchase Thanks - 15 Day Tour	159	3.31%
		9. Purchase Thanks - 10 Day Tour	104	2.17%
		10. Chapter 48: Link Monitoring	87	1.81%

view full report

Finally, clicking on the **view full report** link beneath the table always brings up a more detailed display on the selected metric or dimension.

Chapter Addendum: Behavior Terms Defined

The following are definitions of key dimensions and metrics used to describe user interactions with your website pages.

Pageviews

Pageviews reports the total number of pages (which contain the Google Analytics tracking code) viewed during all sessions by all users. Note that this measure is subject to inflation due to the way that duplicate page views are handled. If, for example, a user clicks reload after reaching a particular page, this is counted as an additional pageview and two pageviews would be recorded. Similarly, if a user navigates to a different page on your site and then returns to the original page, a second pageview is then recorded even though the original page had already been seen.

Unique Pageviews

Unique pageviews represent the number of visits during which a page was viewed at least once, for example:

- If a visitor views the same web page seven times during the same visit, then it will count as seven pageviews but only one unique pageview.

- If the same visitor exits your site, but comes back later after the session expires and views the same web page two more times, the metric will be increased to nine pageviews and two unique pageviews.

Average Time on Page

As the name implies, this metric reports the average amount of time visitors spent viewing a specified page or set of pages (for example, all pages on your website).

Bounce Rate

Bounce Rate is the percentage of single-page visits, that is, visits in which a site user leaves your site from the first page viewed without interacting with that or any other page.

Google Analytics reports both Bounce Rate and % Exit (defined next). While these metrics are very similar, they provide you with different information. A bounce occurs when a user comes to your website and only looks at a single page before leaving the site. When a visitor bounces, he does not visit any other pages on your site, nor does he interact with anything on the single page viewed. The exit rate does not take into consideration how many pages the visitor looked at. It only looks at exits compared to the total visits.

% Exit reports how many people leave your site from a particular page or from the site overall. Google Analytics calculates % Exit for each page of your site by dividing the total number of exits from a page by the total number of pageviews for that particular page.

The % Exit metric is important because it tells you how many people are leaving from each page. If your visitors are leaving the site from a "Thank You" page or after completing a sale, this may be desirable. If they are leaving from other pages, this may reflect a lack of desired information or frustration with that page or their prior experience on the site. Either way, this would lead you to conduct a more detailed analysis to determine the underlying causes.

22

The Behavior Menu:
Site Content and Site Search

This chapter focuses on the information provided through the **Site Content** and **Site Search** submenus in the **Behavior** main menu. We begin with the four options available beneath the **Behavior > Site Content** menu option (see below).

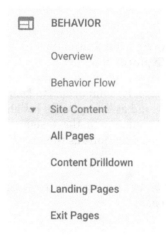

Site Content > All Pages

Clicking on **Behavior > Site Content > All Pages** brings up two different views for data exploration.

Top of Page

The default display for the **Behavior > Site Content > All Pages** option brings up a line chart similar to that shown on the top of page 226. The chart, by default, displays pageviews for the selected time period. Similar to the **Audience > Overview** chart, you can change the data groupings for how the data is displayed (day, week, or month), you can change the charted metric by using the pull-down menu (currently displaying "Pageviews"), or you can chart two metrics simultaneously by selecting a second metric via the **Select a metric** menu. You can also view and create annotations.

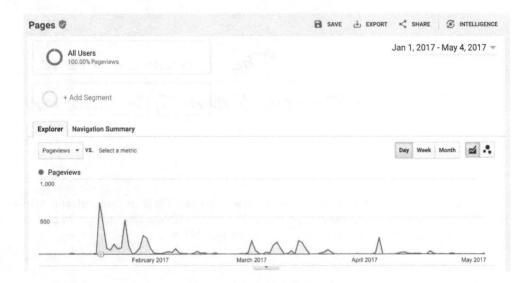

A very powerful option, the **Navigation Summary** link, is located on the top, left-hand side of the chart next to the **Explorer** tab. The Navigation Summary allows you to see the behaviors associated with any page on your site, specifically, what happens before and after users arrive at that page. It is important to keep in mind that this data relates to pageviews and not sessions, and as a result, the insights provided by the Navigation Summary are an excellent compliment to the insights provided by the **Behavior > Behavior Flow** report, which uses sessions as the organizing metric. (Behavior Flow is discussed in Chapter 23.)

Clicking on **Navigation Summary** displays the table shown below, which is placed immediately beneath the line chart.

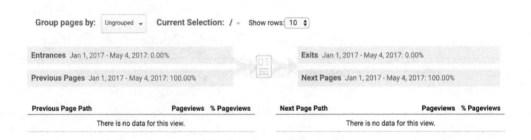

To begin using this option, select the page on which you want to focus using the pull-down menu next to **Current Selection**, in the top, middle of the display (see above). When you pull-down this menu, a list of all your website pages (which contain GATC) are displayed, as shown on the top of page 227.

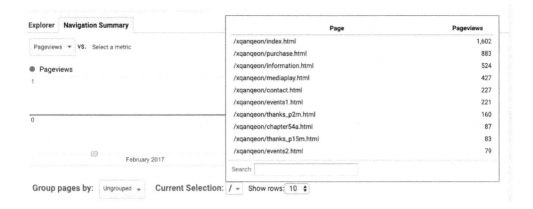

Select the page in which you are interested. When I select my site's contact page the display changes to that shown below. Note that the URL of my contact page is now shown next to "Current Selection."

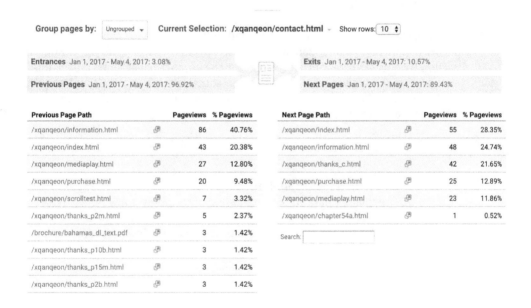

Let's focus on the four grey boxes on the top of the display beneath the URL of my contact page.

- The two grey boxes on the left-hand side tell you how the page is reached. These arrows report the percentage of site users who reach the page directly (**Entrances**) and the percentage of site users who come to the page via another page (**Previous Pages**). In this case, nearly all users viewing the contact page (96.92%) reached the page via another page; few came directly to this page.

- The two grey boxes on the right-hand side tell you want happens when people leave this page. **Exits** reports the percentage of users who leave the site entirely while **Next Pages** reports the percentage who remain on the site and view another page. In this case, most users (89.43%) stay on the site after viewing my contact page.

Beneath the arrows are two columns, one labeled **Previous Page Path** and the other is labeled **Next Page Path**. These columns provide the detail on pages viewed prior to and after the target page. Keep in mind that the base for this percentage is all pageviews prior to or after the target page. Thus, these relative numbers will change as the target page is changed.

What can we learn from each column of data?

- The information shown in the left-hand column (beneath **Previous Page Path**) indicates that most users who access the contact page go directly there from my information page (40.76%) or homepage (20.38%). What is there about these two pages that is driving this behavior? The remainder of paths to the contact page come from a diverse range of prior pages.

- The information shown in the right-hand column (beneath **Next Page Path**) indicates that my "thank you for sending an email page" (thanks_c.html) is reached by only 21.65% of those who visit the contact page. Thus, only a small portion of those viewing the contact page actually send an email and see the thank you page. We need to first determine why; and then, perhaps, redesign the contact page to encourage contact through form completion.

Bottom of Page

The data presented on the bottom of the **Behavior > Site Content > All Pages** report (see top of page 229) provides data in a format similar to tables you've already seen. Here, however, the columns focus on user-page interaction rather than the user characteristics reported in the **Audience** menu. The meaning of each column header was provided in the addendum to the prior chapter.

Of particular importance on this table are the metrics that report **Average Time on Page** and **% Exit**. The former metric provides valuable insights into the level of engagement with a particular page, while the latter metric helps you see the locations from which individuals are leaving the site. When taken together, both metrics help you identify any specific site pages that need revision.

	Page	Pageviews	Unique Pageviews	Avg. Time on Page	Entrances	Bounce Rate	% Exit	Page Value
		4,799 % of Total: 100.00% (4,799)	2,939 % of Total: 100.00% (2,939)	00:00:46 Avg for View: 00:00:46 (0.00%)	904 % of Total: 100.00% (904)	32.60% Avg for View: 32.60% (0.00%)	18.84% Avg for View: 18.84% (0.00%)	$3,700.90 % of Total: 99.97% ($3,701.97)
1.	/xqanqeon/index.html	1,602 (33.38%)	840 (28.58%)	00:01:13	796 (88.05%)	32.04%	25.84%	$2,437.74 (65.87%)
2.	/xqanqeon/purchase.html	883 (18.40%)	396 (13.47%)	00:00:25	45 (4.98%)	40.00%	11.66%	$5,621.46 (151.89%)
3.	/xqanqeon/information.html	524 (10.92%)	307 (10.45%)	00:00:30	21 (2.32%)	28.57%	16.22%	$1,697.88 (45.88%)
4.	/xqanqeon/mediaplay.html	427 (8.90%)	308 (10.48%)	00:01:09	13 (1.44%)	57.14%	20.37%	$1,968.83 (53.20%)
5.	/xqanqeon/contact.html	227 (4.73%)	178 (6.06%)	00:00:29	7 (0.77%)	0.00%	10.57%	$2,509.27 (67.80%)
6.	/xqanqeon/events1.html	221 (4.61%)	177 (6.02%)	00:00:32	3 (0.33%)	0.00%	24.43%	$3,654.52 (98.75%)
7.	/xqanqeon/thanks_p2m.html	160 (3.33%)	89 (3.03%)	00:00:21	2 (0.22%)	0.00%	11.25%	$8,071.91 (218.11%)
8.	/xqanqeon/chapter54a.html	87 (1.81%)	68 (2.31%)	00:00:12	0 (0.00%)	0.00%	4.60%	$5,710.29 (154.29%)
9.	/xqanqeon/thanks_p15m.html	83 (1.73%)	59 (2.01%)	00:00:09	1 (0.11%)	0.00%	14.46%	$10,854.24 (293.29%)
10.	/xqanqeon/events2.html	79 (1.65%)	66 (2.25%)	00:00:10	1 (0.11%)	0.00%	10.13%	$6,059.09 (163.72%)

Show rows: 10   Go to: 1   1 - 10 of 22

By default, pages are ordered by the absolute number of pageviews. Similar to the **Audience** tables you learned about earlier, you can use the charting options on the top of the table to create pie, bar, and percent differential charts.

The chart above lists pages by their URL address. If you can't remember which pages are associated with which URLs, then just click on the **Page Title** option located just above Secondary dimension in the Primary Dimension line. This will change the display to pages ordered by title rather than URL.

Finally, you can focus on a single page by clicking on its URL or title. This is useful when you want to create page specific tables or add a secondary dimension to the report.

Site Content > Content Drilldown

The **Behavior > Site Content > Content Drilldown** report allows you to examine user interaction with your website pages by "drilling down" into the folder structure you've set up on your site. You move from the highest-level directories to the level of terminal pages.

Let's look at a different data set that works well to illustrate this and the remaining metrics. Selecting the **Behavior > Site Content > Content Drilldown** option generates a table similar to that shown on the top of page 230. The column headers provide information on page interaction averaged for all of the pages within a particular directory (listed in the far left-hand column). Given that almost all of my website pages are within the /xxangeon/ directory, it is not surprising that the vast majority of page interactions occur within this directory.

Page path level 1	Pageviews ↓	Unique Pageviews	Avg. Time on Page	Bounce Rate	% Exit
	2,842 % of Total: 100.00% (2,842)	2,045 % of Total: 100.00% (2,045)	00:00:44 Avg for View: 00:00:44 (0.00%)	34.65% Avg for View: 34.65% (0.00%)	37.26% Avg for View: 37.26% (0.00%)
1. ☐ /xxangeon/	2,720 (95.71%)	1,965 (96.09%)	00:00:38	34.15%	37.57%
2. ☐ /vpv/	73 (2.57%)	48 (2.35%)	00:03:17	50.00%	26.03%
3. ☐ /zmscmizzle/	13 (0.46%)	4 (0.20%)	00:01:55	100.00%	15.38%

Clicking on a specific directory allows you to "drilldown" for more detail on page interactions within that directory. Clicking on the /xxangeon/ directory produces the table
shown below. The page with the most pageviews in this directory is my purchase page
(purchasef.html). The data reported for user interactions with this page are generally in line with my overall site averages.

Page path level 2	Pageviews ↓	Unique Pageviews	Avg. Time on Page	Bounce Rate	% Exit
	2,720 % of Total: 95.71% (2,842)	1,965 % of Total: 96.09% (2,045)	00:00:38 Avg for View: 00:00:44 (-13.37%)	34.15% Avg for View: 34.65% (-1.45%)	37.57% Avg for View: 37.26% (0.83%)
1. ☐ /purchasef.html	409 (15.04%)	238 (12.11%)	00:00:23	32.73%	30.56%
2. ☐ /	391 (14.37%)	344 (17.51%)	00:00:56	37.00%	36.57%
3. ☐ /mexico1a.html	250 (9.19%)	137 (6.97%)	00:00:23	7.69%	15.60%
4. ☐ /purchasealt.html	208 (7.65%)	141 (7.18%)	00:00:30	53.90%	67.31%
5. ☐ /purchasec.html	188 (6.91%)	121 (6.16%)	00:00:11	45.76%	64.36%
6. ☐ /contact.html	98 (3.60%)	98 (4.99%)	00:00:25	0.00%	13.27%
7. ☐ /thanks_p.html	95 (3.49%)	92 (4.68%)	00:02:18	0.00%	75.79%
8. ☐ /thanks1.html	83 (3.05%)	34 (1.73%)	00:00:36	28.57%	19.28%
9. ☐ /mediaplay.html	79 (2.90%)	74 (3.77%)	00:00:46	80.00%	48.10%
10. ☐ /thanks_c.html	79 (2.90%)	74 (3.77%)	00:00:13	0.00%	51.90%

The process of clicking on a higher order classification to view lower order pages can be
repeated until a terminal page within the directory is reached. Since my purchasef.
html page is a terminal page, clicking on this page's listing in the table brings up the
following, which repeats and expands upon the data presented in the prior table.

Page	Pageviews ↓	Unique Pageviews	Avg. Time on Page	Bounce Rate	% Exit
	409 % of Total: 14.39% (2,842)	238 % of Total: 11.64% (2,045)	00:00:23 Avg for View: 00:00:44 (-48.66%)	32.73% Avg for View: 34.65% (-5.55%)	30.56% Avg for View: 37.26% (-17.98%)
1. /xxangeon/purchasef.html	409(100.00%)	238(100.00%)	00:00:23	32.73%	30.56%

Finally, you can immediately change the directory and page of interest via the pull-down menus directly beneath **Content Drilldown** at the top of the report page. At the moment, I am examining the `purchasef.html` page within the `/xxangeon/` directory (see below).

I can use the pull-down menus to immediately change the directory (see top figure below) or page being examined (see bottom figure below).

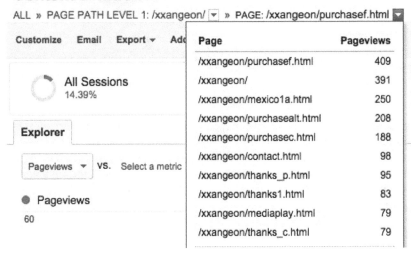

The **Behavior > Site Content > Landing Pages** menu option provides insights into how users enter your site and where they go afterwards. Similar to the **All Pages** report, two data view options are presented, one on the top of the page and the other in tabular form on the bottom of the page.

Top of page

Once again, Google Analytics provides a line chart on the top of the report page. Beyond this chart, there are two things of note, both of which appear as options above the line chart.

The first option, **Entrance Paths**, can be found above the line chart next to the **Explorer** tab (see below)

The **Entrance Paths** option allows you to see the paths a user takes after landing on (i.e., entering) your site via a specified page. Similar to the prior charting options, the insights provided by the **Entrance Paths** report are an alternative way to obtain the insights provided by the **Behavior > Behavior Flow** report (discussed in Chapter 23). Clicking on this option brings up the display shown below.

To begin, use the pull-down menu next to **User started at this landing page** to select the landing page on which you want to focus (see example on the top of page 233). We'll select the main entry page to the site, /xxangeon. However, before leaving this display, it is important for you to note the relative ranking of different landing pages as this will inform you of the extent to which users are following your "ideal" entrance and subsequent paths through your site.

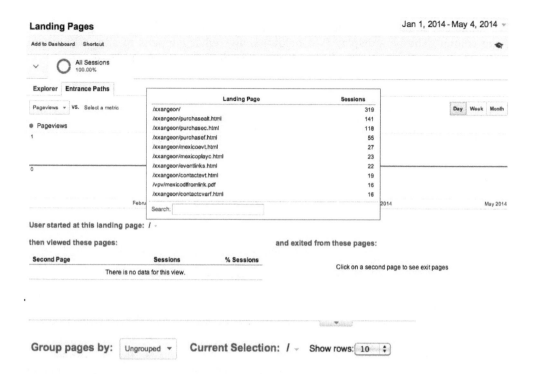

After I select my target landing page, the display changes to that shown below.

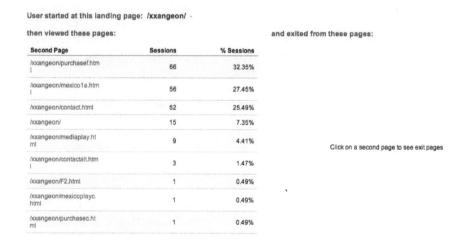

In this example, the column labeled **Second Page** indicates where site users went after entering the site through the site's home page. Interestingly, users tend to go directly to the purchase page (`purchasef.html`) or the Mexico information page (`mexico1a.html`). Is this direct path to the purchase page one which we want to encourage or redesign the site to discourage?

We can begin to answer this question by clicking on the purchase page in the **Second Page** column. The new display (see below) shows what happens to site visitors who enter on the home page and then immediately click through to the purchase page.

User started at this landing page: /xxangeon/

then viewed these pages:				and exited from these pages:		
Second Page	Sessions	% Sessions		Exit Page	Sessions	% Sessions
/xxangeon/purchasef.html	66	32.35%		/xxangeon/thanks_p.html	24	36.36%
/xxangeon/mexico1a.html	56	27.45%		/xxangeon/purchasef.html	20	30.30%
/xxangeon/contact.html	52	25.49%		/xxangeon/mediaplay.html	9	13.64%
/xxangeon/	15	7.35%		/xxangeon/thanks_c.html	5	7.58%
/xxangeon/mediaplay.html	9	4.41%		/xxangeon/	3	4.55%
/xxangeon/contactalt.html	3	1.47%		/xxangeon/contact.html	2	3.03%
/xxangeon/F2.html	1	0.49%		/xxangeon/mexico1a.html	1	1.52%
/xxangeon/mexicoplayc.html	1	0.49%		/xxangeon/mexicocm.html	1	1.52%
/xxangeon/purchasec.html	1	0.49%		/xxangeon/mexicogl.html	1	1.52%

Search:

This site is designed take a user to a "thank you for your purchase" page (/thanks_p. html) after a purchase is made. The second column shows that this is the most common exit page after viewing the purchase page. This is to be expected and indicates that about of 37% of all sessions involve a purchase. But there is bad news. The percentage of users who view the purchase page (in the first column) and then leave from this page (as shown in the second column) is 30.3%. Thus, about one-third of users view the purchase page and then leave the site without any further engagement (including contact or purchase). We would certainly want to examine the characteristics of the purchase page to determine why such a large percentage of users are leaving from this page.

The second option on the top of the **Behavior > Site Content > Landing Pages** report allows you to change the metrics displayed in the bottom of page table. We'll discuss this option after we discuss the data table itself.

Bottom of Page

The table on the bottom of the **Behavior > Site Content > Landing Pages** report rank orders site _entry_ pages on the basis of total sessions within your selected time frame (see table on the top of page 235). As you've seen in other reports, this table provides data in terms of acquisition, behavior and ecommerce metrics.

Landing Page	Acquisition			Behavior			Conversions eCommerce ▼		
	Sessions ↓	% New Sessions	New Users	Bounce Rate	Pages / Session	Avg. Session Duration	Transactions	Revenue	Ecommerce Conversion Rate
	1,098 % of Total: 100.00% (1,098)	**84.79%** Avg for View: 84.79% (0.00%)	**931** % of Total: 100.00% (931)	**34.70%** Avg for View: 34.70% (0.00%)	**2.72** Avg for View: 2.72 (0.00%)	**00:01:23** Avg for View: 00:01:23 (0.00%)	**271** % of Total: 100.00% (271)	**$1,940,200.00** % of Total: 100.00% ($1,940,200.00)	**24.68%** Avg for View: 24.68% (0.00%)
1. /xxangeon/	332 (30.24%)	78.01%	259 (27.82%)	37.65%	3.28	00:01:35	63 (23.25%)	$423,500.00 (21.83%)	18.98%
2. /xxangeon/purchasealt.html	141 (12.84%)	97.87%	138 (14.82%)	53.90%	1.49	00:00:15	61 (22.51%)	$339,900.00 (17.21%)	43.26%
3. /xxangeon/purchasec.html	118 (10.75%)	98.31%	116 (12.46%)	45.76%	1.55	00:00:06	59 (21.77%)	$377,900.00 (19.48%)	50.00%
4. /xxangeon/purchasef.html	55 (5.01%)	74.55%	41 (4.40%)	32.73%	2.22	00:00:23	25 (9.23%)	$182,800.00 (9.42%)	45.45%
5. /xxangeon/mexicoevt.html	27 (2.46%)	66.67%	18 (1.93%)	22.22%	3.59	00:02:14	8 (2.95%)	$116,600.00 (6.01%)	29.63%
6. /xxangeon/mexicoplayc.html	23 (2.09%)	82.61%	19 (2.04%)	26.09%	1.26	00:01:19	0 (0.00%)	$0.00 (0.00%)	0.00%
7. /xxangeon/eventlinks.html	22 (2.00%)	81.82%	18 (1.93%)	9.09%	4.14	00:01:59	20 (7.38%)	$147,800.00 (7.62%)	90.91%
8. /xxangeon/contactevt.html	19 (1.73%)	94.74%	18 (1.93%)	0.00%	2.68	00:00:24	0 (0.00%)	$0.00 (0.00%)	0.00%
9. /xxangeon/scroll6.html	17 (1.55%)	82.35%	14 (1.50%)	0.00%	4.00	00:02:38	0 (0.00%)	$0.00 (0.00%)	0.00%

The prior table presents a lot of data all at once. You can focus on a specific type of data by using the data view options displayed beneath the **Explorer** tab. **Site Usage** will always appear and **Ecommerce** will appear when your site is configured for ecommerce. Additional options will appear as you add goals to your site.

Selecting the **Site Usage** option, for example, changes the metrics to those shown below, allowing you to better focus on just the metrics related to site usage.

Landing Page	Sessions ↓	Pages / Session	Avg. Session Duration	% New Sessions	Bounce Rate
	1,098 % of Total: 100.00% (1,098)	**2.72** Avg for View: 2.72 (0.00%)	**00:01:23** Avg for View: 00:01:23 (0.00%)	**84.79%** Avg for View: 84.79% (0.00%)	**34.70%** Avg for View: 34.70% (0.00%)
1. /xxangeon/	332 (30.24%)	3.28	00:01:35	78.01%	37.65%
2. /xxangeon/purchasealt.html	141 (12.84%)	1.49	00:00:15	97.87%	53.90%
3. /xxangeon/purchasec.html	118 (10.75%)	1.55	00:00:06	98.31%	45.76%
4. /xxangeon/purchasef.html	55 (5.01%)	2.22	00:00:23	74.55%	32.73%
5. /xxangeon/mexicoevt.html	27 (2.46%)	3.59	00:02:14	66.67%	22.22%
6. /xxangeon/mexicoplayc.html	23 (2.09%)	1.26	00:01:19	82.61%	26.09%
7. /xxangeon/eventlinks.html	22 (2.00%)	4.14	00:01:59	81.82%	9.09%
8. /xxangeon/contactevt.html	19 (1.73%)	2.68	00:00:24	94.74%	0.00%
9. /xxangeon/scroll6.html	17 (1.55%)	4.00	00:02:38	82.35%	0.00%

Finally, similar to other tables, you can use the charting options on the top of the table to create pie, bar, and percent differential charts. In addition, clicking on any individual page will bring up a chart displaying just that page. As with other charts, this is useful when you want to add a secondary dimension to the examination of that page.

The **Behavior > Site Content > Exit Pages** menu option provides insights into how users leave your site. Similar to the **Behavior > Site Content > Landing Pages** report two data view options are presented, one on the top of the page and the other in tabular form on the bottom of the page.

The chart on the top of the page presents the line chart you've seen earlier. The chart on the bottom of the page is identical to the **Behavior > Site Content > Landing Pages** report, except here pages are ordered in terms of the number of site users leaving your site after viewing a particular page (see below).

	Page	Exits	↓ Pageviews	% Exit
		1,095 % of Total: 100.00% (1,095)	**2,989** % of Total: 100.00% (2,989)	**36.63%** Avg for View: 36.63% (0.00%)
☐ 1.	/xxangeon/	**147** (13.42%)	396 (13.25%)	37.12%
☐ 2.	/xxangeon/purchasealt.html	**140** (12.79%)	208 (6.96%)	67.31%
☐ 3.	/xxangeon/purchasef.html	**125** (11.42%)	409 (13.68%)	30.56%
☐ 4.	/xxangeon/purchasec.html	**121** (11.05%)	188 (6.29%)	64.36%
☐ 5.	/xxangeon/thanks_p.html	**72** (6.58%)	95 (3.18%)	75.79%
☐ 6.	/xxangeon/thanks_c.html	**41** (3.74%)	79 (2.64%)	51.90%
☐ 7.	/xxangeon/mexico1a.html	**40** (3.65%)	251 (8.40%)	15.94%
☐ 8.	/xxangeon/mediaplay.html	**38** (3.47%)	79 (2.64%)	48.10%
☐ 9.	/xxangeon/mexicoplayc.html	**24** (2.19%)	35 (1.17%)	68.57%

.   .   .   .

Let's now focus on the four data reporting options within the **Behavior > Site Search** menu, as shown on the top of page 237. We'll use data from the Google Store to illustrate the use and interpretation of these metrics.

> ✓ Site search metrics are only displayed in Google Analytics views which have been configured for search. Google provides the resources and direction to take you through the steps required for configuration. See *Set Up Site Search* at https://support.google.com/analytics/answer/1012264.

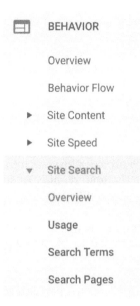

BEHAVIOR

Overview

Behavior Flow

▶ Site Content

▶ Site Speed

▼ Site Search

Overview

Usage

Search Terms

Search Pages

The **Behavior > Site Search > Overview** page is organized similarly to the **Audience > Overview** page. The top of the page displays a line chart and the bottom of the page provides a summary of key dimensions. The most relevant data is provided in the middle of page display, as shown below.

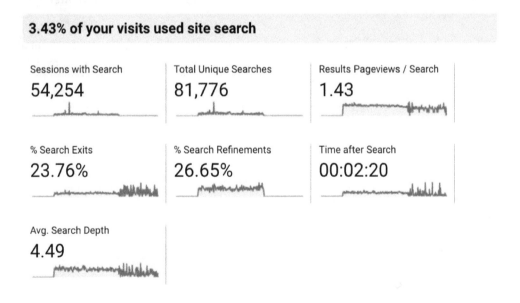

3.43% of your visits used site search

Sessions with Search	Total Unique Searches	Results Pageviews / Search
54,254	81,776	1.43

% Search Exits	% Search Refinements	Time after Search
23.76%	26.65%	00:02:20

Avg. Search Depth
4.49

The very top of the display tells us how many site visits included at least one site search. In this example, 3.43% of visits included a site search.

Site search summary metrics appear next. Each of these metrics is defined as follows:[52]

- *Sessions with Search* represents the total number of sessions that used the site's internal search function at least once.

- *Total Unique Searches* reports the total number of times site search was used. This metric excludes multiple searches on the same keyword during the same session.

- *Results Pageviews/Search* provides insights into site search outcomes and is calculated by dividing the total number of search result pageviews by the total number of unique searches.

- *% Search Exits* reports the percentage of searches made immediately before leaving the site. This metric is calculated by dividing search exits by the total number of unique searches.

- *% Search Refinements* represents the percentage of searches that resulted in a search refinement (which is defined as the number of times a user searched again immediately after performing a search). This metric is calculated by dividing the total number of search refinements by the total number of search results pageviews.

- *Time after Search* reports the average amount of time users spent on the site after performing a search.

- *Ave. Search Depth* represents the average number of pages viewed after performing a search.

With regard to the Google Store data (shown in the figure on page 237), the 3.43% of all site visitors who used site search appear to respond positively to this feature: few leave the site after search (as reflected in the low % Search Exits) while engagement with the site (as reflected in Time After Search and Average Search Depth) is high after a search takes place. An examination of additional metrics will help us to determine if our conclusion regarding the positive impact of internal search use is correct.

Site Search > Usage

This report divides site sessions into two categories: those that included site search and those that did not include search. This split allows you to directly compare the behaviors and outcomes of the people using search to those who didn't use search. The table on the top of page 239 displays the behaviors of these two groups when **Site Usage** is selected from the top of the page, beneath the Explorer tab.

---

[52] *How Site Search Metrics are Calculated* at
https://support.google.com/analytics/answer/1032321

Site Search Status	Sessions	Pages / Session	Avg. Session Duration	% New Sessions	Bounce Rate
	1,581,855	5.44	00:02:23	77.99%	46.01%
	% of Total: 100.00% (1,581,855)	Avg for View: 5.44 (0.00%)	Avg for View: 00:02:23 (0.00%)	Avg for View: 77.92% (0.10%)	Avg for View: 46.01% (0.00%)
1. Visits Without Site Search	1,527,601 (96.57%)	5.15	00:02:16	78.32%	47.43%
2. Visits With Site Search	54,254 (3.43%)	13.78	00:05:34	68.70%	6.11%

Site engagement appears to be much higher for those who used the site's internal search versus those who did not use the search feature. The chart indicates that the average number of pages per session is nearly three times higher for the "Visits With Site Search" group (13.78 versus 5.15), average session duration is more than double (5:34 versus 2:16) and the bounce rate is significantly lower (6.11% versus 47.43%).

The table below displays the behaviors of the "Visits With Site Search" and "Visits Without Site Search" groups when **Ecommerce** is selected from the top of the page, beneath the Explorer tab. Once again, we see important differences between the groups. The advantage of the "Visits With Site Search" group, in terms of engagement, appears to transfer to ecommerce. The "Visits With Site Search" group is much more likely to make a transaction (as evidenced in the ecommerce conversion rate) and their per session value is significantly higher.

Site Search Status	Sessions	Revenue	Transactions	Avg. Order Value	Ecommerce Conversion Rate	Per Session Value
	1,581,855	$3,771,253.34	25,415	$148.39	1.61%	$2.38
	% of Total: 100.00% (1,581,855)	% of Total: 100.00% ($3,771,253.34)	% of Total: 100.00% (25,415)	Avg for View: $148.39 (0.00%)	Avg for View: 1.61% (0.00%)	Avg for View: $2.38 (0.00%)
1. Visits Without Site Search	1,527,601 (96.57%)	$3,445,857.21 (91.37%)	23,283 (91.61%)	$148.00	1.52%	$2.26
2. Visits With Site Search	54,254 (3.43%)	$325,396.13 (8.63%)	2,132 (8.39%)	$152.62	3.93%	$6.00

Site Search > Search Terms

The **Behavior > Site Search > Search Terms** menu option displays the words and phrases that site visitors used when conducting an internal site search. This data provides insights into what visitors are looking for on the site and the effects of each specific search term on engagement and ecommerce outcomes.

The default report for **Behavior > Site Search > Search Terms** is shown on the top of page 240.

Search Term	Total Unique Searches	Results Pageviews / Search	% Search Exits	% Search Refinements	Time after Search	Avg. Search Depth
	81,776 % of Total: 100.00% (81,776)	**1.43** Avg for View: 1.43 (0.00%)	**23.76%** Avg for View: 23.76% (0.00%)	**26.65%** Avg for View: 26.65% (0.00%)	**00:02:20** Avg for View: 00:02:20 (0.00%)	**4.49** Avg for View: 4.49 (0.00%)
1. stickers	**2,400** (2.93%)	1.46	40.75%	4.66%	00:02:03	5.06
2. youtube	**2,085** (2.55%)	2.57	26.76%	5.86%	00:03:44	6.66
3. gopher	**1,993** (2.44%)	1.27	46.21%	4.49%	00:01:32	2.83
4. ingress	**1,917** (2.34%)	1.68	54.20%	4.81%	00:01:52	2.80
5. android	**1,362** (1.67%)	4.04	28.85%	6.45%	00:03:40	6.75
6. chromecast	**874** (1.07%)	1.11	35.35%	16.74%	00:02:11	4.71
7. nexus	**777** (0.95%)	1.07	49.81%	12.68%	00:00:47	1.77
8. YouTube	**755** (0.92%)	2.57	38.81%	5.00%	00:03:22	3.78
9. backpack	**727** (0.89%)	1.57	17.88%	13.52%	00:03:09	7.68

Some key questions that this data helps to answer include:

- *Which search terms are most likely to be used?* In this case, the most common search terms (as shown in the Total Unique Searches column) are "stickers," "youtube" and "gopher." A deeper understanding of what visitors are seeking will help you make stronger strategic decisions with regard to content and content display/organization.

- *How many search results pages did it take for people to find what they were looking for?* In this case, most searchers found what they were looking for on the first page of results (as evidenced in the Results Pageviews/Search column). This is good. Higher numbers in this column indicate either that visitors were searching for something not on the site or that search results are inefficient. It is important to determine which is the case and to identify appropriate strategic responses.

- *How satisfied were visitors with their search results?* Higher percentages in the % Search Exits column indicate higher percentages of visitors who gave up and left the website after a search. In this case, percentages varied across the most common search terms.

  Search satisfaction is also reflected in the data provided in the % Search Refinements column. Higher percentages in this column reflect greater likelihood of conducting sequential searches (when, for example, the initial search results did not provide the desired results).

  Higher averages in either or both of these columns indicate the need to strategically examine the quality of search results and to identify ways to increase the relevancy of search results.

- *Which search queries lead to greater website engagement?* Insights into the answer to this question are provided in the two right-hand columns of the table. Here, higher numbers in either or both columns indicate higher levels of engagement. Search queries with lower numbers should be examined with an eye toward explaining their negative impact on engagement.

The table below examines the relationship between search terms and ecommerce outcomes when **Ecommerce** is selected from the top of the page, beneath the Explorer tab. While all of this data provides important insights, perhaps the most important is the ecommerce conversion rate – whether or not an ecommerce transaction occurred after a specific search. Higher percentages indicate that a search term is more likely to lead to a transaction. Lower percentages indicate the lack of a purchase after use of a specific search term. These latter search terms (and their provided results) should be examined to determine the underlying cause.

Search Term	Total Unique Searches	Revenue	Transactions	Avg. Order Value	Ecommerce Conversion Rate	Per Search Value
	81,776 % of Total: 100.00% (81,776)	$314,033.22 % of Total: 8.33% ($3,771,253.34)	2,031 % of Total: 7.99% (25,415)	$154.62 Avg for View: $148.39 (4.20%)	2.48% Avg for View: .31.08% (-92.01%)	$3.84 Avg for View: $46.12 (-91.67%)
1. stickers	2,400 (2.93%)	$12,393.06 (3.95%)	61 (3.00%)	$203.16	2.54%	$5.16
2. youtube	2,085 (2.55%)	$13,375.50 (4.26%)	114 (5.61%)	$117.33	5.47%	$6.42
3. gopher	1,993 (2.44%)	$1,595.48 (0.51%)	31 (1.53%)	$51.47	1.56%	$0.80
4. ingress	1,917 (2.34%)	$537.62 (0.17%)	16 (0.79%)	$33.60	0.83%	$0.28
5. android	1,362 (1.67%)	$6,092.01 (1.94%)	41 (2.02%)	$148.59	3.01%	$4.47
6. chromecast	874 (1.07%)	$2,604.30 (0.83%)	19 (0.94%)	$137.07	2.17%	$2.98
7. nexus	777 (0.95%)	$135.68 (0.04%)	3 (0.15%)	$45.23	0.39%	$0.17
8. YouTube	755 (0.92%)	$1,525.22 (0.49%)	16 (0.79%)	$95.33	2.12%	$2.02
9. backpack	727 (0.89%)	$5,104.60 (1.63%)	31 (1.53%)	$164.66	4.26%	$7.02

Site Search > Search Pages

The **Behavior > Site Search > Search Pages** menu option displays the pages from which searches were conducted. This data provides insights into website location when visitors decided to use search, perhaps because the current page was not providing the information they desired.

The default table is shown on the top of page 242. Again, while all of this data provides strategic insights, perhaps the most important column is the first column, Total Unique Searches. Pages with greater search sessions may require attention with regard to that page's content, navigation and orientation.

Start Page	Total Unique Searches ↓	Results Pageviews / Search	% Search Exits	% Search Refinements	Time after Search	Avg. Search Depth
	81,776 % of Total: 100.00% (81,776)	**1.43** Avg for View: 1.43 (0.00%)	**23.76%** Avg for View: 23.76% (0.00%)	**26.65%** Avg for View: 26.65% (0.00%)	**00:02:20** Avg for View: 00:02:20 (0.00%)	**4.49** Avg for View: 4.49 (0.00%)
1. /shop.axd/Home	**19,284** (23.58%)	1.04	22.69%	27.49%	00:01:21	2.59
2. /shop.axd/Search	**16,122** (19.71%)	1.84	27.19%	32.95%	00:02:41	4.79
3. (entrance)	**7,420** (9.07%)	1.00	44.88%	8.11%	00:01:18	1.68
4. /shop.axd/Cart	**1,280** (1.57%)	1.32	8.91%	28.21%	00:04:24	8.63
5. /Google+Redesign/Brands/YouTube/home	**1,063** (1.30%)	1.02	32.55%	26.71%	00:01:00	1.60
6. /Google+Redesign/Brands/YouTube/	**1,049** (1.28%)	1.02	32.98%	25.70%	00:00:45	1.35
7. /Google+Redesign/Wearables/Men+s+T-Shirts/	**881** (1.08%)	1.04	14.53%	23.25%	00:02:22	4.17
8. /Google+Redesign/Fun/	**770** (0.94%)	1.10	14.68%	28.39%	00:02:00	4.74
9. /Google+Redesign/Fun/home	**743** (0.91%)	1.10	16.02%	30.20%	00:01:57	4.28

23
The Behavior Menu: Behavior Flow

Chapter 18 discussed how to interpret and apply **Audience > Users Flow** data to strategic decision-making. The **Behavior > Behavior Flow** report is interpreted in exactly the same way, except here the primary goal is to understand how individuals move through the site as a function of different landing pages. We'll recap the Users Flow discussion for you as we explore the **Behavior > Behavior Flow** report.

The table shown below appears when I select **Behavior > Behavior Flow**.

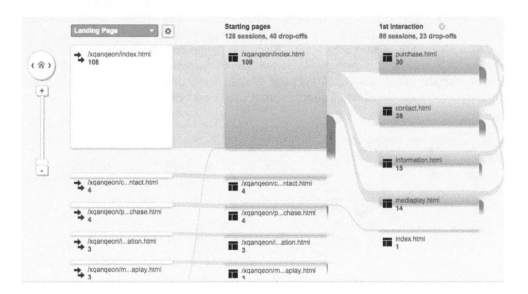

The default chart uses **Landing Page** as the organizing dimension (see the top of the first column). Beneath **Landing Page** is a list of all landing pages ordered by session frequency. In this example, my home page (/xqanqeon/index.html) accounts for the vast majority in initiating site sessions.

Similar to **Audience > Users Flow,** the chart is composed of different sized boxes and grey bands. The size of the individual boxes indicates the relative number of sessions occurring on any individual page. The larger the box, the greater the number of sessions. The grey bands show connections between site pages. The larger the grey band the greater the connection between two pages.

You can see the exact size of the relationship between two pages by placing your cursor over any grey band, as shown below. The pop-up window indicates that 21.9% of all my site traffic involved sessions, which started on the site's home page and moved to the purchase page, `purchase.html`.

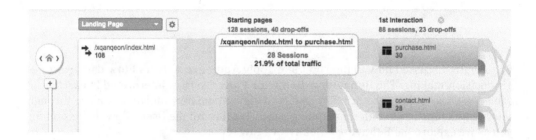

The information provided at the top of the Starting pages column provides important insights into your site's stickiness when looking at all landing pages as a group. Starting page metrics report that overall there were 128 sessions with 40 drop-offs. This means that of all those sessions started on my site (on any page) about one-third "dropped off" or left without any further interaction. Since our home page accounts for the largest number of sessions, it is reasonable to assume that about one-third of sessions are ending after the initial viewing of this page. We can verify this by rolling our cursor over the top green box in the Starting pages column, as shown below.

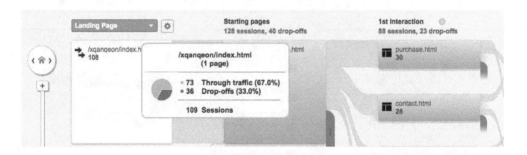

The home page is the starting page for 109 sessions (out of the total 128) and the drop-off rate for this page is about what we would expect (33%). Clearly, we'll need to look at our home page with the goal of reducing this drop-off rate.

Let's take a closer look at those who remain on our site after entering on the home page. We begin by clicking on the green home page box (in the Starting pages column) and then selecting **Highlight traffic through here** in the pop-up window, as shown in the chart on the top of page 245.

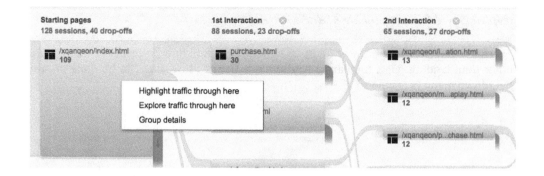

This creates the chart shown below.

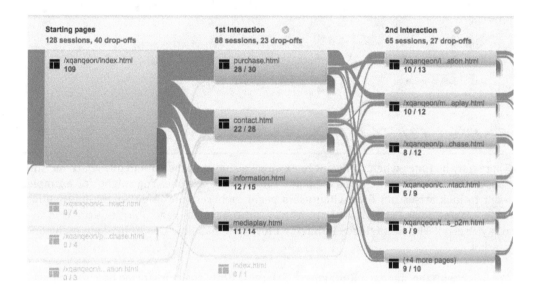

We can see that there is no consistent session flow. Sessions progress from the home (landing) page to each of four other pages, and from these pages session consistency is reduced even more. Additionally, the video page (/xqanqeon/mediaplay.html), in which we invested significant time and resources, is the least visited page from the home landing page. We need to determine how to revise/redesign both the visual and content areas of our site to better lead consumers through the desired path to purchase (rather than going immediately to the purchase page).[53]

---

[53] You might ask why it is unacceptable to have sessions move directly from the home page to the purchase page. The data indicate this path is not in our best interest because few arrive at the purchase confirmation page in the 2nd interaction. This path through our site is unfortunately unlikely to result in a sale.

Changing the organizing dimension

There are times when you may want to look at behavior flow in terms of dimensions other than landing page. Similar to **Audience > Users Flow**, this can be done via the pull-down menu (see below).

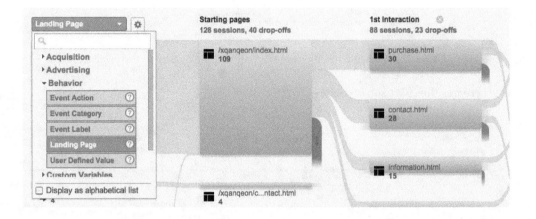

Restricting the data view

There may be times when you want to examine a subset of the data in one chart, but this subset consists of two or three elements rather than just one. You might, for example, want to look at session flow when users begin their session on either the information page (/xqaneqon/information.html) or the video page /xqanqeon/media-play.html). The **Behavior > Behavior Flow** options allow this to be done easily and quickly.

We begin with the standard **Behavior > Behavior Flow** chart organized by landing page, as shown below.

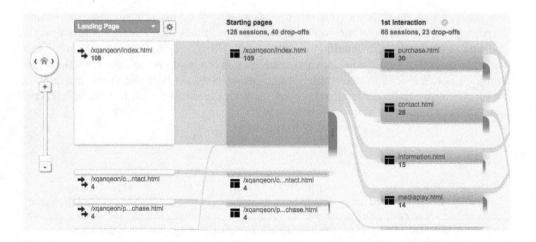

Next, we indicate that we want to restrict the data view to two of these landing pages. We do this by clicking on the small gear symbol to the left of **Landing Page** (see below).

When this is done the popup window shown below appears.

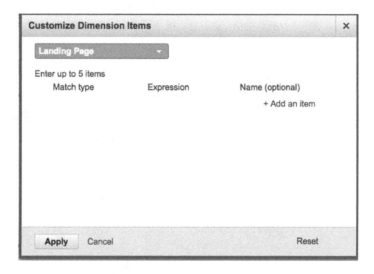

We want to select two landing pages. To begin, we click on **+Add an item** and on the new line displayed we set **Match type** to **matches regex**. We then type the information needed to identify each landing page in the **Expression** box. When we are done, the information provided in the window is as shown below.

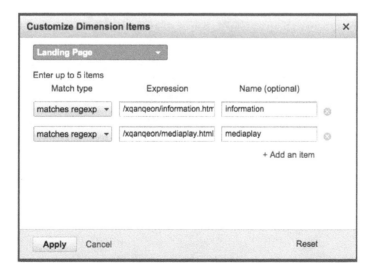

Finally, when we are sure that the information is correct, we press **Apply** and the display changes to include just the two pages of interest, as shown below.

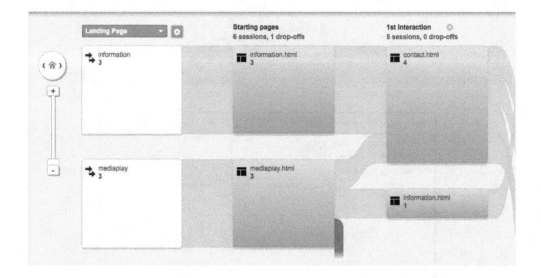

24

The Behavior Menu: Site Speed

Metrics that report how quickly your site overall and specific pages are loading can be found in the **Site Speed** menu beneath the **Behavior** main menu (see below).[54] This information is particularly important when you want to maximize the chances of a positive user experience with your website or blog.

Site Speed provides data on three aspects of site load speed and latency. These are:

- *Page-load time for a subset of site pageviews.* As with metrics we have already discussed, you can view the data across different dimensions to see how quickly your pages loaded from a variety of perspectives (e.g., in different browsers or in different countries). This data can be seen via the **Behavior > Site Speed > Overview** and **Behavior > Site Speed > Page Timings** menu options. No additional configuration of your website or blog is required to collect this data.

- *Execution speed or load time of any discrete hit, event, or user interaction that you want to track* (for example, how quickly images load or response time to button clicks). Data for these metrics is available in the **Behavior > Site Speed > User Timings** report. Google notes that the collection of this data "Requires additional set up that must be completed by a qualified developer."

---

54 Primary sources for this chapter are: *About Site Speed* at
https://support.google.com/analytics/answer/1205784?hl=en and *Interpret Site Speed* at
https://support.google.com/analytics/answer/2383341?hl=en.

- *How quickly the browser parses the document and makes it available for user interaction.* Data for these metrics are available in the **Behavior > Site Speed > Page Timings** report. No additional configuration is required to collect this data.

Site Speed metrics can help you determine how well your site and specific pages perform with regard to how quickly users are able to see and interact with content. You can identify areas that need improvement and then track the extent to which those improvements reduce load times. Finally, when you determine that improvements are necessary, Google provides suggestions through the **Behavior > Site Speed > Speed Suggestions** menu option.

Overview

Behavior > Site Speed > Overview displays summary information for metrics related to site speed and latency. Each of these metrics, as well as others related to site and page speed, are defined in this chapter's addendum.

Top of Page

The chart shown on the top of the **Behavior > Site Speed > Overview** page presents (by default) a line graph of **Average Page Load Time**. When all is working well on your site, the line and peaks should be relatively flat, indicating consistency in this metric. Spikes in the line graph may be an indication of specific site problem(s) and that a page-by-page analysis of load times may be warranted. A drop in the line graph indicates improvement in average site load times and should appear whenever you are successful in modifying pages to reduce load time.

The need to monitor this metric on a daily basis is illustrated in the line graph shown below. We noted a significant rise in **Average Page Load Time** on March 12 and took steps to remedy the problem before it became worse.

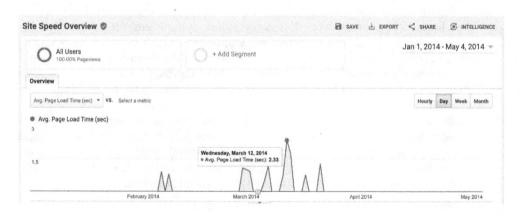

Similar to other line charts, you have the option of changing the displayed metric. The range of speed-related metrics can be found by using the pull-down menu beneath the **Overview** tab, as shown below.

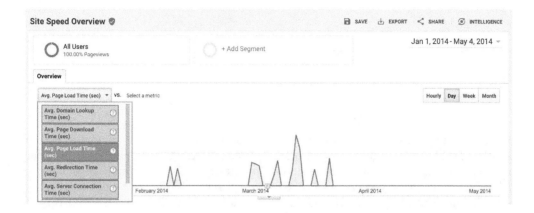

Finally, similar to other line graphs, you can chart two metrics at the same time or you can chart the same metric in two different time periods.

Middle of Page

The data presented in the middle of **Behavior > Site Speed > Overview** display reports site averages for the set of reported speed metrics (see below). Since all of these metrics relate to site speed, lower numbers are better, indicating faster load and connection speeds. The average metrics for my site appear to be quite acceptable.

Keep in mind, however, that these are averages and as such, can be influenced by extreme measures. A high overall average page load time, for example, may be deceptive if its high average is influenced by the extremely high load time of just one or two pages. As a result, while a low number in these metrics is a good sign, higher numbers should be interpreted cautiously and should lead to a more detailed examination of individual page performance, as discussed later in this chapter.

The bottom of the page chart (see below) allows you to examine average page load times by browser, country or page.

Site Speed		Browser	Avg. Page Load Time (sec)
Browser	▶	1. Firefox	0.76
Country		2. Internet Explorer	1.13
Page		3. Chrome	1.74
			view full report

Examination by browser and country (and its subdivisions of city) allows you to isolate any site problems related to these two areas. High load times for a particular browser may indicate that the site needs to be better optimized for that browser. High load times for a particular country may also indicate that optimization should be explored when sending site content to IP addresses located in that country. Clicking **view full report** for these metrics takes you to more detailed tables.

While browser and country insights are important, perhaps the most important link is **Page,** which allows you to see the load times and other speed data for individual pages. Since clicking on **view full report** for this metric takes you to the same display as that obtained through the **Behavior > Site Speed > Page Timings** menu option, we'll discuss **Page Timings** in the next section.

Page Timings

Let's examine some recent data from our travel site.

Selecting the **Behavior > Site Speed > Page Timings** menu option brings up two displays. First, on the top of the page, the same **Average Page Load Time** chart as presented in the **Behavior > Overview** page is displayed. As with the earlier chart, the metric(s) and time frame for the display can be customized to meet your strategic information needs. Options to display additional highly technical metrics appear next to and below the Explorer tab, as shown below.

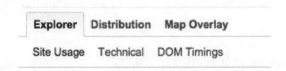

Explorer	Distribution	Map Overlay
Site Usage	Technical	DOM Timings

Data on the bottom of the **Behavior > Site Speed > Page Timings** display shows page load times for individual site pages. Note that if you are taken to the over/under line chart, you can click on the table icon above the chart to display the data as a table. The table icon, which resembles a grid, is on the upper right-hand side of the table and is the first in the row of three icons. The resulting table, organized by page URL, is shown below.

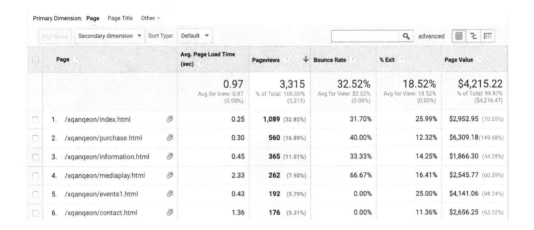

Selecting the **Page Title** option from above the chart (on the left-hand side in the Primary Dimension row) makes the table easier to interpret by listing pages by name rather than URL, as shown below.

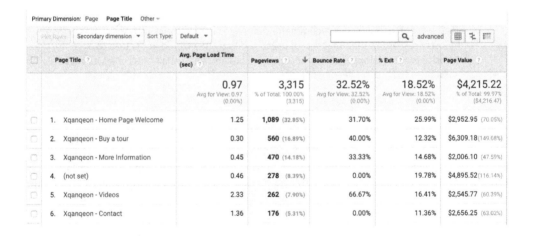

At this point, we are only interested in the first two columns: **Average Page Load Time** and **Pageviews**. Pageviews is important because we don't want to draw conclusions about pages for which there are so few views that the reported load times become unreliable. As a general rule of thumb, we recommend at least 30 pageviews occur before you pay much attention to the Average Page Load Time.

You can use this chart to identify pages with relatively long load times. This can be done easily by clicking on the **Average Page Load Time** column header. Doing so orders all of your pages in terms of load time from high to low. The table below presents all of our pages by title where the pages with the longest average load times are presented first. These are the pages, which may require attention.

In my case, all of my pages seem to load quickly except one (listed in the first position), which is still fast but a bit longer than the others. I can take a look at this page to see how this load time can potentially be reduced. Google Analytics' **Speed Suggestions** might provide some specific guidance.

> Industry guidelines recommend that pages load in three seconds or less. Industry research found that 75% of users said that they would not return to a website that took longer than 4 seconds to load and nearly half of all users expect webpages to load in 2 seconds or less.

Speed Suggestions

Selecting the **Behavior > Site Speed > Speed Suggestions** option displays a list of your site's pages ordered by pageviews. Similar to Average Page Load Time, this display is easier to apply to strategic decision-making if you click on the **Average Page Load Time** column header, which will order your pages from highest to lowest in terms of average load time. As we saw in the previous table, most of our pages are doing quite well. There is only one page with more than 30 pageviews that takes more than two seconds to load (see table on the top of page 255).

	Page	Pageviews	Avg. Page Load Time (sec)	PageSpeed Suggestions	PageSpeed Score
1.	/xqanqeon/	0	2.43	4 total	88
2.	/xqanqeon/mediaplay.html	254	2.33	5 total	87
3.	/xqanqeon/contact.html	169	1.36	4 total	81
4.	/xqanqeon/scrolltest.html	47	0.85	4 total	82
5.	/xqanqeon/thanks_p15b.html	63	0.58	4 total	87
6.	/xqanqeon/thanks_c.html	50	0.54	4 total	88

The table's last column presents a **PageSpeed Score**. This score indicates how much room for improvement a particular page has, with scores nearer to 100 indicating less room for improvement than scores closer to zero. Our one relatively slower page has a score of 87, which indicates that some improvement can be accomplished by following the PageSpeed Suggestions. Clicking on the link for this page in the **PageSpeed Suggestions** column brings up the following display labeled PageSpeed Insights. Notice that the Page Speed Score for Desktop is the same as that shown in the previous table.

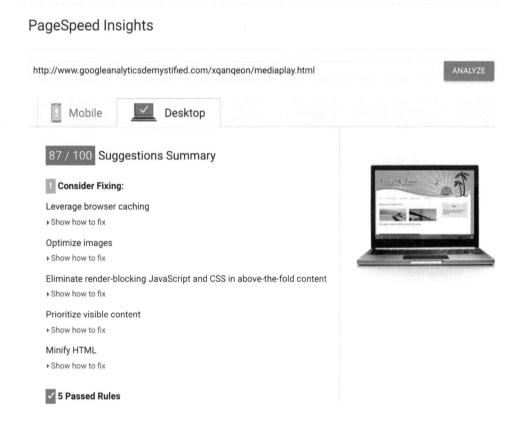

PageSpeed Insights

http://www.googleanalyticsdemystified.com/xqanqeon/mediaplay.html   ANALYZE

Mobile   Desktop

87 / 100 Suggestions Summary

! Consider Fixing:

Leverage browser caching
▸ Show how to fix

Optimize images
▸ Show how to fix

Eliminate render-blocking JavaScript and CSS in above-the-fold content
▸ Show how to fix

Prioritize visible content
▸ Show how to fix

Minify HTML
▸ Show how to fix

✓ **5 Passed Rules**

The good news is that the site has passed five of Google's rules. Clicking on any of the five **Show how to fix** links brings up specific suggestions for the remaining problem areas. The example shown below is the result of clicking on **Show how to fix** for **Optimize images**. Notice how the suggestion communicates both the overall positive effect of following this suggestion (a 21% overall reduction in image size) and the specific detail for each image, which appears on the page.

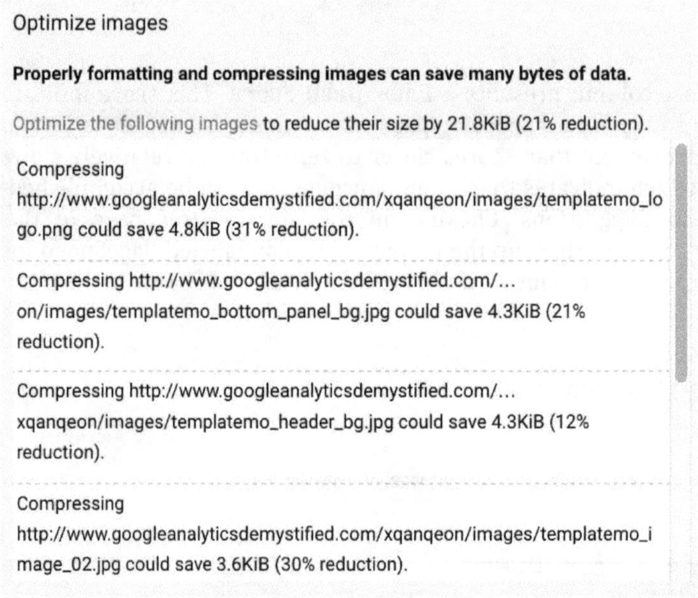

Optimize images

Properly formatting and compressing images can save many bytes of data.

Optimize the following images to reduce their size by 21.8KiB (21% reduction).

Compressing http://www.googleanalyticsdemystified.com/xqanqeon/images/templatemo_logo.png could save 4.8KiB (31% reduction).

Compressing http://www.googleanalyticsdemystified.com/... on/images/templatemo_bottom_panel_bg.jpg could save 4.3KiB (21% reduction).

Compressing http://www.googleanalyticsdemystified.com/... xqanqeon/images/templatemo_header_bg.jpg could save 4.3KiB (12% reduction).

Compressing http://www.googleanalyticsdemystified.com/xqanqeon/images/templatemo_image_02.jpg could save 3.6KiB (30% reduction).

The preceding data and discussion applied to page performance via desktop devices. But, what about sessions where the site is accessed via a mobile device?

Referring back to PageSpeed Insights, you'll notice a tab for Mobile and a tab for Desktop. We can obtain insights into the page's mobile performance by clicking on the **Mobile** link on the suggestions results page. When this is done, the figure on the top of page 257 is shown.

PageSpeed Insights

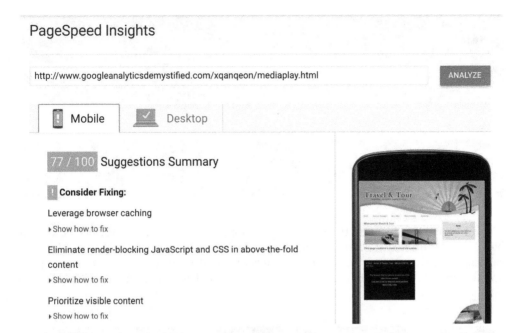

Our page performs more poorly when viewed via a mobile device, as our mobile score is only 77 out of 100 (versus the 87 out of 100 for desktop). As with the desktop display, Google provides specific suggestions for improving the page's download speed.

Additional insights into a mobile user's experience can be obtained by clicking on the link near the top of the PageSpeed Insights display (see below). The link is located at the end of the phrase "try out here."

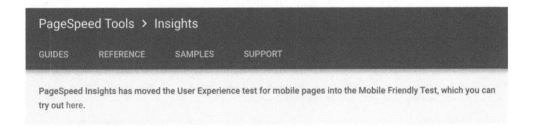

PageSpeed Insights

Selecting this link brings up the display shown on the top of page 258.

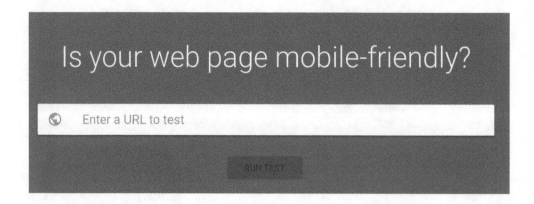

We can type the full URL of the page we've just examined into **the Enter a URL to test** box. Pressing **Run Test** after the URL is typed in the box brings up additional insights relevant to a site visitor's mobile experience with that page. The insights for our page are shown below. Note that all of the areas identified for improvement relate to the mobile visitor's experience.

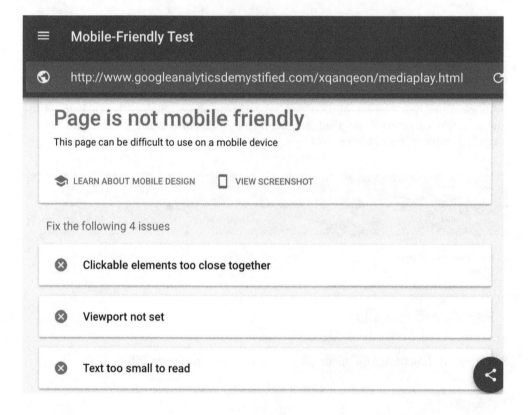

Beyond user experience, improving this page is very important as Google notes that this page is not mobile friendly. This will have a negative impact on our Google search ranking.

Average Page Load Time

Average Page Load time is the average amount of time (in seconds) that it takes for pages in the analytical sample to load. This metric applies to both overall site perform- ance and specific pages. The amount of time calculated for a specific page begins with the initiation of a pageview request (e.g., a click on a page link) and ends when the page is completely loaded in the browser window. The load times for specific pages can be improved via Google Analytics' Speed Suggestions.

Average Page Download Time

This is the average amount of time for a page, or all pages in the site sample, to down- load. This metric is influenced by user connection dynamics (which are out of your con- trol) and the amount of source code on a page (which is within your control). Generally, the greater the amount of source code, the slower the download time. Two easy things to reduce source code are to eliminate in-line styles via CSS and to place all JavaScript in external files.

Average Domain Look-up Time

This metric reports the average amount of time (in seconds) taken in the DNS look-up for a specific page or the average of all site pages included in the sample. If you are finding that DNS look-up is taking an unusual amount of time, then try to DNS diagnos- tics tools at:

`http://mxtoolbox.com/DNSLookup.aspx`

Problems in this area, however, are generally beyond your control.

Average Redirection Time

This metric reports the average amount of time (in seconds) spent in redirects before fetching a particular page or for the site as a whole. If there are no redirects, this metric's value is typically expected to be zero. If you are using redirects on your site, then you will want to minimize the amount of time it takes to accomplish this. At minimum, you

---

[55] Definitions are provided by Google Analytics *Interpret Site Speed* at: https://support.google.com/analytics/answer/2383341?hl=en&ref_topic=1282106. Implications adapted from *Speed Matters; Improve usability with Google Analytics Site Speed Reports* at: http://www.iacquire.com/blog/speed-matters-improve-usability-with-google-analytics-site-speed-reports.

should eliminate any multiple or daisy-chain redirects. You can also use the Rex Swain's HTTP viewer to identify any problems.

The viewer is located at:

`http://www.rexswain.com/httpview.html`

Average Server Connection Time

This the average amount of time (in seconds) spent in establishing a TCP connection for a particular page or for the site as a whole. Slow connection times may be the result of server or hosting problems, and conversations with these individuals may be warranted when server connection times are slow.

Average Server Response Time

The is the average amount of time (in seconds) a site's server takes to respond to a user request, including the network time from the user's location to the server. As with the prior metrics, this metric applies to both overall site performance and specific pages. Vender notes that "A couple of things might be involved here. Your web server can be poorly configured to handle even a basic amount of user connections and processes. If you have an amateur configure your server settings it's very likely that RAM and process allocations are NOT optimized. Get a seasoned web server administrator to configure your web server. Another possibility is that you're running a database-driven site and NOT taking advantage of caching. For example, if you are running a WordPress site and don't use a caching plugin, then you're making your server work way too hard. No matter what CMS you are using, if you have pages that query your database for content BUT that content relatively remains static over a period of time, you should be caching that content so your server only needs to generate that content once over multiple requests."

In-Page Analytics

In-Page Analytics provide important insights into how individuals navigate through your site. The most recent iteration of Google Analytics has, unfortunately, eliminated this data from standard Google Analytics reports. As a result, we provide direction for accessing this data via the Google Chrome Page Analytics extension.

Obtaining and using the Chrome In-Page Analytics extension

The Chrome Page Analytics extension is available for free from the Google Webstore at:

https://chrome.google.com/webstore/detail/page-analytics-by-google/fnbdnhhicmebfgdgglcdacdapkcihcoh

(If this link is too much trouble to type, you can locate the extension through a Google search of "Chrome page analytics extension".)

Just click on the **Add to Chrome** link after you arrive at the webstore.

Once installed, you can view the in-page analytics for any page of your site by:

-   opening the page you wish to view in your Chrome browser; make certain to type the full URL to the page,

-   clicking on the Google Analytics Chrome Extension icon to turn it **On**,

-   (and if no data is displayed) clicking on any link on the page to activate in-page analytics.

If data is still missing from your display, try toggling the display shown opposite on and off. The icon is located near the top on the right-hand side of the page in the control bar.

A page resembling that shown on the top of page 262 should appear once in-page analytics is successfully activated.[56]

---

[56] There is a chance that after initiating in-page analytics subsequent returns to your site will activate this feature. Should this happen, make certain that the extension is set to **OFF** and sign out of your account at Google Analytics. Also note that this extension may be "buggy" and not perform as we describe.

The In-Page Analytics display

Top of page summary

The top of the page summary provides page-related metrics for the page being displayed. These metrics are pulled from a number of different reports, as shown below. All of these metrics have been discussed in prior chapters.

Bottom of page display

The bottom of the report page displays your selected webpage and the click rate for links and other engagement items on this page. The click through rate is the boxed percentage above each link.

The screen shown on the top of page 263, for example, indicates that the five links on the top of my travel site home page are very infrequently used by visitors to this page. Equally disturbing is that fact that 15% of visitors to the home page click the "Home" link while on this page.

Note that hovering your cursor over any percentage or link displays more detailed information, as shown below.

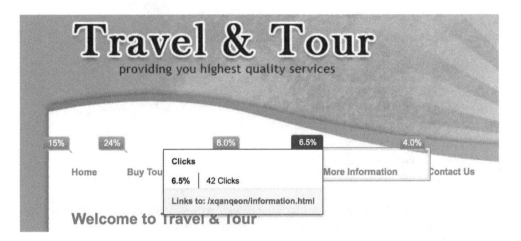

The Control Bar appears between the top of page metric summary and the detailed web page display.

The far left-hand side of the Control Bar presents a calendar pull-down menu. You can use this menu to change the current date range.

The links and pull-down menus on the right-hand side of the Control Bar (see below) allow you to change and customize which metrics are displayed and the form in which they are displayed. These options are discussed next, keeping in mind that the default settings typically allow you to understand key information needed for decision-making.

Show only Clicks ▾ with more than: 0.10% ▾ ▮▮ 💬 Send

The Control Bar contains two pull-down menus. The menu associated with "Clicks" (by default) allows you to select the specific metric to see in the display (see the figure below). Here you can see the standard metrics available as well as goal-related metrics (if any) specific to your site. Note that beyond the ability to select **Clicks**, the specific metrics displayed will vary as a function of what is active on your site.

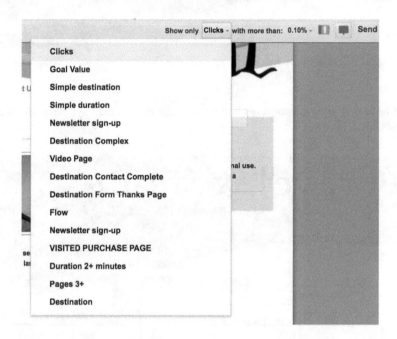

The menu labeled ".10%" (by default) allows you to set a display threshold for the selected metric (see figure below). You can, for example, display data for only those links that are clicked by more than 10% of that page's users.

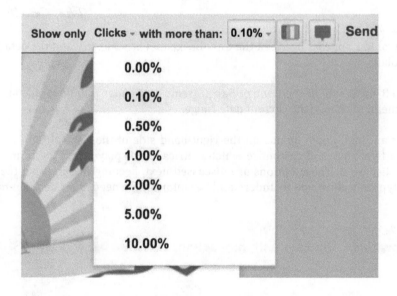

The **Show Color** option, depicted on the Control Bar by the colored bars, just to the right of the percentage, is deselected by default. Selecting this option color codes the displayed percentages to visually highlight differences (see below). The legend used to interpret the colors appears at the top left of the web page.

The icon just to the right of the **Show Color** option toggles the data display on and off.

The **Send** option (on the far right of the control bar) connects you with the extension's Google Plus page.

Pros and cons of In-Page Analytics

Nick Lewis and Krystian Szastok have presented a concise and useful point of view with regard to the pros and cons of Google's In-Page Analytics. Their perspective follows:[57]

> The biggest pro of In-Page Analytics is the ability to see where people click on the page and follow navigation paths through your site. In-Page offers an intuitive visual map that gives instant access to detailed navigation data and in a way that can make necessary on-page optimization and even web design changes more immediately obvious than trying to mentally map dry data onto the page yourself.
>
> Great as In-Page Analytics can be, it's not all roses, and the Devil's in the detail. Where it displays a percentage to represent the proportion of visitors to a page who clicked a certain link, it does so by the target url, rather than the actual link. So for example, if your logo links to your homepage and you also have a home button, it will show the same percentage across both of them rather than telling you whether people clicked the logo or the home button most. Similarly, there is no way of tracking clicks to on-page anchors, meaning that if you have a lot of content on a page, and have used anchors for usability, you can't tell which particular part is prompting people to click.

---

[57] Excerpted from *Pros and Cons of In-Page Analytics* at http://moz.com/ugc/the-pros-and-cons-of-inpage-analytics.

Section VII:
Segments

Our approach to data examination in the **Audience** and **Behavior** menus has focused on the information provided for all website or blog users who pass through any active filters. This approach assumes that we've selected the total sample as the analytical sample. As a consequence, we've deferred addressing many questions. For example:

- How can I best understand the behaviors of those who make a purchase on the first day they visit my site?

- How valuable are our downloadable materials and do they contribute to conversion? Do the conversion or transaction behaviors of those who download materials differ from the behaviors of those who do not?

Questions such as these vary across websites with different content and goals. Regardless of the specific question, the answers typically lie in segmentation: an examination of small subgroups of the total user base.

The three chapters in this section provide insights into the segmentation process and the use of Google Analytics' segments to create small but important subgroups of individuals who will be the specific focus of our analytical efforts.

- Chapter 26 provides an introduction to segmentation and segment creation.

- Chapter 27 provides an example of applying Google Analytics segments to strategic decision-making.

- Chapter 28 describes how to use segments to remove referral spam from existing data.

With this overview in mind, we'll return to segments in upcoming chapters as we apply this approach to website goals, downloadable materials, campaigns, and events.

26

Segmentation and
Google Analytics Segments

Segmentation is the process of dividing a large, heterogeneous group of individuals into smaller, homogeneous groups. A simple segmentation could, for example, divide all website visitors into two groups: those who made a purchase and those who did not. We could then look at the behaviors and characteristics of both groups to see what factors beyond purchase differentiate and explain the behaviors of individuals in each group.

The previous example illustrates the two types of variables used in segmentation. *Classification variables* are the basis for segment formation and can be selected from any of the broad range of Google Analytics dimensions. Classification variable(s) can be a single dimension (such as transaction outcome) or they can entail a combination of dimensions. Additionally, once a dimension is chosen, you can use all or just some of the dimension's values for segment formation. The following, for example, segments website users on the basis of three dimensions: transaction outcome, type of user, and landing page. These classification variables result in the two groups shown below:

Segment 1:   Individuals who made a transaction on their first visit, were new visitors, and entered via the home page

Segment 2:   Individuals who did not make a transaction on their first visit, were new visitors, and entered via the home page

Once classification variables have been used to form segments, one or more *descriptive variables* are used to describe the users within each segment. In this example, we could select *relevant* descriptive variables from the metrics provided in the **Audience** and **Behavior** reports. The table shown on the top of page 270 does just this.

Descriptive Metric	Segment 1 (Purchasers)	Segment 2 (Nonpurchasers)
Time spent on home page (sec)	:58	:11
Ave. home page load time (sec)	1.2	3.2
% Exit from home page	21%	65%
% Viewing media	65%	11%
% Viewing purchase page	100%	8%
Browser		
Chrome	45%	48%
Safari	22	42
Firefox	33%	10

Examining the selected descriptive metrics by segment provides important insights for future strategic discussion and decision-making. We can see that those who make a purchase versus nonpurchasers appear to be highly engaged with the home page, are unlikely to leave the site from this page, view media, and make it to the purchase page. The opposite is true for nonpurchasers. Moreover, the distribution of browser types is different for the two groups, as is home page load time. This data would lead us to explore several issues, among the most important: home page optimization for Safari; how to increase home page engagement/reduce exit rate; and how to increase media page usage.

When to use segmentation

There is no limit to the number of segments that can be formed using Google Analytics data. As a result, it is important that any use of segmentation be grounded in one of the following types of situations, where the segmentation helps you to better understand:

- data patterns and trends provided in the primary reports

- why website goals are/are not being achieved

- opportunities for website improvement, promotion, and targeting

Segment controls

So far, "All site sessions" has served as the sample for our analyses. Confirmation can be found on the top, left-hand side of any page, where "All Sessions 100%" is displayed next to the blue circle (see top of page 271). This indicates that the report presents data on all site sessions for the selected date range.

Audience Overview

All Users
100.00% Sessions

But, this doesn't have to be the case. We can restrict our analysis to one or more segments, where a segment is defined by any single or combination of dimensions and metrics.[58] You access segments via the **+Add Segment** option on the top of almost any page (located next to or beneath the blue circle **All Sessions** identifier, see below).

Audience Overview

All Users
100.00% Sessions

+ Add Segment

When you click **+Add Segment**, the segments page displays, as shown below. Note that this particular display includes segments that are provided by Google Analytics (e.g., "All Users") and segments, which I have created. These latter segments have a "Created" and "Modified" date.

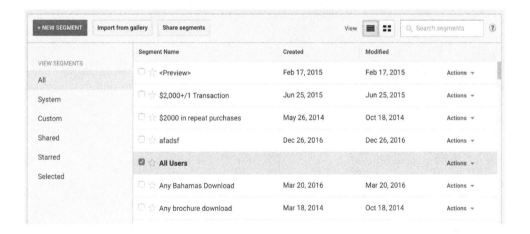

	Segment Name	Created	Modified	
	<Preview>	Feb 17, 2015	Feb 17, 2015	Actions ▾
	$2,000+/1 Transaction	Jun 25, 2015	Jun 25, 2015	Actions ▾
	$2000 in repeat purchases	May 26, 2014	Oct 18, 2014	Actions ▾
	afadsf	Dec 26, 2016	Dec 26, 2016	Actions ▾
✓	All Users			Actions ▾
	Any Bahamas Download	Mar 20, 2016	Mar 20, 2016	Actions ▾
	Any brochure download	Mar 18, 2014	Oct 18, 2014	Actions ▾

VIEW SEGMENTS

All
System
Custom
Shared
Starred
Selected

+ NEW SEGMENT   Import from gallery   Share segments   View   Search segments

---

[58] Both segments and filters restrict data presentation to a specified group of sessions or users. Filters permanently restrict the types of individuals reported while segments are temporary and can be eliminated at any time.

The display's highlighted row (or rows) indicates the segment(s) currently being used, in this case "All Users". This active segment is also checked in the Segment Name list. You can add additional segments by selecting (checking) a segment in the list. When this is done, the segment will appear in the next available **Choose segment from list** box on the top of the display. The display below, for example, illustrates what happens when we add the segment "Any brochure download" to the data view.

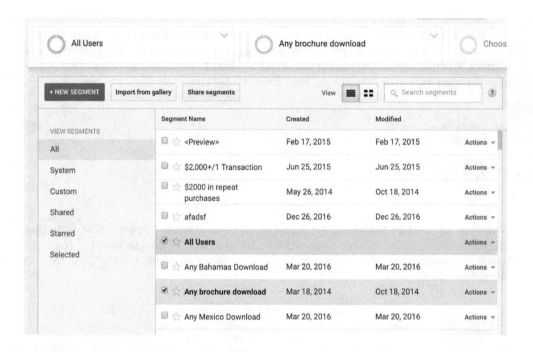

Once a segment is applied to a view, it continues to be applied to all data displays until removed. A segment can be removed from the display by using the pull-down arrow next to its name, as shown below.

The row containing the **+ NEW SEGMENT** button shows segment creation and display options. There are three options on the left-hand side:

- You create a new segment by clicking the **+ NEW SEGMENT** link.

- **Import from gallery** allows you to obtain custom segments created by others.

- **Share segments** takes you to your administrator's page where you can perform sharing, deletion, and related activities.

There are two options on the right-hand side next to **View**. These options determine how segments are displayed. The two figures shown below illustrate what happens when the bar and grid options are selected.

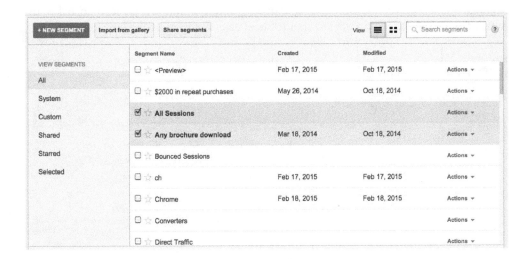

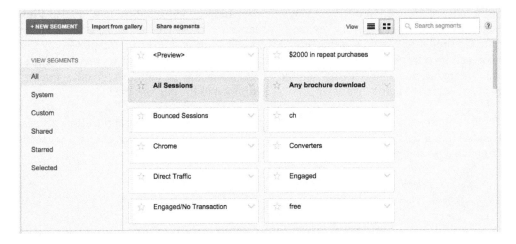

In both cases, moving your mouse over a segment name will display the characteristics that define the segment (see example below).

Segment maintenance, such as editing, copying, and deletion are performed using the **Actions** pull down menu on the left-hand side of each segment listing (see below).

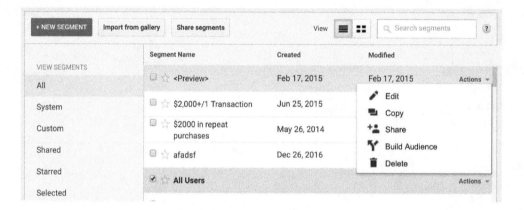

Segments are grouped in different ways, as shown in the left-hand column labeled **View Segments**. "All" displays every segment available to the selected view. "System" displays only the predefined segments provided by Google Analytics. "Custom" displays only segments created by you. "Shared" presents a list of those segments, which you have shared with other accounts or views. "Starred" presents a list of your preferred segments. Finally, "Selected" lists those segments being applied to the current data view.

The two options on the bottom of the page complete the segment application process (see the figure below). **Apply** applies the selected segments to the current data set while **Cancel** leaves things as they were before the segment page was opened.

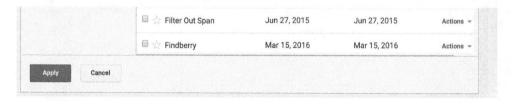

System segments

Google Analytics provides a number of built-in segments, which can be seen when the **System** option is selected in the **View Segments** column. These segments allow you to immediately restrict your data presentation in order to better understand users and sessions defined by the most common types of characteristics and behaviors. The full list of System segments is shown below. The listed names reflect the characteristics of the users or sessions within the segment. "Mobile Traffic," for example, will restrict the data view to only those sessions begun via a mobile device, while "Sessions with Transactions" restricts the data view to only those sessions in which a transaction took place.

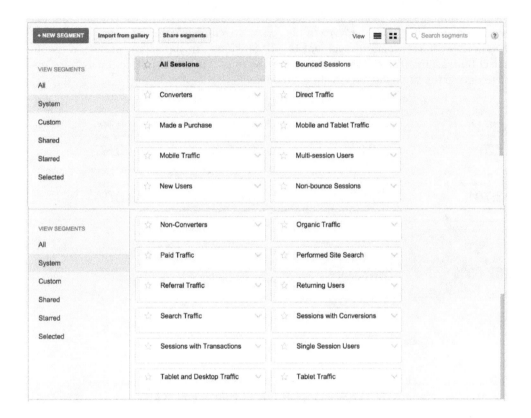

Segment data display

The display of segment data is the same for all types of segments. Let's use a System segment as an example.

Imagine that we want to examine just the segment "Sessions with Transactions." We accomplish this by using the list of segment names to deselect (remove) "All Sessions" and select "Sessions with Transactions." Clicking on **Apply** changes the data presented to only this group of sessions, as shown bon the top of page 276. All the data displays are labeled to indicate that only the segment of "Sessions with Transactions" is reported.

The report shown above displays data for just one segment and this is fine if we want to focus on only a single segment. There are times, however, when we want to compare two segments. We might, for example, want to compare the characteristics of the "Sessions with Transaction" segment to "All Sessions". In this circumstance, we would select both segments from the list of segment names. This would place the data for both segments in the same display, as shown below.

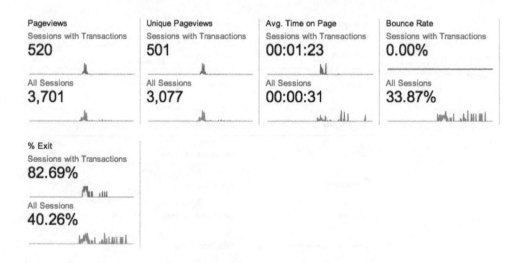

It is important to keep two things in mind with regard to segment data display. First, it not necessary to include "All Sessions" as one of your segments. The table on the top of page 277 displays session information for three segments, none of which is "All Sessions". Here we are examining information related to sessions initiated via different sources: direct, referral and search.

Second, once segments are selected the metrics displayed will change to reflect your current data selection. The report above was generated from the **Audience > Overview** menu, while the report shown below was generated from the **Conversions > Ecommerce > Overview** menu option. Notice how the segments remain constant, but the reported metrics change.

Finally, keep in mind that you can always return to your complete data set by deselecting all segments and then selecting "All Sessions" from the **System** display.

Creating new segments

Google Analytics' **System** segments allow you to explore many different types of questions and information needs. There are times, however, when your site goals or information needs require you to examine a segment of users or sessions, which you define. The process to accomplish this is straightforward.

First, click on the **+Add Segment** option that is located on the top of every report page. Then, when the segment option page appears, click on **+New Segment** on the top of the page. This will take you to the default segment creation page, shown on the top of page 278.

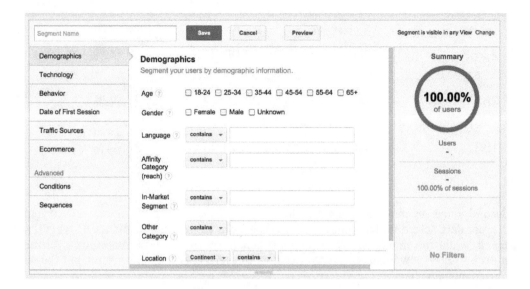

Our first tasks require us to name the segment (in the **Segment Name** text box) and to determine where we want the segment to be visible (i.e., available.) By default, the segment you create will be available in all views. If you want to change this level of availability, select the **Change** option located in the upper right-hand corner of the display (see below).

Clicking **Change** brings up an overlay menu where you can indicate your preference (see below).

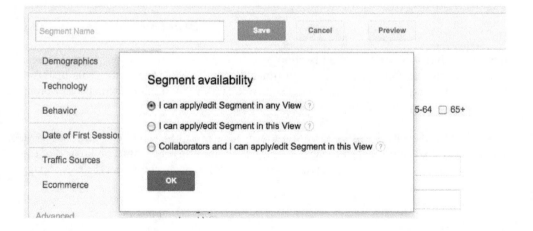

We'll leave the segment name until the end.

The large circle on the right-hand side of the page (see the figure on the top of page 278) indicates current segment size, which at the moment contains 100% of both users and sessions. This is reasonable given that no segment characteristics have been selected. These numbers will update to reflect segment size in terms of both a percent-age and absolute number as segment characteristics are added. Keep an eye on these numbers as you define your segment since the reliability of segment data declines as segment size decreases.

The options on the left-hand side of the display indicate the dimensions available for use in segment creation.

Let's now create a segment. The segment will contain only those users who spent $2,000 or more in their only transaction. This requires us to select from two different dimen-sions. First, we click on **Ecommerce** on the left-hand side of the page, and then complete the form using the pull-down menu options as shown below, where we fill in the field relevant to our segment, in this case revenue.[59] Once the data has been entered, we click anywhere on the form and the data on the right-hand side updates to let us know that 49.58% of all our users satisfy this single criteria (which is shown on the bottom right-hand side of the page). This percentage represents 292 users and 673 sessions (which in turn represent 60.74% of all sessions). At the moment, this segment is large enough so that we can have confidence in the underlying data. Finally, notice the small number 1 next to **Ecommerce** on the left-hand side of the page. This indicates that the current segment consists of a single Ecommerce criterion.

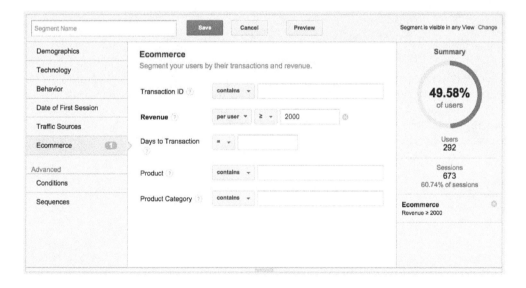

---

[59] Note that the **Ecommerce** menu option appears when your site is configured for ecommerce. Sites configured for Enhanced Ecommerce will have a broader range of segment definitions.

Next, we select **Behavior** from the left-hand menu options and specify that we want to include only those users who made a single transaction. Since this is the last specification, we'll also name this segment (see figure below). Notice how the size of the segment has declined as we added this second criterion. The segment now represents 46.52% of all our users. This percentage represents 274 users and 579 sessions (which in turn represent 52.26% of all sessions). This segment is still large enough to provide confidence in the underlying data. Notice that a small number **1** next to **Behavior** on the left-hand side of the page. This indicates that the current segment consists of a single Behavior criterion. Finally, the lower right-hand side of the page has been updated to reflect the current state of the segment, that is, the two specific defining criteria.

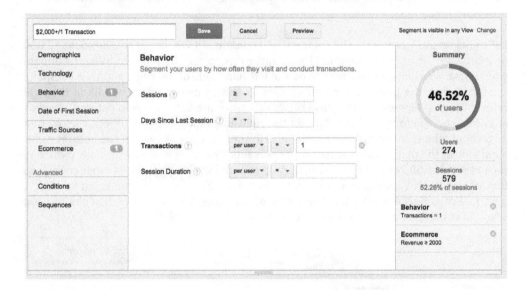

After all criteria have been added we can press **Preview** to see the effect of applying the segment to our data. When we are satisfied with our segment, we select **Save** (which appears on the top of the page). When we revisit the segments page, the new segment will appear in both the "All Segments" and "Custom Segments" lists. The "All Segments" list is shown below.

Now when we select this segment, our data view will contain only the users/sessions contained in this segment, as shown below.

Ecommerce Conversion Rate	Transactions	Revenue	Average Order Value
$2,000+/1 Transaction	$2,000+/1 Transaction	$2,000+/1 Transaction	$2,000+/1 Transaction
47.32%	274	$2,761,900.00	$10,079.93

Unique Purchases	Quantity
$2,000+/1 Transaction	$2,000+/1 Transaction
273	273

Finally, there may be times when you want to create a segment with characteristics that go beyond those available through the **Demographics, Technology, Behavior, Date of First Session, Traffic Sources,** and **Ecommerce** menu options. Two options are available and are discussed in the next two sections.

Creating new segments: Adding conditions

The **Conditions** option is on the lower part of the left-hand menu. This option lets you create a segment according to single or multi-session conditions alone or in conjunction with other types of user or session characteristics. Selecting **Conditions** brings up the display shown below.

Your options for defining the **Conditions** to be used for segment definition are shown on the top, middle of the display just to the right of "Filter. " Here you decide whether to create the segment based on Sessions or Users (via the **Sessions** pull-down menu) and whether the characteristic will be used to Include or Exclude (via the **Include** pull-down menu). Beneath these options is a pull-down menu, which by default, displays **Ad Content**. This menu gives you access to Google Analytics dimensions and metrics, both those defined by Google, as well any goals or related metrics you have created on your own (see figure below).

You build a segment by selecting the appropriate metric and then specifying the criterion. Multiple characteristics can be added by clicking on the **+ Add Filter** link.

We can illustrate this by creating a segment that consists of all site users who (1) came to our site directly (i.e., by using a bookmark or typing the URL into their browser), and (2) visited our special purchase page (`purchasef.html`).

We first identify users who came to our site directly. This is accomplished via the settings shown below.

Conditions

Segment your users and/or their sessions according to single or multi-session conditions.

Filter	Users ▾	Include ▾
Source ▾	contains ▾	(direct)

+ Add Filter

We then click on the **+ Add Filter** button to add the second criterion: a visit to the special purchase page. This is accomplished via the second set of settings shown on the below.

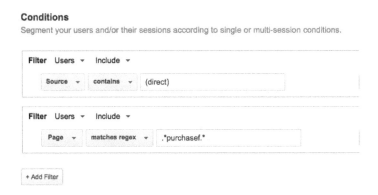

At this point, the full screen resembles that shown below. Note that the size of the group, as reflected in the number of users and sessions, is sufficient for us to have confidence in the data reported for the segment.

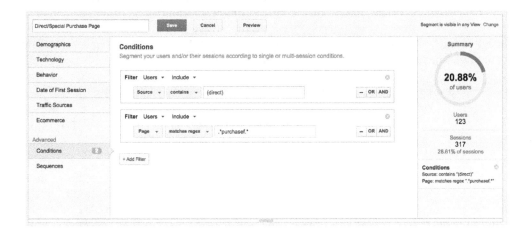

Finally, should you desire, you can always combine selections from the **Conditions** menu with other standard characteristics. We could, for example, further refine the prior sample to specify that the segment also contain those who made a purchase (after visiting our site directly and visiting the special purchase page). We would add this criterion in the way described in the prior section, resulting in the new segment definition screen shown on page 284. Note that as before, adding additional specifications to the segment definition reduces the size of the segment.

Creating new segments: Sequences

The previous example showed how the **Conditions** option allows you to use the full range of Google Analytics dimensions and metrics to define a segment of site users/session. There are times, however, when you want to define a segment in terms of the *sequence* of behaviors displayed during a site visit rather than the cumulative filtering of characteristics. This is accomplished via the **Sequences** option.

Imagine that we've designed our travel website to (ideally) lead a user to purchase. The path to purchase is believed to be:

> View Page `F2.html` -> View Page `F3.html` ->
> View options on Purchase Page (`purchase.html`) ->
> View "Thank You Page" after purchase is made (`thanks.html`)

The **Sequences** option allows us to create a segment that consists only of those individuals who took this exact path to purchase. We begin by selecting this option from the left-hand menu. Next, we select **Include** and **Users** from the **Filter** options. We allow the **Sequence start** to come at any time during a visit (thus leaving the final menu set to **Any user interaction**). Finally, we select **Page** from the green **Behavior** option (by using the pull-down menu which, by default, is labeled **Ad Content**). Finally we identify the first page in our funnel via a regex expression. All of these actions result in the display shown in the figure on the top of page 285.

Sequences

Segment your users and/or their sessions according to sequential conditions.

+ Add Filter

Clicking on **Add Step** allows us to add the second step to the sequence. Here, the process is the same except that the page represented in this second step is F3.html (see below). Notice that we have selected the "is immediately followed by" option. This option creates a sequence in which page F2 must be immediately followed by page F3 with no intervening pages.

Sequences

Segment your users and/or their sessions according to sequential conditions.

+ Add Filter

We follow this same procedure for adding the final two steps to our sequence, as shown below. Note that the regex statement is different than the prior to account for the fact that we have multiple pages which contain "purchase" or "thanks". Once again, because we are looking to form the segment based on a strict sequence of events, we select the "is immediately followed by" option.

Finally, we give the segment a descriptive name and, if all looks well, press **Save**. This new segment then appears on our list of custom segments.[60]

What if we wanted to change the sequence in which the pages are viewed? We might, for example, want the site visitor to start the sequence with page F2, then immediately view page F3, and then make a purchase later (but not necessarily next) in the sequence. This can be accomplished by changing the "followed by" option after Step 2, as shown on the top of page 287.

---

[60] You can always see and delete all user created segments for a particular view via your Administrator's page. Just click on **Segments** in the middle of the right-hand view column.

Sequences

Segment your users and/or their sessions according to sequential conditions.

Importing segments

Beyond **System** and **Custom** segments, there is one additional way for you to define segments. You can view and import segments created by others.

You begin the view/import process by selecting **Import from gallery** on the top of the initial segment display page. When this is done, an overlay page will appear (see page 288) in which a listing of segments for all categories will be shown. You can narrow the display to specific types of segments by selecting and deselecting topics from the left-hand **Filter by category** menu.

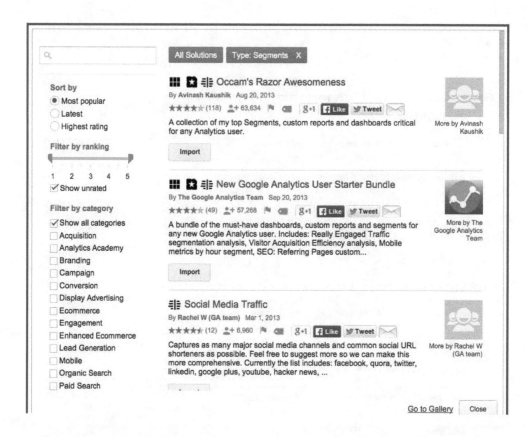

When you are thinking about importing segments, it is important to read the descriptions of the types of segments available, keeping in mind that you are looking for segments relevant to your specific website's characteristics, objectives, and goals. Also keep in mind that a segment that is close to what you need, but needs minor modification, can always be edited after import. Clicking on any title displays more detail on a new page (see top of page 289). You then select the **Import** option on the top of the page. When this is done, you will see a new page, which displays of all items available for import. Since at this point we are only interested in custom segments, we select all of the listed segments and deselect all other items. Finally, we select how we want to use these new segments: either in all views or only the currently active view.

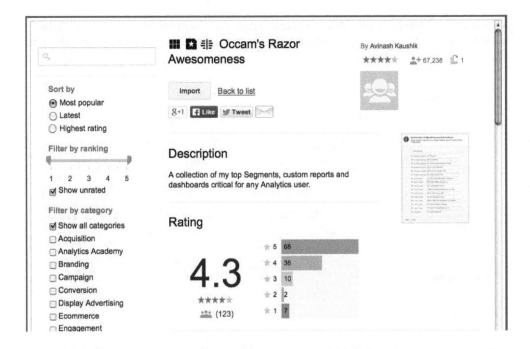

Clicking **Create** takes us to the administrative display where all segments associated with the current view are displayed. We can then modify the list and edit custom and imported segments through the choices in the **Actions** column on the main segment display page.

A note on segment size and interpretation

Whenever you apply a segment to a set of Google Analytics data, the segment's size is shown on the top of the page beneath the segment name. The figure shown below illustrates the application of two segments: one segment reflects site sessions initiated by new site users, while the second segment reflects sessions initiated by returning users. Since all sessions must fit into one of these two segments, the sum of the two segments is 100%.

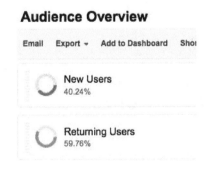

Note that these percentages are the same as shown in the new/returning numeric table, shown below. The percentages agree because both the above summary and the data table below reflect sessions.

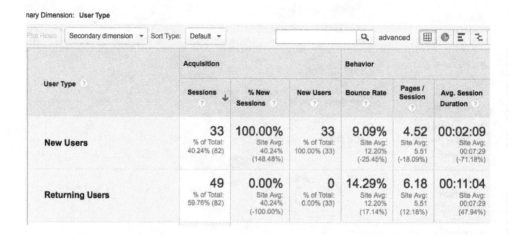

User Type	Acquisition			Behavior		
	Sessions ↓	% New Sessions	New Users	Bounce Rate	Pages / Session	Avg. Session Duration
New Users	33 % of Total: 40.24% (82)	100.00% Site Avg: 40.24% (148.48%)	33 % of Total: 100.00% (33)	9.09% Site Avg: 12.20% (-25.45%)	4.52 Site Avg: 5.51 (-18.09%)	00:02:09 Site Avg: 00:07:29 (-71.18%)
Returning Users	49 % of Total: 59.76% (82)	0.00% Site Avg: 40.24% (-100.00%)	0 % of Total: 0.00% (33)	14.29% Site Avg: 12.20% (17.14%)	6.18 Site Avg: 5.51 (12.18%)	00:11:04 Site Avg: 00:07:29 (47.94%)

When we move to apply these segments to a different type of metric, the relative size of the two segments changes, for example, when we apply these two segments to pages (rather than sessions). The segment summary is shown below. As expected, the two data views agree and the sum of the two segments also equals 100%. However, the percentages reported for each segment have changed because the underlying metric has changed.

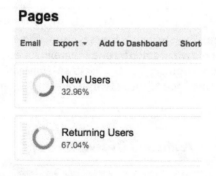

The takeaway from this is straightforward: *Whenever you are using the percentages reported for one or more segments, make certain that you interpret this percentage in terms of the appropriate underlying metric.*

27

Segments and Strategic Planning

Hopefully, you've come to realize that segments, when applied strategically, have great potential to increase the success of web and blog related decisions. Importantly, the value of a segment to assist decision-making is not dependent upon its complexity, but rather reflects it appropriateness for the strategic question that motivated its creation.

This chapter provides a case study to illustrate how segments allow us to make smarter, more successful decisions.

The scenario

Imagine sitting in a meeting that is now approaching two hours. The conversation has taken various forms, but always comes back to the same issue:

Marketing Max: My job is to drive people to the site. Increasing our audience is my number one priority. I don't care how or where they enter the site. We need more bodies ... and if I drive more bodies to the site, then sales will go up. Forget about where they land. It doesn't matter. Give me the money that the web designers are getting to work on our home page ... a waste of money, by the way ... and I guarantee sales will increase.

Designer Deb: What drivel. What a lack of understanding of how things work. Of course we need people to visit, but the site has been designed to move people through its pages in a particular way. We've designed an experience that builds and, like any good story, it's important to start at the beginning. People need to enter the site on the home page. This is really critical. Sales depend on it.

Marketing Max: Prove it!

Designer Deb: You prove it!

By now, you're quite tired of this. You say: "Give me an hour... and I'll prove who is right."

It is important to explicitly state your strategic question prior to creating and applying segments. Without this question, it is impossible to determine the extent to which your segments will allow you to address your strategic information need and it is extremely difficult to isolate relevant data. The question, in this case, is: "To what extent does entering the site on the home page (i.e., landing on the home page) affect site transactions?"

The question implicitly asks us to compare two types of site visitors: those who enter via the home page and those who enter the site on any page other than the home page. Two segments are therefore required.

The first segment, named "Home Landing Page," consists of all sessions whose landing page was the home page, as shown below.

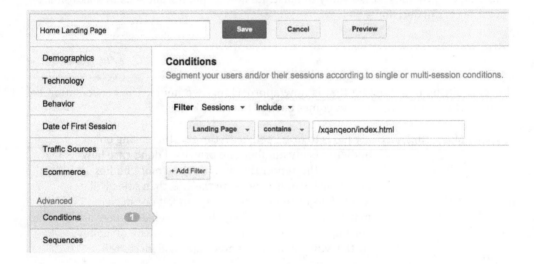

The second segment, named "No Home Landing Page", consists of all sessions whose landing page was any page other than the home page, as shown on the top of page 293. Note that the two segments are defined in terms of just a single condition and are identical except for the role of the landing page in initiating the session. The first segment *includes* all sessions that start on the home page, while the second segment *excludes* all sessions that start on the home page. These two groups are complimentary and mutually exclusive. Together they should equal 100% of all site sessions.

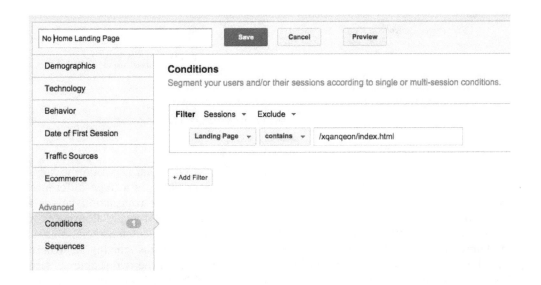

Generating and analyzing the relevant data

Prior to data analysis, it is necessary to verify that you have created and applied the correct segments. You verify this by looking at the segment labels near the Explorer tab on the top of any report page. The labels in this case are shown below.

Both segments are appropriate and together they add to 100%. Everything looks fine, so data analysis can proceed. Your first insight comes directly from this display. You notice that significantly more sessions begin at pages other than the home page (87.58% of all sessions). Marketing Max is getting his wish.

Max and Deb agree that the bottom line for the website is sales. But, this is where the agreement ends. Max and Deb each believe that his/her approach maximizes sales. Only one can be right. You can resolve the issue by comparing ecommerce data for the two segments. The relevant data is shown on the top of page 294.

Ecommerce Conversion Rate	Transactions	Revenue
Home Landing Page	Home Landing Page	Home Landing Page
19.83%	23	$131,000.00
No Home Landing Page	No Home Landing Page	No Home Landing Page
0.86%	7	$47,000.00

The difference between the two segments is striking. Sessions that begin on the home page are significantly more likely to have a transaction. There is a huge difference: 19.83% of sessions that begin on the home page result in a transaction versus a transaction rate of .86% for sessions that begin elsewhere. Moreover, differences in revenue generated by the two segments show a similar pattern: sessions beginning on the home page generate three-times as much revenue as sessions starting elsewhere. This difference is especially noteworthy given the difference in the two segments' size. Sessions beginning on the home page represent only 12.42% of all sessions but account for 73.6% of all revenue.[61] Designer Deb is absolutely correct. Sessions beginning on the home page are significantly more likely to generate a transaction versus sessions beginning anywhere else on the site. Spending funds to drive traffic to site pages other than the homepage is a waste of money as there is a very low probability that a transaction will take place.

Having answered the fundamental strategic question, you try to next determine why this outcome is occurring. You think that it might have something to do with levels of site engagement, so you take a look at this data. Yes, there is evidence to support the belief that sessions starting on a page other than home page are frustrating and/or inappropriate and/or confusing and/or not in accordance with site visitors' needs. The relevant data is shown below. Individuals who land on a page other than the home page spend very little time on the site. This is because they almost immediately leave the site after arrival without any interaction. In fact, nearly all sessions (91.81%) that begin on a page other than the home page end almost immediately without any page engagement.

Avg. Session Duration	Bounce Rate
Home Landing Page	Home Landing Page
00:01:56	29.31%
No Home Landing Page	No Home Landing Page
00:00:19	91.81%

The evidence clearly points to the value of the home page as the site's landing page. This is evidence that would not be available without the application of segments to the analysis.

---

[61] This is calculated as 131,000 ÷ (131,000 + 47,000)

28
Using Segments to Eliminate Referral Spam From Existing Data

Chapter 12 described how referral spam can significantly distort your data and presented approaches for applying filters to eliminate this spam from future data collection. Since filters are not applied retroactively, they are not able to eliminate spam from data collected prior to the creation and application of the filter. You can, however, eliminate referral spam from historical data by creating a segment that eliminates referral spam. This chapter describes how to define this segment using two of the approaches used to create the spam filters in Chapter 12.

Defining the segment's characteristics

The first segment characteristic screens for and includes only traffic from legitimate hostnames. For your convenience, the following recaps the hostname discussion from Chapter 12.

Spammers send spam to random Google Analytics account IDs. Working IDs accept the spam. Since the process is random, spammers don't know the hostname of the website corresponding to a specific Google Analytics property. This means that it is possible to create a segment that only includes traffic sent to legitimate hostnames. The drawback of this approach is that it is easy to accidentally exclude legitimate data from the segment if all relevant hostnames are not included in the segment definition. If, for example, an individual views a page of my site through Google Translate, this will be reported as coming from hostname `translate.googleusercontent.com`. If I want to include the data generated by this visit in the segment's reports, then I need to include this hostname in the segment definition.

The first step in creating this segment definition requires you to identify all legitimate hostnames for your site or blog. You can accomplish this by logging into your Google Analytics account and from the Home page select (click on) the appropriate view. The view's data will then be displayed. Then, from the options on the left-hand side of the page select **Audience > Technology > Network**. On the top of the newly displayed table are two data display options, **Service Provider** and **Hostname** (see below). Click on **Hostname**.

Primary Dimension: **Service Provider**   Hostname

| Plot Rows | Secondary dimension ▼ | | Q   advanced |

A table similar to that shown below will be displayed.

Hostname ?	Acquisition			Behavior			
	Sessions ? ↓	% New Sessions ?	New Users ?	Bounce Rate ?	Pages / Session ?	Avg. Session Duration ?
Hostname	542 % of Total: 35.52% (1,526)	52.03% Avg for View: 82.96% (-37.29%)	282 % of Total: 22.27% (1,266)	56.64% Avg for View: 70.64% (-19.82%)	2.86 Avg for View: 1.78 (60.69%)	00:02:50 Avg for View: 00:01:18 (118.47%)
1. www.googleanalyticsdemystified.com	411 (75.83%)	57.66%	237 (84.04%)	50.12%	3.15	00:03:13
2. co.lumb.co	58 (10.70%)	1.72%	1 (0.35%)	96.55%	1.03	00:00:01
3. googleanalyticsdemystified.com	32 (5.90%)	68.75%	22 (7.80%)	62.50%	3.28	00:02:58
4. www.classmatandread.net	12 (2.21%)	33.33%	4 (1.42%)	25.00%	4.08	00:09:17

With regard to my site, the hostnames shown in lines 1 and 3 are valid and will used to define one of the segment's characteristics. I also need to expand the list so that it includes any hostnames that I think are valid, but that do not appear on my Google Analytics hostname report. Your process will follow these steps for your own hostnames.

Finally, we generate a regular expressions statement that includes all valid hostnames. In my case this statement is:

.*googleanalyticsdemystified.*|.*googleusercontent.*|.*paypal.*|.*youtube.*

Notice how we separate each hostname with the regex "or" symbol: **|**.

Your regex statement will include your valid hostnames.

Finally, we use the regex statement to define the first segment characteristic so that only traffic from valid hostnames will be included in the data reports. This portion of the segment definition looks as follows:

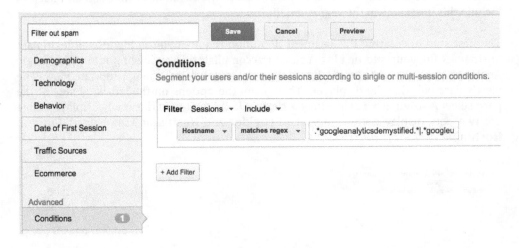

The second component of the segment definition takes advantage of spammers' inability to read your pages' titles.[62] Here, we confirm that the data included in the segment's reports are valid by defining the segment as containing all sessions *except* those where the page title is "(not set)".[63] When you've completed this step, the segment definition will look as shown below. Clicking **Save** concludes the filter creation process by saving the filter.

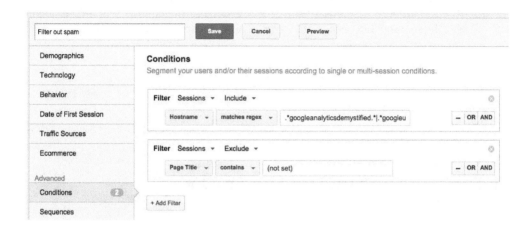

Impact of spam removal

Let's illustrate the importance of filtering referral spam from existing data with some recent data from my site. We'll see how the conclusions we draw, and the actions we take, vary substantially before and after the segment is applied to the data.

The first table shown on page 298 shows site engagement for "All sessions", the typical way to view a report. No segment has yet been applied. The data in this report indicate that:

- the number of sessions is very high (2,565) and far exceeds my goal of 1,500 sessions. My efforts to drive traffic to the site seem to be working well. Nothing more needs to be done in this area.

-

- problems arise immediately upon entering the site, as indicated in the extraordinarily high bounce rate of 76.06%. Three-quarters of our sessions terminate without any site engagement. This is disastrous. A priority is to reduce this metric to below our target of 45% (the benchmark level).

---

[62] This solution is a variation of that proposed by Blackmore Ops, *Three Effective Solutions for Google Analytics Referral Spam* at http://www.blackmoreops.com/2015/05/06/effective-solutions-for-google-analytics-referral-spam/.

[63] This approach filters for "(not set)" rather than the null page title (as described in Chapter 12) because we are post- rather than pre-processing the data.

- problems continue with those visitors who do not leave the site immediately. The number of pages per session and average session duration are both very low. It appears that my site content is failing to hold visitors' attention or meet their information needs. I need to spend considerable time revising my current site content and creating new content in order to improve these metrics.

- individuals leave the site without any desire to return. Almost all sessions (86.2%) are new sessions. Ideally, the revisions to site content will help to lower this figure and encourage users to return. I can't be successful if I have to consistently rely on generating business from new site visitors.

The table below displays the same metrics after the addition of the "Filter out spam" segment. The table makes it easy to compare the metrics reported for "All sessions" with the metrics for the spamless data set. Two things are clear: every one of the previous conclusions drawn about the site were incorrect and that taking the suggested actions would be inappropriate and likely detrimental.

Here is what is really happening on the site. Comments in plain type reflect conclusions drawn from the total data set (i.e., spam inclusive) and comments in italics express the reality of the situation drawn after spam has been excluded:

- the number of sessions is very high (2,565) and far exceeds my goal of 1,500 sessions. *Absolutely wrong. The number of sessions is far below my goal. In fact, we've only reached about one-third of the goal.* My efforts to drive traffic to the site seem to be working well. Nothing more needs to be done in this area. *What I'm doing now isn't working at all. I need to significantly alter my approach to driving people to the site.*

- problems arise immediately upon entering the site, as indicated in the extraordinarily high bounce rate of 76.06%. *The bounce rate is high in an absolute sense (45.13%), but it is not above our benchmark target.* Three-quarters of our sessions terminate without any site engagement. This is disastrous. A priority is to reduce this metric to below our target of 45% (the benchmark level). *It appears that most individuals entering our site have some engagement before leaving.*

- problems continue with those visitors who do not leave the site immediately. *This is incorrect.* The number of pages per session and average session duration are both very low. *Actually, these two engagement metrics are much more positive than initially believed. While it would be good to increase both metrics (in an absolute sense), sessions, on average, do involve a reasonable time on site and number of pages viewed per session.* It appears that my site content is failing to hold visitors' attention or meet their information needs. I need to spend considerable time revising my current site content and creating new content in order to improve these metrics. *Content should always be examined and revised periodically, but the current content is not the disaster indicated by the unfiltered set of metrics.*

- individuals leave the site without any desire to return. Almost all sessions (86.2%) are new sessions. Hopefully, the revisions to site content will help to lower this figure and encourage users to return. *The metrics indicate that sessions are fairly evenly divided between new sessions (53.6%) and returning sessions (46.4%).*[64] I can't be successful if I have to consistently rely on generating business from new site visitors. *I seem to be doing a good job of encouraging past visitors to return to the site at least one more time.*

---

[64] This latter figure is not explicitly reported in the data summary. It is calculated by subtracting the percentage of new users from 100%.

Section VIII:
Goals

So far we've looked at how to use and interpret a wide array of metrics. There are opportunities, however, to supplement these standard metrics with metrics that are uniquely relevant to your website's or blog's specific goals and objectives. The chapters in this and the following two sections illustrate how to accomplish this.

The four chapters in this section demonstrate how to create and apply custom Google Analytics goal metrics to specific strategic needs.

- Chapter 29 introduces you to three types of goals: destination, duration, and view. The chapter provides examples of when and how to apply these types of goals to assess the extent to which website objectives are being achieved.

- Chapter 30 provides instruction for how to read and interpret goal-related metrics.

- Chapter 31 shows how to monitor goal conversions with Real Time reports.

- Chapter 32 shows how to apply goals to the creation of custom segments.

Destination, Duration, and View Goals

Google Analytics provides an easy and powerful way for you to collect information related to your website's or blog's specific goals and objectives. Your ability to make better strategic decisions may, for example, require you to identify and better understand site users who:

- view certain pages, or

- pass through the website in a certain way, or

- spend a minimum amount of time on the site, or

- interact with a predefined number of pages.

The extent to which these and other goals have been achieved can be determined through the creation and analysis of custom goals.

Google Analytics allows you to create four different types of goals. These are:

- **Destination:** A destination goal is achieved when a website user loads (lands upon) a specific page, for example, a "Thank You" page after completing a purchase or contact form.

- **Duration:** A duration goal is achieved when a website user spends a pre-specified amount of time on the site, for example, five minutes or more.

- **Pages/Screens Per Visit:** This goal is achieved when a website user views a pre-specified number of pages or screens, for example, when three or more pages have been loaded.

- **Event:** This goal is achieved when a website user's behavior matches a pre-specified behavior, for example, viewing a video, downloading a PDF file or completing a site registration form.

We'll look at the first three types of goals in this section. Events are discussed in Section X.

You create goals through the **Admin** link on the top of every Google Analytics page. Once you click on this link, you'll see the main Administrator's Page (see below). Make certain that the relevant **Account, Property**, and **View** are displayed. Then click on the **Goals** link in the **View** column. The link to goals is in this column because goals are created specific to a view. Thus, different views for the same property may have different goals.

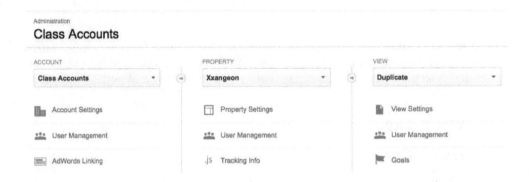

Your goals summary page will be displayed next (see below). Here all of the goals for the current view are displayed. At the moment, we have not yet set up any goals for this view, so this portion of the display is blank.

The critical elements on this screen are:

- **+ NEW GOAL:** A click on this link creates a new goal from scratch.

- **Import from Gallery:** Allows you to import goals that have been created by others. Since Google Analytics best practice requires that goals should be created specific to your site's objectives and organization, we recommend that you use this option to gather ideas but not to directly import goals.

- **Goal:** The names of all goals created for the current view are listed.

- **Past 7 day conversions:** The number of site users who satisfied the goal's parameters within the last week.

- **Recording:** Visuals in this column indicate whether the goal is currently turned "on" or "off". Google Analytics only monitors goals, which are turned "on."

Finally, the note beneath the table reminds us that we can only have 20 goals per view. If we need to create more goals than this we do so with another view since once a goal is created it cannot be deleted even when it is turned "off."

Destination goals

We'll create three destination goals: one simple goal that uses just a single destination page, a more complex goal to which we assign a funnel, and a third destination goal that monitors all pageviews within a specific directory.

Simple Destination Goal

This goal is considered a "conversion"[65] when a user arrives at a pre-specified page.

The travel website is set-up so that a site visitor is sent to a "Thank You" page after the contact form is sent. We can use this "Thank You" page as our destination goal, allowing us to quickly see how many forms have actually been sent. We can also compare contact page views with the number of goal conversions in order to determine the percentage of people who were on the contact page and then actually sent the contact form.

We begin the goal development process by clicking on **+NEW GOAL** which brings up one of two displays, depending upon how the view is configured. You might see the screen shown on the top of page 306. If this is the case, just select **Custom** on the bottom of the display and then click on **Next Step**. This will take you to the second possible display after clicking on **+NEW GOAL**, shown as the second figure on page 306 (beneath the **Next Step** button). This latter display is the one you will use to create the destination goal.

 The numbering system used to identify the various steps to goal creation may vary depending upon your starting screen.

---

[65] Google Analytics uses the term "conversion" to indicate that a goal has been attained, an event has taken place, or a purchase has been made.

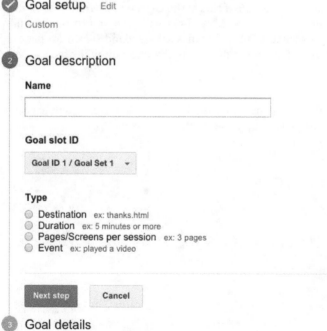

The next step in destination goal creation responds to the information requests for **Goal description**. We name the goal (in this case we'll call the goal "Contact Page Sent") and we indicate that it is a destination goal by selecting the button labeled **Destination**. The screen now appears as shown below.

Note that there is an opportunity to give the goal an identification number and to assign it to a goal set. This is done via the pull-down menu beneath **Goal slot ID**. Google Analytics has the ability to group goals together for purposes of data reporting. Thus, it is typically a good practice to group similar goals together in the same set. We can, for example, put all of our destination goals in Set 1.

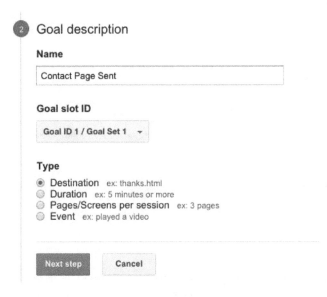

Clicking on **Next step** brings up **Goal details**, as shown below.

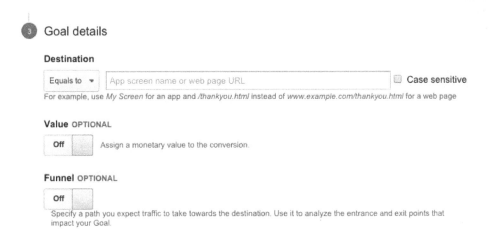

Since this is a **Destination** goal, we need to provide the destination page URL, which is `thanks_c.html`. This URL is typed into the top box, labeled "Destination," using regex to define the page. Note that we also indicate that regex is being used via the pull-down menu. For the moment, we'll leave **Value** and **Funnel** off, as they do not apply in this particular case. When done the screen is as shown below.

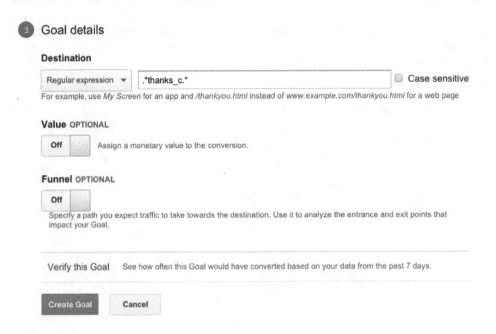

Finally, we'll use the **Verify this Goal** link to confirm that we are doing things properly. We should see the percentage of conversions, assuming any occurred, within the prior seven days. If you receive a 0% conversion message, use the **Content** menus to make certain that this outcome is correct, keeping in mind that a 0% conversion rate can be correct if no one has completed the goal or even visited your site in the past seven days. If everything seems correct, then click on the **Create Goal** button, and your goal will appear in the main goal table, as shown below.

Note two things about this display. First, once created, your goal will automatically begin to collect data unless recording is manually turned "off." Second, the number of available goals reported beneath the table has updated to note that only 19 goals remain available for this view.

Destination Goal With Funnel

This more complex type of goal reports a conversion only when an individual takes a specific path to your destination page.

Goal development with a funnel or destination starts similarly to the previous goal. We click on **+NEW GOAL** from the goal listing page, and then, if necessary, indicate that it is a custom goal. We then name the goal and indicate that it is a destination goal. In this case, the destination is the "Thank You" page following a purchase. The name of the goal is "Purchase Thank You Page".

The next step begins similar to a simple destination goal where we type in the URL of the destination page. One of our travel websites actually contains six "thank you for purchase pages," one for each of the travel packages shown on the purchase page. The URL and names of the thank you pages are:

```
/xanqeon/thanks_2b.html
/xanqeon/thanks_10b.html
/xanqeon/thanks_15b.html
/xanqeon/thanks_2m.html
/xanqeon/thanks_10m.html
/xanqeon/thanks_15m.html
```

Since we are only interested in whether a purchase has been confirmed, we indicate (via regex) that our destination goal is any one of these pages, as follows:

.*thanks_[2|10|15].*

We indicate this by selecting **Regular Expression** from the pull-down menu just to the left of our destination URL (see figure on the bottom of this page).

Beneath the destination page URL there are options to add value and funnel information to this goal. It isn't appropriate to add value information in this case because we will have actual purchase information.

Beyond goal value, you can decide to create a funnel leading to the goal destination page, where a funnel represents the path you expect users to take en route to the destination page. According to Google: "When you specify steps in a Funnel, Analytics can the track where visitors enter and exit the path on the way towards your goal. You may see, for example, a page or screen in a Funnel from which a lot of traffic exits before completing the goal - indicating a problem with that step. You might also see a lot of traffic skipping steps, indicating the path to conversion is too long or contains extraneous steps."

We begin the funnel creation process by clicking on the "On/Off" icon beneath **Funnel OPTIONAL**. Doing so brings up the additional information request shown on the bottom of the figure below.

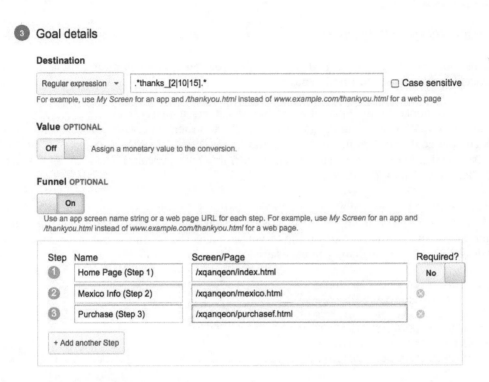

We're going to set up a funnel leading to the purchase "Thank You" page, whose URL was typed into destination box. The funnel reflects our best estimate of how a site user moves from the beginning to the end of the purchase process.

Our best judgment is that a purchase is a four-step process, ending in the "Thank You" goal destination page. The three steps prior to this page (beginning with the first page viewed) are believed to be: `index.html` (the home page), `mexico.html` (the Mexico information page) and `purchasef.html` (the purchase page,). We'll need to type each of these into the funnel activation form, indicating that the first step is not required, that is, it is possible to enter the funnel via pages other than this one. After each step is added, we click the **+Add another Step** icon to extend the funnel to a new page. When we're done, the page displays the figure shown on the top of page 311.

2 Goal details

Destination

| Regular expression ▾ | .*thanks.* | ☐ Case sensitive |

For example, use *My Screen* for an app and */thankyou.html* instead of *www.example.com/thankyou.html* for a web page

Value OPTIONAL

| Off | Assign a monetary value to the conversion. |

Funnel OPTIONAL

| On |

Use an app screen name string or a web page URL for each step. For example, use *My Screen* for an app and */thankyou.html* instead of *www.example.com/thankyou.html* for a web page.

Step	Name	Screen/Page	Required?
1	Home Page (step 1)	/xqanqeon/index.html	No
2	Mexico Info (step 2)	/xqanqeon/mexico.html	⊗
3	Purchase (step 3)	/xqanqeon/purchasef.html	⊗

+ Add another Step

Verify this Goal   See how often this Goal would have converted based on your data from the past 7 days.

Note that only the pages that lead up to the destination are provided above. The final destination page ("Thank You") has already been identified. Once we verify the goal, clicking **Create Goal** (on the bottom of the page) adds the goal to our goal summary page, as shown on below.

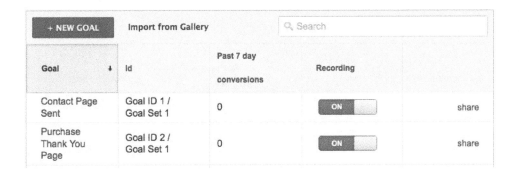

+ NEW GOAL	Import from Gallery		🔍 Search	
Goal ↓	Id	Past 7 day conversions	Recording	
Contact Page Sent	Goal ID 1 / Goal Set 1	0	ON	share
Purchase Thank You Page	Goal ID 2 / Goal Set 1	0	ON	share

Destination is any page within a specified directory

Imagine that we have a website with multiple pages organized by subject matter. We might, for example, have thirty pages of travel photos placed in the /photo subdirectory of our site. The URLs to these pages might be of the form:

```
http://mysite.com/photo/mexico_country.html
http://mysite.com/photo/mexico_north.html
http://mysite.com/photo/bahamas.html
http://mysite.com/photo/carribean.html
```

We want to know whether individuals are visiting the pages within this subdirectory. However, similar to our purchase thank you page, we are not interested in visits to specific pages as this can be determined from the standard data reporting menus. Instead, we are interested in the overall number of people visiting _any_ page within the /photo subdirectory. Goals and regex allow us to collect the appropriate data. As a result, the goal we are creating will be considered a conversion when a visitor reaches any page within the **/photo** subdirectory.

We begin the goal development process as we did in the preceding examples. We click on **+NEW GOAL**, name the goal (in this case "Visit to Photo Subdirectory"), and indicate that it is a destination goal. Clicking on **Next step** brings up the next step, **Goal details**.

As with the prior examples, **Goal details** collects specific goal characteristics (as shown below). Since we decided that this was a **Destination** goal, we need to provide the destination URL. This is typed into the top box. We use regex to indicate that the destination is any page within the /photo subdirectory and have selected **Regular expression** from the pull-down menu. We'll leave **Value** and **Funnel** off, as they do not apply in this particular case. Thus, prior to verifying the goal, the page will look like that shown below.

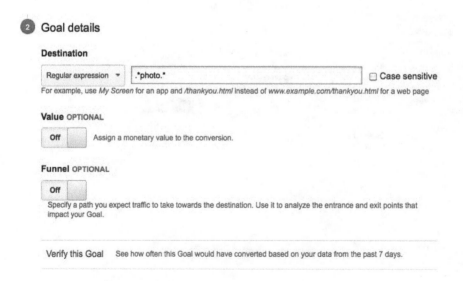

Finally, we'll use the **Verify this Goal** link to confirm that we are doing things properly. We should see the percentage of conversions, assuming any occurred, within the prior seven days. Clicking on the **Create Goal** link saves the goal and takes you back to the goal summary page, shown below.

Goal ↓	Id	Past 7 day conversions	Recording	
Contact Page Sent	Goal ID 1 / Goal Set 1	0	ON	share
Purchase Thank You Page	Goal ID 2 / Goal Set 1	0	ON	share
Visit to Photo Subdirectory	Goal ID 3 / Goal Set 1	0	ON	share

+ NEW GOAL   Import from Gallery   🔍 Search

17 goals left

Duration goals

A duration goal is considered a conversion when a site user has spent a predefined amount of time on your site. You begin creating this goal in the same way as a destination goal: you click on **+NEW GOAL**, name the goal (in this case "Time on site > 2 minutes"), indicate that it is a **Duration** goal, and then click **Next step**. After this, you'll see the display shown below.

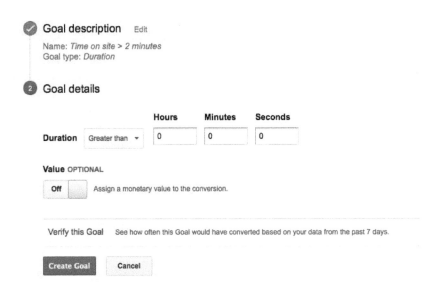

Goal description   Edit

Name: *Time on site > 2 minutes*
Goal type: *Duration*

2 Goal details

	Hours	Minutes	Seconds
Duration Greater than ▾	0	0	0

Value OPTIONAL

Off   Assign a monetary value to the conversion.

Verify this Goal   See how often this Goal would have converted based on your data from the past 7 days.

Create Goal   Cancel

All that remains at this point is to set the minimum amount of time for goal conversion (in this case, two minutes), verify and then create the goal. The goal summary page will update to show the addition of this new goal.

Pages/Screens per session goals

A pages/screens per session goal is very similar to a duration goal, except this goal is considered a conversion when a site user has viewed a predetermined number of pages or screens during a single session. You begin creating this goal in the same way as a destination goal: you click on **+NEW GOAL**, name the goal (in this case "Pages > 4 per session), indicate that it is a **Pages/Screens per session** goal, and then click **Next step**. After this, you'll see the screen shown below.

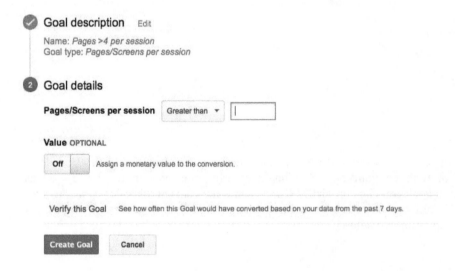

All that remains at this point is to set the minimum number of pages/screens per session for goal conversion (in this case, four), verify, and then create the goal. The goal summary page will update to show the addition of this new goal, as shown on the top of page 315.

+ NEW GOAL	Import from Gallery		🔍 Search		
Goal ↓	Id	Past 7 day conversions	Recording		
Contact Page Sent	Goal ID 1 / Goal Set 1	0	ON		share
Pages >4 per session	Goal ID 5 / Goal Set 1	0	ON		share
Purchase Thank You Page	Goal ID 2 / Goal Set 1	0	ON		share
Time on site > 2 minutes	Goal ID 4 / Goal Set 1	0	ON		share
Visit to Photo Subdirectory	Goal ID 3 / Goal Set 1	0	ON		share

15 goals left

A Caution Regarding Duration and Page View Goals

Tim Ash makes a persuasive case for avoiding duration and pageview goals. Please read his perspective here:

http://blog.kissmetrics.com/pageviews-time-on-site/

Revising an existing goal

It is possible to revise the parameters of an existing goal. Simply go to the goal summary page and click on the name of the goal you wish to revise. But be very careful because Google Analytics will not apply your changes retroactively. As a result, changing the parameters of a goal will mix the conversions for the old parameter with conversions for the revised parameter. It is much better practice to turn the old goal OFF and create a new goal in its place.

Goal value

So far, we haven't assigned a value to any of our goals. We didn't need to assign a value to the goal, which included actual product purchase (Google Analytics records this automatically), and the other goals did not have a value, which was nonaribtrary. How much, for example, is two minutes on site worth? This is not to say, however, that values should never be set for non-ecommerce goals.

Imagine that you have a site that is designed to attract new clients. Each new client, on average, generates $1,000 in revenue. Your site provides a content section, which provides whitepapers and you know from experience that 15% of those downloading a whitepaper will eventually become a client. In situations such as these, you can create a goal, which would be achieved when any whitepaper is downloaded. The value of this goal could be calculated as follows:

Goal Value = Percentage Converting * Average Revenue Generated

Goal Value = .15 * $1,000

Goal Value = $150

Similar logic can be applied to a contact form goal. If you know that 2% of those completing a contact form eventually become clients, then a contact form completion goal can be valued at $2, calculated as:

Goal Value = Percentage Converting * Average Revenue Generated

Goal Value = .02 * $1,000

Goal Value = $2

In sum, assigning a monetary value to a goal gives you a way to compare conversions and measure changes and improvements to your site or app.

30
Goal Reporting:
The Conversions Menu

You'll recall that Google Analytics uses the term "conversion" to indicate that a goal has been achieved. Thus, not surprisingly, the metrics related to goal conversions are found beneath the **Conversions** menu, as shown below.

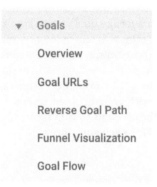

This chapter examines each of these options.

Overview

By default, **Conversions > Goals > Overview** reports two sets of goal-related metrics for the property and view being examined. Some of these metrics are summative, that is, the metrics report the performance of all goals grouped together, while others relate to individual goals. Consider the data reported near the middle of the **Conversions > Goals > Overview** page shown on the top of page 318. The goals represent some of those I created for my travel website.

Goal Completions	Goal Value	Goal Conversion Rate	Total Abandonment Rate
52	$0.00	46.43%	14.75%

More information Mexico goal page (Goal 1 Completions)	Purchase Confirmation (Goal 2 Completions)	Visit to music subdirectory (Goal 3 Completions)	Time on site > 2 minutes (Goal 4 Completions)
11	9	9	5

Pages > 4 / visit (Goal 5 Completions)	Contact Thanks (Goal 7 Completions)
18	0

The top row presents summative metrics. The data indicate that in sum there were 52 total goal completions with an average goal conversion rate of 46.43%. This information is interesting, but relatively useless. Since these are summative measures, they can be skewed by goals that are performing either extremely well or extremely poorly. Furthermore, this metric assumes that all goal conversions are of equal value, but is this is rarely the case. Similarly, the goal completion page table shown on the bottom of the **Conversions > Goals > Overview** page (see below) is relatively useless because it presents the terminal pages for all goals in one table. It is impossible to see which pages are the specific terminal pages for each specific goal.

Goals

Goal Completion Location ▸

Source / Medium

Goal Completion Location	Goal Completions	% Goal Completions
1. /xxangeon/thanks1.html	13	25.00%
2. /xxangeon/thanks_p.html	10	19.23%
3. /xxangeon/mexico1a.html	9	17.31%
4. /xxangeon/music/mandolin.html	6	11.54%
5. /xxangeon/purchasef.html	4	7.69%
6. /xxangeon/index.html	3	5.77%
7. /xxangeon/music/guitar.html	3	5.77%
8. /xxangeon/	2	3.85%
9. /xxangeon/contact.html	1	1.92%
10. /xxangeon/music/oboe.html	1	1.92%

Given the summative nature of the data being reported, the only truly useful information on the **Conversions > Goals > Overview** page is the conversion rate for each goal, which can be found in the row(s) beneath the summative metrics. In this case, the data is presented in the second and third rows of the table shown on the top of this page. These data report the number of completions (i.e., conversions) for each of the goals I've set up for my website. As such, you can use this data for a quick overview of each goal's number of completions.

The problem with these metrics is that we don't have any context for guiding their interpretation. Are eleven completions for Goal 1 good or bad? They are good if eleven represents a significant percentage of sessions; they are bad if eleven represents only a small portion of site sessions. The context for interpreting the absolute number of conversions is easy to find when we manipulate the data presented on the **Conversions > Goals > Overview** page.

The top of the **Conversions > Goals > Overview** report provides a pull-down menu labeled **Goal Option** with the default setting of **All Goals**. This option can be found directly below the **+Add Segment** option (see below).

Selecting this menu displays all goals for the desired view, where goals turned "On" are displayed in blue, underlined, bold type (these are Goals 1 to 5 and 7 below). Goals turned "Off" are displayed in grey scale (as in Goal 6 below).

Selecting any of the active goals revises the overview page to display just the information on the selected goal, as shown below when we select Goal 1 from the pull-down menu.

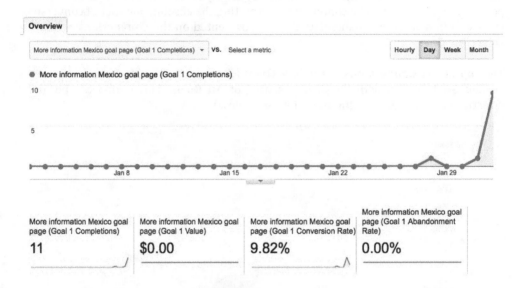

Now we have the context to interpret this goal's conversion rate. Overall slightly less than 10% of site users (exactly 9.82%) converted this goal. Note that both goal value and abandonment rate are both zero. Goal value is zero because we did not assign this goal a value when it was created. Abandonment rate is zero because it is a single page destination goal and therefore there is no place to "abandon" goal acquisition. Thus, as general practice, abandonment rate should be ignored for any goal lacking a prespecified funnel.

> ✅ Keep in mind, that the conversion rate is the result of dividing conversions by sessions for the time period indicated for the report. Thus, conversions will be artificially low if they are started sometime after the start of the reporting period. As a result, make certain that the time period corresponds with the start of goal creation.

The table on the bottom of the goal-specific **Conversions > Goals > Overview** page provides two types of data for the specific goal being examined. First, it tells you the terminal page when the goal was completed. This is useless data for destination goals, as the terminal page is identical to the destination page, as shown below:

Goals		More information Mexico goal page (Goal 1 Completions)	% More information Mexico goal page (Goal 1 Completions)
Goal Completion Location ▶	Goal Completion Location		
Source / Medium			
	1. /xxangeon/thanks1.html	11	100.00%

For Duration and Pages/View goals, the data in this table report where on the site a user was when the goal was achieved. The data for our Duration goal (time on site greater than two minutes) is shown below.

Goals		Goal Completion Location	Time on site > 2 minutes (Goal 4 Completions)	% Time on site > 2 minutes (Goal 4 Completions)
Goal Completion Location	▸			
Source / Medium		1. /xxangeon/	2	40.00%
		2. /xxangeon/mexico1a.html	2	40.00%
		3. /xxangeon/thanks_p.html	1	20.00%

The actionability of this data is relatively low unless there is a desire for the visitor to be on a specific page when the goal was converted.

Goal URLs

The second option in the **Goals** menu (**Conversions > Goals > Goal URLs**) brings up a page that reports both the terminal URL and the number of conversions by terminal URL for all goals (see below). Since these metrics are summative, this data has very little value since all goals are grouped together in a single display.

Goal Completion Location ?	Goal Completions ?	↓ Goal Value ?
	52 % of Total: 100.00% (52)	**$0.00** % of Total: 0.00% ($0.00)
1. /xxangeon/thanks1.html	13 (25.00%)	$0.00 (0.00%)
2. /xxangeon/thanks_p.html	10 (19.23%)	$0.00 (0.00%)
3. /xxangeon/mexico1a.html	9 (17.31%)	$0.00 (0.00%)
4. /xxangeon/music/mandolin.html	6 (11.54%)	$0.00 (0.00%)
5. /xxangeon/purchasef.html	4 (7.69%)	$0.00 (0.00%)
6. /xxangeon/index.html	3 (5.77%)	$0.00 (0.00%)
7. /xxangeon/music/guitar.html	3 (5.77%)	$0.00 (0.00%)
8. /xxangeon/	2 (3.85%)	$0.00 (0.00%)
9. /xxangeon/contact.html	1 (1.92%)	$0.00 (0.00%)
10. /xxangeon/music/oboe.html	1 (1.92%)	$0.00 (0.00%)

Valuable data can be obtained for destination goals when, similar to the preceding example, the data view is set to report metrics for just a single goal. The figure below, for example, displays data for our "Thank You" destination goal, the page displayed after someone downloads a Mexico information PDF.

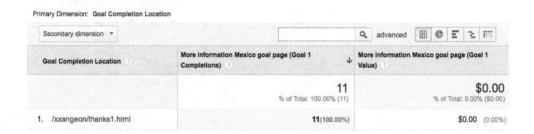

This initial view simply summarizes data we saw on other tables. The value of this table is hidden in the **Secondary Dimension** pull-down menu (upper-left hand side of the display). Selecting this menu allows you to examine the goal conversion process in more detail. Of great value are the **Goal Conversion** options, which allow you to see one, two or three steps prior to goal conversion (see below).

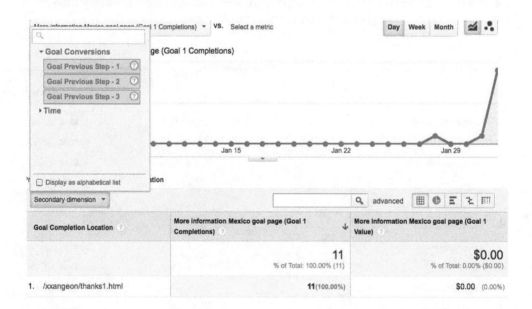

We've set up our site so that the Mexico information download can only be accomplished via our Mexico Information page (`mexico1a.html`). Selecting **Goal Previous Step 1** from the **Secondary dimension** menu displays a table that shows the page viewed immediately prior to conversion (see page 323).

Primary Dimension: Goal Completion Location

Goal Completion Location	Goal Previous Step - 1	More Information Mexico goal page (Goal 1 Completions) ↓	More Information Mexico goal page (Goal 1 Value)
		11 % of Total: 100.00% (11)	$0.00 % of Total: 0.00% ($0.00)
1. /xxangeon/thanks1.html	/xxangeon/mexico1a.html	9 (81.82%)	$0.00 (0.00%)
2. /xxangeon/thanks1.html	(entrance)	2 (18.18%)	$0.00 (0.00%)

The data is quite informative. Nine of the eleven conversions are as expected. These visitors move from the Mexico information page (`mexico1a.html`) to the "Thank You" for downloading page. However, the remaining two conversions reflect access to this page by typing the "Thank You" page URL directly into a browser. Given the relative size of this group, we would want to determine why individuals were taking this path to conversion and how to revise our site so that all individuals who convert this goal have downloaded the target PDF from the Mexico Information page.

Finally, we can obtain even more insights into the path to conversion by selecting **Goal Previous Step 2** and **Goal Previous Step 3** from the **Secondary dimension** menu.

Reverse goal path

The previous data option allowed you to focus on the first, second or third page viewed prior to goal conversion. This focus was achieved by showing only one of these prior steps in the table at one time.

The **Conversions > Goals > Reverse Goal Path** option presents all three steps in a single table. As with the preceding data, this data is best viewed when it is specific to one individual destination goal, as shown on the top of page 324 for the Mexico download "Thank You" page goal.

Goal Option:

Goal 1: More information Mexico goal page ▾

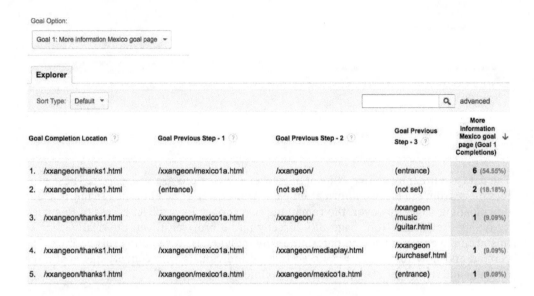

Goal Completion Location ?	Goal Previous Step - 1 ?	Goal Previous Step - 2 ?	Goal Previous Step - 3 ?	More Information Mexico goal page (Goal 1 Completions) ↓
1. /xxangeon/thanks1.html	/xxangeon/mexico1a.html	/xxangeon/	(entrance)	**6** (54.55%)
2. /xxangeon/thanks1.html	(entrance)	(not set)	(not set)	**2** (18.18%)
3. /xxangeon/thanks1.html	/xxangeon/mexico1a.html	/xxangeon/	/xxangeon /music /guitar.html	**1** (9.09%)
4. /xxangeon/thanks1.html	/xxangeon/mexico1a.html	/xxangeon/mediaplay.html	/xxangeon /purchasef.html	**1** (9.09%)
5. /xxangeon/thanks1.html	/xxangeon/mexico1a.html	/xxangeon/mexico1a.html	(entrance)	**1** (9.09%)

Notice how this additional level of detail makes the identification of underlying trends more difficult to see versus the table that presents just the step immediately prior to conversion. The data displayed in the Goal URLs table (discussed on pages 321-323) indicate that mexico1a.html was the last page to be viewed prior to conversion for nine of eleven conversions. The same finding is available from this chart, however now it is not as easy to see because the second step prior to conversion differs. (You can confirm that the outcome is the same by adding all conversions in which mexico1a.html was the last page prior to conversion, that is, Goal Previous Step -1. These are lines 1, 3, 4, and 5.)

Funnel visualization

Funnel visualization (**Conversions > Goals > Funnel Visualization)** is only appropriate for those goals in which you created a funnel during the goal creation process.

Imagine that we create a purchase "Thank You" page, where we believe that the path to purchase and conversion would move through several steps (pages), as shown below :

View Page F2.html (Step One) -> View Page F3.html (Step Two) ->

View Page F4.html (Step Three) -> Make a Purchase ->

Convert on "Thank You Page" (thanks1.html)

Selecting the **Conversions > Goals > Funnel Visualization** option for our Purchase "Thank You" page destination goal displays the chart shown on page 325.

Purchase Confirmation

This Goal was completed in 10 sessions | 38.46% funnel conversion rate

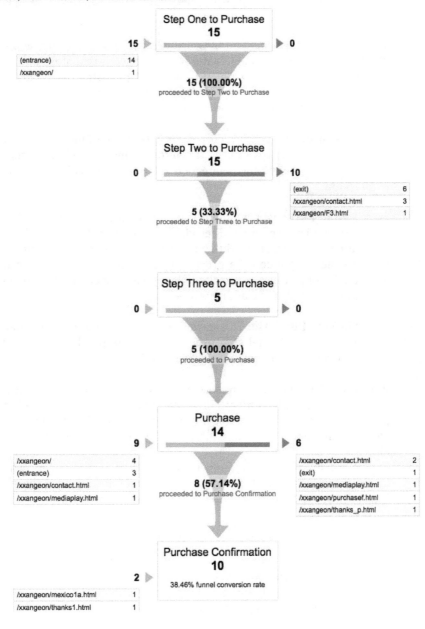

Step One to Purchase	
15	

15

| (entrance) | 14 |
| /xxangeon/ | 1 |

0

15 (100.00%)
proceeded to Step Two to Purchase

Step Two to Purchase	
15	

0

10

(exit)	6
/xxangeon/contact.html	3
/xxangeon/F3.html	1

5 (33.33%)
proceeded to Step Three to Purchase

Step Three to Purchase	
5	

0

0

5 (100.00%)
proceeded to Purchase

Purchase	
14	

9

/xxangeon/	4
(entrance)	3
/xxangeon/contact.html	1
/xxangeon/mediaplay.html	1

6

/xxangeon/contact.html	2
(exit)	1
/xxangeon/mediaplay.html	1
/xxangeon/purchasef.html	1
/xxangeon/thanks_p.html	1

8 (57.14%)
proceeded to Purchase Confirmation

Purchase Confirmation	
10	

2

38.46% funnel conversion rate

| /xxangeon/mexico1a.html | 1 |
| /xxangeon/thanks1.html | 1 |

The first things to notice about the funnel are the funnel and step names. **Purchase Confirmation** in the chart refers to the name we gave this goal during goal creation. Similarly, the names of each step, "Step One to Purchase," "Step Two to Purchase," etc., are the names we gave to each step when specifying funnel characteristics during goal creation.

Each funnel step has an inwardly and outwardly facing arrow. The arrow pointing into the funnel tells you how many people entered the funnel at that stage and from where on the site they came. The arrow pointing outward indicates the number of people leaving the funnel at that point and where they went. With this in mind, we would interpret the first three steps of the funnel as follows:

- **Step One to Purchase:** Fifteen people entered the funnel on this page (which is `F2.html`). All entered the funnel from the site home page. The page seems to be working as intended as no individuals leave the funnel at this point.

- **Step Two to Purchase:** No additional people entered the funnel, but ten people (67%) left the funnel after viewing this page. Clearly, rather than motivating people to proceed to purchase, this page is instead motivating most people to abandon the process. Even worse, the majority of these individuals are exiting the site altogether. Clearly, there is a problem with this page that needs to be addressed.

- **Step Three to Purchase:** This page seems to be working as intended. All who move to this funnel step proceed on to the purchase page. As expected, no new visitors enter the funnel at this point.

- **Purchase:** The data shown here indicate several problems with our assumptions and site content. First, nine individuals have arrived at the purchase page without moving through the funnel. We would want to compare the actual purchases of these individuals versus "funnel purchasers" to see if the funnel is doing more harm than good and, more fundamentally, whether the funnel is needed at all. Second, nearly half of all individuals arriving at this page leave without making a purchase. This is also cause for concern, and the characteristics of this page, would need to be examined with an eye toward revision.

- **Purchase Confirmation**: It's problematic that only 38.46% of all visitors who enter the funnel at some point complete a purchase and are sent to the "Thank You" confirmation page. This is especially worrisome because this percentage is inflated by the two individuals who arrived at the end of the funnel without making a prior purchase.

Taken as a whole, visitors' behaviors along the funnel path indicate a pressing need for further examination, analysis, and website revision.

This is the final option in the **Conversions > Goals** menu. This funnel is interpreted similarly to the **Users Flow** funnel discussed in Chapter 18. Here, however, you select the goal of interest through the top of chart pull-down menu (see below).

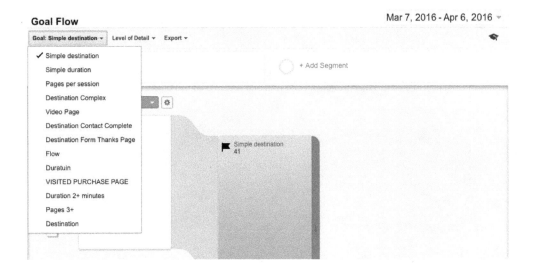

31
Goal Reporting and the Real-Time Menu

The Google Analytics **Real-Time** menu allows you see what is happening on your website or blog at nearly the same time as actions occur. You can see what pages are being visited, how many users are viewing each page, where users are coming from (locations and traffic sources), and goal and event conversions. The **Real-Time** menu is accessed via the **Real-Time** menu option near the top left of every reporting screen (see below).

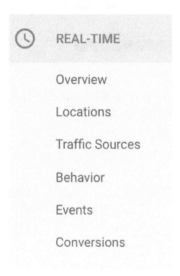

The figure shown on the top of page 330 is the **Real-Time > Overview** display that summarizes key metrics. Perhaps of greatest importance are the number of users currently on the site (in this example there are two, shown as both the numeric and the bars on the top right-hand side) and the pages currently being viewed (shown on the bottom right-hand side).

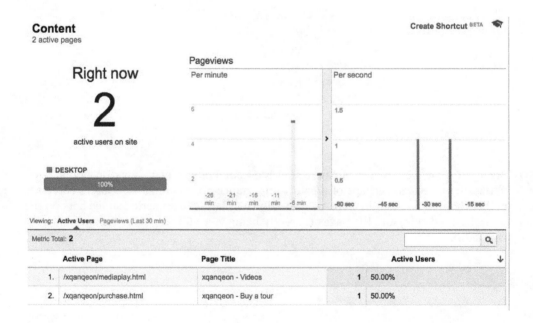

The figure below is the **Real-Time > Content** display that provides more detailed information on current content consumption.

Unfortunately, you'll soon discover that once the novelty of real-time monitoring wears off, this data is only strategically useful for a limited range of situations, one of which is monitoring goal conversions.

Real-Time goal conversions

You can monitor destination goal conversions in real-time via the **Real-Time > Conversions** option.[66] Once this is selected, you'll see a list of all active destination goals and the number of users who have converted each goal. The figure below, for example, shows that each of two goals has been converted by a single active user. Note that selecting the option next to **Active Users** allows you to see goal conversions for the prior 30 minutes. This option is labeled **Goal Hits (Last 30 min)**.

There are two strategic uses for monitoring goal conversion in real time. The first allows you to confirm that your goals are working as intended. The second provides insights into the effectiveness of your marketing campaigns.

Confirming that goals are working as intended

You'll recall that our travel site uses six different pages to confirm a purchase, where each page is specific to a tour selection. We want to monitor each page through the standard content menu. Additionally, we have created a goal that converts whenever *any* of these pages is viewed. This allows us to easily keep track of the total number of purchases. We can use real time to make certain that we have properly created this goal.

---

[66] Only destination goals can be monitored in real time. Goals are available for monitoring immediately after they are created.

First, we select **Real-Time > Conversions** and make certain that the goal of interest is displayed. In our case, the purchase "Thank you" page is the second goal listed (see below).

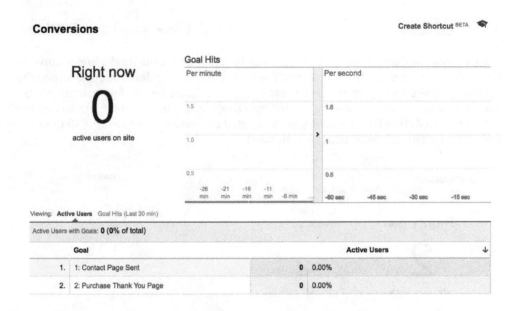

Next, we select the **Real-Time > Content** option. Leaving this display open, we visit our travel site in another browser window or another browser. We make a "purchase" and confirm that the correct thank you page is being displayed. In our case it is, as shown below.

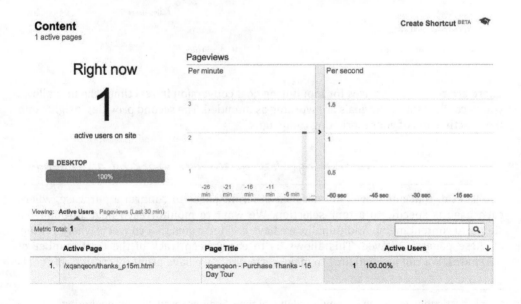

Finally, we again select the **Real-Time > Conversions** option and make certain that the purchase goal has increased by one. This change indicates that our goal is recording as intended (see below).

If you find that a goal is not converting, check to make certain that: (1) there is no misspelling in the URL of the goal destination, (2) the tracking code is present on the destination/conversion page, and (3) the match type in the goal definition is correct.

Monitoring marketing activities

Imagine that you are running a time-sensitive campaign designed to increase membership sign-ups. You have two approaches you want to test: a '10% off' offer and a '14 months for the price of 12' offer. A special web page has been designed for each offer. You have an email list of 15,000 target individuals to whom membership offers will be sent.

One option for executing this promotion simply divides the list in half, sending each half a different offer and monitoring the results in the usual way. However, real time offers an alternative.

First, we set up each membership sign-up page as a goal. One goal converts when someone signs up for 10% off and the second goal converts when someone signs up for 14 months for price of 12. One thousand of each offer are emailed to a randomly selected portion of the total list. You monitor conversions for each offer in real-time knowing that historically the majority of sign-ups will take place within two hours of the email blast. Your next step, at the end of two hours, depends upon the observed real-time trend:

- If neither offer meets the target sign-up goal then no further emails are sent out until new offer(s) are developed.

- If both offers meet the target sign-up goal and the offers are not significantly different from each other in terms of sign-ups, then the remaining list is divided in half, with each half receiving one of the offers.

- If only one offer meets the target sign-up goal or if both meet the goal and one is significantly better than the other, then the entire remainder of the list is emailed the stronger offer.

32

Goals and Custom Segments

Chapters 27 and 28 illustrated how important strategic insights can be obtained through the use of segments, where a segment was formed through the use of one or more Google Analytics provided metrics. As you'll see in this and forthcoming chapters, segments can also be formed on the basis of metrics that you generate specifically for your website. One of these metrics is goal conversion.

Any custom segment can be formed with goal conversion metrics. You can form the segment using only goal conversion metrics, or you can combine goal conversion metrics with other standard metrics. For example:

- a segment can contain only those individuals who converted on Goal 1 (or any other goal).

- a segment can contain only those individuals who converted on both Goal 1 and Goal 2.

- a segment can contain only those individuals who converted on Goal 1 but did not covert on Goal 2.

- a segment can contain only those individuals who converted on Goal 1 and who live outside the United States.

- a segment can contain only those individuals who converted on Goal 1 and who came to the site via a social referral and who made a purchase.

Creating a custom segment using goals

You create a custom segment using goal metrics in the same way you created other custom segments. You access segments via the **+Add Segment** option on the top of almost any page located beneath the blue circle **All Sessions** identifier. When you click **+Add Segment** the segments page displays. You then begin the segment creation process by clicking the **+ New Segment** button. The segment creation page will then display.

Goal metrics are incorporated into a segment's definition via the **Conditions** option, which is shown on the bottom left-hand side of the page. The selection of this option brings up the **Conditions** page, as shown on the top of page 336.

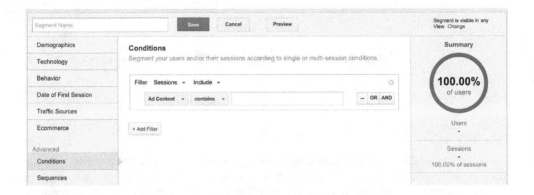

Pulling-down the menu currently labeled **Ad Content** displays both green and blue menu options. Near the bottom of the blue menu options is **Goal Conversions** (as shown below).

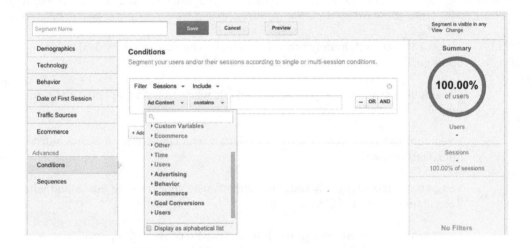

The selection of this menu option results in a listing all of the goals created for the current view.

Let's illustrate the remainder of the segment creation process using this scenario:[67]

Imagine that my travel website has added three new pages to promote Brazil vacations. When we added the pages to the site, we also created a goal that converts whenever any one of these three pages is viewed. The name of the Goal is "Goal 6: Any Numbered Brazil." We want to use custom segments to determine if goal conversion has any impact on purchase behavior.

---

[67] This scenario references goals and pages that are not part of your travel website.

We create the desired segment by selecting "Goal 6: Any Numbered Brazil (Completions)" from the pull-down menu. Selection of this goal changes the display to that shown below, where the goal name is now incorporated into the display.

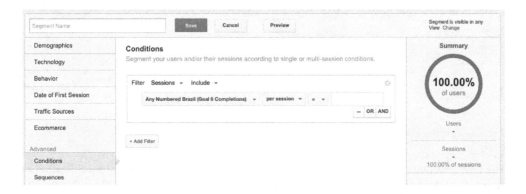

We complete the segment creation process by indicating that we want the segment to filter on users and **include** those users who convert one or more times (as shown below). The segment is also named "Brazil Page Viewed."

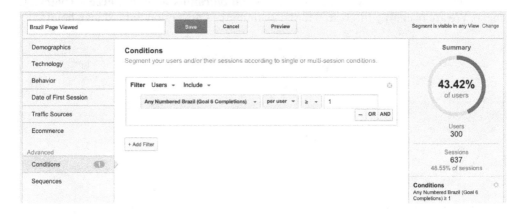

The updated graphic on the right-hand side indicates that the segment represents 43.42% of all users. Lastly, we **Save** the segment.

This segment is now available for use in data analysis, but taking one more step will increase our insights. We initially set up this goal to see if purchase-realated behaviors increased when site users visited one or more of the special Brazil pages. Since it is beneficial to provide context for interpreting the behaviors of this segment, we need to create a second segment consisting of those who did not convert this goal. Thus, we need a second segment to represent those who did not visit any of the special Brazil pages.

We create this segment of "nonconverters" in a manner almost identical to the prior segment. Once again, we select "Goal 6: Any Numbered Brazil (Completions)". We name the segment "No Brazil Page Viewed", set the filter to users, only now we indicate that we want to **Exclude** users who converted (see figure on the top of page 338).

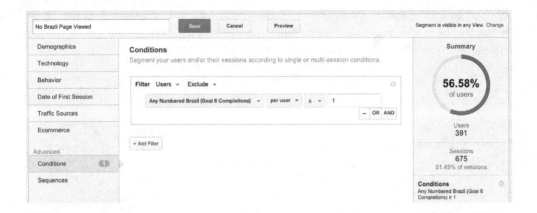

The two segments should account for 100% of site users, as a user must be classified as either converting or not converting the goal. This is in fact the case, as the two segment sizes do add to 100% (43.42 + 56.58). With this confirmation in mind, we **Save** the segment. We can now use the two custom segments to determine any influence of our special Brazil pages on puchase behaviors.

Ecommerce metrics are available through the **Conversions > Ecommerce > Overview** menu. We are primarily interested in the Ecommerce Conversion Rate, shown below.

We can see that the pages promoting the special Brazil vacation were a good idea. Individuals who viewed these pages were significantly more likely to make a purchase versus those who visited the site but did not see these pages.

This is all good news. Should we desire, we can create additional segments to see the impact of specific pages on purchase as well as create segments to determine how the number of pages viewed affected purchase behaviors.

Section IX:
Tracking Downloads

We've seen how Google Analytics provides insights into user characteristics and users' interactions with the different pages on your website. This information is available, for example, in the **Users Flow** report or in the **Site Content** section of the **Behavior** menu. But many websites and blogs offer a broader range of interactions including video and downloadable content such as PDFs, Excel documents, ebooks, etc. Google Analytics can't track these events directly, but with some minor tweaks to your pages' HTML code, you can successfully track visitor interactions with these types of content. This section helps you understand how to track downloads and strategically use these metrics to improve website performance.

- Chapter 33 shows you how to track user interactions with downloadable content and demonstrates how to send relevant data to Google Analytics.

  Note that this chapter's discussion is intended to work with Universal Analytics (analytics.js). If you are using the Global Site Tag tracking code (gtag.js), please read Chapter 33a in the Appendix (pages 665 to 672) before returning to Chapter 34.

- Chapter 34 provides examples of how to go beyond basic download metrics to increase the potential for website success.

- Chapter 35 illustrates how tracked downloads can be used as goals.

The tracking of video interactions is discussed in the context of events in Chapters 44 and 44a (in the appendix).

Tracking Downloads

Note that this chapter's discussion is intended to work with Universal Analytics *(analytics.js)*. If you are using the Global Site Tag tracking code *(gtag.js)*, please read Chapter 33a in the appendix (pages 665 to 672) before returning to Chapter 34.

Google Analytics allows you to treat interactions with downloadable items as if they were regular pageviews. These items can be any form of content: PDFs, Excel files, Word documents, or video. The ability to track these downloads allows you to monitor your site content and to analyze these interactions using all of the same menus and techniques used to analyze actual pageviews.

Let's first see how trackable downloads are reported in Google Analytics. Then we'll see how to implement this activity.

How are downloads reported?

Tracked downloads are reported in exactly the same way as regular pageviews, and as a result, you determine the labels used to identify the download. Thus, it is important for you to organize and name your downloads in a way that makes them easy to find and understand in Google Analytics reports. At minimum, in terms of location, your downloadable content should be placed in a separate subdirectory.[68]

Let's look at a simple example.

Imagine that I have a subdirectory (also called a "folder") with two downloads. The subdirectory is named `/information/` and the two downloads provide tour information for Mexico and the Bahamas. The Mexico document is named `mexico_dl.pdf` and the Bahamas document is named `bahamas_dl.pdf`.

---

[68] We recommend the following readings if you are unfamiliar with how directories and subdirectories are used to organize website content: *Web Style Guide, Site Structure* at http://webstyleguide.com/wsg3/5-site-structure/3-site-file-structure.html; *How to Design a Website* at http://how-to-design-a-website.com/website-usability/website-directory-structure; *Folder Hierarchy Best Practices for Digital Asset Management* at http://www.damlearningcenter.com/resources/articles/best-practices-for-folder-organization/.

The table shown below illustrates the top level of my site's organization and is the table which appears when I select **Behaviors > Site Content > Content Drilldown**. The first listing, **/xqanqeon/,** is the folder which contains all of my site's pages and related content. Thus, it is not surprising that this folder has the greatest number of pageviews.

The above figure also shows two of my folders with downloadable elements. The **/brochure/** folder contains long PDFs, while the **/information/** folder contains short, one page fact sheets. We can see that users are more interested in longer versus shorter downloads, as the **/brochure/** folder has nearly three times as many downloads (as reflected in pageviews) versus the **/information/** folder.

We are interested in the **/information/** folder as it contains the two downloadable PDFs of interest. We can see that in total, there were ten downloads from this folder (again, as evidenced in the pageviews column), and that all of these downloads were initiated by different users. We determine this by dividing *pageviews* by *unique page-views*. The closer this ratio is to 1.0, the greater the proportion of downloads by different users.

Clicking on the **/information/** link in the table above brings up detailed information on each of the two downloads contained within the folder (see the table below).

The metrics in this table inform us of two things with regard to downloads and subsequent behaviors:

- There are equal numbers of Mexico and Bahamas downloads, and all downloads were initiated by different site users.

- Site engagement differs dramatically between the two downloads. Those who downloaded the Mexico PDF stayed on the site and all viewed at least one more page (as evidenced in the **%Exit** of 0% from this page). Those who downloaded the Bahamas PDF had no further site engagement and immediately left the site (as evidenced in the **%Exit** of 100% from this page). Clearly, we would want to explore why those viewing the Bahamas PDFs are behaving in this manner, and then modify the site or the Bahamas PDF's characteristics to reduce or eliminate these behaviors.

Finally, we can always gain deeper insights into download behaviors through the use of secondary dimensions. The chart below, for example, indicates that all of the downloads took place by Irish site users.

Your site's structure and downloadable content

You are the one who ultimately determines the directory structure for your downloads and what the downloads will be named. With regard to structure, you can place all of the downloads in a single directory, choosing, for example, from labels such as:

```
/downloads/
/brochures/
```

or you can use a nested approach, choosing, for example, from labels such as:

```
/brochure/mexico/
/brochure/bahamas/
```

Remember that your specific strategic information needs should be the guide for how downloadable elements are organized on your site and subsequently labeled in Google Analytics reports.

Let's look at another set of downloads on my site. Here, all of my downloads have been placed in the /brochure/ directory. There are two downloads for Mexico named:

```
mexico_dl_image.pdf
mexico_dl_text.pdf
```

It is important to note that each PDF has been named in a way that allows us to easily see the topic country, the fact that it is a download (as indicated by _dl) and the source of the download request (image or text). This type of clear naming makes it much easier to interpret reports when your website offers many downloadable elements.[69]

For the moment, let's just focus on the Mexican PDFs. The full URLs to each of the Mexican PDFs on my site are:

```
http://www.googleanalyticsdemystified.com/xqanqeon/brochure/
mexico_dl_image.pdf
```

```
http://www.googleanalyticsdemystified.com/xqanqeon/brochure/
mexico_dl_text.pdf
```

The two components of download tracking

If you use different browsers, you've seen how the same action is often treated differently. Downloads, for example, are handled differently in Firefox and Chrome. In light of this situation, our approach to tracking downloads is browser independent, and as a result, the appropriate data should be sent to Google Analytics regardless of the browser employed by the site user.

Our approach to tracking downloads requires that you do two things: First, you'll need to incorporate and customize a very small JavaScript script on each page from which you want to track a download. Second, you'll need to make a small addition to the link or image that initiates the download. The following discusses each of these steps.

The JavaScript script

The JavaScript script must be placed in the HTML code on every page from which you want to track one or more downloads. This script does not need to be placed on pages without downloads and it only needs to appear once in a page's HTML code regardless of the number of download options appearing on the page. The script should be placed directly after the Google Analytics tracking code, as shown on the top of page 345 where the Google Analytics tracking code is in the smaller type and the new JavaScript script is in larger type.

---

[69] For simplicity, we use the terms "download," "downloadable element," and PDF interchangeably. However, as mentioned earlier, the tools and techniques discussed for PDFs apply to any downloadable piece of content: video, Excel files, images, etc.

```
<script>
(function(i,s,o,g,r,a,m){i['GoogleAnalyticsObject']=r;i[r]=i[r]||function(){
(i[r].q=i[r].q||[]).push(arguments)},i[r].l=1*new
Date();a=s.createElement(o),
m=s.getElementsByTagName(o)[0];a.async=1;a.src=g;m.parentNode.insertBefore(
a,m)  })
(window,document,'script','//www.google-analytics.com/analytics.js','ga');
ga('create', 'UA-50182280-1', 'googleanalyticsdemystified.com');
ga('send', 'pageview');
</script>

<script>
function download(file)
{
ga('send', 'pageview', file);
alert("Thanks for your download.");
(window.location="YOUR FULL URL HERE"+file);
}
</script>
```

Three instructions are embedded in the script after the JavaScript function is named.

- **ga('send', 'pageview', file)** sends the name of the downloaded file to Google Analytics. This line never needs to be changed.

- **alert("Thanks for your download.")** uses a pop-up window to acknowledge the download. The time lag between the appearance of this window and initiation of the download allows time for all browsers to send the name of the downloaded file to Google Analytics. You can customize the message by changing the text between the quotation marks. Make certain that any changes leave the beginning and ending quotation marks intact.

- **(window.location="YOUR FULL URL HERE"+file)** provides the browser with the full URL to the location of your download.

   Here, you to replace the phrase **YOUR FULL URL HERE** with the URL to your downloads, up to but not including the folder in which they are housed. For example, the PDFs on our site are located in the **/brochure/** folder. On our site, the full URL to one of the downloads is:

   ```
   http://www.googleanalyticsdemystified.com/xqanqeon/
   brochure/mexico_dl_image.pdf
   ```

This step requires that we place within the JavaScript the URL up to but not including the folder containing the PDFs. In my case, the URL in the script appearing between the quotation marks (and which would replace **YOUR FULL URL HERE**) would be:

`http://www.googleanalyticsdemystified.com/xqanqeon`

You need to replace the phrase **YOUR FULL URL HERE** with the full URL that leads to your downloads. Make certain to place this URL between the quotation marks (replacing the indicated phrase) and leave the rest of the line as is. Take care not to leave any spaces between the quotation marks and your URL. Finally, make certain not to end the URL with a slash or period.

When you have made the preceding changes, save the page without changing its name and then proceed to see how to modify the HTML code for the initiating a download via a text or image link.[70]

Tracking a download via a text link

Our approach tracks a download by altering the link, which initiates the download. This alteration puts the JavaScript script into motion, sending data to Google Analytics and sending the requested PDF or other content to the site user. We'll begin with text links and then move on to an image link.

An ordinary HTML text link to a Mexico information PDF would be of the form:

```
<a href="information/mexico.pdf">Click to download more
  information on Mexico</a>
```

Here, the name of the downloadable document is `mexico.pdf`, which is in the `information/` folder. The link text that appears on the web page is: **Click to download more information on Mexico.**

We're going to change the basic form of this text link to the following format:

```
<a href="JavaScript:download('/information/mexico.pdf')">Click
Here</a> to download more information on Mexico
```

You'll use this link format anywhere on your site you want to allow a trackable download to take place via a text link. Leave the link as shown above except for the three elements, which need to be addressed whenever you use this format:

---

[70] You can see trackable text and image links in action at my website at:
http://www.googleanalyticsdemystified.com/xqanqeon/information1.html

- *Mandatory:* Replace /information/mexico.pdf with the location and name of the content to be downloaded when the link is clicked. In this example, for my site, we would change this to: /brochure/mexico_dl_text.pdf to indicate the actual location and name of the file to be downloaded when the link is clicked upon. Note that a slash ("/") now precedes the name of the folder. Keep the beginning and ending single quotation marks intact.

- *Optional:* Replace **Click Here** with the text you want to appear as the active link. You can leave this as is if you desire.

- *Mandatory:* Replace **to download more information on Mexico** with whatever text appropriately completes the sentence. For this example, we will change this text to read: **to obtain a brochure on Mexican travel.**

Once the prior is complete, the trackable download via a text link would be:

```
<a href="JavaScript:download('/brochure/mexico_dl_text.pdf')">
Click Here</a> to obtain a brochure on Mexican travel
```

This link is placed in the page's HTML code at the point where we want the text link to appear.

Tracking downloads via an image link

We can initiate a download by having a user click on an image. An ordinary HTML image link to my Mexico information PDF via an image would be:

```
<a href="information/mexico.pdf"><img src="images/mexico.jpg">
</a>
```

Here, the name of the downloadable document is mexico.pdf, which is in the information/ folder. The image used as a link is named **mexico.jpg** and resides in the images/ directory.

We're going to change the basic form of this text link to the following:

```
<a href="JavaScript:download('/information/mexico.pdf')">
<img src="images/mexico.jpg"></a>
```

This format is nearly identical to that used to create our text link. The only difference is that the text, which appears on the web page has been replaced by an image.

You'll use this link format anywhere on your site you want a trackable download to take place via an image click. Two elements need to be addressed when you use this format:

- *Mandatory:* Replace /information/mexico.pdf with the location and name of the content to be download when the image link is clicked. In this example, we would change this to: /brochure/mexico_dl_image.pdf to indicate the actual location and name of the file to be downloaded when the image link is clicked upon. Note that a slash ("/") now precedes the name of the folder. Keep the beginning and ending single quotation marks intact.

- *Mandatory:* Replace the image name with the image that you want to use as the link. For this example, we've changed the image to `images/mexico1.jpg`.

Once the prior is complete, the trackable download via an image link would be:

```
<a href="JavaScript:download('/brochure/mexico_dl_image.pdf')">
<img src="images/mexico1.jpg"></a>
```

Upload the revised page to your server and then use **Real-Time** to make certain that the link is working as intended.

Confirming that data is being sent to Google Analytics

We saw in Chapter 31 how the Google Analytics **Real-Time** menu can help us see if our goals are working as intended. The **Real-Time** menu can also be used to confirm that our efforts to track downloads are also working. This assumes that you have created and placed trackable downloads on your site.

Using Chrome, access your site's page with the trackable text link. If the link is working, you should see the name of the downloaded PDF in the **Real-Time > Content** display, as shown below for my download. The name of the download is beneath the **Active Page** header on the left-hand side of the display.

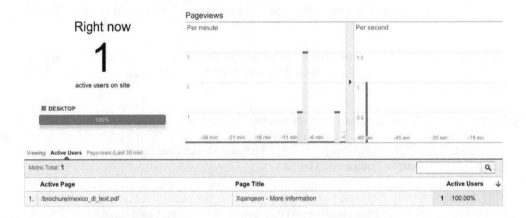

Note that we've tested this approach in Firefox, Chrome and Safari and it has worked in all three browsers, although Safari can at times still be problematic with this and other scripts we'll present later in this book. We recommend testing in Chrome or Firefox. The sporadic problems with Safari should have little impact as Safari's share of usage is estimated to be less than 4%.

34

Applications of Download Tracking

It takes considerable thought and time to create downloads that have perceived value among site users. Once these downloads are created, download tracking helps us evaluate how to best bring these downloads to users' attention and how to evaluate the impact of these downloads on subsequent user interactions and behaviors.

This chapter illustrates two applications of download tracking by addressing two strategic questions relevant to our travel website:

- Are all three methods of initiating a download (text, image, button) equally effective in motivating a download?

- Do the different types of downloads vary in their ability to influence subsequent purchase behaviors?

But, these are not the only questions that can be asked. Depending upon your specific website goals, other questions might be:

- Is there a difference between downloads in terms of motivating a site revisit?

- Are some downloads more effective than others in stimulating contact, registration, or other related behaviors?

- Which download topics are of more/lesser interest to site users?

- To what extent are there differences between downloads in terms of increasing site engagement?

- To what extent do downloads stimulate referrals and trackbacks to the site?

Evaluating differences in download options

We always want to make certain that the format used to initiate a download is the most effective, especially given the time and effort that goes into content creation. As we saw in the previous chapters, we can initiate a download via text, image or button (a specific type of image). Download tracking allows us to determine which of these approaches is the most successful in motivating a download.

The first task is to name and place each download to facilitate interpretation of the relevant Google Analytics reports. All three downloads are placed in the /brochure/ mexico_dl/ folder and we name each download as follows:

mexico_image.pdf

mexico_link.pdf

mexico_button.pdf

We locate the pageviews for each download option through **Behavior > Site Content > Content Drilldown**. Selecting this menu option brings up the top level directory display, as shown below, where on the second line we can see that 32 downloads have taken place in total from this folder.

We click on /brochure/ in the prior display to generate the table shown below. As noted above, the three PDFs (one for each download option) are located within the /mexico_dl/ folder shown on the first line of the table. The Pageviews column for this folder tells us that there have been 17 total downloads from this folder. The 1.0 ratio of pageviews to unique pageviews indicates that each user downloaded only one PDF.

Clicking on the `/mexico_dl/` folder brings up detailed information on each download option, as shown below. The Pageviews column shows a distinct user preference for the button link: about 70% of all downloads were via this link. This information would guide website revision, as we can potentially increase the number of downloads by changing our text and image links to buttons.

Primary Dimension: **Page path level 3**   Page   Other ▾

Secondary dimension ▾ Sort Type:	Default ▾			

Page path level 3 ?	Pageviews ? ↓	Unique Pageviews ?	Avg. Time on Page ?	Bounce Rate ?
	17 % of Total: 9.50% (179)	**17** % of Total: 10.97% (155)	**00:00:09** Site Avg: 00:00:10 (-13.26%)	**0.00%** Site Avg: 0.00% (0.00%)
1. ☐ /mexico_button.pdf	**12** (70.59%)	12 (70.59%)	00:00:10	0.00%
2. ☐ /mexico_link.pdf	**3** (17.65%)	3 (17.65%)	00:00:05	0.00%
3. ☐ /mexico_image.pdf	**2** (11.76%)	2 (11.76%)	00:00:11	0.00%

Evaluating download influence on purchase behavior

Downloads are often used to influence subsequent site behaviors, for example, increasing engagement or motivating a registration, contact or purchase. Let's look at the latter circumstance to see how download tracking can help us determine the extent to which downloads differ in terms of motivating a purchase and purchase amount.

We begin as we did in the prior exercise by naming and placing each download to facilitate interpretation of the relevant Google Analytics reports. All three downloads are placed in the `/brochure/brazil_dl/` folder, and we name each download as follows:

```
brazil1.pdf
brazil2.pdf
brazil3.pdf
```

Each download has different content.

We can examine the relationship between download content and subsequent purchase behaviors by isolating individuals who saw only one of the brochures. Groups are formed via custom segments to reflect the one download viewed. Since we have three downloads, three custom segments will be formed, one for each download.[71]

---

[71] This is the cleanest test of download impact. But, if sample size were sufficient, we could examine not only those who saw only one download, but also those who saw some combination of downloads. The procedure would be the same, except that more segments would be formed

The custom segment creation process begins the same as when other metrics are used for group definition. You access custom segments via the **+Add Segment** option on the top of almost any page, located near the blue circle **All Sessions** identifier. When you click **+Add Segment**, the segments page displays. You then click the **+New Segment** button. The segment creation page will then display.

As with all custom segments based on a specific condition, we begin group definition via the **Conditions** option, which resides on the bottom left-hand side of the page. Since the segment filters for a specific pageview by individual site visitors whenever the site was visited, we set the Filter to "users" and "Include". Next, we use the search box in the pull-down the menu currently labeled **Ad Content** to locate **Page**, as shown below.

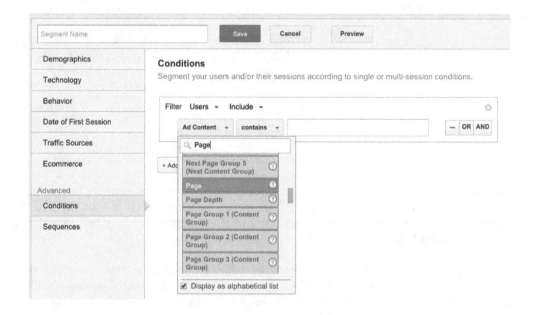

We can now define our first segment. We type in the page of interest in the text box (using regex to indicate the page is `brazil1.pdf`), changing the pull-down menu from **contains** to **matches regex**. This will include in the segment all users who saw `brazil1.pdf`. However, we also want to exclude from this group users who may have seen either `brazil2.pdf` or `brazil3.pdf`. To accomplish this, we add a second filter to this group. This filter excludes any user from this group who viewed `brazil2.pdf` or `brazil3.pdf`. Finally, we name this segment "Saw Only Brazil 1". This results in the screen displayed on the top of page 353. The segment is then saved.

Conditions

Segment your users and/or their sessions according to single or multi-session conditions.

The process is repeated for custom segments two and three (giving each an appropriate name), as illustrated in the following two figures.

Conditions

Segment your users and/or their sessions according to single or multi-session conditions.

Conditions

Segment your users and/or their sessions according to single or multi-session conditions.

We can now use the three custom segments to explore reactions to and impact of the three different downloads.

Reactions to the three different downloads can be seen in the pageview data, obtained via the **Behavior > Site Content > All Pages** menu option. This table (see below) provides two important insights. First, site users appear to be much more likely to download the brazil3.pdf. Clearly, this PDF's topic is of greater interest. Second, the brazil3.pdf is much more likely to keep a user on the site. Only 21.74% of those who downloaded the brazil3.pdf left the site after the download versus nearly half (45.45%) of those who downloaded the brazil1.pdf. All in all, the brazil3.pdf seems to have much better potential for fostering site engagement.

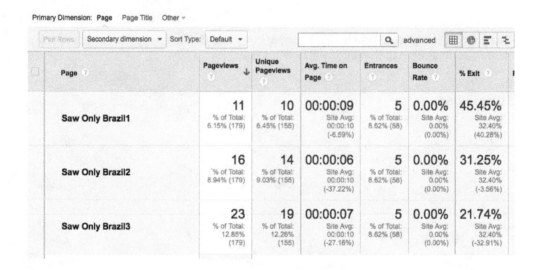

The strength of the brazil3.pdf can be seen in the ecommerce data, obtained through the **Conversions > Ecommerce > Overview** menu option (see top of page 355). This data parallels that of the pageview data and reinforces the conclusions that the strongest download is brazil3.pdf and the weakest download is brazil1.pdf.

When we look at the **Ecommerce Conversion Rate** (which reflects the percentage of sessions that resulted in a transaction, see page 355) we can clearly see the overwhelming superiority of the brazil3.pdf download. Significantly more of those who saw this PDF purchased a tour at a much higher average order value. Based on this data, we would most likely eliminate brazil1.pdf and brazil2.pdf as download options and attempt to create more downloadable content similar to brazil3.pdf.

Ecommerce Conversion Rate	Transactions	Revenue	Average Order Value
Saw Only Brazil1	Saw Only Brazil1	Saw Only Brazil1	Saw Only Brazil1
0.00%	0	$0.00	$0.00
Saw Only Brazil2	Saw Only Brazil2	Saw Only Brazil2	Saw Only Brazil2
40.00%	2	$7,000.00	$3,500.00
Saw Only Brazil3	Saw Only Brazil3	Saw Only Brazil3	Saw Only Brazil3
80.00%	4	$45,000.00	$11,250.00

35

Download Tracking and Goals

The prior chapter illustrated how tracked downloads recorded as pageviews can be used to form custom segments. This chapter illustrates how tracked downloads, similar to any recorded pageview, can also be used to create a goal.

Downloads as goals

This type of goal is considered a "conversion" when a user downloads content such as a PDF. Since we're recording the download as a pageview then we would use the name of the download as the goal destination.

The first step is to have the desired account, property and view displayed on the Administrators page. Next, we click on **Goals** in the View column.

We begin the goal development process by clicking on **+NEW GOAL** which brings up one of two displays, depending upon how the view is configured. You might see the screen shown on the top of page 358. If this is the case, just select **Custom** on the bottom of the display and then click on **Next Step**. This will take you to the second possible display after clicking on **+NEW GOAL**, shown as the second figure on page 358 (beneath the **Next Step** button). This latter display is the one you will use to create the destination goal.

The numbering system used to identify the various steps to goal creation may vary depending upon your starting screen.

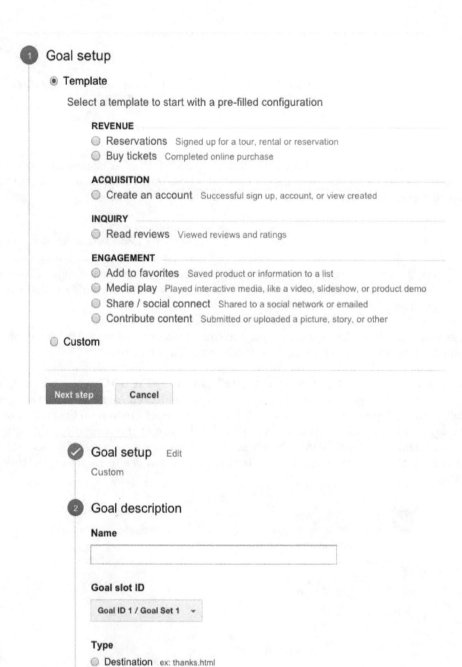

1 Goal setup

● Template

Select a template to start with a pre-filled configuration

REVENUE
○ Reservations Signed up for a tour, rental or reservation
○ Buy tickets Completed online purchase

ACQUISITION
○ Create an account Successful sign up, account, or view created

INQUIRY
○ Read reviews Viewed reviews and ratings

ENGAGEMENT
○ Add to favorites Saved product or information to a list
○ Media play Played interactive media, like a video, slideshow, or product demo
○ Share / social connect Shared to a social network or emailed
○ Contribute content Submitted or uploaded a picture, story, or other

○ Custom

[Next step] [Cancel]

✓ Goal setup Edit
Custom

2 Goal description

Name

[   ]

Goal slot ID

[Goal ID 1 / Goal Set 1 ▾]

Type
○ Destination ex: thanks.html
○ Duration ex: 5 minutes or more
○ Pages/Screens per session ex: 3 pages
○ Event ex: played a video

[Next step] [Cancel]

3 Goal details

The next step in destination goal creation responds to the information requests for **Goal description**. We name the goal (in this case we'll call the goal "Download PDF") and we indicate that it is a destination goal by selecting the button labeled **Destination**. The screen now appears as shown below.

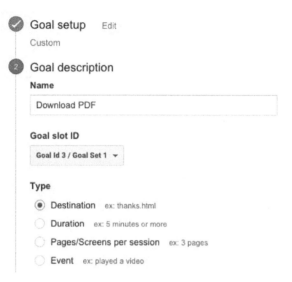

Note that there is an opportunity to give the goal an identification number and to assign it to a goal set. This is done via the pull-down menu beneath **Goal slot ID**. Google Analytics has the ability to group goals together for purposes of data reporting. Thus, it is typically a good practice to group similar goals together in the same set. We can, for example, put all of our destination goals in Set 1.

Clicking on **Next step** brings up **Goal details**, as shown below.

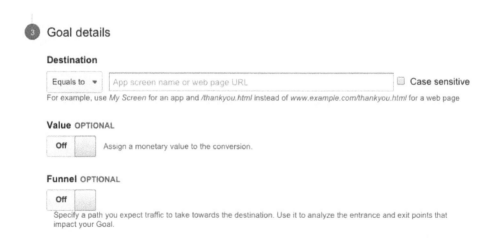

Since this is a **Destination** goal, we need to provide the destination page URL, in this case any page with .pdf. This URL is typed into the top box, labeled "Destination," using regex to define the page. Note that we also indicate that regex is being used via the pull-down menu. We'll leave **Value** and **Funnel** off, as they do not apply in this particular case. When done the screen is as shown below.[72]

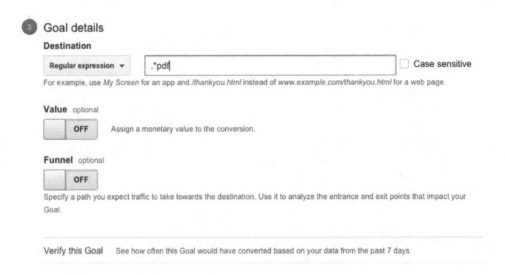

Finally, we'll use the **Verify this Goal** link to confirm that we are doing things properly. We should see the percentage of conversions, assuming any occurred, within the prior seven days. If you receive a 0% conversion message, use the **Content** menus to make certain that this outcome is correct, keeping in mind that a 0% conversion rate can be correct if no one has completed the goal or even visited your site in the past seven days. If everything seems correct, then click on the **Create Goal** button, and your goal will appear in the main goal table, as shown below.

---

[72] This goal converts whenever any PDF is downloaded. The title is not important. We could, however, take a different approach and set up one or more goals that convert when a specific PDF is downloaded.

Section X:
Events

Note that the chapters in this section are intended to work with Universal Analytics (analytics.js). If you are using the Global Site Tag tracking code (gtag.js), please read Chapters 36a to 44a in the Appendix (pages 673 to 738) before returning to Chapter 45 and the remainder of Section XI.

Our discussion of download tracking in Section IX illustrated how Google Analytics can track user-site interactions in more detail than page level reporting. Fortunately, Google Analytics allows us to move beyond tracking a single interaction such as a download to monitor almost any type of user-site interaction. Event tracking is the means used to accomplish this. Event tracking allows us to determine, for example:

-   whether or not a video embedded on our site was played, and if played, whether the video was watched all the way to the end.

-   how much of a specific page was actually read.

-   which elements of a form are roadblocks to completion.

-   which pages/blog entries are responsible for the greatest amount of social sharing.

The nine chapters in this section explore events and demonstrate how critical strategic insights can be obtained from using this feature of Google Analytics.

36

Introduction to Events

Google Analytics explains events as "user interactions with content that can be tracked independently from a web page or a screen load. Downloads, mobile ad clicks, gadgets, Flash elements, AJAX embedded elements and video plays are all examples of actions you might want to track as Events." Additional events that you may want to track include form completions, scroll depth, outbound link tracking, and social sharing interactions.

The tracking of events, similar to the monitoring of downloads, requires us to modify the HTML code to let Google Analytics know the specific event that has been "triggered." Before we address the HTML code itself, it is important to understand the types of information Google Analytics requires in order to track an event. The components of event tracking code are:

ga('send', 'event', 'category', 'action', 'label', value, {'nonInteraction': 1});

where:

- **ga** indicates that this is a Google Analytics command. This element is never modified.

- **send** directs the data to Google Analytics. This element is never modified.

- **event** indicates that the information being sent relates to an event. This element is never modified.

- **category, action, label** and **value** provide details on the event taking place. Only **category** and **action** are required elements. The remaining two elements (**label** and **value**) are optional. The characteristics of each of these is discussed next.

- **{'nonInteraction': 1}** indicates that the event, when activated, should not be treated as a user-site interaction. This is only present when you want the event to be considered a noninteraction.

This chapter discusses each of the components that provide the event's details and the ways in which event information is sent to Google Analytics. Subsequent chapters in this section provide examples of how events can be used to increase insights into user behavior, resulting in more effective strategic analysis and decision-making.

The Category parameter

The **category** parameter represents your highest level of event grouping and is a required element in all event statements. "Downloads", "Videos", and "Social Media Sharing" are examples of category parameters, although you can be as specific or broad as required by your strategic needs. You might, for example, need more specific information on videos viewed than simply collecting all event interactions within the single "Videos" event category. In this case, you could create more specific categories, for example:

- Videos - Movies
- Videos - Music
- Videos - Instructional
- Videos - Testimonial

Similarly, you might want to organize your blog entries and track the extent to which different types of entries are read by site users. Here, rather than having a single category named "Blog", you might create several categories to reflect the content of different blog posts, for example:

- Blog - Metrics
- Blog - HTML coding
- Blog - Research design

We highly recommend that you examine your site's goals and objectives, as well as your own information needs, prior to the creation of categories for use in event tracking. While new categories can always be added, it is a time-consuming process to create and analyze multiple categories and event triggers for essentially the same event. If, for example, you initially call your video tracking category "Video" and later forget and use the plural "Videos", you will have two separate categories for video tracking. A small amount of pre-planning makes a major contribution to ease of analysis and application to decision-making.

The Action parameter

Every event command must contain an **action** parameter that names the specific interaction you are tracking. The action parameter appears right after the category parameter. You might, for example, want to monitor when a video is started as a way of gauging site users' interest in the video's topic. In this circumstance, the **category** would be "video" and the **action** would be "play".

Similar to the category label, while you have complete control over the form and characteristics of the action name, it is always best to develop your naming strategy prior to (rather than during) implementation. In this regard, Google Analytics notes that during the planning process:

- *Action names should be relevant to your strategic information needs.*

Google Analytics' event tracking combines metrics for the same action name across two different categories. If, for example, you associate the action label "Click" with both the "Downloads" category label and the "Videos" category label, the metrics for the "Click" in your reports appears with all interactions tagged with that same name. Thus, you should select different action labels for different categories of events. You might, for example, choose to use the action label "click" for gadget interactions, while reserving the action labels, "Play", "Pause", and "Stop" for video player interactions.

- *Use action names globally to either aggregate or distinguish user interaction.*

For example, you can use "Play" as an action label in the "Videos" category for all videos on your website. In this model, the Google Analytics Top Actions report would provide aggregate data for events with the "Play" action, and you can see how this event for your videos compares to other events for all videos, such as "Pause" or "Stop."

Finally, keep in mind than an action name need not necessarily reflect an overt action. In some cases, such as tracking downloads as an event, the actual event or action name is not as meaningful as other information regarding the event, so you might use the action parameter to track other elements such as a topic or other strategically valuable pieces of information.

The Label parameter

The **label** parameter is an optional component in the event tracking code. Labels allow you to obtain additional information for events that you want to track, such as a video title, the source of the download (for example, text or image) or the video topic. Imagine, for example, that you have three videos on your site. With regard to event tracking, each one of these videos can use the "Videos" category name with the "Play" action, but each could also have a separate identifier (such as the video name or topic) so that they appear as distinct elements in your reports.

The Value parameter

The **value** parameter differs from the previous event command components in that it is a number rather than a word. As such, it is used when you need to assign a numeric value to a tracked event. You could, for example, use this parameter to record the number of seconds it takes for a video to load.

Google Analytics reports an event's values individually as well as its overall average. Imagine, for example, that you are monitoring video download time and that the download times for five unique views were: 5, 5, 8, 10 and 25. Google Analytics would report each of these values as well as the average of 10.3.

The **interaction** parameter is optional. It allows you to determine how you want to calculate the bounce rate for pages on your site that include event tracking.

Google Analytics provides this scenario: Imagine, for example, that "you have a home page with a video embedded on it. It's quite natural that you will want to know the bounce rate for your home page, but how do you want to define that? Do you consider visitor interaction with the home page video an important engagement signal? If so, you would want interaction with the video to be included in the bounce rate calculation, so that sessions including only your home page with clicks on the video are not calculated as bounces. On the other hand, you might prefer a more strict calculation of bounce rate for your home page, in which you want to know the percentage of sessions including only your home page regardless of clicks on the video. In this case, you would want to exclude any interaction with the video from bounce rate calculation."

This where the non-interaction parameter comes into play. Remember that a bounce is defined as a session containing only one interaction hit, such as a single pageview. By default, the event hit sent by the **ga send event** command is considered an interaction hit, which means that it is included in bounce rate calculations. However, when {'**nonInteraction': 1**} is included in the event command, then the event trigger is not considered an interaction hit. Google Analytics notes that "including this command in a session containing a single page tagged with non-interaction events is counted as a bounce - even if the visitor also triggers the event during the session. Conversely, omitting this parameter means that a single-page session on a page that includes event tracking will not be counted as a bounce if the visitor also triggers the event during the same session." Thus, this command should only be used when the event triggers on a noninteraction event, such as an event that takes place when the page loads and therefore requires no active engagement on the part of the site user.[73]

Placing the event HTML code

Let's examine two common uses of event tracking: when a page loads[74] or when a user takes an action such a clicking on a link or starting a video play.

Sending event information when a page loads

Imagine that you want to use events to automatically monitor the characteristics of content entries when each entry is viewed. You want to know, for each piece of content viewed, the author, topic, and month the content was first posted. This information can

---

[73] The source used for the content and quotes in the value and interaction parameter discussion is *Event Tracker Guide* at
https://developers.google.com/analytics/devguides/collection/gajs/eventTrackerGuide.

[74] While this type of event is most commonly associated with page loads, it can also be used to track any type of loading action, for example, the display of a particular image or a video load.

be sent to Google Analytics via an event command when the page loads in a user's browser. The event command would have the following characteristics for a piece of content which discusses analytics and which was authored by Davis in April:

- **category** represents the author "Davis"

- **action** is the blog topic, in this case, "Analytics"

- **label** is the month of the original posting, in this case, "April"

- **value** is not relevant and is omitted

- {**'nonInteraction': 1**} is relevant as this event is triggered when the page loads without any overt user interaction

When an event is activated during a page load, it can be attached to the **<body>** parameter using the **onload** HTML command. This approach makes explicit that event information is being sent when the page first loads. Given these parameters, the complete HTML statement that would activate the event would be:

<body onload = "ga('send', 'event', 'Davis', 'Analytics', 'April', {'nonInteraction': 1});">

The statement would replace the original **<body>** command in my HTML code. When you wish to use this format to send event information when the page loads just substitute your own event information (e.g., category, action etc.) for that shown above.

Sending event information when an interaction occurs

When an event is triggered by an explicit user-site interaction such as a click on a link, the event code is typically attached to the relevant action using the **onClick** command. Let's imagine that you have a number of links that go to sites other than yours, and that you want to create an event whenever your site user clicks on one of these links. This will help you to gauge the relative use and appeal of these links. The event command for one of these links might have the following characteristics:

- **category** identifies the type of action, in this case labeled "Click External Link"

- **action** represents the interaction, in this case, "Click"

- **label** is the link's URL, in this case, "http://www.google.com/analytics"

- **value** is not relevant and is omitted

- {**'nonInteraction': 1**} is not relevant as this event is triggered by an overt user interaction and is omitted

Given these parameters, the complete HTML statement that would activate the event would be:

<a href = "http://www.google.com/analytics" onClick = "ga('send', 'event', 'Click External Link', 'Click', 'www.google.com/analytics'); ">Click here to go to Google Analytics</a>

This link would replace the normal link:

<a href = "http://www.google.com/analytics">Click here to go to Google Analytics</a>

Using JavaScript to send onClick event information

Visit the following page on my travel website:

http://www.googleanalyticsdemystified.com/xqanqeon/chapter36.html

The page automatically sends a set of event information when the page loads. You can see the code for this event by looking at the <body> command within the page's HTML code. Clicking on the link sends you to Google Analytics. However, you'll note that rather than sending you directly, the page informs you that it is redirecting you to the new site. Why don't we send you directly without this notice?

You'll recall from the discussion of download tracking that there are differences across browsers in terms of how they interpret HTML commands. Thus, while the **onClick** command should always send event information directly to Google Analytics, the reality is that depending upon the browser event data may not always be sent. To avoid this problem, an alternative to the **onClick** format is to use JavaScript to send the data associated with an **onClick** event. Similar to the use of JavaScript to track downloads, this approach is browser independent and has a much higher likelihood that your event data initiated by a link click will be sent to Google Analytics.

This approach alters the form of the link and places a small JavaScript script in the <head> section of your page.

The JavaScript script needs to be placed in the HTML code on every page from which you want to track an **onClick** event. This script does not need to be placed on any other pages and it only needs to appear once in a page's HTML code, regardless of the number of **onClick** events appearing on that page. The script should be placed directly after the opening <head> tag, as shown on the top of page 369 (for my site), where the Google Analytics tracking code is in the smaller type and the new JavaScript script is in larger type:

```
<head>

<script>
function redir(category, action, label, value, where)
{
ga('send', 'event', category, action, label, value);
alert("Redirecting");
(window.location=where);
}
</script>

[Additional HTML may appear here]

<script>

(function(i,s,o,g,r,a,m){i['GoogleAnalyticsObject']=r;i[r]=i[r]||function(){
(i[r].q=i[r].q||[]).push(arguments)},i[r].l=1*new
Date();a=s.createElement(o),
m=s.getElementsByTagName(o)[0];a.async=1;a.src=g;m.parentNode.insertBefore(
a,m)  })
(window,document,'script','//www.google-analytics.com/analytics.js','ga');
ga('create', 'UA-50182280-1', 'googleanalyticsdemystified.com');
ga('send', 'pageview');

</script>
```

Note that this script and others we provide do not conflict with each other. As a result, you can include this script and the download tracking script on the same page. Just place one after the other. The order does not matter.

Four instructions are embedded in the script.

- **function redir(category, action, label, value, where)** names the function and information to be collected. This line never needs to be changed.

- **ga('send', 'event', category, action, label, value);** sends the event information to Google Analytics. This line never needs to be changed.

- **alert("Redirecting")** uses a pop-up window to acknowledge the redirect. The time lag between the appearance of this window and the redirect allows time for all browsers to send the information to Google Analytics. You can customize the message by changing the text between the quotation marks. Make certain that any changes leave the beginning and ending quotation marks intact.

- **(window.location=where)** is the redirect location specified in the ink. This line should not be changed.

Next, you'll need to create your link, which will be of the form:

<a href="javascript:redir('category', 'action', 'label', 0,'redirect URL')">Click Here</a>

The link carries all of the event and redirect information. When you use this link, leave all of the wording and punctuation as is except:

- replace the words **category** and **action** with your category and action names. Remember that both names are required. Make certain to leave the ' punctuation.

- replace the word **label** with your label name parameter if one is being used. If you are not using a label parameter, then delete the word **label** leaving the ' punctuation without any spaces.

- leave the 0 if your event has no value; otherwise replace the 0 with your event value.

- replace **redirect URL** with the full URL where the site user is being sent after clicking on the link. As with the prior replacement, make certain to leave the ' punctuation.

You can use this link format anywhere on your site where you want to use **onClick** to trigger an event whose data is sent to Google Analytics. Remember to replace **Click Here** with whatever text you want to appear as the text link.

Let's apply this approach to the situation described previously, where:

- **category** identifies the type of action, in this case labeled "Click External Link"

- **action** represents the interaction, in this case, "Click"

- **label** is location of the redirect, in this case, "google.com/analytics"

- **value** is zero

- **redirect URL** is "http://www.google.com/analytics"

In this case, the link would be:

<a href="javascript:redir('Click External Link', 'Click', 'google.com/analytics', 0,'http://www.google.com/analytics')">Click here to go to Google Analytics</a>

In contrast, if no label parameter were used, the link would be:

<a href="javascript:redir('Click External Link', 'Click','', 0,'http://www.google.com/analytics')"> Click here to go to Google Analytics</a>

Google Analytics places some limits on the collection of event data. Specifically, the first 10 event hits sent to Google Analytics are tracked immediately, after which the tracking rate is limited to one event hit per second.

As the number of events in a session approaches the Google Analytics overall data collection limits, additional events might not be tracked. For this reason, Google recommends that you:

- avoid scripting a video to send an event for every second played and other highly repetitive event triggers,

- avoid excessive mouse movement tracking, and

- avoid time-lapse mechanisms that generate high event counts

37

Events and Content Monitoring

The previous chapter illustrated how events can be used to monitor content consumption and link usage. This chapter and the next address each of these uses of events in more detail. We'll begin with a discussion of content consumption.

We've seen how Google Analytics provides a great deal of page specific information, for example, how often each page is viewed, time on page and bounce rate. This data, however, does not allow us to easily collapse similar types of pages to obtain an overview of how *types* of pages (as a group) are performing in terms of engagement and contribution to goals or transactions. Events allows us to accomplish this.

The scenario

Imagine that our website provides a significant amount of content related to budget travel and travel in Europe, Ireland, and Italy. Each topic is addressed with content created by one of two authors, as shown below:

Davis	Budget
Davis	Europe
Davis	Ireland
Rose	Budget
Rose	Europe
Rose	Italy

Looking across these writers and content, we want to know:

- Regardless of the author, which topics are most viewed and generate the most engagement and positive purchase behaviors?

- Regardless of the topic, which authors are most viewed and generate the most engagement and positive purchase behaviors?

We can use events to answer these strategic questions by placing two events on each page. When this page loads, one event automatically sends author information and the second event sends topic information.

The code used to signal our target events follows standard event code format. The code used to signal a page written by Davis (without worrying about the topic) would be:

ga('send', 'event', 'Written_By','Davis',{'nonInteraction': 1});

while the code for a page written by Rose (again, without worrying about the topic) would be:

ga('send', 'event', 'Written_By','Rose',{'nonInteraction': 1});

Notice that in both of these cases, since we only need to identify the author, the code only provides Category and Action information. No additional information is needed.

Similarly, the code used to signal the content of a specific page (without worrying about the author) would be:

ga('send', 'event', 'Theme','Budget',{'nonInteraction': 1});

ga('send', 'event', 'Theme','Europe',{'nonInteraction': 1});

ga('send', 'event', 'Theme','Ireland',{'nonInteraction': 1});

ga('send', 'event', 'Theme','Italy',{'nonInteraction': 1});

As with the code used to identify the page author, only Category and Action information are required. We also identify each of these events as a noninteraction so as not to distort pageviews and bounce metrics.

Placing the code

We want both author and content information to be sent automatically to Google Analytics once the page loads in a site user's browser. As a result, we attach both event commands to **<body>** using **onload**.

We have six author/topic combinations. The HTML event command for each author/topic combination would be placed on the appropriate page and would be of the form shown in the table on the top of page 375. Notice that there are two event commands attached to **onload**: one to identify the page's author and one to identify the page's topic.

Author/Topic Combination	HTML event code placed on page
Davis/Budget	**<body onload ="ga('send', 'event',** **'Written_By','Davis',{'nonInteraction': 1}); ga('send', 'event',** **'Theme','Budget',{'nonInteraction': 1});">**
Davis/Europe	**<body onload ="ga('send', 'event',** **'Written_By','Davis',{'nonInteraction': 1}); ga('send', 'event',** **'Theme','Europe',{'nonInteraction': 1});">**
Davis/Ireland	**<body onload ="ga('send', 'event',** **'Written_By','Davis',{'nonInteraction': 1}); ga('send', 'event',** **'Theme','Ireland',{'nonInteraction': 1});">**
Rose/Budget	**<body onload ="ga('send', 'event',** **'Written_By','Rose',{'nonInteraction': 1}); ga('send', 'event',** **'Theme','Budget',{'nonInteraction': 1});">**
Rose/Europe	**<body onload ="ga('send', 'event',** **'Written_By','Rose',{'nonInteraction': 1}); ga('send', 'event',** **'Theme','Europe'),{'nonInteraction': 1};">**
Rose/Italy	**<body onload ="ga('send', 'event',** **'Written_By','Rose',{'nonInteraction': 1}); ga('send', 'event',** **'Theme','Italy',{'nonInteraction': 1});">**

Data analysis and insights

We begin by selecting **Top Events** from the **Behavior > Events** menu, which displays all of our event categories (see the table on the top of page 376). The two event category parameters "Theme" and "Written_By" (see lines 8 and 9) correspond to the event categories in our event commands for tracking authors and content, so these are the event categories of interest. Since both the author and theme triggers are sent to Google Analytics at the same time, it is reassuring that both report the same number of events as shown in the **Total Events** column (21 for each in this example). Notice that the number of unique events is almost identical to the number of total events. This reflects the fact that almost all site users read only one blog.

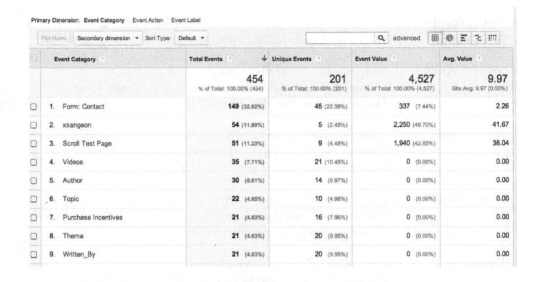

Primary Dimension: Event Category   Event Action   Event Label

	Event Category	Total Events ↓	Unique Events	Event Value	Avg. Value
		454 % of Total: 100.00% (454)	201 % of Total: 100.00% (201)	4,527 % of Total: 100.00% (4,527)	9.97 Site Avg: 9.97 (0.00%)
☐	1. Form: Contact	149 (32.82%)	45 (22.39%)	337 (7.44%)	2.26
☐	2. xxangeon	54 (11.89%)	5 (2.49%)	2,250 (49.70%)	41.67
☐	3. Scroll Test Page	51 (11.23%)	9 (4.48%)	1,940 (42.85%)	38.04
☐	4. Videos	35 (7.71%)	21 (10.45%)	0 (0.00%)	0.00
☐	5. Author	30 (6.61%)	14 (6.97%)	0 (0.00%)	0.00
☐	6. Topic	22 (4.85%)	10 (4.98%)	0 (0.00%)	0.00
☐	7. Purchase Incentives	21 (4.63%)	16 (7.96%)	0 (0.00%)	0.00
☐	8. Theme	21 (4.63%)	20 (9.95%)	0 (0.00%)	0.00
☐	9. Written_By	21 (4.63%)	20 (9.95%)	0 (0.00%)	0.00

The selection of either **Theme** or **Written_By** from the list of Event Categories allows us to see more detailed information on that specific event category. Selecting **Theme** from the list brings up the table below, which shows that across authors Budget travel and Ireland are much more popular topics than Europe (as indicated in the counts in the Total Events column).

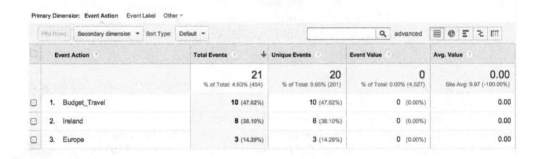

Primary Dimension: Event Action   Event Label   Other ▾

	Event Action	Total Events ↓	Unique Events	Event Value	Avg. Value
		21 % of Total: 4.63% (454)	20 % of Total: 9.95% (201)	0 % of Total: 0.00% (4,527)	0.00 Site Avg: 9.97 (-100.00%)
☐	1. Budget_Travel	10 (47.62%)	10 (47.62%)	0 (0.00%)	0.00
☐	2. Ireland	8 (38.10%)	8 (38.10%)	0 (0.00%)	0.00
☐	3. Europe	3 (14.29%)	3 (14.29%)	0 (0.00%)	0.00

Similarly, the selection of **Written_By** from the initial list of event categories brings up a table that shows that across topics, the materials written by Davis and Rose are read with about equal frequency (see below).

Primary Dimension: Event Action   Event Label   Other ▾

	Event Action	Total Events ↓	Unique Events	Event Value	Avg. Value
		21 % of Total: 4.63% (454)	20 % of Total: 9.95% (201)	0 % of Total: 0.00% (4,527)	0.00 Site Avg: 9.97 (-100.00%)
☐	1. Davis	11 (52.38%)	10 (50.00%)	0 (0.00%)	0.00
☐	2. Rose	10 (47.62%)	10 (50.00%)	0 (0.00%)	0.00

While this information is helpful for future planning, it is not complete. We need to look at our author and content trends in terms of site engagement and subsequent transactions.

Let's return to the page displayed after one of the event categories is selected. The page below is shown when we select **Theme** from the **Behavior > Top Events** data display. On the top of this page, above the line chart (but beneath the **Explorer** tab), are additional data view options: Site Usage and Ecommerce (see below).

Clicking on **Site Usage** brings up the table shown below, in which we see that subsequent site engagement is different for each content area. Budget travel appears to motivate greater site engagement: users who read content on this topic have more Pages/Session and spend more time on the site as reflected in Average Session Duration.

We can conduct the same analysis for authors, which will display the following table. Here, we see mixed results with regard to each author's ability to motivate site engagement. Those who read Davis' content view more site pages, but those who read Rose's content spend more time on the site. (This may simply be a function of Rose's tendency to ramble.)

	Event Action	Sessions	Pages / Session	Avg. Session Duration	% New Sessions
		20 % of Total: 3.12% (642)	4.30 Site Avg: 2.23 (92.51%)	00:00:18 Site Avg: 00:01:18 (-77.06%)	95.00% Site Avg: 84.74% (12.11%)
1.	Davis	10 (50.00%)	5.60	00:00:12	100.00%
2.	Rose	10 (50.00%)	3.00	00:00:24	90.00%

We can conduct a parallel analysis focused on transactions. Selecting **Ecommerce** from the **Explorer** options brings up the following table for the three types of content. Here, we can see that while Budget travel and Ireland are read at nearly equal levels, Budget travel is associated with significantly greater revenue versus the other two content areas.

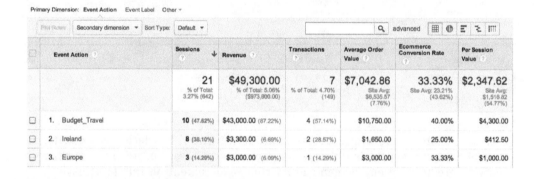

	Event Action	Sessions	Revenue	Transactions	Average Order Value	Ecommerce Conversion Rate	Per Session Value
		21 % of Total: 3.27% (642)	$49,300.00 % of Total: 5.06% ($973,800.00)	7 % of Total: 4.70% (149)	$7,042.86 Site Avg: $8,535.57 (7.76%)	33.33% Site Avg: 23.21% (43.62%)	$2,347.62 Site Avg: $1,516.82 (54.77%)
1.	Budget_Travel	10 (47.62%)	$43,000.00 (87.22%)	4 (57.14%)	$10,750.00	40.00%	$4,300.00
2.	Ireland	8 (38.10%)	$3,300.00 (6.69%)	2 (28.57%)	$1,650.00	25.00%	$412.50
3.	Europe	3 (14.29%)	$3,000.00 (6.09%)	1 (14.29%)	$3,000.00	33.33%	$1,000.00

Conducting a similar analysis for authors, we see that Davis' content has significantly greater association with better transactions versus content created by Rose (see table on page 379). This is especially important since both authors are read at equal rates.

Event Action	Sessions	Revenue	Transactions	Average Order Value	Ecommerce Conversion Rate	Per Session Value
	20 % of Total: 3.12% (642)	$49,300.00 % of Total: 5.06% ($973,800.00)	7 % of Total: 4.70% (149)	$7,042.86 Site Avg: $6,535.57 (7.76%)	35.00% Site Avg: 23.21% (50.81%)	$2,465.00 Site Avg: $1,516.82 (62.51%)
1. Davis	10 (50.00%)	$48,000.00 (97.36%)	5 (71.43%)	$9,600.00	50.00%	$4,800.00
2. Rose	10 (50.00%)	$1,300.00 (2.64%)	2 (28.57%)	$650.00	20.00%	$130.00

All in all, monitoring both authors and themes through events and relating these events to site engagement and purchase behaviors makes a significant contribution to future blog planning. We would likely want to publish relatively more blog entries written by Davis with a focus on budget travel.

Google Analytics Demystified

38

Advanced Events: Link Tracking

Chapter 25 discussed how **In-Page Analytics** tells us how often each link on a page is clicked. However, **In-Page Analytics** cannot help us determine the ultimate effect of different link selections on an outcome variable such as contact, newsletter registration, or purchase. Fortunately, event tracking allows us to transcend this limitation.

This chapter explains how to use events for link tracking.[75]

The scenario

Imagine that we want to learn which of three incentives is most likely to lead to purchase and which of the incentives leads to the highest travel purchase amount. The three incentives, each shown in a different link, are:

- 10% discount on day of purchase,

- free lifetime membership in the travel club, and

- free insurance.

All three incentives appear on the same page.

The JavaScript and HTML event code

Once again, we're going to use a combination of JavaScript and link alteration to ensure that all browsers send the appropriate data to Google Analytics. We follow the same approach as described on pages 368-370.

The JavaScript is placed in the HTML code on the page containing the links we want to track. We place the script (shown on the top of page 382) directly after the Google Analytics tracking code. Note that the alert message now says: **Taking you to your special offer.** as this message is relevant to link action.

---

[75] The techniques discussed in this chapter can be applied to any website link. An event can be created, for example, when a link to a downloadable PDF is selected or a link to an external website is used.

```
<script>
function redir(category, action, label, value, where)
{
ga('send', 'event', category, action, label, value);
alert("Taking you to your special offer");
window.location=where);
}
</script>
```

In this example, the category name is "Purchase Incentives", the action name is "Click" and the label is the name of the special offer. Each link is coded with the same destination page (`purchase.html`). Since we ultimately want to relate link selection with transaction amount event, value is set to zero.

Since there are three options (one for each offer), we will need three links, as shown below.

```
<a href="JavaScript:redir('Purchase Incentives', 'Click', '10% Off',
0,'purchase.html')"> 10% off today</a>
```

```
<a href="JavaScript:redir('Purchase Incentives', 'Click', 'Lifetime membership',
0,'purchase.html')"> Lifetime membership</a>
```

```
<a href="JavaScript:redir('Purchase Incentives', 'Click', 'Free insurance',
0,'purchase.html')"> Free insurance</a>
```

Data analysis and insights

We begin by selecting **Top Events** from the **Behavior > Events** menu, which displays all of our event categories (see below). Since we are interested in looking at link effectiveness we click on "Purchase Incentives", which is the event category parameter.

	Event Category	Total Events	Unique Events	Event Value	Avg. Value
		188 % of Total: 100.00% (188)	**62** % of Total: 93.94% (56)	**4,284** % of Total: 100.00% (4,284)	**22.79** Site Avg: 22.79 (0.00%)
☐	1. xxangeon	54 (28.72%)	5 (8.06%)	2,250 (52.52%)	41.67
☐	2. Scroll Test Page	49 (26.06%)	8 (12.90%)	1,910 (44.58%)	38.98
☐	3. Form: Contact	41 (21.81%)	19 (30.65%)	124 (2.89%)	3.02
☐	4. Purchase Incentives	21 (11.17%)	16 (25.81%)	0 (0.00%)	0.00
☐	5. Download	9 (4.79%)	9 (14.52%)	0 (0.00%)	0.00
☐	6. Videos	8 (4.26%)	4 (6.45%)	0 (0.00%)	0.00
☐	7. Scroll Depth	6 (3.19%)	1 (1.61%)	0 (0.00%)	0.00

The selection of an event category from the list allows us to see the actions associated with that category. In this case, there is only one action associated with the category "Purchase Incentives" (see below).

Clicking upon the **Event Action** "Click" brings up a chart of our three event labels (see below). Here, we can begin to see differences across offers, where "Lifetime Membership" appears to generate the least amount of interest, as reflected in its relatively low number of total and unique events. If you look at the HTML code for each link (see below), you'll notice that event value was set to zero. This decision is reflected in the **Event Value** and **Avg. Value** columns.

We can look at the relationship between offer and transactions by selecting **Ecommerce** from the top of the page just beneath the **Explorer** tab (see below).

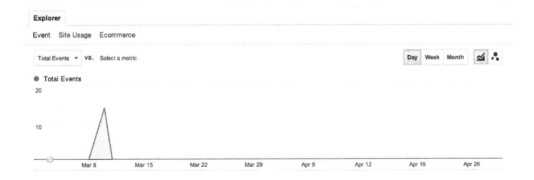

When **Ecommerce** is selected, the table shown below is generated (assuming that you are still on the **Event Label** display). This table shows our three label parameters where we can see significant differences across offers in terms of ultimate purchase behaviors. The number of sessions (equivalent to unique events in the earlier tables) is similar for "Free Insurance" and "10% Off". Both have nearly equal appeal. The effect of these links on purchase behaviors is, however, very different. The "Free Insurance" offer leads to higher overall revenue, more transactions per session, higher average order value, and higher per session value. Clearly this is the more powerful offer and should likely be the only one offered and emphasized.

Primary Dimension: Event Label   Other ▾

Plot Rows | Secondary dimension ▾ | Sort Type: Default ▾ | 🔍 advanced | ▦ ◑ ☰ ⟟ ⊞

Event Label	Sessions ↓	Revenue	Transactions	Average Order Value	Ecommerce Conversion Rate	Per Session Value
	18 % of Total: 2.83% (637)	**$180,100.00** % of Total: 18.49% ($973,800.00)	**30** % of Total: 20.13% (149)	**$6,003.33** Site Avg: $6,535.57 (-8.14%)	**166.67%** Site Avg: 23.39% (612.53%)	**$10,005.56** Site Avg: $1,528.73 (554.50%)
☐ 1. Free_Insurance	8 (44.44%)	$123,900.00 (68.80%)	13 (43.33%)	$9,530.77	162.50%	$15,487.50
☐ 2. 10%_Off	7 (38.89%)	$32,900.00 (18.27%)	11 (36.67%)	$2,990.91	157.14%	$4,700.00
☐ 3. Lifetime_Membership	3 (16.67%)	$23,300.00 (12.94%)	6 (20.00%)	$3,883.33	200.00%	$7,766.67

Event Reporting

The prior chapters introduced you to some of the event-related data reported by Google Analytics. This chapter takes a closer look at this data found within the **Behavior > Events** menu (see below.)

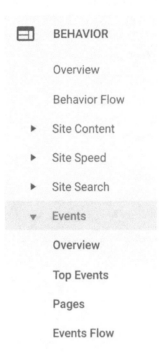

Overview

The **Behavior > Events > Overview** report is organized similar to other overview reports, although the data reported here is focused on events. By default, the line chart on the top of the **Behavior > Events > Overview** page summarizes event activation for the total set of all events that occurred during the specified time period (see the display on the top of page 386). Keep in mind however, that this is summative data that combines all events into a single display and so has very limited usefulness.

Beyond the default display of **Total Events**, you have the option of displaying additional event summary information by using the pull-down menu beneath **Overview** (see below).

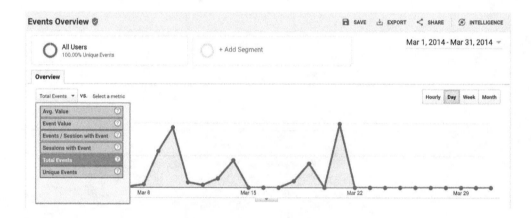

Selecting **Sessions with Event**, for example, displays the chart shown below.

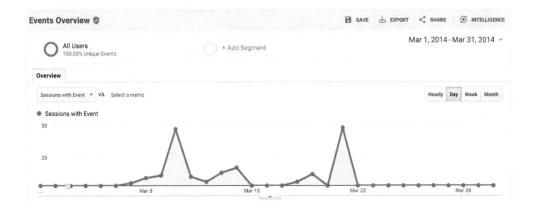

Finally, similar to all line charts, you can chart two dimensions at the same time by using the **Select a Metric** menu option. The chart shown below, for example, simultaneously charts "Sessions with Event" and "Unique Events".

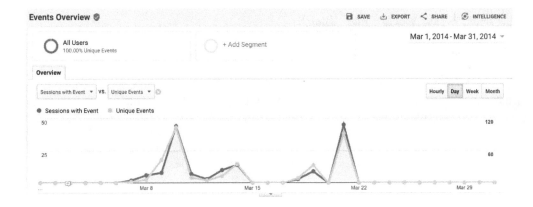

The table on the middle of the **Behavior > Events > Overview** page provides numeric summary information for all events that have taken place during the specified time period (see below). Similar to other **Overview** pages, clicking on any small line graph changes the line chart display to that metric.

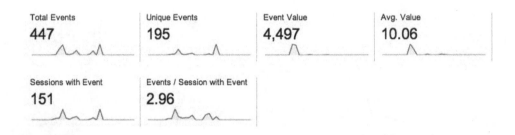

Once again, keep in mind that the preceding data may have limited value because they are summative and not specific to a single event.

You'll recall that you specify an event's category, action, and optional label when you create the event's HTML, for example:

ga('send', 'event', 'Videos', 'Play', 'Blog');

Here, "Videos" is the category, "Play" is the action, and "Blog" is the label.

Google Analytics uses this information to organize your event reports. The chart on the bottom of the **Behavior > Events > Overview** page provides insights into events organized by Category, Action or Label. By default, the display first focuses on events organized by Category parameters. The table shown below, for example, presents my ten categories of events with a percentage distribution by event category. This table is useful when you want to know which event categories are more or less likely to occur.

Top Events		Event Category	Total Events	% Total Events
Event Category	▸	1. Form: Contact	149	33.33%
Event Action		2. xxangeon	54	12.08%
Event Label		3. Scroll Test Page	49	10.96%
		4. Videos	35	7.83%
		5. Author	30	6.71%
		6. Topic	22	4.92%
		7. Purchase Incentives	21	4.70%
		8. Theme	20	4.47%
		9. Written_By	20	4.47%
		10. Download	14	3.13%

view full report

Clicking on the **Event Action** and **Event Label** links on the left-hand side of the table brings up similar charts, only now the charts present Action and Label metrics, as shown in the following two charts.

Top Events		Event Action	Total Events	% Total Events
Event Category		1. field filled	114	25.50%
Event Action	▸	2. scroll reach	103	23.04%
Event Label		3. Davis	52	11.63%
		4. submit	35	7.83%
		5. Play	26	5.82%
		6. Budget	25	5.59%
		7. Click	21	4.70%
		8. Ireland	14	3.13%
		9. Mexico-1	14	3.13%
		10. Budget_Travel	9	2.01%

view full report

Top Events		Event Label	Total Events	% Total Events
Event Category		1. Submit	51	15.89%
Event Action		2. click	35	10.90%
Event Label	▸	3. gender	23	7.17%
		4. http://www.youtube.com/watch?feature=player_embedded&v=ILDxENakeV8	23	7.17%
		5. 10%	19	5.92%
		6. 20%	19	5.92%
		7. 30%	17	5.30%
		8. email	17	5.30%
		9. name	13	4.05%
		10. 40%	10	3.12%

view full report

Top Events

The **Behavior > Events > Top Events** menu option repeats the list of events organized by event category, except now each event category is described not only in terms of total occurrence, but also, in terms of unique occurrence and value (see the table on the top of page 390). Similar to our analysis of pageviews, we can (for any individual event category) divide *total events* by *unique events*. The closer this ratio is to 1.0, the greater the proportion of that event triggered by different users.

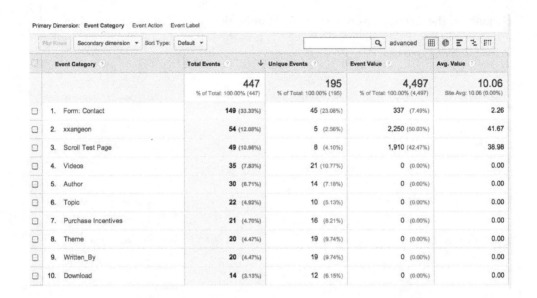

Note that on the top of the above chart **Primary Dimension,** is set to **Event Category**. The other options for selecting the primary dimension allow you to see a chart focused on event actions or event labels, as shown in the table below and on the top of page 391.

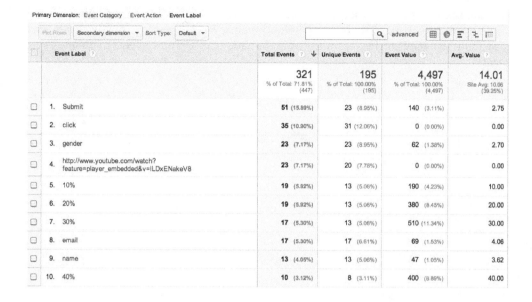

Primary Dimension: Event Category Event Action **Event Label**

Event Label	Total Events ↓	Unique Events	Event Value	Avg. Value
	321 % of Total: 71.81% (447)	**195** % of Total: 100.00% (195)	**4,497** % of Total: 100.00% (4,497)	**14.01** Site Avg: 10.06 (39.25%)
1. Submit	**51** (15.89%)	23 (8.95%)	140 (3.11%)	2.75
2. click	**35** (10.90%)	31 (12.06%)	0 (0.00%)	0.00
3. gender	**23** (7.17%)	23 (8.95%)	62 (1.38%)	2.70
4. http://www.youtube.com/watch?feature=player_embedded&v=ILDxENakeV8	**23** (7.17%)	20 (7.78%)	0 (0.00%)	0.00
5. 10%	**19** (5.92%)	13 (5.06%)	190 (4.23%)	10.00
6. 20%	**19** (5.92%)	13 (5.06%)	380 (8.45%)	20.00
7. 30%	**17** (5.30%)	13 (5.06%)	510 (11.34%)	30.00
8. email	**17** (5.30%)	17 (6.61%)	69 (1.53%)	4.06
9. name	**13** (4.05%)	13 (5.06%)	47 (1.05%)	3.62
10. 40%	**10** (3.12%)	8 (3.11%)	400 (8.89%)	40.00

The advantage of the preceding charts is that they provide information on all events in a single view. The disadvantage, however, is that the presence of multiple events in the same table makes it difficult to see the trends for just one single event category, action or label. Fortunately, this is easy to remedy.

You'll recall that selecting the **Behavior > Events > Top Events** menu option brings up a list of event categories (see the table on the top of the next page). The **Event Category**, "Topic", shown on line 6 of the table, relates to labeling of the topics of content entries that can be read by site users. My site offers multiple content entries addressing both budget travel and Europe. The goal is to see which topic, overall, is the most popular.

Two HTML event commands were used to collect the appropriate metrics:

ga('send', 'event', 'Topic', 'Budget');

ga('send', 'event', 'Topic', 'Europe');

The category "Topic" is the same for both events while the action parameter is used to label the topic as either "Budget" or "Europe."

The table below indicates that there were 22 content entries read (the number of total **Topic** events), with 10 of these being unique events. Thus, it appears that each site user read about two blog entries (as indicated in the ratio of total Topic events to unique Topic events).

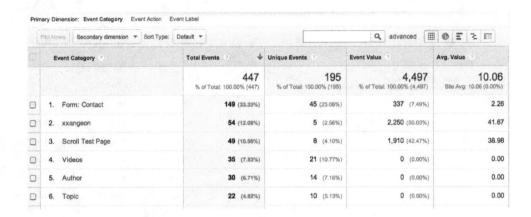

Primary Dimension: Event Category   Event Action   Event Label

	Event Category	Total Events	Unique Events	Event Value	Avg. Value
		447	**195**	**4,497**	**10.06**
		% of Total: 100.00% (447)	% of Total: 100.00% (195)	% of Total: 100.00% (4,497)	Site Avg: 10.06 (0.00%)
1.	Form: Contact	**149** (33.33%)	45 (23.08%)	337 (7.49%)	2.26
2.	xxangeon	**54** (12.08%)	5 (2.56%)	2,250 (50.03%)	41.67
3.	Scroll Test Page	**49** (10.96%)	8 (4.10%)	1,910 (42.47%)	38.98
4.	Videos	**35** (7.83%)	21 (10.77%)	0 (0.00%)	0.00
5.	Author	**30** (6.71%)	14 (7.18%)	0 (0.00%)	0.00
6.	Topic	**22** (4.92%)	10 (5.13%)	0 (0.00%)	0.00

Clicking on the **Topic** category parameter in line 6 of the above table allows us to drill-down into the characteristics of just this one event category. After the category name is selected, a table presenting all actions associated with the category is displayed (see below). The table indicates that while both content topics have been read, there is much more interest in budget versus European travel. Note that the **Event Action** labels are taken directly from the event's HTML commands.

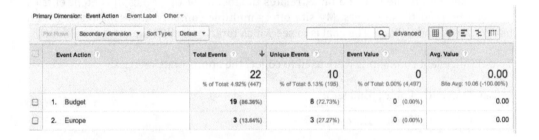

Primary Dimension: Event Action   Event Label   Other ▾

	Event Action	Total Events	Unique Events	Event Value	Avg. Value
		22	**10**	**0**	**0.00**
		% of Total: 4.92% (447)	% of Total: 5.13% (195)	% of Total: 0.00% (4,497)	Site Avg: 10.06 (-100.00%)
1.	Budget	**19** (86.36%)	8 (72.73%)	0 (0.00%)	0.00
2.	Europe	**3** (13.64%)	3 (27.27%)	0 (0.00%)	0.00

Clicking on each link in the **Event Action** column brings up the list of **Event Labels** associated with that action *if* this optional parameter has been used in the HTML code that provides the characteristics of the event. In this case, since no labels were used to describe this event, the resulting table presents no data, as shown below.

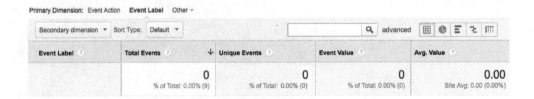

Primary Dimension: Event Action   **Event Label**   Other ▾

Event Label	Total Events	Unique Events	Event Value	Avg. Value
	0	**0**	**0**	**0.00**
	% of Total: 0.00% (9)	% of Total: 0.00% (0)	% of Total: 0.00% (0)	Site Avg: 0.00 (0.00%)

There are times when the same event is triggered from multiple pages. We could, for example, put event links for our special offers on four different pages of the website. In cases such as this, it is important to know the specific pages on which the event is taking place. This information is available though the **Behavior > Events > Pages** menu option, as shown below.

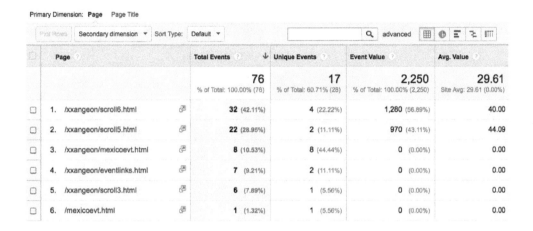

Clicking on the name of any individual page will display metrics for the events that occurred only on that page.

Events flow

The **Events Flow** chart is interpreted similarly to the flow charts discussed earlier, keeping in mind that the data reported here focus on the path to event triggers.

Google Analytics Demystified

Events as Goals

Chapter 39 showed how events are reported as part of the **Behavior > Events** menu option. There are times, however, when you not only want to explore the data available through event reporting, but also, want to consider and examine events as website goals. Google Analytics allows you to do this.

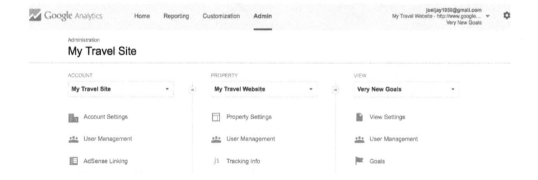

✅ Your HTML code for naming and triggering the event should be present in your web page's HTML code prior to beginning goal creation.

Classifying events as goals

(The beginning of this section recaps the information from the goal creation discussion in Section VIII.)

You create goals through the **Admin** link on the top of every Google Analytics page. Once you click on this link, you'll see your administrator's page (see below). Make certain that the appropriate **Account, Property**, and **View** are displayed, and then click on the **Goals** link in the **View** column.

Your goals summary page will be displayed next (mine is shown below), where all of the goals for the current view are displayed.

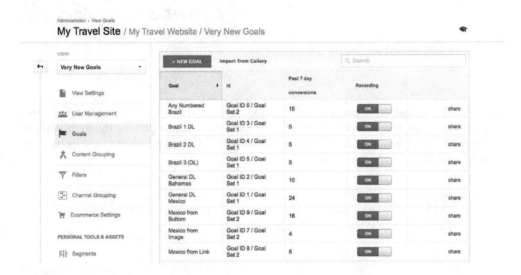

Clicking on **+ New Goal** brings us to the goal creation page (see below). The first step in creating an event-triggered goal is responding to the information requests in **Goal description**. We give the goal a descriptive name by filling in the text box (in this case we'll call the goal "Any Mexico Download") and clicking on **Event** (under **Type**).

Clicking on **Next Step** brings up the display shown on the top of page 397, which collects the target event's characteristics.

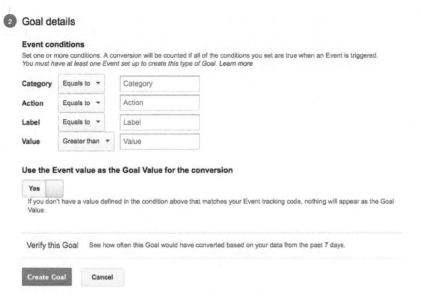

We fill in each text box with the event's characteristics, as shown below. Since there is no value associated with this goal, **Value** is left on the default **Yes**.

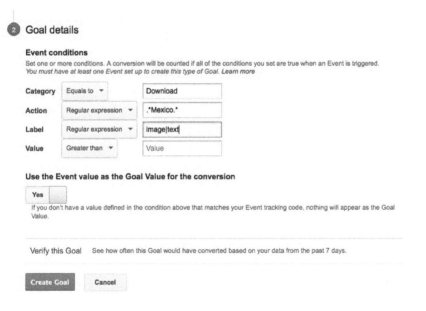

Note that we used regex in two places. First, since we are interested in any download containing the word "Mexico" we use regex to indicate this. Any action parameter containing "Mexico", for example, "Mexico1" or "3cMexico" will satisfy the action condition. Second, we are not interested in differentiating text from image links to the download, so we specify that either one qualifies for inclusion by using the regex | as the "or" statement., in this case "image|text".

Once we verify that all of the information is correct, we click on **Create Goal** to save the goal. The data relevant to this event-triggered goal will be reported identically to any other goals you created.

41

Events and Custom Segments

Chapter 40 discussed how goals can be used to create custom segments and how these segments inform strategic decision-making. Events can be used in a similar way.

Creating a custom segment using events

You create a custom segment using events similarly to the way you created custom segments using goals. You access segments via the **+Add Segment** option on the top of almost any page (located beneath the blue circle **All Sessions** identifier). When you click **+Add Segment**, the advanced segments page displays. You then begin the segment creation process by clicking the **+ New Segment** link. The segment creation page will then display.

Event metrics are incorporated into a segment's definition via the **Conditions** option, which is shown on the bottom left-hand side of the segment creation page. The selection of this option brings up the **Conditions** page, as shown below.

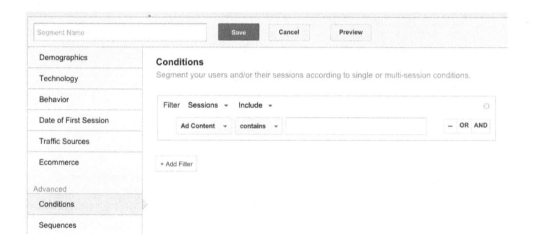

Pulling-down the menu currently labeled **Ad Content** displays both green and blue menu options. Within the green **Behavior** menu are three options related to events: Event Category, Event Action and Event Label (as shown on the top of page 400). The options are more easily found when you order the list alphabetically or use the search box.

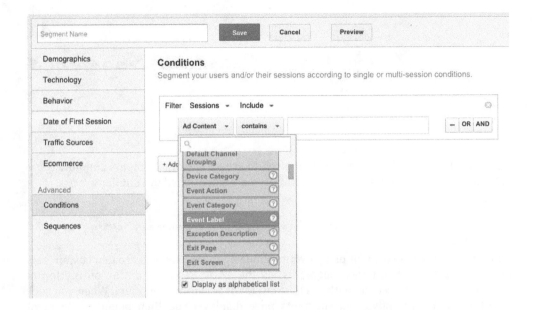

You can select any individual element or combination of elements to create the custom segment.

Let's illustrate the remainder of the process using two different types of events. One event triggers when the page is loaded, and the second event triggers from a link click. Both events have the same category and label:

- **category** is "Travel to Europe"

- **label** is "France"

The **action** for each event is different. The action for the page load event is "Activates on page load", while the action for the link-triggered event is "Activates on link click". We'll use these different actions to define our segments.

Let's create two custom segments based on these events using this scenario:

> Imagine that you have a content page that describes travel to Europe, specifically France. You track those who visit the page through an event that triggers when the page is loaded. The page also provides a link to download a formatted, print-ready PDF of the page's content. You track those who use this link through an event triggered when the link is clicked. Both events have the category, label, and action parameters described above. You want to be able to explore differences between those who visit the page and download versus those who visit the page and do not download.

The first custom segment will include those individuals who visited **both** the page (as this event was triggered automatically by a page visit) and clicked on the download PDF link (as this event was triggered by a user interaction on the same page).

On the initial **Conditions** screen, we begin by selecting **Event Action** from the pull-down menu. Next, we indicate the action that defines a visit to the page as "Activates on page load." Finally, we set the Filters to Users and Include, as shown below:

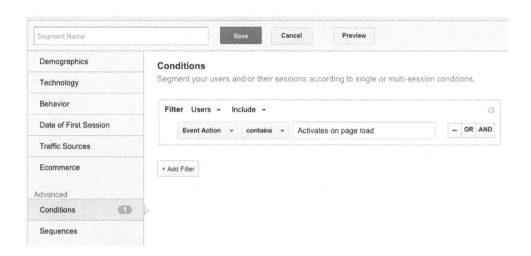

At the moment, the segment consists of all those who visited the page. We now need to restrict this segment to those who also downloaded the PDF. To do this, we click on **+Add Filter** which brings up the display shown below.

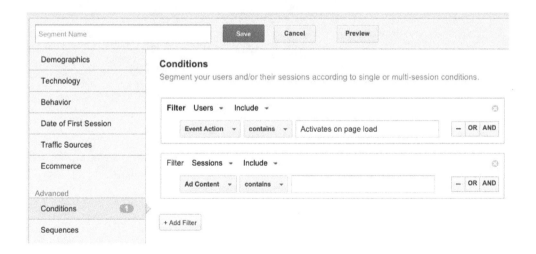

We now add the **Event Action** that signifies a download, i.e., "Activates on link click", as shown below. We again set the filter to **Users** and **Include**. Finally, we name and save the segment.

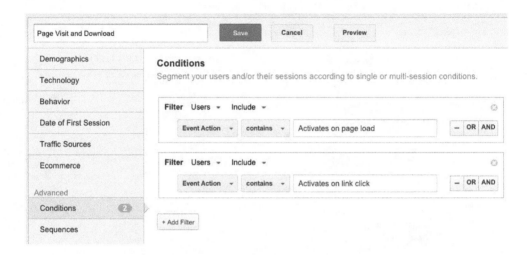

Let's now create the second custom segment. This segment will include all individuals who visited the page, but **did not** click on the link to download the PDF. We begin creating this segment in the same way as the previous segment, identifying all those who visited the page, as shown below.

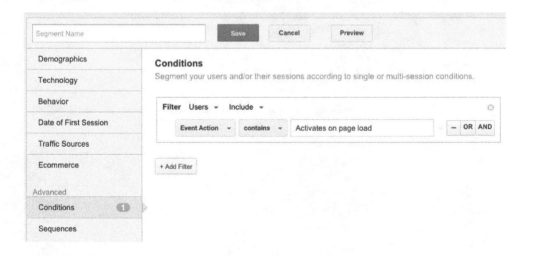

Now we need to restrict this segment to those who did not download the PDF. To do this, we click on **+Add Filter** which brings up the display shown below.

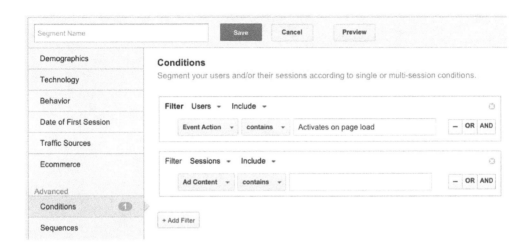

We add the **Event Action** that signifies a download, i.e., "Activates on link click", as shown below.

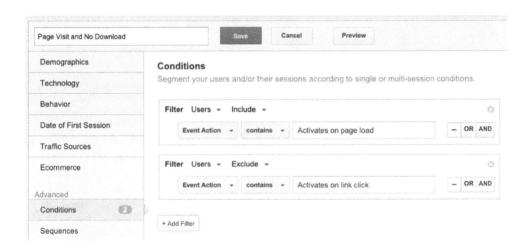

Now, however, while we once again leave **Users** as one of the filters, we select **Exclude**. As a result, the segment will contain only those who visited but did not download. We then name and save the segment.

Once created, event-related custom segments can be used in data analysis in the same way as goal-related custom segments.

42
Advanced Events: Page Scroll

You probably spend a lot of time planning your website or blog content. Ideally, by now you can see how Google Analytics can help you make better content-related strategic decisions by monitoring and reporting users' page and content interactions (for example, pages read, time spent on page, bounce rate, etc.). But without the use of events, Google Analytics cannot tell you *how much* of a page is actually read. This chapter explains how to set up and obtain data on "page scroll depth," the percentage of a page viewed by a site visitor.[76]

This chapter explains how to use events to monitor and analyze page scroll depth.

How the script works

The script first determines the total height of a web page and then divides the page into ten equal parts (10% split). Next, the script finds the height of the site user's browser window and determines how many of those 10% splits the user can see when the page first loads. Finally, the script monitors the user's page scroll. When a user starts to scroll down the page, the script triggers an event when the user reaches each new 10% split.

The event command uses the following code format:

ga('send', 'event', title, 'scroll reach', '10%',10, {'nonInteraction': 1});

Title is the page title that the user is currently on and the 10% changes to reflect the split of the page to which the user has scrolled. The last field is set to **{'nonInteraction': 1}**, which tells Google Analytics to consider each event trigger a non-interaction event. This prevents distorting your pageview, bounce rate and related metrics.

---

[76] We use a script developed by Dave Taylor at http://dave-taylor.co.uk/blog/scroll-reach-tracking-in-google-analytics/) to track scroll depth. We have modified this script, however, to update the event commands to Universal Analytics.

First, you will need to download the following zip file:

http://www.googleanalyticsdemystified.com/resources/google-analytics-scroll-tracking_ua.js.zip

Once obtained and unzipped, upload the file ending in **.js** (not the zip file) to the same directory as your site. Then follow these steps.

1. Select the page you want to monitor. Open the page in your HTML editing program. Make certain your Google Analytics tracking code is present on the page.

2. You need four lines of additional JavaScript on every page for which you want to track scroll depth. The lines are:

   <script src="https://ajax.googleapis.com/ajax/libs/jquery/1.7.2/jquery.min.js">

   </script>

   <script type="text/JavaScript" src="YOUR URL/google-analytics-scroll-tracking_ua.js">

   </script>

   Place these lines just after the opening **<head>** command.

   All that you need to do is replace the phrase **YOUR URL** with the full URL to your site. Make certain that you use the full URL (that is, start with http://) and include the subdirectory, if one is used. My four lines of code would look as follows:

   <script src="https://ajax.googleapis.com/ajax/libs/jquery/1.7.2/jquery.min.js">

   </script>

   <script type="text/JavaScript" src="http://www.googleanalyticsdemystified.com/xqanqeon/google-analytics-scroll-tracking_ua.js">

   </script>

3. Save the page and upload to your server.

Once this is done, you can cut and paste the revised four lines of HTML code to other pages for which you want to track scroll depth. *Make certain that when you use this code on other pages, that you give each new page a descriptive title so that it can be easily identified in your Google Analytics reports.* Additionally, if necessary, you'll need to copy and place the file **google-analytics-scroll-tracking_ua.js** in the same directory/folder as the other pages of your website that you wish to monitor.

We access page scroll data through the **Behavior > Events > Top Events** menu, which brings up a table similar to that shown below. Each website page containing the script will be listed using the page's title. In our case, the only page on which we incorporated the script is titled "Scroll Test Page." This page is shown in line three of the table shown below.

We click on the name of the page of interest to bring up the data related to this category's **Event Action** parameter (see below). The script automatically labels this "scroll reach."

Clicking on **scroll reach** brings up specific scroll information for the page, as illustrated in the table on the top of page 408. Note that the percentages are ordered in terms of **Total Events**, so they may not be listed in strict numeric order.

Because of the way the script works, only some of the data is valuable. The **Average Value** on the right-hand side of the top line reports the average amount of page scrolling. In this case, the average depth of scrolling is 38.04%. So, only a bit more than one-third of the page (on average) is seen. This is not very good at all.

The **Total Events** column provides a distribution of how many individuals reached a certain point on the page. Since this data represents multiple scrolls for each individual, the key column is **Unique Events,** which reports the number of unique users reaching each scroll point. An **Event Label** of 10% or 20% (depending upon a page's total length) typically represents the number of pageviews, as this is the amount of the page that can typically be seen upon page load without the need for scrolling. The numbers decline moving down the **Unique Events** column, representing fewer and fewer individuals who scroll toward the end of the page. We can see that only three individuals read 80% of the page and only two scrolled to the bottom of the page reading 100% of the content. The content is simply not maintaining interest or engagement. We need a revised content strategy to increase the amount of content consumption.

Relating scroll depth to outcome measures

The prior analysis illustrated how scroll depth can help you understand content consumption for any particular page. Scroll depth data can also be used to understand how consumption of a particular page's content is related to important website goals and outcome behaviors. You can, for example, set a goal for a particular scroll depth and then use goal conversion to form custom segments. Or, you can examine how scroll depth is related to important outcome measures such as ecommerce. Let's take a look to see how the latter can be accomplished.

We start with **Events > Top Events** from the left-hand side menu options. This displays a table similar to that shown on the top of page.

Google Analytics Demystified

Primary Dimension: **Event Category** Event Action Event Label

	Event Category ?	Total Events ?	↓ Unique Events ?	Event Value ?	Avg. Value ?
		615	306	6,563	10.67
		% of Total: 100.00% (615)	% of Total: 5.61% (5,451)	% of Total: 100.00% (6,563)	Avg for View: 10.67 (0.00%)
☐	1. Scroll Test Page	147 (23.90%)	21 (6.86%)	5,600 (85.33%)	38.10
☐	2. Form: Xqanqeon - Contact	102 (16.59%)	43 (14.05%)	963 (14.67%)	9.44
☐	3. Video	90 (14.63%)	41 (13.40%)	0 (0.00%)	0.00

The page of interest is "Scroll Test Page" shown on line 1 of the table. We click on **Scroll Test Page,** which displays the table shown below.

	Event Action ?	Total Events ?	↓ Unique Events ?	Event Value ?	Avg. Value ?
		147	21	5,600	38.10
		% of Total: 23.90% (615)	% of Total: 0.39% (5,451)	% of Total: 85.33% (6,563)	Avg for View: 10.67 (256.98%)
☐	1. scroll reach	147 (100.00%)	21 (100.00%)	5,600 (100.00%)	38.10

Clicking on **scroll reach** displays the following table.

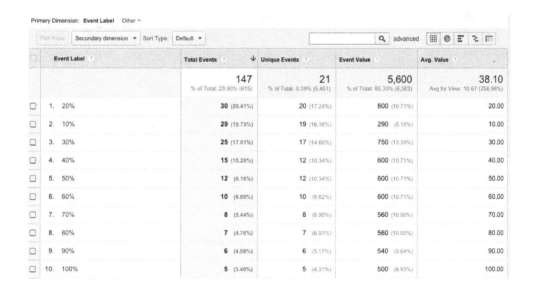

	Event Label ?	Total Events ?	↓ Unique Events ?	Event Value ?	Avg. Value ?
		147	21	5,600	38.10
		% of Total: 23.90% (615)	% of Total: 0.39% (5,451)	% of Total: 85.33% (6,563)	Avg for View: 10.67 (256.98%)
☐	1. 20%	30 (20.41%)	20 (17.24%)	600 (10.71%)	20.00
☐	2. 10%	29 (19.73%)	19 (16.38%)	290 (5.18%)	10.00
☐	3. 30%	25 (17.01%)	17 (14.66%)	750 (13.39%)	30.00
☐	4. 40%	15 (10.20%)	12 (10.34%)	600 (10.71%)	40.00
☐	5. 50%	12 (8.16%)	12 (10.34%)	600 (10.71%)	50.00
☐	6. 60%	10 (6.80%)	10 (8.62%)	600 (10.71%)	60.00
☐	7. 70%	8 (5.44%)	8 (6.90%)	560 (10.00%)	70.00
☐	8. 80%	7 (4.76%)	7 (6.03%)	560 (10.00%)	80.00
☐	9. 90%	6 (4.08%)	6 (5.17%)	540 (9.64%)	90.00
☐	10. 100%	5 (3.40%)	5 (4.31%)	500 (8.93%)	100.00

Now we want to focus on ecommerce data. Beneath the Explorer tab near the top of the page is an option to change the tabular display to ecommerce data (see below).

Explorer

Event   Site Usage   Ecommerce

Clicking on **Ecommerce** changes the prior table to that shown below. The table now reports ecommerce data.

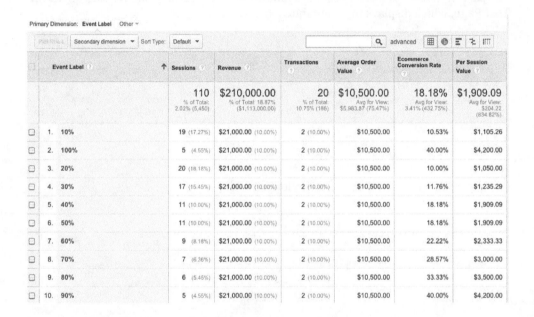

Clicking on the **Ecommerce Conversion Rate** column header changes the table to that shown on the top of page 411, where the lines in the table are ordered by ecommerce conversion rate. Here we can clearly see the effect of the page's content consumption on ecommerce success. Content appears to play an important role since Ecommerce Conversion Rate and Per Session Value both increase in almost direct response to an increase in scroll depth.

Our observation of the data trend seems to indicate a strong relationship between scroll depth and important outcome measures. Should we desire, we can statistically examine this relationship to verify our conclusion. This approach is described in the chapter addendum.

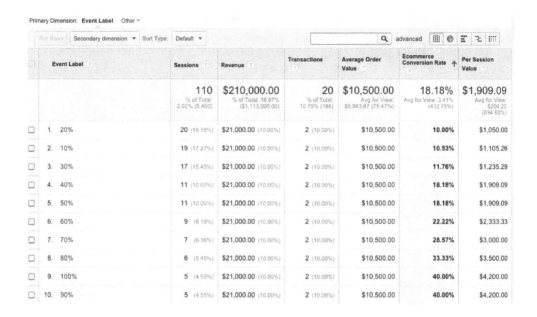

	Event Label ?	Sessions ?	Revenue ?	Transactions ?	Average Order Value ?	Ecommerce Conversion Rate ↑ ?	Per Session Value ?
		110 % of Total: 2.02% (5,460)	$210,000.00 % of Total: 18.87% ($1,113,000.00)	20 % of Total: 10.75% (186)	$10,500.00 Avg for View: $5,983.87 (75.47%)	18.18% Avg for View: 3.41% (432.75%)	$1,909.09 Avg for View: $204.22 (834.82%)
☐ 1.	20%	20 (18.18%)	$21,000.00 (10.00%)	2 (10.00%)	$10,500.00	10.00%	$1,050.00
☐ 2.	10%	19 (17.27%)	$21,000.00 (10.00%)	2 (10.00%)	$10,500.00	10.53%	$1,105.26
☐ 3.	30%	17 (15.45%)	$21,000.00 (10.00%)	2 (10.00%)	$10,500.00	11.76%	$1,235.29
☐ 4.	40%	11 (10.00%)	$21,000.00 (10.00%)	2 (10.00%)	$10,500.00	18.18%	$1,909.09
☐ 5.	50%	11 (10.00%)	$21,000.00 (10.00%)	2 (10.00%)	$10,500.00	18.18%	$1,909.09
☐ 6.	60%	9 (8.18%)	$21,000.00 (10.00%)	2 (10.00%)	$10,500.00	22.22%	$2,333.33
☐ 7.	70%	7 (6.36%)	$21,000.00 (10.00%)	2 (10.00%)	$10,500.00	28.57%	$3,000.00
☐ 8.	80%	6 (5.45%)	$21,000.00 (10.00%)	2 (10.00%)	$10,500.00	33.33%	$3,500.00
☐ 9.	100%	5 (4.55%)	$21,000.00 (10.00%)	2 (10.00%)	$10,500.00	40.00%	$4,200.00
☐ 10.	90%	5 (4.55%)	$21,000.00 (10.00%)	2 (10.00%)	$10,500.00	40.00%	$4,200.00

Real-Time confirmation

You can check to make certain that the scripts are working via Real-Time.

Log into your Google Analytics account and bring up the **Real-Time > Events** display. Click on **Events (last 30 min)**. At the moment the display should be blank as no events have been activated. Now, in a separate browser window (or an entirely different browser, preferably Chrome), visit the page you modified and scroll down the page. In our case the page title is "Scroll Test Page". Revisit your **Real-Time > Events** display where you should see a display similar to that shown below. It is only important that "Scroll Test Page" (or the title of your page) appears in the **Event Category** column.

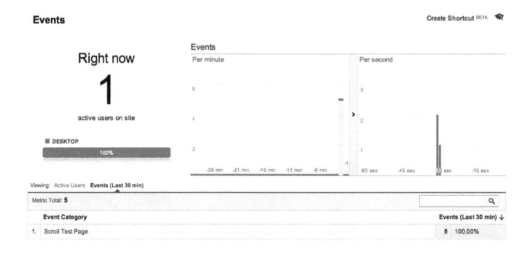

Click on **Scroll Test Page** (or your chosen page title) to bring up the **Event Action** and **Event Label** display (see table below). If data appears in the two columns, then you have successfully monitored scroll depth.

Correlation determines the association between two measures. A common correlation, for example, is that of height and weight. There is a positive correlation between height and weight where taller people tend to be weigh more than shorter people. People of the same height vary in weight, and you can probably think of two people you know where the shorter one weighs more than the taller one. Nevertheless, the average weight of people 5'2" is less than the average weight of people 5'4", and their average weight is less than that of people 5'7", etc. Correlation can tell you the extent to which overall height is related to weight.

Correlations are reported with a measure called a correlation coefficient. This measure ranges from a score of -1 to +1 and consists of two parts.

- The sign of the correlation coefficient, either + or -, indicates the direction of the association.

- The numeric component (which ranges from -1 to + 1 indicates the strength of the association.

If the correlation coefficient equals +1.0 then there is a perfect positive correlation between the two measures. All of the observations fall on a straight line and as one measure increases so does the other. If the correlation coefficient equals -1.0 then there is a perfect negative correlation. Here, all of the observations fall on a straight line but as one measure increases the other decreases. A correlation coefficient of zero indicates a complete absence of a relationship between the two measures.

Let's see how to compute this measure.

First, we'll need to have access to scroll depth and ecommerce measures. Follow the steps described earlier to obtain a table similar to that shown on the top of page 414.

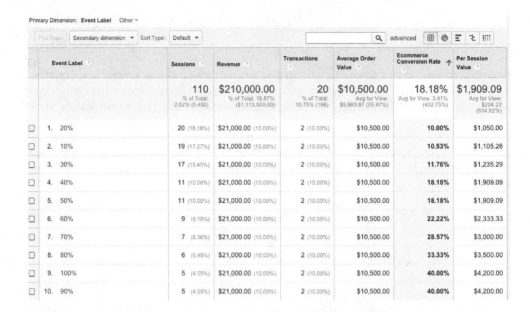

Primary Dimension: Event Label   Other ▾

Event Label	Sessions	Revenue	Transactions	Average Order Value	Ecommerce Conversion Rate ↑	Per Session Value
	110 % of Total: 2.02% (5,450)	$210,000.00 % of Total: 18.87% ($1,113,000.00)	20 % of Total: 10.75% (186)	$10,500.00 Avg for View: $5,983.87 (75.47%)	18.18% Avg for View: 3.41% (432.75%)	$1,909.09 Avg for View: $204.22 (834.82%)
1. 20%	20 (18.18%)	$21,000.00 (10.00%)	2 (10.00%)	$10,500.00	10.00%	$1,050.00
2. 10%	19 (17.27%)	$21,000.00 (10.00%)	2 (10.00%)	$10,500.00	10.53%	$1,105.26
3. 30%	17 (15.45%)	$21,000.00 (10.00%)	2 (10.00%)	$10,500.00	11.76%	$1,235.29
4. 40%	11 (10.00%)	$21,000.00 (10.00%)	2 (10.00%)	$10,500.00	18.18%	$1,909.09
5. 50%	11 (10.00%)	$21,000.00 (10.00%)	2 (10.00%)	$10,500.00	18.18%	$1,909.09
6. 60%	9 (8.18%)	$21,000.00 (10.00%)	2 (10.00%)	$10,500.00	22.22%	$2,333.33
7. 70%	7 (6.36%)	$21,000.00 (10.00%)	2 (10.00%)	$10,500.00	28.57%	$3,000.00
8. 80%	6 (5.45%)	$21,000.00 (10.00%)	2 (10.00%)	$10,500.00	33.33%	$3,500.00
9. 100%	5 (4.55%)	$21,000.00 (10.00%)	2 (10.00%)	$10,500.00	40.00%	$4,200.00
10. 90%	5 (4.55%)	$21,000.00 (10.00%)	2 (10.00%)	$10,500.00	40.00%	$4,200.00

On the top of the page displaying the table is an option to export the table to Excel (see below). Click on **Export** and select your preferred format

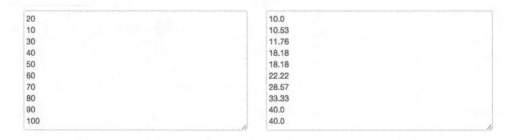

Open the Excel spreadsheet after it downloads to your computer. Note that all of the data from the table is displayed in the Excel download.

We can use the online calculator at pearsoncorrelation.com to compute the correlation coefficient (`http://pearsoncorrelation.com/`). When we arrive at this site, two boxes are displayed. Place the data in the **Event Label** column in the left-hand box, eliminating the percentage sign from the data. You can copy and paste this data from the Excel download or you type the data directly into the box. Next, copy and paste (or retype) the data in the **Ecommerce Conversion Rate** column into the right-hand side box, again eliminating the percentage sign. When you are done, your screen will resemble that shown below, where the data is from the table on the top of this page.

20	10.0
10	10.53
30	11.76
40	18.18
50	18.18
60	22.22
70	28.57
80	33.33
90	40.0
100	40.0

Press the **Calculate Pearson Correlation Coefficient** button beneath the data. Doing so should display a graph of your data as well as the correlation coefficient (shown on the very top of the display page). Remember, a coefficient closer to either -1 or +1 indicates a strong relationship. My data is shown below where the statistical analysis shows a very strong positive relationship between scroll depth and the Ecommerce Conversion Rate. The more people read the more likely they are to make a purchase.

We can perform a similar analysis to explore the relationship between scroll depth and **Per Session Value**. Here, we leave the scroll depth data in the left-hand box alone but we place the Per Session Value data in the right-hand box (eliminating the dollar sign). Pressing the **Calculate Pearson Correlation Coefficient** button beneath the data displays the screen shown below. There is also a very strong positive relationship between these two measures, again indicating that more content consumption is strongly associated with higher per session value.[77]

---

[77] As your interpret your data remember that correction is a measure of association and does not evaluate cause and effect. Correlation indicates the relationship between two measures. A strong positive correlation only indicates that the two variables generally move together in the same direction. Correlation, however, does indicate causation; it does not indicate that one variable causes the movement in the other or that a change in one will result in a change in the other.

43

Advanced Events:
Form Completion Monitoring

Forms are an important way by which a website or blog begins to establish or reinforce a relationship with a site user. Google Analytics can tell us the number of people who send a form as well as the number of people who go to the form page without sending the form. Without events, however, Google Analytics cannot provide any diagnostics for the form itself. The use of events allows us to determine which fields (if any) are problematic and lead to form abandonment.[78]

How the script works

The script examines your form and identifies each field that needs a response. Every time a form user selects a pull-down menu option, clicks on a button or begins to fill in a text field, the script sends an event trigger to Google Analytics telling it that the field had been accessed and some information provided. In a perfect world, the number of page-views for the page containing the form should equal the number of users completing every field on the form and then pressing the Submit button. The greater the discrepancy between the number of pageviews and form field/submit completion, the greater problem with the form. Keep in mind that this script only checks to see if a field has been accessed, it does not check for valid field entries.

Installing the script

First, you will need to download the following zip file:

http://www.googleanalyticsdemystified.com/resources/form-tracking-google-analytics-v2.js.zip

Once obtained and unzipped, upload the file ending in **.js** (not the zip file) to the same directory as your site. Then follow these steps.

---

[78] We will be using a script developed by Dave Taylor at http://dave-taylor.co.uk/blog/form-analytics-plugin-for-google-analytics/ to track form completion. We have modified this script, however, to make the event commands appropriate to Universal Analytics.

1. Select the page you want to monitor. Open the page in your HTML editing program. Make certain your Google Analytics tracking code is present on the page.

2. You need four lines of additional JavaScript on every page for which you want to track form completion. The lines are:

   `<script src="https://ajax.googleapis.com/ajax/libs/jquery/1.7.2/jquery.min.js">`

   `</script>`

   `<script type="text/JavaScript" src="YOUR URL/form-tracking-google-analytics-v2.js">`

   `</script>`

   All that you need to do is replace the phrase **YOUR URL** with the full URL to your site. Make certain that you use the full URL (that is, start with http://) and include the subdirectory, if one is used. My four lines of code would therefore look as follows:

   `<script src="https://ajax.googleapis.com/ajax/libs/jquery/1.7.2/jquery.min.js">`

   `</script>`

   `<script type="text/JavaScript" src="http://www.googleanalyticsdemystified.com/xqanqeon/form-tracking-google-analytics-v2.js">`

   `</script>`

   Place the lines after the opening head tag: **<head>**

3. Save the page and upload to your server.

Once this is done, you can cut and paste the revised code to other pages for which you want to track form completion. *Make certain that when you use this code on other pages, that you give each new page a descriptive title.* Additionally, you'll need to copy and place the file **form-tracking-google-analytics-v2.js** in the same directory/folder as the other pages of your website that contain forms you wish to monitor.

Interpreting the data

The first thing we need to determine is how may unique individuals visited our contact page. We can obtain this information by selecting **Behavior > Site Content > All Pages** from the left-hand side menu options. When we do this, we discover that 26 people visited our contact page (see line 8 and the data presented in the "Unique Views" column in the table shown on the top of page 418).

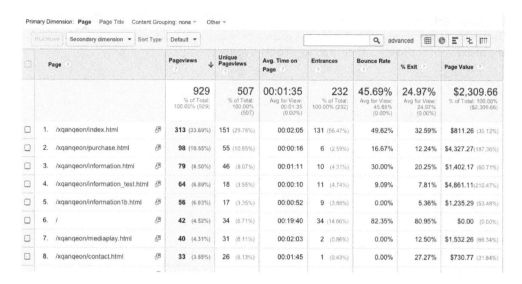

Next, we access form completion data through the **Behavior > Events > Top Events** menu option, which in this case brings up the table shown below.

The script automatically names the event category "Form: [Name of Page]", so in our case we are interested in the information relevant to the "Form: Contact" **Event Category**. Clicking on this link displays the page's **Event Action** table (see below).

We then click on the **field filled** link to bring up the detailed report table (see below). Because site users can fill in, leave and return to revise any field, we are interested in the **Unique Events** column rather than the **Total Events** column.

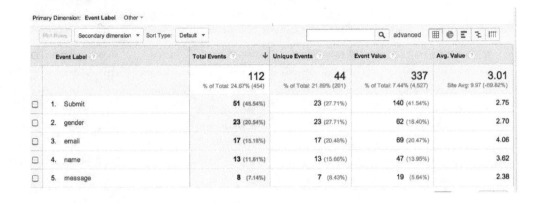

Each of the four fields in our contact form, as well as the submit button, are shown in the table. The data indicate problems with nearly all the form fields. The extent of these problems can be viewed in the context of the 23 people who submitted the form.

- The only information provided by all users was gender. Only about 74% of those submitting the form provided an email address. (This was calculated by dividing 17 by 23.) This is particularly distressing, as there is no opportunity to follow-up without an email address.

- The remaining two form fields, name and message, are even more problematic. Only about half of those submitting the form provided a name and only about one third provided a message.

Clearly our form isn't working. We need to redesign the form to facilitate the sending of complete information.

Real-Time confirmation

You can check to make certain that the scripts are working via Real-Time.

You can confirm that form monitoring is working (that is, triggering when a user completes a form field) by using the **Real-Time** menu's **Events** option. We'll illustrate how this works by using our form, located at:

http://www.googleanalyticsdemystified.com/xqanqeon/contact.html.

Notice how the form contains four fields: gender, name, email, and message.

We begin by logging into our Google Analytics account and bringing up the **Real-Time >
Events** display. Once we arrive, we click on **Events (last 30 min)**. At the moment, the
display is blank as no events have been activated. Now, in a separate browser window we
visit the contact page where we indicate the appropriate gender and move to the email
field.

Now we re-visit our **Real-Time > Events** display where we see the display shown
below, where "Form: Xqanqeon - Contact" is shown in the **Event Category** column.

Clicking on "Form: Xqanqeon - Contact" displays the table shown on the top of page 422,
where the first completed form field (shown in the **Event Label** column) is presented.
(We make certain that we select **Events (Last 30 min)** as the display parameter.)

We now complete the form and press **Submit**. When we revisit the **Real-Time** display we see the table shown below which indicates that all the fields have been completed and the form has been submitted.

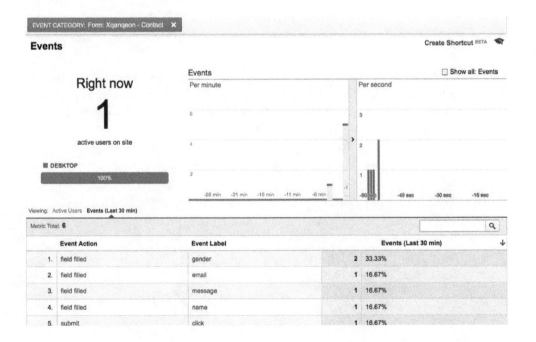

44

Advanced Events: Video Monitoring

We can all see contribution of multimedia to consumer engagement and subsequent website success. While Google Analytics can tell us the number of people who come to a page with video, without the use of events it cannot tell us whether the video was started and how much of the video was viewed. The script described in this chapter can accomplish this.

How the script works

The script monitors a user's interaction with a video embedded on one of your website pages.[79] The script sends an event notification to Google Analytics when the video is started and at 25%, 50%, 75% and 100% of total video time actually viewed. The category label is set to "Video", the action label records the amount viewed, and the event label identifies the video by its YouTube identifier and name.

Installing the script

First, you will need to obtain the following files:

videoscan1.js

videoscan2.js

You can obtain these files by downloading the following zip file:

http://www.googleanalyticsdemystified.com/resources/videomonitor.zip

Once obtained and unzipped, upload the two files ending in **.js** (not the zip file or the unzipped folder) to the same directory as your site. Then follow these steps.

1. Select the page containing the video you want to monitor.

---

[79] The script used to monitor video engagement was written by Stephane Hamel at http://www.cardinalpath.com/youtube-video-tracking-with-gtm-and-ua-a-step-by-step-guide. We have, however, made some modifications to eliminate the use of Google Tag Manager present in the original script in order to send event data to Google Analytics using the **ga (send, event)** command. We have also simplified/reduced the data sent to Google Analytics in an effort to simplify data interpretation. Finally, this script only works with YouTube video.

2. You need six lines of additional JavaScript on every page for which you want to track video viewing. The lines are:

```
<script src="https://ajax.googleapis.com/ajax/libs/jquery/1.7.2/jquery.min.js">

</script>

<script type="text/JavaScript" src="YOUR URL/videoscan1.js">

</script>

<script type="text/JavaScript" src="YOUR URL/videoscan2.js">

</script>
```

All that you need to do is replace the phrase **YOUR URL** with the full URL to your site. Make certain that you use the full URL (that is, start with http://) and include the sub-directory, if one is used. My six lines of code would therefore look as follows:

```
<script src="https://ajax.googleapis.com/ajax/libs/jquery/1.7.2/jquery.min.js">

</script>

<script type="text/JavaScript"
src="http://www.googleanalyticsdemystified.com/xqanqeon/videoscan1.js">

</script>

<script type="text/JavaScript"
src="http://www.googleanalyticsdemystified.com/xqanqeon/videoscan2.js">

</script>
```

Place these lines after the opening head tag: **<head>.**

3. Place the following lines of code at the place in your HTML code where you want the video to appear:

```
<iframe width="420" height="315"
src="http://www.youtube.com/embed/YTubeAddress?enablejsapi=1" frameborder="0"
allowfullscreen></iframe>
```

The commands in this line pull the video from YouTube and place the video on your web page. Replace the phrase "YTubeAddress" with the unique address of the video when it plays at YouTube.

For example, if you view a video at:

`https://www.youtube.com/watch?v=MHgj2UzqMx0`

you would replace "YTubeAddress" with "MHgj2UzqMx0" and the line would read:

**<iframe width="420" height="315"
src="http://www.youtube.com/embed/MHgj2UzqMx0?enablejsapi=1"
frameborder="0" allowfullscreen></iframe>**

Complete this step with the video of your choice. You have the option of altering the width and height of the video player by changing the width and height specifications in the beginning of the line. Leave the remainder of the line untouched.

4. Save the page and upload to your server.

Once this is done, you can cut and paste the revised code from steps 2 and 3 to other pages for which you want to track video viewing. *Make certain that when you use this code on other pages, that you give each new page a descriptive title.* Additionally, you'll need to place the files **videoscan1.js** and **videoscan2.js** in the same directory/folder as the other pages on your website that contain video playback you want to monitor.

Interpreting the data

We access the video interaction data through the **Behavior > Events > Top Events** menu option, which brings up the display shown below. Video play data will always be shown in the line labeled **Video** (which in this case is line 1 of the table). Note that since this script uses "Video" as the category label, you should avoid using this name to label other category events.

Event Category	Total Events	↓ Unique Events	Event Value	Avg. Value
	124 % of Total: 100.00% (124)	59 % of Total: 24.69% (239)	725 % of Total: 100.00% (725)	5.85 Avg for View: 5.85 (0.00%)
1. Video	29 (23.39%)	10 (16.95%)	0 (0.00%)	0.00
2. Scroll Test Page	27 (21.77%)	5 (8.47%)	700 (96.55%)	25.93
3. Davis	14 (11.29%)	9 (15.25%)	0 (0.00%)	0.00

The data presented in the table above is summative; it reports metrics for all of the videos viewed on our site. We can see that there were 10 unique user sessions in which any video was started (as reported in the Unique Events column). Clicking **Video** brings up summary interaction information.

Summary interaction metrics are reported via **Event Action** (see first column in the table below). Again focusing on Unique Events, we can see that of the 10 people starting *any* video (as reported in the first line labeled 0%), only three watched at least 25% (as reported in line two) and only one made it all the way through (as reported in line 4).

Clicking on the Event Label option above the table allows us to see the specific videos viewed (see below).

You can click on the name of any specific video to see viewing data for just that video. Let's focus on the Il Divo video reported on line one. When we click on this video title the report changes to focus on just this one video, as shown in the table on the top of page 427.

Event Action	Total Events ↓	Unique Events	Event Value	Avg. Value
	17 % of Total: 13.71% (124)	7 % of Total: 2.93% (239)	0 % of Total: 0.00% (725)	0.00 Avg for View: 5.85 (-100.00%)
☐ 1. 0%	10 (58.82%)	7 (53.85%)	0 (0.00%)	0.00
☐ 2. 25%	3 (17.65%)	2 (15.38%)	0 (0.00%)	0.00
☐ 3. 50%	2 (11.76%)	2 (15.38%)	0 (0.00%)	0.00
☐ 4. 100%	1 (5.88%)	1 (7.69%)	0 (0.00%)	0.00
☐ 5. 75%	1 (5.88%)	1 (7.69%)	0 (0.00%)	0.00

This video is really failing to hold viewer's attention. Of the seven people who started the video (as shown on line one of the Unique Events column) only two make it to the 25% viewing mark and only one watched the video all the way to the end.

Similar to page scroll depth, we can examine important outcome measures in terms of video viewership. The table below relates this video's viewership to ecommerce metrics (see below). The video not only fails to hold viewers' attention but regardless of the amount viewed, no one exposed to the video made a purchase.

Primary Dimension: **Event Action** Other ▾

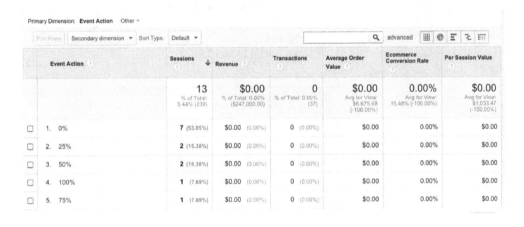

Event Action	Sessions ↓	Revenue	Transactions	Average Order Value	Ecommerce Conversion Rate	Per Session Value
	13 % of Total: 5.44% (239)	$0.00 % of Total: 0.00% ($247,000.00)	0 % of Total: 0.00% (37)	$0.00 Avg for View: $6,675.68 (-100.00%)	0.00% Avg for View: 15.48% (-100.00%)	$0.00 Avg for View: $1,033.47 (-100.00%)
☐ 1. 0%	7 (53.85%)	$0.00 (0.00%)	0 (0.00%)	$0.00	0.00%	$0.00
☐ 2. 25%	2 (15.38%)	$0.00 (0.00%)	0 (0.00%)	$0.00	0.00%	$0.00
☐ 3. 50%	2 (15.38%)	$0.00 (0.00%)	0 (0.00%)	$0.00	0.00%	$0.00
☐ 4. 100%	1 (7.69%)	$0.00 (0.00%)	0 (0.00%)	$0.00	0.00%	$0.00
☐ 5. 75%	1 (7.69%)	$0.00 (0.00%)	0 (0.00%)	$0.00	0.00%	$0.00

Finally, keep in mind that video viewership metrics, like all events, can be used to form custom segments for more in-depth analyses.

Real-Time confirmation

You can use Real-Time to confirm that the scripts are working.

Log into your Google Analytics account and bring up the **Real-Time > Events** display. Click on **Events (last 30 min)**. At the moment, the display should be blank as no events have been activated. Now, in a separate browser window (or an entirely different browser, preferably Chrome), visit the page with the video you want to monitor. Watch the video all the way through. Now, revisit your **Real-Time > Events** display where you should see a display similar to that shown below.

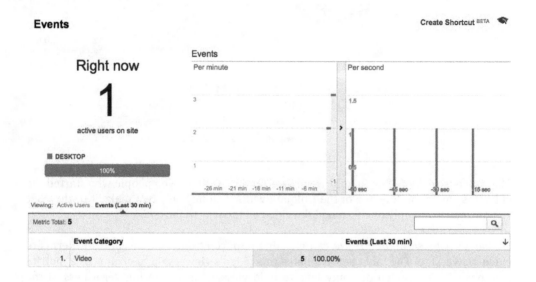

Click on the **Video** link in the **Event Category** column. This should generate a table similar to that shown on below. Here, in the **Event Action** column, you can see that one person started the video (as reflected in the top 0% line), and that one person watched the video all the way to the end (as reflected in the 25%, 50%. 75% and 100% lines). The name of the video being viewed is shown in the **Event Label** column.

Section XI:
Referral and the Acquisition Menu

One of the most powerful aspects of Google Analytics is the ability to track the origin of website users and to relate various origins to the broad range of data provided, including page interactions, goal conversions, conversion paths, user characteristics, and transactions. The chapters in this section help you better understand how to find and apply this data to your own strategic decision-making.

- Chapters 45 to 47 discuss the form, interpretation and application of data available through three **Acquisition** options: Overview, All Traffic, and Search Console.

- Chapter 48 shows you the power of treating your own links as referral sources.

- Chapter 49 shows you how evaluate the relative success of your current and past campaigns.

- Chapter 50 explores Social data in the Acquisition menu.

Google Analytics Demystified

45

The Acquisition Menu: Overview

The **Acquisition** menu provides insights regarding the sources of your website users, as illustrated below. All of the metrics (with the exception of AdWords) provided by the **Acquisition** menu are discussed as follows: The **Overview** option is discussed in this chapter. Subsequent chapters address **All Traffic** (Chapter 46), **Search Console** (Chapter 47), and **Campaigns** (Chapters 49). **Social** is discussed in Chapters 50.

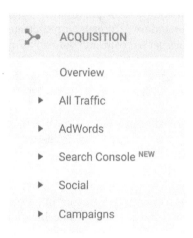

Overview

Acquisition > Overview helps you understand how your website traffic is influenced by broad groupings of referral sources called **Channels**. These default channels are pre-defined by Google Analytics and consist of the following:[80]

Direct   Sessions in which a user typed your website URL directly into his/her browser or who came to your site via a bookmark.

Email   Sessions that are manually tagged with a medium of "email". (Tagging is explained in Chapter 48)

---

[80] Source for channel definitions is "About MCF funnels" at
https://support.google.com/analytics/answer/1191184?hl=en.

Organic Search	Non-paid users to your site whose sessions begin at a search engine. Google tracks organic traffic from itself and most of the major search engines such as Bing and Yahoo. You can, if necessary, add additional search engines.
Paid Search	Traffic from the AdWords Search Network or other search engines identified as "cost per click" or "pay per click."
Referral	Traffic from other websites not identified as social that link to your site.
Social	Traffic from social media sites like Facebook, Linkedin and Twitter. Referrals from links tagged as ads are not considered a social referral.
Display	Interactions with a medium of "display" or "cpm". This channel also includes AdWords interactions with the ad distribution network set to "content" but excluding ad format of "text".
Paid Search	Traffic from the AdWords Search Network or other search engines, with a medium of "cpc" or "ppc" .
Other Advertising	Sessions that are tagged with a medium of "cpc", "ppc", "cpm", "cpv", "cpa", "cpp", "content-text", "affiliate" (excluding paid search).

These existing channels should meet the needs of most websites and blogs. You can, however, visit and edit these channels by selecting **Channel Settings** in the **View** column of your Administrator's page. At this same location, if needed, you can create new channels that reflect your unique information or strategic needs.[81] When you create a Custom Channel Grouping at the user level or create a new Channel Grouping in a view, you:

- Can immediately select it in reports,

- Can apply it retroactively and see historical data classified by your new channel definitions, and

- Change how reports display your data, without changing the data itself.

There are two parts to the **Acquisition > Overview** display. The data on the top of the page provides summary data via pie and line charts (see the top of page 433). By default, the pie chart displays the distribution of site sessions in terms of the default channel groupings, while the line charts display sessions and conversions over time.

---

[81] For guidance on the creation of custom channel groupings see: About Channel Groupings at https://support.google.com/analytics/answer/601009 and Create and Use MCF Groupings at https://support.google.com/analytics/answer/1250116.

The data displayed in these charts are determined by the two pull-down menus on the top left-hand side of the page. The **Primary Dimension** menu allows you to change the data source from Channels to other types of direct and referral traffic, as shown below.

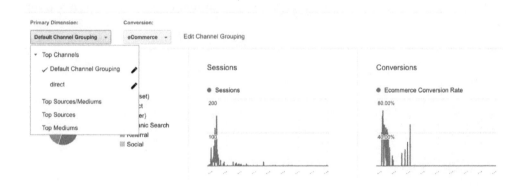

Selecting **Top Sources**, for example, changes the pie chart report to the distribution of specific sources of website traffic (see below).

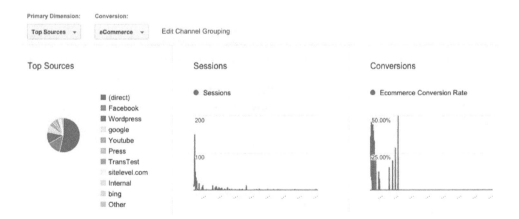

The **Conversion** pull-down menu allows you to change the outcome measure to all goals or any specific goal (see below).

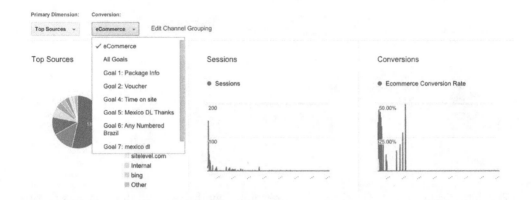

Selecting "Goal 4: Time on site", for example, changes the display to that shown below. This selection changes the line chart shown on the far right-hand side of the page as well as the Conversion data shown in the tables on the bottom of the **Acquisition > Overview** page.

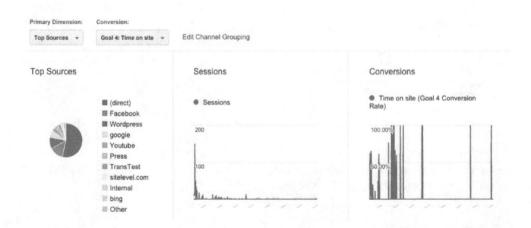

The numeric table shown on the bottom of the **Acquisition > Overview** report provides detailed information on the selected Primary Dimension/Goal Option combination. The table shown on the top of page 435, for example, is the default table reporting the **Default Channel Grouping** (from the **Primary Dimension** pull-down menu) and **Ecommerce** (from the **Conversion** pull-down menu). Three types of information are provided: Acquisition, Behavior and Conversion.

	Acquisition			Behavior			Conversions		
	Sessions	% New Sessions	New Users	Bounce Rate	Pages / Session	Avg. Session Duration	Ecommerce Conversion Rate	Transactio...	Revenue
Hostname	628	83.60%	525	35.99%	2.46	00:00:47	27.71%	174	$1,651,800.00
1 ▪ Direct	337			34.42%			26.41%		
2 ▪ (Other)	228			37.28%			36.84%		
3 ▪ Organic Search	46			43.48%			2.17%		
4 ▪ Referral	12			41.67%			0.00%		
5 ▪ Social	5			0.00%			0.00%		

The top summary line indicates that overall, in terms of **Acquisition**, I've had 628 site sessions of which 83.60% were new sessions. This makes sense given that the vast majority of our site users (525) were new users. The **Behavior** block of data provides information on average bounce rate (35.99%), average pages per session (2.46), and average session duration (47 seconds). Finally, the **Conversions** block of data provides information on total conversions (174), total revenue ($1,651,800), and average ecommerce conversion rate (27.71%).

Beneath the top summary line is a list of each referral source, as defined by the **Primary Dimension** pull-down menu. Since the previous table was defined by the Default Channel Grouping, each top referral channel is shown. Here, we want to compare channels to each other to determine each channel's relative strengths and weaknesses. The table indicates that most of my site traffic is Direct with Organic Search providing some additional secondary support. Very little of my traffic is due to Social or third-party referrals. Whether these levels are good or bad depends upon my specific website goals. In my case, these low levels are unsatisfactory in light of my efforts and goals so, as a result, I need to develop strategies to increase referrals from these sources.

Clicking on the name or bar chart for a channel brings you to the **Acquisition > All Traffic > Channels** report for that specific channel. We discuss the main and channel-specific **Acquisition > All Traffic > Channels** reports in the next chapter.

46

The Acquisition Menu: All Traffic

The **Acquisition > All Traffic** menu option provides access to four types of metrics, as shown below.

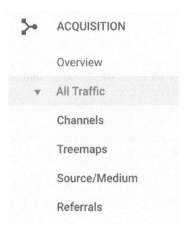

Channels

The **Acquisition > All Traffic > Channels** menu option displays the same broad channels as **Acquisition > Overview**, but more detailed data is provided for each channel grouping. You'll recall that the numeric table on the **Acquisition > Overview** page used bars to indicate relative size. The **Acquisition > All Traffic > Channels** option moves beyond this visual to display the underlying data, as shown below. Note that the three categories of data shown in the **Acquisition > Overview** report are also shown here.

Default Channel Grouping	Acquisition			Behavior			Conversions eCommerce ▼		
	Sessions ↓	% New Sessions	New Users	Bounce Rate	Pages / Session	Avg. Session Duration	Ecommerce Conversion Rate	Transactions	Revenue
Hostname	628 % of Total: 25.66% (2,447)	83.60% Avg for View: 94.24% (-11.29%)	525 % of Total: 22.77% (2,306)	35.99% Avg for View: 73.11% (-50.78%)	2.46 Avg for View: 1.45 (69.39%)	00:00:47 Avg for View: 00:00:30 (59.58%)	27.71% Avg for View: 7.11% (289.65%)	174 % of Total: 100.00% (174)	$1,651,800.00 % of Total: 100.00% ($1,651,800.00)
1. Direct	337 (53.66%)	94.36%	318 (60.57%)	34.42%	2.58	00:01:00	26.41%	89 (51.15%)	$842,400.00 (51.00%)
2. (Other)	228 (36.31%)	74.56%	170 (32.38%)	37.28%	2.17	00:00:18	36.84%	84 (48.28%)	$798,400.00 (48.34%)
3. Organic Search	46 (7.32%)	67.39%	31 (5.90%)	43.48%	2.63	00:00:45	2.17%	1 (0.57%)	$11,000.00 (0.67%)
4. Referral	12 (1.91%)	8.33%	1 (0.19%)	41.67%	3.08	00:04:18	0.00%	0 (0.00%)	$0.00 (0.00%)
5. Social	5 (0.80%)	100.00%	5 (0.95%)	0.00%	4.60	00:00:17	0.00%	0 (0.00%)	$0.00 (0.00%)

Once again, we can see the dominance of Direct as the primary way users initiate site sessions, and we can see the secondary importance of referrals from Organic Search. Now, however, we can examine these findings in more detail. Here's is what we learn from the table (ignoring Social, which has too small a base to allow reliable conclusions to be drawn):

-   Direct is more likely, and Referral and Organic Search are less likely, to consist of new sessions.

-   The bounce rate for Organic Search and Referral is higher than for Direct and (Other).

-   The ecommerce conversion rate for Organic Search and Referral is much lower than for Direct and (Other).

-   In terms of gross revenue, Direct and (Other) are clearly the most important, accounting for nearly all revenue. Organic Search and Referral generate very little additional revenue.

Overall, it seems that Organic Search and Referral traffic are not making a significant contribution to website or business success, especially when we look at metrics such as the Ecommerce conversion rate which is independent of the size of the referral group.

We can focus on one specific aspect of each channel by selecting an option from beneath the Explorer tab. My options, which include the site goals I've created, are shown below.

Selecting **Site Usage** displays the table shown below.

Default Channel Grouping	Sessions	Pages / Session	Avg. Session Duration	% New Sessions	Bounce Rate
Hostname	628 % of Total: 25.66% (2,447)	2.46 Avg for View: 1.45 (69.39%)	00:00:47 Avg for View: 00:00:30 (59.56%)	83.60% Avg for View: 94.24% (-11.29%)	35.99% Avg for View: 73.11% (-50.78%)
1. Direct	337 (53.66%)	2.58	00:01:00	94.36%	34.42%
2. (Other)	228 (36.31%)	2.17	00:00:18	74.56%	37.28%
3. Organic Search	46 (7.32%)	2.63	00:00:45	67.39%	43.48%
4. Referral	12 (1.91%)	3.08	00:04:18	8.33%	41.67%
5. Social	5 (0.80%)	4.60	00:00:17	100.00%	0.00%

The selection of **Ecommerce** from beneath the Explorer tab generates the table shown below.

Default Channel Grouping	Sessions ↓	Revenue	Transactions	Average Order Value	Ecommerce Conversion Rate	Per Session Value
Hostname	628 % of Total: 25.66% (2,447)	$1,651,800.00 % of Total: 100.00% ($1,651,800.00)	174 % of Total: 100.00% (174)	$9,493.10 Avg for View: $9,493.10 (0.00%)	27.71% Avg for View: 7.11% (289.65%)	$2,630.25 Avg for View: $675.03 (289.65%)
1. Direct	337 (53.66%)	$842,400.00 (51.00%)	89 (51.15%)	$9,465.17	26.41%	$2,499.70
2. (Other)	228 (36.31%)	$798,400.00 (48.34%)	84 (48.28%)	$9,504.76	36.84%	$3,501.75
3. Organic Search	46 (7.32%)	$11,000.00 (0.67%)	1 (0.57%)	$11,000.00	2.17%	$239.13
4. Referral	12 (1.91%)	$0.00 (0.00%)	0 (0.00%)	$0.00	0.00%	$0.00
5. Social	5 (0.80%)	$0.00 (0.00%)	0 (0.00%)	$0.00	0.00%	$0.00

Finally, if you have goals created for your site, you can also look at goal-related metrics by selecting the appropriate **Goal Set** from beneath the Explorer tab, as shown below.

Default Channel Grouping	Sessions ↓	Goal Conversion Rate	Per Session Goal Value	Package Info (Goal 1 Conversion Rate)	Voucher (Goal 2 Conversion Rate)	Time on site (Goal 4 Conversion Rate)	Mexico DL Thanks (Goal 5 Conversion Rate)
Hostname	628 % of Total: 25.66% (2,447)	65.29% Avg for View: 25.79% (153.18%)	$2.61 Avg for View: $0.76 (241.91%)	3.18% Avg for View: 0.82% (289.65%)	0.16% Avg for View: 0.04% (289.65%)	35.35% Avg for View: 18.02% (96.15%)	0.00% Avg for View: 0.00% (0.00%)
1. Direct	337 (53.66%)	66.77%	$2.67	2.67%	0.30%	37.39%	0.00%
2. (Other)	228 (36.31%)	54.82%	$2.31	3.95%	0.00%	28.51%	0.00%
3. Organic Search	46 (7.32%)	91.30%	$3.52	4.35%	0.00%	45.65%	0.00%
4. Referral	12 (1.91%)	75.00%	$2.08	0.00%	0.00%	41.67%	0.00%
5. Social	5 (0.80%)	180.00%	$5.00	0.00%	0.00%	100.00%	0.00%

Clicking on the name of a channel brings up a table that displays metrics for only that channel. The metrics displayed are specified by the option selected beneath the Explorer tab. This is the same outcome as clicking on a channel name or metric in the **Acquisition > Overview** table.

Below is the **Acquisition > All Traffic > Channels** summary table.

Default Channel Grouping	Acquisition			Behavior			Conversions eCommerce ▼		
	Sessions ↓	% New Sessions	New Users	Bounce Rate	Pages / Session	Avg. Session Duration	Ecommerce Conversion Rate	Transactions	Revenue
Hostname	628 % of Total: 25.66% (2,447)	83.60% Avg for View: 94.24% (-11.29%)	525 % of Total: 22.77% (2,306)	35.99% Avg for View: 73.11% (-50.76%)	2.46 Avg for View: 1.45 (69.39%)	00:00:47 Avg for View: 00:00:30 (59.58%)	27.71% Avg for View: 7.11% (289.65%)	174 % of Total: 100.00% (174)	$1,651,800.00 % of Total: 100.00% ($1,651,800.00)
1. Direct	337 (53.66%)	94.36%	318 (60.57%)	34.42%	2.58	00:01:00	26.41%	89 (51.15%)	$842,400.00 (51.00%)
2. (Other)	228 (36.31%)	74.56%	170 (32.38%)	37.28%	2.17	00:00:18	36.84%	84 (48.28%)	$798,400.00 (48.34%)
3. Organic Search	46 (7.32%)	67.39%	31 (5.90%)	43.48%	2.63	00:00:45	2.17%	1 (0.57%)	$11,000.00 (0.67%)
4. Referral	12 (1.91%)	8.33%	1 (0.19%)	41.67%	3.08	00:04:18	0.00%	0 (0.00%)	$0.00 (0.00%)
5. Social	5 (0.80%)	100.00%	5 (0.95%)	0.00%	4.60	00:00:17	0.00%	0 (0.00%)	$0.00 (0.00%)

Clicking on **Referral**, for example, brings up a table that provides summary information for Referral traffic organized by Hostname (see below).

Source	Acquisition				Behavior			Conversions eCommerce ▼		
	Sessions ↓	% New Sessions	New Users	Bounce Rate	Pages / Session	Avg. Session Duration	Ecommerce Conversion Rate	Transactions	Revenue
Hostname	12 % of Total: 0.49% (2,447)	8.33% Avg for View: 94.24% (-91.16%)	1 % of Total: 0.04% (2,306)	41.67% Avg for View: 73.11% (-43.01%)	3.08 Avg for View: 1.45 (112.29%)	00:04:18 Avg for View: 00:00:30 (772.98%)	0.00% Avg for View: 7.11% (-100.00%)	0 % of Total: 0.00% (174)	$0.00 % of Total: 0.00% ($1,651,800.00)
1. sitelevel.com	8 (66.67%)	0.00%	0 (0.00%)	62.50%	1.38	00:00:01	0.00%	0 (0.00%)	$0.00 (0.00%)
2. search.freefind.com	2 (16.67%)	50.00%	1 (100.00%)	0.00%	4.50	00:07:40	0.00%	0 (0.00%)	$0.00 (0.00%)
3. ss540.fusionbot.com	2 (16.67%)	0.00%	0 (0.00%)	0.00%	8.50	00:18:02	0.00%	0 (0.00%)	$0.00 (0.00%)

Selecting a different metric such as Ecommerce, from the **Explorer** tab changes the metrics reported. Below are the Ecommerce metrics for Referral Hostnames.

Source	Sessions	↓ Revenue	Transactions	Average Order Value	Ecommerce Conversion Rate	Per Session Value
Hostname	12 % of Total: 0.49% (2,447)	$0.00 % of Total: 0.00% ($1,651,800.00)	0 % of Total: 0.00% (174)	$0.00 Avg for View: $9,493.10 (-100.00%)	0.00% Avg for View: 7.11% (-100.00%)	$0.00 Avg for View: $675.03 (-100.00%)
1. sitelevel.com	8 (66.67%)	$0.00 (0.00%)	0 (0.00%)	$0.00	0.00%	$0.00
2. search.freefind.com	2 (16.67%)	$0.00 (0.00%)	0 (0.00%)	$0.00	0.00%	$0.00
3. ss540.fusionbot.com	2 (16.67%)	$0.00 (0.00%)	0 (0.00%)	$0.00	0.00%	$0.00

As you generate tables, it is important to keep track of the channel data that is being reported and the channel-specific options for additional data reports. Understanding this relationship and its impact on the types of data available/reported will greatly enhance your ability to strategically apply this information. Let's illustrate this for each of the channels driving traffic to my site, primarily focusing on Acquisition and Behavior metrics.

We start with the table that reports default channel metrics.

Default Channel Grouping	Acquisition				Behavior			Conversions eCommerce ▼		
	Sessions ↓	% New Sessions	New Users	Bounce Rate	Pages / Session	Avg. Session Duration	Ecommerce Conversion Rate	Transactions	Revenue
Hostname	628 % of Total: 25.66% (2,447)	83.60% Avg for View: 94.24% (-11.29%)	525 % of Total: 22.77% (2,306)	35.99% Avg for View: 73.11% (-50.78%)	2.46 Avg for View: 1.45 (69.38%)	00:00:47 Avg for View: 00:00:30 (59.56%)	27.71% Avg for View: 7.11% (289.65%)	174 % of Total: 100.00% (174)	$1,651,800 % of Total: 100 ($1,651,80
1. Direct	337 (53.66%)	94.36%	318 (60.57%)	34.42%	2.58	00:01:00	26.41%	89 (51.15%)	$842,400.00 (51
2. (Other)	228 (36.31%)	74.56%	170 (32.38%)	37.28%	2.17	00:00:18	36.84%	84 (48.28%)	$798,400.00 (48
3. Organic Search	46 (7.32%)	67.39%	31 (5.90%)	43.48%	2.63	00:00:45	2.17%	1 (0.57%)	$11,000.00 (0
4. Referral	12 (1.91%)	8.33%	1 (0.19%)	41.67%	3.08	00:04:18	0.00%	0 (0.00%)	$0.00 (0
5. Social	5 (0.80%)	100.00%	5 (0.95%)	0.00%	4.60	00:00:17	0.00%	0 (0.00%)	$0.00 (0

Clicking on **Direct** brings up the Landing Page table shown below. This table provides useful insights into where those directly accessing my site enter the site. As expected, most site sessions begin on my home page. However, the site engagement metrics for these sessions (higher Pages/Session and Avg. Session Duration, lower Bounce Rate) are all more positive than the average. The impact of this outcome on subsequent purchase behavior certainly needs to be investigated. We can use segments and **Behavior > Site Content > Landing Pages** to further explore this phenomenon.

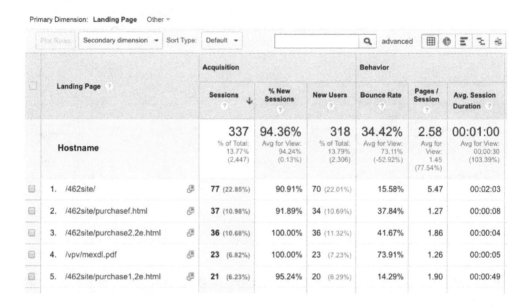

Selecting **Organic Search** from the table on the bottom of page 440 initially displays the organic search results that led to site visits (see below). Lines 2 and 3 both reflect the unique labels used when creating the site.

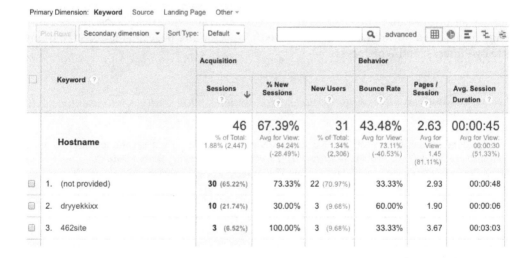

You'll notice that the largest keyword category is **(not provided)**. Google's shift to secure, encrypted search in late 2013 has resulted in many Google Analytics users seeing the largest segment of their Keyword report being **(not provided)**. This is because encrypted Google searches don't pass the keyword data through to websites, eliminating the ability to see which keywords are bringing users to the site or blog.[82]

Two additional options appear on the top of the Organic channel report. **Source** allows you to see which search engines are sending traffic to your site. The table below, for example, indicates that almost all of my organic search referrals are coming via Google search. However, I don't know the relative value of each referral. Selecting Ecommerce from beneath the Explorer tab changes the table to that shown below.

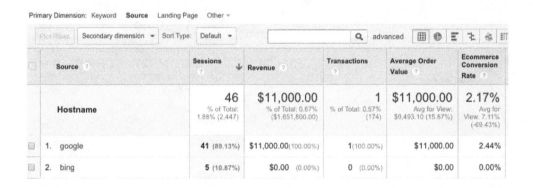

Neither referral source is impressive as reflected in the low number of transactions, Average Order Value and Ecommerce Conversion rate.[83] Organic search typically makes an important contribution to website success, I need to determine why this is not the case for my site. (We'll look at the data provided by the Landing Page option above the table) in the context of Search Engine Optimization, discussed in the next chapter.)

Finally, selecting **Social** from the table on the bottom of page 440 displays the social referrals that led to site visits (see table on the top of page 443). Here, we can see that almost all of my (few) social referrals are coming from Pinterest. Selecting **Landing Page** from above the table allows me to see the specific site pages being referred to my site by Pinterest and Wordpress.

---

[82] Several individuals have proposed workarounds to this problem. Their recommendations can be found at: *Google '(Not Provided)' Keywords: 10 Ways to Get Organic Search Data* at http://searchenginewatch.com/article/2297674/Google-Not-Provided-Keywords-10-Ways-to-Get-Organic-Search-Data; *Smarter Data Analysis of Google's https (not provided) change: 5 Steps* at http://www.kaushik.net/avinash/google-secure-search-keyword-data-analysis/; *How to Unlock Your 'Not Provided' Keywords in Google Analytics* at http://blog.kissmetrics.com/unlock-keyword-not-provided/.

[83] This data is fictitious and is not intended to be interpreted as a reflection of actual performance.

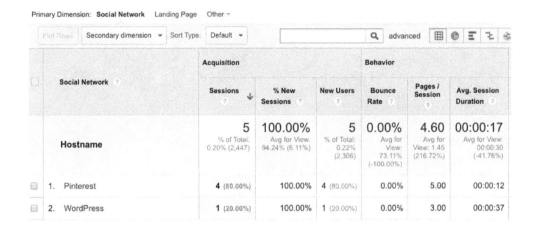

Social Network ?	Acquisition			Behavior		
	Sessions ↓ ?	% New Sessions ?	New Users ?	Bounce Rate ?	Pages / Session ?	Avg. Session Duration ?
Hostname	5 % of Total: 0.20% (2,447)	100.00% Avg for View: 94.24% (6.11%)	5 % of Total: 0.22% (2,306)	0.00% Avg for View: 73.11% (-100.00%)	4.60 Avg for View: 1.45 (216.72%)	00:00:17 Avg for View: 00:00:30 (-41.76%)
1. Pinterest	4 (80.00%)	100.00%	4 (80.00%)	0.00%	5.00	00:00:12
2. WordPress	1 (20.00%)	100.00%	1 (20.00%)	0.00%	3.00	00:00:37

Treemaps

Google explains the value of Treemaps as follows:

"The Treemaps report lets you visually explore trends in your Acquisition channels so you can quickly and intuitively develop hypotheses about your incoming traffic. Treemaps represent data as rectangles. The size and color of each rectangle represent different metrics, so you can combine different aspects of your data into a single visualization. Treemaps are a good hypothesis-generation tool because they can help expose the relative importance of, and the relationship between, different entities."[84]

You access Treemaps via **Acquisition > All Traffic > Treemaps**. This menu option displays a Treemap with the default metrics of Sessions and Pages/Session, as shown on the top of page 444. Each rectangle in the report represents an individual acquisition channel. Given the current metrics selected, the larger the box, the greater the number of sessions initiated via that channel. Additionally, the color of the rectangle shows how the segment performs on the secondary dimension, in this case, Pages/Session. Here the scale runs from green (high) to red (low).[85] The box in the lower right-hand corner, for example, is small but dark green. This indicates that Referrals (the channel represented by the box) is low on the first metric (sessions) because the box is small, but high on the second metric (Pages/ Session) because the box is dark green.

---

[84] This quote and other content in this section are from *Treemaps Reports* at https://support.google.com/analytics/answer/6180144?hl=en.

[85] The scale is reversed for Bounce Rate.

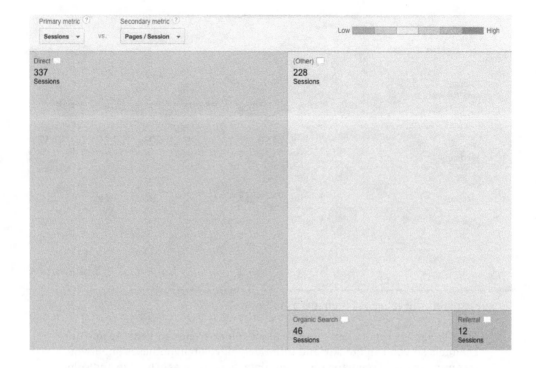

Placing your mouse your over the dialog box icon in any rectangle provides the actual data for the two metrics used to define the Treemap (see below).

Clicking in any specific rectangle provides more detailed information for that specific channel. Clicking in the **Direct** rectangle, for example, provides the display shown on the top of page 445. Here we can see the number of sessions and Pages/Session associated with individual pages with direct site access.

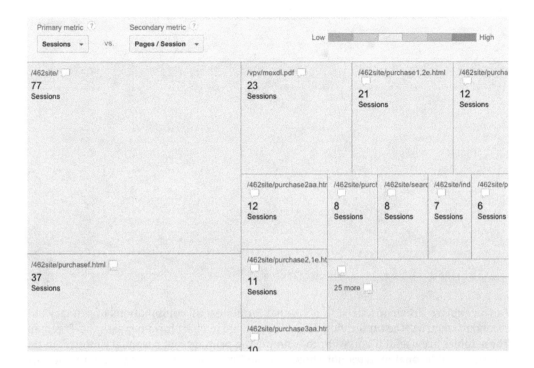

You are not restricted to the primary and secondary metrics displayed in the initial Treemap. There are two pull-down menus at the top of the Treemap display (see below).

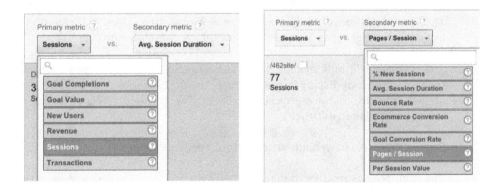

Changing the metric in either menu changes the Treemap display, as shown in the figure on the top of page 446, where the primary metric is Goal Completions and the secondary metric is Average Session Duration.

As you explore Treemaps, keep in mind that for almost all combinations of primary and secondary metrics, the underlying data are available in chart form beneath the Treemap. These tables are useful if you want to examine the primary and secondary metrics in the context of additional metrics not shown in the Treemap. Finally, these data tables are identical to those that can be obtained through the **Acquisition > All Traffic > Channels** reports.

Google notes that there are currently several limitations to the Treemap report:

- The Treemaps report is only available in web reporting views. This report is not available in other types of reporting views, such as mobile app views.

- The treemap will only display up to 16 rectangles at a time. If you have more than 15 entities to display in the treemap, the first 15 appear as individual rectangles, and the rest are grouped together. The grouped category appears as one rectangle labeled "Other".

- Segmentation is not yet supported in the Treemaps report.

- The color scale is relative to the weighted average of all entities. The color spectrum moves from red to green, and the intensity of the color that appears in each rectangle is relative within your report. There are no absolute or fixed values associated with any specific color or shade of color.

The **Acquisition > All Traffic > Source/Medium** report provides user referral metrics categorized by:

- **Source**: This is the search engine or referring domain from which traffic to your site originated, for example, *google* (the search engine) or *google.com* (the domain). Direct traffic that does not originate from search-engine results or a referring link in a domain is identified as *(direct)*.

- **Medium**: This is the type of web content that contained the link to your site. For example, when traffic originates from links in organic search results, then the medium is identified as *organic*; when the traffic originates from links in banner ads, then the medium is identified as *banner*. The medium for direct traffic for which there is no originating link is identified as *(none)*.

We discuss Source/Medium in the context of link tagging and the **Acquisition > All Traffic > Campaign** menu in Chapters 48 and 49.

Referrals

The information in the **Acquisition > All Traffic > Referrals** report (see below) lets you see which domains (and pages in those domains) are referring traffic to your site, how much traffic they're referring, which landing pages are the most popular referral destinations, and the extent to which those referred visitors interact with your site. As a result, this report not only lets you see traffic levels from expected sources, but also lets you see whether there are unexpected sources (such as a review, blog post, or news story) that you didn't know about.

Source		Acquisition			Behavior			Conversions	eCommerce ▾	
		Sessions ↓	% New Sessions	New Users	Bounce Rate	Pages / Session	Avg. Session Duration	Ecommerce Conversion Rate	Transactions	Revenue
Hostname		17 % of Total: 0.69% (2,447)	35.29% Avg for View: 94.24% (-62.55%)	6 % of Total: 0.26% (2,306)	29.41% Avg for View: 73.11% (-59.77%)	3.53 Avg for View: 1.45 (143.01%)	00:03:07 Avg for View: 00:00:30 (533.35%)	0.00% Avg for View: 7.11% (-100.00%)	0 % of Total: 0.00% (174)	$0.00 % of Total: 0.00% ($1,651,800.00)
1.	sitelevel.com	8 (47.06%)	0.00%	0 (0.00%)	62.50%	1.38	00:00:01	0.00%	0 (0.00%)	$0.00 (0.00%)
2.	pinterest.com	4 (23.53%)	100.00%	4 (66.67%)	0.00%	5.00	00:00:12	0.00%	0 (0.00%)	$0.00 (0.00%)
3.	search.freefind.com	2 (11.76%)	50.00%	1 (16.67%)	0.00%	4.50	00:07:40	0.00%	0 (0.00%)	$0.00 (0.00%)
4.	ss540.fusionbot.com	2 (11.76%)	0.00%	0 (0.00%)	0.00%	8.50	00:18:02	0.00%	0 (0.00%)	$0.00 (0.00%)
5.	462site.wordpress.com	1 (5.88%)	100.00%	1 (16.67%)	0.00%	3.00	00:00:37	0.00%	0 (0.00%)	$0.00 (0.00%)

47

The Acquisition Menu:
Search Console

The **Acquisition > Search Console** reports provide information about the performance of Google organic search traffic. These reports help you see search engine queries, the number of times your site URLs appear in search results (impressions), as well as post-click site engagement data such as bounce rate and ecommerce conversion rate. This data can, for example, help you to identify:

- landing pages on your site that have good click-through rates but poor average positions in search results. These could be pages that people want to see, but have trouble finding.

- search keywords for which your site has good average positions, but poor click-through rates. These are search queries for which your pages get attention and where improved content could lead to more visitors.[86]

Prerequisite steps

You can only access **Acquisition > Search Console** metrics after you have both:

- added and verified your site at Google Search Console, and

- configured Search Console reporting from within your Google Analytics account.

Google Search Console

Make certain that you are signed into the Google account you use for Google Analytics. Then, visit Google Search Console at https://www.google.com/webmasters/. Once you have clicked on the **Search Console** button, do the following:

- Click **Add a Property** and then, on the popup form, type the URL of the site you want to add. This should be the same URL as you registered in Google Analytics. Type the entire URL, such as http://www.example. com/mysitefolder. Leave the website identifier as is.

---

[86] These examples and other chapter content are adapted from Google Analytics' *Search Console Reports* at https://support.google.com/analytics/answer/1308626 and https://support.google.com/analytics/answer/1308621.

- Click **Add** and the **Site verification** page will open.

- Select the verification method you want to use, and follow the instructions.

- Click **I am not a robot** and then press **Verify** after you have followed your preferred approach to verification.

After you have successfully completed this process, continue with the next step of configuring Search Console from within your Google Analytics account.

Configuring Search Console with Google Analytics

You can configure Search Console in your Google Analytics account as follows:

- Select **Admin** from the top of any Google Analytics report page. Make certain that the relevant Account, Property, and View are displayed.

- In the **Property** column, click **Property Settings**.

- Scroll down to **Search Console Settings**. You should see the URL of your website, which confirms that the website is verified in Search Console and that you have permission to make changes. If you do not see the URL, return to the prior step and add your site to Search Console.

- Under **Search Console**, select the reporting view(s) in which you want to see Search Console data.

- Click **Save**.

Data Availability

Fortunately, under some circumstances, historical search query data for your website will appear in your Google Analytics reports. Historical data is, however, affected by two factors:

- *The starting date of the Google Analytics view.* As you know, once a website is set up correctly with Google Analytics tracking, one or more views can report data for the site. For each view, the report date begins on the *creation date for the view*. Data from before the view creation date is not available.

- *The starting date of the Search Console collection for the website.* If you have Search Console data collection already set up, the reports will display historical data back to the creation date of the view. If you have just enabled Search Console data collection for your site, data will appear in your reports within 24 hours of site verification. Google Analytics will show any data collected for that site, but historical data previous to site verification may not be available.

Imagine that the following has taken place:

Jan 1 — View A in Analytics set up for your website.

Feb 1 — Search Console data collection set up for your website.

March 1 — View B in Analytics set up for your website.

April 1 — Search reporting enabled for View A and View B.

In this case, the data availability for each view would be:

View A — Search data begins on Feb 1.

View B — Search data begins on March 1.

Available metrics and dimensions

Search Console data is combined with Google Analytics data via the Landing Page dimension. This integration lets you see how pre-click data like queries and impressions correlate with post-click data like bounce rate and transactions. The following data is provided:

- **Queries**: The Google Search queries that generated impressions of your website URLs in Google organic search results.

- **Impressions**: The number of times any URL from your site appeared in search results viewed by a user, not including paid AdWords search impressions.

- **Clicks**: The number of clicks on your website URLs from a Google Search results page, not including clicks on paid AdWords search results.

- **Average Position**: The average ranking of your website URLs for the query or queries. For example, if your site's URL appeared at position 2 for one query and position 6 for another query, the average position would be 4 calculated as $(2 + 6) \div 2$.

- **CTR**: Click-through rate, calculated as (Clicks $\div$ Impressions) x 100.

Note that Search Console data is incompatible with Google Analytics segments. If you apply segments to the Search Console reports, your Google Analytics metrics are segmented, but the Search Console metrics are not, and return values of 0.

The remainder of this chapter discusses these metrics in the context of each **Acquisition > Search Console** report option. We'll illustrate the value and interpretation of these reports by using actual data from this book's promotional website collected during the time of the second edition. The second edition had a slightly different name: *Google Analytics Demystified: A Hands-On Approach*.

The **Acquisition > Search Console > Queries** report "lists the Google Search queries that generated impressions of your website URLs in Google organic search results. Understanding the correlation between how users search and the relevancy of your pages to those queries provides insight into how to optimize your content.

- The number of impressions that each page generates and the average position of impressions let you understand how well the search engine correlates your content to user queries.

- Clicks and click-through rate let you understand how well users correlate search results with their intentions.

To protect user privacy, queries that are made infrequently or that contain sensitive or personal information are grouped together as *(other)*."

With this in mind, let's take a look at the Google search queries that generated the most impressions for my website URLs (see the table on the top of page 453). Each line in the report - except line 1 -notes one of the search queries in which my site URLs appear. You'll notice that Line 1 reports **(not set)** instead of a specific search query. Google's John Mueller explains this aspect of the report as follows:

> "In Search Analytics if you look at the numbers of the queries that you see there, you will sometimes see that we show a top aggregated, maybe a hundred queries, and in a table below if you add the numbers together, you might see 70 queries or something like that. The difference there is essentially queries that we filter out; and in Search Console we don't show them separately and in Google Analytics they chose to call them Not Set. So that is what you are seeing there, not some-thing completely different, its not showing the difference that you'd have to calculate yourself if you calculated the difference yourself."[87]

---

[87] See *Google Analytics Assigns (not set) to Missing Data* at
http://www.analyticsedge.com/2015/10/google-analytics-assigns-not-set-to-missing-data/.

Search Query	Impressions	Clicks	CTR	Average Top Position
	1,023 % of Total: 100.00% (1,023)	**122** % of Total: 100.00% (122)	**11.93%** Avg for View: 11.93% (0.00%)	**14** Avg for View: 14 (0.00%)
1. (not set)	**514** (50.24%)	70 (57.38%)	13.62%	8.5
2. google analytics demystified	**108** (10.56%)	33 (27.05%)	30.56%	2.5
3. google analytics review	**81** (7.92%)	0 (0.00%)	0.00%	45
4. google analtyics review	**73** (7.14%)	0 (0.00%)	0.00%	45
5. google analytics demystified a hands-on approach pdf	**71** (6.94%)	7 (5.74%)	9.86%	5.0
6. google analytics reviews	**49** (4.79%)	0 (0.00%)	0.00%	31
7. google analytics demystified pdf	**38** (3.71%)	4 (3.28%)	10.53%	4.7
8. google analytics demystified: a hands-on approach	**33** (3.23%)	2 (1.64%)	6.06%	3.4
9. analytics demystified	**32** (3.13%)	0 (0.00%)	0.00%	12
10. google analytics demystified: a hands-on approach (second edition)	**15** (1.47%)	5 (4.10%)	33.33%	3.3
11. google analytics strengths and weaknesses	**3** (0.29%)	0 (0.00%)	0.00%	44
12. google analytics book	**2** (0.20%)	0 (0.00%)	0.00%	62
13. book google analytics	**1** (0.10%)	0 (0.00%)	0.00%	46

We can see that three common queries focus on the actual name of the book (lines 2, 5 and 7). The data shown on line 2 is a positive outcome as individuals appear to know the name of the book prior to the search, so other promotion channels appear to be doing their job in generating awareness. Additionally, average position and click-through rates for this search query are also acceptable. Note also the search queries shown on lines 5 and 7. Here, individuals seem to be searching for illicit PDF copies of the book. We can use this information to search out sites that may be allowing copyright-violating downloads.

But, the data also reveals two important problems when we move past the queries directly related to the name of the book. These problems relate to more generalized queries for reviews of "google analytics" (as in lines 3, 4 and 6). Note how each of these queries asks for the same information, only using different spelling in each case.

We can identify and explore this issue by first ordering queries by **Average Top Position** from highest to lowest. We accomplish this by clicking on the Average Position column header. This displays the chart shown on the top of page 454. Our ranking for more generalized queries is horrible! We rank very low. No wonder there is such low traffic originating from these queries. Some significant revision of site content is clearly needed where the goal would be to increase our ranking for more generalized Google analytics or Google analytics book searches.

Search Query	Impressions	Clicks	CTR	Average Top Position
	1,023 % of Total: 100.00% (1,023)	122 % of Total: 100.00% (122)	11.93% Avg for View: 11.93% (0.00%)	14 Avg for View: 14 (0.00%)
1. google analytics book	2 (0.20%)	0 (0.00%)	0.00%	62
2. book on google analytics	1 (0.10%)	1 (0.82%)	100.00%	54
3. book google analytics	1 (0.10%)	0 (0.00%)	0.00%	46
4. google analytics review	81 (7.92%)	0 (0.00%)	0.00%	45
5. google analtyics review	73 (7.14%)	0 (0.00%)	0.00%	45
6. google analytics strengths and weaknesses	3 (0.29%)	0 (0.00%)	0.00%	44
7. www.google analytics	1 (0.10%)	0 (0.00%)	0.00%	39
8. google analytics reviews	49 (4.79%)	0 (0.00%)	0.00%	31
9. google analytics exercises	1 (0.10%)	0 (0.00%)	0.00%	26
10. analytics demystified	32 (3.13%)	0 (0.00%)	0.00%	12
11. (not set)	514 (50.24%)	70 (57.38%)	13.62%	8.5
12. google analytics demystified a hands-on approach pdf	71 (6.94%)	7 (5.74%)	9.86%	5.0
13. google analytics demystified pdf	38 (3.71%)	4 (3.28%)	10.53%	4.7

The data also communicate bad news with regard to click-through rate. When we order **CTR** (Click-Through Rate) from highest to lowest (as shown below) we see that the click-through rate for these generalized searches (lines 10 and 13 in this table) are zero! No one who sees our site in these generalized searches clicks-through to our site. Thus, another task strongly suggested by this data is to determine how to increase click-through for these types of search queries.

Search Query	Impressions	Clicks	CTR ↓	Average Top Position
	1,023 % of Total: 100.00% (1,023)	122 % of Total: 100.00% (122)	11.93% Avg for View: 11.93% (0.00%)	14 Avg for View: 14 (0.00%)
1. book on google analytics	1 (0.10%)	1 (0.82%)	100.00%	54
2. google analytics demystified: a hands-on approach (second edition)	15 (1.47%)	5 (4.10%)	33.33%	3.3
3. google analytics demystified	108 (10.56%)	33 (27.05%)	30.56%	2.5
4. (not set)	514 (50.24%)	70 (57.38%)	13.62%	8.5
5. google analytics demystified pdf	38 (3.71%)	4 (3.28%)	10.53%	4.7
6. google analytics demystified a hands-on approach pdf	71 (6.94%)	7 (5.74%)	9.86%	5.0
7. google analytics demystified: a hands-on approach	33 (3.23%)	2 (1.64%)	6.06%	3.4
8. analytics demystified	32 (3.13%)	0 (0.00%)	0.00%	12
9. book google analytics	1 (0.10%)	0 (0.00%)	0.00%	46
10. google analtyics review	73 (7.14%)	0 (0.00%)	0.00%	45
11. google analytics book	2 (0.20%)	0 (0.00%)	0.00%	62
12. google analytics exercises	1 (0.10%)	0 (0.00%)	0.00%	26
13. google analytics review	81 (7.92%)	0 (0.00%)	0.00%	45

The **Acquisition > Search Console > Landing Pages** report shows your website URLs that have generated the most impressions in Google Search results. You can see how each URL performed in terms of search (Impressions, CTR, etc.), and also in terms of how users engaged with your website content (Bounce Rate, Avg. Session Duration, and Transactions) after they click-through the search listing. Let's focus on search query performance.

The table below shows a portion of the report where landing pages are ordered in terms of **CTR** (Click-Through Rate). Here, the CTRs for my home page (lines 1 and 4), contents page (line 2) and purchase page (line 3) are the highest. Unfortunately, the level of impressions for two of these high CTR pages (contents and purchase) is quite low. Certainly it would be to my advantage to increase the number of impressions for these pages. Additionally, CTRs for the remaining pages are quite low. This is especially problematic for pages that have high impressions, as in my review page (line 9). This issue would also need to be addressed.

Landing Page		Acquisition			
		Impressions	Clicks	CTR ↓	Average Position
		1,107 % of Total: 100.00% (1,107)	124 % of Total: 100.00% (124)	11.20% Avg for View: 11.20% (0.00%)	14 Avg for View: 14 (0.00%)
1. /xqanqeon/		21 (1.90%)	9 (7.26%)	**42.86%**	3.4
2. /text1/contents.pdf		3 (0.27%)	1 (0.81%)	**33.33%**	16
3. /xqanqeon/purchase.html		5 (0.45%)	1 (0.81%)	**20.00%**	3.4
4. /		674 (60.89%)	103 (83.06%)	**15.28%**	5.7
5. /text1/Author.html		9 (0.81%)	1 (0.81%)	**11.11%**	29
6. /text1/about1.html		77 (6.96%)	6 (4.84%)	**7.79%**	9.4
7. /text1/Order.html		13 (1.17%)	1 (0.81%)	**7.69%**	12
8. /text1/FreeSite.html		16 (1.45%)	1 (0.81%)	**6.25%**	12
9. /text1/Review.html		244 (22.04%)	1 (0.81%)	**0.41%**	38

We can examine landing pages in more detail as we move to a second data display. Clicking on the name of a specific page brings up a listing of the search terms that led to just that page. Let's look more deeply at the review page (line 9 in the table above). The table on the top of page 456 shows the search terms that led to the review landing page.

Secondary dimension ▼				
	Acquisition			
Search Query ?	**Impressions** ? ↓	**Clicks** ?	**CTR** ?	**Average Position** ?
	244 % of Total: 22.04% (1,107)	**1** % of Total: 0.81% (124)	**0.41%** Avg for View: 11.20% (-96.34%)	**38** Avg for View: 14 (175.57%)
1. google analytics review	**83** (34.02%)	0 (0.00%)	0.00%	45
2. google analtyics review	**75** (30.74%)	0 (0.00%)	0.00%	45
3. google analytics reviews	**49** (20.08%)	0 (0.00%)	0.00%	31
4. (not set)	**37** (15.16%)	1(100.00%)	2.70%	17

Here we see that more generalized search terms lead to our specific book review page. But, when our review page URL appears in these results, our click-through rate and average position are very poor. Clearly we need to better align this page's content with visitor queries and expectations.

Countries (Location)

The **Acquisition > Search Console > Countries** report provides search query metrics classified by country. Let's again focus on acquisition metrics. The initial data display shows you which countries are generating the most Google search activity and the characteristics of these queries within each county. Thus, this report provides important insights into how search query and response may differ across counties. The portion of our report that focuses on acquisition metrics is shown on the top of page 457. While it is not unexpected that most of the search traffic comes from the United States (line 1) we did find it very surprising that there were so many queries generated internationally. Perhaps we should revise the site's content to respond to a more international mix of site visitors. This might be especially important as the levels of impressions, click-through and average ranking are relatively higher for South Korea and the United Kingdom.

We can look at each country in greater detail. Clicking on the name of any country brings up a table that reports only the search-initiated landing pages for that country. The bottom table on page 457 shows landing pages for United States search-initiated traffic. (Notice the **Landing Page** notation is displayed in dark ink on the top, left-hand side of the table.) Here, we can see that only the home page (primarily line 1) shows acceptable levels of all important measures: impressions, click-through and average position.

Country	Acquisition			
	Impressions ↓	Clicks	CTR	Average Position
	1,107 % of Total: 100.00% (1,107)	**124** % of Total: 100.00% (124)	**11.20%** Avg for View: 11.20% (0.00%)	**14** Avg for View: 14 (0.00%)
1. United States	**477** (43.09%)	44 (35.48%)	9.22%	20
2. India	**104** (9.39%)	9 (7.26%)	8.65%	6.8
3. South Korea	**70** (6.32%)	13 (10.48%)	18.57%	4.8
4. United Kingdom	**48** (4.34%)	13 (10.48%)	27.08%	6.7
5. Italy	**38** (3.43%)	2 (1.61%)	5.26%	9.1
6. Singapore	**34** (3.07%)	0 (0.00%)	0.00%	6.9
7. Canada	**26** (2.35%)	5 (4.03%)	19.23%	5.5
8. Australia	**24** (2.17%)	1 (0.81%)	4.17%	25

Primary Dimension: **Landing Page**   Search Query

Secondary dimension ▼

Landing Page	Acquisition			
	Impressions ↓	Clicks	CTR	Average Position
	477 % of Total: 43.09% (1,107)	**44** % of Total: 35.48% (124)	**9.22%** Avg for View: 11.20% (-17.65%)	**20** Avg for View: 14 (43.88%)
1. /	**218** (45.70%)	32 (72.73%)	14.68%	5.6
2. /text1/Review.html	**194** (40.67%)	1 (2.27%)	0.52%	39
3. /text1/Overview.html	**15** (3.14%)	0 (0.00%)	0.00%	21
4. /xqanqeon/	**11** (2.31%)	6 (13.64%)	54.55%	2.4
5. /text1/about1.html	**9** (1.89%)	2 (4.55%)	22.22%	7.9
6. /text1/FreeSite.html	**6** (1.26%)	1 (2.27%)	16.67%	7.2
7. /text1/Order.html	**5** (1.05%)	1 (2.27%)	20.00%	20

The data displayed in the bottom table on page 457 can be changed by clicking on **Search Query** on the top, left-hand side of the table. When this is done, the table changes to that shown below. The table now displays the search terms in which my site URLs appear *only in the United States*. As with the prior tables, this data provides important insights into how to understand differences in search queries across different countries.

Primary Dimension: Landing Page   **Search Query**

Secondary dimension ▼

Search Query ⑦	Acquisition			
	Impressions ↓ ⑦	Clicks ⑦	CTR ⑦	Average Position ⑦
	477 % of Total: 43.09% (1,107)	**44** % of Total: 35.48% (124)	**9.22%** Avg for View: 11.20% (-17.65%)	**20** Avg for View: 14 (43.88%)
1. (not set)	**202** (42.35%)	31 (70.45%)	15.35%	8.4
2. google analtyics review	**68** (14.26%)	0 (0.00%)	0.00%	45
3. google analytics review	**64** (13.42%)	0 (0.00%)	0.00%	46
4. google analytics demystified	**35** (7.34%)	4 (9.09%)	11.43%	3.0
5. google analytics reviews	**32** (6.71%)	0 (0.00%)	0.00%	31
6. google analytics demystified a hands-on approach pdf	**22** (4.61%)	3 (6.82%)	13.64%	4.6
7. analytics demystified	**17** (3.56%)	0 (0.00%)	0.00%	13
8. google analytics demystified pdf	**13** (2.73%)	2 (4.55%)	15.38%	3.5
9. google analytics demystified: a hands-on approach	**11** (2.31%)	1 (2.27%)	9.09%	3.3

Devices

The **Acquisition > Search Console > Devices** report lets you see which category of devices (desktop, tablet, or mobile) delivers the best search performance and user engagement. If you notice strong search performance but poor user engagement from specific devices (for example, mobile or tablet), then that can be a signal that you need to reevaluate the way you have developed content and/or designed your site for that device.

The acquisition portion of our devices report is shown below. We can see that the vast majority of search queries are made via desktop.

| Device Category | Acquisition | | | |
	Impressions ↓	Clicks	CTR	Average Position
	1,107 % of Total: 100.00% (1,107)	124 % of Total: 100.00% (124)	11.20% Avg for View: 11.20% (0.00%)	14 Avg for View: 14 (0.00%)
1. desktop	1,018 (91.96%)	112 (90.32%)	11.00%	13
2. mobile	87 (7.86%)	11 (8.87%)	12.64%	18
3. tablet	2 (0.18%)	1 (0.81%)	50.00%	3.0

Similar to the **Acquisition > Search Console > Countries** report, clicking on any device category brings up more detailed information related to just that device. Clicking on desktop brings a table displaying just the desktop landing pages (see below). This table can be changed to display desktop search queries by clicking on **Search Query** on the top, left-hand side of the table (see the table on the top of page 460).

Primary Dimension: **Landing Page**   Search Query

Secondary dimension ▼

| Landing Page | | Acquisition | | | | |
		Impressions ↓	Clicks	CTR	Average Position	Sessions
		1,018 % of Total: 91.96% (1,107)	112 % of Total: 90.32% (124)	11.00% Avg for View: 11.20% (-1.78%)	13 Avg for View: 14 (-2.56%)	3 % of Total: 0.08% (3,917)
1. /		616 (60.51%)	94 (83.93%)	15.26%	5.6	2 (66.67%)
2. /text1/Review.html		219 (21.51%)	1 (0.89%)	0.46%	37	0 (0.00%)
3. /text1/about1.html		73 (7.17%)	4 (3.57%)	5.48%	9.5	0 (0.00%)
4. /text1/Overview.html		29 (2.85%)	0 (0.00%)	0.00%	22	0 (0.00%)
5. /xqanqeon/		21 (2.06%)	9 (8.04%)	42.86%	3.4	0 (0.00%)
6. /text1/FreeSite.html		15 (1.47%)	1 (0.89%)	6.67%	8.1	0 (0.00%)
7. /text1/Order.html		12 (1.18%)	0 (0.00%)	0.00%	13	0 (0.00%)
8. /text1/Author.html		9 (0.88%)	1 (0.89%)	11.11%	29	0 (0.00%)

Primary Dimension: Landing Page   **Search Query**

Secondary dimension ▾

	Acquisition			
Search Query ⑦	**Impressions** ↓ ⑦	**Clicks** ⑦	**CTR** ⑦	**Average Position** ⑦
	1,018 % of Total: 91.96% (1,107)	**112** % of Total: 90.32% (124)	**11.00%** Avg for View: 11.20% (-1.78%)	**13** Avg for View: 14 (-2.56%)
1. (not set)	**566** (55.60%)	67 (59.82%)	11.84%	8.1
2. google analytics demystified	**91** (8.94%)	28 (25.00%)	30.77%	2.4
3. google analytics review	**83** (8.15%)	0 (0.00%)	0.00%	45
4. google analytics demystified a hands-on approach pdf	**72** (7.07%)	7 (6.25%)	9.72%	5.1
5. google analtyics review	**50** (4.91%)	0 (0.00%)	0.00%	44

Comparing Search Console and Google Analytics data

Search Console data may differ from the data displayed in other Google Analytics reports. Possible reasons for this include:

- Search Console does some additional data processing, for example, to handle duplicate content and visits from robots.

- Some tools, such as Google Analytics, track traffic only from users who have enabled JavaScript in their browser.

- Google Analytics tracks visits only to pages, which include the correctly configured Analytics JavaScript code. If pages on the site don't have the code, Analytics will not track visits to those pages. Visits to pages without the Analytics tracking code will however, be tracked in Search Console if users reach them via search results or if Google crawls or otherwise discovers them.

- Google Analytics uses the term "keywords" to describe both search engine queries and AdWords paid keywords.[88]

---

[88] *Access Search Console Data in Google Analytics* at
https://support.google.com/webmasters/answer/1120006.

Google provides the following explanation of differences across reports in terms of shared terminology.89

Term	Search Console usage	Google Analytics usage
Impressions	Used for both AdWords impressions and Google Search impressions	Used exclusively for Google Search impressions
Clicks	Used exclusively for Google Search clicks	Used for both AdWords clicks and Google Search clicks
Average Position	Average ranking in Google Search results	Average ranking in Google Search results
CTR	Click-through rate. Clicks/Impressions for Google Search clicks.	Click-through rate. Clicks/Impressions for both AdWords and Google Search clicks.
Keyword	Applies to the key terms used in the written content of the website pages. These terms are the most significant keywords and their variants that Google found when crawling your site. When reviewed along with the Search queries report and your site's listing in actual search results for your targeted keywords, it provides insight into how Google is interpreting the content of your site.	In paid-search or AdWords reports, describes a paid keyword from a search-engine-results page. In the organic-search reports, describes the actual query string a user entered in a web search.
Query	The actual query a user entered in Google search.	Only used in the Search Console reports. Applies to the actual query a user entered in Google search.

---

89 *Search Console Reports* at https://support.google.com/analytics/answer/1308626.

48

Tagging Links

Chapter 38 illustrated how Google Analytics tracks and reports the sources of your website or blog users. While this information helps you assess the relative use and value of different referral sources, it does not provide the depth of data needed to determine the relative value of specific pages or links from individual referral sources. For example, Google Analytics can tell you the number of people visiting your website via your blog, but without your assistance it cannot easily tell you which individual posts are generating relatively more or less referrals. Similarly, without your assistance Google Analytics will have difficulty determining how many visits are generated from different emails or from different links within the same email. Fortunately, this data is easy to collect.

One way that you can help Google Analytics collect more detailed information on referral sources is by tagging your links. This chapter explains the value of tagged links and how to create this type of link.

The value of tagged links

Imagine that email is an important way by which you communicate with current and potential site users. Every week you send out an email that features a different cruise package. There are three links placed at different points in the email (the beginning, middle and end) and all three links take the user to the same page on your website. This page has been specially created to work with the email and is only accessible via the links within the email. You invest a lot of time and money in developing the email promotions, which are designed to drive traffic to the special offer page. Given this goal, you need to answer two strategic questions:

Overall, how effective is the email in generating site visits?

Which link placement is the most effective in generating site visits?

These questions cannot be answered when untagged links are used. A click on a normal (i.e., untagged link) will only bring the email recipient to the appropriate page on your site and Google Analytics will treat all three links in exactly the same way. It will not identify which link was used nor will it give the link in the email credit for the site referral. This is illustrated on the top of page 464, where we are using the **Real-Time > Traffic Sources** menu to see the source of site sessions. A click on an untagged link in an email shows that Google Analytics records this as a direct referral, the same type of referral as when one types the page URL directly into a browser. (This can be seen by the information provided beneath the number of active users on the left-hand side of the display). As a result, this classification does not allow us to answer either of the prior two strategic questions.

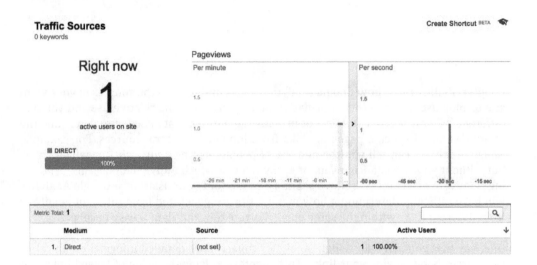

Link tagging allows us to add additional information to a link so that Google Analytics can more precisely track how a site user came to the site. In this example, we can tell Google Analytics to treat each link as if it were part of a marketing campaign, to record that the campaign was conducted via email, and that each link has a specific placement in the email. We'll see how to do this later in this chapter, but for now, let's create these labels for each link using the Google Analytics terms "Source," "Medium", and "Campaign".

Link #1
Source	June 23 Cruise Offer
Medium	Email
Campaign	Top_Placement

Link #2
Source	June 23 Cruise Offer
Medium	Email
Campaign	Middle_Placement

Link #3
Source	June 23 Cruise Offer
Medium	Email
Campaign	Bottom_Placement

Note how all links share common Source and Medium labels. This is because all appear in the same email and all relate to the same cruise offer. We use the campaign slot to label link placement within the email.

The **Real-Time > Traffic Sources** display shown below is what appears when we click on the data related to Link #1. Note how the display has changed from the previous in several important ways. First, Google Analytics notes that the user came to the site as part of a campaign, rather than directly. (This can be seen by the label beneath the number of active users.) Second, our labels for the referral's Medium and Source are shown in the Medium and Source columns. We now know exactly where the user is coming from.

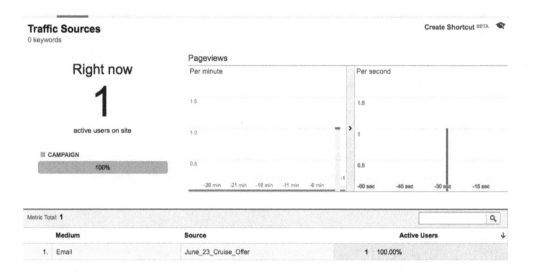

Imagine that email recipients continue to click through to the site, resulting in ten visits, as shown in the figure on the top of page 466. As we continue to monitor this data, we can *begin* to answer the first question posed earlier: "Overall, how effective is the email in generating site visits?" Over the next few days, after more data has been collected, we will examine the data available through the **Acquisition > Campaign** menus to try to definitively answer this question.[90]

---

[90] The next chapter discusses how to access tagged link data from Google Analytics menus and provides direction for the analysis of this data. At the moment we are using Real-Time data just to illustrate the type of data available through tagged links.

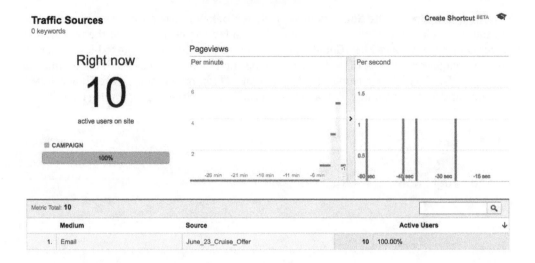

A click on "Email" in the **Medium** column brings up the display shown below.

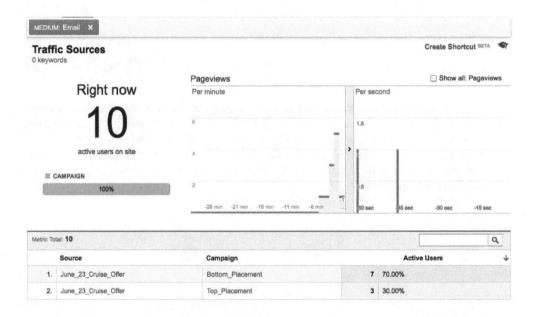

Note that the source of the data, the June 23 cruise offer, is shown in the **Source** column. The **Campaign** column displays link placement. In both cases, the names shown reflect how we labeled each link on page 464. The **Active Users** column shows the distribution of email recipients who clicked on one of the email links. Note: (1) how the link placed on the bottom of the email drives much more traffic to the site and (2) the absence of "Middle Placement" in the list, indicating that no one clicked on the link placed in the middle of the email. As noted earlier, our analysis would continue through the **Behavior > Campaigns** menu option as more data is collected.

As you know, text links typically appear on a digital property as a colored underlined word or phrase. Consider the link "learn about email". You would expect that a click on this link would take you to a page that explains email basics. While "learn about email" is what is displayed, the actual command for taking you to the linked page is hidden in the HTML code. The HTML code for the "learn about email" link would be:

<a href = http://www.mysite.com/email/email.html><learn about email</a>

where the link's destination is: `http://www.mysite.com/email/email.html` and the text that appears on the web page is: **learn about email**.

A Google Analytics UTM tag adds additional information to the end of a standard URL link. All tags in Google Analytics start with a question mark and utm_ followed by the name of the tag, an equal sign, and the tag label.

– UTM parameters are parameters that you can add to *custom* campaigns to correctly track the performance of these campaigns in your Google Analytics reports. An email campaign, as discussed earlier, would be an appropriate use of these tags.

– UTM links do not need to be added to Adwords campaigns.[91] Additionally, there is no need to be add UTM parameters to organic traffic, referral traffic or cost per click traffic. Google can identify all of these sources on its own.

Google Analytics allows a manual tag to contain up to five types of information.

The following table provides the three types of information we will use to tag our links. Since you will have only occasional opportunities to use the remaining two tags, these are omitted from the discussion.

Tag Name	Tag	Definition	Example
Source	utm_source	The marketing vehicle or source of the referral	June Newsletter Wordpress Facebook Pinterest
Medium	utm_medium	The digital medium that conveyed the link	Email Blog post
Campaign	utm_campaign	The identifier for the specific referral source	Spring sale 10% off offer

[91] Manual UTM tagging is appropriate for any non-Adwords campaign. Adwords campaigns are automatically **autotagged** by Google and use a different set of parameters to code the ad's destination URL. The parameter used by Adwords is **gclid =** .

Let's incorporate each of the prior example's link characteristics into this table:

Tag Name	Tag	Definition	Label
Source	utm_source	The marketing vehicle or source of the referral	June 23 cruise offer
Medium	utm_medium	The digital medium that conveyed the link	Email
Campaign	utm_campaign	The identifier for the specific referral source	Top_placement, or Middle_placement, or Bottom_placement

Using this information, Link #1 would appear as follows, where all that the recipient would see is "Visit Now" and selecting the link would take the user to the page at purchase1.html.

<a href = http://www.googleanalyticsdemstified.com/xqanqeon/purchase1.html?utm_source=June_23_cruise_offer&utm_medium=Email&utm_campaign=Top_placement>Visit Now</a>

Fortunately, we don't have to create these links manually. Google provides a link tag generator that allows us to type in our labels and destination URL after which Google generates a fully tagged link. The link tag generator is located at:

https://ga-dev-tools.appspot.com/campaign-url-builder/

This screen provides a text field for you to input the full URL of the link's target page, as well as each of the link parameters you want to use.

> The three parameters discussed earlier are required and are marked with an asterisk. These are campaign source, medium and name. The URL builder does not require that you provide information related to campaign content or campaign term.

The display shown on page 469 illustrates how the link generator form looks when we type in the information for Link #1 from the above example.

Campaign URL Builder

This tool allows you to easily add campaign parameters to URLs so you can track Custom Campaigns in Google Analytics.

Enter the website URL and campaign information

Fill out the required fields (marked with *) in the form below, and once complete the full campaign URL will be generated for you. *Note: the generated URL is automatically updated as you make changes.*

* Website URL	http://www.googleanalyticsdemstified.com/xqanqeon/purchase1.html	The full website URL (e.g. `https://www.example.com`)
* Campaign Source	June_23_cruise_offer	The referrer: (e.g. `google`, `newsletter`)
Campaign Medium	Email	Marketing medium: (e.g. `cpc`, `banner`, `email`)
Campaign Name	Top_placement	Product, promo code, or slogan (e.g. `spring_sale`)
Campaign Term		Identify the paid keywords
Campaign Content		Use to differentiate ads

The bottom of the form will display the tagged link, as shown on the top of page 470. Here you can use the two options beneath the link to either copy the link as it appears or create a shortened link.

Share the generated campaign URL

Use this URL in any promotional channels you want to be associated with this custom campaign

```
http://www.googleanalyticsdemstified.com/xqanqeon/purchase1.html?
utm_source=June_23_cruise_offer&utm_medium=Email&utm_campaign=Top_placement
```

☐ Set the campaign parameters in the fragment portion of the URL (not recommended).

📋 Copy URL   🔗 Convert URL to Short Link

49

The Acquisition Menu: Campaigns

The **Acquisition > Campaigns** menu provides four types of reports (see below). This chapter focuses on **Acquisition > Campaigns > All Campaigns.**[92]

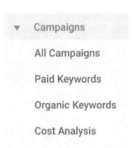

Selecting **Acquisition > Campaigns > All Campaigns** brings up a line chart and data table designed to summarize and provide access to all current and past campaigns. The data table (see below) is the more important of the two displays. Having all campaign data in one place allows you to determine the relative success of each campaign. Clicking on an individual campaign name provides more information for just that campaign.

Campaign	Acquisition			Behavior			Conversions eCommerce ▼		
	Sessions ↓	% New Sessions	New Users	Bounce Rate	Pages / Session	Avg. Session Duration	Ecommerce Conversion Rate	Transactions	Revenue
Hostname	471 % of Total: 14.01% (3,361)	78.34% Avg for View: 91.34% (-14.23%)	369 % of Total: 12.02% (3,070)	41.19% Avg for View: 62.09% (-33.67%)	1.84 Avg for View: 1.72 (6.78%)	00:00:18 Avg for View: 00:00:35 (-48.46%)	37.15% Avg for View: 13.51% (175.06%)	175 % of Total: 38.55% (454)	$1,613,600.0 % of Total: 40.1 ($3,948,981
1. Directexp	137 (29.09%)	81.75%	112 (30.35%)	34.31%	2.26	00:00:08	43.07%	59 (33.71%)	$598,200.00 (37.1
2. DirectPost5	73 (15.50%)	97.26%	71 (19.24%)	49.32%	1.10	<00:00:01	47.95%	35 (20.00%)	$328,500.00 (20.3
3. Direct	62 (13.16%)	87.10%	54 (14.63%)	48.39%	1.44	00:00:22	41.94%	26 (14.86%)	$205,400.00 (12.7
4. Page	35 (7.43%)	31.43%	11 (2.98%)	51.43%	1.40	00:00:02	31.43%	11 (6.29%)	$80,900.00 (5.0
5. Sept	23 (4.88%)	78.26%	18 (4.88%)	52.17%	1.43	00:00:21	47.83%	11 (6.29%)	$65,800.00 (4.0
6. Bahamas	19 (4.03%)	47.37%	9 (2.44%)	52.63%	1.00	00:00:00	47.37%	9 (5.14%)	$146,300.00 (9.0
7. Mexico	19 (4.03%)	42.11%	8 (2.17%)	52.63%	1.11	00:00:06	42.11%	8 (4.57%)	$32,600.00 (2.0
8. Home_page	16 (3.40%)	87.50%	14 (3.79%)	18.75%	2.44	00:00:11	25.00%	4 (2.29%)	$31,000.00 (1.1

---

[92] **Organic Keywords** provides the same information as when the Organic channel is selected in **Acquisition > All Traffic > Channels**. **Paid Keywords** and **Cost Analysis** are omitted, as they are likely to be of interest to only those engaged in paid search.

We'll more fully explore the types of data provided by **Acquisition > Campaigns > All Campaigns** in the context of the following scenario.

The scenario

Consider a situation in which you promote a special offer through your Facebook page, your blog, and an email newsletter. The offer is communicated through a video post that offers individuals a two-cabin upgrade if they buy a tour through the use of one of these links. Each of these links takes the user to a special purchase page. You want to determine which referral source is better at driving traffic to the site and fostering positive purchase behaviors.

You'll monitor each referral source via tagged links that have the following characteristics: the Source tag will be different for each link, but all three links will have the same Medium and Campaign tags. The Source tag identifies the referral source.

Source	utm_source	The marketing vehicle or source of the referral	Facebook, or Blog, or Email
Medium	utm_medium	The digital medium which conveyed the link	Video Post
Campaign	utm_campaign	The identifier for the specific referral source	2 cabin upgrade

All three links are generated with Google's link tag generator as shown below:

<a href =
http://www.googleanalyticsdemstified.com/xqanqeon/sale1.html?utm_source=Facebook
&utm_medium=Video_Post&utm_campaign=2_cabin_upgrade>Visit Now</a>

<a href =
http://www.googleanalyticsdemstified.com/xqanqeon/sale1.html?utm_source=Blog&utm
_medium=Video_Post&utm_campaign=2_cabin_upgrade>Visit Now</a>

<a href =
http://www.googleanalyticsdemstified.com/xqanqeon/sale1.html?utm_source=Email&ut
m_medium=Video_Post&utm_campaign=2_cabin_upgrade>Visit Now</a>

Campaign metrics

Clicking on **Acquisition > Campaigns > All Campaigns** brings up a summary display of all campaigns initiated during the specified time period (see top of page 473).

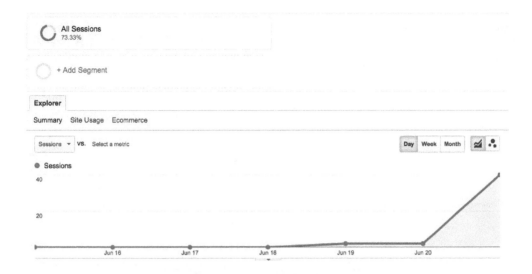

First, the **All Sessions** graphic (on the top, left-hand side of the report) indicates the size of the session base underlying all of the campaign-related data reports. In this case, 73.33% of all site sessions were related to one or more campaigns.

Second, there are three data display options beneath the **Explorer** tab on the left-hand side of the page. Each option changes both the line chart and the tabular data display shown on the bottom of the **Acquisition > Campaigns > All Campaigns** report. All three options present data for each campaign conducted during the specified time period. The **Summary** option summarizes acquisition, behavior and conversion metrics. The **Site Usage** option summarizes site behavior and engagement metrics. Finally, the **Ecommerce** option provides ecommerce-specific metrics.

I've applied each of the prior options to generate the three charts shown on page 474. Taken together, these charts provide important insights into the overall response to the "2 cabin upgrade" campaign.

-   This is the most successful campaign run during this time period. Nearly two thirds of all sessions (29 of 44) were related to this campaign.

-   Almost all sessions (96.55%) were new sessions primarily from new site users.

-   Site engagement generated by the campaign had several positive outcomes, in particular: the number of pages per session was quite high and the bounce rate was quite low.

-   The campaign was by far the most successful in revenue generation. In fact, it was the only campaign to generate revenue.

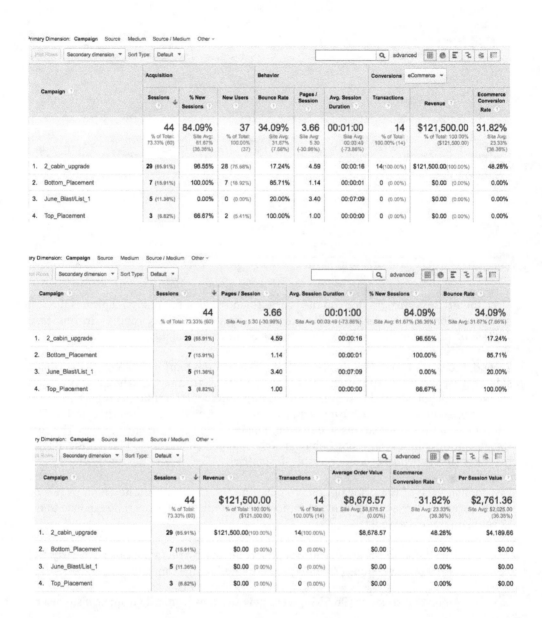

All of these positive outcomes describe overall campaign impact. However, you'll recall that the campaign consisted of three elements: a Facebook post, a blog post, and an email. We need to determine the extent to which *each* of these elements contributed to this campaign's success.

We begin by clicking on the name of the campaign in any of the prior tables. Clicking on the campaign name from the Summary table brings up the summary display for each of the source/medium combinations used in the campaign (see table on top of page 475).

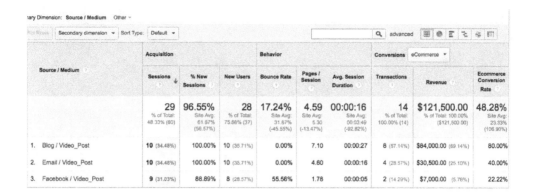

The data in this table indicates that each of the sources resulted in about the same number of sessions, the vast majority of which were new sessions. There were, however, significant differences across the three campaign sources in terms of the campaign objective: cruise purchase. The blog post was clearly the strongest referral source while Facebook was clearly the weakest. Those who came to the website from the blog post had more transactions and generated more revenue. This relationship between campaign source and transactions can be seen in more detail when we select **Ecommerce** from below the **Explorer** tab. This brings up the table shown below, where we can see that average purchase rate, conversion rate, and per session value are all the highest for the blog campaign source.

Selecting **Site Usage** from below the **Explorer** tab provides data that helps to explain this outcome (see below). Individuals who came to site from the blog post were more engaged with site content. These individuals viewed more pages per session, had longer average session duration and a nonexistent bounce rate.

The Acquisition Menu: Social

We saw earlier that the **Acquisition > All Traffic > Channels** menu option provides important information on the role of social channels and specific social platforms in referring users to your site. The **Acquisition > Social** menu options shown below allow you to focus on social referrals in greater depth.

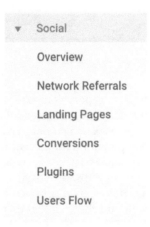

The **Acquisition > Social > Overview** report allows you to quickly see conversion metrics generated from social channels. The default view, shown on the top of page 478, displays total conversions and conversion value, that is, the sum of all ecommerce and goal metrics. This is indicated by the Conversions pull-down menu located on the top right-hand side of the page, which is currently set to "All".

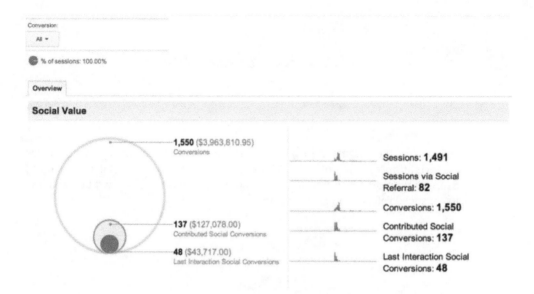

The **Social Value** graph and numeric report compare the total number and monetary value of goal completions and/or ecommerce conversions to those that resulted from social referrals. (The chart above focuses on ecommerce conversions.) Before we look at these metrics, it is important to keep in mind that a visit from a social referral may result in a conversion immediately, or it may assist in a conversion that occurs at a later date. Referrals that generate conversions in the same session as the referral are labeled **Last Interaction Social Conversions**. However, if a referral from a social source does not immediately generate a conversion, but the visitor returns later and converts, the referral is included in **Contributed Social Conversions**. Looking at both types of conversions is essential to understanding the role that social referrals play in helping you to achieve your strategic objectives.

As noted, the display can focus on either goals or ecommerce. When the focus is on goals, we believe that the display has only moderate value because the overall summative measures may mask significant differences across contributing individual goals. Additionally, not all goals may be of equal importance. We recommend, therefore, that you focus this table and subsequent analyses on the specific goals of interest. This is accomplished via the **Conversion** pull-down menu. Selecting this menu (see the top of page 479) allows us to select just ecommerce and/or goals of interest. We just revise the checkmarks to leave only the items(s) of interest checked.

Checking only **Transaction** revises the display to that shown below. Note how the total number of conversions and the two social metrics (**Contributed Social Conversions** and **Last Interaction Social Conversions**) have changed to reflect this narrower focus.

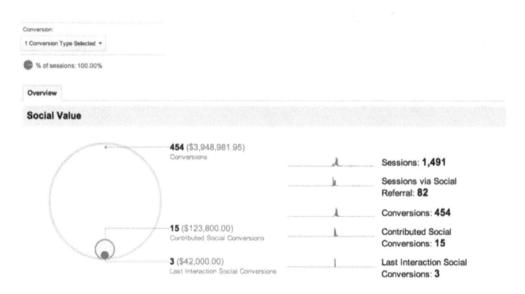

Now we can more clearly see the extent to which social referrals contribute to ecommerce success. Beginning with the data on the right-hand side, we see that of 1,491 total sessions, only 82 were initiated via a social referral. This percentage (5.5%) indicates that social overall plays a minor role in driving traffic to our site. In addition, social's role in conversions is even lower. Social contributed to 15 conversions out of the total 454 (3.3%). Perhaps more importantly, only 18% of all social referrals resulted in a transaction (15 ÷ 82), which is below our site average conversion rate of 30.4% (454 ÷ 1491).

The circular chart on the left-hand side of the previous display provides data related to ecommerce conversion value. Overall, the 454 conversions resulted in just over $3.9 million in sales, of which social contributed $123,800. We can compare social's share of all ecommerce conversions (3.3%) to its share of conversions value (3.1%, calculated as 123,800 ÷ 3,948,982). Thus, social's contribution to sales is about what we would expect given its share of referrals.

Overall, our social efforts appear to be problematic. Our rate of social referral is very low and the overall conversion rate and monetary conversion amounts for social-initiated sessions are very low when compared to our overall site averages. Later, we'll see if this conclusion is reflective of all social networks.

The table on the bottom of **Acquisition > Social > Overview** (see below) presents a list of data selection options (on the left-hand side) and social networks involved in site sessions (on the right-hand side). We can see that sessions have been initiated by four social networks, with Pinterest accounting for the most sessions and Facebook generating the least number of sessions.

Social Sources		Social Network	Sessions	% Sessions
Social Network	▸	1. Pinterest	28	34.15%
Pages		2. YouTube	20	24.39%
Shared URL		3. WordPress	19	23.17%
Social Plugins		4. Facebook	15	18.29%
Social Source				

view full report

Network Referrals

The **Acquisition > Social > Network Referrals** report provides two types of data (see the top of page 481). The line charts on the top of the report allow you to compare the number of sessions via a social referral to the number of all sessions. At first glance, the similarity in the two line charts might lead us to believe that almost all sessions were initiated via social referrals. However, note the scale on the left-hand side of each line chart. The inconsistency in scales makes it very hard to use and interpret these charts.

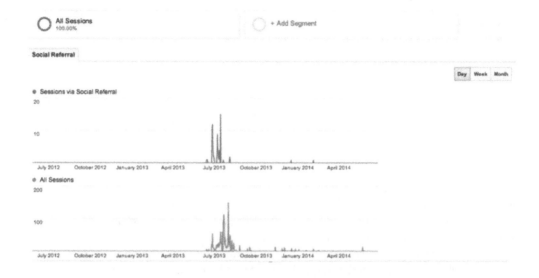

The table on the bottom of the **Acquisition > Social > Network Referrals** report is much more useful and allows you to examine and compare engagement metrics for each social network which has initiated referrals (see below). Here, in addition to the number of sessions, you can see total pageviews, average session duration, and average number of pages/session. These data indicate that user engagement differs across social networks. Users referred by YouTube appear to have the highest engagement with our travel site, while users referred by Facebook appear to have the lowest engagement. Soon we'll examine these metrics in the context of conversions and conversion value.

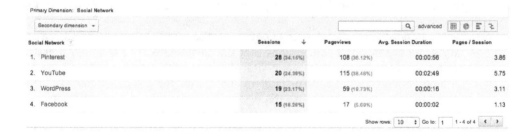

Social Network	Sessions	Pageviews	Avg. Session Duration	Pages / Session
1. Pinterest	28 (34.15%)	108 (36.12%)	00:00:56	3.86
2. YouTube	20 (24.39%)	115 (38.46%)	00:02:49	5.75
3. WordPress	19 (23.17%)	59 (19.73%)	00:00:16	3.11
4. Facebook	15 (18.29%)	17 (5.69%)	00:00:02	1.13

Clicking on the name of any social network displays information on the path taken from the social referrer to your website, as shown for YouTube on the top of page 482. Two things are noteworthy. First, almost all referrals from YouTube are to my site home page. Second, even though the samples are small, it appears that site engagement after a YouTube referral differs depending upon the URL to which the referral took place. We would want to monitor this trend and, if warranted, to try to increase the number of referrals to pages with higher engagement but only if those pages were important contributors to conversions. We can explore that aspect of social referrals via the **Acquisition > Social > Conversions** menu option described next.

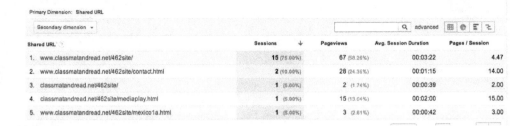

Shared URL	Sessions ↓	Pageviews	Avg. Session Duration	Pages / Session
1. www.classmatandread.net/462site/	**15** (75.00%)	67 (58.26%)	00:03:22	4.47
2. www.classmatandread.net/462site/contact.html	**2** (10.00%)	28 (24.35%)	00:01:15	14.00
3. classmatandread.net/462site/	**1** (5.00%)	2 (1.74%)	00:00:39	2.00
4. classmatandread.net/462site/mediaplay.html	**1** (5.00%)	15 (13.04%)	00:02:00	15.00
5. www.classmatandread.net/462site/mexico1a.html	**1** (5.00%)	3 (2.61%)	00:00:42	3.00

Conversions

The **Acquisition > Social > Conversions** report allows you to move beyond engagement metrics to quantify the monetary value of social network referrals. This report shows the total number of conversions and the monetary value of conversions that occurred as a result of referrals from each social network. Conversions are treated and defined similarly to those on the **Acquisition > Social > Overview** page:[93]

- *First Click Conversions* and *First Click Conversion Value* represent the number and monetary value of sales and conversions the channel initiated. This is the first interaction on a conversion path. The higher these numbers, the more important the channel's role in initiating new sales and conversions.

- *Last Click or Direct Conversions* and *Last Click or Direct Conversion Value* represent the number and monetary value of last click conversions. When someone visits your site from a social network and converts in the same session, the visit is considered a last click. The higher these numbers, the more important the social network's role is in driving completion of sales and conversions.

- *Assisted Conversions* and *Assisted Conversion Value* are the number and monetary value of sales and conversions that the social network assisted. An assist occurs when someone visits your site after a social network referral, leaves without converting, but returns later to convert during a subsequent visit. The higher these numbers, the more important the assist role of the social network is in completing a conversion.

- *Assisted/Last Click or Direct Conversions* and *First/Last Click or Direct Conversions* summarize a social network's overall role. A value close to 0 indicates that the social network functioned primarily in a last click capacity. A value close to 1 indicates that the social network functioned equally in an assist and a last click capacity. The more this value exceeds 1, the more the social network functioned in an assist capacity.

---

[93] *Analyzing channel contribution*
(https://support.google.com/analytics/answer/1191204?hl=en)

The figure shown below is the initial display when **Acquisition > Social > Conversions** is selected. Note that the **Conversions** pull-down menu below the **Explorer** tab (on the top left-hand side) is by default set to "All". Thus, without changing this setting, the report will provide summative measures similar to the default view on the **Acquisition > Social > Overview** page.

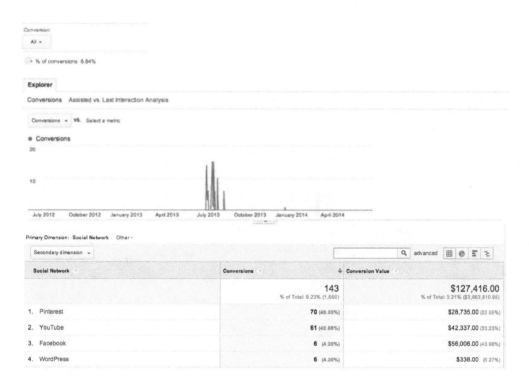

As with the prior **Acquisition > Social > Overview** data, we recommend focusing on ecommerce alone or on specific goals. We can focus on ecommerce by checking only **Transaction**, as shown below.

The display shown below is the result of our focus on ecommerce transactions. The numeric table on this page provides insights into each social network's role in ecommerce conversions. The top summary line chart repeats the data shown on the **Acquisition > Social > Overview** page. Each row beneath this summary provides information on a specific social network, specifically the total number of conversions and the conversion value associated with that network.

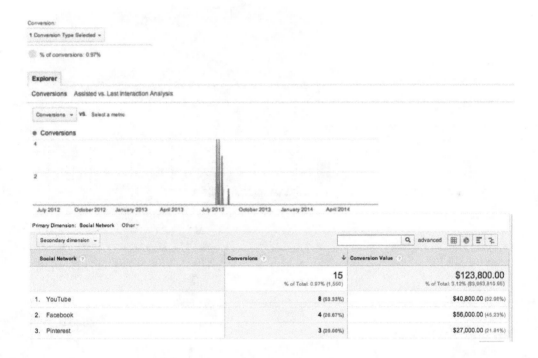

At this point, it is useful to create a summary table of our own. This table puts conversions in context by combining the session information from the **Acquisition > Social > Overview** report with the conversion information in the previous report. We also calculate, for each social network, the percentage of all sessions that resulted in a conversion. This table is shown below.

Network	Sessions	Conversions	% Sessions Converted
Pinterest	28	3	10.7%
YouTube	20	8	40.0%
Wordpress	19	0	0.0%
Facebook	15	4	26.7%

The data in this table indicate that not all social referrals are equally valuable. While Pinterest has the most referrals (i.e., initiates the greatest number of sessions), it has a very low conversion rate, indicating that most people who arrive at our site via Pinterest leave without a purchase. At this point we would conclude that these are not valuable referrals. The conversion rates for Facebook and YouTube are much higher, indicating that these network referrals are more likely to make a purchase. Based on this information, we would conclude that YouTube and Facebook referrals are better, more valuable referrals. Finally, note Wordpress, where the number of sessions is relatively high but the conversion rate is 0%, No one referred by Wordpress made a purchase. Clearly, we would need to examine our Wordpress content strategy to see why this is the case.

We can continue to differentiate referrals from different social networks by modifying the previous table, this time examining conversion value per session and average conversion value. This new table is shown below for the three networks that generated conversions.

Network	Sessions	Conversions	Average Conversion $/ Session[94]	Average $/ Conversion[95]
Pinterest	28	3	$954	$9,000
YouTube	20	8	$2,040	$5,100
Facebook	15	4	$3,733	$14,000

This data indicate that the relative contribution of each social network is more complex than originally thought. As such, each may require a different strategy.

- The conversion rate for Pinterest is indeed quite low (as indicated in the first table) and the resulting **Average Conversion $/Session** is also low as a result. However, when individuals referred by this network do make a purchase, it is a large one. Overall, these are valuable customers, and our goal would be to increase conversions/session.

- YouTube makes a different type of contribution to our ecommerce success and therefore requires a different strategy. Individuals referred by YouTube are the most likely to convert but their financial contribution is relatively low. We can try to increase the number of referrals from YouTube (accepting the current financial contribution) and/or attempt to increase the average purchase amount.

- Facebook referrals have a relatively high conversion rate and they generate the highest **Average Conversion $/Session** and **Average $/Conversion.** These are

---

[94] This metric is calculated by dividing Conversion Value by Sessions.

[95] This metric is calculated by dividing Conversion Value by Conversions.

very valuable customers, and our strategic goal would be to increase referrals from Facebook, assuming that the conversion rate and purchase amount would remain the same.

One last insight into the strategic contribution of different social networks can be found by clicking on the **Assisted Versus Last Interaction** link beneath the **Explorer** tab. This brings up the table shown below.

This table indicates that our current content strategy at YouTube and Pinterest works to drive users to the site, but these users never make a purchase on the same visit. Therefore, we might want to modify content at these sites to encourage a purchase during their initial referred visit. Facebook, on the other hand, sends a different type of individual to our site. These users are much more likely to make a purchase and to make this purchase during their initial referred visit. Thus, when it works, the content appears to be effective. But, the breadth of appeal of this content may be relatively low, as indicated in the low number of overall sessions initiated by Facebook. As a result, our initial hunch is supported - we would want to examine our content strategy to try to increase the referral rate from Facebook (assuming consistency in purchase behaviors once they arrive).[96]

Plugins

The **Acquisition > Social > Plugins Report** focuses on site buttons such as Google +1 and Facebook Like. From a content management perspective, it is important to know which buttons are being clicked and for which content. For example, if you publish articles on your site, you'll want to know which articles are most commonly "liked" or shared, and from which social networks they're being shared (for example, Google+ or Facebook). You can use this information to create more of the type of content that's popular with your visitors. Also, if you find that some buttons are rarely used, you may wish to remove them to reduce clutter.

---

[96] Assisted and last click conversions provide important insights into a social network's contribution to ecommerce success and goal attainment. Attribution allows us to look even more deeply at social network performance and to place this performance in the context of other channels. Attribution is discussed in Section XIV.

Google Analytics notes that no setup is required to track Google +1 interactions that occur on your site, but additional technical setup is required to track other Social interactions.

Landing Pages

Acquisition > Social > Network Referrals allowed us to see the specific landing pages referred to by each individual social network. The **Acquisition > Social > Landing Pages** report (shown below) displays engagement metrics (sessions, pageviews, average session duration, and average pages per session) organized by landing page and summed across all social networks. Keep in mind that because these are summative measures, the overall average may not reflect the characteristics of a specific social network. Note that a metric new to this table is Data Hub Activities, which reports data hub conversations and events associated with each social referral landing page.

Primary Dimension: Shared URL

Shared URL	Sessions ↓	Pageviews	Avg. Session Duration	Data Hub Activities	Pages / Session
1. www.classmatandread.net/462site/	39 (47.56%)	165 (55.18%)	00:01:29	0 (0.00%)	4.23
2. www.classmatandread.net/462site/purchasef.html	13 (15.85%)	15 (5.02%)	00:00:03	0 (0.00%)	1.15
3. www.classmatandread.net/462site/mexico.html	8 (9.76%)	28 (9.36%)	00:01:36	0 (0.00%)	3.50
4. www.classmatandread.net/462site/thanks_p.html	8 (9.76%)	15 (5.02%)	00:00:05	0 (0.00%)	1.88
5. www.classmatandread.net/462site/package.html	5 (6.10%)	22 (7.36%)	00:00:59	0 (0.00%)	4.40
6. www.classmatandread.net/462site/contact.html	2 (2.44%)	28 (9.36%)	00:01:15	0 (0.00%)	14.00
7. www.classmatandread.net/462site/indexa.html	2 (2.44%)	3 (1.00%)	00:00:08	0 (0.00%)	1.50
8. www.classmatandread.net/462site/mediaplay.html	2 (2.44%)	3 (1.00%)	00:02:39	0 (0.00%)	1.50
9. classmatandread.net/462site/	1 (1.22%)	2 (0.67%)	00:00:39	0 (0.00%)	2.00

Social Users Flow

The **Acquisition > Social > Social Users Flow** is identical to other flow charts, except here the focus is on social networks (see the top chart on page 488). Similar to other user flow reports, you can select and highlight the user path for traffic beginning from a single source, in this case a specific social referrer. The bottom chart on page 488, for example, shows users flow for those referred to my site from YouTube.

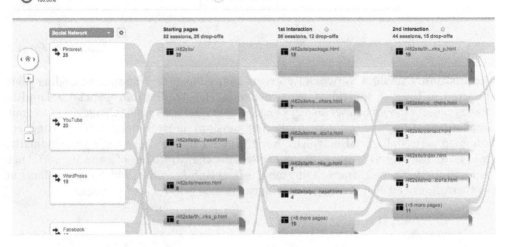

Social Users Flow

May 27, 2012 - Ju

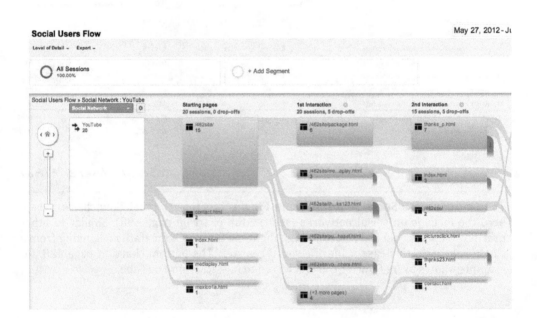

Section XII:
The Ecommerce Menu

Integrating ecommerce functionality into your site can be a daunting task. The task becomes even more complex when you decide to send ecommerce data to Google Analytics. Given the multiple approaches that can be used to accomplish these tasks and the need to customize the approach selected to your specific needs, we are not going to discuss how to install ecommerce on your site. Rather, our focus is on the analysis of ecommerce data, helping you to understand the types of information available and the strategic insights this information provides.

- Chapter 51 describes the process by which ecommerce data is sent to Google Analytics.

  Note that this chapter's discussion is intended to work with Universal Analytics (analytics.js). If you are using the Global Site Tag tracking code (gtag.js), please read Chapter 51a in the Appendix (pages 739 to 740) before returning to Chapter 52 in the main text.

- Chapter 52 discusses the various ways ecommerce data can be viewed, analyzed and applied to strategic decision-making.

Sending Ecommerce Data to Google Analytics

Google Analytics ecommerce tracking allows you to measure the number of transactions and revenue that your website generates. On a typical ecommerce site, after users click the 'purchase' button, their purchase information is sent to the businesses' web server or external shopping cart, which carries out the transaction. If successful, the server or cart typically redirects the purchaser to a 'Thank You' or receipt page with transaction details and a receipt of the purchase. At this point, you can send the ecommerce data from the 'Thank You' page to Google Analytics.[97]

Imagine that our travel website sells six different tours:

Mexico	2 days	$3,500
Mexico	10 days	$9,000
Mexico	15 days	$12,000
Bahamas	2 days	$3,500
Bahamas	10 days	$9,000
Bahamas	15 days	$12,000

The format of the ecommerce transmission to Google Analytics would be identical across all six tour options. The content differs with regard to tour specifics. The source code used to send ecommerce data to Google Analytics for the 10-day Bahamas tour package is shown below and continues on the top of page 492.

```
ga('require', 'ecommerce', 'ecommerce.js');

ga('ecommerce:addTransaction',
{   'id': '1234',                      // Transaction ID. Required.
    'affiliation': 'Travel Tour',      // Affiliation or store name.
    'revenue': '9000.00',              // Grand Total.
    'shipping': '0',                   // Shipping.
    'tax': '0'                         // Tax. });
```

---

[97] More detailed information on sending ecommerce data to Google Analytics can be found at https://developers.google.com/analytics/devguides/collection/analyticsjs/ecommerce#overview

```
ga('ecommerce:addItem',
{    'id': '1234',                        // Transaction ID. Required.
     'name': '10 Day Tour Package',       // Product name. Required.
     'sku': 'B10',                        // SKU/code.
     'category': 'Bahamas',               // Category or variation.
     'price': '9000.00',                  // Unit price.
     'quantity': '1'                      // Quantity. });

ga('ecommerce:send');
```

There are four parts to this code. The first line, ga('require', 'ecommerce', 'ecommerce.js');, sends a request to Google Analytics for the ecommerce javascript necessary to process the data. This line of code is required.

The next large block of code is summary information for the entire transaction, which is normally calculated by the shopping cart. It is common practice to send information that provides the store name, the grand total, shipping, and tax. In our case, because we are only selling tour packages, shipping and tax are set to zero and the total revenue equals the price of the selected tour.

The next block of code is generated for every item placed in the shopping cart, in this case the purchase of a single tour. Google Analytics requires that we provide the transaction ID (which is the same as that reported in the summary information) and the product name. We've named each tour package in terms of the number of tour days. Providing the remaining information in this block of code allows us to look more deeply at our ecommerce outcomes in Google Analytics' ecommerce reports. Each tour is therefore also given a SKU code and category.

- The SKU code indicates the tour destination and number of days. The B10 in this example indicates that the tour is for 10 days in the Bahamas. A code of M02 would indicate a 2 day Mexico tour.

- The category indicates the destination without worrying about days. Two categories are used: Bahamas and Mexico.

Finally, we provide price and quantity information for the specific item.

The last line of code, ga('ecommerce:send'); sends all of the information to Google Analytics. This line of code is required.

As noted earlier, the format remains the same while the specifics change for each tour package. Information on a 15-day tour to Mexico would be sent to Google Analytics as shown on the top of page 493.

```
ga('require', 'ecommerce', 'ecommerce.js');

ga('ecommerce:addTransaction',
{   'id': '1234',                        // Transaction ID. Required.
    'affiliation': 'Travel Tour',        // Affiliation or store name.
    'revenue': '15000.00',               // Grand Total.
    'shipping': '0',                     // Shipping.
    'tax': '0'                           // Tax. });

ga('ecommerce:addItem',
{   'id': '1234',                        // Transaction ID. Required.
    'name': '15 Day Tour Package',       // Product name. Required.
    'sku': 'M15',                        // SKU/code.
    'category': 'Mexico',                // Category or variation.
    'price': '15000.00',                 // Unit price.  '
    'quantity': '1'                      // Quantity. });

ga('ecommerce:send');
```

You'll note that the above transmission does not send credit card information. Google does not want this information because it is personally identifiable.

Ecommerce Metrics and Reporting

Ecommerce reporting options and metrics are found in the **Conversions** menu, shown below.

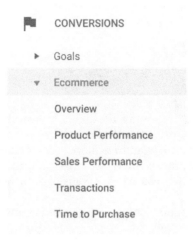

CONVERSIONS

▶ Goals

▼ Ecommerce

    Overview

    Product Performance

    Sales Performance

    Transactions

    Time to Purchase

Overview

The **Conversions > Ecommerce > Overview** display is similar in format to other Overview pages, except here the focus is on ecommerce metrics. The line chart on the top of the Overview report page (see display on the top of page 496) displays one of six core ecommerce metrics for the selected time period. My ecommerce conversion rate by day is displayed. The specific data displayed in this chart are noted just above the line graph.

These data are interesting, informing us that on several days the ecommerce rate exceeded 50%; while on most days, the ecommerce conversion rate was low or nonexistent. We would certainly want to explore this trend in greater depth to see if an explanation could be found; for example, we may want to explore whether or not the lower conversion rates were associated with website or browser problems.

We can use the pull-down menu just beneath the **Overview** tab to explore the trend in other ecommerce metrics (see below).

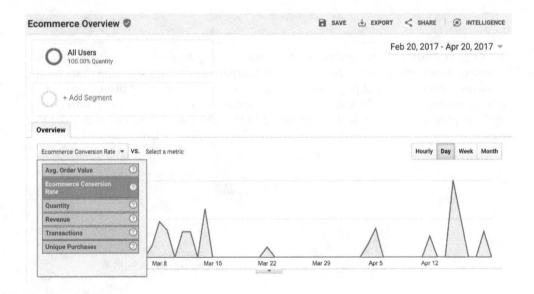

Beneath the line chart are two groups of data. Immediately below the chart are summary ecommerce metrics (see top of figure below). Here, the ecommerce conversion rate, number of transactions, unique purchases, total revenue, and average order value are reported. The bottom table reports names of products sold and the total quantity of each. You can use the options on the left-hand side to change the listing to reflect Product SKU, Product Category, and Source/Medium. The product-related names, SKU, and category come from the ecommerce information sent to Google Analytics, as discussed in Chapters 51 and 51a.

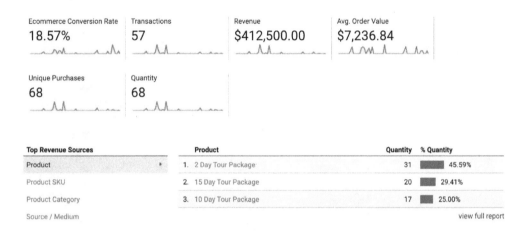

All of the metrics on the top of the display provide important insights into your ecommerce trends. Perhaps the most important is the ecommerce conversion rate, which is calculated as the *percentage of visits that resulted in an e-commerce transaction*. As a result,

Ecommerce Conversion Rate = (# of ecommerce transactions / visits) * 100

As we've seen in previous data displays, ecommerce conversion data is a core part of many data tables. We can, for example, see the ecommerce conversion rate for different locations (**Audience > Geography > Location**) or different types of site visitors (**Audience > Behavior > New Vs. Returning**).

We can also look more closely at the ecommerce conversion rate by combining primary and secondary reporting dimensions. Imagine, for example, that you want to find the mobile ecommerce conversion rate for a cost-per-click (CPC) campaign. Either of the following approaches would provide the relevant data:

- Go to **Audience > Mobile > Overview**. Add a secondary dimension showing Traffic type.

- Go to **Audience > All traffic > Channels**. Add a secondary dimension showing Device Category.

It is often informative to use the **Conversions > Ecommerce > Overview** presentation to compare two time periods. Imagine, for example, that we select the period of February 20, 2017 to April 20, 2017 to compare to the same period a year earlier (which will be our baseline). The figure below shows that this comparison has been selected.

Summary statistics are shown below. The trend is not positive. While average order value increased slightly in the most recent period, all of the other ecommerce measures declined compared to one year ago.

The bottom tabular chart in the **Conversions > Ecommerce > Overview** report (see below) allows us to see the specific source of increased revenue. These data indicate that compared to a year earlier, there was a decline in the number of 2- and 10-day packages, while there was a slight increase in the number of 15-day packages. This in part explains the slight increase in average order value shown in the table above.

Top Revenue Sources	Product	Quantity	% Quantity
Product ▸	1. 2 Day Tour Package		
Product SKU	Feb 20, 2017 - Apr 20, 2017	31	45.59%
Product Category	Feb 20, 2016 - Apr 20, 2016	47	54.02%
Source / Medium	% Change	-34.04%	-15.61%
	2. 15 Day Tour Package		
	Feb 20, 2017 - Apr 20, 2017	20	29.41%
	Feb 20, 2016 - Apr 20, 2016	17	19.54%
	% Change	17.65%	50.52%
	3. 10 Day Tour Package		
	Feb 20, 2017 - Apr 20, 2017	17	25.00%
	Feb 20, 2016 - Apr 20, 2016	23	26.44%
	% Change	-26.09%	-5.43%

The **Conversions > Ecommerce > Product Performance** menu option provides summary ecommerce metrics for each product sold, in our case, the three tours of different durations: 2, 10, and 15 days (see table below). We can see that the 2-day package is the most frequently purchased, while the 15-day package makes the largest contribution to overall revenue (47.86%).

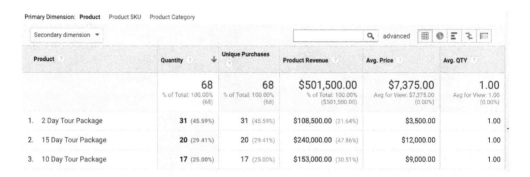

It is often useful to examine ecommerce product data in the context of a secondary dimension. The table shown below, for example, looks at product performance in the context of visitor type: new versus returning. Here we can see that there are distinct differences between the two types of site visitors in terms of the type of tour purchased by each group. Additionally, we can see that across all tour types, significantly more tours were purchased by returning compared to new visitors.

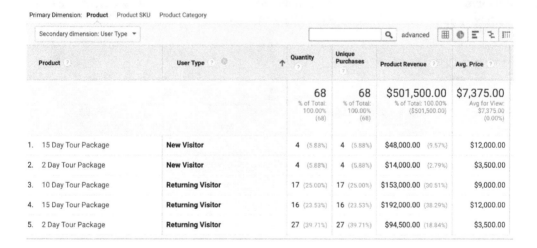

The table below examines product performance in the context of source (which we have placed in alphabetical order by clicking in the **Source** header box). We can see that the vast majority of purchases resulted from those who accessed the site directly.

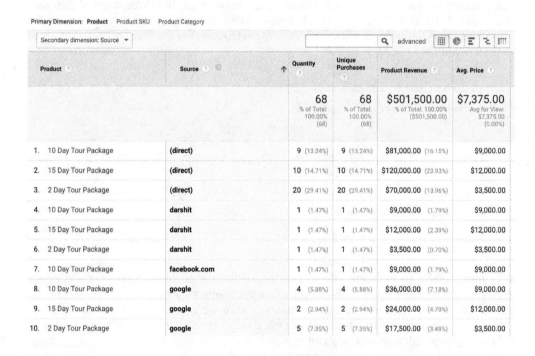

Primary Dimension: **Product**   Product SKU   Product Category

Product	Source	Quantity	Unique Purchases	Product Revenue	Avg. Price
		68 % of Total: 100.00% (68)	**68** % of Total: 100.00% (68)	**$501,500.00** % of Total: 100.00% ($501,500.00)	**$7,375.00** Avg for View: $7,375.00 (0.00%)
1. 10 Day Tour Package	(direct)	9 (13.24%)	9 (13.24%)	$81,000.00 (16.15%)	$9,000.00
2. 15 Day Tour Package	(direct)	10 (14.71%)	10 (14.71%)	$120,000.00 (23.93%)	$12,000.00
3. 2 Day Tour Package	(direct)	20 (29.41%)	20 (29.41%)	$70,000.00 (13.96%)	$3,500.00
4. 10 Day Tour Package	darshit	1 (1.47%)	1 (1.47%)	$9,000.00 (1.79%)	$9,000.00
5. 15 Day Tour Package	darshit	1 (1.47%)	1 (1.47%)	$12,000.00 (2.39%)	$12,000.00
6. 2 Day Tour Package	darshit	1 (1.47%)	1 (1.47%)	$3,500.00 (0.70%)	$3,500.00
7. 10 Day Tour Package	facebook.com	1 (1.47%)	1 (1.47%)	$9,000.00 (1.79%)	$9,000.00
8. 10 Day Tour Package	google	4 (5.88%)	4 (5.88%)	$36,000.00 (7.18%)	$9,000.00
9. 15 Day Tour Package	google	2 (2.94%)	2 (2.94%)	$24,000.00 (4.79%)	$12,000.00
10. 2 Day Tour Package	google	5 (7.35%)	5 (7.35%)	$17,500.00 (3.49%)	$3,500.00

Let's return to the original table displayed when **Conversions > Ecommerce > Product Performance** is selected from the left-hand menu (see below). Above the chart are three display options, where **Product** is currently selected.

Primary Dimension: **Product**   Product SKU   Product Category

Product	Quantity	Unique Purchases	Product Revenue	Avg. Price	Avg. QTY
	68 % of Total: 100.00% (68)	**68** % of Total: 100.00% (68)	**$501,500.00** % of Total: 100.00% ($501,500.00)	**$7,375.00** Avg for View: $7,375.00 (0.00%)	**1.00** Avg for View: 1.00 (0.00%)
1. 2 Day Tour Package	31 (45.59%)	31 (45.59%)	$108,500.00 (21.64%)	$3,500.00	1.00
2. 15 Day Tour Package	20 (29.41%)	20 (29.41%)	$240,000.00 (47.86%)	$12,000.00	1.00
3. 10 Day Tour Package	17 (25.00%)	17 (25.00%)	$153,000.00 (30.51%)	$9,000.00	1.00

Selecting **Product SKU** changes the display to that shown below. This more detailed table tells us which specific products are most popular and each product's contribution to revenue. As with the product names, the SKUs come from the information sent to Google Analytics when a transaction takes place. SKUs beginning with a 'M' refer to Mexico while SKUs beginning with a 'B' refer to the Bahamas. The number after each letter refers to the length of the tour. We can see that the two most popular tours (in terms of the quantity purchased) are the 2- and 15-day Mexican tours. The 15-day Mexican tour makes the greatest contribution to revenue.

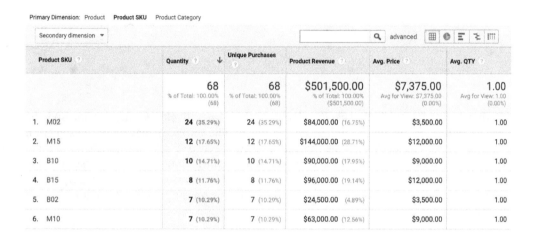

The preference for Mexican tour packages can also be seen when we select **Product Category** from the link options appearing above the table. As shown below, we can see that Mexico packages account for a majority of both sales (63.24%) and revenue (58.03%). We would certainly want to determine the strategic implications of these disproportionate sales.

Let's return one last time to the initial table displayed by the **Conversions > Ecommerce > Product Performance** menu option (see below).

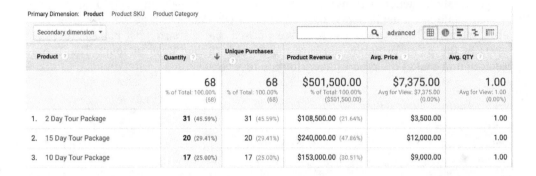

Clicking on the name of any specific product brings up a display of information specific to that product, in this case 10-day tour packages. The initial display after the selection of '10 Day Tour Package' is a table that shows SKU-associated revenue metrics (see table below). Here we can see that there were seven Mexican 10-day tours sold versus ten 10-day Bahamas tours. This information is summarized in terms of product category in the bottom table below. This table is generated by clicking on the **Product Category** link on the top of the table.

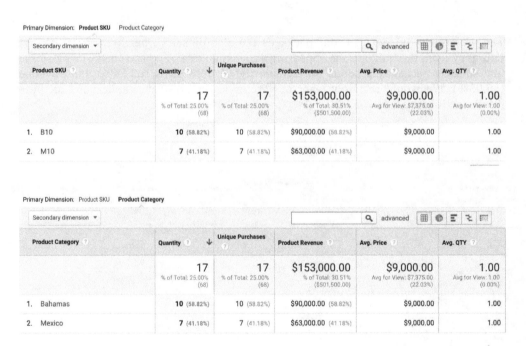

Selecting **Conversions > Ecommerce > Sales Performance** generates a table similar to that shown below. Here, revenues by day of sale are placed in descending order based on revenue generated.

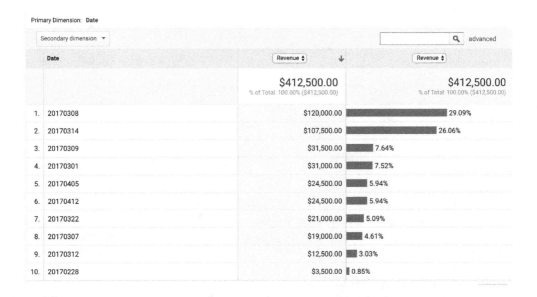

This chart can be organized by descending or ascending date, as shown in the chart below. This view is particularly useful for helping you see how revenue grows or declines over time. We put the dates in sequence by clicking in the **Date** box on the top of the table.

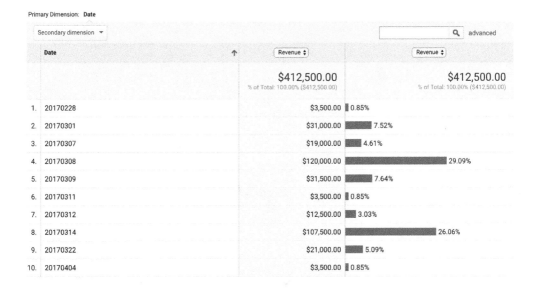

Transactions

The **Conversions > Ecommerce > Transactions** menu option is similar to the previous display, except now revenues are reported in terms of your Transaction ID, which as discussed in Chapters 52 and 52a is sent to Google Analytics as part of the ecommerce data transmission. There is only one Transaction ID listed in the chart, as all of our transactions are hardcoded to use the same ID.

Transaction ID	Revenue ↓	Tax	Shipping	Quantity
	$412,500.00 % of Total: 100.00% ($412,500.00)	$0.00 % of Total: 0.00% ($0.00)	$0.00 % of Total: 0.00% ($0.00)	68 % of Total: 100.00% (68)
1. 1234	$412,500.00 (100.00%)	$0.00 (0.00%)	$0.00 (0.00%)	68 (100.00%)

Time to Purchase

Finally, the **Conversions > Ecommerce > Time to Purchase** menu option provides two data displays. The specific display is selected via the options presented beneath the **Distribution** tab.

Days to Transaction reports the number of days that pass between the initial site session and an ecommerce transaction. This table shown below)] indicates that most transactions are either made immediately (i.e., zero days to transaction) or after a significant time lag (i.e., 28+ days to transaction).

Distribution		

Days to Transaction   Sessions to Transaction

Transactions

57
% of Total: 100.00% (57)

Days to Transaction	Transactions	Percentage of total
0	15	26.32%
1	2	3.51%
6	4	7.02%
7-13	5	8.77%
14-20	1	1.75%
28+	30	52.63%

Sessions to Transaction reports the number of sessions that pass between the initial site session and the session with a transaction. When interpreted in conjunction with the previous table, this table (see below) reinforces the interpretation that transactions are made either soon after first site access or after a significant number of site sessions.

Distribution

Days to Transaction   Sessions to Transaction

Transactions
57
% of Total: 100.00% (57)

Sessions to Transaction ?	Transactions ?	Percentage of total
1	9	15.79%
2	9	15.79%
3	6	10.53%
4	4	7.02%
5	6	10.53%
6	11	19.30%
7-25	12	21.05%

Section XIII:
The Conversions Menu

In today's digital world, consumers encounter a number of touch points on their way to a conversion (for example, purchasing a product). A typical consumer might first learn about a product via an email, then read reviews, then read about the product on several blogs, then visit the product's website, then read more reviews, then see an AdWords ad, and then finally purchase the product. Attribution is the process by which a marketer assigns a value to each of these touch points in order to determine the relative contribution of each touch point to the final conversion. The four chapters in this section lead you through the process of working with and applying attribution models.

- Chapter 53 discusses conversions and assisted conversions in the context of multi-channel funnels.
-
- Chapter 54 discusses the strengths and weaknesses of the primary types of attribution models.

- Chapter 55 illustrates how to obtain and apply Google Analytics attribution data to your own strategic information needs.

- Chapter 56 illustrates how attribution can help you better understand your return on investment in various marketing channels.

53

Multi-Channel Funnels

Multi-Channel Funnels provide detailed insights into the goal of ecommerce conversions. The chapter begins with a discussion of Multi-Funnel Channel characteristics and interpretation. This is followed by a focus on the data reporting options available for Multi-Channel Funnels (see below).[98]

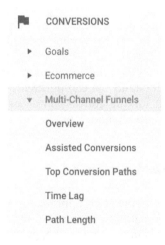

A complicated path to conversion

You'll recall that there are many types of conversions in Google Analytics. A site visitor can convert, for example, when a specific goal is achieved or when an ecommerce transaction is completed. Google Analytics, by default, gives all the credit to the last traffic source touch point encountered prior to the conversion.

Imagine, for example, Betsy's search for a new espresso machine:

- Betsy starts by reading reviews in her favorite online food blogs. She begins to create a list of brands in which she is interested. One of the blogs has a link to a review site, which Betsy visits.

---

[98] You must have set goals and/or ecommerce tracking in order to use Multi-Channel Funnels. The absence of goals/ecommerce tracking will result in an absence of data.

- The next day, Betsy does a Google search for 'espresso machines' and for each of the brands on her list. She clicks on several of the organic search terms, as well as several of the paid ads.

- Betsy narrows her list to two brands. She does another search to focus on just these two brands. The results show that there are YouTube videos related to each brand. She views the videos. Later that same day, while visiting her favorite food websites, she sees display advertising that describes a sale currently occurring at Best Buy. An espresso machine is featured in one of the ads. She clicks on the ad to visit the Best Buy site.

- Finally, Betsy decides on the brand she wants. She does another Google search to find the best price. She clicks on a paid search ad that takes her to Best Buy's website, where she buys a $500 machine.

Clearly, Betsy has had multiple touch points prior to her conversion. It really doesn't make sense to give all the credit for the conversion to her last touch point: paid search.

This is where multi-channel funnels and attribution come into play. Multi-channel funnels allow us to better understand the complicated path to conversion. Attribution allows us to spread the credit for the conversion across multiple touch points. Let's begin with an exploration of multi-channel funnels. The next two chapters then extend this discussion to attribution.

What are multi-channel funnels?

Multi-channel funnels are Google Analytics' approach to helping you better understand site visitors' often complicated paths to conversion by evaluating the interaction and contribution of multiple channels in the conversion/purchase cycle.

Google Analytics defines the journey through channels to conversion as the *conversion path*.

In order to create conversion paths, Google Analytics keeps track of all the touch point interactions a site visitor encounters prior to conversion. By default, only interactions within the prior 30 days are included, although you always have the option of shortening or lengthening this period.

Google Analytics' conversion paths monitor and analyze all of the standard channels available in other analytics reports. Thus, all of the default channel labels that you see in the Multi-Channel Funnel reports are defined by Google as part of the Multi-Channel Grouping. The default channels are:

Direct	Sessions in which a user typed your website URL directly into his/her browser or who came to your site via a bookmark.
Email	Sessions that are manually tagged with a medium of 'email'. (Tagging is explained in Chapter 48.)

Organic Search	Non-paid users to your site whose sessions begin at a search engine. Google tracks organic traffic from itself and most of the major search engines such as Bing and Yahoo. You can, if necessary, add additional search engines.
Paid Search	Traffic from the AdWords Search Network or other search engines identified as 'cost per click' or 'pay per click.'
Referral	Traffic from other websites not identified as social that link to your site.
Social	Traffic from social media sites like Facebook, Linkedin and Twitter. Referrals from links tagged as ads are not considered a social referral.
Display	Interactions with a medium of 'display' or 'cpm'. This channel also includes AdWords interactions with the ad distribution network set to 'content' but excluding ad format of 'text'.
Other Advertising	Sessions that are tagged with a medium of 'cpc', 'ppc', 'cpm', 'cpv', 'cpa', 'cpp', 'content-text', 'affiliate' (excluding paid search).

These existing channels should meet the needs of most websites and blogs. You can, however, visit and edit these channels by selecting **Channel Settings** in the **View** column of your Administrator's page. At this same location, if needed, you can create new channels that reflect your unique information or strategic needs. This will allow you to create your own custom channel grouping(s) in addition to the prior default channel groupings. Custom channel groups can be used immediately and can be applied to historical data.

Let's see how these channels are incorporated into Multi-Channel Funnel reports.

Overview

The **Conversions > Multi-Channel Funnels > Overview** menu option provides summary data. There are three parts to the data display.

The display on the top of the page (see the top of page 512) presents both data and a means to focus the data display. Prior to proceeding with data analysis, make certain that you set the options on the top of display to ensure that you are viewing the correct data set.

Conversion Segments   Shortcut

Conversion: Type: Lookback Window:

All ▾ | **All** | AdWords | Set [30] days prior to conversion ⑦

🥧 % of conversions: 100.00%

| Overview |

Conversions ▾ | **vs.** Select a metric

● Conversions

100

50

April 2015 ——— May 2015 ——— June 2015 ——— July 2015 ——— August 2015

The pull-down menu beneath **Conversion** (see the top right-hand side above and the pull-down menu below) allows you to focus the data display on all conversions (both goals and ecommerce), only ecommerce conversions, all goal conversions, or a subset of goal conversions. Make certain that you only check the conversions of interest.

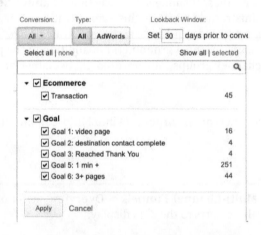

The center menu option, **Type** (which appears next to **Conversion**), allows you to select the source of the conversion. You can select either All conversions or specifically focus on AdWords conversions.

The **Lookback Window** (which appears next to **Type**) is an adjustable period of up to 90 days prior to each conversion. Only impressions and interactions occurring within this period are included in the data displayed.

You can move to the center of page data display once you've made your choices in the prior options.

An example center data display is shown below. This display focuses on ecommerce transactions conducted over the prior 30 days for the period ending January 31, 2016.

There were 188 total conversions of which 97 were assisted. Thus, about half of our ecommerce conversions (97 ÷ 188) involved at least two touch points.[99]

We can see the channels that took part in our conversion paths through the Multi-Channel Conversion Visualizer shown on the bottom of the **Conversions > Multi-Channel Funnels > Overview** display (see below).

Multi-Channel Conversion Visualizer

See the percentage of conversion paths that included combinations of the channels below. Select up to four channels.

Direct & Referral & Organic Search: 3.19% (6)

Channel	% of total conversions
☑ ⬤ Direct	97.87%
☑ ⬤ Referral	16.49%
☑ ⬤ Organic Search	8.51%

---

[99] In this context, an assisted conversion is one where one channel or traffic source appeared on the conversion path but was not the final conversion interaction, that is, the conversion was completed through another traffic source. In other words, an assisted conversion occurs when one traffic source results in a later goal completion through another traffic source.

There are two parts to this display. The table on the left-hand side displays all of the channels involved in any of our conversion paths. In my case, the conversion path can include up to three channels where Direct (primarily) and Referral (secondarily) were involved in the highest percentage of conversions. This is important for me to know because it has direct implications for evaluating how successful I've been in incorporating various channels in the path to an ecommerce conversion.

The Venn diagram on the right-hand side of the display visually shows the overlap across channels in the conversion path. The diagram on the bottom of page 513, for example, shows that all three touch points were involved in 3.19% of all transactions. We can move our cursor any single or combination of channels to see their individual or combined impact, as illustrated below. Here, we see that Direct and Organic Search worked together in 6.38% of conversions.

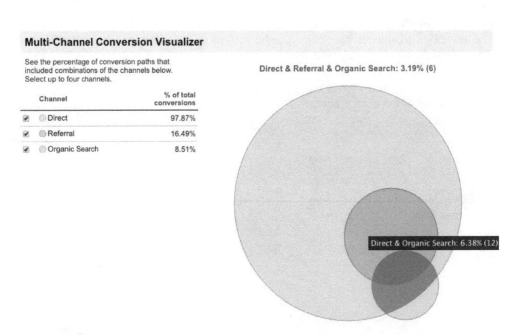

Finally, you can change the channels displayed in the Venn diagram by checking or unchecking channels in the left-hand side table.

Assisted Conversions

The **Conversions > Multi-Channel Funnels > Assisted Conversion** report summarizes the roles and contributions of each channel on the conversion path. A channel can play one of three roles in a conversion path:

- *Last interaction* is the interaction that immediately precedes the conversion.

- *Assist interaction* is any interaction that is on the conversion path but is not the last interaction.

- *First interaction* is the first interaction on the conversion path; it's one form of assist interaction.

Google Analytics calculates the metrics in the **Conversions > Multi-Channel Funnels > Assisted Conversion** by examining all the conversion paths for the conversions you're analyzing, as follows:

- *Assisted Conversions* and *Assisted Conversion Value*: This is the number (and monetary value) of sales and conversions the channel assisted. If a channel appears anywhere, except as the final interaction, on a conversion path, it is considered an assist for that conversion. The higher these numbers, the more important the assist role of the channel.

- *Last Click or Direct Conversions* and *Last Click or Direct Conversion Value*: This is the number (and monetary value) of sales and conversions the channel closed or completed. The final click or direct traffic before a conversion gets last interaction credit for that conversion. The higher these numbers, the more important the channel's role in driving completion of sales and conversions.

- *First Click Conversions* and *First Click Conversion Value*: The number (and monetary value) of sales and conversions the channel initiated. This is the first interaction on a conversion path. The higher these numbers, the more important the channel's role in initiating new sales and conversions.

- *Assisted/Last Click or Direct Conversions* and *First/Last Click or Direct Conversions*: These ratios summarize a channel's overall role. A value close to 0 indicates that a channel completed more sales and conversions than it assisted. A value close to 1 indicates that the channel equally assisted and completed sales and conversions. The more this value exceeds 1, the more the channel assisted sales and conversions.[100]

An example **Conversions > Multi-Channel Funnels > Assisted Conversion** report is shown on the top of page 516. The most valuable data is shown in the MCF channel report shown on the bottom table.

- Direct is the most important source of ecommerce sales, playing a role in most longer paths to conversion (i.e., assisted conversions) and especially as the final touch point (last click or direct conversions). The .59 in the last column (given that it is closer to one than zero) indicates that Direct equally assisted and completed sales and conversions.

---

[100] *Analyze Channel Contribution* at https://support.google.com/analytics/answer/1191204.

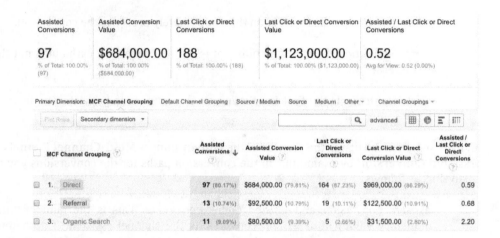

MCF Channel Grouping	Assisted Conversions ↓	Assisted Conversion Value	Last Click or Direct Conversions	Last Click or Direct Conversion Value	Assisted / Last Click or Direct Conversions
1. Direct	97 (80.17%)	$684,000.00 (79.81%)	164 (87.23%)	$969,000.00 (86.29%)	0.59
2. Referral	13 (10.74%)	$92,500.00 (10.79%)	19 (10.11%)	$122,500.00 (10.91%)	0.68
3. Organic Search	11 (9.09%)	$80,500.00 (9.39%)	5 (2.66%)	$31,500.00 (2.80%)	2.20

- The Referral channel shows a similar pattern, although this channel is a part of far fewer conversions overall. Increasing the number and quality of referrals should have a positive impact on ecommerce success.

- The Organic Search channel is an 'assist' rather than 'closing' channel. While this channel was a part of both assisted and last click conversions, the data trend as well as the number in the last column (2.20) indicate that this channel is much more likely to be a part (but not end) of the conversion path.

Top Conversion Paths

The **Conversions > Multi-Channel Funnels > Top Conversion Paths** shows all of the unique conversion paths (i.e., sequences of channel interactions) that led to conversions, as well as the number of conversions from each path and the value of those conversions (see below for the top seven paths). This allows you to see how channels interact along your conversion paths, thereby expanding on the insights obtained from the **Conversions > Multi-Channel Funnels > Assisted Conversion report.**

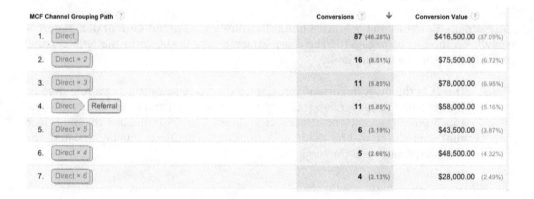

MCF Channel Grouping Path	Conversions ↓	Conversion Value
1. Direct	87 (46.28%)	$416,500.00 (37.09%)
2. Direct × 2	16 (8.51%)	$75,500.00 (6.72%)
3. Direct × 3	11 (5.85%)	$78,000.00 (6.95%)
4. Direct ▷ Referral	11 (5.85%)	$58,000.00 (5.16%)
5. Direct × 5	6 (3.19%)	$43,500.00 (3.87%)
6. Direct × 4	5 (2.66%)	$48,500.00 (4.32%)
7. Direct × 6	4 (2.13%)	$28,000.00 (2.49%)

This display confirms the conclusions drawn from the **Conversions > Multi-Channel Funnels > Assisted Conversion** report. Direct is a part of each of the top seven paths to conversion, playing a role either alone (as last click) or as part of a longer referral path (as in the path shown on line 4).

The **Conversions > Multi-Channel Funnels > Time Lag** report shows you the amount of time that has elapsed between a visitor's original session and a goal conversion (in this case, an ecommerce conversion).

Distribution

Conversions

188
% of Total: 100.00% (188)

Conversion Value

$1,123,000.00
% of Total: 100.00% ($1,123,000.00)

Time Lag in Days	Conversions	Conversion Value	Percentage of total Conversions	Conversion Value
0	119	$598,500.00	63.30%	53.29%
1	3	$27,500.00	1.60%	2.45%
2	7	$47,000.00	3.72%	4.19%
3	4	$28,000.00	2.13%	2.49%
4	6	$26,500.00	3.19%	2.36%
5	3	$24,500.00	1.60%	2.18%
8	1	$3,500.00	0.53%	0.31%
9	2	$15,500.00	1.06%	1.38%
12-30	43	$352,000.00	22.87%	31.34%

Thus, it appears that we have two types of transactions: those that take place during an initial session and those that take place in a session after a significant delay, in this case, 12 days or more. Both types of transactions make an important contribution to site revenue. Using segments, we would want to take a more detailed look at both of these types of transactions.

Conversions > Multi-Channel Funnels > Path Length allows us to focus in on how many steps preceded the conversion (see below). Note that the path-to-purchase conversion is quite short, with most users seeing only one page prior to making a purchase. This is consistent with the data that we've seen in the prior reports. We could use the **Conversions > Goals** reports to determine the specific pages viewed prior to purchase to better understand the overall purchase process.

Path Length in Interactions	Conversions	Conversion Value	Percentage of total Conversions / Conversion Value
1	91	$439,000.00	48.40% / 39.09%
2	27	$133,500.00	14.36% / 11.89%
3	12	$90,000.00	6.38% / 8.01%
4	5	$48,500.00	2.66% / 4.32%
5	6	$43,500.00	3.19% / 3.87%
6	6	$43,500.00	3.19% / 3.87%
7	2	$15,500.00	1.06% / 1.38%
8	3	$16,000.00	1.60% / 1.42%
9	1	$9,000.00	0.53% / 0.80%
10	2	$15,500.00	1.06% / 1.38%
12+	33	$269,000.00	17.55% / 23.95%

54

Attribution Models

Chapter 50 described how we determine which (if any) social networks served as a referral source immediately prior to a site session. But for many sites and blogs, the path to visitation or conversion is longer, containing many different channels in addition to social media (e.g., paid and organic search, display advertising, and email).

Let's take another look at Betsy's search for a new espresso machine, as described in the previous chapter:

- Betsy starts by reading reviews in her favorite online food blogs. She begins to create a list of brands in which she is interested. One of the blogs has a link to a review site, which Betsy visits.

- The next day, Betsy does a Google search for 'espresso machines' and for each of the brands on her list. She clicks on several of the organic search terms, as well as several of the paid ads.

- Betsy narrows her list to two brands. She does another search to focus on just these two brands. The results show that there are YouTube videos related to each brand. She views the videos. Later that same day, while visiting her favorite food websites, she sees display advertising that describes a sale currently occurring at Best Buy. An espresso machine is featured in one of the ads. She clicks on the ad to visit the Best Buy site.

- Finally, Betsy decides on the brand she wants. She does another Google search to find the best price. She clicks on a paid search ad that takes her to Best Buy's website, where she buys a $500 machine.

This is a complicated but not unrealistic path to conversion. We have two options for determining the contribution of each channel or digital encounter to the final sale (i.e., conversion). On the one hand, we can decide that the last click prior to conversion gets all the credit for the conversion. Since Betsy's last click prior to conversion was the paid ad, Best Buy would give all the credit for the sale to this ad. But this just doesn't feel right because it ignores all of the exposure and influence of everything Betsy saw prior to the purchase. On the other hand, we can spread out credit for the conversion to all channels encountered prior to the conversion. This is much more reasonable and is what attribution modeling allows us to do.

Attribution models are a way to distribute the value of a conversion across all of the channels or touch points an individual encountered prior to the conversion. In Betsy's case, the $500 she spent on the espresso machine would be distributed across the following channels: social, organic search, paid display advertising, and direct site access.

Attribution models make us strategically smarter about individual channel contributions to the path to conversion, which in turn helps us determine whether our efforts and associated spending to influence consumers reflect consumers' actual behaviors. Once we know this, we can answer marketers' most fundamental question: What is our return on investment across all of the digital channels in which we are engaged? (This topic is explored in Chapter 56.)

Google Analytics performs three of the data-intensive jobs that allow us to accomplish a distribution of conversion credit across digital channels:

- it tracks consumers' journey to purchase;

- for each consumer, it records exposure to different channels during that journey; and

- it does the math that allocates conversion value across channels.

Our very important job is to tell Google Analytics how to perform the allocation. We accomplish this through the selection of one or more attribution models.

We begin by determining which attribution model(s) make the most sense for our brand, website, or blog. The model(s) we select represent our current understanding of the value of each sequential digital encounter during the consumers' path to conversion. Google Analytics provides seven predefined models from which we can choose.[101] We'll illustrate each model with the path to conversion shown below. We'll update this path as we discuss each attribution model available in Google Analytics.

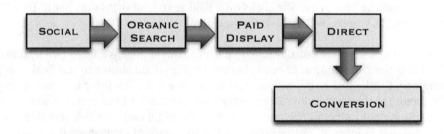

---

[101] We explore six of these models, ignoring the AdWords-focused model as this model applies only to AdWords advertisers.

This model assumes that only one channel influences the conversion and that this channel was the one encountered immediately preceding the conversion. No channel other than the one immediately prior to conversion is believed to exert any influence.

It is now almost universally understood that this attribution model oversimplifies the conversion process and distorts the influence of all channels encountered prior to the conversion. As a result, this model has extremely limited usefulness and should only be used when it is assumed that:

- the path to conversion is short, with little to no consideration or evaluation taking place prior to conversion, and

- all channels are believed to exert the same level of influence when they occur immediately prior to the conversion.

The Last Interaction attribution model is illustrated below where 100% of the credit for the conversion is given to direct site access. The influence of all other channels encountered prior to this access are ignored to reflect the assumption that the consumer decided to access the site directly without being influenced by any other channels.

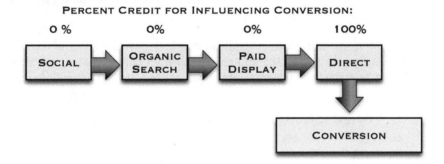

Last Non-Direct Click attribution model

This is a variation of the Last Interaction model. This model assumes that:

- direct site access and a subsequent conversion represent consumers who have already been influenced through a different channel prior to direct site access; and

- the conversion can be attributed entirely to the last channel encountered prior to direct site access; and

- all channels are believed to exert the same level of influence when they occur immediately prior to the conversion.

This model is illustrated below, where 100% of the credit for the conversion is given to paid display, the last channel encountered prior to direct site access. The influence of all other channels prior to paid display are ignored. This is the default model when attributing conversion values in non-Multi-Channel Funnel reports.

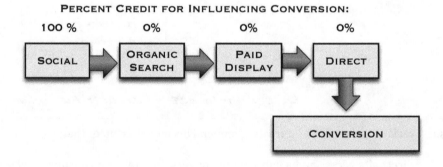

First Interaction attribution model

This model is a mirror image of the Last Interaction model and, as a consequence, reflects an opposite set of assumptions. The First Interaction attribution model assumes that only the first channel encountered in the path to conversion exerts any influence, regardless of the length of that path.

The First Interaction attribution model is illustrated below where 100% of the credit for the conversion is given to Social. The influence of all other channels are ignored because no channel other then the first one encountered is believed to exert any influence.

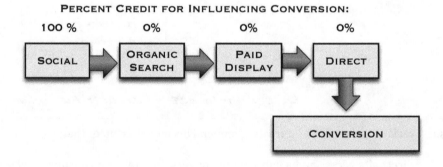

Linear Attribution model

This model deviates from the previous models in its belief that each channel deserves an equal amount of credit for the conversion. Here, it is assumed that all channels prior to a conversion are important and that every channel exerts an equal amount of influence.

The Linear Attribution model is illustrated below where credit for the conversion is allocated equally across all four channels encountered prior to the conversion, resulting in each channel being given 25% of the credit for the conversion.

PERCENT CREDIT FOR INFLUENCING CONVERSION:

| 25 % | 25% | 25% | 25% |

SOCIAL → ORGANIC SEARCH → PAID DISPLAY → DIRECT → CONVERSION

In the absence of other strategic information to inform your judgment regarding influences on the path to conversion, this and the next model are the recommended models to apply to your conversion data.

Time Decay model

The Time Decay model, illustrated below, assumes that all channels encountered prior to conversion exert some influence, *and* that this influence increases as the consumer moves closer to the conversion. Thus, channels encountered closer to the conversion are given relatively more credit for that conversion.

PERCENT CREDIT FOR INFLUENCING CONVERSION:

| 10 % | 20% | 30% | 40% |

SOCIAL → ORGANIC SEARCH → PAID DISPLAY → DIRECT → CONVERSION

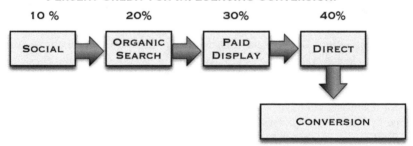

Google Analytics explains this model as follows: 'This model is based on the concept of *exponential decay* and most heavily credits the touch points [i.e. channels] that occurred nearest to the time of conversion. The Time Decay model has a default *half-life* of 7 days, meaning that a touch point occurring 7 days prior to a conversion will receive 1/2 the credit of a touch point that occurs on the day of conversion. Similarly, a touch point occurring 14 days prior will receive 1/4 the credit of a day-of-conversion touch point.'

Position Based model

This hybrid model reflects the assumptions of several of the previously discussed models. This model assumes that:

- all channels prior to a conversion are important, but

- the first and last encounter are relatively more important and therefore,

- the first and last encounter deserve to be given most of the credit for the conversion.

The Position Based model is illustrated below, where the first and last channels encountered are each given 40% of the credit for the conversion, while the remaining credit is distributed across the remaining channels.

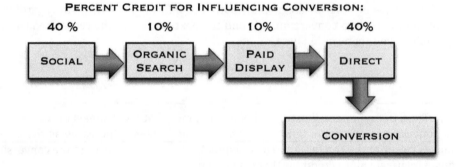

Attribution in practice

Once we specify a model, Google Analytics does all of the number crunching. Specifically, Google Analytics keeps track of every site users' path to conversion and then applies the selected model's credit allocation framework to that path.

Imagine, for example, that we want to use the Last Interaction attribution model to evaluate contributions to conversion. For simplicity, we'll apply this model to two site users, each of whom bought a $100 tour. Each user, however, took a different path to conversion, as shown on the top of page 525.

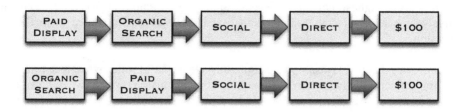

In each case, Google Analytics would by default, allocate 100% of the credit for the conversion to the last channel encountered, which in both cases is Direct. Our Google Analytics report would state that $200 of the total $200 conversion value should be given to Direct. We would then assume that we don't need to invest in any other channels, as all of our sales are credited to Direct.

This outcome illustrates the flaw in the Last Interaction attribution model. Notice that multiple channels are encountered prior to conversion, and that Social always precedes conversion. Certainly, these channels, especially Social, deserve some credit. We can see the influence of the channels encountered prior to conversion by changing our model to the Time Decay attribution model. This model would result in the following credit to each channel:

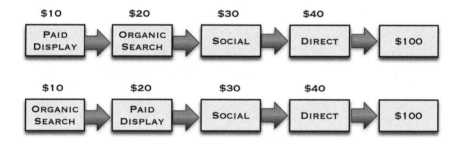

Adding the allocations for each channel results in the following:

Channel	Total $ Allocation	% of Total
Direct	$80	40%
Social	$60	30%
Paid Display	$30	15%
Organic Search	$30	15%

This outcome seems much more reasonable. Direct is given the most credit relative to the other channels, because it is the channel encountered immediately prior to the final conversion. Social's important role in always leading to the final channel is reflected in its high, but not highest, conversion credit. Finally, both Paid and Organic Search show relatively low levels of conversion credit given their relative distance from the final conversion.

The take away from this example is hopefully clear. The model we select to allocate credit for conversions has a direct impact on the conclusions we draw. Our use of the Last Interaction attribution model would lead us to believe that no channels other than Direct have any value to our business success. This conclusion would likely lead to disaster. The Time Decay attribution model, on the other hand, is much more likely to lead to business success, where we acknowledge the importance of Direct as the final channel encounter, but also note how Social plays an important role in leading to this final channel encounter and ultimate conversion.

55

Working With Attribution Models

We access Google Analytics attribution data from the **Conversions > Attribution > Model Comparison** menu option, shown below.

Clicking on **Model Comparison** brings up the display shown below. Before examining the data however, we need to make certain that all of the settings are appropriate to our strategic information needs.

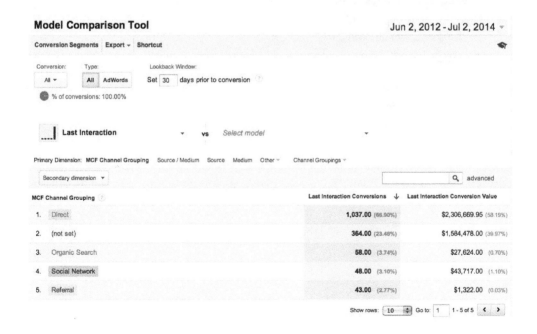

The very top of the page presents three options for data examination (see below).

- Within the **Conversion** pull-down menu (currently labeled 'All') is a list of all web site goals and ecommerce transactions. Use this menu to select only those items of interest. In our case, we'll focus on ecommerce transactions.

- The middle display, labeled **Type**, asks you to select the data of interest. Here you can decide to examine all data or to isolate the data associated with your AdWords campaigns. We'll leave the default as is and will select **All**.

- **Lookback Window** is the final option. This setting determines the amount of time Google Analytics will track channel encounters prior to the conversion. You can increase or decrease the Lookback Window by clicking in the numeric display window (which is set by default to 30) and then using the resulting slider bar to increase or decrease the window to reflect your assumptions as to the length of the consideration phase leading to conversion (see below). A window of 30 days is the generally accepted time frame.

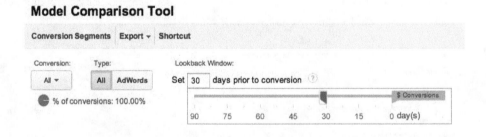

Once these settings are finalized, you can move on to interacting with the attribution models.

The initial data displayed after selecting **Conversions > Attribution > Model Comparison** is generated using the assumptions inherent in the Last Interaction attribution model (see below).

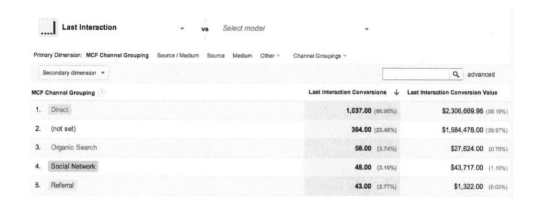

We know that the data represents the Last Interaction model because of the label immediately above the data display as well as the labels for the two data columns. This chart is interpreted as follows:

-   The first column, labeled **MCF Channel Grouping**, shows all of the channels encountered prior to purchase. In our case, users encountered our site directly, and also used organic search, social networks, and referrals. Note that '(not set)' means that Google Analytics could not determine a specific channel.

-   The middle column, labeled **Last Interaction Conversions**, reports the number of times each channel was given credit as the last channel encountered prior to conversion.

-   The last column, labeled **Last Interaction Conversion Value**, presents the allocated conversion dollar value for each channel, where this amount is allocated according to the assumptions of the model selected. In this case, each channel is given 100% of its conversion value when it was the last channel encountered prior to conversion.

The data derived in this model would lead to the conclusion that only Direct is important and that it is a waste of time to place any effort in other channels.

We can test this conclusion by altering the model used to generate the data. Above the table (on the left-hand side) is a chart description currently labeled **Last Interaction**. This is actually a pull-down menu (see below) that allows you to change the model.

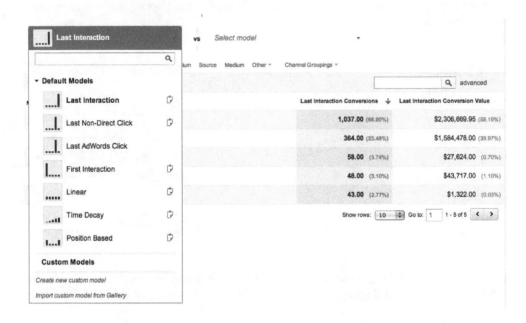

Selecting **Position Based**, for example, changes the data display to that shown below.

The outcomes derived from this model's assumptions appear (not unexpectedly) to be different than those shown in the **Last Interaction** model. However, it's hard to keep all the numbers in your head to make a direct comparison. Fortunately, Google Analytics simplifies this task for you.

In the previous section we saw how Google Analytics allows you to change the model being displayed. We can use this same portion of the display to simultaneously select, view, and compare two or three models in the same display.

To the right of the currently selected model name is a pull-down menu labeled **Select Model**. You can see this option just to the right of the **Last Interaction** label in the display shown below.

This pull-down menu labeled 'Select model' also displays a list of attribution models (see below).

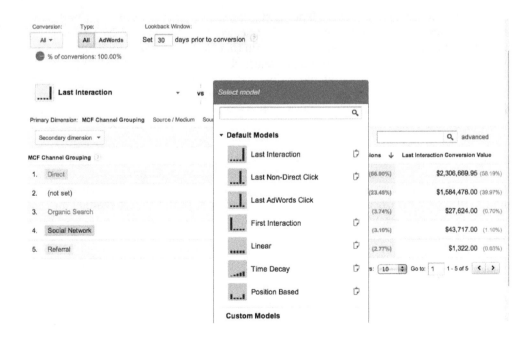

Selecting a model from this list, in this case **Position Based**, changes the data display to that shown below. Note that the names of both of the selected attribution models are now displayed above the numeric table.[102]

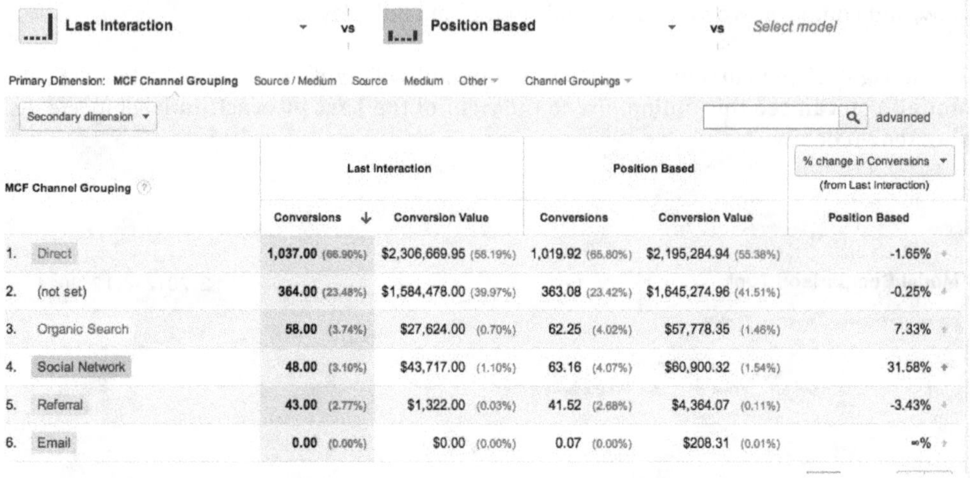

	Last Interaction		Position Based		% change in Conversions ▾ (from Last Interaction)
MCF Channel Grouping ⑦	**Conversions** ↓	**Conversion Value**	**Conversions**	**Conversion Value**	**Position Based**
1. Direct	1,037.00 (66.90%)	$2,306,669.95 (58.19%)	1,019.92 (65.80%)	$2,195,284.94 (55.38%)	-1.65% ↗
2. (not set)	364.00 (23.48%)	$1,584,478.00 (39.97%)	363.08 (23.42%)	$1,645,274.96 (41.51%)	-0.25% ↗
3. Organic Search	58.00 (3.74%)	$27,624.00 (0.70%)	62.25 (4.02%)	$57,778.35 (1.46%)	7.33% ↗
4. Social Network	48.00 (3.10%)	$43,717.00 (1.10%)	63.16 (4.07%)	$60,900.32 (1.54%)	31.58% ↗
5. Referral	43.00 (2.77%)	$1,322.00 (0.03%)	41.52 (2.68%)	$4,364.07 (0.11%)	-3.43% ↗
6. Email	0.00 (0.00%)	$0.00 (0.00%)	0.07 (0.00%)	$208.31 (0.01%)	∞% ↗

The table simultaneously presents data generated from both attribution models. The format is the same as the single model display. The first column displays channels encountered on the path to conversion, while the next two pairs of columns present conversions and conversion amounts for each attribution model. The last column allows us to compare the outcomes of the two models.

At the moment, the last column is labeled **% Change in Conversions** via a pull-down menu, and this change is relative to our first selected model: **Last Interaction**. Given how this comparison is calculated, make certain that the attribution model that you are using as your frame of reference is always selected first. Notice how changing the model changes the conclusions we draw about the relative contribution of different channels. Direct remains the most important channel, but the number of conversions attributed to organic search and especially social network referral increased substantially when we shift to the **Position Based** model.

We can change the right-hand comparison from conversions to conversion value by selecting the pull-down menu currently labeled **% Change in Conversions** and selecting **% Change in Conversion Value**. This changes the previous display to that shown on the top of page 533. Once again, we see the importance of the Direct channel, but the remaining channels are now significantly more important in terms of their contribution to conversion amount.

Here we can see how the model we select has a direct influence on how we interpret the success of our efforts and formulate subsequent strategic decisions.

---

[102] This example compares two models. You can, however, compare three models at the same time by using the Select Model pull-down menu to add a third model to the display,

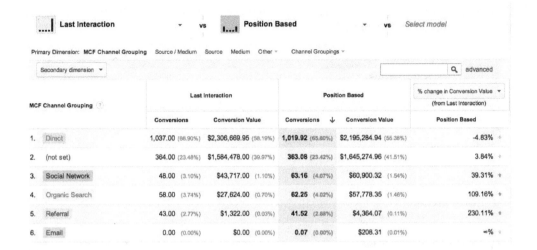

| MCF Channel Grouping ⑦ | Last Interaction | | Position Based | | % change in Conversion Value ▾ (from Last Interaction) |
	Conversions	Conversion Value	Conversions ↓	Conversion Value	Position Based
1. Direct	1,037.00 (86.90%)	$2,306,669.95 (58.19%)	1,019.92 (65.80%)	$2,195,284.94 (55.38%)	-4.83% ◢
2. (not set)	364.00 (23.48%)	$1,584,478.00 (39.97%)	363.08 (23.42%)	$1,645,274.96 (41.51%)	3.84% ◢
3. Social Network	48.00 (3.10%)	$43,717.00 (1.10%)	63.16 (4.07%)	$60,900.32 (1.54%)	39.31% ◢
4. Organic Search	58.00 (3.74%)	$27,624.00 (0.70%)	62.25 (4.02%)	$57,778.35 (1.46%)	109.16% ◢
5. Referral	43.00 (2.77%)	$1,322.00 (0.03%)	41.52 (2.68%)	$4,364.07 (0.11%)	230.11% ◢
6. Email	0.00 (0.00%)	$0.00 (0.00%)	0.07 (0.00%)	$208.31 (0.01%)	∞% ◢

Custom attribution models

After you work with Google Analytics standard attribution models for a while, you may decide that you need to create your own model, one that reflects your own unique business situation and your specific customers' paths to conversion. Fortunately, Google Analytics makes this easy to accomplish.

Let's imagine that the standard **Position Based** attribution model best fits your analytical needs, but that it could nevertheless be fine-tuned to better describe your customers' paths to conversion. You begin the customization process by activating the pull-down menu attached to the current attribution model's name, as shown on below.

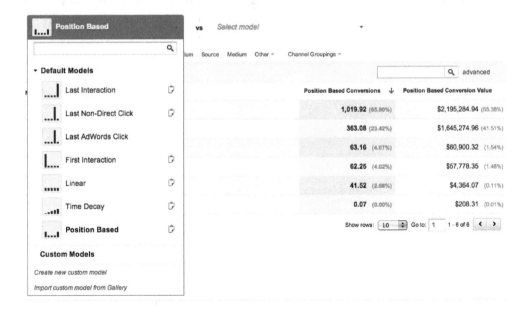

On the very bottom of the menu is a link labeled **Create new custom model**. Clicking on this link brings up the display shown below.

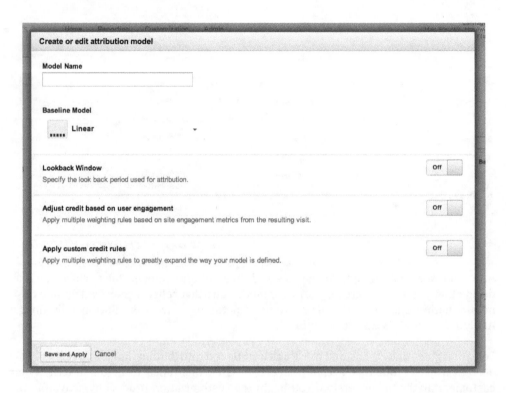

We'll name the file 'Modified Position Based Model' and select **Position Based** from the **Baseline Model** pull-down menu. The display then changes to items relevant to the Position Based model, as shown page 535.

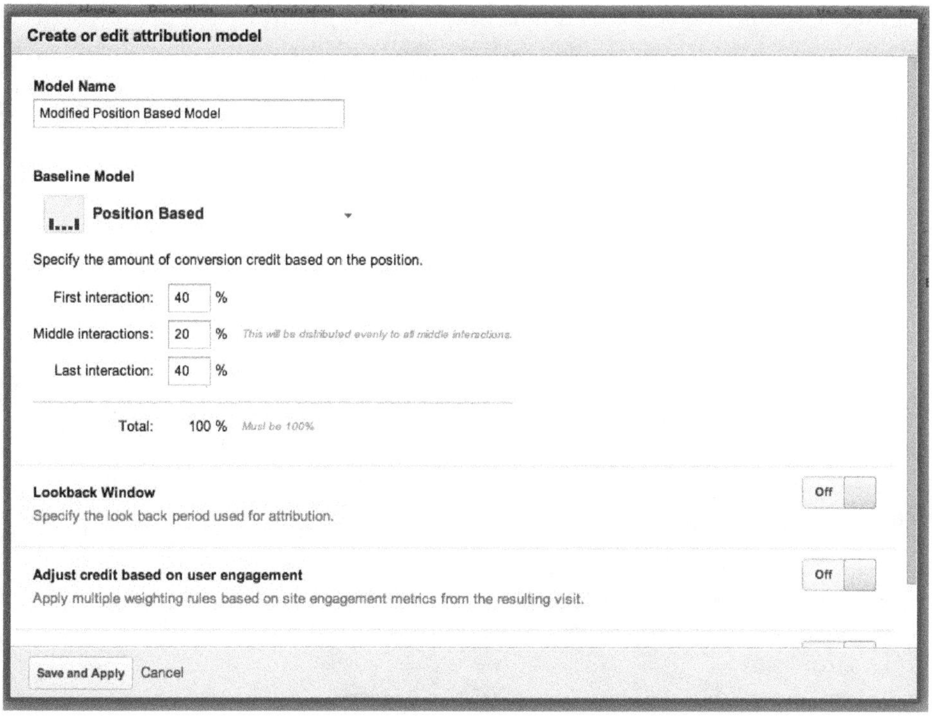

Create or edit attribution model

Model Name

Modified Position Based Model

Baseline Model

I...I   Position Based   ▾

Specify the amount of conversion credit based on the position.

First interaction: [40] %

Middle interactions: [20] %   *This will be distributed evenly to all middle interactions.*

Last interaction: [40] %

Total: 100 %   *Must be 100%*

Lookback Window   [Off]
Specify the look back period used for attribution.

Adjust credit based on user engagement   [Off]
Apply multiple weighting rules based on site engagement metrics from the resulting visit.

[Save and Apply]   Cancel

The standard Position Based model's assumptions for distributing conversion credit are shown in the middle of the display. The model currently uses a 40 - 20 - 40 percent distribution. But, we want this new model to distribute conversion credit as 50 - 35 - 15 percent. So, we change the percentages shown to these new percentages. Next, we turn the **Lookback Window** 'On' and then use the slider or text box to indicate 30 days. Finally, we leave the last two settings turned 'Off'. All of these settings are shown on the top of page 536. When we are satisfied with our settings, we click **Save and Apply**. The custom attribution model is then applied to the current data set.

The table below and the table on the top of page 537 compare our Modified Position Based model to the standard Position Based model. Both tables indicate that our change in how conversion credit is allocated affects both conversion credit (the table below) and especially conversion amount (the table on the top of page 537).

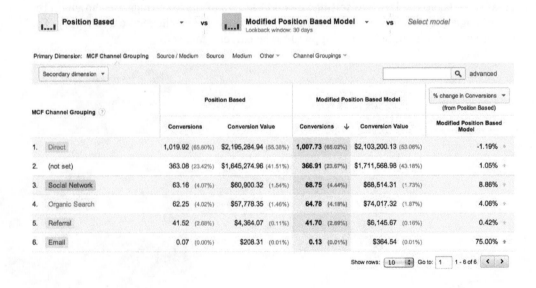

MCF Channel Grouping ⑦	Position Based		Modified Position Based Model		% change in Conversions ▾ (from Position Based)
	Conversions	Conversion Value	Conversions ↓	Conversion Value	Modified Position Based Model
1. Direct	1,019.92 (65.80%)	$2,195,284.94 (55.38%)	1,007.73 (65.02%)	$2,103,200.13 (53.06%)	-1.19% ◦
2. (not set)	363.08 (23.42%)	$1,645,274.96 (41.51%)	366.91 (23.67%)	$1,711,568.98 (43.18%)	1.05% ◦
3. Social Network	63.16 (4.07%)	$60,900.32 (1.54%)	68.75 (4.44%)	$68,514.31 (1.73%)	8.86% ◦
4. Organic Search	62.25 (4.02%)	$57,778.35 (1.46%)	64.78 (4.18%)	$74,017.32 (1.87%)	4.06% ◦
5. Referral	41.52 (2.68%)	$4,364.07 (0.11%)	41.70 (2.69%)	$6,145.67 (0.16%)	0.42% ◦
6. Email	0.07 (0.00%)	$208.31 (0.01%)	0.13 (0.01%)	$364.54 (0.01%)	75.00% ◦

Show rows: 10 ▾ Go to: 1 1 - 6 of 6 < >

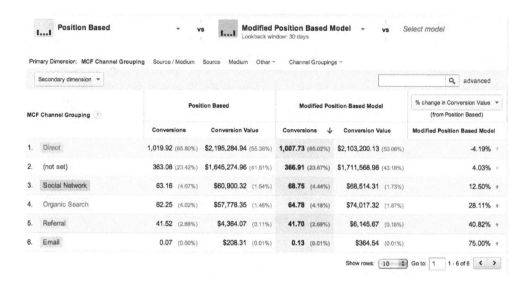

You can select, edit, or share custom attribution models by using the attribution model pull-down menu and scrolling down (if necessary) to **Custom Models**, as shown below.

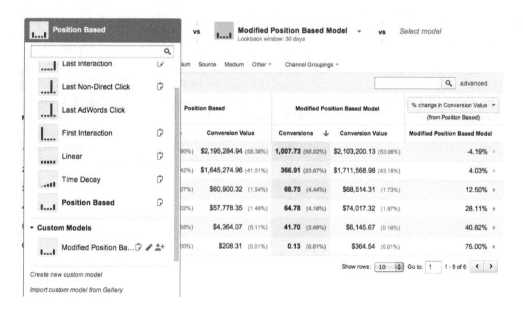

We don't need to end model customization with just the percentage allocation for conversion credit and conversion value. We can select and give extra credit to a channel that we believe deserves extra credit regardless of its position in the conversion path. Imagine, for example, that we think the Social channel exerts an important influence at any point in the conversion path in which it appears; and as a result, we want our model to take this into account when calculating credit for conversions and conversion amounts.

We begin by selecting **Create new custom model** in the model pull-down menu (see the bottom of the lower figure on page 537). This model begins the same as the previous model, only this time with a new name. We'll call this new model 'Social Bonus Modified Position Based'. Next, we select Position Based as our baseline model, change the percentages shown to 50 - 35 – 15, turn the **Lookback Window** 'On', and then use the slider or text box to indicate 30 days. Finally, we scroll to the bottom of the page and turn **Adjust custom credit rules** 'On'. The figure shown below will then appear.

The top pull-down menu (currently labeled **Position in Path**) allows us to choose the type of interaction to which we want to allocate extra credit. We select **MCF Channel Grouping** from this menu and **Social Network** from the menu to its immediate right. Then, on the bottom of the display we set the credit display to '10' to indicate that we want Social Network to have ten times the credit of other channels in the path to conversion (see below). When done, we select **Save and Apply** from the bottom of the page (which is not shown below).

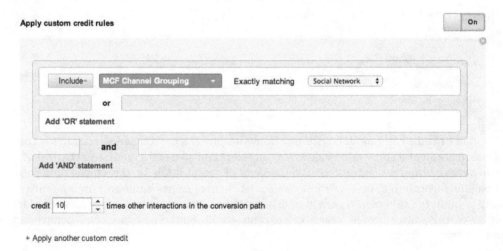

The table below displays the conversion amount credit assigned by the original **Position Based** model and the **Social Bonus Modified Position Based** model. Notice how all channels are affected, some much more than others, as we change the underlying assumptions of the model. This is why, from a strategic perspective, it is so important to develop a model that fits your unique set of conversion circumstances.

Position Based vs Social Bonus Modified Positi... vs Select model

Primary Dimension: **MCF Channel Grouping** Source / Medium Source Medium Other Channel Groupings

Secondary dimension | advanced

MCF Channel Grouping	Position Based		Social Bonus Modified Position Based		% change in Conversion Value (from Position Based)
	Conversions	Conversion Value	Conversions	Conversion Value	Social Bonus Modified Position Based
1. Direct	1,019.92 (65.80%)	$2,195,284.94 (55.38%)	982.27 (63.37%)	$2,089,385.24 (52.71%)	-4.82%
2. (not set)	363.08 (23.42%)	$1,645,274.96 (41.51%)	365.99 (23.61%)	$1,698,799.35 (42.86%)	3.25%
3. Social Network	63.16 (4.07%)	$60,900.32 (1.54%)	97.55 (6.29%)	$95,171.78 (2.40%)	56.27%
4. Organic Search	62.25 (4.02%)	$57,778.35 (1.46%)	63.02 (4.07%)	$74,003.58 (1.87%)	28.08%
5. Referral	41.52 (2.68%)	$4,364.07 (0.11%)	41.05 (2.65%)	$6,123.64 (0.15%)	40.32%
6. Email	0.07 (0.00%)	$208.31 (0.01%)	0.11 (0.01%)	$327.37 (0.01%)	57.15%

Refining the data

We can not only change the underlying assumptions of an attribution model, but we can also change the data to which the model is applied.

It is often useful to restrict the data displayed after an attribution model is selected. These restrictions allow you to more precisely focus on specific aspects of the path to conversion. This is accomplished by using the **Conversion Segments** pull-down menu just below the page title. Selecting a single option from this menu restricts the data set to only those paths to conversion that match your selected criteria. Clicking on this box brings up the display shown below where 'All Conversions' is checked by default.

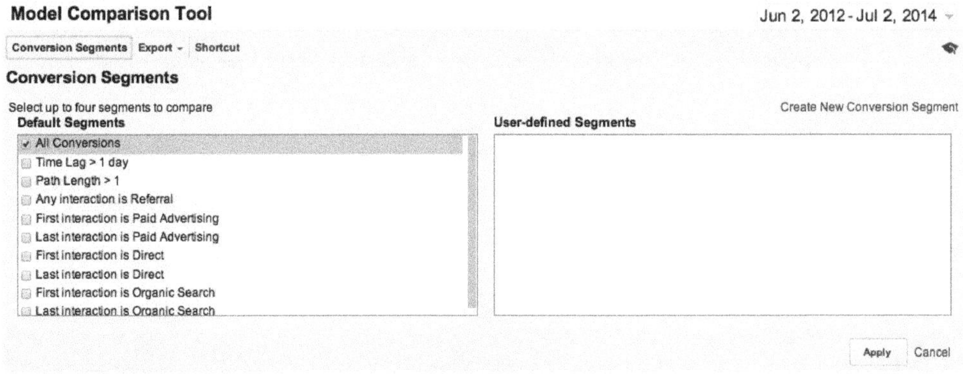
Model Comparison Tool
Jun 2, 2012 - Jul 2, 2014
Conversion Segments
Export
Shortcut
Conversion Segments
Select up to four segments to compare
Default Segments
All Conversions
Time Lag > 1 day
Path Length > 1
Any interaction is Referral
First interaction is Paid Advertising
Last interaction is Paid Advertising
First interaction is Direct
Last interaction is Direct
First interaction is Organic Search
Last interaction is Organic Search
User-defined Segments
Create New Conversion Segment
Apply
Cancel

As an example, I can choose to view conversion values for any path beginning with Organic Search or only those paths that are longer than a single encounter. Let's explore the first option.

Checking 'First Interaction is Organic Search' and unchecking 'All Conversions' in the pull-down menu restricts the data being analyzed to just the paths to conversion that begin with Organic Search. The data is shown below for the First Interaction attribution model.

Here we learn that there were 66 conversions in which the path to conversion began with Organic Search. These conversions were worth $87,919. But how did these paths end? We can answer this question by adding the Last Interaction Attribution Model to the table. This new table is shown below.

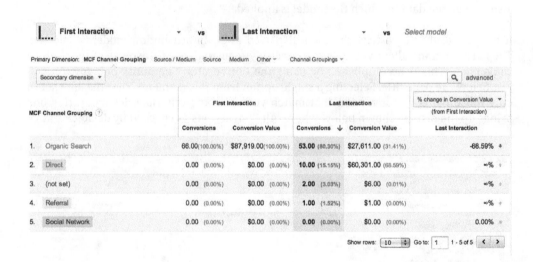

With this chart, we acquire a very important insight into the path to conversion when the path begins with Organic Search. Of the 66 conversions begun with Organic Search, 53 of these ended with organic search, indicating a path length of just this single encounter. However, 10 of the remaining paths begun with Organic Search ended with Direct. While this might seem a small number, look at the conversion column. The ten paths involving Direct as the final encounter generate significantly more revenue than when Organic Search is the only channel encountered. We would certainly want to explore this trend to determine how we can capitalize on the Organic Search to Direct path to conversion.

56

Attribution Data and Return on Investment

Attribution data provides the information marketers need to determine the return from their time and financial investment overall and in different channels. This chapter begins with a basic discussion of the return on investment calculation. It then moves on to an illustration of how this calculation can be performed using attribution data. Finally, the chapter closes with a discussion of the strategic application of this calculation to channel support. This discussion illustrates how you can conduct your own Return on Investment analysis.

Return on Investment defined

Return on Investment (ROI) is a calculation that places the revenue you receive from marketing efforts in the context of how much you spent to obtain those revenues. ROI is calculated as follows:

First, calculate your Net
Revenue (NR) by subtracting
Total Costs from Total Revenue: NR = Total Revenue – Total Costs

Next, divide NR by Total Costs to
obtain percent gain/loss (%GL) %GL = (NR ÷ Total Costs)

Finally, obtain ROI by multiplying
%GL by 100 and adding the
percent sign ROI = %GL * 100

Imagine, for example, that your total marketing expenditures for the year are $100,000 and that total revenues for the period are $250,000. Your return on investment would be calculated as follows:

First, calculate your Net Revenue (NR) by subtracting Total Costs from Total Revenue:	NR = Total Revenue – Total Costs	NR = 250,000 - 100,000 = **150,000**
Next, divide NR by Total Costs to obtain percent gain/loss (%GL)	%GL = NR / Total Costs	%GL = 150,000 ÷ 100,000 = **1.5**
Finally, obtain ROI by multiplying %GL by 100 and adding the percent sign	ROI = %GL * 100	ROI = 1.5 * 100 = **150%**

The ROI in this example indicates that we have made a 150% return on investment, that is, for every dollar spent we made $1.50. Thus, interpreting an ROI calculation is straight forward: a positive ROI means that we made money, a negative ROI means that we lost money.

Overall ROI

Our goal is to determine both overall and channel specific ROI. We'll use the data collected by Google Analytics to represent revenue. With this information, we'll calculate overall ROI first.

Two pieces of data are required for the computation of overall ROI: total revenues and total costs. We'll use the **Conversions > Ecommerce > Overview** report to find total revenue, which is $3,948,981.95 (this is the same number as adding the individual channels in the Conversion Value column in any of the **Conversions > Attribution > Model Comparison** reports). We'll round total revenues to $3,950,000. Our marketing expenditures for the same time period for all channels and activities were, in total, $3,750,000. We calculate overall ROI as follows:

First, calculate your Net Revenue (NR) by subtracting Total Costs from Total Revenue:	NR = Total Revenue – Total Costs	NR = ($3,950,000 - 3,750,000) = **200,000**
Next, divide NR by Total Costs to obtain percent gain/loss (%GL)	%GL = NR / Total Costs	%GL = 200,000/3,750,000 = **.05333**
Finally, obtain ROI by multiplying %GL by 100 and adding the percent sign	ROI = %GL * 100	ROI = .05333 * 100 = **5.33%**

Overall, not a great year for ROI. The revenue generated by all of our marketing activities just very barely exceeded our marketing expenditures.

The overall ROI results are pretty discouraging. An examination of ROI by channel may provide insights into this outcome.

In order to examine ROI by channel, we need to determine channel-specific expenditures and revenue for each channel. Channel-specific expenditures come from our internal records. Channel-specific revenues come from our selected attribution model report. We'll use the Social Bonus Modified Position Model created in Chapter 54 shown below.

Social Bonus Modified Positi... vs Select model

Primary Dimension: MCF Channel Grouping Source / Medium Source Medium Other Channel Groupings

Secondary dimension advanced

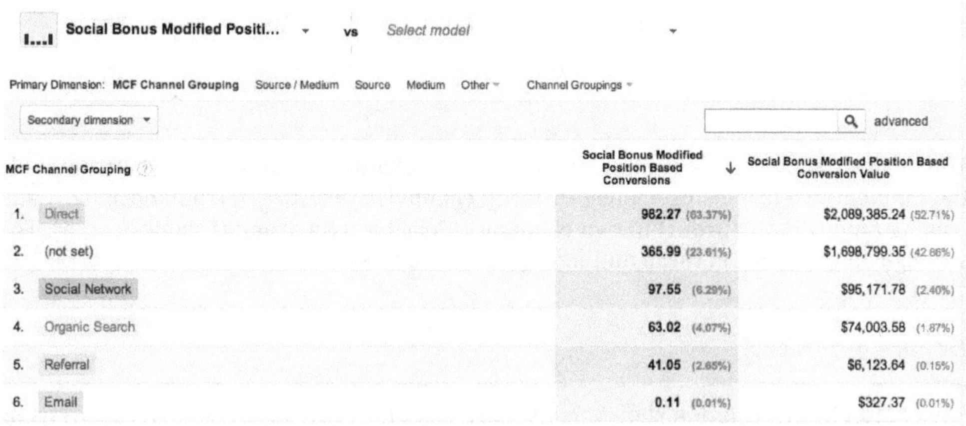

MCF Channel Grouping	Social Bonus Modified Position Based Conversions	Social Bonus Modified Position Based Conversion Value
1. Direct	982.27 (63.37%)	$2,089,385.24 (52.71%)
2. (not set)	365.99 (23.61%)	$1,698,799.35 (42.86%)
3. Social Network	97.55 (6.29%)	$95,171.78 (2.40%)
4. Organic Search	63.02 (4.07%)	$74,003.58 (1.87%)
5. Referral	41.05 (2.65%)	$6,123.64 (0.15%)
6. Email	0.11 (0.01%)	$327.37 (0.01%)

First, we create a table that provides revenues, expenditures, and net revenues by channel. Note that: (1) we include only those channels for which we have revenue estimates, (2) the **(not set)** channel grouping has been eliminated as we don't know the specific channel(s) that are reported here, and (3) the total of these channel expenditures does not equal the total expenditures shown in the previous section because those expenditures included activities beyond these specific channels. This table is shown below where all revenue numbers have been rounded.

Channel	Expenditures	Revenue	Net Revenue
Direct	$2,500,000	$2,089,390	- $410,610
Social Network	$50,000	$95,170	+ $45,170
Organic Search (for SEO)	$30,000	$74,000	+ $44,000
Referral	$9,000	$6,120	- $2,880
Email	$1,000	$330	- $670

All that remains is to use the ROI formula presented earlier to calculate ROI by channel. The results of these calculations have been added to the prior table, as shown below.

Channel	Expenditures	Revenue	Net Revenue	Channel ROI
Direct	$2,500,000	$2,089,390	- $410,610	-16.4%
Social Network	$50,000	$95,170	+ $45,170	+90.3%
Organic Search (for SEO)	$30,000	$74,000	+ $44,000	+146.7%
Referral	$9,000	$6,120	- $2,880	-32.0%
Email	$1,000	$ 330	- $670	-67.0%

The analysis shows that investments in different channels have different outcomes. At the moment, we are losing money in three channels (Direct, Referral, and Email) and making money (i.e., a profit) in two channels (Social Network and Organic Search). The strategic implications of these findings are discussed next.

Strategic ROI

The overall ROI calculation shows that we are just breaking even. The above analysis by channel shows us how well each channel is performing. The ROI by channel analysis also provides insights into how overall ROI can be improved.

- Direct conversions comprise the overwhelming majority of sales. But, the negative ROI indicates that we are losing money on this channel. We can use the **Conversions > Ecommerce > Overview** menu option combined with custom segments to discover that our conversion rate (18.6%) and average sale ($3,200) for this channel are both relatively low. We need to develop a strategic plan to increase both of these metrics. Beyond this, we need to become more efficient with regards to our marketing efforts in this channel. Decreasing expenditures while improving conversion rate and increasing average sale amount should reverse the negative ROI observed in this channel.

- Two channels, Social Network and Organic Search, show significant promise. At the moment, the overall dollar revenue from these channels is relatively low, but their ROI is very high. Investing marketing support in these channels, given their high ROI, should help our overall ROI improve. This is especially true given that these channels' conversion rates are very high (34.5% and 42.8%, respectively) as are their average sales ($5,100 and $6,500, respectively). Clearly, a strategic plan that provides greater support for these two channels is needed.

- Two channels, Referral and Email, appear to negatively impact our overall ROI. Revenue from these two channels is not only very low, but there also appears to be little motivation for us to invest in these channels given their negative ROI. Marketing support for these two channels should probably be eliminated and these funds should instead be invested in other areas where there is a greater likelihood of a positive return..

Section XIV:
Experiments

We often use our best informed judgment to make decisions with regard to site design and content. There are times, however, where important insights and direction come from a more objective source - data gathered via an experiment. An experiment allows us to ask a question, manipulate appropriate stimuli, and then collect data to see how the manipulations affect the outcome. We could, for example, develop three alternative versions of our home page and use judgment to pick the 'best.' Or, we could conduct an experiment, expose the pages to site visitors in a systematic way, and then use Google Analytics data to see the relationship between alternative page design and subsequent conversions. The latter approach is more likely to lead to a better decision.

The three chapters in this section introduce you to experiments and explain how you can conduct experiments with Google Analytics.

- Chapter 57 provides an introduction to experiments and experimental planning.

- Chapter 58 leads you through the steps required to create an experiment with Google Analytics.

- Chapter 59 discusses how to manage experiments and interpret the data collected through experiments.

Introduction to Experiments

The process of website or blog development typically begins with informed judgment. We apply what we know about our business, competitors, and target audience to decisions related to design and content. Google Analytics provides descriptive data that facilitates insights into the strengths and weaknesses of these decisions.

There are times and situations, however, when descriptive data is not enough, especially when we need the answers to 'how does' questions, for example:

- How does moving our sharing icons from the right- to left-hand side of the page affect the percentage of site visitors clicking to share?

- How does changing the placement of our 'Register Now' button affect registration rate?

- How does changing the length and style of our home page headline affect bounce rate?

- How does changing our call-to-action from text to image affect the rate of contact?

- How does altering our check-out process from three steps to two steps affect shopping cart abandonment and transaction completion?

- How does changing the images on our tour selection page from places to people affect transaction completion and amount?

All of these questions imply that we are seeking to determine causality - the effect of changes in one area on one or more other areas. The best way to determine causality is through an experiment.

The use of experiments to determine causality makes a significant contribution to successful website or blog planning and revision. Fortunately, Google Analytics provides an easy way to conduct experiments. Before discussing the specific types of experiments that can be conducted, however, one additional insight into experimental planning is necessary.

The planning stage of an experiment is crucial to the experiment's ability to provide insightful, actionable information. Thus, when planning an experiment it is necessary to explicitly answer the following questions prior to initiating the experiment:

- What is the background, that is, what concerns or information needs are motivating the experiment?

- What do we need to manipulate?

- How will we measure the outcome of the manipulation?

- Is the manipulation reasonable, that is, why do we believe that there is a relationship between what we are manipulating and what we are measuring as the outcome(s)?

The use of these questions in experimental planning is illustrated below.

What is the background and how does this lead to what we specifically need to learn?	The bounce rate of our home page is unacceptably high (42%) and has consistently remained at this level over the past three months. It has been proposed that the font used on this page is both too small and too dense in layout, discouraging visitors from staying and engaging with the content. We need to learn whether altering the type appearance on the home page reduces the bounce rate.
What do we need to manipulate?	We need to manipulate the type style and density. Specifically, we will increase the type size from 9-point to 12-point and at the same time we will move from single to double spacing. Content will remain unchanged.
How will we measure the outcome of the manipulation?	We will evaluate the effect of the manipulation in terms of bounce rate, comparing the bounce rate of the original page to that of the revised page. Data on both pages will be collected at the same time, keeping the effect of any external influences on the outcome consistent across both pages.
Is the manipulation reasonable?	It is believed that the effect of type size and density on bounce rate is reasonable, as competitive sites all use less dense approaches to content presentation.

An A/B experiment is the simplest form of experimental design.

An A/B test evaluates the effect of a **single** revision or change on your outcome measure(s), where 'A' refers to your original stimulus and 'B' refers to your altered stimulus. An A/B test, for example, might alter the color of a 'register now' button while leaving placement and all other page elements the same. Alternatively, an A/B test might alter the headline on the page, once again leaving all other elements the same. Thus, in an A/B test it is crucial that only one revision be made at a time, allowing any differences in outcome between the A and B versions to be attributed to the single change. Given a single change, the execution of an A/B test is straightforward, as illustrated in the above figure: half of site visitors are randomly assigned to view the 'A' version while the remaining half view the 'B' version.

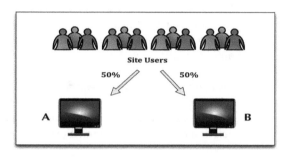

Every A/B test is unique in that it is designed to satisfy a specific set of strategic information needs. However, across websites and blogs, the following are commonly addressed issues:

- the wording, size, color and placement of calls to action

- the placement and size of sharing icons

- the wording and appearance of a headline or product description

- the layout of page functional elements such as menus, content, and images

- form layout and field sequence

- types, size and placement of images

There are better and worse ways to conduct an A/B test. .[103]

Things to do:

- *Know how long to run a test.* Ending the test too early can lead to false conclusions because you may have gotten different results had you waited a little longer to obtain more data from a larger sample. Ending the test too late isn't good either, because poorly performing variations could cost you conversions and sales. You can estimate how long to run a test by using a calculator like the

---

[103] Adapted from Smash Magazine, http://www.smashingmagazine.com/2010/06/24/the-ultimate-guide-to-a-b-testing/

one provided by Visual Website Optimizer[104] or you can keep running the test until you find a statistically significant difference between the A and B variations.

- *Show repeat visitors the same variations.* You should have a mechanism for remembering which variation a visitor has seen. This prevents visitor confusion when, for example, the same visitor is shown different visuals, prices, offers, or content on different visits.

- *Make your A/B test consistent across the whole website.* If you are testing a sign-up button that appears in multiple locations, then a visitor should see the same variation everywhere. Showing one variation on your home page and another variation on the registration page will confuse the visitor and skew the results.

Things not to do:

- *Never wait to test the variation until after you've tested the original.* Always test both versions simultaneously. If you test one version one week and the second variation the next week, extraneous variables may be the real influence on the outcome. It's possible, for example that the 'B' version is actually less effective than the 'A' version in motivating sales, but you had better sales while testing it because a huge snowstorm kept people indoors during use of this version. Always split traffic between two versions at the same time.

- *Don't surprise regular visitors.* If you are testing a core part of your website, include only new visitors in the test. This can be done through the use of cookies outside of Google Analytics. You want to avoid shocking regular visitors, especially because the variations may not ultimately be implemented.

- *Don't let your gut feeling overrule test results.* The winners in A/B tests are often surprising or counter-intuitive. On a green-themed website, a stark red button could emerge as the winner, even if the red button isn't easy on the eye. Don't reject an outcome simply because you disagree with or predicted different results.

Finally, there are two important things to keep in mind with regard to A/B testing. First, A/B tests are not restricted to websites. You can use the same approach to test the comparative impact of alternative approaches within email, blog posts, and similar digital communications. Second, it is possible to test three (or more) variations of the same change at the same time. Imagine, for example, that you wanted to test the impact of photos of people (the original) versus pets (revision 'B') versus scenery (revision 'C'). Since only one element is changing across variations (i.e., image subject matter), this would simply be an A/B/C test.

---

[104] See http://visualwebsiteoptimizer.com/ab-split-test-duration/

A/B tests explore the effect of a single revision on one or more outcome measures. Sometimes, though, it is necessary to simultaneously measure the effects of two manipulations at the same time. We choose this approach when we think that there may be some interaction or interplay between the two manipulations. Let's illustrate this approach with an example.

Imagine a home page with a high bounce rate. This page is visually quite dense, with a display that includes many small pictures and uses very small type. You want to know whether a change in just pictures *or* just type *or* both pictures and type at the same time will affect the bounce rate. This information need can be answered with a factorial design.

Once the planning questions have been answered, a factorial design experiment begins with the identification of factors and levels. A factor is a manipulation. We have two factors in this example, pictures and text. Each factor consists of two or more levels (also referred to as options), which represent the actual manipulations. In this case, each factor has two levels. The levels for pictures will be Eight (the number of pictures on the current home page) and Four (the number of pictures on the revised page). The levels for text will be Small (as on the current page) and Large (as on the revised page).

The number of stimuli needed for a factorial design experiment is determined by multiplying the numbers of levels across all factors. In this case we would need four stimuli (obtained by multiplying 2 x 2; 2 levels of pictures x 2 levels of type). We then create one stimuli for each combination of levels. This is illustrated in the grid shown below where the numbers refer to variation numbers.

	Small Type	**Large Type**
Eight pictures	1	2
Four pictures	3	4

The four numbered variations in the grid will have the following characteristics:

Variation 1:	Small type, Eight pictures
Variation 2:	Large type, Eight pictures
Variation 3:	Small type, Four pictures
Variation 4:	Large type, Four pictures

This experiment would be executed similarly to an A/B test, except here site visitors would be randomly assigned to view one of the four test stimuli, keeping in mind and applying the do's and don'ts for A/B testing discussed earlier.

58

Creating an Experiment With Google Analytics

Our experiment will test the relative effectiveness of two different pages on ecommerce revenue.

Before launching a Google Analytics experiment, it is necessary to have all stimulus pages loaded on your server and accessible online. Once stimulus materials are ready, you begin the process by selecting **Behavior > Experiments**. Selecting this option brings you to the page that lists all of your experiments. The page shown below will display if you have not yet created any experiments.[105]

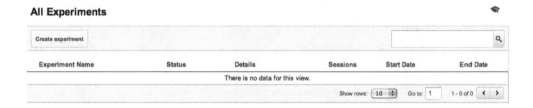

The display changes after you create your first experiment. Now, all of your current and past experiments are listed, as shown on the top of page 558 for the experiments being conducted on my website. When examining the list, keep in mind that experiments are view specific, so an experiment will only be shown in the view in which it was created.

---

[105] Note that Google has developed a new free platform for creating and running experiments. The platform, named Optimize, can be accessed by selecting Optimize from your sign-in page at http://www.google.com/analytics. For an in-depth guide to using Optimize see Joel Davis, *Google Optimize Demystified*. The current platform described here remains available but may be depreciated in the future.

Notifications:

Picture Test has finished | View report |

Create experiment						
Experiment Name	Status	Details		Sessions	Start Date	End Date
sfkdnisdik	● Running			--	Apr 15, 2014	Still running
Picture Test	● Ended	Time limit reached		206	Mar 1, 2014	May 30, 2014
Untitled experiment	● Ended	Stopped manually		53	Feb 28, 2014	Mar 1, 2014
Untitled experiment	○ Setup	Step 1		--	--	--

Experiments are initiated by clicking on **Create experiment**. The next display (see below) presents an overview of the four steps we need to go through to create an experiment.

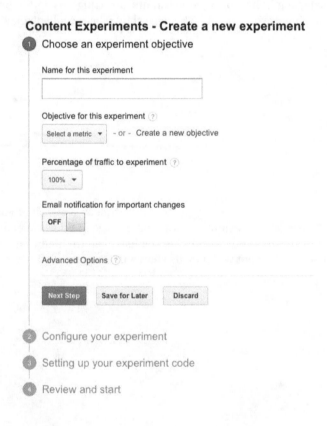

This first step asks you to provide a descriptive name for the experiment (we'll call ours 'Purchase Page Image Test') and to identify your outcome measure via the pull down **Select a metric** menu. We'll choose **Revenue** within the **Ecommerce** menu, keeping in mind that an outcome measure does not have to be transactions or, in fact, any ecommerce measure. Different experimental objectives might require the use of a goal as the outcome measure. Next, we determine the percentage of website traffic we want to participate in the experiment. The greater the percentage, the quicker results can be obtained. However, if your experiment involves drastic or risky changes, you might want to include only a small proportion of your site's traffic in the experiment. We'll set this parameter to 100%, allowing all site visitors to participate. Since we don't need any email notifications we leave this set to 'Off' and select **Next Step**.

Step 2 asks us to identify the test materials (see the display below). We type in the full URL to our current and test page and give each page a descriptive name. We use the displayed images to confirm that the correct pages have been selected. Since we are running a simple A/B test, just the two pages shown are required. If we were running an experiment with more variations, we would click on the **+Add Variation** link to add additional test variations. In either case, when done we select the **Next Step** link.

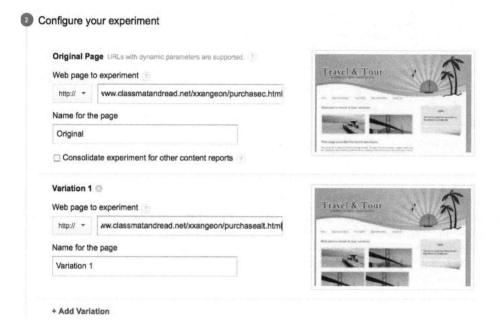

Step 3 asks us how we want to handle the tracking code necessary for the experiment to run and for Google Analytics to collect data (see below).

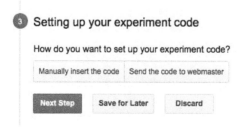

Since we are doing this ourselves, we click on **Manually insert the code**, after which we see the display shown below.

Adding script code to your page ⑦

1. Make sure your original and variation pages have Google Analytics tracking code installed.
2. Then, paste this experiment code immediately after the opening head tag at **the top** of your original page.

```
<!-- Google Analytics Content Experiment code -->
<script>function utmx_section(){}function utmx(){}(function(){var
k='80466313-19',d=document,l=d.location,c=d.cookie;
if(l.search.indexOf('utm_expid='+k)>0)return;
function f(n){if(c){var i=c.indexOf(n+'=');if(i>-1){var j=c.
indexOf(';',i);return escape(c.substring(i+n.length+1,j<0?c.
length:j))}}}var x=f('__utmx'),xx=f('__utmxx'),h=l.hash;d.write(
'<sc'+'ript src="'+'http'+(l.protocol=='https:'?'s://ssl':
'://www')+'.google-analytics.com/ga_exp.js?'+'utmxkey='+k+
'&utmx='+(x?x:'')+'&utmxx='+(xx?xx:'')+'&utmxtime='+new Date().
valueOf()+(h?'&utmxhash='+escape(h.substr(1)):'')+
'" type="text/javascript" charset="utf-8"><\/sc'+'ript>')})();
</script><script>utmx('url','A/B');</script>
<!-- End of Google Analytics Content Experiment code -->
```

Additional information for your experiment code:

Experiment ID: PYfum_W_SmePjEH6teDzCQ
Experiment Key: 80466313-19

Publish experiment pages

Publish your original and variation pages to the web.
When you're done - Click **Next Step** to continue.

The directions ask us to place the code shown in the box immediately after the opening <head> tag of our original page, which in this case is **purchasec.html**. Only the original page contains the experiment-specific code. We open the page in our HTML editor, paste the code into the page where directed, upload the page to the server, and then press **Next Step**. Note that this page now contains both the GATC code and the above experiment-specific code. It can also contain any of the javascript discussed in the context of events.

If all has gone well, we'll then see the confirmation shown on the top of page 561. Clicking on **Start Experiment** activates data collection and begins the experiment.

④ Review and start

Experiment Code Validation

✓ **Original: Two Pictures:** Experiment code found. Google Analytics code found.
✓ **Test: Six Pictures:** Google Analytics code found.

Notes for this experiment

```
┌─────────────────────────────────────────┐
│                                         │
│                                         │
│                                         │
│                                         │
│                                        ◢│
└─────────────────────────────────────────┘
```

[Start Experiment]   [Save for Later]   [Discard]

Random assignment to experimental groups

A typical experiment uses pure random assignment to determine which variation an individual will see. Thus, in a typical A/B/C test, each respondent will have a 33.3% chance of being assigned to each group.

Google Analytics experiments use a different random assignment technique. You can read about this approach here:

https://support.google.com/analytics/answer/
2844870?hl=en&ref_topic=2844866

59

Managing Experiments and Interpreting Outcomes

After your first experiment has been created, selecting **Behavior > Experiments** takes you to the experiment summary page, as shown below for my experiments.

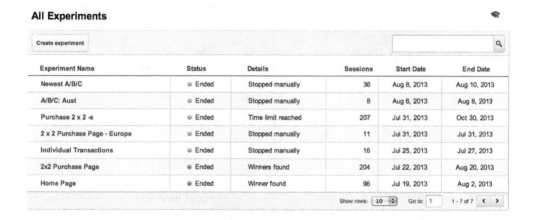

Summary information is provided for each current and past experiment associated with the current view. The display provides information regarding status (in development, running, or ended), outcome details (stopped manually, time limit reached, or winner found), number of sessions, and start/end date. Clicking on the name of any specific experiment brings up a detailed data display for that experiment.

Let's look at the types of data provided and data analysis for A/B and factorial experiments.

The background and specifics of this A/B test are as follows::

What is the background and how does this lead to what we specifically need to learn?	When we look at all site users and the average revenue per session, we find an average of about $3,000 per user over the past six months. The goal is to raise this average amount. It has been proposed that by adding additional pictures to the purchase page, users will be subconsciously motivated to purchase longer vacations.
What do we need to manipulate?	We need to manipulate the number of pictures on the page, increasing the number from two to six. Other content and the purchase process will remain unchanged.
How will we measure the outcome of the manipulation?	We will evaluate the effect of the manipulation in terms of average transaction per session.
Is the manipulation reasonable?	We have observed significantly more pictures on competitive sites, especially on the purchase page. As a result, we believe that there may be a relationship between picture quantity and average transaction amount.

Given this situation, we'll create one new version of the purchase page (with six pictures) and test this page against the current purchase page (which has two pictures). For purposes of labeling within Google Analytics reporting, we'll call the original page 'Original: Two Pictures' and the alternative version 'Test: Six Pictures'. We can access current reports of experimental results by selecting **Behavior > Experiments** and then, on the experiments summary page, clicking on the name of the experiment.

The report shown on the top of page 565 is the default view shown when we first access our experiment's data. Since the focus is on conversions, these data can always be viewed by selecting the **Conversions** link on the top of the page (beneath the **Explorer** tab). The top and side of the page provide important context for data interpretation:

- The message in the center of the display indicates that we stopped the experiment manually before Google Analytics chose a 'winner.' In our view, the data trend indicated that we would cause significant harm to our company by continuing the research.

- The data on the upper right-hand side of the display indicates that the outcome represents 91 days of data collection during which there were 206 experimental sessions.

There are two sets of data displayed: the upper line chart and the bottom tabular data. We ignore the line chart on the top of the page and focus on the data reported in the bottom table.

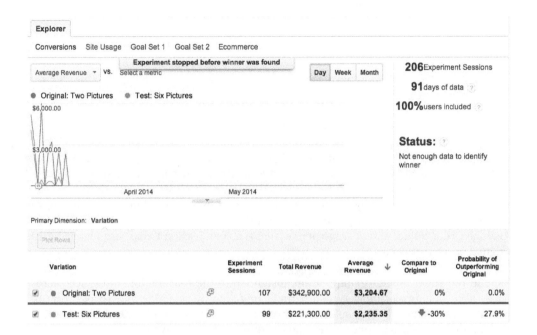

The two-line table on the bottom of the page presents conversion data on our original purchase page (the top line of the table) and the test page (the bottom line of the table). We can see that the number of Experiment Sessions for each page are roughly equivalent. With regard to Average Revenue (calculated by dividing Total Revenue by Experiment Sessions), we find that while the original page is equivalent to the historical average (about $3,000), the test page is performing significantly less well, generating about 30% less revenue per session. This metric, rather than Total Revenue, is the more meaningful, as it adjusts for different numbers of sessions on the original and test page. Finally, Google Analytics predicts that there is a very low probability that the test page will eventually outperform the original.

Selecting **Ecommerce** from beneath the **Explorer** tab displays additional detail on the ecommerce performance of the original and test page, as shown below.

Primary Dimension: Variation

Plot Rows

Variation		Experiment Sessions ↓	Revenue	Transactions	Average Order Value	Ecommerce Conversion Rate	Per Session Value
☑ ● Original: Two Pictures	🔗	107	$342,900.00	52	$6,594.23	48.60%	$3,204.67
☑ ● Test: Six Pictures	🔗	99	$221,300.00	48	$4,610.42	48.48%	$2,235.35

This table repeats several of the metrics reported in the **Conversions** table, with slight changes in how the metrics are named.

- Experiment Sessions are reported with the same label.

- The Revenue column reports the same data as the Total Revenue column in the **Conversions** table.

- Per Session Value reports the same data as the Average Revenue in the **Conversions** table.

The table also reports three valuable new metrics. The Transactions and Ecommerce Conversion Rate columns provide the absolute number of transactions and more importantly, the percentage of sessions resulting in a transaction. In this experiment, these metrics are equivalent across the original and test page. In both cases, about half of all sessions resulted in a sale. The final metric, Average Order Value, reports the average sales amount (calculated by dividing Total Revenue by Transactions). Once again, the original purchase page is outperforming the test page. In fact, both the average sale (i.e., Average Order Value) and average per session (i.e., Per Session Value) are higher for the original purchase page.

Beyond the experimental manipulation, insights into the reasons for differences across pages used in an experiment can sometimes be found by selecting **Site Usage** from beneath the **Explorer** tab. This selection results in the table shown below, which indicates that, in this case, engagement metrics did not differ across the two pages.

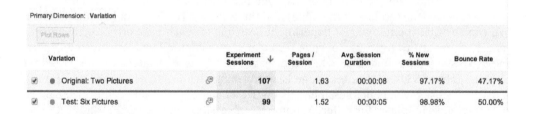

Primary Dimension: Variation

Variation	Experiment Sessions ↓	Pages / Session	Avg. Session Duration	% New Sessions	Bounce Rate
☑ ● Original: Two Pictures	107	1.63	00:00:08	97.17%	47.17%
☑ ● Test: Six Pictures	99	1.52	00:00:05	98.98%	50.00%

In sum, the experiment demonstrated that our hypothesis with regard to the effect of number of pictures on the purchase page was not validated. Our current page is the more powerful design when compared to the page with additional pictures. While the conversion rate for the two pages is nearly identical, the Average Order Value and Average Session Value for our current page is significantly higher than that of the test page. It's best that we keep our current page as is and run another experiment to determine if a stronger page can be designed.

Our factorial experiment will examine the simultaneous influence of two factors on engagement, conversion, and transaction metrics. The first factor explores the influence of picture type with two levels: pictures of people and pictures of scenery. The second factor looks at type of call to action (i.e., the link to purchase), again with two levels: image and text. The factorial design for this experiment is summarized below.

		Factor 1: Type of Picture	
		People	Scenery
	Image	1	2
Factor 2: Call to Action			
	Text	3	4

Similar to all experiments, we access the data for this experiment through the list of experiments displayed after **Experiments** is selected from the **Behavior** menu. Clicking on the name of the experiment first brings up the data summary shown below. Note that the data relates to transactions, as this was set as our primary outcome measure when we created the experiment.

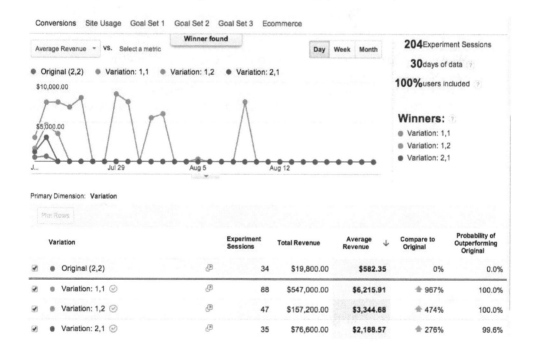

Variation		Experiment Sessions	Total Revenue	Average Revenue ↓	Compare to Original	Probability of Outperforming Original
☑ ● Original (2,2)		34	$19,800.00	$582.35	0%	0.0%
☑ ● Variation: 1,1 ⊘		88	$547,000.00	$6,215.91	⬆ 967%	100.0%
☑ ● Variation: 1,2 ⊘		47	$157,200.00	$3,344.68	⬆ 474%	100.0%
☑ ● Variation: 2,1 ⊘		35	$76,600.00	$2,188.57	⬆ 276%	99.6%

The characteristics of each stimulus shown in the previous table are provided below.

	People	Scenery
Image	1 (1,1)	2 (2,1)
Text	3 (1,2)	4 (2,2)

Variation (1,1):	People in picture, image call to action
Variation (1,2):	People in picture, text call to action
Variation (2,1):	Scenery in picture, image call to action
Original (2,2):	Scenery in picture, text call to action

Let's first look at what the reported results tell us about our experimental manipulations. First, the experiment has run long enough and has collected enough data for Google Analytics to declare a winner, which is noted on the top right-hand side of the page. This decision was made after 204 experimental visits took place over a 30-day period. The report indicates that:

- All three variations performed significantly better than the original, in both a practical and statistical sense, as reflected in the data reported in the Average Revenue column. In all three cases, our confidence that each variation outperformed the original in terms of average revenue generated per session is at or near 100%. (Typically, any confidence level over 95% is considered statistically significant.)

- While all three variations outperformed the original, there do appear to be important differences within the set of three variations. The average transaction generated by Variation (1,1) appears to be much higher than the average transaction generated by the remaining two variations, which are quite close to one another.

We can look at these trends from a different perspective if we put the Average Revenue per session amounts within each cell of our table, as shown below.

	People	Scenery
Image	$6,216	$2,189
Text	$3,345	$582

The data, when examined in this way, provides three important insights.

- First, regardless of the type of call-to-action, pictures of people generated higher average revenue versus pictures of scenery.

- Second, regardless of the type of picture, an image call-to-action always resulted in higher revenue versus a text call-to-action.

- Finally, there seems to be an interaction or cumulative effect of the factors tested. The combination of people + image call-to-action shows that both elements work together to produce a result that is much stronger than the contribution of each factor independently. This latter insight is only available through a factorial design, and would not occur if we conducted two sequential A/B tests (one test to explore pictures and a second test to explore the call-to- action).

Selecting the **Ecommerce** option beneath the **Explorer** tab displays the chart shown below. While the **Per Session Value** is the same as the prior table, note the data reported in the **Average Order Value** column. The superiority of the people + image approach (Variation 1,1) is again apparent: the **Ecommerce Conversion Rate** and **Average Order Value** for this variation are significantly higher than the other variations, especially the original home page.

Variation		Experiment Sessions	Revenue	Transactions	Average Order Value	Ecommerce Conversion Rate	Per Session Value
☑ ● Original (2,2)		34	$19,800.00	13	$1,523.08	38.24%	$582.35
☑ ● Variation: 1,1 ⊘		80	$547,000.00	39	$14,025.64	48.75%	$6,837.50
☑ ● Variation: 1,2 ⊘		47	$157,200.00	18	$8,733.33	38.30%	$3,344.68
☑ ● Variation: 2,1 ⊘		35	$76,600.00	13	$5,892.31	37.14%	$2,188.57

Section XV:
Advanced Metrics: User Level Data

All of the information we've seen so far has been aggregated. This data represents groups of individuals. While this data can be incredibly useful, it is often the case that additional insights can be obtained when we examine unaggregated data that reports the characteristics and behaviors of each individual site visitor.

The two chapters in this section focus on individual user data.

- Chapter 60 describes the types of data and analyses made possible by the new Google Analytics feature: User Explorer.

- Chapter 61 extends the discussion of user level data analysis and interpretation.

The **Audience > User Explorer** report lets you isolate and examine individual rather than aggregate user characteristics and behaviors. This level of analysis is important whenever you want to see if there are ways to better personalize or improve the user experience/path to conversion or when you want to form segments that reflect a specific user's characteristics/behaviors.

Google Analytics associates individual user behavior with either a Client-ID or User-ID. A User-ID is set and communicated to Google Analytics by the website or app, for example, after a site visitor signs-in. A Client-ID, on the other hand, is set automatically by Google Analytics and represents a unique browser or device. This chapter focuses on the **Audience > User Explorer** reports that use Client-ID (since this is available by default to all Google Analytics users), keeping in mind that the discussion and examples apply equally well to User-ID.[106]

The initial display

Selecting **Audience > User Explorer** displays a table similar to the one shown below. The far left-hand column displays each site visitor's Client-ID. The rows are ordered by Sessions. The visitor shown on line 1, for example, initiated 37 sessions while the visitor on line 10 initiated 7 sessions. Google Analytics limits you to the metrics shown in the remaining columns: average session duration, bounce rate, revenue, transactions and goal conversion rate (the next chapter shows you how to expand these metrics).

Client Id	Sessions	Avg. Session Duration	Bounce Rate	Revenue	Transactions	Goal Conversion Rate
1. 1876202093.1455743019	37 (5.92%)	00:07:52	21.62%	$86,000.00 (16.12%)	11 (15.07%)	32.43%
2. 510566204.1417637647	34 (5.44%)	00:01:22	73.53%	$0.00 (0.00%)	0 (0.00%)	0.00%
3. 918278306.1450463460	21 (3.36%)	00:09:44	9.52%	$70,500.00 (14.86%)	9 (12.33%)	14.29%
4. 1438794505.1465287199	10 (1.60%)	00:01:15	90.00%	$0.00 (0.00%)	0 (0.00%)	100.00%
5. 677153654.1435401677	10 (1.60%)	00:00:56	60.00%	$0.00 (0.00%)	0 (0.00%)	20.00%
6. 1231923752.1459454247	8 (1.28%)	00:08:50	12.50%	$15,500.00 (3.27%)	2 (2.74%)	50.00%
7. 970294918.1465058157	8 (1.28%)	00:12:06	62.50%	$0.00 (0.00%)	0 (0.00%)	12.50%
8. 396445747.1457711839	7 (1.12%)	00:00:02	85.71%	$0.00 (0.00%)	0 (0.00%)	100.00%
9. 669115477.1457638373	7 (1.12%)	00:02:17	42.86%	$3,500.00 (0.74%)	1 (1.37%)	28.57%
10. 997303680.1457901590	7 (1.12%)	00:07:25	28.57%	$0.00 (0.00%)	0 (0.00%)	0.00%

---

[106] Primary sources for this chapter are *User Explorer* at https://support.google.com/analytics/answer/6339208 and *New in Google Analytics: User Explorer Report* at http://www.ganotes.com/new-in-google-analytics-user-explorer-report/.

This table often proves useful information when you want to identify trends and issues that require additional analysis. In this case, we might ask about the pattern displayed by the visitor shown on line 2: 'What inferences can we draw about the user experience and motivations of one or more individuals who have initiated multiple sessions, but have very low average session duration, a high bounce rate, and no transactions?'

	Client Id ⑦	Sessions ⑦ ↓	Avg. Session Duration ⑦	Bounce Rate ⑦	Revenue ⑦	Transactions ⑦	Goal Conversion Rate ⑦
1.	1876202093.1455743019	37 (5.92%)	00:07:52	21.62%	$86,000.00 (18.12%)	11 (15.07%)	32.43%
2.	510566204.1417637647	34 (5.44%)	00:01:22	73.53%	$0.00 (0.00%)	0 (0.00%)	0.00%
3.	918278306.1450463460	21 (3.36%)	00:09:44	9.52%	$70,500.00 (14.86%)	9 (12.33%)	14.29%
4.	1438794505.1465287199	10 (1.60%)	00:01:15	90.00%	$0.00 (0.00%)	0 (0.00%)	100.00%
5.	677153654.1435401677	10 (1.60%)	00:00:56	60.00%	$0.00 (0.00%)	0 (0.00%)	20.00%
6.	1231923752.1459454247	8 (1.28%)	00:08:50	12.50%	$15,500.00 (3.27%)	2 (2.74%)	50.00%
7.	970294918.1465058157	8 (1.28%)	00:12:06	62.50%	$0.00 (0.00%)	0 (0.00%)	12.50%
8.	396445747.1457711839	7 (1.12%)	00:00:02	85.71%	$0.00 (0.00%)	0 (0.00%)	100.00%
9.	669115477.1457638373	7 (1.12%)	00:02:17	42.86%	$3,500.00 (0.74%)	1 (1.37%)	28.57%
10.	997303680.1457901590	7 (1.12%)	00:07:25	28.57%	$0.00 (0.00%)	0 (0.00%)	0.00%

Show rows: 10   Go to: 1   1 - 10 of 391   < >

Additional questions/issues can be identified when the data is reordered by a column other than Sessions. The table below, for example, orders the rows in the table by the number of transactions. Here we can see that our visitors divide into two distinct groups. The first four rows represent one group: individuals who made multiple transactions across a large number of sessions. The second group represents those who make a single transaction in relatively few (or even a single) session. What can we infer about the differences in user experiences and the paths to conversion that distinguish these two groups? How can we apply these insights to future strategic decisions?

	Client Id ⑦	Sessions ⑦	Avg. Session Duration ⑦	Bounce Rate ⑦	Revenue ⑦ ↓	Transactions ⑦	Goal Conversion Rate ⑦
1.	1876202093.1455743019	37 (5.92%)	00:07:52	21.62%	$86,000.00 (18.12%)	11 (15.07%)	32.43%
2.	160163757.1462247018	6 (0.96%)	00:00:17	0.00%	$75,500.00 (15.91%)	7 (9.59%)	16.67%
3.	918278306.1450463460	21 (3.36%)	00:09:44	9.52%	$70,500.00 (14.86%)	9 (12.33%)	14.29%
4.	1231923752.1459454247	8 (1.28%)	00:08:50	12.50%	$15,500.00 (3.27%)	2 (2.74%)	50.00%
5.	1160454689.1450712253	1 (0.16%)	00:02:38	0.00%	$12,000.00 (2.53%)	1 (1.37%)	100.00%
6.	1235936797.1458244716	1 (0.16%)	00:01:06	0.00%	$12,000.00 (2.53%)	1 (1.37%)	100.00%
7.	1612701903.1458260032	2 (0.32%)	00:01:04	0.00%	$12,000.00 (2.53%)	1 (1.37%)	50.00%
8.	1730554120.1458971062	3 (0.48%)	00:12:17	66.67%	$12,000.00 (2.53%)	1 (1.37%)	100.00%
9.	231050153.1458549128	1 (0.16%)	00:00:10	0.00%	$12,000.00 (2.53%)	1 (1.37%)	100.00%
10.	575725710.1456195369	2 (0.32%)	00:00:56	50.00%	$12,000.00 (2.53%)	1 (1.37%)	0.00%

You can click on a visitor's Client-ID (in the initial display) to focus on the behaviors of that specific individual. Let's imagine that we are interested in the individual reported on the first line of the table shown on the bottom of page 574. This individual has the highest number of both sessions and transactions, so it is important to understand how this individual moves through the site and to infer his/her motivations. When we click on this individual's Client-ID the table shown below is displayed.

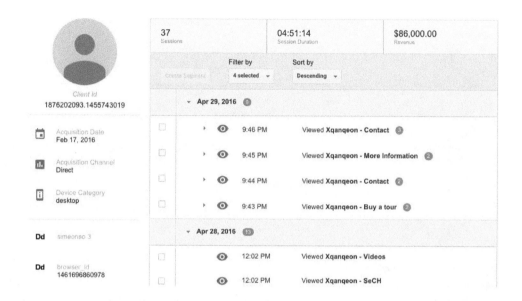

The left-hand column provides background information on the individual, specifically, when s/he first visited the site (the Acquisition Date), how s/he first reached the site (the Acquisition Channel), and the technology used to reach the site (the Device Category). The two pieces of information labeled **Dd** represent custom dimensions associated with this individual.

The top row of the table repeats two of the data points from the initial table (Sessions and Revenue) and substitutes Total Session Duration for Average Session Duration. By default, the center portion of the table displays information related to pageviews, goals, ecommerce and events, each of which is identified by a different icon..

There are two ways to customize this display. First, we can change the range of information displayed, in order to focus on fewer aspects of the individual's behaviors. We accomplish this by checking and unchecking the boxes in the **Filter by** pull-down menu (see display on the top of page 576). Second we can change the order in which data is presented, placing the oldest data on the top of the display. This is accomplished by using the **Sort by** pull-down menu (see second display on page 576). The goal of both displays is to facilitate a better understanding of how one site visitor moves through the site (hopefully) on the way to a conversion or transaction.

Creating segments

The prior data display makes it easy to create segments based on one visitor's behaviors, in essence asking the question, 'How do we examine the behaviors of other individuals who exhibit the same behaviors of interest as this individual?'

You begin the segment creation process by first clicking on the Client-ID of the individual of interest. This will then display the individual's characteristics and behaviors, as illustrated in the prior section. Next, you click (in the left-hand side boxes) the behaviors of interest (as shown on the top of page 577). The desired behaviors will be highlighted in blue. Clicking the **Create Segment** button on the top of the display brings up the bottom figure on page 577. Note how the selected characteristics have been autofilled in the form. All that remains to be done is name the segment, apply it to the current User Explorer table, and press **Save**.

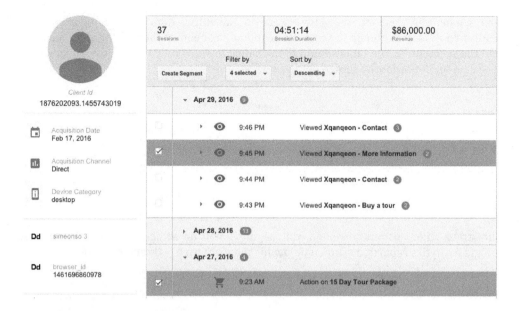

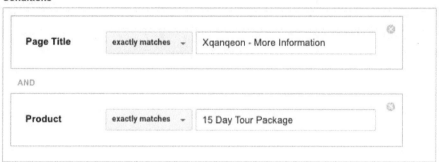

Create Segment

Name

More Info and Bought 15 Day

Conditions

Page Title	exactly matches ▾	Xqanqeon - More Information

AND

Product	exactly matches ▾	15 Day Tour Package

Enable Views

○ Any View

◉ Current View

☐ Apply the segment to User Explorer Report after saving.

[Save]   [Cancel]

The segment is then created. Move back to the initial data display by clicking on **Audience > User Explorer** to see if the segment has been applied. If not, then manually add the segment.[107] The table should then change to show only those individuals who fit the segment definition, as shown below.

Client Id	Sessions	Avg. Session Duration	Bounce Rate	Revenue	Transactions	Goal Conversion Rate
1. 1876202093.1455743019	37 (50.68%)	00:07:52	21.62%	$86,000.00 (33.14%)	11 (36.67%)	32.43%
2. 918278306.1450463460	21 (28.77%)	00:09:44	9.52%	$70,500.00 (27.17%)	9 (30.00%)	14.29%
3. 1231923752.1459454247	8 (10.96%)	00:08:50	12.50%	$15,500.00 (5.97%)	2 (6.67%)	50.00%
4. 160163757.1462247018	6 (8.22%)	00:00:17	0.00%	$75,500.00 (29.09%)	7 (23.33%)	16.67%
5. 1235936797.1458244716	1 (1.37%)	00:01:06	0.00%	$12,000.00 (4.62%)	1 (3.33%)	100.00%

Similar to other custom segments, this segment will be available for use in all other Google Analytics reports, as shown below for the **Audience > Overview** report.

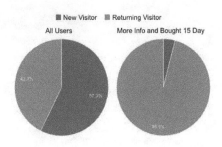

Application of Client-ID data

Google Analytics provides several examples for the use of this type of data.

Respond to specific behavior within a segment

If other reports indicate noteworthy behavior by a particular segment, you can examine specific users within that segment to get a more detailed understanding of what's going on. For example, if the **Audience > Overview** report indicates that the 18-24 segment

---

[107] See Chapter 32 if you've forgotten how to create and apply custom segments.

has an unusually high bounce rate or low average session duration compared to other age groups, you can apply that segment to **Audience > User Explorer**, and then take a look at some individual users to see whether they're bouncing or exiting from the same page or group of pages.

A closer examination of your content might reveal that while the graphics and copy might work well for other age groups, they're not especially relevant to the 18-24 segment. For example, you might have different age groups buying the same sneaker that has been in production for 100 years, but for entirely different reasons. The 18-24 segment might be responding to what is suddenly a unique design relative to everything else in the market, while their parents are buying nostalgia. In a case like this, you want to support those different segments with site content that is relevant to their motivations for buying.

In a case like this, you can create each segment in Google Analytics, apply it to the report, and export the IDs for that segment. You can then personalize the site experience based on ID, and direct each group to the relevant content from your ads.

Upsell

As you develop ongoing relationships with your customers, you also want to develop opportunities to move them to higher levels of conversion. When you understand how your higher level customers purchase, you have the opportunity to lead the next tier of customers along that same path. For example, if you're a travel agency that books 8, 10, and 15-day tours, it might require only modest effort to encourage customers who routinely purchase 10-day tours to upgrade to 15 days.

The **Audience > User Explorer** report lets you examine how your more valuable users engage with your site, the paths they follow, where they spend their time, which promotions they click. With that information in hand, you can start to personalize the site experience for your middle-tier customers to include the same content and offers your top-tier customers enjoy most.

In this case, create two segments: one of your middle-tier customers and one of your top-tier customers. Apply the top-tier segment to the **Audience > User Explorer** report, and examine the session behavior to see how those users engage with your site, which content they interact with most, and which content leads to conversions. Then apply the segment of middle-tier customers and export their IDs. Use that list of IDs to personalize their site experience to more closely match the experience of your top-tier customers. You can also use that list of IDs you export to build an audience of those middle-tier customers and serve them ads for those higher-end tour packages.

Remarketing

By examining individual session behavior, you can see when your users fall short of completing goals. For example, you can see when they add items to their carts, but don't go on to complete the transactions, or when they purchase one item but not the complementary item they also viewed (e.g., they purchased the hat but not the scarf). In these cases, you have perfect opportunities to remarket to those users with specific information related to their experiences. For example, you can remind users of exactly which items they left in their carts; or if a user has purchased a hat, you can follow up with ads for the matching scarf.

You can create segments based on the relevant behavior you identify in the **Audience > User Explorer** report, and then use those segments as the basis for new remarketing audiences.

Personalize customer service

If your business offers high-touch customer service, the **Audience > User Explorer** report let's you see a detailed history of each user so your CSRs can understand context and offer informed guidance. For example, if you handle custom property rentals, then a CSR can see which properties users have rented in the past, and which properties they might have been looking at before they called customer service.

Identify personas

If you develop personas as part of your marketing, investigate the behavior of different segments so that those personas are based on how users engage with your site. For example, you can create segments of male users 18-34 that each fall into different interest categories (e.g., Avid Investors, Sports Fans, Music Lovers), apply those segments to the report, and then look through the session activity to see things like which products they only view versus which ones they purchase, or which goals they tend to complete more often.'[108]

---

[108] *User Explorer* at https://support.google.com/analytics/answer/6339208.

61
Extended User Level
Analysis and Application

The last chapter described the process by which you can obtain and draw insights from the individual user data provided by Google Analytics. This chapter describes additional considerations and approaches to the analysis and application of this data.

Examining the data in Excel

Google Analytics allows you to download any tabular data to Excel. An examination of data in this format (as we will do in this chapter) often leads to insights beyond those obtained from the tables initially provided by Google Analytics. You can download the table that reports individual user data to Excel by following these steps:

1. Log into Google Analytics and select the desired data view.

2. Select **Audience > User Explorer** from the left-hand menu. The User Explorer data table will display.

3. Beneath the table is an indicator of the total number of rows in the table, as illustrated below. My table has 240 rows, where each row represents a unique site user.

4. Use the pull-down **Show rows** menu to select a number greater than the total number of rows. In this example, I would select 250 (see below). The table will change to display all rows.

5. On the top of the Google Analytics page beneath the User Explorer label are four options (see below). Use the pull-down **Export** menu to download the data in your preferred Excel format.

User Explorer

Email   Export ▾   Add to Dashboard   Shortcut

Now let's see how we can manipulate and examine this data in order to increase insights and inform strategic planning.

Calculating additional measures

You'll recall from the prior chapter that Google Analytics only reports six measures on the **Audience > User Explorer** report: sessions, average session duration, bounce rate, revenue, transactions, and goal conversion rate. The types of metrics reported can be increased using Excel's calculation function. You can, for example, easily create any of the following to assist in exploring individual visitor behaviors:

Total session duration = Average Session Duration * Sessions

Average revenue per session = Revenue ÷ Sessions

Average order value = Revenue ÷ Transactions

Average number of transactions per session = Transactions ÷ Sessions

Determining the 'goodness' of averages shown in other Google Analytics reports

Almost of all the data reported by Google Analytics are summary data using either totals or averages. Let's focus on averages.

The table shown below uses averages to report Ecommerce Conversion Rate (7.66%) and Average Order Value ($7,131.58).

Ecommerce Conversion Rate	Transactions	Revenue	Average Order Value
7.66%	38	$271,000.00	$7,131.58

There is no question that these two averages are calculated correctly. The question, though, is: 'To what extent can we have confidence that the average is actually a good descriptor of the distribution it's intended to summarize?'

Exploring data on the individual level allows us to answer this important question.

We'll illustrate this concept with data obtained (and downloaded to Excel) from the **Audience > User Explorer** report. We'll compare two groups: Purchases made from an initial visit to the site and purchases made after two or more visits to the site. Our analysis will be guided by the following:

> *An average is a good summary of the underlying data distribution when most of the data points in the distribution are close to the average. An average is misleading when it does not accurately describe the underlying distribution, that is, when relatively few data points fall close to the average.*

Let's examine the transaction amounts of those making a purchase in their first visit to the site. This is illustrated in the graph shown below, which we generated from the data provided in the **Audience > User Explorer** report.[109] This chart resembles a typical bell curve where most of the data points cluster around the average transaction amount of $12,940. In this case, it would be acceptable to base our strategic planning on the belief that the average transaction is a good descriptor/representation of this group of individuals' behaviors and that the typical (average) purchase amount is just short of $13,000.

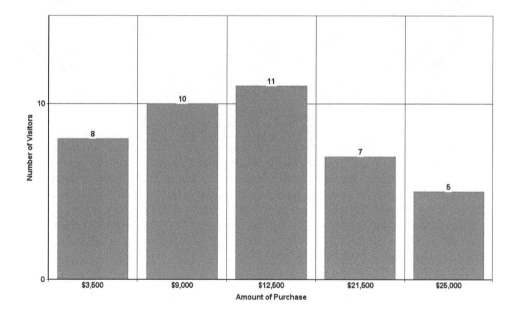

---

[109] The chart is created as follows: We first use segments to focus the Google Analytics data tables on individuals of interest. Next, after downloading the tabular **Audience > User Explorer** data to Excel (for each of the two segments) we use the Excel Sort function to order transaction amount from lowest to highest. Next, we use the Excel Count function to count the number of individuals at each transaction level. Finally, we create the chart using the online chart generator at http://www.onlinecharttool.com.

Now let's examine the purchase behaviors of those who visited the site two or more times. The average purchase amount for this group is nearly the same as the last group: $12,912 (versus $12,940). The distribution of actual purchase amount for this group is shown below. But in this case the average is misleading. Very few transactions are actually of average value. We have many low and many high transactions, with very few falling near the average. It would be incorrect and misleading to claim that the average purchase amount of $12,912 accurately represents the behaviors of individuals in this group.

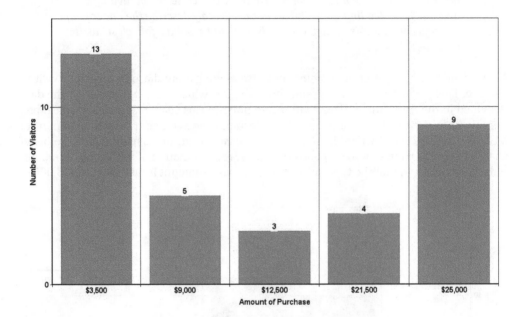

In sum, we have two groups with the same average but very different underlying distributions. It would be quite problematic to conclude that, based on the averages, the transaction behaviors of the two groups are the same. In the first example, our strategic planning could draw the correct conclusion that the average transaction was about $13,000. In the second case, our strategic planning would be better off ignoring the average and concluding that there are two distinct segments of individuals within this larger group: one segment, which has a very low transaction amount, and a second segment, which has a very high transaction amount.[110]

Individual user data also helps us determine the extent to which an average is deceptively high or low due to one (or a few) extreme measures. Let's illustrate this with average session duration, another measure provided by **Audience > User Experience**.

---

[110] Note that while this discussion focused on transaction amount, it is equally appropriate for other measures such as sessions, average order value, average session duration, and goal conversions.

Average session duration is reported through **Audience > Overview**, as shown below. Here we can see that the average session duration for our site is just over three minutes, an amount of time we're happy with. Using this metric, we would conclude that site engagement is fine.

Now let's look at the **Audience > User Explorer** report ordered by average session duration (see below).

Client Id	Sessions	Avg. Session Duration ↓	Bounce Rate	Revenue	Transactions	Goal Conversion Rate
1. 677153654.1435401677	5 (3.91%)	00:35:09	0.00%	$24,500.00 (22.27%)	3 (23.08%)	700.00%
2. 1914197976.1461990891	5 (3.91%)	00:34:58	0.00%	$24,500.00 (22.27%)	3 (23.08%)	660.00%
3. 1253515664.1465879309	1 (0.78%)	00:18:06	0.00%	$0.00 (0.00%)	0 (0.00%)	500.00%
4. 970294918.1465058157	3 (2.34%)	00:04:55	33.33%	$0.00 (0.00%)	0 (0.00%)	400.00%
5. 842492425.1465998669	2 (1.56%)	00:04:43	0.00%	$33,000.00 (30.00%)	3 (23.08%)	600.00%
6. 1123641339.1466619470	1 (0.78%)	00:01:36	0.00%	$0.00 (0.00%)	0 (0.00%)	600.00%
7. 723093199.1465411541	1 (0.78%)	00:01:07	0.00%	$0.00 (0.00%)	0 (0.00%)	400.00%
8. 156048912.1466438558	1 (0.78%)	00:00:57	0.00%	$24,500.00 (22.27%)	3 (23.08%)	800.00%
9. 571323276.1466136833	1 (0.78%)	00:00:16	0.00%	$3,500.00 (3.18%)	1 (7.69%)	400.00%
10. 710901142.1465642967	1 (0.78%)	00:00:16	0.00%	$0.00 (0.00%)	0 (0.00%)	300.00%

Something seems off. There are no data points falling around the average of three minutes. This leads us to suspect that the reported average of about three minutes is misleading. In this case, however, the average is not distorted by the distribution but rather by the few individuals who lie on the highest end of the distribution. (Individuals shown on lines 1, 2 and 3.) The guideline that we use here is:

> *Averages can be distorted due to the presence of a few high or low outlier data points. In these cases, it is acceptable to recalculate an average that eliminates these points.*

Since we've downloaded the data to Excel, it is easy to recalculate average session duration eliminating these three 'outliers.' When this is done, average session duration drops to about twelve seconds! Our conclusion is now the opposite of where we began. Site engagement is very low and this problem needs to be immediately addressed. We would have made inappropriate strategic decisions with regard to site engagement had we not recalculated this metric.

Imagine that we run a one-week promotion that began on February 15 and ended on February 22. The promotion's goal was to increase the average order amount versus the prior week. One approach to determining the effect of the promotion would be to set two time periods (for example, the week of the promotion and the prior week) and then compare total sales across the two periods. The sales data from these two weeks is summarized below:

February 15 to 21   vs.   February 8 to 14

Average
Order Amount $6,243 $5,221

The data seem to indicate that the promotion was successful as total revenue increased during the promotional period (as compared to the prior week). Based on this data we'd conclude that the promotion met its goal and should be used again when the strategic goals are similar.

But, is this conclusion correct?

The most precise way to determine if group differences are real and meaningful is through the use of statistical significance. In this example, the calculation of statistical significance would be a quantitative way to determine whether a difference in average order amount between the two periods is due to chance or is real, that is, a result of the promotion. This is important because we only want to make strategic decisions based on real differences.

Statistical significance is evaluated via a probability level (represented as p). A probability level of .05 or less indicates that we can be 95% (or more) certain that the difference between the two groups is real and not due to chance.

Individual level data would allow us to calculate statistical significance, as follows:

1. Restrict the date range to the week prior to the promotion.

2. Download (to Excel) the data from the **Audience > User Explorer** table.

3. Copy the column of data from the Revenue column eliminating the dollar sign if present.

4. Go to http://www.socscistatistics.com/tests/studenttest/Default2.aspx. Paste the data in the top box labeled Treatment 1 (X). Keep this browser window open.

5. Change the date range to the week of the promotion.

6. Download (to Excel) the data from the **Audience > User Explorer** table.

7. Copy the column of data from the Revenue column eliminating the dollar sign if present.

8. Go to http://www.socscistatistics.com/tests/studenttest/Default2.aspx.
   Paste the data in the top box labeled Treatment 2 (X). Note that you do not need an equal number of data points in each box.

9. Leave **Significance Level** set to .05. Set **One-Tailed or two-tailed hypothesis** to two-tailed.

10. Click **Calculate T and P Values**.

The next page will display a lot of data. Scroll to the very bottom of the page where you will see either:

> The result *is* significant at p < .05.

> The result is *not* significant at p < .05.

The first sentence, when present, indicates that the difference between the two groups is real and that there is less than a 5% change that the difference is due to chance. Put another way, you can be 95% confident that the difference is real. If the second statement appears, then it becomes far less likely that difference is real and far more likely that the difference between the two groups is due to chance. In this latter case, the averages for the two groups should be considered to be essentially the same and the difference between the two groups should be ignored.

When we run our sales data for the two periods through the analysis we find that **the result is *not* significant at p < .05**. Thus, our conclusion that the promotion was effective and should be used again was erroneous and could have led to significant problems should it have been used another time. Statistical significance testing saved us from implementing an ineffective promotion.

Section XVI:
Data Management and the
Customization Menu

There is no shortage of data in Google Analytics. Therefore, it is important for you to manage your data in a way that allows you to focus on important issues and facilitates application to strategic decision-making. The six chapters in this section discuss techniques that can help you manage your data.

- Chapter 62 discusses two types of Google Analytics intelligence events: diagnostic notifications and custom alerts.

- Chapter 63 discusses shortcuts, exports, and downloads, and their use in easing data management and analysis burdens.

- Chapters 64 and 65 discuss two options in data presentation: custom reports and dashboards.

- Chapter 66 shows you how to move beyond standard metrics through the creation of your own calculated metrics.

- Chapter 67 discusses asset sharing.

- Chapter 68 explains Google Analytics' Intelligence questions and insights.

62

Diagnostic Notifications and Custom Alerts

Diagnostic notifications are designed to highlight and bring to your attention a situation, which Google Analytics perceives to be an important problem, for example:

- when your current tracking code is not present, configured properly and/or readable, or

- when there are odd data trends, such as when conversions stop occurring.

Notifications are view-specific, so you may see different notifications for different views within the same property.

Diagnostic notifications are accessed through the 'bell' on the upper right-hand side of any report page by any user with at least Edit permission. If there are new diagnostic notifications available, you'll see a number over the notification bell, which is located just above the date range (see below).

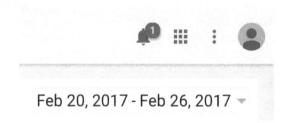

When there is a number on the bell, as in this example, clicking on the bell brings up a list of current and archived notifications (see the figure on the top of page 592).[111]

---

[111] Source for this section is *Diagnostics Messages* at
https://support.google.com/analytics/answer/6006306.

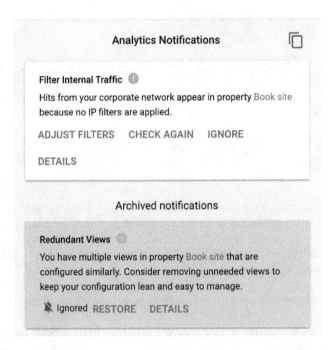

The color of the number on the bell indicates the type of problem identified.

- Red notifications are the highest priority and typically relate to issues such as untagged pages, bad filters, abundance of self-referrals, (not set) in AdWords Reports, and double-tagging.

- Yellow notifications (the next priority level) relate to unresolved issues including AdWords clicks vs. sessions discrepancies, duplicate campaign parameters, auto-tagging disabled, and an oversized 'Other' channel.

- Blue notifications (lowest priority) feature recommendations such as creating a goal, excluding internal IPs, linking to Webmaster Tools, using remarketing, using segmentation, and using annotations.

Note that the number on the bell only shows you the highest priority notification. If, for example, you have 5 red, 2 yellow and 3 blue notifications, you will see only a red 5 on the bell notification, but when you click on the bell you will see all of ten notifications.[112]

Each new notification includes a description of the problem, a likely solution, and links to the following:

- **Check again** allows you to check this issue again during the next Diagnostics run to see whether you have resolved the problem.

---

[112] *Google Analytics Diagnostics* at http://online-behavior.com/analytics/diagnostics

- The Analytics page on which you can address the problem (e.g., Adjust goals, Configure AdWords preferences).

- **Ignore** the issue and do not issue further notifications.

- **Details**. Learn more about the problem and possible solutions. The figure below illustrates more detail for the 'Filter Internal Traffic' problem shown on the prior page.

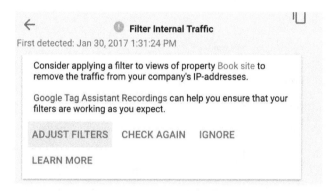

As shown above, you have several options on the Details display.

- **Learn more** links to relevant education material for that problem (e.g., a Help Center or Google Developers article).

- If you take steps to fix a problem, you can then click **Check again** to have Diagnostics reexamine the issue to determine whether your approach solved the problem. If the problem was solved, you won't receive any further notifications. If the problem persists, Diagnostics reminds you again after the next evaluation of your Google Analytics implementation.

- If you **Ignore** a notification, it is archived, and Diagnostics makes no further checks or warnings of that problem. However you always have the option to restore the notification to its original state.

As indicated above, the Details page, as well as the initial notification, provide an option to enact a problem-specific solution. The figure shown on the top of page 594 illustrates the problem-specific solutions provided for each potential problem.

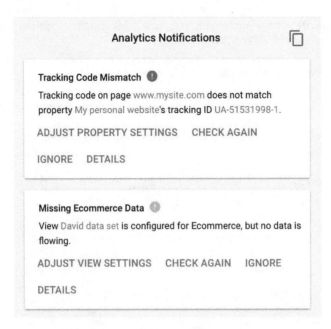

Finally, keep in mind that In order to evaluate your Analytics implementation, Diagnostics crawls your web pages as Googlebot and does so in a way that minimizes any inflation of traffic data. Google notes however, that

> "many websites are configured to recognize that GoogleBot is not a real user, and so GoogleBot traffic is not included in any site statistics. In addition, under normal circumstances, GoogleBot does not trigger false ad clicks and the consequential false hit data getting sent to Analytics. However, if you send your ad traffic through a third-party before it arrives at your site, that third party may record a hit. Savvy third parties recognize that GoogleBot is not a real user and not a legitimate generator of traffic data, and so rerouting through third parties does not usually inflate statistics. However, Diagnostics has no way to guarantee the sophistication of those third parties, and cannot categorically guarantee that there is no inflation of traffic statistics."

Custom alerts

Custom Alerts allow you to identify a set of conditions related to user characteristics and behaviors. Google Analytics then posts to your Google Analytics account or sends you an email when one of your specified conditions is met.

Imagine, for example, that the bounce rate of your home page has been an ongoing problem, and that you have just redesigned the page in an effort to reduce the bounce rate. You can set up a custom alert that would have Google Analytics inform you whenever something good or something bad happens on this page, for example, a decrease or an increase of 10% or more in the page's bounce rate.

There are two different circumstances in which custom alerts are very valuable. First, alerts can be used to provide ongoing monitoring of website health. Second, alerts can be created to monitor the results of a specific campaign. We'll look at custom alerts for both situations later in this chapter.

Creating custom alerts

Custom alerts are view-specific, that is, the alert will only appear within that view or any other views with which you share the alert.

You begin the custom alert creation process by selecting **Custom Alerts** from the Customization menu (see below).

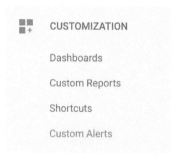

This will display a page listing custom alert messages, which have been created during the currently selected time period (see below). Since we have not yet created any alerts the page is blank.

Clicking on **Manage custom alerts** brings up the alert creation display shown on the top of page 596. Here, all current alerts are displayed. Note that you can also reach this display through your Administrator's page by clicking on **Custom Alerts** located near the bottom of the view column.

You create a new custom alert by clicking on **+NEW ALERT** on the top left-hand side of the display. When you do so, the display shown below appears. This is where you will specify the alert parameters.

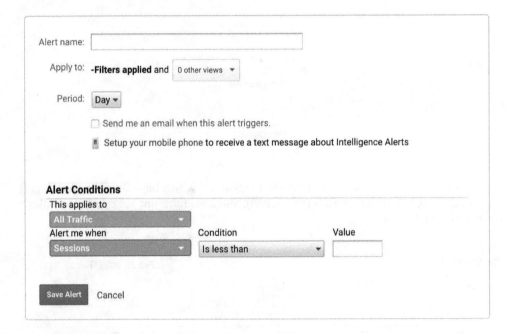

This form is completed as follows.

- You enter a descriptive name for your custom alert in the **Alert Name** text box.

- The **Apply to:** field is used to indicate the view(s) for which you want to apply the alert. The current view is shown by default in bold type. If you want to apply the alert to additional views, use the pull-down menu and check each view to which you want to apply the alert. The alert is then available to you in any of the other views you select. Nothing needs to be done if you want the custom alert to only apply to the current view.

- Use the **Period** pull-down menu to indicate the frequency at which the alert should be generated. You can select Day, Week, or Month.

- Use the next set of check boxes to indicate how (if at all) you want to be notified when the custom alert is generated. Note that when you choose to receive a notice by email, you can have others informed at the same time.

- You use the green and blue pull-down menus to specify the alert's conditions. The top (green) pull-down menu allows you set the focus of the alert (options are shown on the left, below), while the bottom (blue) pull-down menu allows you select the metric of interest (options are shown on the right, below).

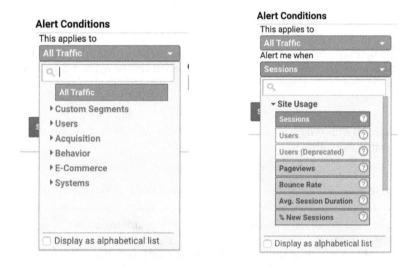

- Finally, specify the **Condition** and **Value**, and when all looks right, click **Save Alert**. If there are no errors, Google Analytics will indicate that the alert was successfully created.

Accessing alert-relevant data

Google will, if you have selected the notification option, notify you when a custom alert triggers. You can see alert-relevant data by clicking on **Custom Alerts** in the Customization menu. This will bring up a listing of all alerts triggered during the currently selected time period (see below).

Each alert is accompanied by **a Details** option, shown in far right-hand column. Clicking on this link brings up the relevant data display (see example below).

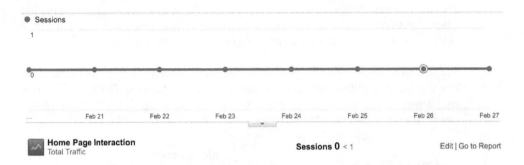

Note that this display provides two additional options (provided in the lower right-hand corner). **Edit** allows you to change the alert's characteristics while **Go to Report** takes you to the full data display relevant to the alert.

The remainder of this chapter discusses situations in which custom alerts provide important strategic insights.[113]

Using custom alerts to monitor website health

Unfortunately, we don't always know when there are problems on our site, for example, when the server is down or when other network issues prevent access. A **daily** custom alert can be used to monitor the site and inform you when there are access issues as reflected in an absence of traffic. The parameters shown in the display on the top of page 599 shows how this custom alert can be created.

---

[113] Source material and further examples can be found at: *Top 15 Google Analytics Custom Alerts* at http://www.6smarketing.com/blog/top-15-google-analytics-custom-alerts-to-set-up/; *55 Google Analytics Custom Alerts* at http://www.lunametrics.com/blog/2012/09/24/55-google-analytics-custom-alerts-check-engine-light-data/.

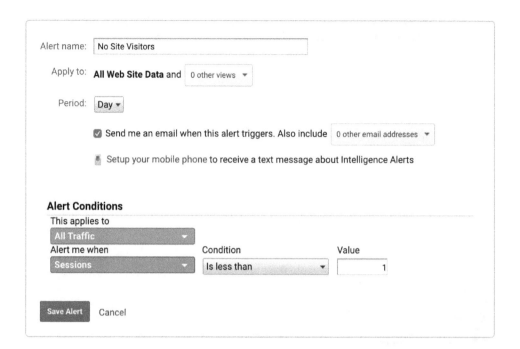

Custom alerts are an excellent way to monitor key user characteristics related to your strategic objectives, for example, monitoring changes in returning visitors and visitor location. The examples on pages 600 and 601 show how **weekly** custom alerts are created for each of these situations. In both cases:

- the time period is set to weekly because we don't want the alert to be influenced by random daily fluctuations.

- we create two alerts for each situation, one to signal a positive trend and the second to signal a negative trend.

- each alert looks at relative percentage change rather than an absolute percentage.

The displays below show the parameters of two custom alerts created to monitor *new site sessions*. The first alert triggers with a significant increase in sessions, while the second alert triggers with a significant decrease.

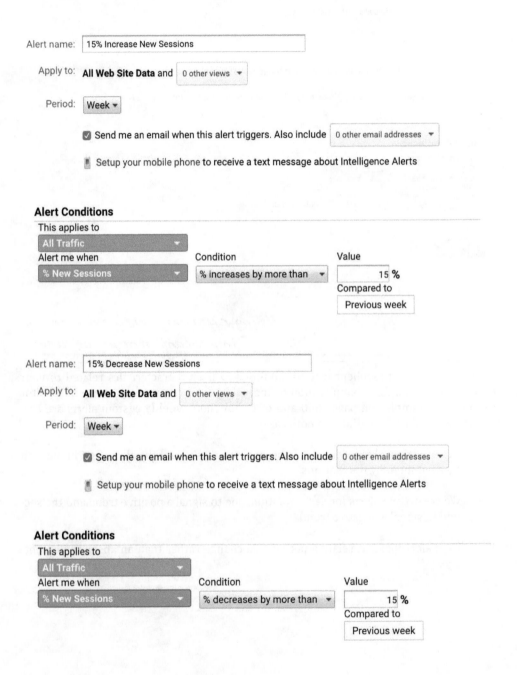

The displays below show the parameters of two custom alerts created to monitor *new site visitors from England*, one of our important geographic source of sales. Again, we create one alert that triggers on a significant increase, and another alert that triggers on a significant decrease.

Strategic planning is always facilitated when you understand how users find your website. Imagine that you have made a significant investment in search engine optimization, specifically Google and Bing. You can monitor the impact of this investment by creating a custom alert that monitors changes in referrals from these sources to your site. You can create an alert to monitor search referrals as a group (shown in the first figure below) or referrals from a specific source (shown in the second figure below).

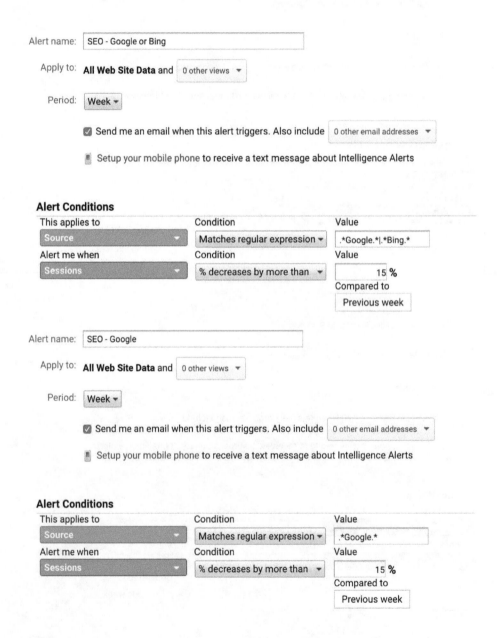

Custom alerts are appropriate for tracking changes in site engagement. You can, for example, look at changes in your bounce rate and average visit duration. However, you are not limited to overall site metrics. You can monitor the bounce rate or other engagement metrics for one or more specific pages.

The example below shows how we monitor the bounce rate for an individual page, in this case, our purchase page. Since the alert is looking at bounce rate, we are only interested in knowing when bounce rate increases beyond the absolute level we consider acceptable.

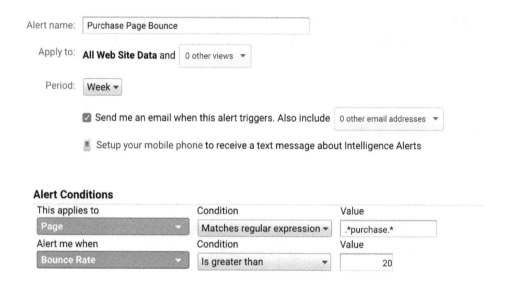

We can use custom alerts to monitor changes in important metrics such as revenue, purchase conversion rate, and total revenue. The two figures shown on page 604 illustrate the creation of two custom ecommerce alerts. The first (top figure) alerts us when total revenue drops by 15% or more. The second (bottom figure) alerts us when revenue generated by a specific category, in this case Bahamas tours, declines more than 15%. Both comparisons are on a week-to-week basis.

63

Shortcuts and Exports

Shortcuts and exports are two powerful ways to reduce your data-related workload.

Creating shortcuts

A shortcut is a quick way for you to access the Google Analytics reports you use most often. Creating a shortcut to a report uses the same logic as keyboard shortcuts, that is, they are a way of accomplishing more by doing less.

Below is a typical Google Analytics report, in this case a focus on new versus returning users.

There are two relevant links. **Shortcut** appears beneath the chart title (see below). This option allows you to create a new shortcut. **Shortcuts** are also a part of the **Customization** menu. This link takes you to a list of all of the shortcuts you created.

New vs Returning

| Customize | Email | Export ▾ | Add to Dashboard | Shortcut |

Let's look at each of these options.

You create a shortcut directly from the data report of interest by clicking on the **Short-cut** link beneath the report title. Doing so brings up an overlay where you can accept the proposed name or rename the shortcut (see below).

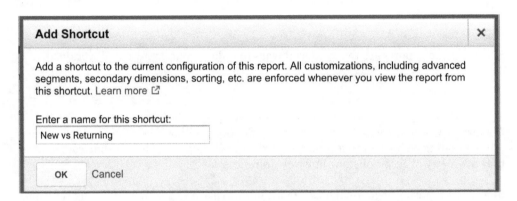

Clicking **OK** creates the shortcut. You can access this and all other shortcuts by clicking on the **Shortcuts** link in the **Customization** menu. This will display a page similar to that shown below. Clicking on the name of any shortcut will take you to the relevant data display.

While shortcuts allow you to instantly access frequently used reports, their real power comes from the additional information that is saved as part of the shortcut. Google notes that:

> Any setting you apply to a report, like adding an advanced segment or a new metric, stays applied in a shortcut until you manually change the settings. The settings are saved even if you sign out and sign back in to your account. All report customizations and settings are saved in a shortcut except for the date range. Check the dates each time you use a shortcut to make sure the time period you need is applied.[114]

---

[114] *Shortcuts* at https://support.google.com/analytics/answer/2676996.

As a result, you do not have to repeat time-consuming actions in order to drill-down into important metrics. All of the drill-down behaviors are saved along with the shortcut. In addition, you can create short-cuts to any custom reports and tables you've created.

Managing shortcuts

As noted earlier, you manage all your shortcuts through the Shortcuts link in the Customization menu. This takes you to a display of all your shortcuts, similar to that shown below.

Shortcuts

Name	Creation Date	
Engagement	Feb 8, 2017	Actions ▾
Audience Overview	Feb 9, 2017	Actions ▾
New vs Returning	Feb 28, 2017	Actions ▾

On the far right hand side there is an **Actions** menu for each shortcut. Pulling-down this menu displays shortcut management options that you can use to view the report, rename, or delete the shortcut (see below).

Shortcuts

Name	Creation Date	
Engagement	Feb 8, 2017	Actions ▾
Audience Overview	Feb 9, 2017	View
New vs Returning	Feb 28, 2017	Rename
		Delete

Exporting reports

You have two options with regard to exporting Google Analytics reports. You can download the report to view and manipulate offline or you can email the report to others.

Downloading a report

At the top of almost every report is an option to export the report. This option, labeled **Export**, is on the line directly beneath the report title (on the same line as the **Shortcut** link). Selecting the **Export** menu shows the formats in which data can be downloaded (see below).

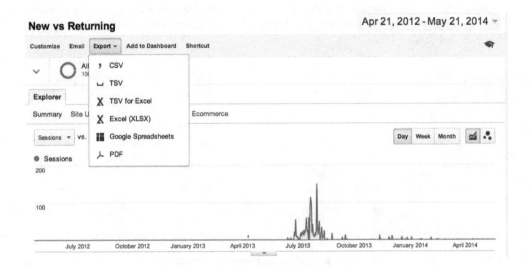

Note that the PDF download is an exact representation of the data displayed in the online view and that this download contains a link back to the original online report.

Emailing a report

The option to email a report or its underlying data, labeled **Email**, is located to the left of the **Export** option (beneath the chart title). Selecting this link brings up the overlay shown on the top of page 609. Your email address and subject are automatically filled in the form. You'll need to fill out the rest of the parameters (recipient, attachment format, email frequency, and day of the week to email). Once this is done, just click **Send** to initiate the email process.

Emails will continue to be sent until canceled. If you know in advance how long you want the emails sent, select the appropriate time period from the email form's **ADVANCED OPTIONS**.

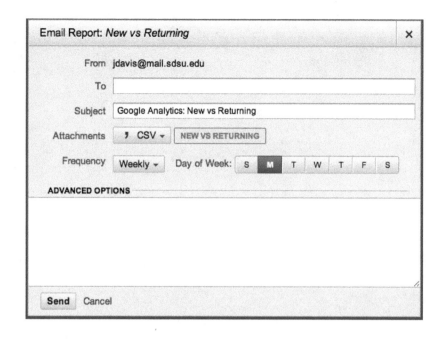

64

Custom Reports

As users of analytic tools, much of the data we spend time reviewing is merely suggestive. However, this is not always the data we want to analyze and from which we want to draw insights. There is so much data available to us, but only a fraction of it will lead us to better business decisions. This most pragmatic, relevant, actionable data can be found through Custom Reports.[115]

This chapter reviews the fundamental elements and application of Custom Reports.

Google Analytics provides you with the option to create and manage custom reports. A custom report is a report that you create to suit your own information needs by combining all relevant metrics in a single display. The content of these reports is unique to your business goals and thus, makes it easier to analyze the data and extract the most pragmatic insights. You could, for example, create a custom report that combines metrics from audience, behavior and conversion dimensions.

A custom report allows you to choose (a) the dimensions and metrics that you are most interested in and (b) the visual manner in which the data is presented. This ability to customize and build your own reports according to your own business goals is what makes these reports among the most useful features in Analytics.

The good news? Analytics experts have already created templates for custom reports they believe to be most valuable; and these reports are accessible to users through the Solutions Gallery. Though these expert reports are useful to reference, it is best to start simple and create a basic report, which you can add layers to later.

Overview

We'll illustrate how to create a custom report with data from my travel site. Let's begin by creating a report that looks at traffic and conversions by channel: something that is useful to most e-commerce sites.

You begin the creation of a custom report by navigating to the **Customization** tab and clicking on **Custom Reports > + New Custom Report**, as shown on the top of page 612.

---

[115] Information in this section adapted from: https://conversionxl.com/12-google-analytics-custom-reports/

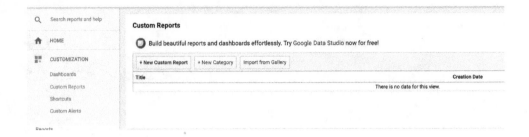

The first step is to create a relevant title for the report (i.e. E-Commerce Report) as shown below.

Report Tabs

From there, you need to add tab(s). Each tab can look at a different piece of data based on what you are interested in reporting. Every custom report will have at least one tab, but you can add more. When you add more tabs, all the following information applies to the tab that's currently highlighted.

For my E-Commerce Report, I titled the first tab 'Browser Usage' and chose metrics that will help evaluate how users on different browsers interact with my website (see below).

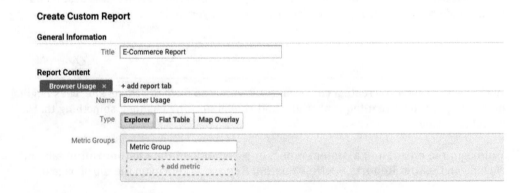

Selecting a Report Type

The next step is to select a report type (Explorer, Flat Table, or Map Overlay). You will select a new report type for each tab you create. Keep in mind that each tab can have a different report type. For example, you may create one tab as a Flat Table and another tab as a Map Overlay. In doing so, you create multiple tabs with different data visualizations, all in one custom report.

Each report type provides us with a different visual presentation:

The **Explorer** report is the standard Analytics report, which includes a line graph and a data table underneath with dynamic elements like a 'search/sort' option as well as secondary dimensions (see example below).

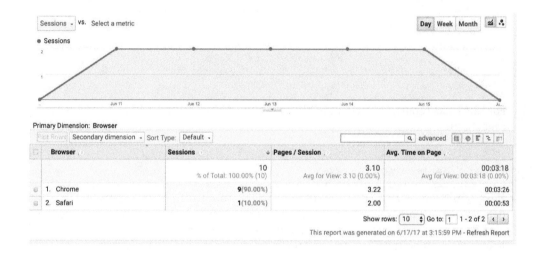

The **Flat Table** is a static, sortable table, which presents data in rows.

The **Map Overlay** presents the data based on geographic location. The information is presented as a map of the world, where different countries and regions will display in a range of colors based on volume of engagement and traffic (see top of page 614).

Continent	Sessions	↓ Pages / Session	Avg. Time on Page
	10	3.10	00:03:18
	% of Total: 100.00% (10)	Avg for View: 3.10 (0.00%)	Avg for View: 00:03:18 (0.00%)
1. Americas	5(50.00%)	5.00	00:03:26
2. Asia	3(30.00%)	1.00	00:00:00
3. Europe	2(20.00%)	1.50	00:00:53

For this basic report, I selected the Explorer report type, as this is the standard Analytics report type.

Selecting metric groups

Next, you need to choose the metrics in which you are most interested. This will be determined by your specific business goals. For my Browser Usage tab, I selected three metrics: sessions, pages per session, and average time on page. Each of these metrics helps me to understand how my customers are interacting with my website.

If at any time, you decide you want to delete a metric group you've created, simply click on the **X** located at the right-hand side of the Metric Groups box (see below).

To add an additional metric group to your custom report, click on the **+ Add metric group** button and repeat the same selection process as explained previously.

Selecting dimensions

In order to further break down the data you're interested in, you can select certain dimensions to add to your report. These dimensions will be displayed as individual rows in the final custom report.

For the Browser Usage tab of my custom report, the most important dimension for me to add was Browser type. To add a dimension, you click the **+ add dimension** button and select whichever dimension you are interested in including in your report.

I selected **Browser** from the dropdown menu. By doing so, I was able to 'drilldown' my website's session metrics and gain deeper insights as to how various browser users were interacting with my website.

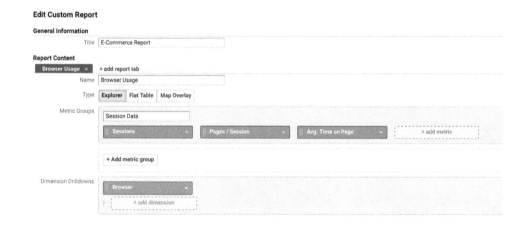

At this point, you can **Save** this Custom Report, as you have selected all of the required fields to create a Custom Report.

When you click **Save**, you will be taken to your custom report. After clicking **Save**, my Custom Report looked like that shown below.

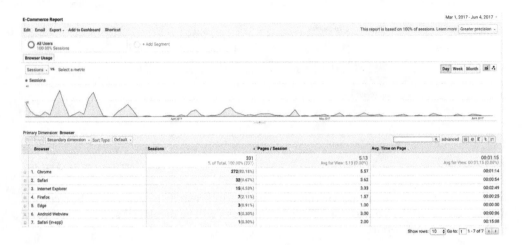

Based on my report you can see that over 80% of my website sessions are using Chrome. Thus, if I am considering which browsers I should focus on when looking to enhance desktop experience or mobile experience, I would likely start with Chrome.

Additionally, when looking at Average Time on Page, I notice that users accessing my website with Internet Explorer are spending much longer on a page than any other browser user (2:49 minutes). This could be an opportunity for my company to investigate in order to better understand this anomaly in the data.

Custom report management

Clicking on the Custom Reports tab on the left-hand side of your Analytics screen will bring you to a menu with all of the Custom Reports you've created so far. Here is what my Custom Reports page looks like, hosting just my E-Commerce Report:

If you want to adjust or delete any custom report you've created, you can do so easily.

On the Custom Reports page, there will be an **Actions** button to the right of each custom report you've created. You can click on this button and a dropdown menu will appear with the options to **Edit, Copy, Share**, or **Delete** that custom report.

Editing your custom report is accessed through the Actions button as well. For example, after saving my report, I decided I wanted to add a filter to my E-Commerce Report. I clicked **Actions > Edit** to do so. This brings me back to the page you see below.

From here, you have the option to **+ add filter**. This will narrow the data down to specific subset of data you are interested in, or conversely, can eliminate a set of data that you are not interested in. [116]

For example, you may filter the data by country to better understand where your conversions are coming from geographically (**+ add filter > Users > Country**); or by device to see how your e-commerce site is performing on mobile versus desktop (**+ add filter > Users > Device Category**).

I did not choose to add a filter to my report. However, you can use this feature to limit your data even further based on whatever elements of your website or campaign are most pertinent to your business at any given time. This is a key benefit of custom reports: they allow us to view our data according to very specific goals.

---

[116] For reference, an in-depth discussion of filters was discussed in Chapters 9, 10, 11, and 12.

Our custom report is now complete. We will press **SAVE** and the report will resemble the figure shown below.

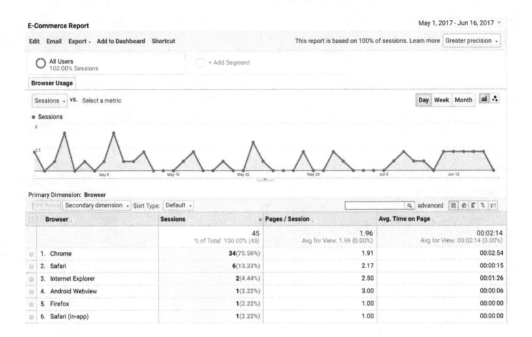

✔ Be sure to adjust the date range on the Custom Report to the appropriate settings for your business goals. For my custom report, I selected a custom date range of May 1st, 2017 – Jun 16, 2017, which was the length of a campaign I was evaluating.

Deleting filters

To delete a filter you have added to your custom report, click **Edit** on the left hand side of the bar toward the top of the report. From there, click the **x** on the right hand side of the text box next to your selected filter, as shown below.

Filters - optional

| Include ▾ | Referral Path ▾ | Exact ▾ | | ⊗ |

and

+ add filter ▾

From here, you can explore and interpret the data in your report: looking for trends, patterns, and anomalies. For example, you may find that the bounce rate from organic traffic is higher than other channels. This could illustrate a problem with your landing, age, such as a lack of mobile-optimization.

Additionally, this custom report also allows you to determine which sources are performing best. If traffic from Facebook is producing most revenue, then perhaps this justifies greater budget spending on Facebook advertising.

Sharing custom reports

When shared, custom reports allow you to deliver more focused relevance to those interested in the data. The custom reports feature allows you to create different reports when reporting to different people, clients, etc.

For example, you may consider minimizing specific details in reports for individuals who solely want top-level information, so as not to distract them from the big picture. Similarly, you can set up filtered reports for individuals working on specific marketing and advertising channels such as email marketing, social media marketing, and search engine optimization (SEO).

You can share your Custom Report in one of two ways: through a template link (to send via e-mail) or through the Solutions Gallery (to share publicly). [117] In order to share your custom report via e-mail, you can click E-mail at the top of your Custom Report, as shown on the top of page 620.

---

[117] To see examples of reports that other Google Analytics users and experts have created and shared in the Solutions Gallery, visit the following links:
http://barker.co.uk/gahours
https://www.koozai.com/blog/analytics/setting-up-and-using-custom-reports-in-google-analytics/
https://www.google.com/analytics/web/importing/?authuser=0&utm_source&utm_medium&utm_term&utm_content&utm_campaign#importing/a47792028w79131574p81823498/%3F_.objectId%3DSgdpUI30RIOnVL3bMJBC9A%26_.selectedProfile%3D/

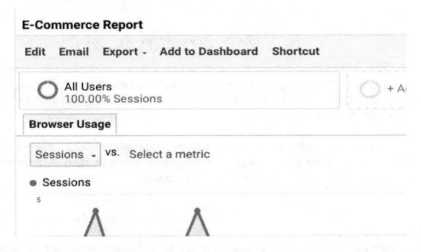

A screen will then appear, where you can enter in the recipient's address that you wish to receive the report (see below).

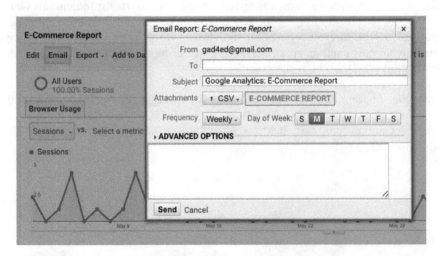

In addition to sharing Custom Reports via a template link or the Solutions Gallery, you can also export the report to your device. The **Export** option is also in the tool bar above your Custom Report, alongside the options to **Edit**, **Email**, **Add to Dashboard**, and **Shortcut**.

A dashboard is a visual display of metrics that relate to a specific strategic information need, property goal, or strategic objective. You can, for example, create a dashboard that focuses on the conversion of specific goals, the outcome of a specific marketing campaign, ecommerce data, referral sources, site health, or website or blog engagement. This chapter discusses the procedures for creating and editing your own dashboards as well as for acquiring dashboards created by others.[118]

You access dashboards through the **Dashboards** link that is part of the Customization menu (see opposite). Selecting this link brings you to a list of all dashboards currently available in the selected view (see below).

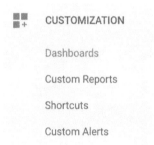

CUSTOMIZATION

Dashboards

Custom Reports

Shortcuts

Custom Alerts

Dashboards

CREATE		All	Shared	Private	Search

Name	Creation Date	↑	Type
Mobile Ecommerce Dashboard	Mar 18, 2014		Private
Site Performance Dashboard	Mar 18, 2014		Private

Show rows 10 ▾   1 - 2 of 2 ‹ ›

Let's look at the 'Site Performance Dashboard' in order to see a dashboard's primary components.

An example dashboard

The dashboard shown on the top of page 622 focuses on website health. Note how each displayed metric is relevant to this topic.

---

[118] Google has an alternative free platform for creating dashboards and other visual reports of your data. Select Data Studio when you sign into your account at http://www.google.com/analytics.

Dashboards can be used to track any time period, but are best used when they display recent data, typically either the past week or previous day. Since the maintenance of site health is of critical importance, we've set up this dashboard to report only the prior day's data.

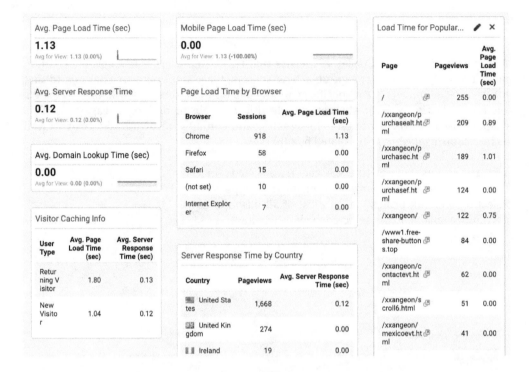

Creating a dashboard

Let's create a dashboard from scratch. This will allow us to see the options for data selection and visual appearance. Our dashboard will focus on website engagement for the previous seven days. This time range is easily set through the use of the pull-down menu in the date range settings (see below).

The first step to dashboard creation is clicking on **Customization > Dashboards** and then (on the next page displayed) selecting **CREATE**. Next, the layout option page will be shown (see the figure on the top of the next page).

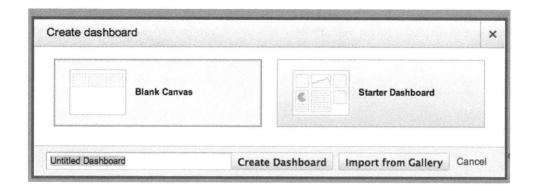

Here we select 'Blank Canvas' to create an entirely customized new dashboard. We name the dashboard 'Site Engagement' and press **Create Dashboard**. (We'll discuss the **Import from Gallery** option later in this chapter.) At this point, the name of the new dashboard is added to the **Dashboards > Private** menu options and the overlay screen shown below is displayed. Note that 'New Widget' is the default name that will remain until you rename the dashboard element.

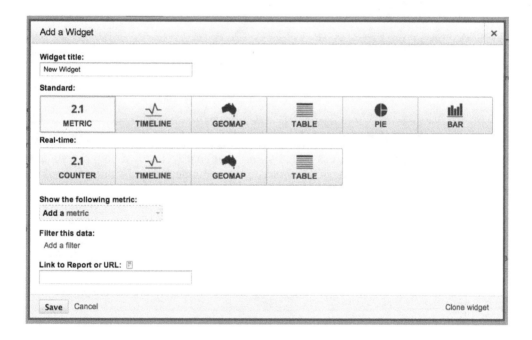

There are two rows of available metrics: **Standard** and **Real-Time**. **Standard** metrics are displayed for a requested time period while **Real-Time** metrics pull data to reflect what is happening now. Your choice of metrics depends upon your strategic information needs. Our site engagement dashboard will only use **Standard** metrics.

We begin by clicking in the **2.1 Metric** box in the **Standard** row, thereby indicating that we want to display a single numeric metric. The desired metric is selected through the use of the pull-down menu beneath **Show the following metric**. Our first engagement metric is **Average Session Duration**. When we select this metric from the menu, the screen changes to that shown below. Note that the widget name has automatically been changed to reflect our selection.

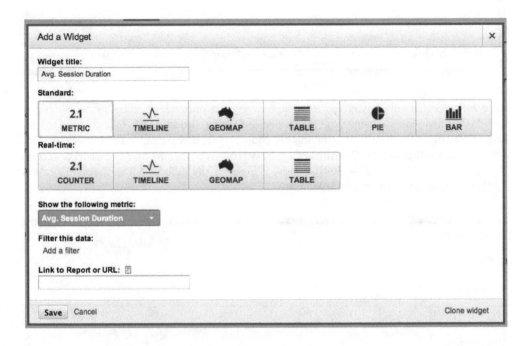

When we press **Save,** the metric is added to our dashboard as shown below. Note how the data includes both the numeric summary for the time period and a line graph of the underlying data.

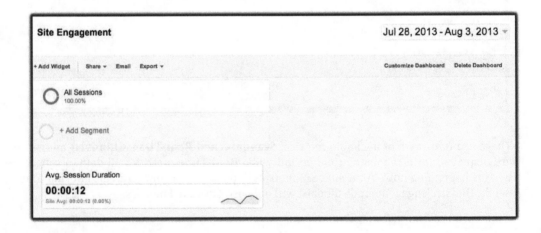

Once our first metric is added to the dashboard, additional metrics can be added by clicking on **+Add Widget** on the top left of the display. (Each item displayed in the dashboard is called a 'widget'.) The preceding process then repeats. The figure shown below illustrates dashboard appearance after adding two more engagement metrics in the same way as just described.

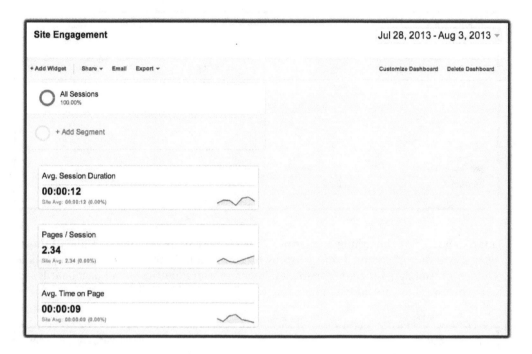

After the addition of several metrics to the dashboard, it is often beneficial to modify the dashboard's visual appearance by rearranging the widgets. We accomplish this as follows: First we click on the **Customize Dashboard** option on the top of the dashboard. This brings up the overlay page shown opposite that allows us to determine the number and size of columns in which widgets are displayed.

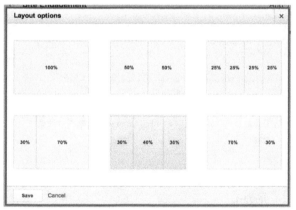

Selecting the bottom row middle option (and then pressing **Save**) returns us to our original dashboard display.

We now have the option of moving metric displays into one of three rows and manipulating the order if desired. To move a widget, we simply click in the line containing the widget's name, and then drag and drop the widget into its desired place, as shown below.

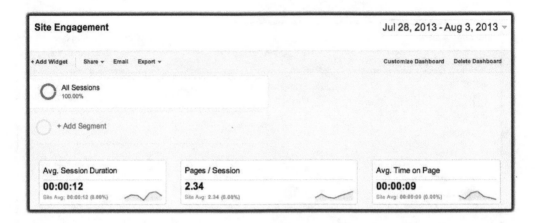

So far so good, but something is missing. There is no context to interpret any of these metrics. Are they based on 1,000 sessions or 10 sessions? 100 users or 5 users? As a result, we recommend including both sessions and users metrics on all dashboards, as shown below. These are added in the same way as the previous metrics.

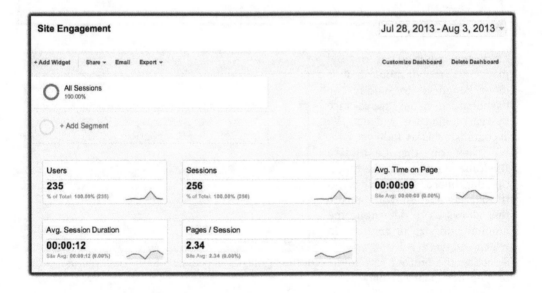

Let's add one last single metric. As before, we click on **+Add Widget** to add a metric and then, on the overlay, we add **Goal Conversion Rate** as an additional 2.1 Metric. Now that we know the overall conversion rate, let's see the trend that relates goal conversion rate to the overall number of goals started. We can look at the relationship between two metrics by clicking in the **TIMELINE** box made available after **+Add Widget** is selected. This changes the display to that shown below.

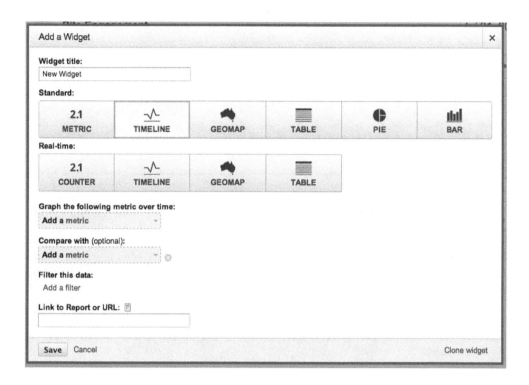

Notice how the selection options have changed to reflect our desire to create a timeline. We can look at the relationship between goal conversions and goal starts by first selecting **Goal Conversion** rate from the **Graph the following metric over time:** pull-down menu and by selecting **Goal Starts** from the **Compare with (optional)** pull-down menu. This adds the timeline data to our dashboard, as shown on the top of page 628.

The timeline display for the two selected metrics is shown in the second row of the dashboard (on the top of page 628). Note how displaying both the average conversion rate metric and the timeline provides insights beyond those provided by each individually. The **Goal Conversion Rate** metric is high at 51.17%, indicating that just over half of all goals started are completed. This is good, but because it is an average, it is important to look at the underlying data, which are provided by the timeline. You can see that early in the week, the number of goal starts was quite low, and the conversion rate was declining. We then tried to improve both measures in the middle of the week. The next day (August 1) both measures improved, after which the conversion rate remained very high, but the number of goals started significantly declined. We appear to have overcompensated and need to determine a way to increase goal starts while maintaining the high goal completion rate.

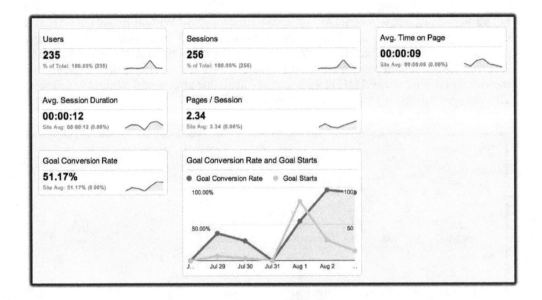

We'll skip the **GEOMAP** display since all of our visitors are from the United States and we are not interested in engagement by geographic region.

The **TABLE** option allows us to display tables similar to those provided in standard Google Analytics reports. When we click in the **TABLE** box, the following is displayed. Note how the metric selection options have changed again to reflect that we are constructing a table.

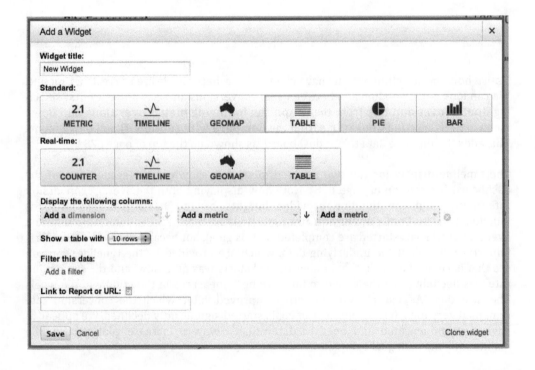

The engagement behaviors of new versus returning users have always been a concern, so we are going to construct a table that looks at this relationship. As illustrated below, we select our dimension of interest (in this case **User Type** from the first pull-down menu) and our two metrics of interest from the middle and right pull-down menus (in this case, the two engagement metrics **Avg. Time on Page** and **Avg. Session Duration**).

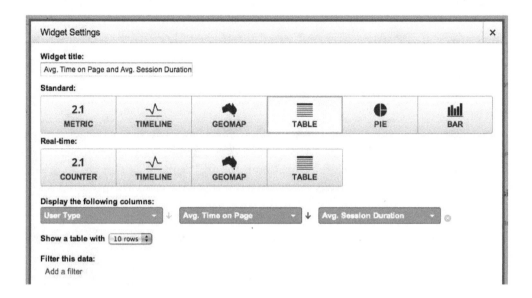

Pressing **Save** adds the table to our dashboard, which, after rearranging the display, appears on the bottom of the middle column, as shown below.

We can continue our focus on new versus returning visitors by selecting the **PIE** chart option, as shown below. Notice, that once again the options have changed to reflect **PIE** chart selection.

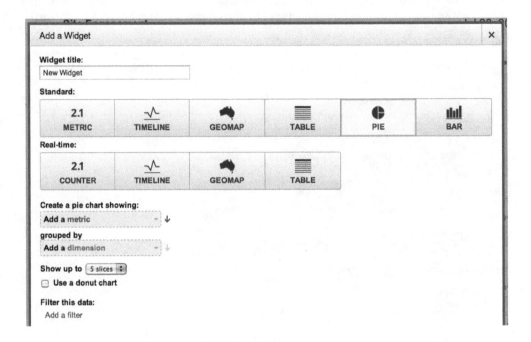

We select our engagement metric, **Unique Pageviews**, from the top pull-down menu and **User Type** from the bottom pull-down menu, as shown below.

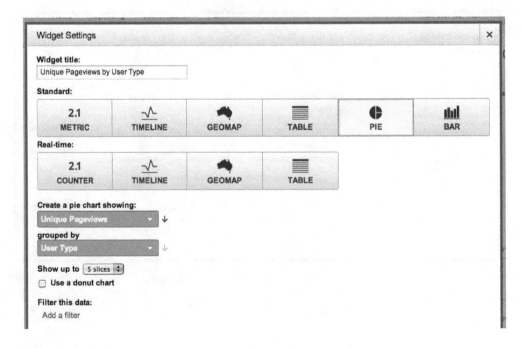

Pressing **Save** adds the pie chart to our dashboard, which, after rearranging the display, appears on the bottom of the right-hand column as shown below.

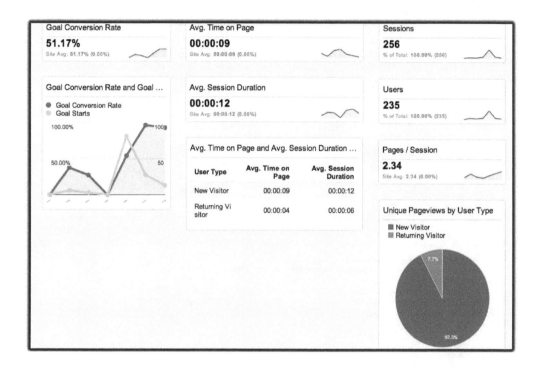

BAR charts are the last metric display option. When we select this option, similar to the other display choices, the options change to reflect bar chart creation (see the top of page 632). We need to specify the metric we want displayed and the grouping dimension. This is accomplished through the use of two pull-down menus, where the metric is selected from the top **Create a bar chart showing:** pull-down menu and the grouping dimension is selected from the **grouped by** pull-down menu.[119]

---

[119] There are many more options for widget display beyond the basics we discuss in this chapter. We encourage you to play with these options, keeping in mind that any widgets created but unwanted can be edited or deleted, as discussed shortly.

Pressing **Save** adds the table to our dashboard, which, after rearranging the display, appears on the bottom of the first column, as shown on the top of page 633.

Our dashboard is now complete. We've added all the core metrics to allow us to quickly evaluate site engagement on a rolling seven-day basis. However, one final observation on the dashboard's organization is needed. This dashboard, similar to others you create, should allow for the quick observation of related measures. As a result, metrics should be displayed in a logical way. In our case, we've grouped related measures within the same column. The left-hand column presents measures related to conversion rate; the middle column presents timing and view measures; and the right-hand column provides information related to new versus returning users.

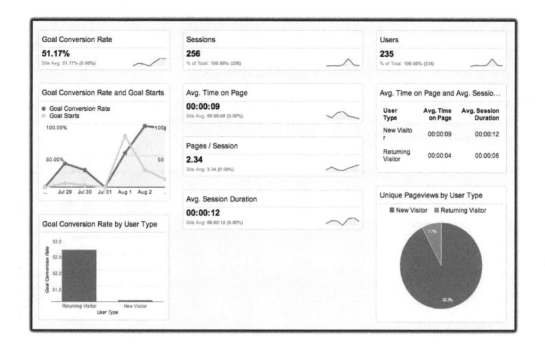

You can edit or delete any dashboard display.

As shown opposite, every display contains an edit option (the pencil) and a delete option (the 'x') that appear when you roll your mouse over the display's title.

Clicking on the 'x' initiates the deletion process, which is finalized when you confirm the deletion. Clicking on the pencil takes you to the same overlay page in which the display was created. Here, any of the display options can be edited.

You can edit the name of a dashboard by clicking in the dashboard's title frame, as shown below. Then, just type the new name and press **Save**.

| Campaign Evaluation Dashboard | Save | cancel | | Jun 29, 2014 - Jul 29, 2014 |

Custom segments can be applied to a dashboard by clicking on **+Add a Segment**, which appears on the top of the page just beneath **All Sessions**.

The figure below shows the addition of the custom segment, **Sessions with Transactions**, to the dashboard display. Note how each widget now reports data for both all sessions and sessions with transactions.

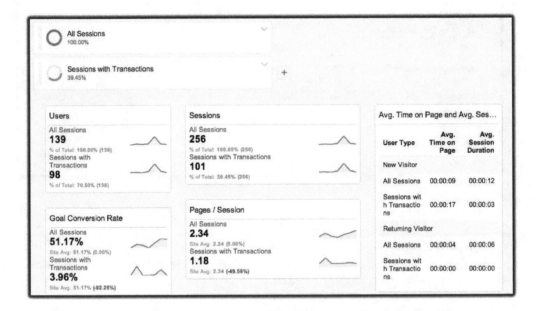

This display, however, feels a bit crowded. We can make things easier to read and better focused on the segment of interest by eliminating the **All Sessions** data. This allows the display to present only the data relevant to **Sessions with Transactions**, as shown on the top of page 635. This display allows us to easily focus on the characteristics of just this segment of site users.

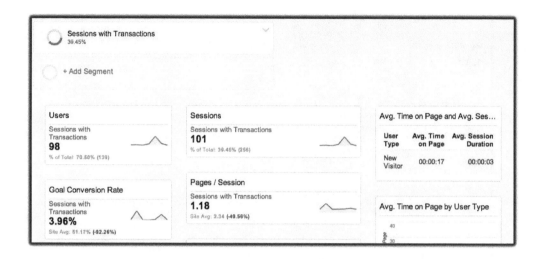

One very beneficial use of applying custom segments to dashboards is the monitoring of marketing campaigns. You'll recall that we can tag campaigns with source, medium, and campaign parameters (see Chapters 48 and 49). We can create a dashboard designed to present key metrics related to campaigns, and then use custom segments to focus the dashboard on the campaign of interest. This is accomplished as follows.

Determine the link tags

Campaign links are tagged so that Google Analytics can identify the source of the referral. Imagine that we are going to send out a campaign with the following characteristics:

Tag Name	Tag	Definition	Label
Source	utm_source	The marketing vehicle or source of the referral	May 10% off offer
Medium	utm_medium	The digital medium that conveyed the link	Facebook
Campaign	utm_campaign	The identifier for the specific referral source	Video post

Create the dashboard

We create a dashboard that focuses on the essential metrics needed to evaluate the campaign. This dashboard is shown on the top of page 636. Note that any data shown in the dashboard reflect the current time period and not the upcoming campaign.

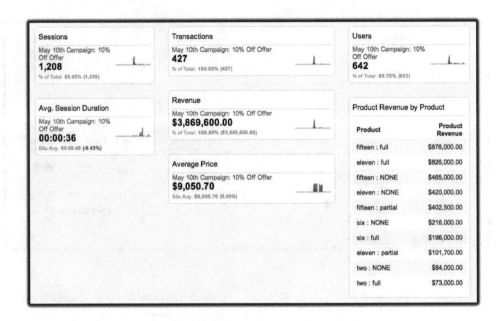

Create a custom segment to identify users referred by the campaign.

We click on **+Add Segment** (on the top of the dashboard page) and then **+New Segment** to begin the segment creation process. On the next screen we click on **Traffic Sources** to define our segment in terms of the upcoming campaign. This brings up the display shown below.

We'll define the segment by using the **Source** and **Medium** parameters provided on page 636. Adding these parameters and naming the segment results in the display shown below. Clicking **Save** stores the segment and adds the segment to our list of available segments.

Apply the segment to the dashboard

Once the campaign starts, we load the **Dashboards > Private > Campaign Evaluation Dashboard** and then apply the custom segment. In our case, this results in the dashboard shown below, where we can quickly examine the campaign's effect on generating traffic and sales.

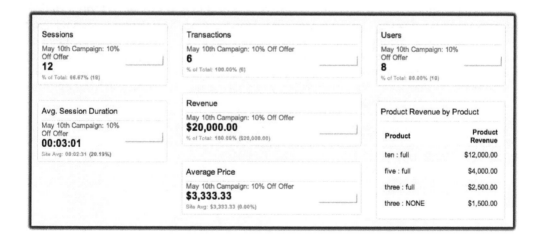

We noted earlier that dashboards are, by default, available only within the view in which they were created and are viewable only by the person who created the dashboard. You have two options, however, for sharing your dashboards with others who have account access.

On the top of the dashboard, next to **+Add Widget**, is a sharing pull-down menu with three options (as shown below). The options are displayed when **Share** is selected.

The **Share Object** option allows everyone with access permission to the current view to see the dashboard. These individuals merely go to **Dashboards > Shared** and click on the dashboard name to view the data for the selected date range. The figure opposite shows my two shared dashboards.

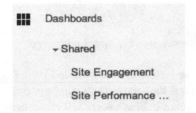

The second option in the **Share** pull-down menu, **Share template link,** allows you to share the dashboard with any Google Analytics user. Clicking on **Share template link** brings up an overlay page with a custom link. You can send the link to others whom you want to be able to see the dashboard. When they click on this link the display shown on the top of page 639 is shown. This display asks the individual to assign the dashboard to one of his/her views via the **Select a view** pull-down menu. Selecting a view adds the dashboard to that view. Note that when you share a dashboard in this way only the display is shared; your data remains confidential.

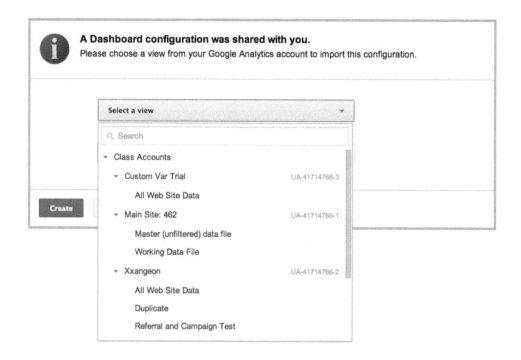

The final way to share a dashboard is through the **Share in Solutions Gallery** option. This option places your dashboard in the Google Analytics Solution Gallery for anyone to use. As with the link sharing option, only your dashboard configuration is shared; your data remains confidential and is not shared.

Importing dashboards

While you may wish to share your dashboards with others via the Google Analytics Solutions Gallery, other Google Analytics users have already decided to share their dashboards with you. You can import dashboards from the Google Analytics Solutions Gallery by selecting **Import from Gallery** when the initial create dashboard window is displayed. You will then see the dashboards that are available for import.

Finally, there are dashboards available for import outside of the Google Analytics Solutions Gallery. The following are excellent sources of dashboard ideas, all of which can be imported and then edited to meet your specific strategic information needs.

- Econsultancy:
  `https://econsultancy.com/blog/62828-10-useful-google-analytics-custom-dashboards#i.ie2lm07nwewwyz`

- Dashboardjunkie: `http://www.dashboardjunkie.com/`

- Zeta:
  `http://www.zeta.net/10-free-google-analytics-dashboards/`

66
Calculated Metrics

Calculated Metrics are user-defined metrics that are created from existing metrics. Calculated Metrics provide more options in data collection by allowing you to perform basic calculations with the metrics right in the Google Analytics interface – without having to export the data into Excel or other external programs.

Although Analytics provides dozens of default metrics about our site users and visitors, there are going to be some metrics that we are interested in that are not provided. This is where Calculated Metrics assist us by providing us flexibility and customization in the data we collect through the creation of new metrics that reflect our own site's goals.

It's important to note that Calculated Metrics are different from Custom Metrics. Unlike Custom Metrics, Calculated Metrics are configured at the **View** level, not the **Property** level. Calculated metrics also differ from custom metrics in the way that they are collected and processed.

Creating a Calculated Metric

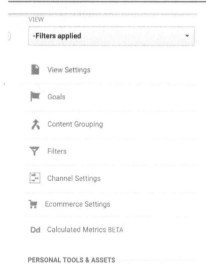

Let's use an example from my travel site to illustrate how Calculated Metrics can be applied to an ecommerce site.

Imagine that after expending extra funds toward updating my Information page, I wanted to know whether or not my visitors were actually engaging with the new content. I specifically wanted to evaluate how engaged our site visitors were with our travel brochure PDFs each time they came to our page.

One way to evaluate engagement with my brochures is by tracking downloads per session. However, there is no default metric in Analytics that satisfies this information need; so I need to create a Calculated Metric.

You can access the Calculated Metrics tool through your **Admin page**. Toward the bottom of your View menu, you will see the Calculated Metric tool link, just before the Personal Tools & Assets menu begins (see above).

From here, click **+ NEW CALCULATED METRIC** and begin filling out the required fields to create a metric personalized to your business goals, needs, & inquiries. Each of these fields is explained in the next section.

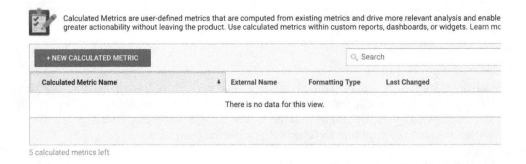

5 calculated metrics left

Only 5 calculated metrics are available per view, unless you have Google Analytics Premium, in which case you will have 50 available calculated metrics per view

Four elements of Calculated Metrics

A Calculated Metric is made up of the following four required fields:

Name

The metric **Name** is the user interface name or the web view name. This is how the calculate metric is identified in a Google Analytics report. You will want to use descripttive names for the calculated metrics you create so that any reader of your report can easily understand what data is being reported. For my information need, I wanted to know how engaged our site visitors were with our travel brochure PDFs each time they came to our page, so I created a calculated metric and named it *PDF Downloads Per Session* (see below).

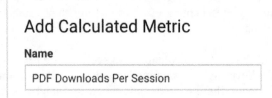

You can change the web view name of a calculated metric at any time.

External Name

As you enter a Name for your calculated metric, a unique **External Name** will be created for you. This is the API name of the calculated metric. You can edit the External Name if you choose, but it is not necessary to do so and you cannot change the name once the calculated metric is created. The external (API) name for our PDF Downloads Per Session would be: ***calcMetric_PDFDownloadsPerSession***

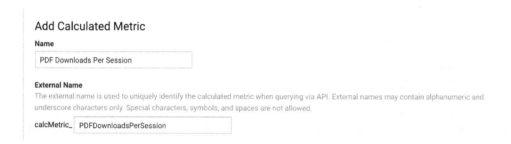

Formatting Type

This setting is used to determine the format in which Analytics should report the values of your calculated metric. There are 5 formatting types available: float, integer, currency (decimal), time, and percent. Select the one that best communicates the desired calculated metric value. You will select the format of your data from the Formatting Type drop down menu.

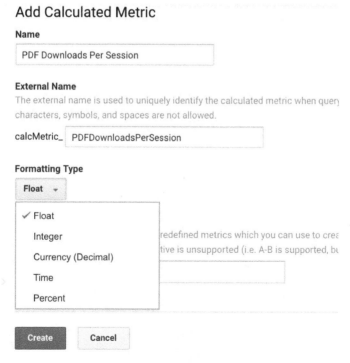

Formula

This is where the calculations begin. The **Formula** field will include the metrics you want to use in the calculation and the arithmetic expressions you will use to carry out the calculation. As you begin typing in the fields you are interested in, Google will suggest metrics to you based on what you have typed so far. Accepted arithmetic expressions include:

> Plus (+)
> Minus (-)
> Divided by (/)
> Multiplied by (*)
> Parenthesis
> Positive cardinal numbers (0-9), can include decimals

For my calculated metric, I had already created a Goal to evaluate whether or not site users were downloading documents from my Information page (*Goal 8 - Downloaded at least one document from Information page*). Thus, my formula would then be: **{{Downloaded at least one document from Information page (Goal 8 Completions)}} / {{Sessions}}**. See image below.

Once you are finished, press **Create**. If done successfully, you will see something similar to the image shown on the top of page 645.

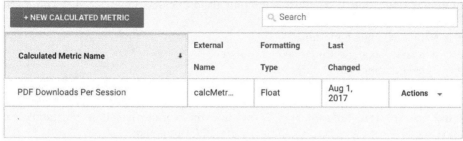

Calculated Metric Name	↓	External Name	Formatting Type	Last Changed	
PDF Downloads Per Session		calcMetr...	Float	Aug 1, 2017	Actions ▾

4 calculated metrics left

If you need to Copy or Delete your newly created Calculated Metric, you can do so by selecting the appropriate option from the **Actions** drop down menu.

Calculated Metric Name	↓	External Name	Formatting Type	Last Changed	
PDF Downloads Per Session		calcMetr...	Float	Aug 1, 2017	Actions ▾

4 calculated metrics left

✔ 'Using the minus operator as a negative is not supported (i.e. A-B is supported, but -B+A is not). Formulas are limited to 1024 characters. Up to 5 (Standard) and 50 (360) calculated metrics are supported at the view level. Using another custom calculated metric in the creation of a new calculated metric is not supported.' [120]

Additional Calculated Metrics

There are dozens of Calculated Metrics that have already been created by Google Analytics users that you may consider using for your own information needs. Below are just a few examples for you to consider:

Revenue After Refunds: Google Analytics do not show a total revenue amount that accounts for refunds – but you can get that in the interface with a custom metric:
- Name: Revenue After Refunds
- External Name: (automatically populated)
- Formatting Type: Currency (Decimal)
- Formula: {{Revenue}} – {{Refund Amount}}

---

[120] A primary source for this chapter is Google Analytics:
https://support.google.com/analytics/answer/6121409?hl=en

Revenue per User: One of the most commonly used calculated metrics for e-commerce sites[121]:
- Name: Revenue per User
- External Name: (automatically populated)
- Type: Currency (Decimal)
- Formula: {{Revenue}} / {{Users}}

Revenue per Session: How much did you make on average, based on the number of user sessions. This is a great metric for analyzing PPC campaigns:
- Name: Revenue per Session
- External Name: (automatically populated)
- Type: Currency (Decimal)
- Formula: {{Revenue}} / {{Sessions}}

Searches per User: a useful metric for sites where search plays a vital role:
- Name: Searches per User
- External Name: (automatically populated)
- Type: Float
- Formula: {{Total Unique Searches}} / {{Users}}

Using Calculated Metrics

Once created, your calculated metrics can be found in the following Google Analytics fields:

> Custom Dashboards (Chapter 65)
> Custom Reports (Chapter 64)
> Analytics Reporting APIs

You can incorporate your calculated metrics into any of the above Analytics fields. Whether it be including a calculated metric a Custom Report that you share with colleagues or clients; or whether you add it to your dashboard, Calculated Metrics allow you to customize your Analytics data to your exact business needs.

✅ In order to access a calculated metric via API, all constituent metrics must also be available by API.

---

[121] Additional examples of Calculated Metrics can be found here:
https://thenextweb.com/insider/2016/09/27/24-examples-google-analytics-calculated-metrics/#.tnw_MqLveCOm
http://blog.analytics-toolkit.com/2015/guide-calculated-metrics-google-analytics/
http://www.lunametrics.com/blog/2015/10/22/calculated-metrics-universal-analytics/

Sharing Assets

In Google Analytics, assets are the tools you use to customize your data analysis. Assets are both created and managed at the reporting view level, and can be shared easily with others.

The Share Assets feature allows you to share all or a selection of the following Google Analytics tools:

- Custom segments
- Custom reports
- Custom channel groupings
- Custom attribution models
- Dashboards
- Goals

The **Share Assets** feature is an easy way to share and view all segments, dashboards, and custom reports in one place. This feature can be extremely valuable if you have several people in your company with individual access to your Google Analytics data. You may, for example, believe that the information in one of your custom reports would be beneficial to send to the IT team at your business; or you may want to share a specific dashboard with a social media consultant who works remotely.

Additionally, this feature will be useful if you are working as a consultant and you need to share a different report or segment with each of your different clients. All such instances provide great opportunities to use the Share Assets feature.

In order to use the Share Assets feature, you need **Edit** permission, as you need to be able to perform administrative and report-based functions for your Google Analytics account.

The Share Assets feature is accessed through your **Admin** page. Click the Admin Icon on the bottom left hand side of your webpage to access. Next, you will want to select the **View** for which you are interested in sharing information. I've selected '-Filters applied'.

Finally, navigate down to the **Personal Tools and Assets** menu. Click **Share Assets**, which appears just below the Shortcuts option on the bottom of the column (see below).

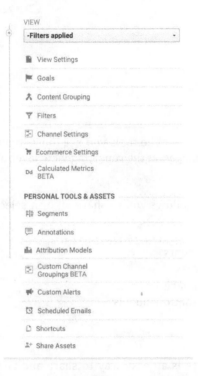

'When you share an asset, only the configuration information is copied and shared. None of your Analytics account data or personal information is shared, so you maintain control over your privacy and data.'[122]

Once you have clicked on **Share Assets**, an entire list of assets, including reports, channel groupings, and segments will show up on your screen (see image on the top of page 649). You can sort this Asset list the by any of following characteristics:

- Name
- Creation Date
- Type

I chose to sort my Share Assets menu by the type of asset.

---

[122] A primary source for this chapter is Google Analytics:
https://support.google.com/analytics/answer/1326774?hl=en

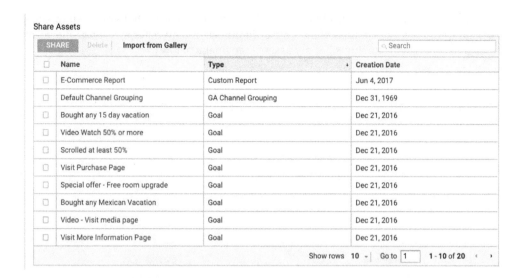

From here, you can select any of the reports, dashboards or segments that you would like to share. Based on your business needs, you have two options when it comes to sharing assets: you can either (a) share one asset at a time from a specific asset menu, or (b) you can share multiple assets at the same time.

If you decide to share all of the Assets within your Google Analytics account, you can tick the checkbox that appears besides the sort parameters discussed above.

Share Assets

	Name	Type	Creation Date
☑	E-Commerce Report	Custom Report	Jun 4, 2017
☑	Default Channel Grouping	GA Channel Grouping	Dec 31, 1969
☑	Bought any 15 day vacation	Goal	Dec 21, 2016
☑	Video Watch 50% or more	Goal	Dec 21, 2016
☑	Scrolled at least 50%	Goal	Dec 21, 2016
☑	Visit Purchase Page	Goal	Dec 21, 2016
☑	Special offer - Free room upgrade	Goal	Dec 21, 2016
☑	Bought any Mexican Vacation	Goal	Dec 21, 2016
☑	Video - Visit media page	Goal	Dec 21, 2016
☑	Visit More Information Page	Goal	Dec 21, 2016

Show rows 10 ▾ | Go to 1   1 - 10 of 20 ‹ ›

Otherwise, you can tick the checkboxes for the particular Assets that you wish to share. For example, I decided just to share my E-Commerce Custom Report with one of my colleagues, instead of sharing all of my assets (see image below).

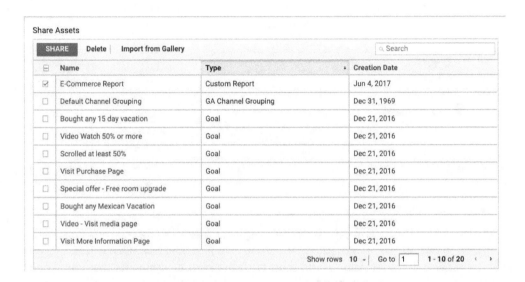

Once you have ticked the relevant checkboxes you would like to share with others, it will enable the red-colored **Share** button. When you click on this option, a pop-up will appear with two options, as seen below:

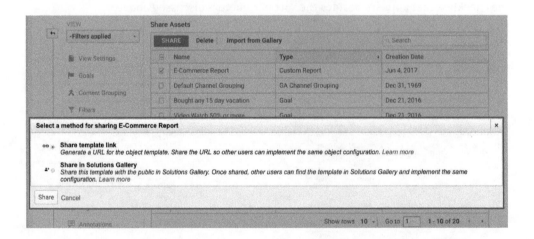

You have two options when it comes to sharing your assets with others. The first option is to share a template link. By selecting this option, Google Analytics will generate a unique URL that an account owner can share with other users. You will want to select this option if you intend to share the asset with only certain people.

Once you have selected the template link option and clicked **Share**, an additional pop-up will appear with a uniquely generated URL, along with a message that asks you to copy the link.

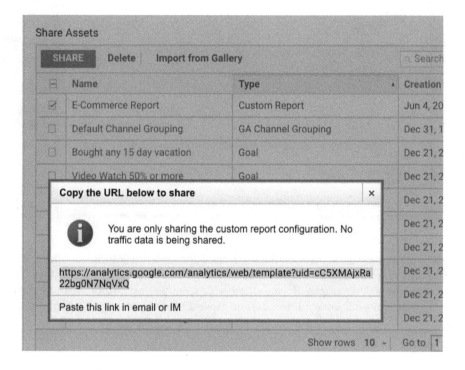

From here, you can copy the URL and insert it into an e-mail, document, etc. in order to share your data with those who will benefit.

Sharing in the solutions gallery

If you would like to share your asset(s) with everyone (publicly), you have the ability do so in the Google Gallery (see figure on the top of page 652).

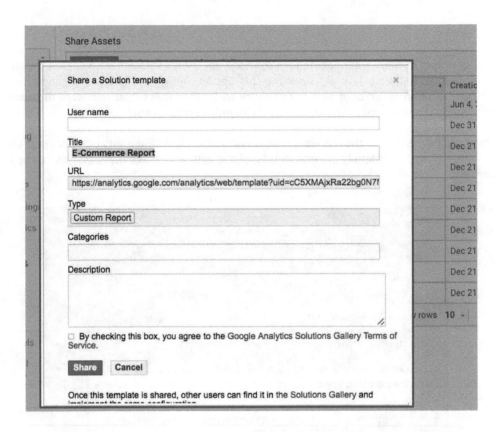

Keep in mind: only configuration data is shared through the Solutions Gallery. When you create and share an asset, your personal information and Analytics data stays private in your account. For example, if you share a Custom Report, other Analytics users can import that report to analyze the data in their Analytics account, but cannot see your data.

To Import an asset from the Analytics Solutions Gallery, simply press Import from Gallery. From here, a pop-up screen will appear, with different shared assets (custom reports, custom segments, etc.) from other Analytics users that you may import into your own report and apply to your own company's data (see figure on the top of page 653).

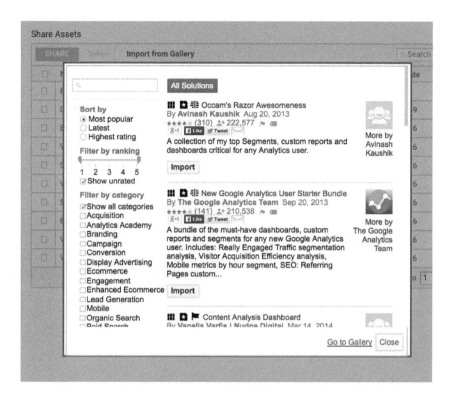

You can search the Solutions Gallery by:

- Most popular, Latest, Highest rating
- Ranking (on a scale of 1-5)
- Category (i.e. Acquisition, Branding, Conversion, Ecommerce, etc.)

Share asset management

From this table, you can also **Delete** an asset or **Import from Gallery** (i.e. import assets from the Solutions Gallery[123]).

To delete an asset, simply tick which asset you would like to remove, which will make the **Delete** button available for you **to** press (see page 654).

---

[123] More information on the Solutions Gallery can be found here:
https://support.google.com/analytics/answer/3314024

Share Assets

| SHARE | Delete | Import from Gallery | | Search |

	Name	Type	⌄ Creation Date
☑	E-Commerce Report	Custom Report	Jun 4, 2017
☐	Default Channel Grouping	GA Channel Grouping	Dec 31, 1969
☐	Bought any 15 day vacation	Goal	Dec 21, 2016
☐	Video Watch 50% or more	Goal	Dec 21, 2016
☐	Scrolled at least 50%	Goal	Dec 21, 2016
☐	Visit Purchase Page	Goal	Dec 21, 2016
☐	Special offer - Free room upgrade	Goal	Dec 21, 2016
☐	Bought any Mexican Vacation	Goal	Dec 21, 2016
☐	Video - Visit media page	Goal	Dec 21, 2016
☐	Visit More Information Page	Goal	Dec 21, 2016

Show rows 10 ⌄ Go to 1 1 - 10 of 20 ‹ ›

Intelligence Questions and Insights

We've all become used to asking our smartphone for information or guidance. These questions or requests can be simple, 'Navigate to the nearest Home Depot,' or complex, 'Which baseball team was the last team to have the best regular season record and not play in the World Series?' Google has brought a similar capability to Google Analytics.

Google Analytics Intelligence is a set of features recently added to Google Analytics that use machine learning to help you better understand and act on your data. The process is similar to that used on your smartphone – you ask a question and Analytics Intelligence searches your data to find the most relevant answer. You can ask simple or complex questions, for example: 'Which channel drove the most traffic to my site in January, 2017?' or 'Did the bounce rate on my home page (index.html) change in January, 2017 compared to December, 2016?'

This chapter will help you understand two aspects of Analytics Intelligence: Questions and Insights.[124]

Questions

Analytics Intelligence provides relevant answers to the vast majority of questions asked about your data. You access this aspect of Analytics Intelligence by clicking on the **Intelligence** link, which appears on the top right-hand side of most reports just above the date range (see below).

Oct 4, 2017 - Oct 10, 2017 ▾

---

[124] A third aspect of Analytics Intelligence powers Smart Goals, Smart Lists, and Session Quality which use machine learning to model conversions and build audiences. You can find information on these aspects of Analytics Intelligence at: *Smart Goals*, https://support.google.com/analytics/answer/6153083; *Smart Lists*, https://support.google.com/analytics/answer/4628577; and Session Quality, https://support.google.com/analytics/answer/7303153.

Selecting this option brings up the Analytics Intelligence interface shown opposite.

You type your question in the top box (currently labeled 'What data are you looking for?') and the most relevant answer will appear below.

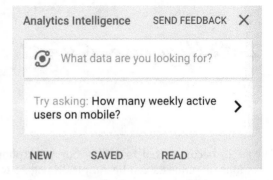

For example, asking 'Which channel drove the most traffic to my site in January, 2017?' results in the answer shown opposite. Our question is answered.

There are three additional options beneath the answer.

- The **Go to report** link takes you to the report from which the data was retrieved.

- The **Related Answers** link provides options (generated by Google) to ask additional questions focused on the same or related data.

- The number of sessions upon which the data is based. Make certain that the report is based on a sufficient number of sessions.

Top 10 Medium by Sessions

Jan 1–31, 2017

Medium	Sessions
referral	212
(none)	176
organic	56
Post	38

📄 Go to report

Related Answers

Based on 100.00% of sessions.

Types of Questions You Can Ask

You can ask questions related to:

- _basic data reporting_. These questions typically focus on a single dimension and metric for example:

'What was our bounce rate yesterday?'

'What channel resulted in the greatest number of sales last month?'

'What country accounted for the greatest number of visits last week?'

- *goals and site performance.* These questions typically focus on conversions for prespecified goals and events as well as site performance, for example:

  'How many Goal 3 conversions did we have last week?'

  'Which product had the greatest number of transactions last month?'

  'Which channel had the highest amount of dollar sales last year?'

  'Which pages had the highest bounce rate last week?'

- *trends.* These questions typically reports/compares two metrics during the same time period or a single metric over two time periods, for example:

  'What is the trend in visitors and transactions during the past month?'

  'What is the conversion rate for referrals versus organic search during the past week?'

  'Did the number of visitors increase in January, 2017 versus January 2016?'

- *focused outcomes.* These questions typically focus on a very specific data request, for example:

  'What percent of all sessions in the United States are generated from social?'

  'What share of all sessions is generated by women?'

  'Which blog entries had over 200 unique views?'

Beyond these question types, Analytics Intelligence can also answer complex question or questions that don't fall into one of the prior categories, for example:

  'How did conversions for Goal 4 compare in January, 2017 versus January 2016 for those who access the site using Firefox or Chrome?'

  'Compare total dollar sales in Ireland and the United States in 2016 among those via direct?'

Tips for Asking Questions[125]

As illustrated earlier, you can specify a date range in your question, for example: 'What were my most popular pages February 1-24, 2017?' or 'What was the share of sessions from Canada last week?'. Keep in mind that if you don't specify a date range, Analytics Intelligence assumes a default date range of the previous 30 days.

You may also see autocomplete options while typing in Analytics Intelligence. These are entities (metrics, dimensions, or dimension values) that exist for your profile and match what you're typing.

Limitations

Analytics Intelligence will attempt to answer the vast majority of questions. It will, however, be unable to answer questions that inquire about data which is not available or for which your site is not currently configured. These latter cases might relate to goals and events, which have not yet been activated, or for time ranges in which data was not collected. Analytics Intelligence is also unable to answer questions related to:

- General support (e.g., 'How do I build a segment?')

- Explanations (e.g., 'Why is my bounce rate increasing?')[126]

- Strategic advice (e.g., 'Which campaign should I invest in?')

- General search (e.g., 'How's the weather?')

Insights

Analytics Intelligence will crawl through your data to discover insights on major changes or opportunities that it believes should be brought to your attention. Insights might, for example, point out that a certain landing page is performing better than normal.

Google explains that 'Insights are classified into New, Saved, and Read feeds. Over time, Analytics Intelligence learns which insights you're most interested in and ranks your New insights using a machine-learning algorithm. The insights in your feed are personalized to your interests, and may differ from the insights other users see in the same view.'

---

[125] This and the following discussion adapted from Google, _About Analytics Intelligence_ at https://support.google.com/analytics/answer/7347597.

[126] These types of questions may be answered in the future.

You'll be notified of unread insights via the Intelligence link on the top of almost all report pages. The number of unread notices will appear in a blue circle. In this case, we have more than 9 unread insights (see below).

New/unread insights will appear when you access Analytics Intelligence, as shown below.

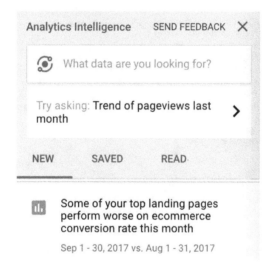

Clicking on the Insight provides access to four types of information (see figure on the top of page 660).

- The very top of the insight provides the original insight, more detail on the evaluation criteria, and the relevant time frame.

- Data tables or charts displaying the relevant data are presented next.

- A link to the full report from which the data has been obtained appears next.

- The bottom of the insight presents recommendations and questions for further consideration.

Some of your top landing pages perform worse on ecommerce conversion rate this month

Sep 1 - 30, 2017 vs. Aug 1 - 31, 2017

Some of your top landing pages performed >25% worse on ecommerce conversion rate this month.

Landing Page	Sessions	Ecommerce Conversion Rate
/home	54.4K,+37.00%	2.11%,-42.67%
/google+redesign /nest/nest-usa	2.4K,+50.83%	13.73%,-26.66%
/google+redesign /shop+by+brand/ waze/waze+pack +of+9+decal+set. axd	1.4K,+22.59%	0.00%,-100.00%
/google+redesign /apparel	1.1K,-13.70%	1.05%,-44.58%

 Go to report

Recommendations

Over this time period, the overall ecommerce conversion rate of your site was *2.1%*. If these pages improved to match their previous performance, your overall ecommerce conversion rate would have been *3.13%*, a *49.21%* improvement.

If there have been changes in the traffic sources to these pages, have you made sure the content is relevant to that traffic?

If you changed the content on these pages, did you notice a change in user behavior?

Once you've read an insight, you can choose to either save or delete it via the three dots to the right of the insight title, as shown below.

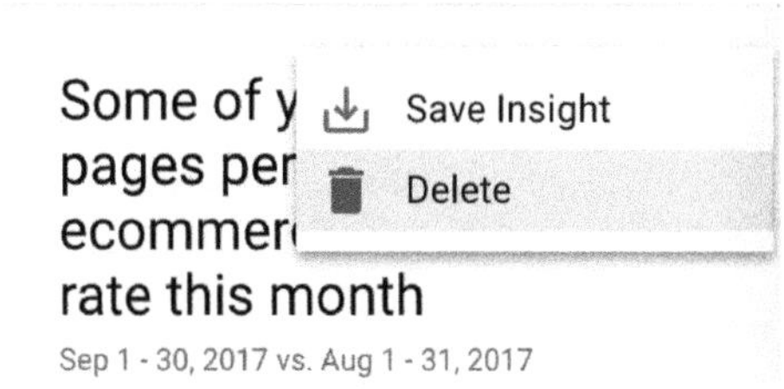

Some of y [Save Insight icon] Save Insight
pages per [Delete icon] Delete
ecommer
rate this month

Sep 1 - 30, 2017 vs. Aug 1 - 31, 2017

Appendix

The chapters in this appendix provide direction for using Global Site Tag tracking code (gtag.js) to send pageview, event, and ecommerce data to Google Analytics. They replace the corresponding chapters in the book that use Universal Analytics tracking code (analytics.js) to perform these functions.

Once you have completed the chapter(s) in this section, return to the next chapter (in sequence) in the text.

Tracking Downloads
Using Global Site Tag Tracking Code

Note that this chapter's discussion is intended to work with Global Site Tag tracking code (gtag.js). If you are using this version of the tracking code, please read this chapter and then continue with Chapter 34 in the main text.

Google Analytics allows you to treat interactions with downloadable items as if they were regular pageviews. These items can be any form of content: PDFs, Excel files, Word documents, or video. The ability to track these downloads allows you to monitor your site content and to analyze these interactions using all of the same menus and techniques used to analyze actual pageviews.

Let's first see how trackable downloads are reported in Google Analytics. Then we'll see how to implement this activity.

How are downloads reported?

Tracked downloads are reported in exactly the same way as regular pageviews, and as a result, you determine the labels used to identify the download. Thus, it is important for you to organize and name your downloads in a way that makes them easy to find and understand in Google Analytics reports. At minimum, in terms of location, your downloadable content should be placed in a separate subdirectory.[127]

Let's look at a simple example.

Imagine that I have a subdirectory (also called a 'folder') with two downloads. The subdirectory is named /information/ and the two downloads provide tour information for Mexico and the Bahamas. The Mexico document is named mexico_dl.pdf and the Bahamas document is named bahamas_dl.pdf.

---

[127] We recommend the following readings if you are unfamiliar with how directories and subdirectories are used to organize website content: *Web Style Guide, Site Structure* at http://webstyleguide.com/wsg3/5-site-structure/3-site-file-structure.html; *How to Design a Website* at http://how-to-design-a-website.com/website-usability/website-directory-structure; *Folder Hierarchy Best Practices for Digital Asset Management* at http://www.damlearningcenter.com/resources/articles/best-practices-for-folder-organization/.

The table shown below illustrates the top level of my site's organization and is the table which appears when I select **Behaviors > Site Content > Content Drilldown**. The first listing, **/xqanqeon/,** is the folder which contains all of my site's pages and related content. Thus, it is not surprising that this folder has the greatest number of pageviews.

The above figure also shows two of my folders with downloadable elements. The **/brochure/** folder contains long PDFs, while the **/information/** folder contains short, one page fact sheets. We can see that users are more interested in longer versus shorter downloads, as the **/brochure/** folder has nearly three times as many downloads (as reflected in pageviews) versus the **/information/** folder.

We are interested in the **/information/** folder as it contains the two downloadable PDFs of interest. We can see that in total, there were ten downloads from this folder (again, as evidenced in the pageviews column), and that all of these downloads were initiated by different users. We determine this by dividing *pageviews* by *unique page-views*. The closer this ratio is to 1.0, the greater the proportion of downloads by different users.

Clicking on the **/information/** link in the table above brings up detailed information on each of the two downloads contained within the folder (see the table below).

The metrics in this table inform us of two things with regard to downloads and subsequent behaviors:

- There are equal numbers of Mexico and Bahamas downloads, and all downloads were initiated by different site users.

- Site engagement differs dramatically between the two downloads. Those who downloaded the Mexico PDF stayed on the site and all viewed at least one more page (as evidenced in the **%Exit** of 0% from this page). Those who downloaded the Bahamas PDF had no further site engagement and immediately left the site (as evidenced in the **%Exit** of 100% from this page). Clearly, we would want to explore why those viewing the Bahamas PDFs are behaving in this manner, and then modify the site or the Bahamas PDF's characteristics to reduce or eliminate these behaviors.

Finally, we can always gain deeper insights into download behaviors through the use of secondary dimensions. The chart below, for example, indicates that all of the downloads took place by Irish site users.

Your site's structure and downloadable content

You are the one who ultimately determines the directory structure for your downloads and what the downloads will be named. With regard to structure, you can place all of the downloads in a single directory, choosing, for example, from labels such as:

```
/downloads/
/brochures/
```

or you can use a nested approach, choosing, for example, from labels such as:

```
/brochure/mexico/
/brochure/bahamas/
```

Remember that your specific strategic information needs should be the guide for how downloadable elements are organized on your site and subsequently labeled in Google Analytics reports.

Let's look at another set of downloads on my site. Here, all of my downloads have been placed in the **/brochure/** directory. There are two downloads for Mexico named:

```
mexico_dl_image.pdf
mexico_dl_text.pdf
```

It is important to note that each PDF has been named in a way that allows us to easily see the topic country, the fact that it is a download (as indicated by _dl) and the source of the download request (image or text). This type of clear naming makes it much easier to interpret reports when your website offers many downloadable elements.[128]

For the moment, let's just focus on the Mexican PDFs. The full URLs to each of the Mexican PDFs on my site are:

http://www.googleanalyticsdemystified.com/xqanqeon/brochure/mexico_dl_image.pdf

http://www.googleanalyticsdemystified.com/xqanqeon/brochure/mexico_dl_text.pdf

The two components of download tracking

If you use different browsers, you've seen how the same action is often treated differently. Downloads, for example, are handled differently in Firefox and Chrome. In light of this situation, our approach to tracking downloads is browser independent, and as a result, the appropriate data should be sent to Google Analytics regardless of the browser employed by the site user.

Our approach to tracking downloads requires that you do two things: First, you'll need to incorporate and customize a very small JavaScript script on each page from which you want to track a download. Second, you'll need to make a small addition to the link or image that initiates the download. The following discusses each of these steps.

The JavaScript script

The JavaScript script must be placed in the HTML code on every page from which you want to track one or more downloads. This script does not need to be placed on pages without downloads and it only needs to appear once in a page's HTML code regardless of the number of download options appearing on the page. The script should be placed directly *before* the Google Analytics tracking code, as shown on the top of page 669 where the Google Analytics tracking code is in the smaller type and the new JavaScript script is in larger type.

---

[128] For simplicity, we use the terms 'download,' 'downloadable element,' and PDF interchangeably. However, as mentioned earlier, the tools and techniques discussed for PDFs apply for any downloadable piece of content: video, Excel files, images, etc.

```
<script>
function download(file)
{
gtag('config', 'YOUR GOOGLE ACCOUNT NUMBER' , {'page_path': file});
alert("Thanks for your download.");
(window.location="YOUR FULL URL HERE"+file);
}
</script>

<!-- Global site tag (gtag.js) - Google Analytics -->
<script async src='https://www.googletagmanager.com/gtag/js?id=UA-55850388-1'></script>
<script>
 window.dataLayer = window.dataLayer || [];
 function gtag(){dataLayer.push(arguments);}
 gtag('js', new Date());
gtag('config', 'UA-55850388-1');
</script>
```

Three instructions are embedded in the script after the JavaScript function is named. Each is on a separate line.

- **gtag('config', ' YOUR GOOGLE ACCOUNT NUMBER' , {'page_path': file})** identifies your account and sends the name of the downloaded file to Google Analytics. You need to substitute your full Google Analytics account number (starting with UA-) in the space now labeled 'YOUR GOOGLE ACCOUNT NUMBER'. Make certain to place your account number between the ' marks. This is all that needs to be modified on this line. When you are done, the line will resemble that shown below:

  gtag('config', ' UA-55850388' , {'page_path': file});

- **alert("Thanks for your download.")** uses a pop-up window to acknowledge the download. The time lag between the appearance of this window and initiation of the download allows time for all browsers to send the name of the downloaded file to Google Analytics. You can customize the message by changing the text between the quotation marks. Make certain that any changes leave the beginning and ending quotation marks intact.

- **(window.location="YOUR FULL URL HERE"+file)** provides the browser with the full URL to the location of your download.

  Here, you replace the phrase **YOUR FULL URL HERE** with the URL to your downloads, up to but not including the folder in which they are housed. For example, the PDFs on our site are located in the **/brochure/** folder. As a result, the full URL to one of the downloads is:

```
http://www.googleanalyticsdemystified.com/xqanqeon/
brochure/mexico_dl_image.pdf
```

This step requires that we place within the JavaScript the URL up to but not including the folder containing the PDFs. In my case, the URL in the script appearing between the quotation marks (and which would replace **YOUR FULL URL HERE**) would be:

```
http://www.googleanalyticsdemystified.com/xqanqeon
```

You need to replace the phrase **YOUR FULL URL HERE** with the full URL that leads to your downloads. Make certain to place this URL between the quotation marks (replacing the indicated phrase) and leave the rest of the line as is. Take care not to leave any spaces between the quotation marks and your URL. Finally, make certain not to end the URL with a slash or period.

When you have made the preceding changes, save the page without changing its name and then proceed to see how to modify the HTML code for the initiating a download via a text or image link.

Tracking a download via a text link

Our approach tracks a download by altering the link, which initiates the download. This alteration puts the JavaScript script into motion, sending data to Google Analytics and sending the requested PDF or other content to the site user. We'll begin with text links and then move on to an image link.

An ordinary HTML text link to a Mexico information PDF would be of the form:

```
<a href="information/mexico.pdf">Click to download more
  information on Mexico</a>
```

Here, the name of the downloadable document is `mexico.pdf`, which is in the `information/` folder. The link text that appears on the web page is: **Click to download more information on Mexico.**

We're going to change the basic form of this text link to the following format:

```
<a href="javascript:download('/information/mexico.pdf')">Click
Here</a> to download more information on Mexico
```

You'll use this link format anywhere on your site you want to allow a trackable download to take place via a text link. Leave the link as shown above except for the three elements, which need to be addressed whenever you use this format:

- *Mandatory:* Replace `/information/mexico.pdf` with the location and name of the content to be downloaded when the link is clicked. In this example, for my site, we would change this to: `/brochure/mexico_dl_text.pdf` to indicate the actual location and name of the file to be downloaded when the link is clicked upon. Note that a slash ('/') now precedes the name of the folder. Keep the beginning and ending single quotation marks intact.

- *Optional:* Replace **Click Here** with the text you want to appear as the active link. You can leave this as is if you desire.

- *Mandatory:* Replace **to download more information on Mexico** with whatever text appropriately completes the sentence. For this example, we will change this text to read: **to obtain a brochure on Mexican travel.**

Once the prior is complete, the trackable download via a text link would be:

```
<a href="javascript:download('/brochure/mexico_dl_text.pdf')">
Click Here</a> to obtain a brochure on Mexican travel
```

This link is placed in the page's HTML code at the point where we want the text link to appear.

Tracking downloads via an image link

We can initiate a download by having a user click on an image. An ordinary HTML image link to my Mexico information PDF via an image would be:

```
<a href="information/mexico.pdf"><img src="images/mexico.jpg">
</a>
```

Here, the name of the downloadable document is mexico.pdf, which is in the information/ folder. The image used as a link is named **mexico.jpg** and resides in the images/ directory.

We're going to change the basic form of this text link to the following:

```
<a href="javascript:download('/information/mexico.pdf')">
<img src="images/mexico.jpg"></a>
```

This format is nearly identical to that used to create our text link. The only difference is that the text, which appears on the web page has been replaced by an image.

You'll use this link format anywhere on your site you want a trackable download to take place via an image click. Two elements need to be addressed when you use this format:

- *Mandatory:* Replace /information/mexico.pdf with the location and name of the content to be download when the image link is clicked. In this example, we would change this to: /brochure/mexico_dl_image.pdf to indicate the actual location and name of the file to be downloaded when the image link is clicked upon. Note that a slash ('/') now precedes the name of the folder. Keep the beginning and ending single quotation marks intact.

- *Mandatory:* Replace the image name with the image that you want to use as the link. For this example, we've changed the image to `images/mexico1.jpg`.

Once the prior is complete, the trackable download via an image link would be:

```
<a href="javascript:download('/brochure/mexico_dl_image.pdf')">
<img src="images/mexico1.jpg"></a>
```

Upload the revised page to your server and then use **Real-Time** to make certain that the link is working as intended.

Confirming that data is being sent to Google Analytics

We saw in Chapter 31 how the Google Analytics **Real-Time** menu can help us see if our goals are working as intended. **Real-Time** can also be used to confirm that download tracking is working.

Using Chrome, access your site's page with the trackable text or image link. If the link is working, you should see the name of the downloaded PDF in the **Real-Time > Overview** display, as shown below for my download. The name of the download is beneath the **Top Active Pages** header in the bottom center of the display.

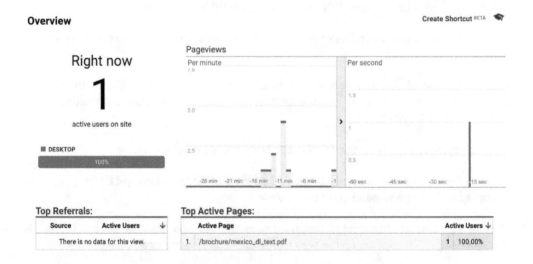

Note that we've tested this approach in Firefox, Chrome and Safari, and it has worked in all three browsers. However, Safari can at times still be problematic with this and other scripts we present in this book. We recommend testing in Chrome or Firefox. The sporadic problems with Safari should have little impact, as its share of usage is estimated to be less than 4%.

Introduction to Events
Using Global Site Tag Tracking Code

Google Analytics explains events as *user interactions with content that can be tracked independently from a web page or a screen load. Downloads, mobile ad clicks, gadgets, Flash elements, AJAX embedded elements and video plays are all examples of actions you might want to track as Events.*

Google's Global Site Tag allows for both predefined (also referred to as 'recommended') and customized events. Predefined events are primarily related to ecommerce behaviors and allow you to effortlessly track the product search and purchase processes. Customized events allow you to track all other user interactions with your website and its content; for example, form completions, scroll depth, outbound link tracking, video content consumption, and social sharing interactions. This chapter and the following chapters focus on customized events.[129]

The tracking of events, similar to the monitoring of downloads, requires us to modify the HTML code to let Google Analytics know that a specific event has been 'triggered.' Before we address the HTML code itself, it is important to understand the types of information Google Analytics requires in order to track a customized event. The components of customized event tracking are shown in the following statement:[130]

```
gtag('event', 'event name', {
            'event_category' : 'category name',
            'event_action'   : 'action name',
            'event_label'    : 'label name',
            'value'          : value amount,
            'non_interaction' : true
});
```

---

[129] Your understanding of customized events provides the basis for the use of predefined events. Additional information on the specific predefined events available through Global Site Tag can be found at
https://developers.google.com/analytics/devguides/collection/gtagjs/events.

[130] This is the full event statement. We'll soon see that not all of these parameters are required. Note that regardless of the number of items in the statement, the last item is not followed by a comma.

The event statement's components are interpreted as follows:

- **gtag** indicates that this is a Google Analytics Global Site Tag command. This element is never modified.

- **event** directs the data to Google Analytics and indicates that the data is related to an event. This element is never modified. **event name** is replaced by your name for the event. You can name the event anything you like.

- **event_category, event_action, event_label** and **value** indicate the type of information being sent to Google Analytics. Only **event_ action** is a required element. The remaining elements (**event_category, event_label** and **value**) are optional. This is the standard form of these parameters and is unchanged when used. The characteristics of each are discussed next.

- **category name, action name, event name** and **value amount** are the labels for each event component. As discussed next, you provide these labels.

- **non_interaction : true** indicates that the event, when triggered, should not be treated as a user-site interaction. This parameter is only present when you want the event to be considered a noninteraction.

This chapter discusses each of these parameters. Chapters 37a to 44a in this appendix provide examples of how events can be used to increase insights into user behavior, resulting in more effective strategic analysis and decision-making.

The event and event name parameters

The **event** parameter is associated with **event name** and is used to provide a global label for the category and other parameters associated with this particular type of event. You provide your desired name for this parameter in place of **event name** in the event command shown on page 673. We suggest that you select a name that both makes sense given the eventual strategic use of the event data and that will be clear to all who will be examining and applying the data to future strategic decisions.

The event_category and category name parameters

The **event_category** parameter is associated with **category name** and represents your highest level of event grouping. It is a required element in all event statements. You provide your desired name for this parameter in place of **category name** in the event command shown on page 673. 'Downloads', 'Videos', and 'Social Media Sharing' are examples of event names, although you can be as specific or broad as required by your strategic needs. You might, for example, need more specific information on videos viewed than simply collecting all event interactions within the single 'Videos' event category. In this case, you could create more specific event name categories, for example:

- Videos - Movies
- Videos – Music
- Videos - Personal

Similarly, you might want to organize your blog entries and track the extent to which different types of entries are read by site users. Here, rather than having a single category named 'Blog', you might create several categories to reflect the content of different blog posts, for example:

- Blog - Metrics
- Blog - HTML coding
- Blog - Research design

We highly recommend that you examine your site's goals and objectives, as well as your own information needs, prior to the creation of categories for use in event tracking. While new categories can always be added, it is a time-consuming process to create and analyze multiple categories and event triggers for essentially the same event. If, for example, you initially call your video tracking category 'Video' and later forget and use the plural 'Videos', you will have two separate categories for video tracking. A small amount of pre-planning makes a major contribution to ease of analysis and application to decision-making.

The event_action and action name parameters

Every event command must contain an **event_action** parameter that names the specific interaction you are tracking. You provide your desired name for this parameter in place of **action name** in the event command shown on page 673. You might, for example, want to monitor when a video is started as a way of gauging site users' interest in the video's topic. In this circumstance, the **category name** would be 'video' and the **action name** would be 'play'.

While you have complete control over the form and characteristics of the **action name**, it is always best to develop your naming strategy prior to (rather than during) implementation. In this regard, Google Analytics notes that during the planning process:

- *Event **action names** should be relevant to your strategic information needs.*

   Google Analytics' event tracking combines metrics for the same action name across different categories. If, for example, you associate the action name 'Click' with both the 'Downloads' category name and the 'Videos' category name, the metrics for 'Click' in your reports appears with all interactions tagged with that same name. Thus, you should select different action names for different categories of events. You might, for example, choose to use the action name 'click' for gadget interactions, while reserving the action name, 'Play', 'Pause', and 'Stop' for video player interactions.

- *Use **action names** globally to either aggregate or distinguish user interaction.*

   For example, you can use 'Play' as an action name in the 'Videos' category for all videos on your website. In this model, the Google Analytics Top Actions report would provide aggregate data for events with the 'Play' action, and you can see how this event for your videos compares to other events for all videos, such as 'Pause' or 'Stop.'

Finally, keep in mind than an action name need not necessarily reflect an overt action. In some cases, such as tracking downloads as an event, the actual event or action name is not as meaningful as other information regarding the event, so you might use the action name parameter to track other elements such as a topic or other strategically valuable pieces of information.

The event_label and label name parameters

The **label name** parameter is an optional component in the event tracking statement. Label names allow you to obtain additional information for events that you want to track, such as a video title, the source of the download (for example, text or image) or the video topic. You provide your desired name for this parameter in place of **label name,** in the event command shown on page 673. Imagine, for example, that you have three videos on your site. With regard to event tracking: each one of these videos can use the 'Videos' category name with the 'Play' category action name; but each could also have a separate label name identifier (such as the video name or topic) so that they appear as distinct elements in your reports.

The value and value amount parameters

The **value** parameter differs from the previous event components in that it is a positive (not negative) number rather than a word or phrase. As such, it is used when you need to assign a numeric value to a tracked event. You could, for example, use **value amount** to record the number of seconds it takes for a video to load.

Google Analytics reports an event's values individually as well as its overall average. Imagine, for example, that you are monitoring video download time and that the download times for five unique views were: 5, 5, 8, 10 and 25. Google Analytics would report each of these values as well as the average of 10.3.

The non_interaction parameter

The **non_interaction: true** parameter is optional. It allows you to determine how you want to calculate the bounce rate for pages on your site that include event tracking.

Google Analytics provides this scenario: Imagine, for example, that 'you have a home page with a video embedded on it. It's quite natural that you will want to know the bounce rate for your home page, but how do you want to define that? Do you consider visitor interaction with the home page video an important engagement signal? If so, you would want interaction with the video to be included in the bounce rate calculation, so that sessions including only your home page with clicks on the video are not calculated as bounces. On the other hand, you might prefer a more strict calculation of bounce rate for your home page, in which you want to know the percentage of sessions including only your home page, regardless of clicks on the video. In this case, you would want to exclude any interaction with the video from bounce rate calculation.'

This where the **non_interaction : true** parameter comes into play. Remember that a bounce is defined as a session containing only one interaction hit, such as a single pageview. By default, the event hit sent by the **gtag** command is considered an interaction hit, which means that it is included in bounce rate calculations. However, when **non_interaction : true** is included in the event statement, then the event trigger is not considered an interaction hit. Google Analytics notes that 'including this command in a session containing a single page tagged with non-interaction events is counted as a bounce - even if the visitor also triggers the event during the session. Conversely, omitting this parameter means that a single-page session on a page that includes event tracking will not be counted as a bounce if the visitor also triggers the event during the same session.' Thus, this command should only be used when the event triggers on a noninteraction event, such as an event that takes place when the page loads and therefore requires no active engagement on the part of the site user.[131]

Placing the event HTML code

Let's examine two common uses of event tracking: when a page loads[132] or when a user takes an action such a clicking on a link or starting a video play.

Sending event information when a page loads

Imagine that you want to use events to automatically monitor the characteristics of content entries when each entry is viewed. You want to know, for each piece of content viewed, the author, topic, and month the content was first posted. This information can be sent to Google Analytics via an event command when the page loads in a user's browser. The event command would have the following characteristics for a piece of content which discusses analytics and which was authored by Davis in April:

- **event name** is set to 'BlogMonitoring'

- **category name** is set to represent the author 'Davis'

- **action name** is the blog topic, in this case, 'Analytics'

---

[131] The source used for the content and quotes in the value and interaction parameter discussion is *Event Tracker Guide* at https://developers.google.com/analytics/devguides/collection/gajs/eventTrackerGuide.

[132] While this type of event is most commonly associated with page loads, it can also be used to track any type of loading action, for example, the display of a particular image or a video load.

- **label name** is the month of the original posting, in this case, 'April'

- **value** is not relevant and is omitted

- **non_interaction : true** is relevant and included as this event is triggered when the page loads without any overt user interaction

When an event is activated during a page load, the corresponding event statement can be attached to the **<body>** parameter using the **onload** HTML command. Given these parameters, the complete HTML statement that would activate the event would be:[133]

```
<body onload = "gtag('event', 'BlogMonitoring', {
        'event_category'  : 'Davis',
        'event_action'    : 'Analytics',
        'event_label'     : 'April',
        'non_interaction' : true
});">
```

The statement would replace the original **<body>** command in the HTML code. When you wish to use this format to send event information when the page loads just substitute your own event information (e.g., category, action and label names) for that shown above.

Sending event information when an interaction occurs

When an event is triggered by an explicit user-site interaction, such as a click on a link, the event code is typically attached to the relevant action using the **onClick** command. Let's imagine that you have a number of links that go to sites other than yours, and that you want to create an event whenever your site user clicks on one of these links. This will help you to gauge the relative use and appeal of these links. The event command for one of these links might have the following characteristics:

- **category name** identifies the type of action, in this case labeled 'External Link'

- **action name** represents the interaction, in this case, 'Click'

- **label name** is the link's URL, in this case, 'http://www.google.com/analytics'

- **value** is not relevant and is omitted

- **non_interaction: true** is not relevant as this event is triggered by an overt user interaction and is omitted

---

[133] Note that the extra spaces were added for the sake of visual clarity. They can either remain or be eliminated to reflect your preference. In addition, there are other ways to transmit this event information, for example, incorporating the event statement into the Global Site Tag tracking code. We prefer this approach because it makes it easier to see the event statement being used.

Given these parameters, the complete HTML statement that would activate the event would be:

```
<a href = "http://www.google.com/analytics" onClick =
        "gtag('event', 'External Link', {
        'event_category' : 'Click',
        'event_action'    : 'Analytics',
        'event_label'     : 'http://www.google.com/analytics'
});">Click here to go to Google Analytics</a>
```

This link would replace the normal link:

```
<a href = "http://www.google.com/analytics">Click here to go to Google Analytics</a>
```

Using JavaScript to send onClick event information

Visit the following page on our travel website:

```
http://www.googleanalyticsdemystified.com/xqanqeon/chapter36a.html
```

The page automatically sends a set of event information when the page loads. You can see the code for this event by looking at the **<body>** command within the page's HTML code. Clicking on the link sends you to Google Analytics. However, you'll note that rather than sending you directly, the page informs you that it is redirecting you to the new site. Why don't we send you directly without this notice?

You'll recall from the discussion of download tracking that there are differences across browsers in terms of how they interpret HTML commands. Thus, while the **onClick** command should always send event information directly to Google Analytics, the reality is that depending upon the browser event data may not always be sent. To avoid this problem, an alternative to the **onClick** format is to use JavaScript to send the data associated with an **onClick** event. Similar to the use of JavaScript to track downloads, this approach is browser independent and has a much higher likelihood that your event data initiated by a link click will be sent to Google Analytics.

This approach alters the form of the link and places a small JavaScript script in the **<head>** section of your page.

The JavaScript script (see the top of page 680) needs to be placed in the HTML code on every page from which you want to track an **onClick** event. This script does not need to be placed on any other pages and it only needs to appear once in a page's HTML code, regardless of the number of **onClick** events appearing on that page. The script should be placed immediately after the opening **<head>** tag in your HTML code:

```
<script>
function redir(category, action, label, value, where)
{
gtag('event', 'Link', {
'event_category':category,
'event_action':action,
'event_label': label,
'value': value
});
alert("Redirecting");
(window.location=where);
}
</script>
```

Note that this script and others we provide do not conflict with each other. As a result, you can include this script and the download tracking script on the same page. Just place one after the other. The order does not matter.

Four instructions are embedded in the script.

- **function redir(category, action, label, value, where)** names the function and information to be collected. This line never needs to be changed.

- **gatag** and following event parameters take the information provided in your link. Replace (if you desire) the event name 'Link' with the event name of your choice. The remaining event parameters should be left unchanged.

- **alert("Redirecting")** uses a pop-up window to acknowledge the redirect. The time lag between the appearance of this window and the redirect allows time for all browsers to send the information to Google Analytics. You can customize the message by changing the text between the quotation marks. Make certain that any changes leave the beginning and ending quotation marks intact.

- **(window.location=where)** is the redirect location specified in the ink. This line should not be changed.

Next, you'll need to create your link, which will be of the form:

<a href="javascript:redir('category name', 'action name', 'label name', 0, 'redirect URL')">Click Here</a>

The link carries all of the event and redirect information. When you use this link, leave all of the wording and punctuation as is except:

- replace the words **category name** and **action name** with your category and action names. Both names are recommended. If you are not using a category parameter, then delete the phrase **category name** leaving the ' punctuation without any spaces. Make certain the leave the ' punctuation for your action name.

- replace the words **label name** with your label name parameter if one is being used. If you are not using a label parameter, then delete the phrase **label name** leaving the ' punctuation without any spaces.

- leave the 0 if your event has no value; otherwise replace the 0 with your event value.

- replace **redirect URL** with the full URL where the site user is being sent after clicking on the link. As with the prior replacement, make certain to leave the ' punctuation.

You can use this link format anywhere on your site where you want to use **onClick** to trigger an event whose data is sent to Google Analytics. Remember to replace **Click Here** with whatever text you want to appear as the text link.

Let's apply this approach to the situation described previously, where:

- **category name** identifies the type of action, in this case labeled 'Click External Link'

- **action name** represents the interaction, in this case, 'Click'

- **label name** is location of the redirect, in this case, 'google.com/analytics'

- **value** is zero

- **redirect URL** is 'http://www.google.com/analytics'

In this case, the link would be:

`<a href="javascript:redir('Click External Link', 'Click', 'google.com/analytics', 0, 'http://www.google.com/analytics')">Click here to go to Google Analytics</a>`

In contrast, if no label parameter were used, the link would be:

`<a href="javascript:redir('Click External Link', 'Click', '', 0, 'http://www.google.com/analytics')"> Click here to go to Google Analytics</a>`

Google Analytics places some limits on the collection of event data. Specifically, the first 10 event hits sent to Google Analytics are tracked immediately, after which the tracking rate is limited to one event hit per second.

As the number of events in a session approaches the Google Analytics overall data collection limits, additional events might not be tracked. For this reason, Google recommends that you:

- avoid scripting a video to send an event for every second played and other highly repetitive event triggers,

- avoid excessive mouse movement tracking, and

- avoid time-lapse mechanisms that generate high event counts.

Events and Content Monitoring
Using Global Site Tag Tracking Code

The previous chapter illustrated how events can be used to monitor content consumption and link usage. This chapter and the next address each of these uses of events in more detail. We'll begin with a discussion of content consumption.

We've seen how Google Analytics provides a great deal of page specific information, for example, how often each page is viewed, time on page and bounce rate. This data, however, does not allow us to easily collapse similar types of pages to obtain an overview of how *types* of pages (as a group) are performing in terms of engagement and contribution to goals or transactions. Events allows us to accomplish this.

The scenario

Imagine that our website provides a significant amount of content related to budget travel and travel in Europe, Ireland, and Italy. Each topic is addressed with content created by one of two authors, as shown below:

Davis	Budget
Davis	Europe
Davis	Ireland
Rose	Budget
Rose	Europe
Rose	Italy

Looking across these writers and content, we want to know:

- Regardless of the author, which topics are most viewed and generate the most engagement and positive purchase behaviors?

- Regardless of the topic, which authors are most viewed and generate the most engagement and positive purchase behaviors?

We can use events to answer these strategic questions by placing two events on each page. When this page loads, one event automatically sends author information and the second event sends topic information.

The code used to signal our target events follows standard event code format. The code used to signal a page written by Davis (without worrying about the topic) would be:

```
gtag('event', 'BlogMonitoring', {
'event_category' : 'Written_By',
'event_action'    : 'Davis',
'non_interaction' : true });
```

while the code for a page written by Rose (again, without worrying about the topic) would be:

```
gtag('event', 'BlogMonitoring', {
'event_category' : 'Written_By',
'event_action'    : 'Rose',
'non_interaction' : true });
```

Notice that in both of these cases, since we only need to identify the author, the code only provides **category** and **action names**. No additional information is needed.

Similarly, the code used to signal the content of a specific page (without worrying about the author) would be:

```
gtag('event', 'BlogMonitoring1', {
'event_category' : 'Theme',
'event_action'    : 'Budget',
'non_interaction' : true });
```

As with the code used to identify the page author, only **category** and **action names** are required. We also identify each of these events as a noninteraction so as not to distort pageviews and bounce metrics.

Placing the code

We want both author and content information to be sent automatically to Google Analytics once the page loads in a site user's browser. As a result, we attach *both* event commands to <**body**> using **onload**.

We have six author/topic combinations. The HTML event command for each author/topic combination would be placed on the appropriate page and would be of the form shown in the table on the top of page 685. Notice that there are two event commands attached to **onload**: one to identify the page's author and one to identify the page's topic.

Author/Topic Combination	HTML event code placed on page

Davis/Budget	<body onload ="gtag('event', 'BlogMonitoring', {
	'event_category' : 'Written_By',
	'event_action' : 'Davis',
	'non_interaction' : true });
	gtag('event', 'BlogMonitoring1', {
	'event_category' : 'Theme',
	'event_action' : 'Budget',
	'non_interaction' : true });">

Rose/Europe	<body onload ="gtag('event', 'BlogMonitoring', {
	'event_category' : 'Written_By',
	'event_action' : 'Rose',
	'non_interaction' : true });
	gtag('event', 'BlogMonitoring1', {
	'event_category' : 'Theme',
	'event_action' : 'Europe',
	'non_interaction' : true });">

Data analysis and insights

We begin by selecting **Top Events** from the **Behavior > Events** menu, which displays all of our event categories (see the table on the top of page 686). The two event category parameters 'Theme' and 'Written_By' (see lines 8 and 9) correspond to the names in our event commands for tracking authors and content, so these are the event categories of interest. Since both the author and theme triggers are sent to Google Analytics at the same time, it is reassuring that both report the same number of events as shown in the **Total Events** column (21 for each in this example). Notice that the number of unique events is almost identical to the number of total events. This reflects the fact that almost all site users read only one blog.

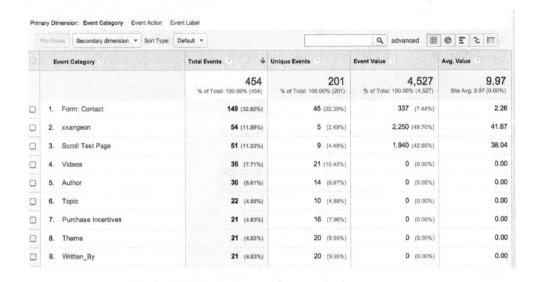

Event Category	Total Events ↓	Unique Events	Event Value	Avg. Value
	454 % of Total: 100.00% (454)	201 % of Total: 100.00% (201)	4,527 % of Total: 100.00% (4,527)	9.97 Site Avg: 9.97 (0.00%)
1. Form: Contact	149 (32.82%)	45 (22.39%)	337 (7.44%)	2.26
2. xxangeon	54 (11.89%)	5 (2.49%)	2,250 (49.70%)	41.67
3. Scroll Test Page	51 (11.23%)	9 (4.48%)	1,940 (42.85%)	38.04
4. Videos	35 (7.71%)	21 (10.45%)	0 (0.00%)	0.00
5. Author	30 (6.61%)	14 (6.97%)	0 (0.00%)	0.00
6. Topic	22 (4.85%)	10 (4.98%)	0 (0.00%)	0.00
7. Purchase Incentives	21 (4.63%)	16 (7.96%)	0 (0.00%)	0.00
8. Theme	21 (4.63%)	20 (9.95%)	0 (0.00%)	0.00
9. Written_By	21 (4.63%)	20 (9.95%)	0 (0.00%)	0.00

The selection of either **Theme** or **Written_By** from the list of Event Categories allows us to see more detailed information on that specific event category. Selecting **Theme** from the list brings up the table below, which shows that across authors Budget travel and Ireland are much more popular topics than Europe (as indicated in the counts in the Total Events column).

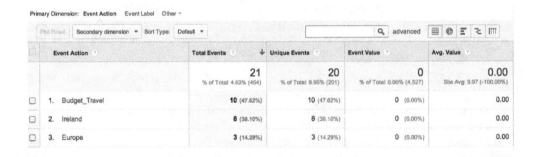

Event Action	Total Events ↓	Unique Events	Event Value	Avg. Value
	21 % of Total: 4.63% (454)	20 % of Total: 9.95% (201)	0 % of Total: 0.00% (4,527)	0.00 Site Avg: 9.97 (-100.00%)
1. Budget_Travel	10 (47.62%)	10 (47.62%)	0 (0.00%)	0.00
2. Ireland	8 (38.10%)	8 (38.10%)	0 (0.00%)	0.00
3. Europe	3 (14.29%)	3 (14.29%)	0 (0.00%)	0.00

Similarly, the selection of **Written_By** from the initial list of event categories brings up a table that shows that across topics, the materials written by Davis and Rose are read with about equal frequency (see below).

Event Action	Total Events ↓	Unique Events	Event Value	Avg. Value
	21 % of Total: 4.63% (454)	20 % of Total: 9.95% (201)	0 % of Total: 0.00% (4,527)	0.00 Site Avg: 9.97 (-100.00%)
1. Davis	11 (52.38%)	10 (50.00%)	0 (0.00%)	0.00
2. Rose	10 (47.62%)	10 (50.00%)	0 (0.00%)	0.00

While this information is helpful for future planning, it is not complete. We need to look at our author and content trends in terms of site engagement and subsequent transactions.

Let's return to the page displayed after one of the event categories is selected. The page shown appears when we select **Theme** from the **Behavior > Top Events** data display. On the top of this page, above the line chart (but beneath the **Explorer** tab), are additional data view options: Site Usage and Ecommerce (see below).

Event Action ?	Total Events ?	Unique Events ?	Event Value ?	Avg. Value ?
	21 % of Total: 4.63% (454)	20 % of Total: 9.95% (201)	0 % of Total: 0.00% (4,527)	0.00 Site Avg: 9.97 (-100.00%)
1. Budget_Travel	10 (47.62%)	10 (47.62%)	0 (0.00%)	0.00
2. Ireland	8 (38.10%)	8 (38.10%)	0 (0.00%)	0.00
3. Europe	3 (14.29%)	3 (14.29%)	0 (0.00%)	0.00

Clicking on **Site Usage** brings up the table shown below in which we see that subsequent site engagement is different for each content area. Budget travel appears to motivate greater site engagement: users who read content on this topic have more Pages/Session and spend more time on the site as reflected in Average Session Duration.

Event Action ?	Sessions ?	Pages / Session ?	Avg. Session Duration ?	% New Sessions ?
	21 % of Total: 3.27% (642)	4.29 Site Avg: 2.23 (91.87%)	00:00:17 Site Avg: 00:01:18 (-77.80%)	95.24% Site Avg: 84.74% (12.39%)
1. Budget_Travel	10 (47.62%)	5.00	00:00:29	90.00%
2. Ireland	8 (38.10%)	3.75	00:00:08	100.00%
3. Europe	3 (14.29%)	3.33	00:00:06	100.00%

We can conduct the same analysis for authors, which will display the following table. Here, we see mixed results with regard to each author's ability to motivate site engagement. Those who read Davis' content viewed more site pages, but those who read Rose's content spent more time on the site. This may simply be a function of Rose's tendency to ramble.

We can conduct a parallel analysis focused on transactions. Selecting **Ecommerce** from the **Explorer** options brings up the following table for the three types of content. Here, we can see that while Budget travel and Ireland are read at nearly equal levels, Budget travel is associated with significantly greater revenue, versus the other two content areas.

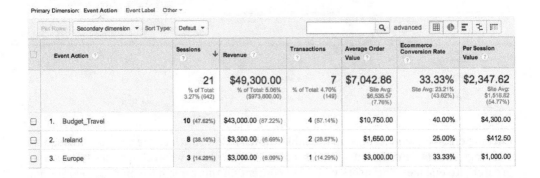

Conducting a similar analysis for authors, we see that Davis' content has significantly greater association with better transactions versus content created by Rose (see table on the top of page 689). This is especially important since both authors are read at equal rates.

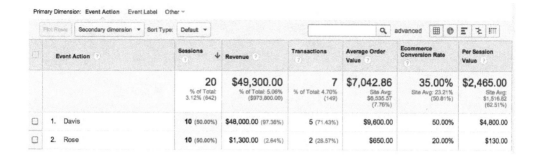

	Event Action ?	Sessions ↓ ?	Revenue ?	Transactions ?	Average Order Value ?	Ecommerce Conversion Rate ?	Per Session Value ?
		20 % of Total: 3.12% (642)	**$49,300.00** % of Total: 5.06% ($973,800.00)	**7** % of Total: 4.70% (149)	**$7,042.86** Site Avg: $6,535.57 (7.76%)	**35.00%** Site Avg: 23.21% (50.81%)	**$2,465.00** Site Avg: $1,516.82 (62.51%)
☐	1. Davis	**10** (50.00%)	$48,000.00 (97.36%)	5 (71.43%)	$9,600.00	50.00%	$4,800.00
☐	2. Rose	**10** (50.00%)	$1,300.00 (2.64%)	2 (28.57%)	$650.00	20.00%	$130.00

All in all, monitoring both authors and themes through events, and relating these events to site engagement and purchase behaviors, makes a significant contribution to future blog planning. We would likely want to publish more blog entries written by Davis with a focus on budget travel.

Advanced Events: Link Tracking
Using Global Site Tag Tracking Code

Chapter 25 discussed how **In-Page Analytics** tells us how often each link on a page is clicked. However, **In-Page Analytics** cannot help us determine the ultimate effect of different link selections on an outcome variable such as contact, newsletter registration, or purchase. Fortunately, event tracking allows us to transcend this limitation.

This chapter explains how to use events for link tracking.[134]

The scenario

Imagine that we want to learn which of three incentives is most likely to lead to purchase and which of the incentives leads to the highest travel purchase amount. The three incentives, each shown in a different link, are:

- 10% discount on day of purchase,

- free lifetime membership in the travel club, and

- free insurance.

All three incentives appear on the same page.

The JavaScript and HTML event code

Once again, we're going to use a combination of JavaScript and link alteration to ensure that all browsers send the appropriate data to Google Analytics. We follow the same approach as described on pages 679 to 681.

The JavaScript is placed in the HTML code on the page containing the links we want to track. We place the script (shown on the top of page 692) directly after the Google Analytics Global Site Tag tracking code. Note that the alert message now says: **Taking you to your special offer.** as this message is relevant to link action. You may change this if desired, but leave the remainder of the script unchanged.

---

[134] The techniques discussed in this chapter can be applied to any website link. An event can be created, for example, when a link to a downloadable PDF is selected or a link to an external website is used.

```
<script>
function redir(category, action, label, value, where)
{
gtag('event', 'Offer', {
'event_category':category,
'event_action':action,
'event_label': label,
'value': value
});
alert("Taking you to your special offer");
(window.location=where);
}
</script>
```

In this example, the category name is 'Purchase Incentives', the action name is 'Click' and the label name is the name of the special offer (i.e., 10% off today, lifetime membership, and free insurance). Each link is coded with the same destination page (`purchase.html`). Since we ultimately want to relate link selection with transaction amount event, value is set to zero.

Since there are three options (one for each offer), we will need three links, as shown below.

```
<a href="javascript:redir('Purchase Incentives', 'Click', '10% Off', 0,
'purchase.html')"> 10% off today</a>

<a href="javascript:redir('Purchase Incentives', 'Click', 'Lifetime membership', 0,
'purchase.html')"> Lifetime membership</a>

<a href="javascript:redir('Purchase Incentives', 'Click', 'Free insurance', 0,
'purchase.html')"> Free insurance</a>
```

Data analysis and insights

We begin by selecting **Top Events** from the **Behavior > Events** menu, which displays all of our event categories (see figure on the top of page 693). Since we are interested in looking at link effectiveness, we click on 'Purchase Incentives', which is the event category parameter.

	Event Category	Total Events	↓ Unique Events	Event Value	Avg. Value
		188 % of Total: 100.00% (188)	**62** % of Total: 93.94% (66)	**4,284** % of Total: 100.00% (4,284)	**22.79** Site Avg: 22.79 (0.00%)
☐ 1.	xxangeon	**54** (28.72%)	5 (8.06%)	2,250 (52.52%)	41.67
☐ 2.	Scroll Test Page	**49** (26.06%)	8 (12.90%)	1,910 (44.58%)	38.98
☐ 3.	Form: Contact	**41** (21.81%)	19 (30.65%)	124 (2.89%)	3.02
☐ 4.	Purchase Incentives	**21** (11.17%)	16 (25.81%)	0 (0.00%)	0.00
☐ 5.	Download	**9** (4.79%)	9 (14.52%)	0 (0.00%)	0.00
☐ 6.	Videos	**8** (4.26%)	4 (6.45%)	0 (0.00%)	0.00
☐ 7.	Scroll Depth	**6** (3.19%)	1 (1.61%)	0 (0.00%)	0.00

The selection of an event category from the list allows us to see the actions associated with that category. In this case, there is only one action associated with the category 'Purchase Incentives' (see below).

	Event Action	Total Events	↓ Unique Events	Event Value	Avg. Value
		21 % of Total: 4.64% (453)	**16** % of Total: 8.00% (200)	**0** % of Total: 0.00% (4,527)	**0.00** Site Avg: 9.99 (-100.00%)
☐ 1.	Click	**21** (100.00%)	16 (100.00%)	0 (0.00%)	0.00

Clicking upon the **Event Action** 'Click' brings up a chart of our three event labels (see below). Here, we can begin to see differences across offers, where 'Lifetime Membership' appears to generate the least amount of interest, as reflected in its relatively low number of total and unique events. If you look at the HTML code for each link (see below), you'll notice that event value was set to zero. This decision is reflected in the **Event Value** and **Avg. Value** columns.

	Event Label	Total Events	↓ Unique Events	Event Value	Avg. Value
		21 % of Total: 11.17% (188)	**16** % of Total: 24.24% (66)	**0** % of Total: 0.00% (4,284)	**0.00** Site Avg: 22.79 (-100.00%)
☐ 1.	Free_Insurance	**10** (47.62%)	8 (44.44%)	0 (0.00%)	0.00
☐ 2.	10%_Off	**7** (33.33%)	7 (38.89%)	0 (0.00%)	0.00
☐ 3.	Lifetime_Membership	**4** (19.05%)	3 (16.67%)	0 (0.00%)	0.00

We can look at the relationship between offer and transactions by selecting **Ecommerce** from the top of the page just beneath the **Explorer** tab (see below).

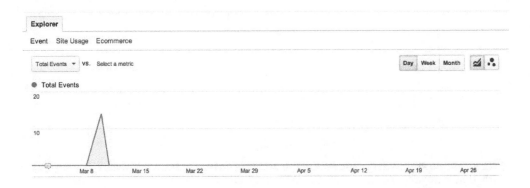

When **Ecommerce** is selected, the table shown below is generated (assuming that you are still on the **Event Label** display). This table shows our three label parameters where we can see significant differences across offers in terms of ultimate purchase behaviors. The number of sessions (equivalent to unique events in the earlier tables) is similar for 'Free Insurance' and '10% Off'. Both have nearly equal appeal. The effect of these links on purchase behaviors is, however, very different. The 'Free Insurance' offer leads to higher overall revenue, more transactions per session, higher average order value, and higher per session value. Clearly this is the more powerful offer and should likely be the only one offered and emphasized.

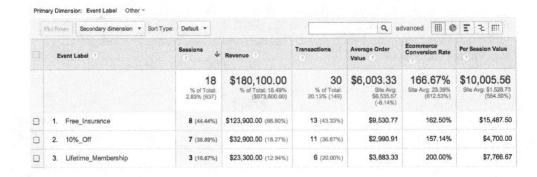

Primary Dimension: Event Label Other ▾

Event Label	Sessions	Revenue	Transactions	Average Order Value	Ecommerce Conversion Rate	Per Session Value
	18 % of Total: 2.83% (637)	$180,100.00 % of Total: 18.49% ($973,600.00)	30 % of Total: 20.13% (149)	$6,003.33 Site Avg: $6,535.57 (-8.14%)	166.67% Site Avg: 23.39% (612.53%)	$10,005.56 Site Avg: $1,528.73 (554.50%)
1. Free_Insurance	8 (44.44%)	$123,900.00 (68.80%)	13 (43.33%)	$9,530.77	162.50%	$15,487.50
2. 10%_Off	7 (38.89%)	$32,900.00 (18.27%)	11 (36.67%)	$2,990.91	157.14%	$4,700.00
3. Lifetime_Membership	3 (16.67%)	$23,300.00 (12.94%)	6 (20.00%)	$3,883.33	200.00%	$7,766.67

Event Reporting
Using Global Site Tag Tracking Code

The prior chapters introduced you to some of the event-related data reported by Google Analytics. This chapter takes a closer look at this data found within the **Behavior > Events** menu (see below.)

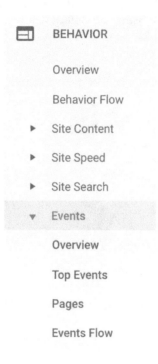

Overview

The **Behavior > Events > Overview** report is organized similar to other overview reports, although the data reported here is focused on events. By default, the line chart on the top of the **Behavior > Events > Overview** page summarizes event activation for the total set of all events that occurred during the specified time period (see the display on the top of page 696). Keep in mind, however, that this is summative data that combines all events into a single display and so has very limited usefulness.

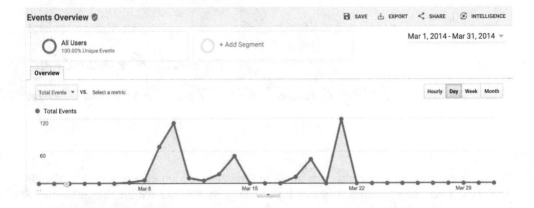

Beyond the default display of **Total Events**, you have the option of displaying additional event summary information by using the pull-down menu beneath **Overview** (see below).

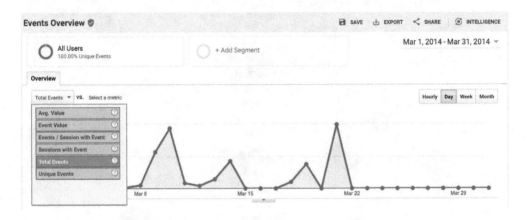

Selecting **Sessions with Event**, for example, displays the chart shown below.

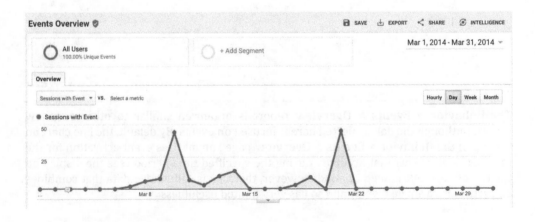

Finally, similar to all line charts, you can chart two dimensions at the same time by using the **Select a Metric** menu option. The chart shown below, for example, simultaneously charts 'Sessions with Event ' and 'Unique Events'.

The table on the middle of the **Behavior > Events > Overview** page provides numeric summary information for all events that have taken place during the specified time period (see below). Similar to other **Overview** pages, clicking on any small line graph changes the line chart display to that metric.

Once again, keep in mind that the preceding data may have limited value because they are summative and not specific to a single event.

You'll recall that you specify an event's names when you create the event statement, as shown below where 'Visuals' is the event name, 'Videos' is the category name, 'Play' is the action name, and 'Blog' is the label name.

```
gtag('event', 'Visuals', {
'event_category: 'Videos',
'event_action': 'Play',
'event_label': 'Blog'
});
```

Google Analytics uses this information to organize your event reports. The chart on the bottom of the **Behavior > Events > Overview** page provides insights into events organized by Category, Action or Label. By default, the display first focuses on events organized by Category parameters. The table shown below, for example, presents my ten categories of events with a percentage distribution by event category. This table is useful when you want to know which event categories are more or less likely to occur.

Top Events		Event Category	Total Events	% Total Events
Event Category	▸	1. Form: Contact	149	33.33%
Event Action		2. xxangeon	54	12.08%
Event Label		3. Scroll Test Page	49	10.96%
		4. Videos	35	7.83%
		5. Author	30	6.71%
		6. Topic	22	4.92%
		7. Purchase Incentives	21	4.70%
		8. Theme	20	4.47%
		9. Written_By	20	4.47%
		10. Download	14	3.13%

view full report

Clicking on the **Event Action** and **Event Label** links on the left-hand side of the table brings up similar charts, only now the charts present Action and Label metrics, as shown in the chart shown below and on the top of page 699.

Top Events		Event Action	Total Events	% Total Events
Event Category		1. field filled	114	25.50%
Event Action	▸	2. scroll reach	103	23.04%
Event Label		3. Davis	52	11.63%
		4. submit	35	7.83%
		5. Play	26	5.82%
		6. Budget	25	5.59%
		7. Click	21	4.70%
		8. Ireland	14	3.13%
		9. Mexico-1	14	3.13%
		10. Budget_Travel	9	2.01%

view full report

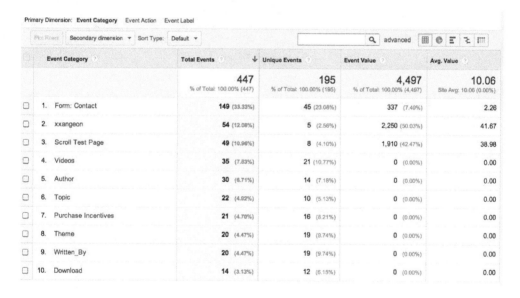

Top Events	Event Label	Total Events	% Total Events
Event Category	1. Submit	51	15.89%
Event Action	2. click	35	10.90%
Event Label ▶	3. gender	23	7.17%
	4. http://www.youtube.com/watch?feature=player_embedded&v=ILDxENakeV8	23	7.17%
	5. 10%	19	5.92%
	6. 20%	19	5.92%
	7. 30%	17	5.30%
	8. email	17	5.30%
	9. name	13	4.05%
	10. 40%	10	3.12%

view full report

Top Events

The **Behavior > Events > Top Events** menu option repeats the list of events organized by event category, except now each event category is described not only in terms of total occurrence, but also, in terms of unique occurrence and value (see the table below). Similar to our analysis of pageviews, we can (for any individual event category) divide *total events* by *unique events*. The closer this ratio is to 1.0, the greater the proportion of that event triggered by different users.

Primary Dimension: **Event Category** Event Action Event Label

	Event Category	Total Events	Unique Events ↓	Event Value	Avg. Value
		447 % of Total: 100.00% (447)	**195** % of Total: 100.00% (195)	**4,497** % of Total: 100.00% (4,497)	**10.06** Site Avg: 10.06 (0.00%)
☐ 1.	Form: Contact	149 (33.33%)	45 (23.08%)	337 (7.49%)	2.26
☐ 2.	xxangeon	54 (12.08%)	5 (2.56%)	2,250 (50.03%)	41.67
☐ 3.	Scroll Test Page	49 (10.96%)	8 (4.10%)	1,910 (42.47%)	38.98
☐ 4.	Videos	35 (7.83%)	21 (10.77%)	0 (0.00%)	0.00
☐ 5.	Author	30 (6.71%)	14 (7.18%)	0 (0.00%)	0.00
☐ 6.	Topic	22 (4.92%)	10 (5.13%)	0 (0.00%)	0.00
☐ 7.	Purchase Incentives	21 (4.70%)	16 (8.21%)	0 (0.00%)	0.00
☐ 8.	Theme	20 (4.47%)	19 (9.74%)	0 (0.00%)	0.00
☐ 9.	Written_By	20 (4.47%)	19 (9.74%)	0 (0.00%)	0.00
☐ 10.	Download	14 (3.13%)	12 (6.15%)	0 (0.00%)	0.00

Note that on the top of the above chart, **Primary Dimension** is set to **Event Category**. The other options for selecting the primary dimension allow you to see a chart focused on event actions or event labels, as shown in the two tables on the top of page 700.

Event Action	Total Events	↓ Unique Events	Event Value	Avg. Value
	447 % of Total: 100.00% (447)	**195** % of Total: 100.00% (195)	**4,497** % of Total: 100.00% (4,497)	**10.06** Site Avg: 10.06 (0.00%)
☐ 1. field filled	**114** (25.50%)	**44** (18.41%)	**337** (7.49%)	2.96
☐ 2. scroll reach	**103** (23.04%)	**13** (5.44%)	**4,160** (92.51%)	40.39
☐ 3. Davis	**52** (11.63%)	**36** (15.06%)	**0** (0.00%)	0.00
☐ 4. submit	**35** (7.83%)	**31** (12.97%)	**0** (0.00%)	0.00
☐ 5. Play	**26** (5.82%)	**20** (8.37%)	**0** (0.00%)	0.00
☐ 6. Budget	**25** (5.59%)	**14** (5.86%)	**0** (0.00%)	0.00
☐ 7. Click	**21** (4.70%)	**16** (6.69%)	**0** (0.00%)	0.00
☐ 8. Ireland	**14** (3.13%)	**14** (5.86%)	**0** (0.00%)	0.00
☐ 9. Mexico-1	**14** (3.13%)	**12** (5.02%)	**0** (0.00%)	0.00
☐ 10. Budget_Travel	**9** (2.01%)	**9** (3.77%)	**0** (0.00%)	0.00

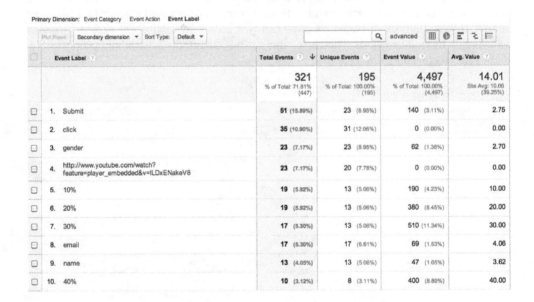

Event Label	Total Events	↓ Unique Events	Event Value	Avg. Value
	321 % of Total: 71.81% (447)	**195** % of Total: 100.00% (195)	**4,497** % of Total: 100.00% (4,497)	**14.01** Site Avg: 10.06 (39.25%)
☐ 1. Submit	**51** (15.89%)	**23** (8.95%)	**140** (3.11%)	2.75
☐ 2. click	**35** (10.90%)	**31** (12.06%)	**0** (0.00%)	0.00
☐ 3. gender	**23** (7.17%)	**23** (8.95%)	**62** (1.38%)	2.70
☐ 4. http://www.youtube.com/watch?feature=player_embedded&v=ILDxENakeV8	**23** (7.17%)	**20** (7.78%)	**0** (0.00%)	0.00
☐ 5. 10%	**19** (5.92%)	**13** (5.06%)	**190** (4.23%)	10.00
☐ 6. 20%	**19** (5.92%)	**13** (5.06%)	**380** (8.45%)	20.00
☐ 7. 30%	**17** (5.30%)	**13** (5.06%)	**510** (11.34%)	30.00
☐ 8. email	**17** (5.30%)	**17** (6.61%)	**69** (1.53%)	4.06
☐ 9. name	**13** (4.05%)	**13** (5.06%)	**47** (1.05%)	3.62
☐ 10. 40%	**10** (3.12%)	**8** (3.11%)	**400** (8.89%)	40.00

The advantage of the preceding charts is that they provide information on all events in a single view. The disadvantage, however, is that the presence of multiple events in the same table makes it difficult to see the trends for just one single event category, action or label. Fortunately, this is easy to remedy.

You'll recall that selecting the **Behavior > Events > Top Events** menu option brings up a list of event categories (see the table on the bottom of page 699). The **Event Category,** 'Topic', shown on line 6 of the table, relates to labeling of the topics of content entries that can be read by site users. Our site offers multiple content entries addressing both budget travel and Europe. The goal is to see which topic, overall, is the most popular.

Two HTML event commands were used to collect the appropriate metrics:

```
gtag('event', 'Blog', {
'event_category': 'Topic',
'event_action': 'Budget'
});

gtag('event', 'Blog', {
'event_category': 'Topic',
'event_action': 'Europe'
});
```

The category name 'Topic' is the same for both events while the action name parameter is used to label the topic as either 'Budget' or 'Europe.'

The table below indicates that there have been 22 content entries read (the number of total **Topic** events), with 10 of these being unique events. Thus, it appears that each site user read about two blog entries (as indicated in the ratio of total Topic events to unique Topic events).

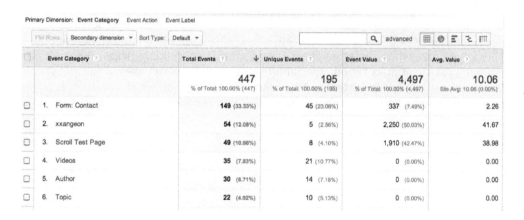

Primary Dimension: Event Category Event Action Event Label

Event Category	Total Events	Unique Events	Event Value	Avg. Value
	447	**195**	**4,497**	**10.06**
	% of Total: 100.00% (447)	% of Total: 100.00% (195)	% of Total: 100.00% (4,497)	Site Avg: 10.06 (0.00%)
1. Form: Contact	**149** (33.33%)	**45** (23.08%)	337 (7.49%)	2.26
2. xxangeon	**54** (12.08%)	**5** (2.56%)	2,250 (50.03%)	41.67
3. Scroll Test Page	**49** (10.96%)	**8** (4.10%)	1,910 (42.47%)	38.98
4. Videos	**35** (7.83%)	21 (10.77%)	0 (0.00%)	0.00
5. Author	**30** (6.71%)	14 (7.18%)	0 (0.00%)	0.00
6. Topic	**22** (4.92%)	10 (5.13%)	0 (0.00%)	0.00

Clicking on the **Topic** category parameter in line 6 of the above table allows us to drill-down into the characteristics of just this one event category. After the category name is selected, a table presenting all actions associated with the category is displayed (see table on the top of page 702). The table indicates that while both content topics have been read, there is much more interest in budget versus European travel. Note that the **Event Action** labels are taken directly from the event's HTML commands.

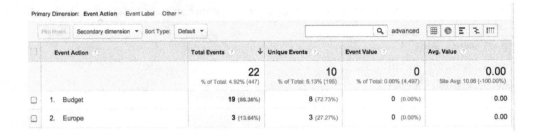

Clicking on each link in the **Event Action** column brings up the list of **Event Labels** associated with that action *if* this optional parameter has been used in the HTML code that provides the characteristics of the event. In this case, since no labels were used to describe this event, the resulting table presents no data, as shown below.

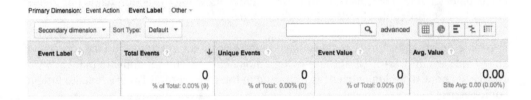

Pages

There are times when the same event is triggered from multiple pages. We could, for example, put event links for our special offers on four different pages of the website. In cases such as this, it is important to know the specific pages on which the event is taking place. This information is available though the **Behavior > Events > Pages** menu option, as shown below.

Clicking on the name of any individual page will display metrics for the events that occurred only on that page.

The **Events Flow** chart is interpreted similarly to the flow charts discussed earlier, keeping in mind that the data reported here focus on the path to event triggers.

Events as Goals
Using Global Site Tag Tracking Code

Chapter 39a showed how events are reported as part of the **Behavior > Events** menu option. There are times, however, when you not only want to explore the data available through event reporting, but also, want to consider and examine events as website goals. Google Analytics allows you to do this.

✅ Your HTML code for naming and triggering the event should be present in your web page's HTML code prior to beginning goal creation.

Classifying events as goals

(The beginning of this section recaps the information from the goal creation discussion in Section VIII.)

You create goals through the **Admin** link on the top of every Google Analytics page. Once you click on this link, you'll see your administrator's page (see below). Make certain that the appropriate **Account, Property**, and **View** are displayed, and then click on the **Goals** link in the **View** column.

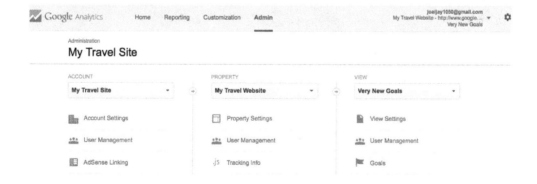

Your goals summary page will be displayed next (mine is shown below), where all of the goals for the current view are displayed.

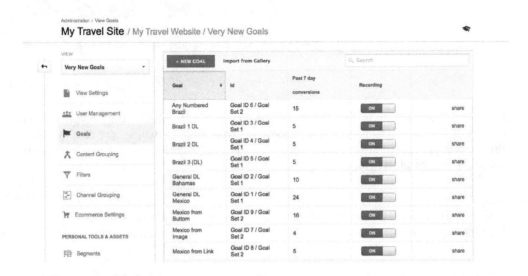

Clicking on **+ New Goal** brings us to the goal creation page (see below). The first step in creating an event-triggered goal is responding to the information requests in **Goal description**. We give the goal a descriptive name by filling in the text box (in this case we'll call the goal 'Any Mexico Download') and clicking on **Event** (under **Type**).

Clicking on **Next Step** brings up the display shown on the top of page 707, which collects the target event's characteristics.

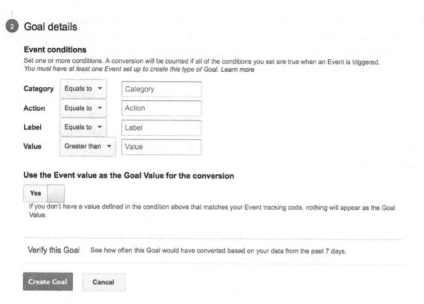

We fill in each text box with the event's characteristics, as shown below. Since there is no value associated with this goal, **Value** is left on the default **Yes**.

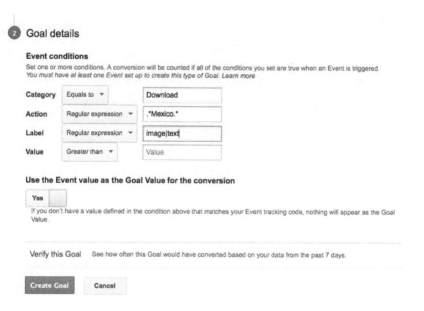

Note that we used regex in two places. First, since we are interested in any download containing the word 'Mexico' we use regex to indicate this. Any action parameter containing 'Mexico', for example, 'Mexico1' or '3cMexico' will satisfy the action condition. Second, we are not interested in differentiating text from image links to the download, so we specify that either one qualifies for inclusion by using the regex | as the 'or' statement., in this case 'image|text'.

Once we verify that all of the information is correct, we click on **Create Goal** to save the goal. The data relevant to this event-triggered goal will be reported identically to any other goals you created.

Events and Custom Segments
Using Global Site Tag Tracking Code

Chapter 40a discussed how goals can be used to create custom segments and how these segments inform strategic decision-making. Events can be used in a similar way.

Creating a custom segment using events

You create a custom segment using events similarly to the way you created custom segments using goals. You access segments via the **+Add Segment** option on the top of almost any page (located beneath the blue circle **All Sessions** identifier). When you click **+Add Segment**, the advanced segments page displays. You then begin the segment creation process by clicking the **+ New Segment** link. The segment creation page will then display.

Event metrics are incorporated into a segment's definition via the **Conditions** option, which is shown on the bottom left-hand side of the segment creation page. The selection of this option brings up the **Conditions** page, as shown below.

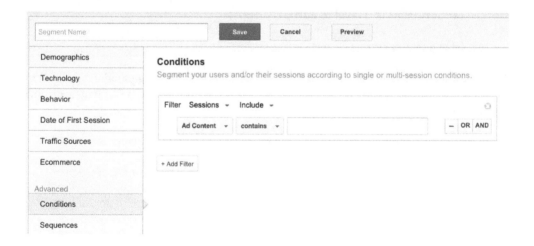

Pulling-down the menu currently labeled **Ad Content** displays both green and blue menu options. Within the green **Behavior** menu are three options related to events: Event Category, Event Action and Event Label (as shown on the top of page 710). The options are more easily found when you order the list alphabetically or use the search box.

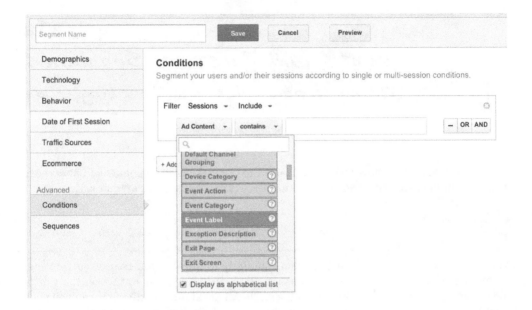

You can select any individual element or combination of elements to create the custom segment.

Let's illustrate the remainder of the process using two different types of events. One event triggers when the page is loaded, and the second event triggers from a link click. Both events have the same category and label:

- **category name** is 'Travel to Europe'

- **label name** is 'France'

The **action name** for each event is different. The action for the page load event is 'Activates on page load', while the action for the link-triggered event is 'Activates on link click'. We'll use these different actions to define our segments.

Let's create two custom segments based on these events using this scenario:

> Imagine that you have a content page that describes travel to Europe, specifically France. You track those who visit the page through an event that triggers when the page is loaded. The page also provides a link to download a formatted, print-ready PDF of the page's content. You track those who use this link through an event triggered when the link is clicked. Both events have the category, label, and action parameters described above. You want to be able to explore differences between those who visit the page and download versus those who visit the page and do not download.

The first custom segment will include those individuals who visited **both** the page (as this event was triggered automatically by a page visit) and clicked on the download PDF link (as this event was triggered by a user interaction on the same page).

On the initial **Conditions** screen, we begin by selecting **Event Action** from the pull-down menu. Next, we indicate the action that defines a visit to the page as 'Activates on page load.' Finally, we set the Filters to Users and Include, as shown below:

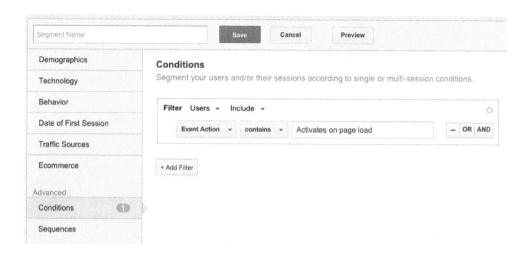

At the moment, the segment consists of all those who visited the page. We now need to restrict this segment to those who also downloaded the PDF. To do this, we click on **+Add Filter** which brings up the display shown below.

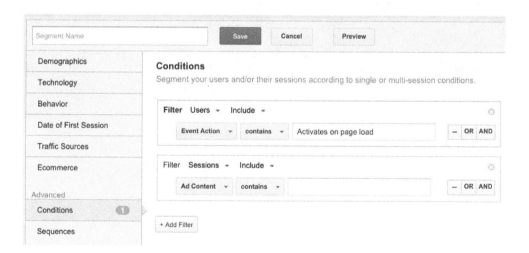

We now add the **Event Action** that signifies a download, i.e., 'Activates on link click', as shown below. We again set the filter to **Users** and **Include**. Finally, we name and save the segment.

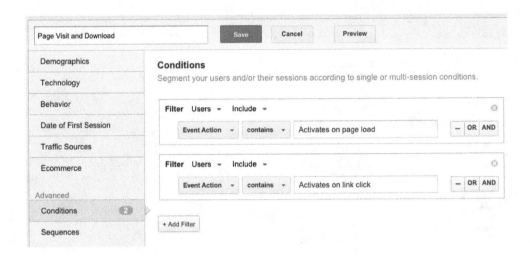

Let's now create the second custom segment. This segment will include all individuals who visited the page, but **did not** click on the link to download the PDF. We begin creating this segment in the same way as the previous segment, identifying all those who visited the page, as shown below.

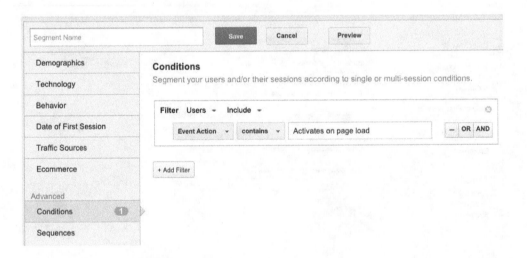

Now we need to restrict this segment to those who did not download the PDF. To do this, we click on **+Add Filter** which brings up the display shown below.

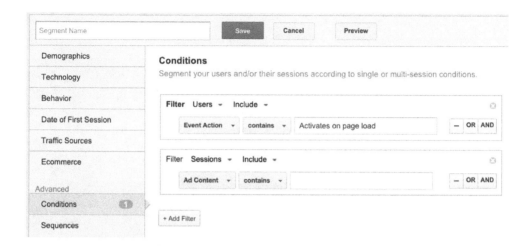

We add the **Event Action** that signifies a download, i.e., 'Activates on link click', as shown below.

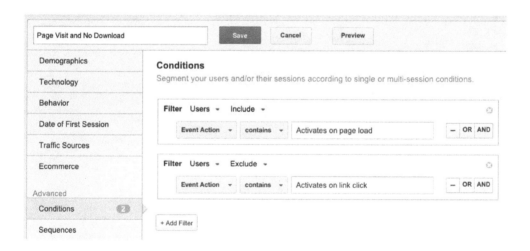

Now, however, while we once again leave **Users** as one of the filters, we select **Exclude**. As a result, the segment will contain only those who visited but did not download. We then name and save the segment.

Once created, event-related custom segments can be used in data analysis in the same way as goal-related custom segments.

Advanced Events: Page Scroll
Using Global Site Tag Tracking Code

You probably spend a lot of time planning your website or blog content. Ideally, by now you can see how Google Analytics can help you make better content-related strategic decisions by monitoring and reporting users' page and content interactions (for example, pages read, time spent on page, bounce rate, etc.). But without the use of events, Google Analytics cannot tell you *how much* of a page is actually read. This chapter explains how to set up and obtain data on 'page scroll depth,' the percentage of a page viewed by a site visitor.[135]

This chapter explains how to use events to monitor and analyze page scroll depth.

How the script works

The script first determines the total height of a web page and then divides the page into ten equal parts (10% split). Next, the script finds the height of the site user's browser window and determines how many of those 10% splits the user can see when the page first loads. Finally, the script monitors the user's page scroll. When a user starts to scroll down the page, the script triggers an event when the user reaches each new 10% split.

The event command uses the following code format:

```
gtag('event', 'ScrollDepth', {
        'event_category' : title,
        'event_action'   : 'scroll reach',
        'event_label'    : '10%',
        'value'          : 10,
        'non_interaction' : true
});
```

Title is the page title that the user is currently on and the 10% changes to reflect the split of the page to which the user has scrolled. The last field is set to **nonInteraction : true**, which tells Google Analytics to consider each event trigger a non-interaction event. This prevents any distortion of your pageview, bounce rate or related metrics.

---

[135] We use a script originally developed by Dave Taylor (http://dave-taylor.co.uk/blog/scroll-reach-tracking-in-google-analytics/) and modified by Evan Sharp. We have further revised the script to update the event commands to work with Global Site Tag.

First, you will need to download the following zip file:

http://www.googleanalyticsdemystified.com/resources/google-analytics-scroll-tracking_gtag5.js.zip

Once obtained and unzipped, upload the file ending in **.js** (not the zip file) to the same directory as your site. Then follow these steps.

1. Select the page you want to monitor. Open the page in your HTML editing program. Make certain your Google Analytics tracking code is present on the page.

2. You need four lines of additional JavaScript on every page for which you want to track scroll depth. The lines are:

   < script src="https://ajax.googleapis.com/ajax/libs/jquery/1.7.2/jquery.min.js">

   </script>

   < script type="text/javascript' src='YOUR URL/google-analytics-scroll-tracking_gtag5.js">

   </script>

   Place these lines just after your Global Site Tag tracking code.

   All that you need to do is replace the phrase **YOUR URL** with the full URL to your site. Make certain that you use the full URL (that is, start with http://) and include the subdirectory, if one is used. My four lines of code would look as follows:

   < script src="https://ajax.googleapis.com/ajax/libs/jquery/1.7.2/jquery.min.js">

   </script>

   < script type="text/JavaScript"
   src="http://www.googleanalyticsdemystified.com/xqanqeon/google-analytics-scroll-tracking_gtag5.js">

   </script>

3. Save the page and upload to your server.

Once this is done, you can cut and paste the revised four lines of HTML code to other pages for which you want to track scroll depth. *Make certain that when you use this code on other pages, that you give each new page a descriptive title so that it can be easily identified in your Google Analytics reports.* Additionally, if necessary, you'll need to copy and place the file **google-analytics-scroll-tracking_gtag5.js** in the same directory/folder as the other pages of your website that you wish to monitor.

We access page scroll data through the **Behavior > Events > Top Events** menu, which brings up a table similar to that shown below. Each website page containing the script will be listed using the page's title. In our case, the only page on which we incorporated the script is titled 'Scroll Test Page.' This page is shown in line three of the table below.

We click on the name of the page of interest to bring up the data related to this category's **Event Action** parameter (see below). The script automatically labels this 'scroll reach.'

Clicking on **scroll reach** brings up specific scroll information for the page, as illustrated in the table on the top of page 718. Note that the percentages are ordered in terms of **Total Events**, so they may not be listed in strict numeric order.

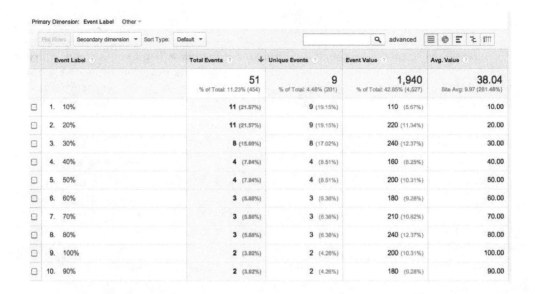

Event Label ?	Total Events ?	↓ Unique Events ?	Event Value ?	Avg. Value ?
	51 % of Total: 11.23% (454)	**9** % of Total: 4.48% (201)	**1,940** % of Total: 42.85% (4,527)	**38.04** Site Avg: 9.97 (281.48%)
☐ 1. 10%	11 (21.57%)	9 (19.15%)	110 (5.67%)	10.00
☐ 2. 20%	11 (21.57%)	9 (19.15%)	220 (11.34%)	20.00
☐ 3. 30%	8 (15.69%)	8 (17.02%)	240 (12.37%)	30.00
☐ 4. 40%	4 (7.84%)	4 (8.51%)	160 (8.25%)	40.00
☐ 5. 50%	4 (7.84%)	4 (8.51%)	200 (10.31%)	50.00
☐ 6. 60%	3 (5.88%)	3 (6.38%)	180 (9.28%)	60.00
☐ 7. 70%	3 (5.88%)	3 (6.38%)	210 (10.82%)	70.00
☐ 8. 80%	3 (5.88%)	3 (6.38%)	240 (12.37%)	80.00
☐ 9. 100%	2 (3.92%)	2 (4.26%)	200 (10.31%)	100.00
☐ 10. 90%	2 (3.92%)	2 (4.26%)	180 (9.28%)	90.00

Because of the way the script works, only some of the data is valuable. The **Average Value** on the right-hand side of the top line reports the average amount of page scrolling. In this case, the average depth of scrolling is 38.04%. So, only a bit more than one-third of the page (on average) is seen. This is not very good at all.

The **Total Events** column provides a distribution of how many individuals reached a certain point on the page. Since this data represents multiple scrolls for each individual, the key column is **Unique Events,** which reports the number of unique users reaching each scroll point. An **Event Label** of 10% or 20% (depending upon a page's total length) typically represents the number of pageviews, as this is the amount of the page that can typically be seen upon page load without the need for scrolling. The numbers decline moving down the **Unique Events** column, representing fewer and fewer individuals who scroll toward the end of the page. We can see that only three individuals read 80% of the page and only two scrolled to the bottom of the page reading 100% of the content. The content is simply not maintaining interest or engagement. We need a revised content strategy to increase the amount of content consumption.

Relating scroll depth to outcome measures

The prior analysis illustrated how scroll depth can help you understand content consumption for any particular page. Scroll depth data can also be used to understand how consumption of a particular page's content is related to important website goals and outcome behaviors. You can, for example, set a goal for a particular scroll depth and then use goal conversion to form custom segments. Or, you can examine how scroll depth is related to important outcome measures such as ecommerce. Let's take a look to see how the latter can be accomplished.

We start with **Events > Top Events** from the left-hand side menu options. This displays a table similar to that shown below.

The page of interest is 'Scroll Test Page' shown on line 1 of the table. We click on **Scroll Test Page,** which displays the table shown below.

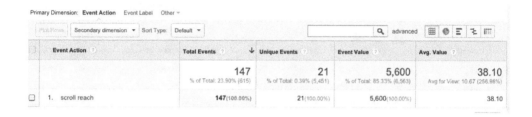

Clicking on **scroll reach** displays the following table.

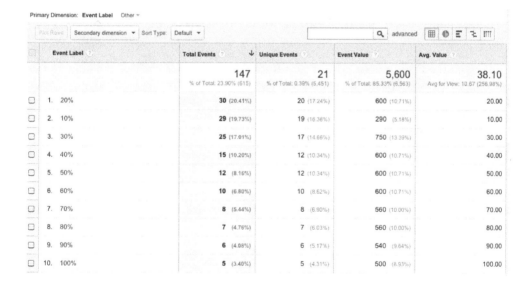

Now we want to focus on ecommerce data. Beneath the Explorer tab near the top of the page is an option to change the tabular display to ecommerce data (see below).

Clicking on **Ecommerce** changes the prior table to that shown below. The table now reports ecommerce data.

Clicking on the **Ecommerce Conversion Rate** column header changes the table to that shown on the top of page 721, where the lines in the table are ordered by ecommerce conversion rate. Here we can clearly see the effect of the page's content consumption on ecommerce success. Content appears to play an important role since Ecommerce Conversion Rate and Per Session Value both increase in almost direct response to an increase in scroll depth.

Our observation of the data trend seems to indicate a strong relationship between scroll depth and important outcome measures. Should we desire, we can statistically examine this relationship to verify our conclusion. This approach is described in the chapter addendum.

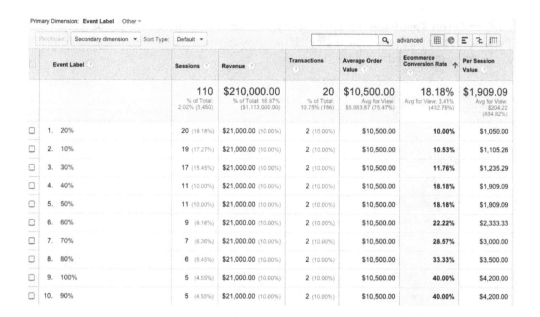

Event Label ?	Sessions ?	Revenue ?	Transactions ?	Average Order Value ?	Ecommerce Conversion Rate ↑ ?	Per Session Value ?
	110 % of Total: 2.02% (5,450)	**$210,000.00** % of Total: 18.87% ($1,113,000.00)	**20** % of Total: 10.75% (186)	**$10,500.00** Avg for View: $5,983.87 (75.47%)	**18.18%** Avg for View: 3.41% (432.75%)	**$1,909.09** Avg for View: $204.22 (834.82%)
☐ 1. 20%	20 (18.18%)	$21,000.00 (10.00%)	2 (10.00%)	$10,500.00	10.00%	$1,050.00
☐ 2. 10%	19 (17.27%)	$21,000.00 (10.00%)	2 (10.00%)	$10,500.00	10.53%	$1,105.26
☐ 3. 30%	17 (15.45%)	$21,000.00 (10.00%)	2 (10.00%)	$10,500.00	11.76%	$1,235.29
☐ 4. 40%	11 (10.00%)	$21,000.00 (10.00%)	2 (10.00%)	$10,500.00	18.18%	$1,909.09
☐ 5. 50%	11 (10.00%)	$21,000.00 (10.00%)	2 (10.00%)	$10,500.00	18.18%	$1,909.09
☐ 6. 60%	9 (8.18%)	$21,000.00 (10.00%)	2 (10.00%)	$10,500.00	22.22%	$2,333.33
☐ 7. 70%	7 (6.36%)	$21,000.00 (10.00%)	2 (10.00%)	$10,500.00	28.57%	$3,000.00
☐ 8. 80%	6 (5.45%)	$21,000.00 (10.00%)	2 (10.00%)	$10,500.00	33.33%	$3,500.00
☐ 9. 100%	5 (4.55%)	$21,000.00 (10.00%)	2 (10.00%)	$10,500.00	40.00%	$4,200.00
☐ 10. 90%	5 (4.55%)	$21,000.00 (10.00%)	2 (10.00%)	$10,500.00	40.00%	$4,200.00

Real-Time confirmation

You can check to make certain that the scripts are working via Real-Time.

Log into your Google Analytics account and bring up the **Real-Time > Events** display. Click on **Events (last 30 min)**. At the moment the display should be blank as no events have been activated. Now, in a separate browser window (or an entirely different browser, preferably Chrome), visit the page you modified and scroll down the page. In our case the page title is 'Scroll Test Page'. Revisit your **Real-Time > Events** display where you should see a display similar to that shown below. It is only important that 'Scroll Test Page' (or the title of your page) appears in the **Event Category** column.

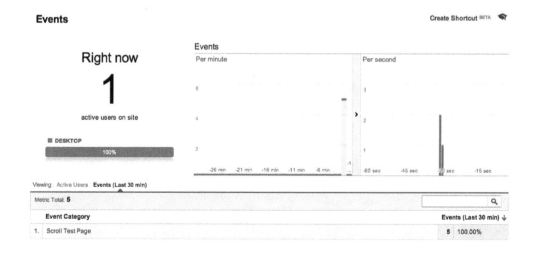

Click on **Scroll Test Page** (or your chosen page title) to bring up the **Event Action** and **Event Label** display (see table below). If data appears in the two columns, then you have successfully monitored scroll depth.

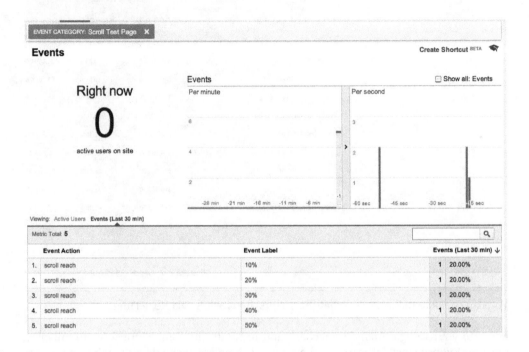

Correlation determines the association between two measures. A common correlation, for example, is that of height and weight. There is a positive correlation between height and weight where taller people tend to be weigh more than shorter people. People of the same height vary in weight, and you can probably think of two people you know where the shorter one weighs more than the taller one. Nevertheless, the average weight of people 5'2" is less than the average weight of people 5'4", and their average weight is less than that of people 5'7", etc. Correlation can tell you the extent to which overall height is related to weight.

Correlations are reported with a measure called a correlation coefficient. This measure ranges from a score of -1 to +1 and consists of two parts.

- The sign of the correlation coefficient, either + or -, indicates the direction of the association.

- The numeric component (which ranges from -1 to + 1 indicates the strength of the association.

If the correlation coefficient equals +1.0 then there is a perfect positive correlation between the two measures. All of the observations fall on a straight line and as one measure increases so does the other. If the correlation coefficient equals -1.0 then there is a perfect negative correlation. Here, all of the observations fall on a straight line but as one measure increases the other decreases. A correlation coefficient of zero indicates a complete absence of a relationship between the two measures.

Let's see how to compute this measure.

First, we'll need to have access to scroll depth and ecommerce measures. Follow the steps described earlier to obtain a table similar to that shown on the top of page 724.

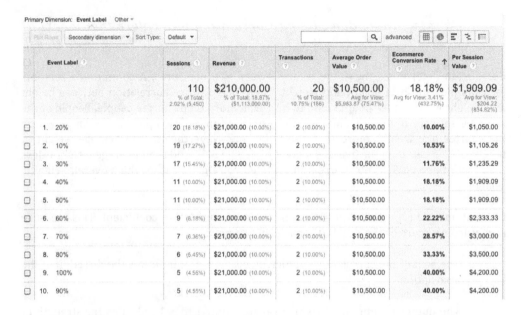

Event Label ?	Sessions ?	Revenue ?	Transactions ?	Average Order Value ?	Ecommerce Conversion Rate ↑ ?	Per Session Value ?
	110 % of Total: 2.02% (5,450)	$210,000.00 % of Total: 18.87% ($1,113,000.00)	20 % of Total: 10.75% (186)	$10,500.00 Avg for View: $5,983.87 (75.47%)	18.18% Avg for View: 3.41% (432.75%)	$1,909.09 Avg for View: $204.22 (834.82%)
1. 20%	20 (18.18%)	$21,000.00 (10.00%)	2 (10.00%)	$10,500.00	10.00%	$1,050.00
2. 10%	19 (17.27%)	$21,000.00 (10.00%)	2 (10.00%)	$10,500.00	10.53%	$1,105.26
3. 30%	17 (15.45%)	$21,000.00 (10.00%)	2 (10.00%)	$10,500.00	11.76%	$1,235.29
4. 40%	11 (10.00%)	$21,000.00 (10.00%)	2 (10.00%)	$10,500.00	18.18%	$1,909.09
5. 50%	11 (10.00%)	$21,000.00 (10.00%)	2 (10.00%)	$10,500.00	18.18%	$1,909.09
6. 60%	9 (8.18%)	$21,000.00 (10.00%)	2 (10.00%)	$10,500.00	22.22%	$2,333.33
7. 70%	7 (6.36%)	$21,000.00 (10.00%)	2 (10.00%)	$10,500.00	28.57%	$3,000.00
8. 80%	6 (5.45%)	$21,000.00 (10.00%)	2 (10.00%)	$10,500.00	33.33%	$3,500.00
9. 100%	5 (4.55%)	$21,000.00 (10.00%)	2 (10.00%)	$10,500.00	40.00%	$4,200.00
10. 90%	5 (4.55%)	$21,000.00 (10.00%)	2 (10.00%)	$10,500.00	40.00%	$4,200.00

On the top of the page displaying the table is an option to export the table to Excel (see below). Click on **Export** and select your preferred format

Top Events

ALL » EVENT CATEGORY: Scroll Test Page ▾ » EVENT ACTION: scroll reach ▾

Customize   Email   Export ▾   Add to Dashboard   Shortcut

Open the Excel spreadsheet after it downloads to your computer. Note that all of the data from the table is displayed in the Excel download.

We can use the online calculator at pearsoncorrelation.com to compute the correlation coefficient (http://pearsoncorrelation.com/). When we arrive at this site, two boxes are displayed. Place the data in the **Event Label** column in the left-hand box, eliminating the percentage sign from the data. You can copy and paste this data from the Excel download or you type the data directly into the box. Next, copy and paste (or retype) the data in the **Ecommerce Conversion Rate** column into the right-hand side box, again eliminating the percentage sign. When you are done, your screen will resemble that shown below, where the data is from the table on the top of this page.

20	10.0
10	10.53
30	11.76
40	18.18
50	18.18
60	22.22
70	28.57
80	33.33
90	40.0
100	40.0

Press the **Calculate Pearson Correlation Coefficient** button beneath the data. Doing so should display a graph of your data as well as the correlation coefficient (shown on the very top of the display page). Remember, a coefficient closer to either -1 or +1 indicates a strong relationship. Our data is shown below where the statistical analysis shows a very strong positive relationship between scroll depth and the Ecommerce Conversion Rate. The more people read the more likely they are to make a purchase.

We can perform a similar analysis to explore the relationship between scroll depth and **Per Session Value**. Here, we leave the scroll depth data in the left-hand box alone but we place the Per Session Value data in the right-hand box (eliminating the dollar sign). Pressing the **Calculate Pearson Correlation Coefficient** button beneath the data displays the screen shown below. There is also a very strong positive relationship between these two measures, again indicating that more content consumption is strongly associated with higher per session value.[136]

---

[136] As your interpret your data remember that correction is a measure of association and does not evaluate cause and effect. Correlation indicates the relationship between two measures. A strong positive correlation only indicates that the two variables generally move together in the same direction. Correlation, however, does indicate causation; it does not indicate that one variable causes the movement in the other or that a change in one will result in a change in the other.

43a
Advanced Events:
Form Completion Monitoring
Using Global Site Tag Tracking Code

Forms are an important way by which a website or blog begins to establish or reinforce a relationship with a site user. Google Analytics can tell us the number of people who send a form as well as the number of people who go to the form page without sending the form. Without events, however, Google Analytics cannot provide any diagnostics for the form itself. The use of events allows us to determine which fields (if any) are problematic and lead to form abandonment.[137]

How the script works

The script examines your form and identifies each field that needs a response. Every time a form user selects a pull-down menu option, clicks on a button, or begins to fill in a text field, the script sends an event trigger to Google Analytics telling it that the field had been accessed and some information provided. In a perfect world, the number of pageviews for the page containing the form should equal the number of users completing every field on the form and then pressing the Submit button. The greater the discrepancy between the number of pageviews and form field/submit completion, the greater the problem with the form. Keep in mind that this script only checks to see if a field has been accessed, it does not check for valid field entries.

Installing the script

First, you will need to download the following zip file:

http://www.googleanalyticsdemystified.com/resources/form-tracking-google-analytics-gtag1.js.zip

Once obtained and unzipped, upload the file ending in **.js** (not the zip file) to the same directory as your site. Then follow these steps:

---

[137] We will be using a script developed by Dave Taylor at http://dave-taylor.co.uk/blog/form-analytics-plugin-for-google-analytics/ to track form completion. We have modified this script to make the event commands appropriate to Global Site Tag.

1. Select the page you want to monitor. Open the page in your HTML editing program. Make certain your Google Analytics tracking code is present on the page.

2. You need four lines of additional JavaScript on every page for which you want to track form completion. The lines are:

   ```
   <script src="https://ajax.googleapis.com/ajax/libs/jquery/1.7.2/jquery.min.js">

   </script>

   <script type="text/JavaScript' src='YOUR URL/form-tracking-google-analytics-gtag1.js">

   </script>
   ```

   All that you need to do is replace the phrase **YOUR URL** with the full URL to your site. Make certain that you use the full URL (that is, start with http://) and include the subdirectory, if one is used. My four lines of code would therefore look as follows:

   ```
   <script src="https://ajax.googleapis.com/ajax/libs/jquery/1.7.2/jquery.min.js">

   </script>

   <script type="text/JavaScript"
   src="http://www.googleanalyticsdemystified.com/xqanqeon/form-tracking-google-
   analytics-gtag1.js">

   </script>
   ```

   Place the lines after your Global Site Tag tracking code.

3. Save the page and upload to your server.

Once this is done, you can cut and paste the revised code to other pages for which you want to track form completion. *Make certain that when you use this code on other pages, that you give each new page a descriptive title.* Additionally, you'll need to copy and place the file **form-tracking-google-analytics-gtag1.js** in the same directory/folder as the other pages of your website that contain forms you wish to monitor.

Interpreting the data

The first thing we need to determine is how many unique individuals visited our contact page. We can obtain this information by selecting **Behavior > Site Content > All Pages** from the left-hand side menu options. When we do this, we discover that 26 people visited our contact page (see line 8 and the data presented in the 'Unique Views' column in the table shown on the top of page 729).

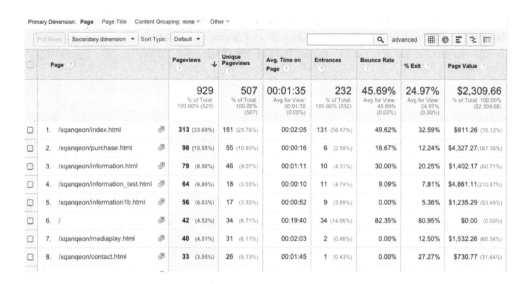

Primary Dimension: **Page**   Page Title   Content Grouping: none ▾   Other ▾

	Page ?		Pageviews ↓ ?	Unique Pageviews ?	Avg. Time on Page ?	Entrances ?	Bounce Rate ?	% Exit ?	Page Value ?
			929 % of Total: 100.00% (929)	**507** % of Total: 100.00% (507)	**00:01:35** Avg for View: 00:01:35 (0.00%)	**232** % of Total: 100.00% (232)	**45.69%** Avg for View: 45.69% (0.00%)	**24.97%** Avg for View: 24.97% (0.00%)	**$2,309.66** % of Total: 100.00% ($2,309.66)
☐	1.	/xqanqeon/index.html	**313** (33.68%)	**151** (29.78%)	00:02:05	131 (56.47%)	49.62%	32.59%	$811.26 (35.12%)
☐	2.	/xqanqeon/purchase.html	**98** (10.55%)	**55** (10.85%)	00:00:16	6 (2.59%)	16.67%	12.24%	$4,327.27(187.36%)
☐	3.	/xqanqeon/information.html	**79** (8.50%)	**46** (9.07%)	00:01:11	10 (4.31%)	30.00%	20.25%	$1,402.17 (60.71%)
☐	4.	/xqanqeon/information_test.html	**64** (6.89%)	**18** (3.55%)	00:00:10	11 (4.74%)	9.09%	7.81%	$4,861.11(210.47%)
☐	5.	/xqanqeon/information1b.html	**56** (6.03%)	**17** (3.35%)	00:00:52	9 (3.88%)	0.00%	5.36%	$1,235.29 (53.48%)
☐	6.	/	**42** (4.52%)	**34** (6.71%)	00:19:40	34 (14.66%)	82.35%	80.95%	$0.00 (0.00%)
☐	7.	/xqanqeon/mediaplay.html	**40** (4.31%)	**31** (6.11%)	00:02:03	2 (0.86%)	0.00%	12.50%	$1,532.26 (66.34%)
☐	8.	/xqanqeon/contact.html	**33** (3.55%)	**26** (5.13%)	00:01:45	1 (0.43%)	0.00%	27.27%	$730.77 (31.64%)

Next, we access form completion data through the **Behavior > Events > Top Events** menu option, which in this case brings up the table shown below.

Primary Dimension: **Event Category**   Event Action   Event Label

	Event Category ?	Total Events ↓ ?	Unique Events ?	Event Value ?	Avg. Value ?
		454 % of Total: 100.00% (454)	**201** % of Total: 100.00% (201)	**4,527** % of Total: 100.00% (4,527)	**9.97** Site Avg: 9.97 (0.00%)
☐	1. Form: Contact	**149** (32.82%)	**45** (22.39%)	337 (7.44%)	2.26
☐	2. xxangeon	**54** (11.89%)	**5** (2.49%)	2,250 (49.70%)	41.67
☐	3. Scroll Test Page	**51** (11.23%)	**9** (4.48%)	1,940 (42.85%)	38.04
☐	4. Videos	**35** (7.71%)	**21** (10.45%)	0 (0.00%)	0.00
☐	5. Author	**30** (6.61%)	**14** (6.97%)	0 (0.00%)	0.00
☐	6. Topic	**22** (4.85%)	**10** (4.98%)	0 (0.00%)	0.00

The script automatically names the event category 'Form: [Name of Page]', so in our case we are interested in the information relevant to the 'Form: Contact' **Event Category**. Clicking on this link displays the page's **Event Action** table (see below).

Primary Dimension: **Event Action**   Event Label   Other ▾

	Event Action ?	Total Events ↓ ?	Unique Events ?	Event Value ?	Avg. Value ?
		149 % of Total: 32.82% (454)	**45** % of Total: 22.39% (201)	**337** % of Total: 7.44% (4,527)	**2.26** Site Avg: 9.97 (-77.32%)
☐	1. field filled	**114** (76.51%)	**44** (58.67%)	337(100.00%)	2.96
☐	2. submit	**35** (23.49%)	**31** (41.33%)	0 (0.00%)	0.00

We then click on the **field filled** link to bring up the detailed report table (see below). Because site users can fill in, leave and return to revise any field, we are interested in the **Unique Events** column rather than the **Total Events** column.

Event Label	Total Events	Unique Events	Event Value	Avg. Value
	112 % of Total: 24.67% (454)	44 % of Total: 21.89% (201)	337 % of Total: 7.44% (4,527)	3.01 Site Avg: 9.97 (-69.82%)
1. Submit	51 (45.54%)	23 (27.71%)	140 (41.54%)	2.75
2. gender	23 (20.54%)	23 (27.71%)	62 (18.40%)	2.70
3. email	17 (15.18%)	17 (20.48%)	69 (20.47%)	4.06
4. name	13 (11.61%)	13 (15.66%)	47 (13.95%)	3.62
5. message	8 (7.14%)	7 (8.43%)	19 (5.64%)	2.38

Each of the four fields in our contact form, as well as the submit button, are shown in the table. The data indicate problems with nearly all the form fields. The extent of these problems can be viewed in the context of the 23 people who submitted the form.

- The only information provided by all users was gender. Only about 74% of those submitting the form provided an email address. (This was calculated by dividing 17 by 23.) This is particularly distressing, as there is no opportunity to follow-up without an email address.

- The remaining two form fields, name and message, are even more problematic. Only about half of those submitting the form provided a name and only about one third provided a message.

Clearly our form isn't working. We need to redesign the form to facilitate the sending of complete information.

Real-Time confirmation

You can check to make certain that the scripts are working via Real-Time.

You can confirm that form monitoring is working (that is, triggering when a user completes a form field) by using the **Real-Time** menu's **Events** option. We'll illustrate how this works by using our form, located at:

http://www.googleanalyticsdemystified.com/xqanqeon/contact.html.

Notice how the form contains four fields: gender, name, email, and message.

We begin by logging into our Google Analytics account and bringing up the **Real-Time > Events** display. Once we arrive, we click on **Events (last 30 min)**. At the moment, the display is blank as no events have been activated. Now, in a separate browser window we visit the contact page where we indicate the appropriate gender and move to the email field.

Now we re-visit our **Real-Time > Events** display where we see the display shown below, where 'Form: Xqanqeon - Contact' is shown in the **Event Category** column.

Clicking on 'Form: Xqanqeon - Contact' displays the table shown on the top of page 734, where the first completed form field (shown in the **Event Label** column) is presented. (We make certain that we select **Events (Last 30 min)** as the display parameter.)

We now complete the form and press **Submit**. When we revisit the **Real-Time** display we see the table shown below which indicates that all the fields have been completed and the form has been submitted.

Advanced Events: Video Monitoring
Using Global Site Tag Tracking Code

We can all see contribution of multimedia to consumer engagement and subsequent website success. While Google Analytics can tell us the number of people who come to a page with video, without the use of events it cannot tell us whether the video was started and how much of the video was viewed. The script described in this chapter can accomplish this.

How the script works

The script monitors a user's interaction with a video embedded on one of your website pages.[138] The script sends an event notification to Google Analytics when the video is started and at 25%, 50%, 75% and 100% of total video time actually viewed. The category label is set to 'Video', the action label records the amount viewed, and the event label identifies the video by its YouTube identifier and name.

Installing the script

First, you will need to obtain the following files:

videoscan1a.js

videoscan2a.js

You can obtain these files by downloading the following zip file:

http://www.googleanalyticsdemystified.com/resources/videomonitor_gtag.zip

Once obtained and unzipped, upload the two files ending in **.js** (not the zip file or the unzipped folder) to the same directory as your site. Then follow these steps.

1. Select the page containing the video you want to monitor.

---

[138] The script used to monitor video engagement was written by Stephane Hamel at http://www.cardinalpath.com/youtube-video-tracking-with-gtm-and-ua-a-step-by-step-guide. We have, however, made some modifications to eliminate the use of Google Tag Manager present in the original script in order to send event data to Google Analytics using Global Site Tag commands. We have also simplified/reduced the data sent to Google Analytics in an effort to simplify data interpretation. Finally, this script only works with YouTube video.

2. You need six lines of additional JavaScript on every page for which you want to track video viewing. The lines are:

```
<script src="https://ajax.googleapis.com/ajax/libs/jquery/1.7.2/jquery.min.js">

</script>

<script type="text/JavaScript' src='YOUR URL/videoscan1a.js">

</script>

<script type="text/JavaScript' src='YOUR URL/videoscan2a.js">

</script>
```

All that you need to do is replace the phrase **YOUR URL** with the full URL to your site. Make certain that you use the full URL (that is, start with http://) and include the sub-directory, if one is used. My six lines of code would therefore look as follows:

```
<script src="https://ajax.googleapis.com/ajax/libs/jquery/1.7.2/jquery.min.js">

</script>

<script type="text/JavaScript"
src="http://www.googleanalyticsdemystified.com/xqanqeon/videoscan1a.js">

</script>

<script type="text/JavaScript"
src="http://www.googleanalyticsdemystified.com/xqanqeon/videoscan2a.js">

</script>
```

Place these lines after Global Site Tag tracking code.

3. Place the following lines of code at the place in your HTML code where you want the video to appear:

```
<iframe width="420" height="315"
src="http://www.youtube.com/embed/YTubeAddress?enablejsapi=1" frameborder="0"
allowfullscreen></iframe>
```

The commands in this line pull the video from YouTube and place the video on your web page. Replace the phrase 'YTubeAddress' with the unique address of the video when it plays at YouTube.

For example, if you view a video at:

`https://www.youtube.com/watch?v=MHgj2UzqMx0`

you would replace 'YTubeAddress' with 'MHgj2UzqMx0' and the line would read:

**<iframe width='420' height='315'
src='http://www.youtube.com/embed/MHgj2UzqMx0?enablejsapi=1' frameborder='0'
allowfullscreen></iframe>**

Complete this step with the video of your choice. You have the option of altering the width and height of the video player by changing the width and height specifications in the beginning of the line. Leave the remainder of the line untouched.

4. Save the page and upload to your server.

Once this is done, you can cut and paste the revised code from steps 2 and 3 to other pages for which you want to track video viewing. *Make certain that when you use this code on other pages, that you give each new page a descriptive title.* Additionally, you'll need to place the files **videoscan1a.js** and **videoscan2a.js** in the same directory/folder as the other pages on your website that contain video playback you want to monitor.

Interpreting the data

We access the video interaction data through the **Behavior > Events > Top Events** menu option, which brings up the display shown below. Video play data will always be shown in the line labeled **Video** (which in this case is line 1 of the table). Note that since this script uses 'Video' as the category label, you should avoid using this name to label other category events.

The data presented in the table above is summative; it reports metrics for all of the videos viewed on our site. We can see that there were 10 unique user sessions in which any video was started (as reported in the Unique Events column). Clicking **Video** brings up summary interaction information.

Summary interaction metrics are reported via **Event Action** (see first column in the table below). Again focusing on Unique Events, we can see that of the 10 people starting *any* video (as reported in the first line labeled 0%), only three watched at least 25% (as reported in line two) and only one made it all the way through (as reported in line 4).

Clicking on the Event Label option above the table allows us to see the specific videos viewed (see below).

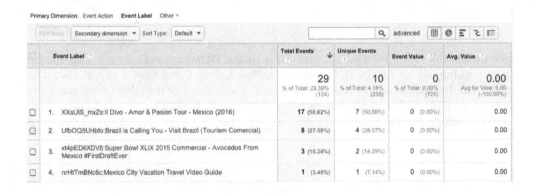

You can click on the name of any specific video to see viewing data for just that video. Let's focus on the Il Divo video (reported on line 1). When we click on this video title the report changes to focus on just this one video, as shown in the table on the top of page 737.

Event Action ?	Total Events ?	↓ Unique Events ?	Event Value ?	Avg. Value ?
	17 % of Total: 13.71% (124)	7 % of Total: 2.93% (239)	0 % of Total: 0.00% (725)	0.00 Avg for View: 5.85 (-100.00%)
☐ 1. 0%	10 (58.82%)	7 (53.85%)	0 (0.00%)	0.00
☐ 2. 25%	3 (17.65%)	2 (15.38%)	0 (0.00%)	0.00
☐ 3. 50%	2 (11.76%)	2 (15.38%)	0 (0.00%)	0.00
☐ 4. 100%	1 (5.88%)	1 (7.69%)	0 (0.00%)	0.00
☐ 5. 75%	1 (5.88%)	1 (7.69%)	0 (0.00%)	0.00

This video is really failing to hold viewer's attention. Of the seven people who started the video (as shown on line one of the Unique Events column), only two make it to the 25% viewing mark and only one watched the video all the way to the end.

Similar to page scroll depth, we can examine important outcome measures in terms of video viewership. The table below relates this video's viewership to ecommerce metrics (see below). The video not only fails to hold viewers' attention, but regardless of the amount viewed, no one exposed to the video made a purchase.

Event Action ?	Sessions ?	↓ Revenue ?	Transactions ?	Average Order Value ?	Ecommerce Conversion Rate ?	Per Session Value ?
	13 % of Total: 5.44% (239)	$0.00 % of Total: 0.00% ($247,000.00)	0 % of Total: 0.00% (37)	$0.00 Avg for View: $6.675.68 (-100.00%)	0.00% Avg for View: 15.48% (-100.00%)	$0.00 Avg for View: $1,033.47 (-100.00%)
☐ 1. 0%	7 (53.85%)	$0.00 (0.00%)	0 (0.00%)	$0.00	0.00%	$0.00
☐ 2. 25%	2 (15.38%)	$0.00 (0.00%)	0 (0.00%)	$0.00	0.00%	$0.00
☐ 3. 50%	2 (15.38%)	$0.00 (0.00%)	0 (0.00%)	$0.00	0.00%	$0.00
☐ 4. 100%	1 (7.69%)	$0.00 (0.00%)	0 (0.00%)	$0.00	0.00%	$0.00
☐ 5. 75%	1 (7.69%)	$0.00 (0.00%)	0 (0.00%)	$0.00	0.00%	$0.00

Finally, keep in mind that video viewership metrics, like all events, can be used to form custom segments for more in-depth analyses.

Real-Time confirmation

You can use Real-Time to confirm that the scripts are working.

Log into your Google Analytics account and bring up the **Real-Time > Events** display. Click on **Events (last 30 min)**. At the moment, the display should be blank as no events have been activated. Now, in a separate browser window (or an entirely different browser, preferably Chrome), visit the page with the video you want to monitor. Watch the video all the way through. Now, revisit your **Real-Time > Events** display where you should see a display similar to that shown below.

Click on the **Video** link in the **Event Category** column. This should generate a table similar to that shown on below. Here, in the **Event Action** column, you can see that one person started the video (as reflected in the top 0% line), and that one person watched the video all the way to the end (as reflected in the 25%, 50%. 75% and 100% lines). The name of the video being viewed is shown in the **Event Label** column.

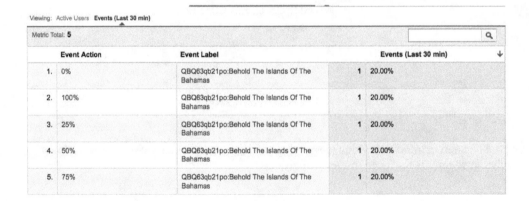

Sending Ecommerce Data to Google Analytics

This chapter illustrates how to send product purchase information to Google Analytics via Global Site Tag. Additional product-related information, such as adding and removing products from a customer's shopping cart and measuring product detail views, can be accomplished using a similar approach.[139]

Google Analytics ecommerce tracking allows you to measure the number of transactions and revenue that your website generates. On a typical ecommerce site, after users click the 'purchase' button, their purchase information is sent to the businesses' web server or external shopping cart, which carries out the transaction. If successful, the server or cart typically redirects the purchaser to a 'Thank You' or receipt page with transaction details and a receipt of the purchase. At this point, you can send the ecommerce data from the 'Thank You' page to Google Analytics.

Imagine that our travel website sells six different tours:

Mexico	2 days	$3,500
Mexico	10 days	$9,000
Mexico	15 days	$12,000
Bahamas	2 days	$3,500
Bahamas	10 days	$9,000
Bahamas	15 days	$12,000

The format of the ecommerce transmission to Google Analytics would be identical across all six tour options. The content differs with regard to tour specifics. The source code used to send ecommerce data to Google Analytics for the 10-day Bahamas tour package is shown on the top of page 740.[140]

---

[139] It is necessary to enable "Enhanced Ecommerce" before Google Analytics (using gtag.js) will accept and display ecommerce data. See *Enhanced Ecommerce with gtag.js* at https://developers.google.com/analytics/devguides/collection/gtagjs/enhanced-ecommerce. This resource also provides additional examples of ecommerce communications with Google Analytics.

[140] Source for this code is the same as shown in footnote 137.

```
gtag('event', 'purchase', {
 'transaction_id': '1234',
 'affiliation': 'Travel Tour',
 'value': 9000.00,
 'currency': 'USD',
 'tax': 0.00,
 'shipping: 0.00
 'items': [
  {
   'id': 'B10',
   'name': 'Ten Day Tour Package',
   'quantity': 1,
   'price': 9000.00
 } ]});
```

There are three parts to this code. The first line, **gtag('event', 'purchase', {** indicates that ecommerce purchase data is being sent to Google Analytics. This line of code is required.

The next large block of code is summary information for the entire transaction, which is normally calculated by the shopping cart. It is common practice to send information that provides the store name, the total value, shipping, and tax. In our case, because we are only selling tour packages, shipping and tax are set to zero and the total value equals the price of the selected tour.

The next block of code is generated for every item placed in the shopping cart: in this case, the purchase of a single tour. Google Analytics requires that at minimum we provide either a product ID or a product name. We've provided both to facilitate different types of analyses in Google Analytics. The remaining information in this block of code provides additional information on the purchase.

Finally, you'll note that the above transmission does not send credit card information. Google does not want this information because it is personally identifiable.

Index

Percent exit (defined), 223

Percent new sessions (defined), 132

Permissions
    Assigning, 46
    Confirming, 49
    Creating at account level, 46 - 48
    Hierarchy, 48 - 49
    Modifying, 49 - 50
    Settings, 28
    Types and levels, 45 - 46

Predefined filters (defined), 54 - 55
    and historical data, 54
    Overview, 53 - 54
    Screen for IP address, 55 - 58
    Screen for referral source (YouTube),
        58 - 61
    Screen for subdirectory, 61 - 64
    Verification (Exclude), 66 - 67
    Verification (Include), 65 - 66
    Verification (overview), 64 – 65

Property (see also Account Management)
    Adding additional to account, 36 - 37
    Creating new, 34 - 36
    Definition, 27
    Deleting, 41 - 42
    Relationship to account, 29 - 30

Real-Time display
    and download tracking, 347 - 348
    and form completing monitoring,
        420 - 421
    and goal reporting, 329 - 334
    and page scroll – See Page Scroll
    and video monitoring, 427 - 428
    Verifying tracking code, 11 - 13

Regex - See Regular Expressions

Regular expressions
    Additional commands, 77 - 78
    Combining "Or" and wildcard, 74 - 75
    Groups of items, 73
    Literals, 75 - 76
    Numeric and alphabetical spans, 76 - 77
    Optional characters ("?"), 71- 72
    "Or" expression, 70 - 71
    Overview, 69 - 70
    Wildcard expression, 73 - 74

Return on Investment (ROI)
    by channel, 545 – 546
    Defined, 543 – 544
    Overall, 544
    Strategic, 546 - 547

Scope, 111 - 113

Search Console
    Available data, 451
    Comparing to analytics, 460
    Data availability, 450 - 451
    Devices, 458 - 460
    Landing pages, 455 - 456
    Location, 456 - 458
    Prerequisite steps, 449 - 450
    Queries, 452 – 454
    Terminology and Adwords, 461

Secondary dimensions, 145 - 147

Segmentation
    Defined, 269 - 270
    When to use, 270

Segments
    and dashboards, 634 - 635
    and events, 399 - 403
    and goals, 335 - 338
    and User Explorer, 576 - 578
    Application to strategy, 291 - 294
    Controls, 270 - 274
    Creating, 277 - 281, 576-578
    Creating with Conditions, 281 - 284
    Creating with Sequences, 284 - 287
    Data display, 275 - 277
    Eliminating spam from existing data,
        295- 299
    Importing, 287 - 289
    Size and interpretation, 289 - 290
    System Segments, 275, 277
    Strategic Planning, 291 - 294

Sessions (defined), 130 - 132

Sharing Assets
    Overview, 647 - 649
    Share asset management, 653 – 654
    Share template link, 651
    Sharing in the solutions gallery,
        651 – 653
    Single Asset vs. Multiple Assets,
        649 – 650

CPSIA information can be obtained
at www.ICGtesting.com
Printed in the USA
LVHW04s1742120718
583538LV00003B/166/P